ROME

EVERYMAN GUIDES

● Encyclopedia section

■ **NATURE** The natural heritage: species and habitats characteristic to the area covered by the guide, annotated and illustrated by naturalist authors and artists.

HISTORY, LANGUAGE AND RELIGION The impact of international historical events on local history, from the arrival of the first inhabitants, with key dates appearing in a timeline above the text.

ARTS AND TRADITIONS Customs and traditions and their continuing role in contemporary life.

ARCHITECTURE The architectural heritage, focusing on style and topology, a look at rural and urban buildings, major civil, religious and military monuments.

AS SEEN BY PAINTERS A selection of paintings of the city or country by different artists and schools, arranged chronologically or thematically.

AS SEEN BY WRITERS An anthology of texts focusing on the city or country, taken from works of all periods and countries, arranged thematically.

▲ Itineraries

Each itinerary begins with a map of the area to be explored.

✪ **SPECIAL INTEREST** These sites are not to be missed. They are highlighted in gray boxes in the margins.

★ **EDITOR'S CHOICE** Sites singled out by the editor for special attention.

INSETS On richly illustrated double pages, these insets turn the spotlight on subjects deserving more in-depth treatment.

◆ Practical information

All the travel information you will need before you go and when you get there.

USEFUL ADDRESSES A selection of the best hotels and restaurants compiled by an expert.

PLACES TO VISIT A handy table of addresses and opening hours.

APPENDICES Bibliography, list of illustrations and general index.

MAP SECTION Maps of all the areas covered by the guide, followed by an index; these maps are marked out with letters and figures making it easy for the reader to pinpoint a town, region or site.

◆ VATICAN, TRASTEVERE

◆ VATICAN, TRAS

Each map in the map section is designated by a letter. In the itineraries, all the sites of interest are given a map reference (for example: **F** B2).

The mini-map pinpoints the itinerary within the wider area covered by the guide.

The itinerary map shows the main sites, the editor's choices and the places of special interest.

✪ This symbol indicates places of special interest.

▲ TRASTEVERE

From early times Trastevere (which means "across the Tiber") was primarily a working-class quarter. In the 2nd and 3rd centuries it was the main center for communities belonging to

◉ One day
◆ D01-B4-C3-C4-03-04
E C1-E1

1. ISOLA TIBERINA
2. PALAZZO AND TOUR ANGUILLARA
3. CHURCH OF SAN CRISOGONO
4. BASILICA OF SANTA CECILIA
5. CHURCH OF THE MADONNA DELL'ORTO
6. OSPEDALE SAN MICHELE
7. PORTA PORTESE
8. CHURCH OF SAN FRANCESCO A RIPA
9. SYRIAN SANCTUARY OF THE JANICULUM
10. EXCUBITORIUM
11. BASILICA OF SANTA MARIA IN TRASTEVERE
12. CHURCH OF SAN PIETRO IN MONTORIO
13. ACQUA PAOLA
14. JANICULE
15. CHURCH OF SANTA MARIA DEI SETTE DOLORI
16. CHURCH OF SANTA MARIA DELLA SCALA
17. PORTA SETTIMIANA
18. PIAZZA TRILUSSA
19. PONTE SISTO
20. PALAZZO CORSINI
21. FARNESINA
22. MONASTERY OF SANT'ONOFRIO

oriental religions ● 252. The early presence of Christians in this area led to the foundation of three titular churches in the 4th century: Santa Maria in Trastevere, San Crisogono and Santa Cecilia. After the period of decline following the great invasions and repeated sacking of the city ● 30, the population was concentrated around these buildings.
EXPANSION. From the 10th and 11th centuries, like the rest of the city, the neighborhood experienced rapid expansion, marked by the development of the new river port known as Ripagrande or the Ripa Romea. Then in the middle of the 13th century Trastevere was integrated into the administrative system of the city of Rome, which brought the number of Rome's districts or *rioni* up to thirteen. A few noble families

(including the Stefaneschi, Papareschi and Alberteschi) lived in the area, but of their homes only those belonging to the Anguillara and the Mattei have survived from that period (both heavily restored). When the papacy returned from Avignon, for a little while Trastevere became the seat of the Studium Urbis university. At that time, there were only two points of communication with the left bank of the Tiber: the Isola Tiberina (Tiber island) and from 1475 the Ponte Sisto, which was intended to give pilgrims access to St Peter's.
ACCESS ROUTES. Until the 14th century no great town planning initiatives affected this district, its population being concentrated close to the Tiber.

Numerous churches were built or renovated during the 16th century, but very few palazzi were constructed. In this period the Via della Lungara took shape, running parallel to the Tiber to provide an easier link with the Borgo (the *rione* of St Peter's ▲ 232). But it was not until the 19th century that the main avenues were built: the Viale di Trastevere running through the middle of the district, and the Lungotevere skirting the river.
A LIVELY QUARTER ★. Trastevere remained a predominantly working-class area until the 1960's, when it increasingly came to be seen as a neighborhood of restaurants and nightlife. But in the morning it retrieves some of its traditional character, and the *vicoli* (small streets) around Santa Maria in Trastevere offer a glimpse of the daily life of the past. The true spirit of the district is revealed in the month of July

THE TRASTEVERE, THE QUARTER OF THE NIGHT ✪
Having attracted travelers and artists since antiquity, the Trastevere is Rome's bohemian quarter par excellence. Today it is frequented most especially by night owls, rivaling the Via Veneto ▲ 302, symbol of *la dolce vita*, and the Piazza Navona ▲ 276 in the number of establishments that stay open until the early hours. It has lost much of its original character after housing speculation in the 1960s drove out the craftsmen, the small local shops and the ordinary working people. However, something of its old spirit returns in July during the Festa de Noiantri ("our own feast"), when restaurant tables invade the sidewalks and processions, concerts, theatrical performances and firework displays fill the small squares and narrow streets.

THE TRASTEVERINI
With their own dialect, in the city of Rome, the people of Trastevere had always considered themselves the descendants of the ancient Romans. The quarter was frequently a source of uprisings; consequently the Trastevere. In 1849 this was the area that continued to defend the short-lived Republic of Rome to the very end.

350

351

At the beginning of each itinerary, the distance, the suggested means of travel and the time it will take to cover the area are indicated beneath the maps:
🚶 On foot
⛵ By boat
⏱ Duration

★ The star symbol signifies sites singled out by the editor for special attention.

● ▲ ◆
The above symbols within the text provide cross-references to a place or a theme discussed elsewhere in the guide.

03

Front endpaper Sites not to be missed
Back endpaper Rome
02 How to use this guide
06 Introduction to the itineraries
07 The authors

● **Encyclopedia section**

15 Nature
16 The Tiber
18 Flora and fauna of the ruins
20 Villa Doria Pamphilj
22 The Pineta Sacchetti
24 The trees of Rome

25 The History of Rome
26 Chronology
34 The institutions of Antiquity
36 The sack of Rome
38 The apostolic Church of Rome
40 Archeology in Rome
42 The Roman language

45 Arts and traditions
46 Legends and traditions
48 Festivals
50 The Order of Malta
52 Pontifical ceremonies
54 Restoration work
56 Food: *Carciofi alla Romana*
60 Roman specialties

59 Architecture
60 The development of the city
62 Building materials and techniques
64 Roman arches and vaults
66 Buildings for entertainment
68 Water in the ancient town
70 Temples and commemorative
   monuments
72 Medieval towers and dwellings
74 Churches of the Middle Ages
76 The Roman marble cutters
78 Counter-Reformation architecture
80 Churches: Baroque innovations
82 The art of "trompe-l'œil"
84 Baroque stage effects
86 Renaissance and Baroque
   palaces
88 Villas and gardens
90 Neoclassicism and Eclectism
92 Fascism and the postwar period
94 The classical orders

95 Rome as seen by painters

105 Rome as seen by writers

▲ Itineraries in Rome

127 The Capitol, the Forum and the Palatine
132 The Capitoline museums
136 The Roman Forum
147 The Palatine

153 From the Forum Holitorium to the Coliseum
162 The imperial forums
170 The Coliseum

175 Circus Maximus and the Aventine

185 The Coelian Hill
193 San Clemente
196 The Latran

201 The Vatican
209 St Peter's Basilica
218 The Sistine Chapel
222 The Raphael Rooms
224 The Vatican museums

237 From Ponte Sant'Angelo to the Ghetto
240 Via Giulia
247 Around Campo de'Fiori
252 The Ghetto

255 The Campo Marzio from the Gesù to Palazzo Madama
257 The Church of the Gesù
262 The Domes of Rome
264 The Pantheon
270 San Luigi dei Francesi

273 Around Piazza Navona

287 The Quirinal
292 Galleria Nazionale d'Arte Antica
298 Fontana di Trevi

303 Il Tridente
313 Piazza di Spagna
315 The Villa Medici

317 Via Appia Antica
319 The Baths of Caracalla
324 The Catacombs

331 From the Baths of Diocletian to San Pietro in Vincoli
336 National Roman Museum
342 Basilica Santa Maria Maggiore

349 Trastevere
352 Isola Tiberina
363 The Janiculum

367 From Villa Giulia to the Foro Italico
370 Villa Giulia
372 Villa Borghese

379 Rome outside the walls
384 Cinecittà

389 Tivoli and Palestrina
400 The Nile mosaic

403 Ostia
408 The corporations' mosaics

◆ Practical information

418 Getting there
420 Staying in Rome from A to Z
428 Hotels
432 Roman cuisine
434 Restaurants
441 Cafés, bars, nightclubs
445 Shopping
447 Useful words and phrases
448 Places to visit
468 Bibliography
472 List of illustrations
480 Glossary
482 Biographical index
491 General index

501 Map section
502 Street index
  A Monte Mario
  B Villa Borghese
  C Villa Ada, Villa Torlonia
  D Vatican, Trastevere
  E Campo Marzio, Celio
  F Pantheon, Quirinale
  G Around Stazione Termini
  H Testaccio, Ostiense
  I Via Appia Antica
526 Metro plan
528 Bus map of the city center

CAPITOL, FORUM, AND PALATINE ▲ 127
The hub of Roman civilization, between the Capitol, center of political power, and the Palatine, cradle of the city.

THE QUIRINAL ▲ 28[
From the corridors of power in the presidential palace to echoes of *la dolce vita* on Via Veneto and the dazzling Fontana di Trevi.

FORUM HOLITORIUM TO THE COLISEUM ▲ 153
In the heart of imperial Rome, from the forums to the finest amphitheater in the Roman world.

IL TRIDENTE ▲ 303
A place for strolling a shopper's paradise and the district of luxury hotels, today Il Tridente is the product of 19th-century rebuilding.

CIRCUS MAXIMUS AND THE AVENTINE
▲ 175 With its public and monastic gardens, the Aventine is an oasis of quiet and calm, removed from the bustle of the city.

VIA APPIA ANTICA ▲ 317
This road, 330 miles long, constitutes a necropolis outside the city walls, with columbariums, altars and catacombs.

THE COELIAN HILL
▲ 185 The vineyards and orchards on the Coelian Hill are the legacy of the religious orders who settled there in the Middle Ages.

BATHS OF DIOCLETIAN TO SAN PIETRO IN VINCOLI ▲ 331
A fine example of the great sweep of the centuries that is Rome's fascination.

THE VATICAN ▲ 201
The greatest concentration of artistic treasures in the world in the smallest state in Europe, the very center of Christianity.

TRASTEVERE ▲ 349
A center of nightlife the quarter "across the Tiber" retains its working class spirit in the streets around the Basilica of Santa Maria in Trastevere.

PONTE SANT'ANGELO TO THE GHETTO ▲ 237
In Campo Marzio, the colorful stalls of Campo dei Fiori, Renaissance palazzi and the narrow streets of the Ghetto.

VILLA GIULIA TO FORO ITALICO ▲ 36[
From the Villa Borghese, Rome's green lung, and a cluster of museums to Fascism's great sports complex.

GESÙ TO PALAZZO MADAMA ▲ 255
Admiring the achievements of Roman builders and genius of architects of the Counter-Reformation.

ROME OUTSIDE THE WALLS ▲ 379
Memories of Early Christian martyrs, dreams of stardom at Cinecittà and symbols of Fascist Rome at EUR.

PIAZZA NAVONA AND AROUND ▲ 273
The finest of piazzas, shaped like a Roman circus, showcase of the genius of the Baroque masters Bernini and Borromini.

TIVOLI, PALESTRINA AND OSTIA ▲ 389, 398, 403
A visit to Roman towns, with their fine mosaics, and th Villa d'Este, with its 500 fountains.

→ **NUMEROUS SPECIALISTS AND ACADEMICS HAVE CONTRIBUTED TO THIS GUIDE.**

MASTERWORK: CLAUDIA MOATTI

● Encylopedia section

■ **NATURE**
Guido Prola, Livia Tedeschini
■ **HISTORY**
Massimo Bray, Jean-Louis Fournel,
Claudia Moatti, Daniel Nony
■ **LANGUAGE**
Raffaele Simone
■ **ARTS AND TRADITIONS**
Corinne Paul, Simone Pelizzoli,
Mauro Quercioli
■ **ARCHITECTURE**
Oliver Bonfait, Catherine Brice,
Stéphane Guégan, Étienne Hubert
■ **ROME AS SEEN BY PAINTERS**
Antonio del Guercio
■ **ROME AS SEEN BY WRITERS**
Lucinda Gane

▲ Itineraries in Rome

Noëlle de La Blanchardière,
Catherine Brice (modern times),
Filippo Coarelli (Antiquity),
Étienne Hubert (Middle Ages),
Christian Michel (modern times),
Claudia Moatti

◆ Practical information

Grégory Leroy, Corinne Paul,
Angela and Francesca Catello,
Laure Raffaëlli-Fournel. Special thanks
to Paul Betts of the *Financial Times*

ROME
Original French-language edition

Editors
Laure Raffaëlli-Fournel *assisted by* Jean-Louis
Malroux, Corinne Paul, Nathalie Salis, Clarisse
Deniau (architecture)
Layout
Riccardo Tremori,
Michèle Bisgambiglia (nature)
Picture research
William Fischer *assisted by* Caterina D'Agostino
and Perrine Henri
Coordination
Eglal Errera
Research
Laure Raffaëlli-Fournel

ILLUSTRATIONS
Nature : Anne Bodin, Jean Chevallier,
François Desbordes, Claire Felloni, Jean-Michel
Kacédan, Pascal Robin, John Wilkinson
Architecture : Pierre Boutin, Nicolette Castle,
Hugh Dixon, Sandra Doyle, Jean-Marie Guillou,
Jean-Benoit Héron, Olivier Hubert,
Pierre de Hugo, Roger Hutchins, Jean-Michel
Kacédan, Philippe Lhez, Philippe Mignon, Pierre
Poulain, Claude Quiec, Jean-Claude Sénée, Jean-
Louis Serret, Jean-Michel Sinier,
Mike Shœbridge, Tony Townsend
Itineraries : Hubert Goger, Jean-Marie Guillou,
Olivier Hubert, Claude Quiec, Bruno Lenormand,
Jean-Pierre Pontcabare
Maps : Édigraphie, Éric Gillion,
Eugène Flurey and Catherine Totem (color)
Computer graphics: Paul Coulbois

PHOTOGRAPHY
Araldo De Luca, Antonello Idini, Marzio Marzot,
Gabriella Peyrot

WE WOULD ALSO LIKE TO THANK
Dominique Fernandes, Francoise Gaultier, Pierre
Gros, Jean Héritier, Louis Marcelin-Rice, Catherine
Metzger, Claire Sotinel, Florence Valdès-Forain and
the École Française de Rome

Encyclopedia section

15 Nature
25 The history of Rome
45 Arts and Traditions
59 Architecture
95 Rome as seen by painters
105 Rome as seen by writers

In 1477 the market which for decades had been held in Piazza del Campidoglio and the adjacent streets was moved to Piazza Navona, where it remained and operated every day until 1869. In acquiring the equivalent function of a Piazza del Comune or a Piazza del Duomo, from the 15th century Piazza Navona became the true heart of Rome.

"I was in Rome in 1791. At the time, the city still had 166,000 inhabitants,…everything…had an air of grandeur and opulence. Today I entered Rome by the same route, and instead of horses and carriages it was filled with flocks of sheep, oxen, and half-wild horses; behind, black-eyed shepherds herded them along."

F. Lullin de Châteauvieux

Founded on the left bank of the Tiber, Rome has straddled the river since the Imperial age. From antiquity to the 19th century, when the *muraglioni* (high embankments) were constructed, frequent flooding forced the Romans to build dikes, dredge the riverbed, and build numerous bridges to connect the two banks. These included ancient structures such as the Pons Sublicius (the oldest on record), the Pons Aemilius (the first stone bridge) and the Pons Aelius (the forerunner of the Ponte Sant'Angelo). The newest bridges are the Ponte Duca d'Aosta (opposite the Foro Italico) and the Ponte Principe Amadeo.

Nature

16 The Tiber
18 The flora and fauna
    of the ruins
20 Villa Doria Pamphilj
22 The Pineta Sacchetti
24 The trees of Rome

EEL
So common that the city's last professional
fishermen make their living from eels.

Nicknamed *"il Biondo Tevere"* ("the Blond
Tiber") because of the silt that tinges its waters,
the river, now channeled between embankments, is still a
natural space that shelters a wide range of fish (including carp,
rudd, and eels) and birds (among them cormorants, kingfishers
and various kinds of gulls). On the other hand, there is very
little vegetation apart from the occasional clump of greenery
that the attentive observer wandering along the riverbanks will
notice, where willows or poplars have spontaneously reappeared
on abandoned land.

It was only at the end of the 19th century
that embankments were built in Rome to
channel the Tiber.

MALLARD
A few couples nest regularly on the little
islands in the river.

LITTLE GREBE
These can be seen in winter, especially near
Ponte Sant'Angelo.

At dusk and dawn some eight hundred great cormorants fly over the town, going to or from their roosts.

GREAT CORMORANT
Despite the pollution, in winter it fishes on the river in the very heart of the town.

GREY WAGTAIL
A very useful permanent resident, as it feeds on insects and mosquitoes in the summer.

BROWN RAT
So aggressive even cats fear it, this haunts the sewers, cellars, and streets.

COYPU
Having escaped from a farm in the 1950's, they bred so vigorously on the Tiber they can now be found in the center of Rome.

CARP
This fish was introduced into Europe by the Romans.

PIKE PERCH
Introduced into the Tiber in 1965 and 1966, it has thrived so well that it is now a threat to the native species.

CATFISH
Also an introduced species, it tolerates polluted waters with a low oxygen content.

HERRING GULL
This gull has nested for some years now on the rooftops of palazzi and churches in the city.

BLACK-HEADED GULL
Mainly winter visitors, but a small number now nest on the Tiber.

summer   winter

17

THE FLORA AND FAUNA OF THE RUINS

SICILIAN LIZARD
Also known as "the lizard of the ruins", it sometimes feeds on the remains of tourists' picnics.

The archeological sites all over Rome are protected environments favorable to the development of unusual flora and fauna. Common plant species such as the fig tree and the caper bush (indigenous to the rocks of the Mediterranean) flourish side by side among the ruins. Orchids also frequently grow there. A number of bird species find a choice refuge in ancient Rome.

LITTLE OWL
Particularly common in the forums, where it hunts rodents.

HOOPOE
Sometimes nests on the Palatine, but is being disturbed by the flow of tourists.

BLACK REDSTART
These birds build their nests among the ruins, away from tourists.

Cats are without doubt the most commonly found mammals in the forums.

The Forum is one of the best places to find original flora and fauna, firmly established in the walls and among the ruins.

GREEN LIZARD
This large, relatively uncommon lizard eats insects and sometimes fledglings too.

JACKDAW
Nests in the Coliseum, but is now less common as it is being driven out by crows.

BLUE ROCK THRUSH
A few couples of this superb species nest in the Coliseum and in the tallest ruins of the forums.

CISALPINE SPARROW
This Italian variety of house sparrow can be identified by its brown skullcap.

KESTREL
Nests in bell towers and ruins, where it even hunts bats.

CAPER
This thorny bush with pretty white flowers grows on walls and in crevices between stones.

FIG
Common in the forums. It bears fruit at the end of the summer.

SPLEENWORT
This small fern grows mainly in the cracks between the blocks of stone in the forums.

WALL PELLITORY
Abundant at the foot of walls, this plant swiftly overruns neglected spots.

BUTTERFLY ORCHID
This magnificent orchid is found during April on all dry and chalky ground.

"Ruin-of-Rome" – a tiny and aptly named plant.

VILLA DORIA PAMPHILJ

EUROPEAN POND TORTOISE
This reptile can occasionally be
observed in the villa's largest lake,
resting on half-submerged branches.

Since antiquity the Romans have been masters of the art of designing superb gardens and country villas, though many of them have been swallowed up by the city. Rome's public parks are an example of these Italian-style gardens where allées, squares, and flowerbeds, bordered by yew, box, or evergreen oak, alternate with groves of such exotic trees as cedars or palms, or with islands of wilder vegetation whose fauna is every bit as interesting as that around various ponds and lakes.

RED FOX
At dusk foxes sometimes come to scavenge in the larger parks, but are not very common.

Despite its well-kept Italian-style gardens, the Villa Doria Pamphilj offers shelter to wild flora and fauna that have adapted remarkably well to urban conditions.

HEDGEHOG
Being shy creatures, hedgehogs only come out at night to hunt for insects and earthworms.

MOORHEN
These birds nest in thick vegetation around the ponds and lakes of Villa Doria Pamphilj.

NUTHATCH
With great agility it creeps down tree trunks, head first.

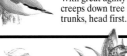

NARROW-LEAVED CEPHALANTHERA
In May and June this discreet orchid flowers in shady places.

VIOLET BIRDS'-NEST ORCHID
A large orchid that grows in sunny patches of undergrowth on poor soil.

MAGPIE
Never far from man, the magpie population is increasing, especially in Rome's villas.

GREY HERON
Herons visit the small lakes of the Villa Doria Pamphilj in winter to fish.

SPIDER ORCHID
This lovely orchid, which blooms from the month of April, grows on very chalky soil.

PURPLE ORCHID
Twenty-nine species of orchid are found in Rome. This one is fairly common.

EVERGREEN OR HOLM OAK
Unlike other oaks, this tree keeps its leaves all year round.

■ THE PINETA SACCHETTI

Even today the Pineta Sacchetti still serves as grazing land for sheep, at the very gates of Rome.

Pineta Sacchetti

Vatican City

The Pineta Sacchetti owes its name to the copses of umbrella pines planted on its heights. It stretches along a valley hollowed out by water, the Valle d'Inferno, to the nearby hills a few minutes from the heart of the city. This protected site gives a fairly accurate idea of the original natural environment of Rome. In fact the city developed in a transitional zone, something between a strictly Mediterranean environment, characterized by forests of evergreen trees, and that of the hills farther inland forested with deciduous trees.

EUROPEAN BEE-EATER
This bird has nested in the Pineta Sacchetti for many years. It makes its nest at the bottom of a tunnel hollowed out in sandy soil.

PHILLYREA LATIFOLIA
This bush grows in the sunny Mediterranean scrubland known as the *macchia* or maquis.

MYRTLE
The flowers give off a most distinctive sweet scent.

TREE HEATHER
This tall heather thrives on the flinty soil of the *macchia*.

SARSAPARILLA
This "creeper" clings to plants or bushes in order to grow.

ARBUTUS
The fruits, which ripen in the fall, are sometimes used to make a liqueur.

BARRED WOODPECKER
It often builds its nest in crevices in the trunks of dead poplars.

TAWNY OWL
It hoots in September and October to establish its territory.

RED ADMIRAL
This butterfly migrates seasonally. It is most in evidence in Rome in the fall.

GREEN TOAD
The damp valley that traverses the Pineta provides an ideal habitat for this toad.

PRAYING MANTIS
These insects are often seen in sunny meadows at the end of the summer, when they lay their eggs.

THE TREES OF ROME

A large number of popes, princes, and great men have sought to leave a reminder of their power in the city by planting trees chosen from among the most exotic or majestic species. Nevertheless, in Rome it is difficult to distinguish between self-sown trees and ones that have been planted.

CYPRESS
Planted by Michelangelo in the Baths of Diocletian when he worked there on the Basilica of Santa Maria degli Angeli.

ORANGE TREE
The orange tree planted by St Dominic at the Basilica of Santa Sabina on the Aventine is almost 1,000 years old.

PLUM TREE
One of Garibaldi's soldiers died at the foot of the plum tree in Villa Glori.

JUDAS TREE
This is supposed to be the kind of tree on which Judas hung himself after betraying Jesus.

Palm trees were often planted to complement Liberty (Art Nouveau) architecture.

BAY
The bay tree in the gardens of the Farnesina was donated by the poet Pascarella in 1934.

EUROPEAN OAK
Torquato Tasso and St Philip Neri rested in the shade of the "Quercia del Tasso" ▲ 365.

UMBRELLA PINE
Also called Italian pine or "pine-kernel pine", this is the king of trees in Rome. It has been associated with the Roman countryside since antiquity. Over the centuries it has inspired countless painters, as well as Ottorino Respighi's orchestral suite *The Pines of Rome*.

The history of Rome

26 Chronology
34 The institutions of Antiquity
36 The sack of Rome
38 The apostolic Church
    of Rome
40 Archeology in Rome
42 The Roman language

THE HISTORY OF ROME

Foundation rites.

ROME'S ORIGINS AND THE AGE OF THE KINGS

THE END OF THE 2ND MILLENNIUM
There is evidence of exchanges between the Mycenaean world and the shores of Italy.

ABOUT 800 BC
The beginning of the Etruscan civilization in Tuscany.

Romulus and Remus.

ABOUT 750 BC
The Greeks found Cumae (in Campania).

ABOUT 600 BC
Marseilles founded by the Greeks, and Capua by the Etruscans.

496 BC
Roman victory over the Latins at Lake Regillus.

Stele dedicated to Romulus (right).

494 BC
Secession of the plebs; creation of tribunes of the people.

396 BC
The Etruscan city of Veii captured by the Romans.

390 BC
The Gauls briefly take possession of Rome.

THE LEGEND. Fleeing Troy, Aeneas, son of Aphrodite and the mortal Anchises, reached the delta of the Tiber in the land of the Latins. He married Lavinia, the daughter of their king, and founded Lavinium. Romulus and Remus were born from the union of the Vestal Virgin Rhea Silvia with the god Mars. The twins, flung into the Tiber by their great-uncle, a usurper, were washed up at the foot of the Palatine Hill, where they were suckled by a she-wolf and discovered by shepherds. When they grew up they founded Rome, on April 21, 753 BC: Romulus plowed a furrow to mark out the sacred precinct of the newly founded town and in a quarrel killed Remus, who had jeeringly jumped over it. Shortly afterward he had the Sabine women kidnapped to provide wives for his companions. From 616 there was a succession of three Etruscan kings (Servius Tullius and the two Tarquins). In 509, after the expulsion of Tarquinius Superbus (Tarquin the Proud), the Republic came into being, with annually elected magistrates called consuls and a temple dedicated to Jupiter, Juno and Minerva on the Capitoline Hill.

ARCHEOLOGY. In the 8th century BC villages covered the hills surrounding the marshy hollow of the Forum. Around the end of the 7th century they gradually gave way to a city that had Latin as its language, Latin gods (Jupiter, Mars and Quirinus) and a temple on the citadel of the Capitol, dominating the Forum. However, it was the Etruscans who turned it into in a town with walls, sewers, aristocratic dwellings and public institutions (including sacred laws, a senate and an army). At the beginning of the 5th century their domination faded, and Rome no longer participated in Mediterranean exchanges.

A POWERFUL ITALIAN REPUBLIC

Pyrrhus.

THE CONQUEST OF THE PENINSULA. Rome took control of the Latins and loosened the grip of the Etruscans. It then exerted pressure in the direction of Campania, with war after war against the Samnites, and eventually had to face the elephants of Pyrrhus, King of Epirus, who had answered the call of the Greeks, alarmed by the advance of Rome. With a multitude of treaties of alliance and by annexing territories, founding colonies and building strategic roads, Rome ensured its hegemony over the Italian peninsula.

PATRICIANS AND PLEBEIANS. The patricians claimed to be the descendants of the first senators and wanted to keep for themselves the right to be magistrates (praetors or consuls)

A Roman patrician.

and priests. In protest the rest of the city's population (the plebs) withdrew to the Aventine, elected their own magistrates and built a sanctuary. Subsequent reconciliations made it possible to draft a common code of law, the Law of the Twelve Tables, allowing plebeians to be consuls and recognizing the inviolable power of the tribunes as well as the validity of the *consilium plebis* and its *plebiscita* (laws voted for by the plebs). From then on, power was shared by the great landowners, the patricians and the plebeians.

323 BC
Death of Alexander the Great.

295 BC
The Romans conquer the Gauls, the Etruscans, and finally the Samnites at Sentinum.

272 BC
The Romans capture Tarentum.

THE CONQUEST OF THE WORLD AND THE CIVIL WARS

THE DOMINATION OF THE MEDITERRANEAN. This took place over two centuries, and Rome often preferred client-states to provinces under direct administration. The Punic wars, at the expense of Carthage, led to the conquest of Sicily, Sardinia and Corsica, then the Iberian peninsula, and finally part of North Africa. The Gauls of the Po plain were forced

Hannibal in Italy (center).

264–241 BC
First Punic War.

219–202 BC
Second Punic War. Scipio Africanus defeats Hannibal.

192–188 BC
Wars in Greece and Asia.

to submit; then the other Gauls, conquered by Julius Caesar, who advanced as far as the Rhine and the North Sea. On the other side of the Adriatic, Rome quelled the Greek world, wiping out the kingdoms of Alexander's successors.

SOCIAL TENSIONS. Rome changed radically during the 1st century. Its religion was enriched with new cults. Latin became a literary language and a national theater was founded. But above all, the conquests brought a flow of money and slaves into Italy. The rich increased their properties, while small landowners lost their land and moved to the towns. The senators were intent on retaining their power, challenged as they were by the *equites* (knights), by other great landowners and by the *publicani* (tax farmers administering the resources of the State). In the army, to which Marius had admitted proletarians, the legionaries began to show greater loyalty to their generals than to the State. Burdened by increasingly heavy taxes, the Italian provinces under Rome's control obtained Roman citizenship after rebelling in 91 to 88 BC. The political unity of Italy was henceforth achieved.

146 BC
Destruction of Carthage (end of Third Punic War) and Corinth.

The Senate.

27

81–79 BC
Sulla's dictatorship. He reforms the constitution.

THE DEATH OF THE REPUBLIC. The end of the Republic witnessed the development of two factions within the ruling class: the *optimates* (the conservative aristocrats) and the *populares* ("friends of the people"), who championed reforms which they obtained in an atmosphere of violence. Nevertheless, the senatorial government dealt successfully with the slaves' revolt led by Spartacus and with Catilina's conspiracy. But after Sulla, who twice marched on Rome, political authority was seized by the generals: in 60 BC Pompey, Crassus and Julius Caesar joined forces in a triumvirate that monopolized power. After conquering Gaul, Caesar crossed the Rubicon, marched on Rome, assumed dictatorial powers, and eliminated Pompey and his supporters. His assassination, on March 15, 44 BC, sparked another civil war: Mark Antony and Octavian (the future Augustus) defeated the tyrannicides Brutus and Cassius before becoming bitter enemies. Octavian's naval victory at Actium over Antony and Cleopatra enabled him to seize power and to annex Egypt. By 30 BC the whole of the Mediterranean had become Roman.

Caesar's murder.

73–71 BC
Spartacus' revolt.

63 BC
Cicero's consulship. The Catiline conspiracy.

THE MAJESTY OF THE "PAX ROMANA"

27 BC
Octavian becomes Augustus.

ABOUT 30 AD
Crucifixion of Jesus

47 AD
The census shows six million Romans.

THE JULIO-CLAUDIAN DYNASTY. In forty-five years of power Augustus laid the foundations for the government of the Roman Empire for four centuries. Forums, aqueducts and temples were built, in addition to other public works. Police and fire brigades and food-distribution facilities were organized in the city, and legions were dispatched to the frontiers. The last great conqueror Augustus vanquished the peoples of the Alps and extended the Empire as far as the right bank of the Danube, though he failed to keep Germany. Tiberius consolidated the Imperial autocracy during his painstaking reign of twenty-two years. Italians and people in the provinces converted to the cult of the emperor, thus demonstrating their loyalty to a regime that had brought peace to the Mediterranean world. Thanks to Caligula and his successors the games became a State institution – to the delight of the Roman plebs, who also benefited from distribution of free food. Under

Augustus of Prima Porta.

A votive shield (centre).

SENATVS
POPVLVSQVEROM
IMPCAESARIDIVIFA
COSVIII DEDIT CLV
VIRTVTIS CLEME
IVSTITIAE PIETATIS
DEOS PATRIAM

64 AD
Great fire of Rome.

68–69 AD
The last revolts of the Gauls.

Uniforms of the
Roman army.

Claudius, the port of Ostia was enlarged in order to improve
the capital's food supply. After a devastating fire Nero
embarked on town planning on a vast scale, a trend that
lasted fifty years and culminated in the building of Trajan's
Forum ▲ 165.

PEACE IN THE 2ND CENTURY.

After Augustus until the time of Septimius Severus new
provinces were created, but from London to Arabia most of
these were former client-states. This transformation
frequently encountered harsh resistance, especially in Judaea.
Although the conquests continued under Trajan with his
annexation in 107 of Dacia on the right bank of the Danube,
Hadrian had to give up Mesopotamia in 117. Antagonism
between the Empire's two cultures was lessened thanks to this
Greek-loving emperor, and a number of the Greek elite were
included in the Imperial administration. By Caracalla's Edict
of 212 AD Roman citizenship, previously granted to the
notables of the cities and tribes and to the auxiliary soldiers,
was finally granted to all free men throughout the Empire.

FIERCE RESISTANCE TO THE BARBARIANS.
In the same
period the Empire passed from the offensive to the defensive.
Encouraged by interior crises, the army chose emperors such
as Maximinus the Thracian, a common soldier brought to
power in 235. However, despite a series of epidemics and
several rebellions, the Empire remained prosperous and its
government stable. The millennium of Rome was
celebrated in 248 by Philip the Arab. Then,
in 260 Valerian was captured by the
Parthians. Despite pressure from the
barbarians, the Romans' sense of
solidarity, together with Gallienus' genius,
enabled them to stem the advance of the
Visigoths as far as Greece. But a
miscellany of rival generals succeeded him,
and eventually in 293 Diocletian
attempted to divide up the Imperial power
between two Augustuses and two Caesars.

THE CHRISTIAN EMPIRE.
This tetrarchy
did not last. In 313, to his own advantage, Constantine started
to build a bureaucratic monarchy based on divine right,
endowed with a well-organized religion, Christianity, and a
new capital, Constantinople. Within a century State
paganism vanished, despite its restoration under the
Emperor Julian (361–3). The soldier-emperors returned,
and on the death of one of them, Theodosius, in 395 the
division of the Empire became final. In 406 the Rhine
front gave way under pressure from the Suevi and the
Vandals. In 410 Rome was sacked by the Visigoths, and
in 455 by the Vandals. Puppet emperors succeeded one
another in the Western Empire, which was devastated by
the barbarians. Germans and Romans formed alliances to
repel Attila's Huns, who attempted to invade first Gaul and
then Italy. Finally in 476 Odoacer, King of the Heruli,
deposed the Emperor of the West, Romulus Augustulus
(right), and recognized the fictitious authority of the Emperor
of Constantinople. The Western Empire had ceased to exist.

69–71 AD
*Revolt of Judaea and
the destruction of the
temple of Jerusalem.*

79 AD
*Eruption of Vesuvius
destroys Herculaneum
and Pompeii.*

161–80 AD
*Marcus Aurelius repels
the Parthians and
Marcomanni.*

271–5 AD
*Construction of the
Aurelian Wall.*

303–4 AD
*The last major
persecutions of
Christians.*

325 AD
*The Council of
Nicaea.*

330 AD
*Foundation of
Constantinople.*

Rome attacked by the
Goths.

391 AD
*Theodosius bans
pagan worship.*

29

THE MAKING OF THE HOLY ROMAN EMPIRE

Gregory I the Great .

476
Odoacer deposes the Emperor of the West in Ravenna.

554
Justinian asserts Byzantine authority in Italy, with Ravenna as its capital.

751
Resumption of Lombard expansion. End of the Ravenna exarchate.

962
Otto the Great, King of Germany, is crowned Emperor.

Charlemagne crowning his son.

FROM THE FALL OF THE EMPIRE TO POPE GREGORY THE GREAT.

When the last Emperor of the West was overthrown, Rome was still the most important metropolis in the western world. It emerged barely recognizable from the war (535–55) waged by Justinian, Emperor of Byzantium, who sought to assert Imperial authority over Italy. But from 568 the peninsula was partially lost to the Lombard invasion. In Rome there were rapid changes: the Senate, the last vestige of the ancient order, disappeared. Pope Gregory the Great (590–604) took control, in place of the amorphous Byzantine regime, and laid the foundations of the popes' temporal power.

CAROLINGIAN SUPPORT.

The Lombard threat led the Pope to form an alliance with the Franks. The pontiff claimed the territories of Rome and Ravenna. Charlemagne recognized his power, and by having himself crowned in Rome restored the city's prestige as the ideal center of the Christian West.

1075–1122
The War of the Investitures is ended by the Concordat of Worms.

NOBILITY, POPE AND EMPEROR.

A long period followed during which the city came under the sway of the great Roman feudal and noble families – the dukes of Spoleto (9th century), the Theophylacts, the Crescentii, then the counts of Tusculum (9th to 10th centuries) – who profited from the weakening of the Carolingians and then from the crisis of pontifical authority and the absence of the Germanic Holy Roman Emperors. In the 11th century a conflict flared up between the Pope and the Emperor. In 1075 Gregory VII referred to a decree banning the Empire's interference in the affairs of the Church, which he intended to reform. In 1084 the Emperor Henry IV responded: he besieged Rome and abducted him. Robert Guiscard, summoned by the Pope, repelled the Emperor and partially destroyed Rome.

THE AGE OF THE COMMUNE

1154–83
Wars between Frederick Barbarossa and the communes. Recognition of the rights of the communes by the Peace of Constance.

THE FIRST STEPS.

In 1143 a popular revolt against the Pope led to the creation of a Senate independent from the Church and the nobility; thus a commune emerged that was soon to find an ardent champion in Arnaldo da Brescia. The Emperor Frederick Barbarossa had this ringleader executed and restored to the Pope his sovereignty over Rome, which formally recognized the commune.

1266
Charles d'Anjou establishes an Angevine kingdom in southern Italy.

STRUGGLES BETWEEN LAY AND CHURCH AUTHORITIES.

After a flourishing period for the commune in the early 13th century, the post of the only senator in Rome created in 1191 was granted to Charles d'Anjou (1263), before the position

Pope Gregory XI
returning to Avignon.

became a papal appendage. The
failure of the Crusades made
Rome the Christians' first holy
town. But the exile of the popes
to Avignon soon began (1309–77).
The town's institutions benefited by
their banishment. However, as in the
previous century, Rome continued to
be torn by the feuds between two
noble families, the Orsini and the Colonna. Inspired
by the myth of Republican Rome, between 1347 and 1354
Cola di Rienzo ● XV endeavored to restore the Republic and
took very severe measures against the nobility. The Pope had
scarcely returned to Rome when the great schism of the West
(1378–1417) undermined his power and caused war to break
out throughout the Church's territory. Rome was left in the
hands of Ladislas of Durazzo.

1339
*Beginning of the
Hundred Years War.*

Cola di Rienzo.

1348
*The Black Death in
Europe.*

THE RENAISSANCE

1453
*The Turks capture
Constantinople.*

1454
*Peace of Lodi between
the great Italian States.*

1494
*Charles VIII sets out to
conquer the Kingdom
of Naples: start of the
Wars of Italy.*

RESTORATION OF PAPAL AUTHORITY. The year 1420
marked the return of the sovereign pontiffs to Rome. During
their absence the city had fallen into decline. It was
unhealthy, short of food and depopulated. The popes
transformed this decaying city into a capital worthy of their
mission and reimposed their authority. The commune of the
people, the nobility, and pontifical power: these were the
poles of Roman political life for three centuries. The popes
opted for an anti-commune policy that provoked violent
reactions during the 15th century and installed a bureaucracy
capable of governing the city directly. The Pope and the
College of Cardinals headed a complex administration (the
Curia) consisting of five councils. The great families vied to
join it, while their nepotism led the popes to keep key posts
for their own relations. Alexander VI was even tempted to
carve out a State in central Italy for his son, Cesare Borgia.

A PERIOD OF SPLENDOR. A policy of large-scale building
was initiated at the end of the 15th century. For two centuries
Rome, whose population was increasing, became a vast
building site. The pontifical court was the main center of
humanist culture, and the town welcomed the great
Renaissance artists. The popes of the day (Alexander VI,
Julius II, Leo X, Clement VII) became great princes who
took part in the alliances of Italy's wars, encouraging France

Pope Julius II.

1517
*Beginning of the
Lutheran Reformation.*

1530
*Charles V is
consecrated Emperor
in Bologna.*

The Sack of Rome
(left).

or its adversaries in turn. The Sack of Rome ● 36 (1527)
seemed likely to put an end to this splendor. But the
pontificate of Paul III and preparations for the Council of
Trent restored Rome's cultural and political importance.

1545–63
*The Council of Trent.
Counter-Reformation.*

THE COUNTER-REFORMATION

1559
Treaty of Cateau Cambrésis: France relinquishes Italy.

THE ALL-POWERFUL PAPACY AND THE FRAGILITY OF THE STATE. Nevertheless, the disruption created by Protestantism in the Christian world and the transfer of the great trading centers from the Mediterranean to the Atlantic and Northern Europe forced Rome to somewhat reduce its universal ambitions. The Pontifical State owed its survival less to real strength than to the logic of the Counter-Reformation, which found a powerful ally in the Spanish monarchy. But the Pope reigned as a king, and the Curia saw its role in local affairs increase. The former cooperation between the aristocracy and the high-ranking clergy lasted until the end of the 17th century – leaving little room for the bourgeoisie, who therefore asserted their position in other capitals.

POVERTY AND GRANDEUR. The popes – especially Sixtus V (left), Paul V and Urban VIII, who between them commissioned many of Rome's Baroque treasures – pursued an active policy of promoting the arts. Patronage encouraged culture while censure stifled it. Opulence and misery rubbed shoulders in this densely populated town: aristocrats, prelates and powerful foreigners measured their prestige according to the number of poor who knocked at their doors and the quantity of servants and peasants they employed.

TO THE NAPOLEONIC AGE

1618–48
The Thirty Years War.

1702–12
The War of the Spanish Succession.

1796–7
Napoleon's Italian campaign.

1799
The Austrians occupy much of the peninsula.

1800–1
French victory at Marengo. The Peace of Lunéville puts the peninsula back under French hegemony.

IMMOBILISM AND CONFORMITY. Clement XI seemed for a time to wish to involve the Pontifical State in the War of the Spanish Succession. But the military and political impotence of the Holy See obliged it to remain neutral. Cut off from mainstream European politics, Rome was forced to content itself with its religious, artistic and archeological prestige.

THE NAPOLEONIC HURRICANE. The French Revolution and its repercussions were to revive political life. In 1798 the French occupied the town. A Roman republic was born, and the Pope was exiled. On his return to Rome in 1800, he accepted all the arrangements. In 1808 French troops again occupied Rome and dismantled the former administration. The following year, his temporal power abolished, the Pope was again forced into exile. Finally on May 24, 1814, he regained the Papal States, and in 1815 the Congress of Vienna restored their former frontiers.

FROM THE RESTORATION TO ITALIAN UNITY

1806
Napoleon proclaimed Emperor of Rome. Proclamation of the Kingdom of Italy.

1814
The fall of the Empire.

Pius IX (right).

THE FIRST WAR OF INDEPENDENCE. Political liberalism, patriotic aspirations and social claims made headway in the first half of the 19th century. In the revolutionary outburst of 1848 temporary governments flourished in several Italian cities, including Rome. For two years it seemed that Pius IX wished to be the spokesman for these new aspirations. However, he recalled his troops

Giuseppe Garibaldi.

involved in the First War of Independence and left his State. On February 9, 1849, Mazzini's supporters proclaimed the abolition of temporal power and the Roman Republic. In reply, France intervened in the Pope's favor and occupied Rome.

ROME BECOMES THE CAPITAL.

In 1859, at the end of the Second War of Independence, the new Kingdom of Italy extended to within a few miles of Rome. France occupied the city, blocking the Roman question, and Garibaldi twice tried in vain to take it. Finally, when the French troops were evacuated, the Piedmontese entered the city on September 20, 1870. Annexed by plebiscite on October 2, Rome as proclaimed the capital of the kingdom.

1848
Revolutions in Europe. First War of Italian Independence. Defeat by the Austrians.

1860
The King of Piedmont is declared King of Italy.

The first Italian flag.

1861
Proclamation of the Kingdom of Italy.

FROM UNITY TO THE PRESENT DAY

THE RISE OF FASCISM IN ROME. Having inherited an extremely weak economy in 1870, the new capital experienced various difficulties until World War One, despite the laws in its favor introduced by the Giolitti government. The Fascist government, which assumed power two years after the March on Rome, as to bring about both a rhetorical rehabilitation of the Eternal City and a reconciliation with the Church by signing the Lateran Treaty, thus putting an end to dissension between the Church and the State.

1915
Italy enters the war on the side of the Allies.

The March on Rome (center).

1924
The Assassination of Matteotti.

1924–43
The Fascist regime.

1933
Hitler comes to power in Germany.

1946
The first Italian Republic.

Pope John XXIII.

FROM WORLD WAR TWO TO TODAY. The Fascist government abandoned the city as soon as the armistice was declared on September 8, 1943. Caught between its status as an open city and the Nazi occupation, Rome's inhabitants began intense underground activity, and the city served as one of the two headquarters of the National Liberation Committee until June 1944. The signing of the Treaty of Rome (1957), the Holy Years (1950 and 1975) and the Olympic Games (1960) brought Rome into the limelight. This city where the service sector is so dominant has been a victim of its own sudden growth: it lacks basic amenities and exists in a state of urban chaos, which the municipality has been unable to remedy despite efforts made since 1975.

"PROVOCO"
"I appeal to the people" was the ritual formula that a citizen (on the left) condemned to death by a magistrate (center) had to pronounce in Republican times to place himself under the protection of the people.

In 509 BC a revolution rid Rome of its kings and established a government that entrusted the State to the Senate and the Roman people, as well as to a body of magistrates. The oligarchic Republic continued until the end of the 1st century AD, despite the expansion of the City-State and the birth of a gigantic empire. In 27 BC power passed into the hands of a single man, the *princeps* or Emperor. The Roman Empire remained undivided until the 4th century AD. Subsequently, due to the threat of barbarian invasions, a division of authority was imposed – which led to the collapse of the Western Empire in 476, while in the East the Byzantine State was asserting itself.

The augurs, recognizable by their sacred crook (the *lituus*), interpreted the omens (*auspicae*) before any public act, such as elections or war.

THE COMITIUM
An approximate reconstruction. The layout of the Comitium admirably reflected the political institutions of the Republic. The Curia housed the sessions of the Senate, which possessed great authority. Assemblies of the people (*populus*) were held on the circular tiers of steps; although theoretically sovereign, they were only permitted to gather to vote when summoned by the superior magistrates. Finally, the magistrates (consuls, praetors, tribunes of the people, etc.) harangued the crowd from the *rostra* ▲ *140*, which faced the Curia.

THE CENSUS OF CITIZENS
Under the Republic this took place every five years. First the father of the family (standing on the left) declared his assets. Then he was assigned his status in the social and military hierarchies (second scene). A religious ceremony accompanied by a sacrifice concluded the process.

> "In this constitution…everything was organized in such an equitable manner that it was impossible to say whether the regime was aristocratic, democratic or monarchic."
>
> Polybius

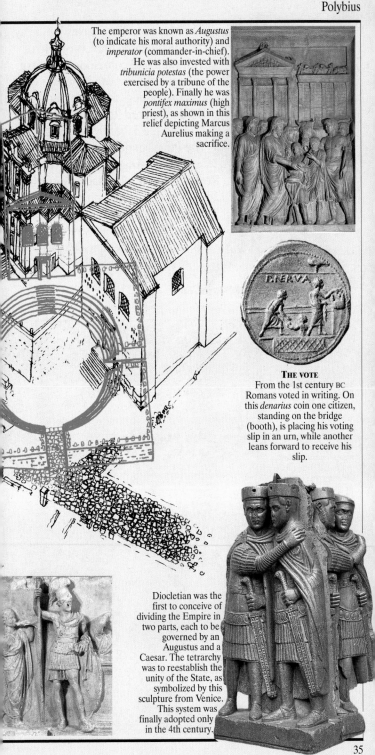

The emperor was known as *Augustus* (to indicate his moral authority) and *imperator* (commander-in-chief). He was also invested with *tribunicia potestas* (the power exercised by a tribune of the people). Finally he was *pontifex maximus* (high priest), as shown in this relief depicting Marcus Aurelius making a sacrifice.

THE VOTE
From the 1st century BC Romans voted in writing. On this *denarius* coin one citizen, standing on the bridge (booth), is placing his voting slip in an urn, while another leans forward to receive his slip.

Diocletian was the first to conceive of dividing the Empire in two parts, each to be governed by an Augustus and a Caesar. The tetrarchy was to reestablish the unity of the State, as symbolized by this sculpture from Venice. This system was finally adopted only in the 4th century.

THE SACK OF ROME

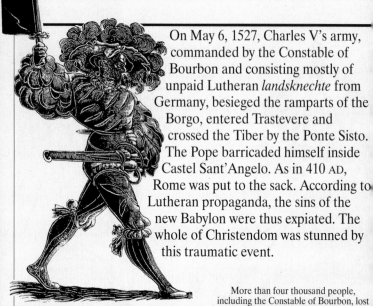

On May 6, 1527, Charles V's army, commanded by the Constable of Bourbon and consisting mostly of unpaid Lutheran *landsknechte* from Germany, besieged the ramparts of the Borgo, entered Trastevere and crossed the Tiber by the Ponte Sisto. The Pope barricaded himself inside Castel Sant'Angelo. As in 410 AD, Rome was put to the sack. According to Lutheran propaganda, the sins of the new Babylon were thus expiated. The whole of Christendom was stunned by this traumatic event.

More than four thousand people, including the Constable of Bourbon, lost their lives in combat and during the siege.

THE LOOTING
For several weeks the city was systematically plundered by the troops.

THE PEACE TREATY
In Madrid, Emperor Charles V feigned regret over the conduct of his troops by not holding victory celebrations, but he knew full well how to reap the profits and only agreed to meet Clement VII to sign a peace treaty on June 20, 1529, in Barcelona.

THE POPE IN CASTEL SANT'ANGELO

n June 6, 1527, the Pope capitulated and agreed to pay a very high ransom, but the Spaniards
kept him prisoner in Castel Sant'Angelo until December 8. In spite of the plague that was
mating both the inhabitants and the army, the destruction of the city continued for six months.

THE GRAFFITI
Frescoes and the walls
of palazzi still bear
traces of the soldiers'
graffiti ▲ 360.

Tu es Petrus et super hanc petram aedificabo ecclesiam meam … Tibi dabo claves caelorum ("You are Peter and on this rock I will build my Church … I will give you the keys of the kingdom of heaven," *Matthew* 16:18–19). As Peter's successor, the Pope is the basis of the community of believers, the head of the Roman Church (*Ecclesia romana*). Originally he was aided by deacons (who administered the charitable works of the Church), the parish priests of Rome and the bishops of the suburbicarian dioceses (Ostia, Albano, Palestrina, Frascati, Sabina and Porto). These prelates, who were the Pope's close advisers, constituted the original College of Cardinals, which since the 12th century has had the task of electing the Pope. As successors to the apostles, the bishops (*episcopoi*) used to be elected by the religious community; today they are appointed by the Pope.

CARDINAL
Appointed by the Pope to assist in governing the Church.

BISHOP
"Prophet, pontiff and pastor", responsible for the Christians in a diocese.

PRIEST
Ordained by the bishop, who invests him with his powers. He assists the bishop in his tasks, particularly in administering the sacraments.

THE POPE
Elected in conclave
by the cardinals, he
heads the community
of believers.

WOMEN'S ORDERS
Nuns who dedicate themselves to the
Christian life are today active in the field of
health care and education in missions in the
Third World.

THE REGULAR CLERGY
In the monastic tradition they follow a Rule
established by a founder. The Cistercian
shown here belongs to the Order founded by
St Bernard in 1098.

Despite the endless destruction it suffered, Rome never stopped
producing innumerable masterpieces that were to influence
European thought, arouse passions and fashions, provoke
debate and research. Through medieval guide books, the
Mirabilia Urbis, and the research of collectors and artists that
opened the way to archeology, one discovers a real defiance of
the passage of time.

THE DOMUS AUREA ▲ *174*

At a time when explorers were discovering
new worlds, feverish excavations were being
carried out in Rome. Some ambitious
projects date from that period (including
the archeological map begun by Raphael)
and important discoveries were made. One
of these was the Domus Aurea, entirely
decorated with "grotesques" that were to
have a major influence on Renaissance
artists. Nero's palace contained
innumerable sculptures, one of which was
the *Laocoön*, discovered in 1506. It
illustrates the story in the second book of
the *Aeneid*, where a priest from Troy and
children are suffocated by two of Apollo's
serpents. Julius II had this remarkable
group moved to the Octagonal Courtyard
the Vatican ▲ *224*.

**A CHANGE OF
MENTALITY**
Until the end of the
18th century
excavations had
sought mainly to
discover buried
treasure; from that
time archeological
digs focused on
unearthing ruins, and
even on restoring
large complexes.
The French played
a considerable role
in these
developments. They
funded numerous
digs and created a
variety of institutions
with directors such as
Canova, Giuseppe
Valadier and the
Prefect of Tournon.
Napoleon associated
himself with efforts to
embellish the city by
opening the Pincio
promenade.

TOWARD SCIENTIFIC ARCHEOLOGY
In the 19th century some great research institutions were
arted, like the Institute for Archeological Correspondence,
created in 1829, whose aspirations are symbolized in this
engraving.

SUBTERRANEAN ROME
When De Rossi rediscovered the catacombs
▲ *324* and founded Christian archeology,
there was a revival of religious fervor.

THE FIRST HISTORY OF ART
Johann Joachim
Winckelmann came
to Rome in 1755 to
be Cardinal Albani's
librarian. This
Prussian with a
passion for antiquity
maintained that "the
only way to achieve
art is to imitate the
Ancients". Inspired
by this neoclassical
principle, he
established a
chronology of
ancient works of art
that became a
seminal source for art
historians.

Religious ceremonies were once again
celebrated in the underground basilicas,
attracting thousands of pilgrims. Pius
IX is seen here visiting the Crypt of the
Popes ▲ *326*.

SPADES AND PICKAXES
Seeing themselves as the heirs to the Roman Empire, the Fascists
exalted archeology. Their desire to renew the capital also destroyed
it: ancient Rome vanished under "the pickaxe of the regime".

THE ROMAN LANGUAGE

ORIGINS

Latin was spoken locally in Rome before it became the language of a huge state. It died when the civilization that disseminated it went into decline. By the end of the Empire the Latin spoken in the city had already undergone profound changes. The classical forms had already given way to the popular ones (low Latin) that were to lead to the so-called "vulgar" romance languages. Thus in a 9th-century church one reads graffiti used as reminders to the priests, such as: *Non dicere ille secrita a bboce* ("Do not repeat secrets out loud"). Two centuries later, a graffiti commentary was added to a picture of one of St Clement's miracles in the beautiful basilica that bears his name ▲ *193*; the commentary is in vulgar Latin with deeply plebeian

expressions, but the saint speaks on in classical Latin! "Romanesco" (the dialect of Rome) was already fixed in the 13th century, when the first literary texts began to appear. At that time it possessed the unmistakable characteristics of a central-southern Italian dialect. One finds, for instance, *quanno* for *quando* (when) with the *nd* = *nn* assimilation typical of central and southern Italy.

FLORENTINE VERSUS ROMAN

The 15th century saw the start of the most important linguistic process to have taken place in Rome since the decline of Latin. This process, known as the *seconda fase* ("second phase") or "Tuscanization" of the Roman language was to distinguish it from the other dialects of the region. The phenomenon was partly due to the growing prestige of the Florentine language and partly to the arrival in Rome of intellectuals and officials from Tuscany (among them Leon Battista Alberti, Enea Silvio Piccolomini and Pietro Bembo). Since many of them became members of the Curia, which was the cradle of all the most important cultural activity in Rome, Vatican documents from then on tended to be written in Tuscan or at least strongly imbued with it. Furthermore, the Sack of Rome in 1527 ● *36* marked the start of a major linguistic upheaval: already the home of many foreigners, the city was now overrun by refugees. It is estimated that in 1550 about 75 percent of Rome's population consisted of immigrants or children of immigrants. This situation helped the Florentine language to become the one used by the nobles. Rome thus lost the opportunity of giving a single language base to the whole of Italy.

ROME, THE OPEN CITY

The presence of many foreigners is still one of Rome's characteristics. Throughout the 20th century residents from the provinces have flooded into Rome, especially from central and southern Italy, and the Roman language is no longer

Signature of Cola di Rienzo.

perceived as a dialect. A large number of newspapers and magazines are produced in Rome, national television and radio are an important presence, and the cinema has made use of many Roman actors – such as Alberto Sordi, Vittorio Gassman, Anna Magnani, Aldo Fabrizi and Marcello Mastroianni, to name but a few. All these factors have contributed to making Roman speech less of a dialect and to the introduction of Roman expressions into current Italian usage. If you look at the works of Giuseppe Gioacchino Belli, Cesare Pascarella and Trilussa (Carlo Alberto Salustri) ▲ *363* the three greatest Roman-dialect poets, whose writings range from the beginning of the 19th century to the first half of the 20th – you will notice the progressive Italianization of their language. However, this has not prevented the survival of specifically Roman forms of speech and the development of a strictly local dialect, popularly called Romanaccio, spoken by the humbler classes. To give you an idea of it, *abbiamo* (we have) is *amo* in Romanaccio; *facciamo* (we make or do) is *famo*; *diciamo* (we say) is *dimo*; and *quello stupido* (that idiot) becomes *uoo stupido*.

THE GREAT ROMAN WRITERS
The greatest exponent of the use of Roman dialect in literature was Giuseppe Gioacchino Belli (1791–1863), who wrote more than two thousand sonnets. These form a prodigious fresco of the life of the humbler people of Rome and constitute an exceptional documentation of the Roman dialect of the time. Other Italian authors have successfully used Romanaccio, the most important and famous of these being Pier Paolo Pasolini (1922–75) and Carlo Emilio Gadda (1893–1973).

ANNA MAGNANI
Although when she made her début in the theater her strong personality attracted attention, Anna Magnani (1908–73) was only "discovered" by the Roman cinema in 1934. It then took her twelve years to achieve stardom, with Roberto Rossellini's *Roma, città aperta* (1945). Working with directors such as Visconti, Pasolini, Renoir and Cukor, she became without question one of the greatest Italian film actresses. The crowning reward of her career came with the Oscar she received in 1955 for her role in *The Rose Tattoo*.

43

● THE ROMAN LANGUAGE

ROMANESCO AND ITALIAN

Today Romanesco (the Roman language) is so widespread that it has deeply penetrated the Italian language, enriching it with a great number of words – such as *palazzinaro* (real-estate speculator), *benzinaro* (service-station attendant), *tassinaro* (taxi driver), *ragazzo/ragazza* (boy/girlfriend), *ragazzino* (child), *fasullo* (bogus, fake), *malloppo* (loot), *bustarella* (money offered as a bribe) and *fregarsene* (not to give a damn about something). Most of the swear words and strong language in modern Italian came from Romanesco – starting with *stronzo* (turd) – and mainly spread via the movies. Although the cosmopolitan character of the population of modern Rome has reduced the usage of Roman dialect in everyday life, popular songs have helped ensure its partial survival.

PLACE NAMES

The Roman dialect has often given places nicknames: the dome of St Peter's, for example, is currently dubbed *er cupolone*; Piazza della Rotonda (in front of the Pantheon) is called *a ritonna*; and the Palazzo di Giustizia is *er palazzacio*. In the historic center of Rome the street names of entire neighborhoods still recall the traditions and terminology of the Middle Ages – among them Via dei Chiavari (locksmiths' street), Via dei Giubbonari (tailors' street), Via dei Capellari (hatters' street), Via dei Pettinari (wool carders' street), Via dei Sediari (chair makers' street) and Via dei Coronari (goldsmiths' street).

FAMILY NAMES

Among typical Roman names, Proietti indicates a foundling in the family long ago; Orsini a link with the noble family of that name; Sargenti or Sargentini a military rank; Sbardella the job of ostler or groom; and Solfanelli a connection with an ancient craft that no longer exists.

"Most of all, I love watching the Roman urchins in the poor streets. Sprawling in dark doorways, young mothers are overrun by swarms of children, like tranquil bitches who let their sharp-toothed puppies play and fight all over them. The most beautiful are the most serious, with their luxuriant curly hair and long eyelashes, and a disdainful mouth above a small, mischievous chin."

Colette, *Nocturnes*

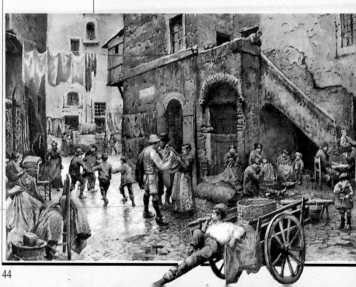

Arts and traditions

46 Legends and traditions
48 Festivals
50 The Order of Malta
52 Pontifical ceremonies
54 Restoration work
56 Food
58 Roman specialties

Rome had its share of oracles as well as ghosts, and in troubled times certain statues even began to "talk". It became customary, under the cover of nightfall, to post mocking epigrams, pamphlets and satires criticizing the government on these "talking statues". This practice, of Venetian origin, found fertile soil in the papal city, which was hardly renowned for its tolerant attitudes.

PASQUINADES
In the 16th century Aretino (1492–1556) had been forced to flee the city because of his satirical sonnets, or "pasquinades", written on the occasion of the election of the new pope. In the 18th century crimes of opinion were still severely punishable by the law, and one of Benedict XIII's edicts threatened "the death penalty, the confiscation of assets and the vilification of the name...of anyone who...writes, prints or distributes...libels of the kind known as pasquinades". However, the death penalty was rarely applied.

PASQUINO AND OTHERS
Several ancient statues were used for the posting of libels. Such was the fate of Pasquino (right) ▲ 279, who gave his name to these dissenting tracts but is in reality a fragment from a group depicting Menelaus and Patroclus. The Abate Luigi, thus named due to his resemblance to a ridiculous deformed sacristan of the Church of the Sudario, is actually a portrait of a Roman consul, magistrate or orator; and Marforio (above) is a representation of a river god.

CAGLIOSTRO AND LORENZA

It is said that on certain misty nights, a strange figure can be seen skirting the walls of the vicoli in Trastevere ▲ *349*, crossing Ponte Garibaldi and making its way to Piazza di Spagna. With a peel of sardonic laughter, the name "Lorenza!" then booms out. Could this not be the ghost of Lorenza Feliciani, who denounced her husband, Count Cagliostro, whose real name was Giuseppe Balsamo? After his arrest in Piazza di Spagna he was imprisoned in the San Leo fortress. Far from gaining her freedom, his wife was shut away in a Trastevere convent and conveniently forgotten.

THE BOCCA DELLA VERITÀ

Beneath the portico of Santa Maria in Cosmedin ▲ *155* there is the enormous face of a Triton, which came from a fountain. Its large mouth was thought in the Middle Ages to be the mouth of an oracle, but it was mainly used for submitting liars to the judgment of God. Forced to put their hand into the orifice, the innocent escaped unharmed while the guilty lost their hand. It is said that the judges may have "helped" God to pass judgment when they were convinced that the accused was guilty.

MADAMA LUCREZIA

This is the only female figure in the congregation of *spiriti arguti* ("witty spirits"), as the family of talking statues are called in Rome.

This gigantic female bust could be either the goddess Isis or Lucrezia, the very beautiful mistress of King Alfonso of Aragon.

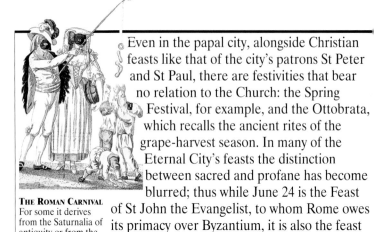

THE ROMAN CARNIVAL
For some it derives from the Saturnalia of antiquity or from the feasts dedicated to Sol Invictus of the late Empire. For others it is simply linked to the Christian calendar. It disappeared at the end of the 19th century when freedom of expression was stifled because of social unrest.

Even in the papal city, alongside Christian feasts like that of the city's patrons St Peter and St Paul, there are festivities that bear no relation to the Church: the Spring Festival, for example, and the Ottobrata, which recalls the ancient rites of the grape-harvest season. In many of the Eternal City's feasts the distinction between sacred and profane has become blurred; thus while June 24 is the Feast of St John the Evangelist, to whom Rome owes its primacy over Byzantium, it is also the feast of the summer solstice.

CARNIVAL REVELS AND DISGUISES

Revelers wore nose masks during the Roman Carnival, which ended with the Festa dei Moccoletti, when everyone tried to snuff out everyone else's candles. The smaller-scale Ronciglione Carnival has *nasi rossi* (red noses) instead.

THE FEAST OF SAN GIUSEPPE

This has become the feast of the Trionfale quarter, just behind St Peter's Basilica. Today the traditional stalls that sell deep-fried *bignè* (fritters) on March 19 compete with the traffic, parked cars and other stalls, which sell things all year round.

THE FEAST OF SAN GIOVANNI

Certain scholars link this feast to the grain-harvest festivals of antiquity, during which sacrifices were offered to Ceres. "On the eve one goes to St John the Lateran to pray and to eat snails … Outside the walls, near the Salita degli Spiriti, there was a witches' tavern where we would dine." (Gigi Zanazzo)

THE SPRING FESTIVAL

This is not so much a feast as a general decoration of the city each year in the month of April. The Spanish Steps are turned into a cascade of azaleas.

OTTOBRATA

...e 19th century ...rape harvests ...celebrated with ...s during which ...s in Romanesco ...were sung and *...altarello* was ...ed.

The eight points of the Maltese cross represent the eight Beatitudes. Also, eight powerful European states presided over the Order's creation, namely Provence, Auvergne, France, Italy, Aragon, England, Germany and Castile.

Rome is the only city in the world that can claim to be a capital three times over. Besides being the capital of Italy, it contains the Vatican State and the Sovereign Order of the Knights of Malta. Created to welcome and care for pilgrims arriving in the Holy Land, the Order of Hospitalers of St John of Jerusalem received papal recognition in 1113 and was given the task of defending the Holy Sepulcher by Calixtus II in 1120. Its original vocation thus became overlaid by a military function, like that of other orders of knighthood.

FROM JERUSALEM TO RHODES

First established in Jerusalem, the Order was transferred to St John of Acre in 1187. After being defeated by the Sultan of Egypt, it left the Holy Land and settled in Cyprus in 1290, then moved to Rhodes, which it captured in 1310.

FROM RHODES TO MALTA

Chased from Rhodes by Sultan Suleiman's Turks, in 1523 the Order petitioned the Pope for a new base and was granted Malta. This was confirmed in 1530 by a treaty between the Pope and Charles V. The Order exercised sovereignty over the island for several centuries.

FROM MALTA TO ROME

In 1798 Napoleon seized the island without opposition on his way to Egypt. Lacking a home, the Order moved to Russia and then various places in Italy before settling in Rome in 1834.

"IT TAKES A PIRATE AND A HALF TO BEAT A PIRATE!"

This was the rallying cry of the Order of the Knights of Malta, who reacted blow by blow to the Moorish and Turkish offensives. In fact, their methods and objectives were similar to those of the Barbary Coast pirates.

SOVRANO MILITARE ORDINE DI MALTA
POSTE MAGISTRALI

SOVRANO MILITARE ORDINE DI MALTA
POSTE MAGIST... 10 SCUDI

25 TARÌ

8 SCUDI

15 GRANI

375 GRANI

A JOY FOR PHILATELISTS
No stamp collector worth his salt can ignore Order of Malta issues.

A SOVEREIGN STATE
Although it has given up all hope of recovering its rule over Malta, since 1962 the Sovereign Order of Malta has succeeded in re-establishing stable and recognized institutions. Its headquarters at No. 68 Via Condotti and its property on the Aventine ▲ *180* are extraterritorial. Like the Vatican, the Order issues its own stamps and mints its own coins; it also has a diplomatic service and issues its own passports. Branches of the Order exist in some ninety countries.

A SYMBOLIC CURRENCY
The monetary system of the Order of Malta is founded on the scudo, which is worth 12 tari or 240 grani (1 scudo = $0.32, £0.17 or €0.24). Having lost the island of Malta in 1798, the Order could no longer issue this currency. In 1961, however, it started minting coins of gold, silver and bronze again, to the delight of numismatists.

51

The Pope is the Bishop of Rome and as successor to St Peter he is the head of the Christian community. He is assisted in this capacity by the Sacred College of cardinals (which elects and advises him), together with the Roman Curia, which embraces the Vatican's entire governmental organization. This includes the Congregations (like ministries, responsible for important issues), law courts (since the Pope has episcopal jurisdiction over all baptized Catholics), secretariats, commissions and other institutions.

L'ILLUSTRATION

SAMEDI 6 JANVIER 1886

HOLY YEARS
The Holy Door, the one on the extreme right of the five doors of the four major basilicas, is only opened every twenty-five years for the duration of the Holy Year (1975, 2000 and so on).

THE TIARA
This is the most obvious symbol of papal sovereignty. The long white stole worn by the Pope is also a symbol of his power.

PAPAL AUDIENCES
The Pope grants a general audience to pilgrims every Wednesday. This is held in the Papal Audience Hall built by Pier Luigi Nervi in 1974. Every Sunday at noon the Pope recites the Angelus and addresses all those present in Piazza San Pietro from a window in the apostolic palace. In the summer he does the same from a window of his summer residence in Castel Gandolfo.

THE "URBI ET ORBI" BLESSING
It is from the great central loggia of St Peter's that the Pope grants his blessing "Urbi et Orbi" (to the city and to the world).

THE "FISHERMAN'S RING"
At the pontifical enthronement, the master of ceremonies presents the Pope with the *anello piscatorio* (the "fisherman's ring"). The name of the ring alludes to the primacy granted, according to St John's Gospel, to St Peter, who had been a fisherman.

THE "SEDIA APOSTOLICA GESTATORIA"
This chair, which most probably dates from the 5th century and symbolizes the spiritual and the material supremacy of the head of the Church, was still used in 1978 by Pope John Paul I. In the past, the Pope used to make his way from the Sistine Chapel to St Peter's seated on this chair, preceded by the College of Cardinals and the pontifical court.

ELECTING A POPE
When the College of Cardinals goes into conclave to elect a new pope, they cast four votes a day. Only the smoke rising from the Sistine Chapel, where the voting takes place, provides an indication of the results. Black smoke means that no candidate has received the necessary two-thirds majority; white smoke indicates that a new pope has been elected.

"HABEMUS PAPAM"
The president of the Sacred College proclaims the election of a pope by pronouncing the hallowed formula "*Habemus papam*". Not long after, the new pontiff appears clad in white. His consecration takes place a few days later.

Today restoration work is based on scientific research. Sophisticated technologies are used to determine the state of preservation of a work of art and to discover the techniques that were used in creating it. Observations are carefully classified and analyzed by computers. After restoration, the details of the operation are recorded. All this data is filed for future reference in case further restoration is required at a later date. Methods such as these have been used for the many restoration operations carried out in Rome in recent years.

MARCUS AURELIUS' STATUE
Set in the middle of a busy piazza, this statue had been exposed to all the insidious effects of pollution, and its structure had been weakened by oxidation, corrosion, rain and vibrations. In addition, it had been damaged by earlier attempts at restoration.

Its recent restoration was carried out by the Istituto Centrale del Restauro. First, various analyses, including a thermal scan to determine degree of condensation were carried out. Its cleaning was a very delicate process because of the layer of gold leaf. Corrosive substances and particles deposited by the atmosphere had to be removed. Because of gold's incompatibility with anticorrosive treatments, the statue had to be protected by a film of acrylic resin before being placed in a protective glass case.

Before frescoes can be restored, chemical testing is required. Color samples are needed in order to determine which pigments were originally used, and to discover what parasitical materials have been deposited on the surface of the painting.

THE SISTINE CHAPEL

layers of greasy dust, soot from candles used in ceremonies and especially a film of animal glue had altered and seriously darkened the colors. Furthermore, certain figures had been retouched when this varnish was applied to protect them. Finally, the infiltration of rainwater from the roof had left whitish saline deposits on the ceiling. The restoration, carried out by Vatican experts, was undertaken when it was discovered that microclimatic variations were contracting the varnish in such a way that it was lifting the painted surface in certain places. The operations were minimal; in fact the main work consisted in cleaning the frescoes, for which the solvent AB 57 was used. The frescoes have now been restored to their original colors.

FONTANA DI TREVI

The fountain was suffering from static problems due to the materials from which it was made, and also from general degradation associated with a highly polluted environment (such as grained dirt and disintegration due to polluting agents).

In particular, it was covered with calcium deposits and algae formations. After general strengthening and cleaning work (sandblasting and ultrasound), plus localized biocidal cleansing, it was equipped with a water processing unit.

Roman cuisine combines the country cooking of Lazio and the Abruzzi region with popular culinary traditions featuring pasta, fresh and dried vegetables, salt cod, offal and pork. Although some of the recipes of antiquity have been handed down (mainly dishes blending sweet and savory flavors), the character of Roman cooking is largely due to the use of condiments (garlic, herbs and spices), sometimes combined with *pecorino* (a sharp sheep cheese), which give a delightful texture, taste and smell to even the simplest dishes.

2. Remove the toughest leaves and cut off the stems.

3. Using a small sharp knife, pare the artichokes into a conical shape.

7. Season them again with a little salt and let them simmer uncovered over low flame. When they are half done, turn the artichokes onto their sides.

6. Place the artichokes prepared in this way on their bases in a pan or dish. Cover with the glasses of water (according to the number of artichokes) and half a glass of olive oil.

> "A country's cuisine is the only reliable proof
> of its civilization."
>
> Marcel Rouff

INGREDIENTS
2 small artichokes per person, lemon juice, salt, pepper, garlic, *mentuccia* (fresh peppermint), 2 glasses of water, half a glass of olive oil.

1. Wash the peppermint and chop the garlic finely.

4. Trim the tips into a point and rub the artichokes all over with a little lemon juice to prevent them from discoloring.

5. Spreading the leaves of the artichokes slightly, insert the salt, pepper, garlic and peppermint leaves between them.

8. When they are cooked, serve them upright in a dish. If the liquid in which they have cooked has not thickened sufficiently, reduce it over a gentle flame. Serve them hot or cold, according to taste, accompanied by a white Castelli wine such as Frascati, Colli Albani or Velletri.

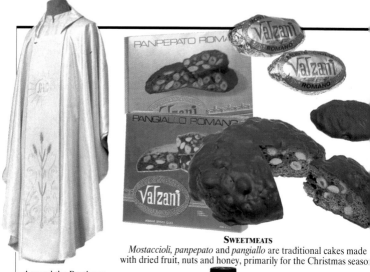

SWEETMEATS
Mostaccioli, panpepato and *pangiallo* are traditional cakes made with dried fruit, nuts and honey, primarily for the Christmas season.

Around the Pantheon and the Borgo Pio there are lots of small shops specializing in ecclesiastical clothing, rosaries and religious souvenirs.

SAMBUCA
A liqueur with an aniseed taste. Romans often float a coffee bean on the surface and light it for added flavor.

CASTELLI WINES
The vineyards of the Colli Albani, to the southeast of Rome, produce delicious white wines, the best known being Frascati.

JEWISH PASTRIES
A delicious combination of candied fruit, raisins and marzipan, these are only found in the patisseries of the Ghetto.

NEWSPAPERS IN ROME
Il Messaggero has a daily column in Romanesco (*Avventure in città*). Do not miss the Thursday edition of *La Repubblica*, which has a supplement (*Trovaroma*) listing the cultural events of the week to come.

"FIACCOLE"
On festive occasions these little lights flicker on Roman monuments.

Architecture

60 The development of the city
62 Building materials and techniques
64 Roman arches and vaults
66 Buildings for entertainment
68 Water in the ancient town
70 Temples and commemorative
    monuments
72 Medieval towers and dwellings
74 Churches of the Middle Ages
76 The Roman marble cutters
78 Counter-Reformation
    architecture
80 Churches: Baroque innovations
82 The art of "trompe l'oeil"
84 Baroque stage effects
86 Renaissance and Baroque palaces
88 Villas and gardens
90 Neoclassicism and eclecticism
92 Fascism and the postwar period
94 The classical orders

THE DEVELOPMENT OF THE CITY

The population of Rome has varied considerably – from a million in the 1st century AD, to 30,000 after the Sack of Rome, to almost three million today – and the size and shape of its inhabited area have not ceased to fluctuate. The town has survived the ravages of history with admirable continuity: the fourteen "regions" of Augustus' time formed the basis for the medieval and modern *rioni* (quarters), and the ancient aqueducts still feed its fountains.

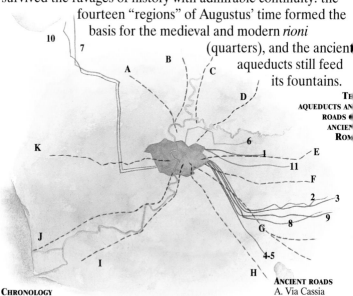

THE AQUEDUCTS AND ROADS OF ANCIENT ROME

CHRONOLOGY OF THE AQUEDUCTS
1. Aqua Appia, 312 BC
2. Anio Vetus, 272 BC
3. Aqua Marcia, 144 BC
4. Aqua Tepula, 125 BC
5. Aqua Iulia, 33 BC
6. Aqua Virgo, 19 BC
7. Aqua Alsietina, 2 BC
8. Aqua Claudia, 38–52 AD
9. Anio Novus, 38–52 AD
10. Aqua Traiana, 109 AD
11. Aqua Alexandriana, 226 AD

ROMAN AQUEDUCTS
"The aqueducts bring so much water to Rome … that almost every house has a great number of tanks, tubes and pipes." So wrote Strabo, the geographer, during the time of Augustus. At the beginning of the 2nd century AD their total capacity amounted to about 250,000 cubic gallons per day.

ANCIENT ROADS
A. Via Cassia
B. Via Flaminia
C. Via Salaria
D. Via Nomentana
E. Via Tiburtina
F. Via Prenestina
G. Via Latina
H. Via Appia
I. Via Ostiense
J. Via Portuense
K. Via Aurelia

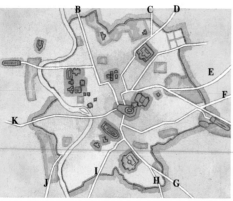

LEISURE AND ENTERTAINMENT ANCIENT ROME
As the political role of the people diminished, the emperor organized more facilities where leisure time could be spent, including porticos (covered walks), baths, and buildings where games were held (circus, theaters, amphitheaters, stadiums, odeons, etc.).

MEDIEVAL ROME

During the late Middle Ages, with the decrease in population, a major part of the area within the Aurelian Wall fell into disuse. The Vatican, fortified in 854, became the political and religious center. From the 10th century to the end of the 13th century, the inhabited area was concentrated around the Tiber as well as the Forum. In the 14th century catastrophes and epidemics decimated the population, but it soon increased again due to a surge of immigration.

THE TOWN PLANNING OF SIXTUS V

During the five years of his pontificate, with Domenico Fontana as his chief architect, Sixtus V (1585–90) implemented a huge urban plan which was to make Rome Europe's first modern city.

BUILDING UNDER SIXTUS V

The Pope had new palaces and religious buildings erected, constructed important roads such as the Via Felice, and created vast squares decorated with columns, fountains and obelisks.

ROME THE CAPITAL

1870: When Rome became the capital, there were only - 00,000 inhabitants.
1910: Its new role accelerated building activity. The city spread mainly eastward, and the popular neighborhood of Testaccio sprang up in the south.
1930: Rome's expansion gathered momentum. Suburbs developed far from the center, isolated in the countryside.
1960: The great parks were now the only areas free from buildings.

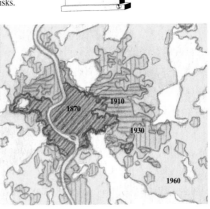

Roman architecture relied for a long time on the assembly of large quadrangular blocks, but masonry characterized by the difference between its facing materials and its internal composition appeared at an early date. The fill, or *opus caementicium*, made of rubble mixed with lime mortar, was highly resistant but rather ungainly. At first it was faced with *opus incertum*; then with *opus reticulatum*, which was soon replaced by *opus testaceum*, a brick facing rapidl adopted for all Roman walls.

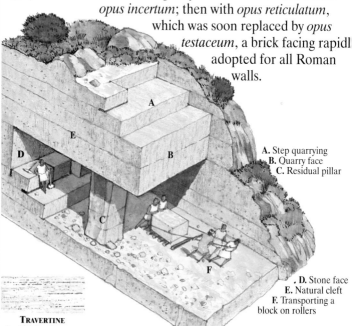

A. Step quarrying
B. Quarry face
C. Residual pillar
D. Stone face
E. Natural cleft
F. Transporting a block on rollers

TRAVERTINE
A whitish calcareous stone from the Tivoli area.

TUFA
A compound of volcanic rocks of varying colors.

QUARRYING FOR STONE
Once the soil covering the rock had been stripped away, the quarrymen scored the rough outline of the blocks on the stone so that, while it was being extracted, it could be hewn into the shape and size required by the architect.

A ROMAN LEWIS

HOIST
A winch operated by a lever was used to lift and position stones.

TECHNIQUES FOR TRANSPORTING AND POSITIONING THE BLOCKS

1. Tenons (projections) were left on the face of the stone so ropes could be attached.

2. Small cavities were carved symmetrically in the blocks so they could be lifted by GRIPS.

3. A dovetail cavity was sunk into the top of the block so a LEWIS could be inserted.

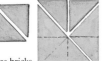

RICKS

andard square bricks
ere designed for the facing of *opus ementicium* walls. Lines were scored on em to facilitate their division into cing elements. Each one, depending on size, could be divided into two, four, eight or eighteen triangular cing bricks.

BRICK COLUMNS
The Romans even used bricks to build columns. They sometimes gave the columns a fluted appearance, and often coated them with stucco.

LIME KILNS
These were in the shape of a flattened cone built on a circular base. Above the combustion chamber stood a cone of heat-resistant bricks, with vents, over which the lime clay was placed. The kilns were fed with firewood and dry grasses through an opening in the base of the combustion chamber.

STAMPS
Roman tile and brick manufacturers marked their products by stamping the damp clay with a seal before it was fired. From the end of the 1st century AD and throughout the 2nd century the most common stamp was in the shape of a *lunula* (crescent).

Quick lime

Slaked lime

4
5
6

A
B
C

OPUS
1. Caementicium
2. Incertum
3. Quasi reticulatum
4. Reticulatum
5. Testaceum
6. Quadratum

OPUS MIXTUM
A. Corner reinforcements of large stone quoins.
B. Corner reinforcements of brick wall.
C. Brick wall with a travertine door frame.

● Roman Arches and Vaults

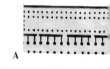

The major achievements of architecture in imperial Rome – diversifying forms and expanding the volume of interiors – are inseparable from the progress made in the design and construction of arches, vaults and cupolas. The most significant advance was the introduction of vaults built in *opus caementicium* together with the increased use of *opus testaceum*, which gave these vaults a strength and flexibility that allowed for unprecedented boldness. Once freed from the constraints of a system relying on rhythmic supports (columns and pillars), ancient classical architecture was able to create structures that contained the seeds of all the future developments of Christian and Islamic architecture.

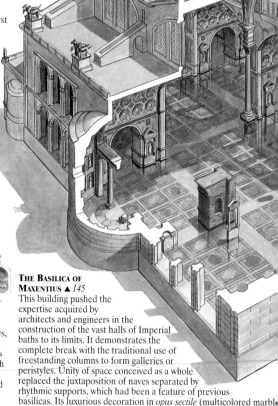

AN ARCHED BAY IN THE TABULARIUM
▲ *141*
This is one of the first examples of a rhythmic system to have a long-lasting effect. The vaulted architecture assumes the weight-bearing functions, while the noble order of the colonnade is used decoratively. Later this type of façade was frequently used for theaters and amphitheaters.

CROSS-SECTION OF THE BASILICA OF MAXENTIUS
As this section shows, the skylight with "thermal" windows (the arches of which echo those of the vaults) is supported by buttresses.

THE BASILICA OF MAXENTIUS ▲ *145*
This building pushed the expertise acquired by architects and engineers in the construction of the vast halls of Imperial baths to its limits. It demonstrates the complete break with the traditional use of freestanding columns to form galleries or peristyles. Unity of space conceived as a whole replaced the juxtaposition of naves separated by rhythmic supports, which had been a feature of previous basilicas. Its luxurious decoration in *opus sectile* (multicolored marble paving and paneling) has now disappeared.

C   D

THE ANCIENT BASILICAS

In the time of Augustus the system used for the Tabularium is adopted for the façades of the monumental Aemilia ▲ *136* (A) and Julia ▲ *141* (B) basilicas. The central nave of the Basilica Ulpia ▲ *165* (C), the largest ever built, was covered by a strong timbered roof; vaults constructed in *opus caementicium* spanned the full width of its great lateral exedras.

These were reinforced with metal struts embedded in the masonry.

The Basilica of Maxentius (D) exploited the full potential of the concrete vault: its inner volume, freed from the constraint of rows of columns, was able to expand into a vast area with exedras.

a

THE SUPPORT

A temporary support for vaults and arches was needed during construction. Consisting of at least two semicircular wooden frames strengthened with struts and trusses, the support would receive stone blocks or bricks (**a**), or poured cement and rubble (**b**).

1

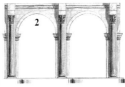

2

THE ARCHITRAVE AND THE ARCHIVOLT

From the 3rd century BC the Romans had been building weight-bearing arches using the classical architrave (**1**). This technique was soon to be replaced by the archivolt (**2**), which rapidly found an application in buildings of all types.

b

EXEDRA
Semicircular apse or portico, with seating.

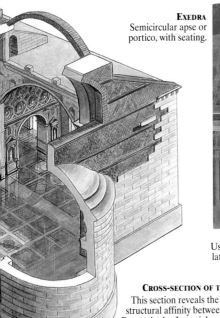

LATERAL EXEDRA
Used to buttress the pillars subject to lateral pressure from the main vault.

CROSS-SECTION OF THE BATHS OF CARACALLA ▲ *319*

This section reveals the structural affinity between Roman baths, Imperial reception halls and basilicas, although designed for very different purposes. They were all built according to a similar principle of weight distribution, due to the introduction of cement vaults and cupolas in the 2nd century AD.

● BUILDINGS FOR ENTERTAINMENT

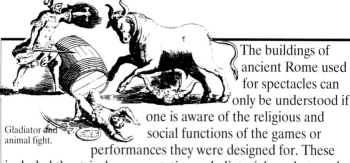

Gladiator and animal fight.

The buildings of ancient Rome used for spectacles can only be understood if one is aware of the religious and social functions of the games or performances they were designed for. These included theatrical representations, gladiatorial combats and chariot races, and most of them already existed in Rome before buildings were designed specifically for them. Although there had been dramatic art in Rome since the 3rd century BC, theaters as such were only built at the end of the Republic.

AMPHITHEATERS

These were a typically Roman invention. The elliptical (or nearly elliptical) shape of the arena enabled a vast crowd of spectators to watch a number of different gladiatorial combats taking place at the same time.

STRUCTURE

The eighty radial walls, the walkways, the stairs, the balcony, the half columns and the external arcades together serve as a shell for the enormous spread of the *cavea* (stone steps).

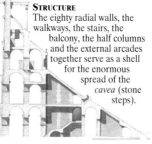

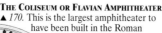

SEATS

The building contains two semicircular range of seats or *maenianae* facing each othe ("*theatrum*", like its Greek equivalent, means a place for spectators to sit).

THE COLISEUM OR FLAVIAN AMPHITHEATER

▲ 170. This is the largest amphitheater to have been built in the Roman world. Travertine pillars alternating with arches provide a solid frame for its walls made of brick, stone blocks and concrete. The carved blocks were assembled without mortar and secured with metal fixings. The whole structure is made up nearly identical modules (A) erected side by s

ACCESS

At ground level, arcades provided access to the different sections of the *cavea* (tiers of steps) allocated to the various social classes (A). In addition, movement inside the Coliseum was regulated by a complex network of ramps and corridors, while compulsory routes to reach assigned seats determined the entrance to be used. The "games" were thus an opportunity for Roman society to demonstrate its sense of hierarchy and cohesion.

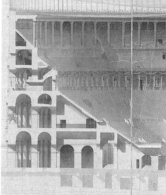

CIRCUSES

These were less costly structures than amphitheaters, and their technical requirements were more modest. The Circus Maximus and Circus Flaminius fulfilled an important role in the Rome of the 4th and 3rd centuries BC due to their link with the triumphal rituals.

CROSS-SECTION AND PLAN OF THE CIRCUS OF MAXENTIUS ▲ *328*
Circuses were built with a long, low central wall, the *spina* ▲ *178*, around which the chariots raced. Each end was marked by a turning point known as a *meta*.

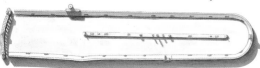

THEATERS

Roman theaters were modeled on theaters of the Hellenistic period in Sicily and southern Italy. But whereas the Greek theaters were left open, facing the natural landscape, with their *cavea* resting on the slope of a hill, Roman ones were enclosed buildings erected on architectural substructures with monumental stage fronts.

STAGE FRONT AND CROSS-SECTION OF POMPEY'S THEATER ▲ *248*

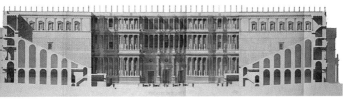

3

OUTER WALLS

In amphitheaters and theaters the external façade of the *cavea* consisted of superimposed arcades framed by engaged columns and separated by friezes.

4

The three lower levels of the Coliseum's façade are made up of (from the bottom) Tuscan Doric, Ionic and Corinthian columns. The fourth level is blind and is decorated with pilasters.

PLAN OF THE COLISEUM
These drawings show the internal and external structure.

PLAN OF MARCELLUS' THEATER ▲ *157*
The *cavea* of Roman theaters never went beyond a semicircle.

In Imperial times, Marcellus' theater served as a model for theaters in the Western Provinces.

● WATER IN THE ANCIENT TOWN

The control and regular distribution of water to large cities was one of Rome's most remarkable urban innovations. Nothing brought a more radical modification to lifestyles than the abundance of running water in towns, with all the public and private infrastructures this implied. Roman engineers were not the inventors of aqueducts, but the challenges Rome had to face in order to harness sometimes quite remote water sources gave rise to the construction of some remarkable buildings.

"CASTELLUM DIVISORIUM" (WATER TOWER)
This enabled water to be distributed within the town. A circular basin was constructed to receive the water, through a grating, from the aqueduct. Lead piping carried the water from the basin to different parts of the town.

PIPES
Water pipes were generally made out of lead sheets rolled around a caliber and welded with a lead seal secured by a strip of clay. The Roman architects Vitruvius and Frontinus established precise standards for their calibration.

BATHS
In the *tepidaria* and *caldaria* the floor and the bottom of the swimming pools were supported by small terracotta pillars around which air heated by an oven could circulate. This space was called the *hypocaustum*. Beneath the marble facing of the walls a very thick coating of cement covered rectangular ceramic piping (*tubuli*), which served as vents for hot air or steam.

CROSS-SECTION OF AN AQUEDUCT

From the spring (*sorgente*) to the *castellum divisorium*, raised sections with arches alternated with underground sections. The latter could be maintained and examined through inspection vents (*lumina*) at regular intervals. Settling sumps (*piscinae liminariae*) allowed the water of the *specus*, as the channel of the aqueduct was called, to be purified before it reached the town. Steep dips in the terrain were traversed by means of siphons, but generally the aim was, wherever possible, to avoid supplying water under pressure.

A. *Sorgente* (spring)
B. *Lumina* (inspection vents)
C. *Piscina liminaria* (settling sump)
D. *Sifone rovescio* (siphon)
E. *Castellum divisorium* (water tower)

PUBLIC FOUNTAINS

These were rarely more than 260 feet apart, so that no one ever lived more than 130 feet away from one. The lead supply pipe came up through a stone fixed in the sidewalk and flowed into a basin made of stone slabs set in the street.

"DOMUS"

This Pompeian *domus* is a good example of a sophisticated house with an *atrium* and a peristyle laid out as a garden.

"INSULA"

This *insula* ▲ *410* in Ostia is one of the most remarkable examples of a large multistoried apartment building with a staircase that opens on to a central courtyard with arcades. It has the unusual feature of a thermal bath connected to it for the use of residents.

It was situated opposite a public fountain and possessed an *impluvium* (1), or cistern, for the collection of rainwater. Some houses were even equipped with running water and had a decorative fountain in the peristyle (2).

THE DISPOSAL OF WASTE WATER

Not all Roman towns had a network of underground sewers. In Rome the main sewer, the *cloaca maxima* ▲ *156*, which is very ancient, remained an open sewer for a long time. It permitted all the water in the city to be drained into the Tiber.

THE TROPHIES OF MARIUS
These figures displayed reproductions of arms and armor stripped from Rome's enemies as a symbol of victory.

In Rome, as in all the great cities of the Empire, the religious buildings gave the urban landscape a sense of order and hierarchical significance. They were the richest and most diverse buildings in the whole array of ancient monuments. Triumphal arches, which were another characteristic of Roman towns, stood at each of the key points in the metropolis. Great mausoleums also adorned the city, commemorating the emperors as if they were Hellenistic sovereigns.

ETRUSCAN TEMPLES
The most ancient temples belonged to the Italo-Etruscan tradition, of which the venerable Temple of Jupiter Capitolinus ▲ 128 was the best example. Three halls of worship (*cellae*) opened onto a deep portico with widely spaced columns.

QUADRANGULAR TEMPLES OF HELLENIC ORIGIN
These made use of all the Greek architectural resources in an essentially decorative form, as can be seen in the Temple of Portunus ▲ 155.

ROUND TEMPLES
The Temple of Vesta ▲ 155 in the Forum Boarium is the oldest instance in Rome of an entirely Greek design (the *tholos periptera*).

TRIUMPHAL ARCHES
The most striking examples of these symbols of Rome's military supremacy have three bays, like the Arch of Constantine ▲ 169. This displays all the traditional signs of solemnity: the bays are framed by Corinthian columns on pedestals, a high attic crowns the whole structure, and every available space is decorated with reliefs.

A. Plan of the Temple of Jupiter Capitolinus.

 B. Plan of the Temple of Portunus.

 C. Plan of the Temple of Venus and Rome.

 D. Plan of the Temple of Vesta.

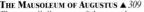

THE MAUSOLEUM OF AUGUSTUS ▲ 309

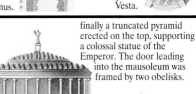

The overall diameter of the tumulus was about 285 feet. It had three levels: a vast cylindrical podium planted as a "sacred forest", the cylindrical drum of the mausoleum itself surrounded by a colonnade, and finally a truncated pyramid erected on the top, supporting a colossal statue of the Emperor. The door leading into the mausoleum was framed by two obelisks.

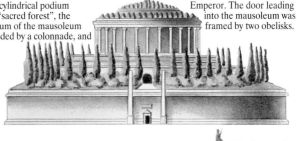

THE "CELLAE"
Porphyry, polychrome marbles and gilded coffers adorned the *cellae*.

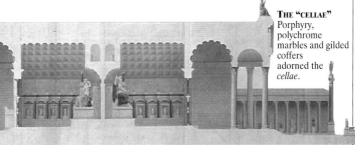

THE TEMPLE OF VENUS AND ROME ▲ 146
This double sanctuary was made up of two temples placed back to back along a longitudinal axis. It was the largest religious building in the Graeco-Roman world.

THE PLAN OF THE PANTHEON
The vast rotunda is preceded by a great quadrangular portico (*pronaos*) with sixteen majestic columns.

THE INTERIOR OF THE PANTHEON ▲ 264
The monumental rigor of this building is due to the harmonious juxtaposition of two simple geometrical figures: the cylinder and the hemisphere.

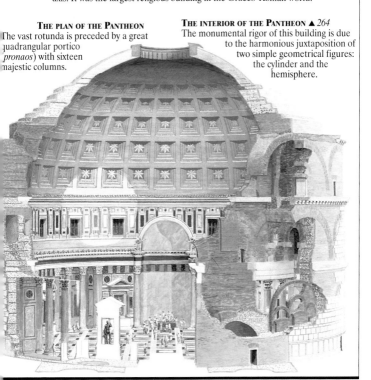

MEDIEVAL TOWERS AND DWELLINGS

During the 11th and 12th centuries the Roman nobility developed an architectural idiom that combined fortifications, towers and ramparts with dwellings. Palaces, surrounded by the houses of relatives and servants, and towers (the military scope of which soon became merely emblematic), were the homes of the grandees until the end of the Middle Ages.

CASA DEI CRESCENZI
This house was built in the 11th century by Nicolò di Crescenzio with a view to "reviving the ancient setting of Rome", as an inscription set above the door proclaims. It is a good example of the reuse of classical architectural and decorative materials and elements within the medieval, domestic, architectural idiom.

TORRE ANGUILLARA ▲ *356*
This 13th-century tower in Trastevere was rebuilt around 1455. Its crenelations are the product of a 19th-century restoration.

THE TOMB OF CECILIA METELLA
▲ *330* Certain tombs on the Via Appia were used as foundations for medieval fortifications.

THE FORTIFICATION OF THE MAUSOLEUM
The Tomb of Cecilia Metella is a vast two-floored structure. In 1302 it was turned into a gigantic dungeon by Pietro Caetani. The Ghibelline crenelations were added at that time. However, its spacious balcony and broad windows make this fortress less severe.

TORRE DELLE MILIZIE ▲ *168*
This very tall tower, the symbol of "Roma turrita", was erected at the beginning of the 13th century on the ruins of Trajan's market. The 1348 earthquake destroyed its upper floors.

TORRE DEI CAPOCCI
This was built in the 13th century as a part of one of the largest fortified complexes, using building materials and bricks from

A MEDIEVAL TOWN HOUSE
The house standing at No. 14 Via dell'Atleta (a delightful street in Trastevere ▲ *353*) is one of the best examples of Roman medieval architecture. Its brick and tufa-rubble façade is adorned with a loggia with a twin arcade supported by marble columns, while above, a frieze of smaller ogival arches rests on travertine corbels.

PLAN OF THE FORTIFIED COMPLEX
The Tomb of Cecilia Metella was surrounded by a rectangular wall originally buttressed by sixteen protruding quadrangular guard towers. It extended over both sides of the Via Appia, which it controlled. The layout of the buildings within these battlements indicates the degree to which the highway had been "privatized", with the castle on one side of the road and its chapel, San Nicola da Bari, on the other.

A STRATEGIC POSITION
Many ancient monuments that were turned into citadels in the Middle Ages had strategic advantages. The Tomb of Cecilia Metella afforded control over an important route into the city.

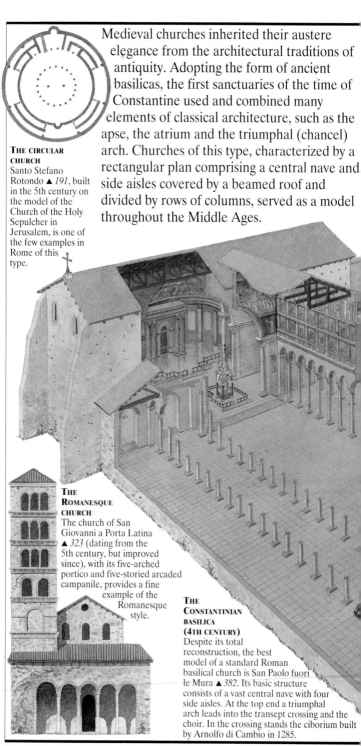

Medieval churches inherited their austere elegance from the architectural traditions of antiquity. Adopting the form of ancient basilicas, the first sanctuaries of the time of Constantine used and combined many elements of classical architecture, such as the apse, the atrium and the triumphal (chancel) arch. Churches of this type, characterized by a rectangular plan comprising a central nave and side aisles covered by a beamed roof and divided by rows of columns, served as a model throughout the Middle Ages.

THE CIRCULAR CHURCH
Santo Stefano Rotondo ▲ *191*, built in the 5th century on the model of the Church of the Holy Sepulcher in Jerusalem, is one of the few examples in Rome of this type.

THE ROMANESQUE CHURCH
The church of San Giovanni a Porta Latina ▲ *323* (dating from the 5th century, but improved since), with its five-arched portico and five-storied arcaded campanile, provides a fine example of the Romanesque style.

THE CONSTANTINIAN BASILICA (4TH CENTURY)
Despite its total reconstruction, the best model of a standard Roman basilical church is San Paolo fuori le Mura ▲ *382*. Its basic structure consists of a vast central nave with four side aisles. At the top end a triumphal arch leads into the transept crossing and the choir. In the crossing stands the ciborium built by Arnolfo di Cambio in 1285.

At Santa Sabina ▲ 179 the twenty-six windows in the nave and three in the apse let in abundant light, which is filtered through panes of selenite (a type of gypsum) held in frames composed of elaborate geometrical shapes.

ARCHITRAVES AND CAPITALS
The redeployment of Corinthian capitals and of friezes with intricate plant motifs, used as architraves, brought classical perfection into Christian buildings.

CUSHIONED CAPITALS
The cushioned capitals of Santa Maria Antiqua ▲ 142 reflect the oriental influence apparent in Roman art from the 6th to the 7th centuries.

THE SPATIAL ORGANIZATION OF A CHRISTIAN BASILICA
Each of these has a narthex in the form of a portico reserved for catechumens and penitents, who were not allowed to enter the sanctuary.

The major basilicas have a quadrangle with a colonnade, known as the *paradisus*, which was conceived as a transition between the public and sacred areas. Inside, one's gaze is focused on the end of the nave by the brilliant mosaics in the apse. The choir, which is divided from the nave by a rail, to indicate that it is reserved for the clergy, encloses the altar.

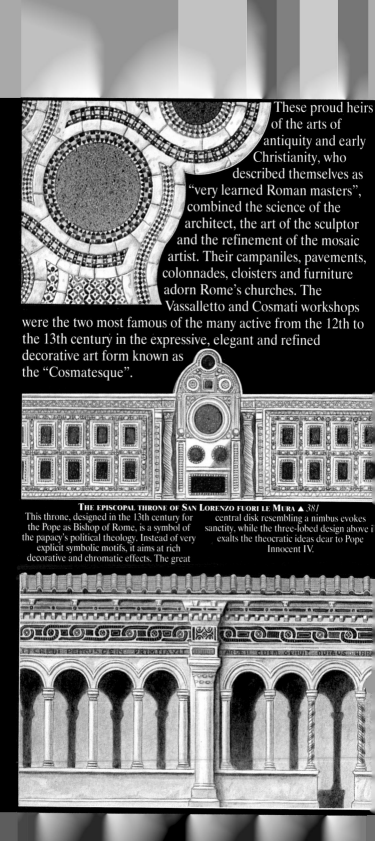

These proud heirs of the arts of antiquity and early Christianity, who described themselves as "very learned Roman masters", combined the science of the architect, the art of the sculptor and the refinement of the mosaic artist. Their campaniles, pavements, colonnades, cloisters and furniture adorn Rome's churches. The Vassalletto and Cosmati workshops were the two most famous of the many active from the 12th to the 13th century in the expressive, elegant and refined decorative art form known as the "Cosmatesque".

THE EPISCOPAL THRONE OF SAN LORENZO FUORI LE MURA ▲ 381
This throne, designed in the 13th century for the Pope as Bishop of Rome, is a symbol of the papacy's political theology. Instead of very explicit symbolic motifs, it aims at rich decorative and chromatic effects. The great central disk resembling a nimbus evokes sanctity, while the three-lobed design above it exalts the theocratic ideas dear to Pope Innocent IV.

DETAIL OF INLAID FRIEZE IN THE CLOISTER OF SAN PAOLO FUORI LE MURA
Polychrome decorations, geometrical designs and mosaics emphasize the architectural features, which glitter with marble, porphyry and serpentine taken from the ruins of antiquity.

COLUMNS FROM THE CLOISTER OF SAN PAOLO FUORI LE MURA
The Roman marble cutters explored every possibility in the decoration of columns, ranging from the rectilinear to the twisted and entwined, enhancing their rhythm with inlaid patterns.

THE CLOISTER OF SAN PAOLO FUORI LE MURA ▲ 382
This cloister, probably designed by one of the Vassalletti, is among the great architectural and decorative achievements of the 13th century in Rome. Each of its four galleries consists of four or five arcades separated by pilasters topped by a pseudo-Corinthian capital.

CARVED MARBLE PASCHAL CANDELABRA

● COUNTER-REFORMATION ARCHITECTURE

Coat of arms of the order of Jesuit fathers.

The rapid development of religious architecture was given a further impetus by the Council of Trent (1545–63), under the militant leadership of newly founded Orders such as the Society of Jesus (the Jesuits). The perfection of the centrally planned church was renounced in reconciling it with the Latin-cross layout, which was better suited to the Church's new liturgical priority: the promotion of preaching. The design of the Gesù, the building of which began in 1568, was based on the total integration of the nave, transept and choir. In the 17th century, church architecture also reaped the benefits of Bernini, Cortona and Borromini's liberating experiments with curves and dynamic effects.

THE GESÙ
▲ 257
For the Jesuits' first large church, Vignola adapted a layout made famous by Alberti's Church of Sant'Andrea, in Mantua. He set off the vast nave with a huge cupola, abundantly lit by the bays in the drum. The wide nave blends into a non-protruding transept, creating a grandiose space of spectacular unity that contributes greatly to the effect of services and sermons by emphasizing the majesty of the choir. The church's minimal decorations – marble altars and frescoes on the cupola and pendentives – were copiously enriched at the end of the 17th century.

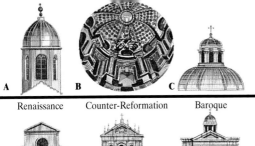

Renaissance   Counter-Reformation   Baroque

A   B   C

B. SANT'IGNAZIO
▲ *261* The layout and façade of the Gesù were virtually copied when this church was constructed in 1626. Only its lavish decorations distinguished it from its model, built in the austere spirit of the Counter-Reformation, before the innovations of the 17th century.

C. SANT'ANDREA AL QUIRINALE ▲ *296*
In this small elliptical church Bernini developed elegant dynamic effects by means of contrasting curves and the tension created by his use of limited space.

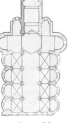

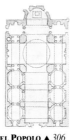

A. SANTA MARIA DEL POPOLO ▲ *306*
This church's ground plan in the shape of a Latin cross and its façade divided into three sections reflect the internal layout of a nave with two aisles, reminiscent of the pure Renaissance style of Santa Maria Novella in Florence, the façade of which was designed by Alberti in 1458.

THE FAÇADE OF THE GESÙ
In the rational tradition of the early Renaissance, Giacomo Della Porta's façade, with its two levels linked by consoles, reflects the interior layout of the church. Three doors open into the single nave. The lateral sections contain chapels. This particular feature is echoed on the first level by the grouping of the pilasters and the projection of the columns supporting the main door's double pediment. The longitudinal axis is thus emphasized.

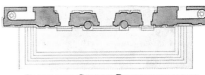

PROFILE OF A COUNTER-REFORMATION FAÇADE
Unlike later, Baroque churches, the Gesù has a flush façade with only slight projections.

THE PANTHEON ▲ *264*
This cupola (2nd century AD) became the model for the "concrete vault". The extrados (outer surface) serves as a complete covering.

While Bernini and Borromini shared the same classical and Renaissance background and pursued a similar goal in seeking to give life to the principles of composition, they differed in their manner of interpreting these traditions – the one theatrical and the other architectural.

The cupola, or dome, was the essential element in the new challenges of religious architecture and underwent unprecedented variations in this period.

THE CUPOLA OF SANT'IVO
The drum supports a stepped cupola surmounted by a lantern at the apex of powerful ribs. A spiral enhances the upward movement.

SANT'IVO ALLA SAPIENZA ▲ *272*
In Borromini's masterpiece, begun in 1642, the dynamic tension generated by the contrasting concave and convex surfaces is brought to a climax. Externally the hexagonal drum appears even more powerful because it inverts the design of the façade, whose curve is extended by the two arcades of the courtyard. Inside, six apses facing each other in pairs, in accordance with the building's interplay of contrasts, reveal the star-shaped ground plan.

The papal emblems of the *monti* decorate the parapet of the façade.

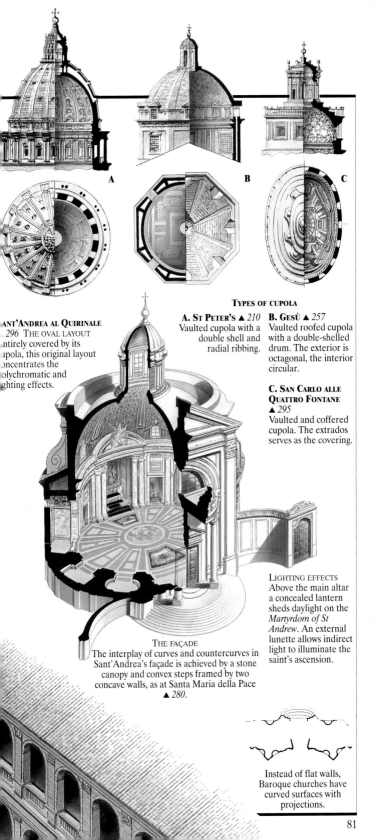

TYPES OF CUPOLA

A. ST PETER'S ▲ *210*
Vaulted cupola with a double shell and radial ribbing.

B. GESÙ ▲ *257*
Vaulted roofed cupola with a double-shelled drum. The exterior is octagonal, the interior circular.

C. SAN CARLO ALLE QUATTRO FONTANE ▲ *295*
Vaulted and coffered cupola. The extrados serves as the covering.

SANT'ANDREA AL QUIRINALE ▲ *296* THE OVAL LAYOUT entirely covered by its cupola, this original layout concentrates the polychromatic and lighting effects.

LIGHTING EFFECTS
Above the main altar a concealed lantern sheds daylight on the *Martyrdom of St Andrew*. An external lunette allows indirect light to illuminate the saint's ascension.

THE FAÇADE
The interplay of curves and countercurves in Sant'Andrea's façade is achieved by a stone canopy and convex steps framed by two concave walls, as at Santa Maria della Pace ▲ *280*.

Instead of flat walls, Baroque churches have curved surfaces with projections.

Preparatory cartoon showing the *trompe l'oeil* effect on a squared surface, with a central vanishing point.

In the 17th century many Roman ceilings were covered with princely apotheoses, celestial glories and *quadrature* (painted architectural elements). Cupolas reveal Baroque cloud formations that sweep architecture, paintings and sculptures up into their luminous vortex. One of the most spectacular masterpieces of this art of illusion, the absolute mastery of the rules of perspective, is the Church of Sant'Ignazio ▲ *261*, where Andrea Pozzo painted a *trompe l'oeil* cupola and, in the nave, a magnificent fresco in which earthly architecture seems to reach heavenly heights.

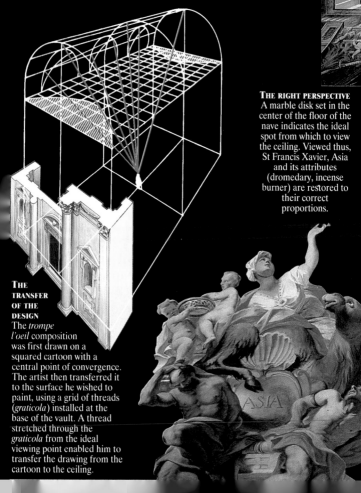

THE RIGHT PERSPECTIVE
A marble disk set in the center of the floor of the nave indicates the ideal spot from which to view the ceiling. Viewed thus, St Francis Xavier, Asia and its attributes (dromedary, incense burner) are restored to their correct proportions.

THE TRANSFER OF THE DESIGN
The *trompe l'oeil* composition was first drawn on a squared cartoon with a central point of convergence. The artist then transferred it to the surface he wished to paint, using a grid of threads (*graticola*) installed at the base of the vault. A thread stretched through the *graticola* from the ideal viewing point enabled him to transfer the drawing from the cartoon to the ceiling.

GENERAL VIEW OF THE CEILING
The swarms of figures in this composition could only be included thanks to the false architectural perspective, which blends naturally into this sublime apotheosis of the Jesuit Missionary Order.

THE PROJECTION OF A CIRCLE
One might perhaps guess that to create the illusion of perfect circles Pozzo had to paint vertical ovals, and that the seemingly gigantic columns are only a few inches tall.

DISTORTED VISION
If you move away from the ideal viewpoint, all this beauty becomes distorted and seems to be in danger of an eternal fall.

Bernini (1598–1680) defined unity as the harmony of opposit rather than as static composition. Because they shared a common theatrical purpose, different arts came together in h conception of architecture to create a dramatic effect that demanded the faithful participate as spectators. Indeed his ai was to convince people of the truth of the Faith and the grandeur of Rome by making full use of the ambiguities produced by a rhetorical ordering of space, light and figurativ elements.

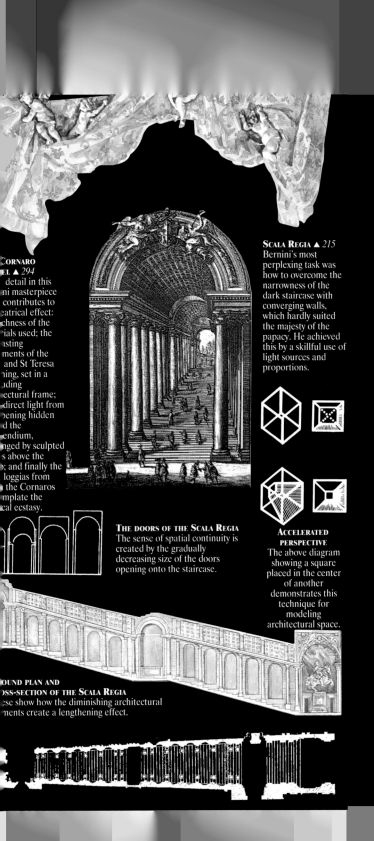

**CORNARO
...EL ▲ 294**
... detail in this
...ni masterpiece
... contributes to
...eatrical effect:
...chness of the
...rials used; the
...asting
...ments of the
... and St Teresa
...ning, set in a
...uding
...ectural frame;
... direct light from
...pening hidden
...d the
...endium,
...nged by sculpted
...s above the
...; and finally the
... loggias from
... the Cornaros
...mplate the
...cal ecstasy.

SCALA REGIA ▲ 215
Bernini's most
perplexing task was
how to overcome the
narrowness of the
dark staircase with
converging walls,
which hardly suited
the majesty of the
papacy. He achieved
this by a skilful use of
light sources and
proportions.

THE DOORS OF THE SCALA REGIA
The sense of spatial continuity is
created by the gradually
decreasing size of the doors
opening onto the staircase.

**ACCELERATED
PERSPECTIVE**
The above diagram
showing a square
placed in the center
of another
demonstrates this
technique for
modeling
architectural space.

**...OUND PLAN AND
...OSS-SECTION OF THE SCALA REGIA**
...ese show how the diminishing architectural
...nents create a lengthening effect.

Following the example of the popes, during the Renaissance Roman nobles and cardinals began to build grandiose palaces that were symbols of the power they wielded in the city. Not all of these possess the austere grandeur of Palazzo Farnese – their principal model – but from the 15th to the 17th centuries they generally followed a similar layout: a quadrilateral building with a central *cortile* (courtyard) surrounded by a gallery with arcades. Their façades testify to the rigorous approach of Roman architects.

THE CANCELLERIA ▲ 249. The highly rational character of this masterpiece of Renaissance architecture (1483–1513), long thought to have been designed by Bramante and whose proportions respect the Golden Section, should not make one overlook its innovative elements, such as the use of corner bay extensions to maximize the building's horizontal potential.

THE CLASSICAL ORDERS ▲ 94
In the courtyard of Palazzo Farnese the three classical orders, Doric, Ionic and Corinthian, are displayed in the superimposed arcades as in the Coliseum. Precise proportional ratios govern these architectural features.

Doorway, by the architect Serlio (1475–1554), making use of the Golden Section.

PALAZZO FARNESE ▲ 244
Modeled on the Florentine tradition, Antonio da Sangallo's design featured a quadrangular ground plan and an austere façade without columns, adorned only by alternating window pediments and moldings. Inside, on the other hand, the vestibule with high coffered vaulting and the original elevation of the courtyard (1513–46) recall the architecture of ancient Rome.

THE STUCCOWORK ON THE FAÇADE OF PALAZZO SPADA

The exuberant ornamental effects contrast with the rigorous classicism of the façade's overall design. The Mannerist richness of these stucco decorations (1556–60) is possibly the first Roman emulation of de Rosso's inventive moldings at Fontainebleau.

PALAZZO SPADA ▲ 246
PALAZZO SPADA
The façade of this palazzo, built at the very beginning of the Counter-Reformation period, has a strictly classical design with bossage decorations between the *piano nobile* and the attic.

BAROQUE WINDOW
The dynamics of this window by Carlo Maderno in Palazzo Barberini are due to the interplay of light and shade and to a hint of perspective worthy of Bernini.

THE LAYOUT OF PALAZZO FARNESE

The main entrance leads to an inner courtyard, from which a grand staircase provides access to the *piano nobile*. The reception rooms are on this floor. The ground floor rooms are reserved for household services, while the upper floors and the loggia contain the living quarters.

ATTIC WINDOW IN PALAZZO BARBERINI
▲ 291. This early work by Borromini includes all the elements of his mature style: the dynamics of the details create a strange tension in a window that has an otherwise classical design.

The villa, which had been a major feature of classical architecture, came into its own again in Florence a little before 1500. But it was in Rome, inspired by ancient examples such as Hadrian's Villa and Pliny's descriptions, that the ideal constructions of the humanist period were built. Bramante's Belvedere, Raphael's Farnesina and Villa Madama and Vignola's Villa Giulia and Villa Caprarola were designed as refined places of *otium*, or contemplative leisure, and were soon imitated all over Europe. Their terraces, loggias and belvederes provided viewpoints from which to gaze at an exalted vision of Nature with which Man fell in perfect harmony.

THE CORTILE DEL BELVEDERE IN THE VATICAN (C. 1505)
This courtyard ▲ *214* was designed as a terraced garden. Its lowest level could be used for a variety of entertainments, particularly aquatic jousting tournaments.

VILLA FARNESINA (1509–10)
▲ *360* Built for Agostino Chigi by Peruzzi, a Tuscan who did not share Bramante's and Raphael's passion for archeology, this became one of the Farnese properties. It was one of Rome's first suburban Renaissance villas.

GROUND PLAN OF THE FARNESINA
The loggia with two projecting wings and the division between winter reception rooms facing south and other living rooms facing north, as well as the painted *trompe l'oeil* perspectives overlooking vast landscapes, were all standard in subsequent villas.

VILLA D'ESTE (1560–C. 1570) ▲ *392*
Like many other villas, this one stands on the slope of a hill, all the better to dominate its wonderful gardens and to view the entire western horizon. The steepness of the ground also ensured a constant water supply to the fountains and offered the visitor, who originally entered the property from below, a carefully stage-managed approach to the building. The walk through these enchanting gardens, quite unlike traditional geometrical parterres, was conceived as a journey of discovery, with innumerable paths winding through coppices, grottoes and nymphaeums.

VILLA MEDICI (C. 1564–75) ▲ 315
This was built on the site of the gardens of
...cullus for Cardinal Ricci di Montepulciano
and was later embellished by Cardinal
...erdinando de' Medici. Today's inner façade

was originally the villa's main entrance. Its
principal features are its grandiose porch
loggia, overlooking the gardens, and the
abundance of classical decorations, which
make it look like a Roman triumphal arch.

THE SITE OF VILLA D'ESTE
...he steep slope of the hill determined both the internal layout of the
...uildings and the landscaping of the gardens, in a spirit characteristic
of the transition from the Renaissance to the Baroque. Many
travelers, from Montaigne to Liszt, praised this villa's charms.

DIANA OF EPHESUS
This copy of a
classical statue
from the
Farnese
collection,
portraying the
goddess of nature,
is the key element in
one of the Villa
d'Este's fountains.

**THE FOUNTAINS
OF THE VILLA
D'ESTE**
By following the
paths criss-crossing
the gardens (the only
way to go) visitors will
discover the Fontana
dell'Organo Idraulico and
the Rometta ("little
Rome") fountain. This

ballet of water, greenery,
masks and statues takes
place under the watchful
eye of Mother Earth, with
her thousand breasts, in a
blend of learned classical
iconographic references to
the myth of Hercules, the
legendary founder of the
Este family, and to the
garden of the Hesperides.

It was not until the French occupation, in 1808, that the neoclassical style established itself in Rome. Later, with the build-up to the unification of Italy in 1861, or even before, a debate began over the "national style", which led to a period of eclecticism and a revival of earlier architectural idioms. The neo-Renaissance style rapidly came to the fore in both private and public buildings, while "Liberty" (Italian Art Nouveau) also became popular and Neoclassicism survived in a rather ponderous and bastardized form. Cast iron and glass, however, was rarely used in the architecture of the city.

PIAZZA DEL POPOLO AND THE PINCIO (1813–20)
Giuseppe Valadier (1762–1839), the great neoclassical architect of Rome, was responsible for terracing the Pincio ▲ *316* and for the layout of the two semicircular areas of Piazza del Popolo ▲ *306*.

THE BOCCONI BUILDING (RINASCENTE) ▲ *267*
The façade of this neo-Renaissance building (1885–7) highlights the use of glass. Inside, cast-iron columns support the various floors, which overlook a vast central space, in conformity with the conventional design of European department stores.

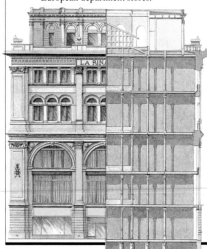

GALLERIA SCIARRA (1885–6) ▲ *301*
The design of this *galleria* of shops, with its Liberty frescoes influenced by Pompeian and pre-Raphaelite paintings, had to overcome the problem of how to provide light. Its architect, Giulio de Angelis, made use of cast-iron structures to lighten the whole ensemble and support a glazed roof.

TESTACCIO ▲ *184*

In this popular area built at the beginning of the 20th century, the apartment blocks lining the streets were given large open courtyards. The idea was to allow air to circulate around the blocks and to relieve the solid monotony of the façades.

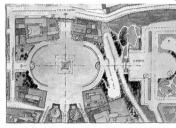

The layout of Piazza del Popolo and the Pincio as they are today.

THE VITTORIANO (1885–1911) ▲ *160*

This weighty symbol of post-Unification monumental architecture is a supreme example of the mixture of styles prevailing at the end of the 19th century. Basically a neoclassical project, it has its roots in the Hellenistic tradition, as much through its use of white marble as through its grandiose composition of colonnades and steps, recalling the altar in Pergamon or the temple in Praeneste ▲ *402*. A rather heavy neo-Realist statue of the king was added before the completion of the planned sculpted decorations, which are much more in the symbolist vein.

The Vittoriano's appearance earned it the nickname of "the typewriter".

● FASCISM AND THE POSTWAR PERIOD

Fascist architecture has a dual
nature. Mussolini's regime was a
blend of the most modern trends with a nostalgia
for Rome's glorious past. Both rationalism and historical
references were therefore encouraged in architecture by the
Fascists, who saw them as a means of pleasing everyone. The
return to classical antiquity was suited to the staging of mass
rallies, while the rationalist style seemed ideal for housing
developments and functional buildings. It is from the rationalist
movement that most postwar architecture evolved.

SAN PIETRO E PAOLO, EUR (1938–55) ▲ 388

✝ This church with strictly geometrical
volumes, built by Arnaldo Foschini, is
designed in the shape of a Greek cross
and was modeled on the churches of
the Renaissance. Its vast dome
(over 235 feet), decorated with
coffers and resting on a drum with
oculi, is a reference to the styles
of classical antiquity.

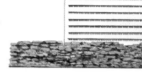

PALAZZO DELLA CIVILTÀ DEL LAVORO, EUR (1938–43) ▲ 387

This is one of the finest monuments of the rationalist school
designed for the Universal Exhibition of 1941–2 ▲ 386. It was
built by the architects Giovanni Guerrini, Ernesto Bruno La
Padula and Mario Romano.

THE FACING

Its reinforced-concrete
structure consists of five
floors with rectangular bays
supported by pillars. It is
faced with a succession of
false travertine arches,
whose rhythmic repetition
was intended to evoke that
of the Coliseum ▲ 170.

FASCIST SCULPTURE

With typical Fascist
overstatement this group
recalls the classical
theme of the
Dioscuri
(Castor and
Pollux) with
their mounts.

STADIO DEI MARMI (1932)

Part of a huge sports complex, the Foro Italico ▲ 377, which epitomized the regime's values and its cult of youth, strength and sport. Its ascetic shunning of every form of decoration is in keeping with modernism, while the starkness of its surfaces and the whiteness of the marble statues, contrasting with the stadium's ocher façades, contribute to the monumental effect of the ensemble.

THE FORO ITALICO "OBELISK" (1932)

A gigantic marble monolith, weighing 330 tons and nearly 60 feet tall, marks the entrance to the Foro Italico. This obelisk of the new Rome, erected by Costantino Costantini, still bears an inscription dedicated to Mussolini, which was never chiseled away.

STAZIONE TERMINI (1938–50) ▲ 338

The rebuilding of Rome's main station spanned the Fascist period and the postwar years. It provides a good illustration of the transition of architectural styles during this period of political change. The two rigid lateral buildings with false arches faced in Travertine were the first to be built, and evoke the paintings of Giorgio De Chirico ▲ 387 in no uncertain way. The grandiose main hall (opened in 1950), on the other hand, is striking because of the dynamic use of materials in its powerfully ribbed undulating roof.

PALAZZETTO DELLO SPORT (1956–8)

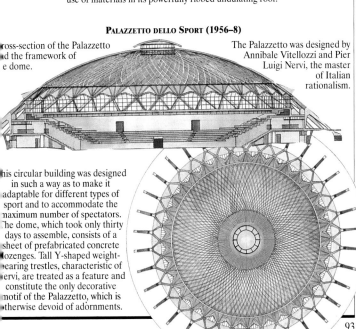

Cross-section of the Palazzetto and the framework of the dome.

The Palazzetto was designed by Annibale Vitellozzi and Pier Luigi Nervi, the master of Italian rationalism.

This circular building was designed in such a way as to make it adaptable for different types of sport and to accommodate the maximum number of spectators. The dome, which took only thirty days to assemble, consists of a sheet of prefabricated concrete lozenges. Tall Y-shaped weight-bearing trestles, characteristic of Nervi, are treated as a feature and constitute the only decorative motif of the Palazzetto, which is otherwise devoid of adornments.

THE CLASSICAL ORDERS

 2 **3** **4** **5**

Using an architecture of columns, the Greeks developed the Doric, Ionic and Corinthian styles, which provided aesthetic solutions to every kind of building. In Rome during the 1st century BC Vitruvius formulated a theory concerning the classical orders at a time when the development of the arch and the vault had reduced columns to a more decorative function. These styles and their variants were destined to become the basic orders of western architecture.

SUPERIMPOSED ORDERS

In all periods the orders were always superimposed in the same sequence. From the bottom: Doric or Tuscan (**1** and **2**), Ionic (**3**), Corinthian (**4**) and Composite (**5**).

Doric capital with ovolo molding.

II. ENTABLATURE

1. Architrave: smooth in the Doric style, but divided into three bands or *fasciae* in the Ionic and Corinthian.
2. Taenia (fillet).
3. Frieze: (left to right)
– Ionic, sometimes omitted from the entablature, sometimes plain.
– Doric, always consisted of alternating metopes (**a**) and triglyphs (**b**), each crowned by a mutule and anchored under the taenia by a *regula* with *guttae*.
– Corinthian, could be adorned with figurative motifs (**c**), animals or plants.
4. Cornice.

III. COLUMNS

Columns have three parts: the base (**a**), the shaft (**b**), which can be smooth or fluted, and the capital (**c**). Their proportions and decorations vary according to the order they belong to:
1. Doric (normally has no base).
2. Tuscan Doric (with a base).
3. Ionic.
4. Corinthian.
5 and 6. Composite.

I. PEDIMENT AND ROOF

1. Tympanum. 2. Raking cornices.
3. Bases for gable and angle *acroteria*: these often took the form of sculptures.

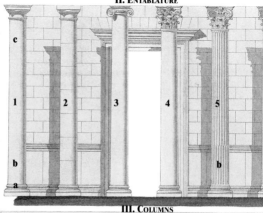

I. PEDIMENT

II. ENTABLATURE

III. COLUMNS

IV. SUBSTRUCTURE

1. Bases flanking steps. 2. Podium: unlike the Greeks, the Romans generally erected temples on massive stone platforms.

Rome
as seen by painters

Both a painter and an architect, GIOVANNI PAOLO PANNINI (c. 1691–1765), was one of the most representative artists of the 18th century. Like many of his contemporaries, he used painting as a means to show reality: cities, palaces, the private apartments of the nobility and the dwellings of the common people. In h[is] *Galleries of Views of Ancient Rome* (1) an[d]

> "At each step, a palace, a ruin, a garden, a desert, a little house, a stable, a triumphal arch, a colonnade, and all these so close together that one could draw them on a small sheet of paper."
>
> Goethe

alleries of Views of odern Rome (2) his ocumentary passion d him to paint intings. Set amid e fabulous decor of ome's Baroque ilazzi, these views rm a perfect nthology of the ome of the Grand ur and pay homage it. Such works sily found eager yers; but, apart m their commercial pects, they were also expression of the ientific quest for

true representation that was eventually to lead to photography.

Even when he decided to portray a real place, as in this *View of the French Academy in Rome* (1), GUSTAVE MOREAU (1826–98) never forgot his overriding artistic aim: to suggest more than the visible. Built up in monochrome masses, the various parts of this picture (trees, flowerbed, buildings) amount to a "vision" rather than a "view". A very well known place, painted many times, thus acquires a certain mystery, which the time of day chosen by Moreau – a gentle twilight – accentuates and makes more magical.

Although as a writer Goethe (1749–1832) offers a totally romantic idea of Rome and Italy, during his visit to Rome in 1784 he admired David's *The Oath of the Horatii*, a pictorial manifesto of neoclassicism. In contrast, David's *The Pyramid of Caius Cestius in Rome* (2) – a nocturnal view of a strangely eerie and exotic place – clearly belongs to the poetry of the ruins which Mantegna had already explored in the 15th century and which the Romantics made their own.

Corot

With *The Coliseum seen from the Farnese Gardens* (1), painted in 1826, Jean-Baptiste Corot (1796–1875) reveals the very essence of his art, in which natural light combines with a geometry free from cumbersome narrative detail. This picture, with its complex composition, has a classical clarity: beyond the foliage in the foreground the view stretches to the distant horizon, visible behind the broken circle of the Coliseum.

Before becoming a Futurist, Giacomo Balla (1871–1958) was a Divisionist, like so many other artists of his generation. At the beginning of the 20th century he painted *The Villa Borghese* many times (2) in pointillist style. In this evocative view, the last echoes of 19th-century art combine with a framework influenced by photography.

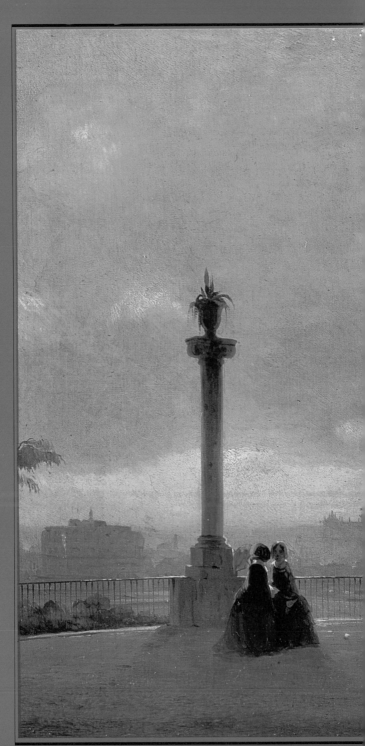

"The dome of St Peter's 'is silhouetted against the purest tint of an orange sunset, while overhead a few stars begin to appear in the sky'."

Stendhal

Corot's long sojourns in Italy did not fail to influence certain Italian painters at the beginning of the 19th century. This was demonstrated in particular by their abandonment of documentary views in favor of a freer and more basic treatment of a mass of structural forms, devoid of anecdotal secondary detail. Ippolito Caffi (1809–66) was one of the artists who succeeded in making the most of Corot's lesson. Caffi painted several Roman landscapes, including this *View of Rome from the Pincio Gardens*, which is suffused with a romantic atmosphere to a greater degree than most of his works. Nevertheless, the twilight composition, in which the suggestion of ghostly figures contrasts with the distant reddish silhouette of St Peter's seen against the flaming sky of the sunset, is no less faithful to the new ideas that Corot's example inspired.

ROME AS SEEN BY PAINTERS

The colors of Rome, red in particular, fired Yves Brayer (1907–90) with enthusiasm. His spontaneous gouaches and more carefully studied oil paintings made him an ironic witness of Roman life in the 1930's, as this picture of *German Seminarians on the Ponte Sant'Angelo* shows.

Rome
as seen by writers

REMINDERS OF THE PAST

ANCIENT RUINS

Visitors to Rome are constantly struck by the echoes of history resounding in the stones of the city. Michel Eyquem de Montaigne (1533–92), the French moralist and essayist, visited Rome at a time when the physical evidence of the Roman Empire was often stumbled upon by builders digging the foundations for new buildings.

❝It would often happen to one digging deep in the earth to come upon the capital of a lofty column which still stood on its base far below; and builders were wont to seek for their erections no other foundations than some mass of ancient masonry, or on arches such as are commonly seen in that of old the road all the way from Rome to Ostia ran past the habitations of men. Amongst other ruins we saw, about midway and on our left, a very beautiful tomb of a Roman prætor with an inscription quite perfect thereon. In Rome, the ruins, as a rule, only manifest themselves to us by th[e] massive solidity of their construction. The ancients built thick walls of brick, an[d] these they lined either with strips of marble or some other white stone, or with [a] kind of cement, or with thick tiles set thereupon. This outside crust, on which th[e] inscriptions were written, has almost everywhere been ruined by the lapse of year[s] wherefore we have now but little knowledge as to all these matters. Inscriptions sti[ll] remain where the walls were originally built in solid fashion. The approaches t[o] Rome in almost every case have a barren and uncultivated look, whether throug[h] the unfitness of the soil for cultivation, or whether, as seems more likely, throug[h] the absence of husbandmen and handicraftsmen in the city. On my journey hither [I] met divers troops of villagers from the Grisons and Savoy on their way to seek wor[k] in the Roman vineyards and gardens, and they told me they gained this wage eve[ry] year. The city is all for the court and the nobility, every one adapting himself to th[e] ease and idleness of ecclesiastic surroundings. There are no main streets of trade[;] what there are would seem small in a small town, palaces and gardens take up a[ll] the space.**❞**

MICHEL EYQUEM DE MONTAIGNE, *THE JOURNAL OF MONTAIGNE'S TRAVELS [IN] ITALY BY WAY OF SWITZERLAND AND GERMANY IN 1580 AND 158[1.] JOHN MURRAY, LONDON, 190[0]*

CLASSICAL ANTIQUITY

William Beckford (1760–1844), the traveler, collector and English member [of] parliament, perceived in Rome a fanciful atmosphere in which spirits from classic[al] antiquity still run free.

❝A spring flowed opportunely into a marble cistern close by the way; two cypress[es] and a pine waved over it. I leaped out, poured water upon my hands, and the[n] lifting them up to the sylvan Genii of the place, implored their protection. I wishe[d] to run wild in the fresh fields and copses above the Vatican, there to hav[e] remained, till fauns might peep out of the concealments, and satyrs begin to touc[h]

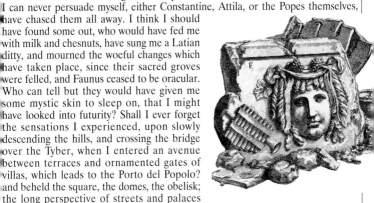

their flutes in the twilight; for the place looks still so wonderous classical, that I can never persuade myself, either Constantine, Attila, or the Popes themselves, have chased them all away. I think I should have found some out, who would have fed me with milk and chesnuts, have sung me a Latian ditty, and mourned the woeful changes which have taken place, since their sacred groves were felled, and Faunus ceased to be oracular. Who can tell but they would have given me some mystic skin to sleep on, that I might have looked into futurity? Shall I ever forget the sensations I experienced, upon slowly descending the hills, and crossing the bridge over the Tyber, when I entered an avenue between terraces and ornamented gates of villas, which leads to the Porto del Popolo? and beheld the square, the domes, the obelisk; the long perspective of streets and palaces opening beyond, all glowing with the vivid red of sun-set? You can imagine how I enjoyed my beloved tint, my favourite hour, surrounded by such objects.**"**

WILLIAM BECKFORD, *THE GRAND TOUR OF WILLIAM BECKFORD*,
PENGUIN BOOKS, LONDON, 1986

THE SACK OF ROME

The autobiography of Benvenuto Cellini (1500–71) is an extraordinarily vivid account of the events of his time. In the following passage he describes the sack of Rome by the Imperialist army under Constable of Bourbon in 1527.

"Having got into the castle in this way, I attached myself to certain pieces of artillery, which were under the command of a bombardier called Giuliano Fiorentino. Leaning there against the battlements, the unhappy man could see his poor house being sacked, and his wife and children outraged; fearing to strike his own folk, he dared not discharge the cannon, and flinging the burning fuse upon the ground, he wept as though his heart would break, and tore his cheeks with both his hands. Some of the other bombardiers were behaving in like manner; seeing which, I took one of the matches, and got the assistance of a few men who were not overcome by their emotions. I aimed some swivels and falconets at points where I saw it would be useful, and killed with them a good number of the enemy. Had it not been for this, the troops who poured into Rome that morning, and were marching straight upon the castle, might possibly have entered it with ease, because the artillery was doing them no damage. I went on firing under the eyes of several cardinals and lords, who kept blessing me and giving me the heartiest encouragement. In my enthusiasm I strove to achieve the impossible; let it suffice that it was I who saved the castle that morning,

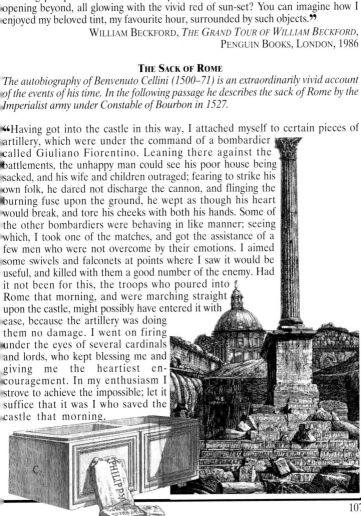

and brought the other bombardiers back to their duty. I worked hard the whole of that day; and when the evening came, while the army was marching into Rome through the Trastevere, Pope Clement appointed a great Roman nobleman named Antonio Santacroce to be captain of all the gunners. The first thing this man did was to come to me, and having greeted me with the utmost kindness, he stationed me with five fine pieces of artillery on the highest point of the castle, to which the name of the Angel specially belongs. This circular eminence goes round the castle, and surveys both Prati and the town of Rome. The captain put under my orders enough men to help in managing my guns, and having seen me paid in advance he gave me rations of bread and a little wine, and begged me to go forward as I had begun. I was perhaps more inclined by nature to the profession of arms than to the one I had adopted, and I took such pleasure in its duties that I discharged them better than those of my art. Night came, the enemy had entered Rome, and we who were in the castle (especially myself, who have alwa[ys] taken pleasure in extraordinary sights) stayed gazing on the indescribable scene [of] tumult and conflagration in the streets below. People who were anywhere else b[ut] where we were, could not have formed the least imagination of what it was. I w[ould] not, however, set myself to describe that tragedy, but will content myself wit[h] continuing the history of my own life and the circumstances which properly belon[g] to it.**"**

THE LIFE OF BENVENUTO CELLIN[I]
TRANS. JOHN ADDINGTON SYMONDS, MACMILLAN, LONDON 192[?]

AROUND THE COLOSSEUM
The city's history impressed itself most forcefully on American novel[ist] Theodore Dreiser (1871–1945) as he wandered around the Colosseum.

"Being new to Rome, I was not satisfied with what I ha[d] seen, but struck forth again ... only to find myself short[ly] thereafter and quite by accident in the vicinity of th[e] Colosseum.... It was exactly as th[e] pictures have represented it – ova[l,] many-arched, a thoroughly ponderou[s] ruin. I really did not gain a suggestio[n] of the astonishing size of it until [I] came down the hill, past tin cans th[at] were lying on the grass – a sign of th[e] modernity that possesses Rom[e] – and entered through one [of] the many arches. Then it cam[e] on me – the amazing thickness [of] the walls, the imposing size an[d] weight of the fragments, the va[st] dignity of the uprising flights [of] seats, and the great space no[w] properly cleared, devoted to th[e] arena. All that I ever knew or hear[d] of it came back as I sat on the co[ld] stones and looked about me.... It wa[s] a splendid afternoon.... Small patche[s] of grass and moss were detectab[le]

everywhere, growing soft and green between the stones. The five thousand wild beasts slaughtered in the arena at its dedication, which remained as a thought from my high-school days, were all with me. I read up as much as I could, watching several workmen lowering themselves by ropes from the top of the walls, the while they picked out little tufts of grass and weeds beginning to flourish in the earthy niches. Its amazing transformations from being a quarry for greedy popes by whom most of its magnificent marbles were removed, to its narrow escape from becoming a woolen-mill operated by Sixtus V, were all brooded over here. It was impossible not to be impressed by the thought of the emperors sitting on their especial balcony; the thousands upon thousands of Romans intent upon some gladiatorial feat; the guards outside the endless doors, the numbers of which can still be seen, giving entrance to separate sections and tiers of seats; and the vast array of civic life which must have surged about. I wondered whether there were vendors who sold sweets or ⎯od and what their cries were in Latin. One could could think of the endless ⎯ocession that wound its way here on gala days. Time works melancholy ⎯anges.**"**

THEODORE DREISER, *A TRAVELLER AT FORTY*,
GRANT RICHARDS, LONDON, 1914

⎯HE GRANDEUR OF ROME

THE CATACOMBS OF SAN SEBASTIANO

⎯e churches of Rome tend to inspire feelings of awe; in the case of Lady Anna ⎯ller (1741–81) this was transformed into panic when she had an unfortunate ⎯cident. She describes the incident here in a letter to a friend written during her visit 1770–71.

⎯The catacombs are the vastest, and the most noted in the neighbourhood of ⎯ome. We explored them accompanied by a ragged ill-looking fellow, whose ⎯siness is to sweep the church, and shew these silent mansions of the dead.... We ⎯re provided with little wax candles, and descended the stair-case, each carrying a ⎯hted *Bougie* ... Having, at length, reached the bottom, after no very agreeable ⎯scent, we found ourselves in a labyrinth of very narrow passages, turning and ⎯nding incessantly; most of these are upon the slope, and, I believe, go down into ⎯e earth to a considerable depth. They are not wider than to admit one person at a ⎯ne but branch out various ways like the veins in the human body; they are also ⎯tremely damp, being practised in the earth, and caused our candles to burn blue. ⎯ the side niches are deposited the bodies (as they say) of more than seventy-four ⎯ousand martyrs. These niches are mostly closed by an upright slab of marble, ⎯ich bears an inscription descriptive of their contents. Several are also buried ⎯der these passages, whose graves are secured by iron grates. We followed our ⎯ttered guide for a considerable time through the passages; at last he stopt, and ⎯ld M —— if he would go with him to a certain *Souterrain* just by, he would shew ⎯m a remarkable catacomb. At that moment I was staring about at the ⎯scriptions, and took it for granted that M —— was really very near, but after ⎯me moments I asked the footman who was standing at the entrance if he saw his ⎯aster; he replied in the negative, nor did he hear any voice: this alarmed me; I bid ⎯m go forward a little way, and that I would wait where I was, for I feared losing ⎯yself in this labyrinth in attempting to get out, not knowing which way they had ⎯rned. I waited a little time, and finding the servant did not return, called out as loud as I could, but, to my great disappointment, perceived that I scarce made a noise; the sound of my voice, from the dampness of the air, or the lowness of passages, remaining (as it were) with me. I trembled all over, and perceived that *Bougie* was near its end; I lighted another with some difficulty, from the shaking my hands ... but figure to yourself the horror that seized me, when, up attempting to move, I perceived myself forcibly held by my clothes from behi and all the efforts I made to free myself ineffectual. My heart, I believe, cease beat for a moment, and it was as much as I could do to sustain myself from fall down upon the ground in a swoon. However, I summoned all my resolution to aid, and ventured to look behind me, but saw nothing. I then again attempted move, but found it impracticable.... I made more violent efforts, and in strugglin at last discovered, that there was an iron grate, like a trap-door, a little open beh me, one of the pointed bars of which had pierced through my gown, and held me the manner I have related. I soon extricated myself, and walking forward, luckily the right path, found M —— who was quietly copying an inscription, the gu lighting him, and the servant returning towards me with the most unconcern aspect imaginable.**99**

LADY ANNA MILLER, *LETTERS FROM ITALY IN THE YEARS 1770 AND 17*
EDWARD AND CHARLES DILLY, LONDON, 17

TRANSFORMATION
The character Dorothea Brooke, in "Middlemarch" by George Eliot (1819–80) ha disastrous honeymoon in Rome but still feels strongly moved by the city itself.

66Ruins and basilicas, palaces and colossi, set in the midst of a sordid prese where all that was living and warm-blooded seemed sunk in the deep degeneracy a superstition divorced from reverence; the dimmer but yet eager Titantic gazing and struggling on walls and ceilings; the long vistas of white forms who marble eyes seemed to hold the monotonous light of an alien world: all this v wreck of ambitious ideals, sensuous and spiritual, mixed confusedly with the si of breathing forgetfulness and degradation, at first jarred her as with an elect shock, and then urged themselves on her with that ache belonging to a glut confused ideas which check the flow of emotion. Forms both pale and glowing to possession of her young sense, and fixed themselves in her memory even when s was not thinking of them, preparing strange associations which remained throu her after years. Our moods are apt to bring with them images which succeed ea other like the magic-lantern pictures of a doze; and in certain states of dull forlornness Dorothea all her life continued to see the vastness of St. Peter's, the huge bronze canopy, the excited intention in the attitudes and garments of the prophets and evangelists in the mosaics above, and the red drapery which was being hung for Christmas spreading itself everywhere, like a disease of the retina.**99**

GEORGE ELIOT, *MIDDLEMARCH*, LONDON, 1871-2

ST PETER'S
Charles Dickens (1812–70) was impressed by the pomp and pageantry of High Mass at St Peter's.

66On Sunday, the Pope assisted in the performance of High Mass at St. Peter's. The effect of the Cathedral on my mind, on that second visit, was exactly what it was at first, and what it remains after many visits. It is not religiously impressive or affecting. It is an immense edifice with no one point for the mind to rest upon; and it tires itself with wandering

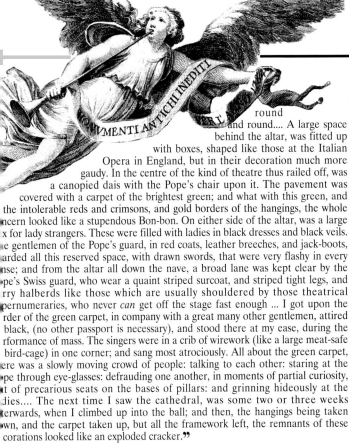

round and round.... A large space behind the altar, was fitted up with boxes, shaped like those at the Italian Opera in England, but in their decoration much more gaudy. In the centre of the kind of theatre thus railed off, was a canopied dais with the Pope's chair upon it. The pavement was covered with a carpet of the brightest green; and what with this green, and the intolerable reds and crimsons, and gold borders of the hangings, the whole concern looked like a stupendous Bon-bon. On either side of the altar, was a large box for lady strangers. These were filled with ladies in black dresses and black veils. The gentlemen of the Pope's guard, in red coats, leather breeches, and jack-boots, guarded all this reserved space, with drawn swords, that were very flashy in every sense; and from the altar all down the nave, a broad lane was kept clear by the Pope's Swiss guard, who wear a quaint striped surcoat, and striped tight legs, and carry halberds like those which are usually shouldered by those theatrical supernumeraries, who never *can* get off the stage fast enough ... I got upon the border of the green carpet, in company with a great many other gentlemen, attired in black, (no other passport is necessary), and stood there at my ease, during the performance of mass. The singers were in a crib of wirework (like a large meat-safe or bird-cage) in one corner; and sang most atrociously. All about the green carpet, there was a slowly moving crowd of people: talking to each other: staring at the Pope through eye-glasses: defrauding one another, in moments of partial curiosity, out of precarious seats on the bases of pillars: and grinning hideously at the ladies.... The next time I saw the cathedral, was some two or three weeks afterwards, when I climbed up into the ball; and then, the hangings being taken down, and the carpet taken up, but all the framework left, the remnants of these decorations looked like an exploded cracker.**"**

CHARLES DICKENS, *PICTURES FROM ITALY,*
CHAPMAN AND HALL, LONDON, 1846

THE SISTINE CHAPEL

Stendhal (1783–1842), the writer otherwise known as Henri Beyle, was less impressed by his experience of mass, this time in the Sistine Chapel.

"I am just come from the celebrated *Capella Sestino:* I was present at the Pope's mass, and was in one of the best places to the right, behind Cardinal Gonsalvi. I heard all those famous sopranos of the *Sestino,* never was *charivari* more disgusting; it is the most offensive noise I have heard in ten years. For two hours, that this mass lasted, I passed one and a half in ceaseless astonishment, feeling myself, examining myself, to discover whether I was not ill, or in interrogating my neighbours. Unluckily, they were almost all English, to whom music is a mere dead letter; my interrogations were addressed to their feelings, they answered me by passages from Dr. Burney.**"**

STENDHAL, *ROME, NAPLES AND
FLORENCE IN 1817,*
HENRY COLBURN,
LONDON, 1818

A MONSTER CHURCH

It was not so much the grandeur as the size of St Peter's th
overwhelmed the narrator of "The Innocents Abroad" by Ma
Twain (1835–1910). The book is a humorous account of a na
American tourist traveling round the Mediterranean, and
established Twain's reputation as a leading wit of his day.

"Of course we have been to the monster Church of
Peter, frequently. ... When we reached the door, a
stood fairly within the church, it was impossible
comprehend that it was a *very* large building
had to *cipher* a comprehension of it. I had
ransack my memory for some more similes.
Peter's is bulky. Its height and size wou
represent two of the Washington capitol
one on top of the other – if the capitol we
wider; or two blocks or two blocks and a half
ordinary buildings set one on top of the oth
St. Peter's was that large, but it could a
would not look so. The trouble was th
everything in it and about it was on suc
scale of uniform vastness that there were
contrasts to judge by – none but t
people, and I had not noticed the
They were insects. The statues
children holding bases of holy wat
were immense, according to the tables
figures, but so was every thing else arou
them. The mosaic pictures in the dome were huge, and were made of thousan
and thousands of cubes of glass as large as the end of my little finger, but the
pictures looked smooth, and gaudy of color, and in good proportion to the don
Evidently they would not answer to measure by. Away down toward the far end
the church (I thought it was really clear at the far end, but discovered afterwa
that it was in the centre, under the dome,) stood the thing they call the *baldacchi*
– a great bronze pyramidal frame-work like that which upholds a mosquito bar.
only looked like a considerably magnified bedstead – nothing more. Yet I knew
was a good deal more than half as high as Niagara Falls. It was overshadowed by
dome so mighty that its own height was snubbed. The four great square piers
pillars that stand equidistant from each other in the church, and support the roo
could not work up to their real dimensions by any method of comparison. I kn
that the faces of each were about the width of a very large dwelling-house fro
(fifty or sixty feet,) and that they were twice as high as an ordinary three-sto
dwelling, but still they looked small. I tried all the different ways I could think of
compel myself to understand how large St. Peter's was, but with small success. T
mosaic portrait of an Apostle who was writing with a pen six feet long seemed on
an ordinary Apostle.**"**

MARK TWAIN, *THE INNOCENTS ABROAD*, HARTFOR
CONNECTICUT, 18

LIFE IN ROME

LODGINGS

Lady Mary Wortley Montagu (1689–1762) lived in France and Italy with h
ambassador husband for almost twenty-three years and wrote many letters back to h
friends and family in England. This extract comes from a letter of October 22, 1740,
the Countess of Pomfret.

DEAR MADAM, – I flatter myself that your ladyship's goodness will give you some pleasure in hearing that I am safely arrived at Rome. It was a violent transition from your palace and company to be locked up all day with my chambermaid, and sleep at night in a hovel; but my whole life has been in the Pindaric style. I am at present settled in the lodging Sir Francis Dashwood recommended to me. I liked that Mr. Boughton mentioned to me . ... much better; 'tis two zechins per month cheaper, and at least twenty more agreeable; but the landlord would not let it, for a very pleasant reason. It seems your gallant knight used to lie with his wife; and as he had no hopes I would do the same, he resolves to reserve his house for some young man. The only charm belonging to my present habitation is the ceiling, which is finer than that of the gallery; being all painted by the proper hand of Zucchero, in perfect good preservation. I pay as much for this small apartment as your ladyship does for your magnificent palace; 'tis true I have a garden as large as your dressing-room. I walked last night two hours in that of Borghese, which is one of the most delightful I ever saw. **"**

THE LETTERS AND WORKS OF LADY MARY WORTLEY MONTAGU,
ED. BY LORD WHARNCLIFFE, RICHARD BENTLEY, LONDON, 1837

ROME IN DECAY

In the same year, 1740, Horace Walpole (1717–97) wrote from Rome to his friend Robert West that he found the city and its nobility to be in a state of decay and impecunity.

"I am very glad that I see Rome while it yet exists; before a great number of years are elapsed, I question whether it will be worth seeing. Between the ignorance and poverty of the present Romans, every thing is neglected and falling to decay; the villas are entirely out of repair, and the palaces so ill kept, that half the pictures are spoiled by damp.... The Cardinal Corsini has so thoroughly pushed on the misery of Rome by impoverishing it, that there is no money but paper to be seen. He is reckoned to have amassed three millions of crowns. You may judge of the affluence the nobility live in, when I assure you, that what the chief princes allow for their own eating is a testoon a day; eighteenpence: there are some extend their expense to five pauls, or half a crown: Cardinal Albani is called extravagant for laying out ten pauls for his dinner and supper. You may imagine they never have any entertainments: so far from it, they never have any company. The princesses and duchesses particularly lead the dismallest of lives. Being the posterity of popes, though of worse families than the ancient nobility, they expect greater respect than my ladies the countesses and marquises will pay them; consequently they consort not, but mope in a vast palace with two miserable tapers, and two or three monsignori, whom they are forced to court and humour, that they may not be entirely deserted. **"**

HORACE WALPOLE, *LETTER TO RICHARD WEST*, 1740

"DIRTY CREATURES"

Another critical view of Romans appears in a letter from Tobias Smollett (1721-71), written in 1765. The English novelist, poet and journalist published a collection of hi[s] letters under the title of "Travels through France and Italy". It is an acerbic work whic[h] earned him the nickname "Smelfungus" from his contemporaries.

❝Nothing can be more agreeable to the eyes of a stranger, especially in the heats [of] summer, than the great number of public fountains that appear in every part [of] Rome, embellished with all the ornaments of sculpture, and pouring fort[h] prodigious quantities of cool, delicious water, brought in aqueducts from differen[t] lakes, rivers, and sources, at a considerable distance from the city. These works ar[e] the remains of the munificence and industry of the antient Romans, who wer[e] extremely delicate in the article of water: but, however, great applause is also du[e] to those beneficent popes who have been at the expence of restoring and repairin[g] those noble channels of health, pleasure, and convenience. This great plenty [of] water, nevertheless, has not induced the Romans to be cleanly. Their streets, an[d] even their palaces, are disgraced with filth. The noble Piazza Navona, is adorne[d] with three or four fountains, one of which is perhaps the most magnificent i[n] Europe, and all of them discharge vast streams of water: but notwithstanding th[is] provision, the piazza is almost as dirty as West Smithfield, where the cattle are sol[d] in London. The corridores, arcades, and even staircases of their most elegan[t] palaces, are depositories of nastiness, and indeed in summer smell as strong a[s] spirit of hartshorn. I have a great notion that their ancestors were not much mor[e] cleanly. If we consider that the city and suburbs of Rome, in the reign of Claudiu[s] contained about seven millions of inhabitants, a number equal at least to the su[m] total of all the souls in England; that great part of antient Rome was allotted [to] temples, porticos, basilicæ, theatres, thermæ, circi, public and private walks an[d] gardens, where very few, if any, of this great number lodged; that by far the greate[r] part of those inhabitants were slaves and poor people, who did not enjoy th[e] conveniencies of life; and that the use of linen was scarce known; we must natural[ly] conclude they were strangely crouded together, and that in general they were a ve[ry] frowzy generation. ... What seems to prov[e] beyond all dispute, that the antient Romans wer[e] very dirty creatures, are these two particular[s] Vespasian laid a tax upon urine and ordure, o[n] pretence of being at great expence in clearing th[e] streets from such nusances; an imposition whic[h] amounted to about fourteen pence a year for ever[y] individual; and when Heliogabalus ordered all th[e] cobwebs of the city and suburbs to be collected, the[y] were found to weigh ten thousand pounds. This wa[s] intended as a demonstration of the great number [of] inhabitants; but it was a proof of their dirt, rathe[r] than of their populosity. I might likewise add, th[e] delicate custom of taking vomits at each other[s] houses, when they were invited to dinner, o[r] supper, that they might prepare their stomach[s] for gormandizing; a beastly proof of the[ir] nastiness as well as gluttony.**❞**

TOBIAS SMOLLETT, *TRAVELS THROUGH FRANC[E] AND ITALY*, OXFORD UNIVERSITY PRESS, 19[00]

THE SCENTS OF ROME

Hester Piozzi (1741–1821) married an Italia[n] musician in 1784 amid much opposition fro[m] friends and family. Her opinion of Romans w[as] not high, however, and she agrees with Smolle[tt] about the odor of the city.

❝Nothing can equal the nastiness at one's entrance to this magazine of perfection [the Barberini Palace]; but the Roman nobles are not disgusted with all sorts of scents, it is plain. These are not what we should call perfumes, indeed, but certainly *odori* – of the same nature as those one is obliged to wade through before Trajan's Pillar can be climbed. That the general appearance of a city which contains such treasures should be mean and disgusting, while one literally often walks upon granite and tramples red porphyry under one's feet, is one of the greatest wonders to me in a town of which the wonders seem innumerable; that it should be nasty beyond all telling, all endurance, with such perennial streams of the purest water liberally dispersed and triumphantly scattered all over it, is another unfathomable wonder; that so many poor should be suffered to beg in the streets when not a hand can be got to work in the fields, and that those poor should be permitted to exhibit sights of deformity and degradations of our species, to me unseen till now, at the most solemn moments, and in churches where silver and gold and richly-arrayed priests scarcely suffice to call off attention from the squalid miseries, I do not try to comprehend. That the palaces which taste and expense combine to decorate should look quietly on while common passengers use their noble vestibules, nay stairs, for every nauseous purpose; that princes, whose incomes equal those of our Dukes of Bedford and Marlborough, should suffer their servants to dress other men's dinners for hire, or lend out their equipages for a day's pleasuring, and hang wet rags out of their palace-windows to dry, as at the mean habitation of a pauper, while, looking in at those very windows, nothing is to be seen but proofs of opulence and scenes of splendour, will not undertake to explain. Sure I am that whoever knows Rome will not condemn this *ébauche* of it.**❞**

HESTER PIOZZI, *GLIMPSES OF ITALIAN SOCIETY IN THE 18TH CENTURY*,
SEELEY AND CO., LONDON, 1892

SENSORY PLEASURES

In the 20th century, the air in Rome is full of exhaust fumes but there are many sensory pleasures in store for the visitor, according to William Sansom (1912–76), the English travel writer and novelist.

❝Although the traffic in Rome is still so loud that a large aeroplane can be seen passing apparently soundless above, it is not as bad as it was in the era of the scooter and moto; you can still tell what that was like by crossing to the poorer quarter of Trastevere where the scooter tends to survive both in bulk and at speed. Every year, in fact, more Italians own cars, and thus does the traffic get slower and quieter. Huge motionless phalanxes are formed. Meanwhile, through the gas of motorised curses and petrol vapour, we can still get a glimpse of a Barberini bee or two, or of the once avant-garde motifs of a Borromini church; and escape into small and inexpensive restaurants where sucking-lamb with rosemary is a dream (how we all, and the bambino-loving Italians, love eating babies) and where a single wood-strawberry irradiates a whole fruit salad. Alas to report that the Taverna Margutta, friend for years of painters true and false, has now become an antique shop: but oldtimers like Ranieri, the Caffè Greco, and the Casina Valadier with its splendid view over this golden-brown city pimpled with a rich fungus of domes – these continue. The present drive is still towards Trastevere, where Roast Umbrian Pigling and Giant Tyrrhenian Shrimps (not-too-grown-up port and prawns) in a gas-lit atmosphere may well be eaten. One of the troubles about Rome is that the wealth of sight-seeables is so great you cannot take bus or taxi between them, or you would miss one or the other. The only thing is to walk. After a day of the papal renaissance and baroque, and of the great ancient walls of brick which being o brick often look as though they are not ruins but being built now by builders gone on strike – all one desires is a bidet of *caffè granita* to bathe the feet in.**"**

WILLIAM SANSOM, *GRAND TOUR TODAY*
HOGARTH PRESS, LONDON, 196

PIGEONS AND RATS

The Italian novelist Italo Calvino (1923–85) writes in his novel "Palomar" about the city's wildlife.

"'Shoo! Shoo!' Mr Palomar rushes on to the terrace to drive away the pigeons, who eat the leaves of the gazania, riddle the succulent plants with their beaks, cling with their claws to the cascade of morning-glories, peck at the blackberries, devour leaf by leaf the parsley planted in the box near the kitchen, dig and scratch in the flowerpots, spilling dirt and baring the roots, as if the sole purpose of their flight were devastation. The doves whose flying once cheered the city's squares have been followed by a degenerate progeny, filthy and infected, neither domestic nor wild but integrated into the public institutions and, as such, inextinguishable. The sky of Rome has long since fallen under the dominion of the over-population of these lumpen-fowl, who make life difficult for every other species of bird in the area and oppress the once free and various kingdom of the air with their monotonous moulting, lead-gray livery.

Trapped between the subterranean hordes of rats and the grievous flight of the pigeons, the ancient city allows itself to be corroded from below and from above, offering no more resistance than it did in the past to the barbarian invasions, as if saw not the assault of external enemies but the darkest, most congenital impulse of its own inner essence.

The city has also another soul – one of the many – that lives on the harmony between old stones and ever-new vegetation, sharing the favors of the sun.**"**

ITALO CALVINO, *MR PALOMAR*, TRANS. WILLIAM WEAVER
SECKER & WARBURG, LONDON, 198

VISITING ROME

EXPENSES

Tobias Smollett here gives advice to 18th-century visitors to the city.

Having given our names at the gate, we repaired to the dogana, or custom-house, where our trunks and carriage were searched; and here we were surrounded by a number of servitori de piazza, offering their services with the most disagreeable importunity. Though I told them several times I had no occasion for any, three of them took possession of the coach, one mounting before and two of them behind; and thus we proceeded to the Piazza d'Espagna, where the person lived to whose house I was directed. Strangers that come to Rome seldom put up at public inns, but go directly to lodging houses, of which there is great plenty in this quarter. The Piazza d'Espagna is open, airy, and pleasantly situated in a high part of the city immediately under the Colla Pinciana, and adorned with two fine fountains. Here most of the English reside: the apartments are generally commodious and well furnished; and the lodgers are well supplied with provisions and all necessaries of life. But, if I studied œconomy, I would choose another part of the town than the Piazza d'Espagna, which is, besides, at a great distance from the antiquities. For a decent first floor and two bed-chambers on the second, I payed no more than a scudo (five shillings) per day. Our table was plentifully furnished by the landlord for two and thirty pauls, being equal to sixteen shillings. I hired a town-coach at the rate of fourteen pauls, or seven shillings a day; and a servitore di piazza for three pauls, or eighteen-pence. The coachman has also an allowance of two pauls a day. The provisions at Rome are reasonable and good, the vitella mongana, however, which is the most delicate veal I ever tasted, is very dear, being sold for two pauls, or a shilling, the pound. Here are the rich wines of Montepulciano, Montefiascone, and Monte di Dragone; but what we commonly drink at meals is that of Orvieto, a small white wine of an agreeable flavour.**

TOBIAS SMOLLETT, *TRAVELS THROUGH FRANCE AND ITALY*,
OXFORD UNIVERSITY PRESS, 1907

SIGHTSEEING

William Beckford (1760–1844) worried about the number of sights to be seen in Rome and despaired of doing them justice.

**I absolutely will have no antiquary to go prating from fragment to fragment, and tell me, that were I to stay five years in Rome, I should not see half it contained. The thought alone, of so much to look at, is quite distracting, and makes me resolve to view nothing at all in a scientific way; but straggle and wander about just as the spirit chuses. This evening it led me to the Coliseo, and excited a vehement desire in me to break down and pulverize the whole circle of

saints' nests and chapels, which disgrace the arena. You recollect, I dare say,
vile effect of this holy trumpery, and would join with all your heart in kicking th
into the Tyber. A few lazy abbots were at their devotion before them; such as wo
have made a lion's mouth water; fatter I dare say, than any saint in the wh
martyrology, and ten times more tantalizing. I looked first, at the dens where w
beasts used to be kept, to divert the magnanimous people of Rome w
devastation and murder; then, at the tame cattle before the altars. Heave
thought I to myself, how times are changed! Could ever Vespasian have imagi
his amphitheatre would have been thus inhabited? I passed on, making th
reflections, to a dark arcade, overgrown with ilex. In the openings which time a
violence have made, a distant grove of cypresses discover themselves; spring
from heaps of mouldering ruins, relieved by a clear transparent sky, strewed wit
few red clouds. This was the sort of prospect I desired, and I sat down o
shattered frieze to enjoy it … Next, directing my steps to the arch of Constantin
surveyed the groups of ruins which surrounded me. The cool breeze of the even
played in the beds of canes and oziers, which flourished under the walls of
Coliseo: a cloud of birds were upon the wing to regain their haunts in its crevic
and, except the sound of their flight, all was silent; for happily no carriages w
rattling along. I observed the palace and obelisk of Saint John of Lateran, a
distance; but it was too late to take a nearer survey; so returning leisurely hom
traversed the Campo Vaccino, and leaned a moment against one of the colum
which supported the temple of Jupiter Stator. Some women were fetching wa
from the fountain hard by, whilst another group had kindled a fire under the shr
and twisted fig-trees, which cover the Palatine hill. Innumerable vaults and arc
peep out of the vegetation. It was upon these, in all probability, the splendid pal
of the Cæsars was raised. Confused fragments of marble, and walls of l
terraces, are the sole traces of its antient magnificence. A wretched rabble w
roasting their chesnuts, on the very spot, perhaps, where Domitian convene
senate, to harangue upon the delicacies of his entertainment.**"**

The Grand Tour of William Beckfo
Penguin Books, London, 1

Majesty

*In 1818 the English poet Percy Bysshe Shelley (1792–1822) left England to settle i
Italy. The following extract is from a letter to Thomas Love Peacock in Decemb
1818.*

"I have seen the ruins of Rome, the Vatican, St. Peter's, and all the miracles
of ancient and modern art contained in that majestic city. The impression
of it exceeds anything I have ever experienced in my travels.… We visited
the Forum and the ruins of the Coliseum every day. The Coliseum is unlike
any work of human hands I ever saw before. It is of enormous height and
circuit, and the arches built of massy stones are piled on one another, and
jut into the blue air, shattered into the forms of overhanging rocks. It has
been changed by time into the image of an amphitheatre of
rocky hills overgrown by the wild olive, the myrtle, and the
fig-tree, and threaded by little paths, which wind among its
ruined stairs and immeasurable galleries.… The interior is all
ruin. I can scarcely believe that when encrusted with
Dorian marble and ornamented by columns of Egyptian
granite, its effect could have been so sublime and so
impressive as in its present state. It is open to the sky, and
it was the clear and sunny weather of the end of
November in this climate when we
visited it, day after day.**"**

*Letters of Percy Bysshe
Shelley,* edited by R.
Ingpen, London, 1909

17TH-CENTURY ROME

e influence of the 17th century should not be overlooked by visitors to
me, according to Edith Wharton (1862–1937), the American novelist
d short-story writer.

t might be well for the purist to consider what would be lost if the
ُenteenth-century Rome which he affects to ignore were actually
otted out. The Spanish Steps would of course disappear, with the
lace of the Propaganda; so would the glorious Barberini palace, and
rnini's neighbouring fountain of the Triton; the via delle Quattro
ontane, with its dripping river-gods emerging from their grottoes,
d Borromini's fantastic church of San Carlo at the head of the
eet, a kaleidoscope of whirling line and ornament, offset by the
licately classical circular cortile of the adjoining monastery. On the
ُirinal hill, the palace of the Consulta would go, and the central
rtal of the Quirinal (a work of Bernini's), as well as the splendid
teway of the Colonna gardens. The Colonna palace itself, dull
d monotonous without, but within the very model of a
agnificent pleasure-house, would likewise be effaced; so
ould many of the most characteristic buildings of the
orso – San Marcello, the Gesù, the Sciarra and Doria
laces, and the great Roman College. Gone, too, would be
e Fountain of Trevi, and Lunghi's gay little church of San
ıcenzo ed Anastasio, which faces it so charmingly across the
uare; gone the pillared court-yard and great painted galleries
the Borghese palace, and the Fontana dei Termini with its
autiful group of adjoining churches; the great fountain of the
azza Navona, Lunghi's stately façade of the Chiesa Nuova, and
orromini's Oratory of San Filippo Neri... But even those who
main unconverted, who cannot effect the transference of
rtistic and historic sympathy necessary to a real
understanding of seventeenth-century architecture, should
at least realize that the Rome which excites a passion of
devotion such as no other city can inspire, the Rome
or which travellers pine in absence, and to which they
eturn again and again with the fresh ardour of discovery, is, externally at least, in
reat part the creation of the seventeenth century.**

EDITH WHARTON, *ITALIAN BACKGROUNDS*,
MACMILLAN & CO., LONDON, 1905

OFF-SEASON

John Cheever (1912–82) recommended visiting Rome out of season – but
cautioned readers to take an umbrella.

**I still cook breakfast in my underwear in this Palace of Justice or
Haunted Public Library and at nightfall the combination
of dim-lamps and Roman gin makes me feel very
peculiar. The gin is terrible. They make it in Torino. The
city seems mercurial and while it is lovely in the sun with
the fountains sparkling it looks, in the rain, like that old
movie-shot: European Capital On Eve Of War. Everyone carries a wet umbrella, there are anxious crowds
around every news stand, the consulate ante-rooms are
full of Egyptian evacuees asking for news or mail, and
the atmosphere of anxiety
and gloom is dense. Then
the sun comes out and
everything seems fine. This
place isn't much good for

entertaining because you can't HEAR anybody or else they echo. I pretend to wo
in the mornings and visit ruins in the afternoon. Castel San Angelo is my favor
but I like the Forum which is very near here. It's a good time of year for sig
seeing because we seem to be the only tourists left. Now and then you run into
cluster of determined Germans but they are infrequent and seem autumnal an
little sad like the honking of geese. The art galleries are empty and so dark that y
can walk for a mile without picking out the shape of a foot.**"**

THE LETTERS OF JOHN CHEEVER, SIMON & SCHUSTER, NEW YORK, 19

TOMBS

*Bernard Berenson (1865–1959), the American art historian and philosoph
recommends a visit to Santa Maria del Popolo. The following diary entries were writ
on November 7, 1952, and October 31, 1950.*

"An hour in Santa Maria del Popolo. Poked about in corridors, sacristies, close
as well as in the church itself. What variety! Early and late Renaissance tombs, t
of them done by the incumbent in his lifetime. They knew better than to trust th
heirs. Choir with ceiling by Pinturicchio at his best, and tombs by Andr
Sansovino anticipating schemes adopted later by Michelangelo for the sepulchre
Julius II at San Pietro in Vincoli. The chapel with frescoes by Pinturicchio again
his best; the recumbent bronze by Vecchietta, the two Caravaggios placed in such
way as to suggest that those who ordered them did not think too highly of the
The charming Jonah in the Chigi Chapel delighted me again. But what impress
me most this time was the tomb of an Odescalchi lady, who died at twenty-two
her third childbirth, made in 1772 or thereabouts. That such a masterpie
rivalling the best Chinese art for expression of energy in leaves, in the eagle, t
tree trunk, the sweep of the drapery, not to speak of the colour, had been done
late, only just before the collapse into the 'art nouveau' which we know as 'Empir
amazed me.**"**

" I first came to Rome in the autumn of 1888 and spent the following months
my feet from early morning till bedtime....Except for [a] group of artists I kn
nobody, nor did it occur to me to want to know anybody. Looking was enough a
reading, but mostly looking. Here, as in Paris and London, I lived more
inwardly than outwardly, although I was active enough. What went on
inside me, not always perceived by me, counted as real and
satisfactory.**"**

BERNARD BERENSON, *THE PASSIONATE SIGHTSEER*,
THAMES & HUDSON, LONDON, 1960

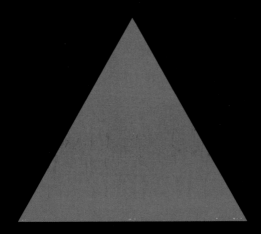

Itineraries in Rome

127 The Capitol, the Forum and
the Palatine
153 From the Forum Holitorium
to the Coliseum
175 Circus Maximus and the Aventine
185 The Coelian Hill
201 The Vatican
237 From Ponte Sant'Angelo
to the Ghetto
255 Campo Marzio from the Gesù to
Palazzo Madama
273 Around Piazza Navona
287 The Quirinal
303 Il Tridente
317 Via Appia Antica
331 From the Baths of Diocletien to
San Pietro in Vincoli
349 Trastevere
367 From Villa Giulia to the
Foro Italico
379 Rome outside the walls
389 Tivoli and Palestrina
403 Ostia

▲ Rome seen from the Janiculum.

▲ Via della Conciliazione.

The Palazzo della Civiltà del Lavoro in EU

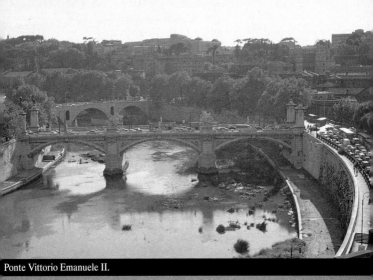

Ponte Vittorio Emanuele II.

The Coliseum.　　　　　　　　　The Fountain of Neptune in Piazza Navona. ▼

▲ An ice-cream shop in Trastevere.

▲ Metro sign.

Monks and nuns at the Vatican. ▼

Market stall near Campo de' Fiori.

The Campo de' Fiori flower market.

Carabinieri. ▼

▲ Via Appia Antica.　　　　　　　　　The colors of Rome. ▼

▼ Ecclesiastical clothes shop at the Vatican.

The Capitol, the Forum and the Palatine

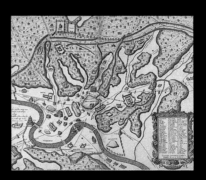

128 The Capitol
132 The Capitoline Museums
136 The Roman Forum
146 The Palatine

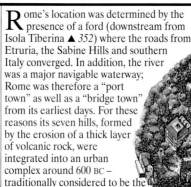

Rome's location was determined by the presence of a ford (downstream from Isola Tiberina ▲ *352*) where the roads from Etruria, the Sabine Hills and southern Italy converged. In addition, the river was a major navigable waterway; Rome was therefore a "port town" as well as a "bridge town" from its earliest days. For these reasons its seven hills, formed by the erosion of a thick layer of volcanic rock, were integrated into an urban complex around 600 BC – traditionally considered to be the time of Tarquinius Priscus, the first Etruscan king of Rome. The city's first ramparts, a few vestiges of which are still visible, are attributed to his successor, Servius Tullius. Severa hundred years later, under Aurelian (270–5 AD), the threat of barbarian invasions made the construction of new fortifications necessary; large sections of his 12-mile wall have been preserved.

THE TARPEIAN ROCK
Tarpeia was seduced by King Titus Tatius, who besieged the Capitol after the rape of the Sabine women ▲ *177*. She offered to

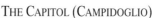

THE CAPITOL (CAMPIDOGLIO)

The hill has two crests separated by a depression (the Asylum), which is now Piazza del Campidoglio. On the northern summit the *arx* ("fortress"), a kind of fortified refuge, was dominated by the Temple of Juno Moneta, standing near the Tarpeian Rock (or Saxum). On the souther summit stood the Temple of Jupiter Capitolinus, the largest temple in Rome, reputedly founded by Tarquinius Priscus though only inaugurated at the beginning of the Republic. Some vestiges of its foundations can still be seen beneath the Palazzo dei Conservatori, while under the Palazzo Senatorio there are remains of the Temple of Veiovis, a very ancient evi deity. Other gods had sanctuaries on the hill, but almost nothing is left of these. Apart from its religious function, the Capitol was the center of political power; part of the state archives were kept in the Tabularium, which dominated the Forum. The Capitol was also the center for the most important ceremonies, such as the investiture of the consuls on January 1, and above all the Triumph. This supreme honor given to generals under the Republic and later to the emperors, was the occasion for a long procession leading to the steps of the Temple of Jupiter. The Capitol's importance has endured throughout the history of Rome. In the Middle Ages the Tabularium, which had been fortified by Rome's powerful noble families, became the seat of the new Roman Senate. This hill houses the main municipal institutions, and it has been a center for Roman art since the 16th century.

open the gates of the citadel in exchange for his favors. Tatius feigned consent, but once inside got his soldiers to crush her to death with their shields. The rock from which traitors were hurled to death was thus called the Tarpeian Rock.

Piazza del Campidoglio ★

This was Rome's first modern piazza, conceived as a great terrace overlooking the city. When Charles V visited Rome in 1536, Pope

Half a day

◆ E B2-B3-C2-C3

Paul commissioned Michelangelo to design a monumental complex worthy of the papal capital. After the artist's death in 1564 the work continued, until 1654, under the direction of Giacomo della Porta, Martino Longhi the Elder and Girolamo Rainaldi, all of whom modified the original plans. As a result the façades of the three palaces are not exactly in accordance with Michelangelo's design, but they were given admirable unity by the pilasters which adorn them and by the balustrades supporting the statues on the cornices.

1. Capitol ✪
2. Santa Maria of Aracoeli
3. Mamertine prison
4. Santi Luca e Martina
5. Forum ✪
6. Basilica of Maxentius
7. Palatine ✪

The Triumph
The victor paraded in a chariot drawn by four white horses, with his soldiers in a long procession bearing the booty plundered from the vanquished, including prisoners in chains and even models of the conquered cities. To remind him of his humble human condition, he was accompanied by a slave who kept repeating the words "Remember that you are only a mortal!".

129

The marble statues of Castor and Pollux, Roman copies of Greek originals that once graced the Temple of Circus Flaminius, stand at the top of the flight of steps designed by Michelangelo.

THE CAPITOL, "CAPUT MUNDI" ✪
The Piazza del Campidoglio, which was designed by Michelangelo, contains a complex of museums that are among the oldest in Europe. As part of Jubilee 2000, the Capitoline museums have undergone an extensive program of restoration: buildings have been renovated, exhibition spaces reorganized and artefacts cleaned. The remains of the Tabularium and of the Temple de Veiovis (beneath the Palazzo Senatorio) are now accessible and the underground gallery interlinking the various palazzi in the piazza has reopened.

THE STATUE OF MARCUS AURELIUS
This equestrian statue, thought to depict Constantine, stood at the Lateran throughout the Middle Ages. It was brought to the Capitol in 1538 and placed on a pedestal designed by Michelangelo.

THE STATUE OF MARCUS AURELIUS. The design of the piazza was almost entirely determined by the equestrian statue of the Emperor Marcus Aurelius (161–80 AD), the focal point of both the oval pattern of the paving stones and the trapezium formed by the façades of the palaces. Since its restoration at the end of the 1980s it has been replaced by a copy. The original is in one of the rooms of the Capitoline Museum.

THE PALACES. The PALAZZO SENATORIO stands at the back of the piazza. Its left wing incorporates the tower of Martino V (c. 1427), and the right wing one of Boniface IX's (1389–1404) towers. The façade is aligned with the central bell tower by Martino Longhi il Vecchio (1578–82) and Michelangelo's twin converging flights of steps. In front of the steps statues of the Nile and the Tiber from the Baths of Constantine on the Quirinal Hill stand on either side of an ancient porphyry statue of Minerva, transformed into the goddess Rome. The symmetrical façades of the PALAZZO DEI CONSERVATORI (on the right), rebuilt between 1564 and 1576, and the CAPITOLINE MUSEUM (on the left), built between 1603 and 1655, conceal buildings of very different dimensions. (Go up the short flight of steps to the right of the Capitoline Museum).

SANTA MARIA IN ARACOELI ★. According to legend the Virgin and Child appeared to the Emperor Augustus, who then built an altar (*ara*) here. In the 13th century the Franciscans built the present church, which became the official church of the *comune* of Rome. Above the door is a beautiful mosaic of the Cavallini school portraying the *Virgin and Child*. At the end of the Black Death, in 1348, the Roman people built the steep monumental flight of marble steps in front of the church, which is dedicated to the Virgin Mary. The church served as the burial place of many members of noble Roman families, whose carved

ombstones are embedded in a fine Cosmatesque ● 76 avement dating from the 13th to 14th century. Not to be nissed is the Chapel of San Bernardino di Siena (first on the ight), decorated with splendid frescoes by Pinturicchio around 1486). Rome's much venerated statue of the Child esus (15th century) is preserved in a small chapel beside the acristy. In September 2000 a fresco attributed to Pietro Cavallini (18th century) was uncovered in the Chapel of an Pasquale di Baylon. (For a magnificent view of the Forum nd the Palatine Hill, descend the Via del Campidoglio, to he right of the Palazzo Senatorio. Walk around the Palazzo enatorio and go down toward the Forum).

MAMERTINE PRISON. The former Tullianum, which has a ravertine façade dating from 40 BC, is built over a Roman lungeon consisting of two rooms. The circular hole in the tone floor of the upper room was originally the only access to he prison below. This was where prisoners of State, such as ugurtha and Vercingetorix, were incarcerated and strangled; ut the medieval legend claiming that St Peter was mprisoned here is unfounded. Above the prison stands the Church of San Giuseppe dei Falegnami (1597–1663).

SANTI LUCA E MARTINA. In 1588 the Church of Santa Martina vas given to the Accademia di San Luca ▲ 299, and thus acquired the name of the patron saint of the arts. The liscovery of the body of St Martin during restoration work in 634 by Pietro da Cortona, the "prince" of the academy, xcited the interest of Pope Urban VIII and his nephew, Cardinal Francesco Barberini. The two prelates herefore commissioned him to build a new church on he site of the old one. Despite its sober decoration, his is one of Rome's finest 7th-century churches. The entrance to he Forum is in Via dei Fori mperiali.)

In the courtyard of the Palazzo dei Conservatori stand fragments of a colossal statute of Constantine found at the Basilica of Maxentius ▲ 145 in 1487. The head measures 8½ feet, the foot 6½ feet.

THE LEGEND OF THE "SANTO BAMBINO"
This statue of the Child Jesus, said by some to be made of olive wood from the Garden of Gethsemane and believed by others to be the work of a saint, is endowed with miraculous powers. In Rome beautiful children are still referred to as *"bello come il pupo dell'Aracoeli"* (pretty as the Aracoeli babe).

The Museo Capitolino – the oldest museum in
Europe – and the Palazzo dei Conservatori, wit
its various sections (the Appartamento dei
Conservatori, Museo del Palazzo dei Conservato
Braccio Nuovo, Museo Nuovo and Pinacoteca
Capitolina), contain rich collections of classical
antiquities as well as some major
European paintings from t
16th and 17th
centuries.

CONSTANTINE
This colossal head
(8 feet 6 inches
high) from the
Basilica of
Maxentius
belonged to a
seated figure of
the Emperor
(325–6 AD).

FUNERARY STELE
This fragment of an
Ionic funerary stele
(late 6th century BC)
depicts a young girl
holding a bird
belonging to the
deceased.

**"THE BOY
WITH THE
THORN"**
The
Spinarius
depicts a
boy sitting
on a rock
extracting a thorn
from his foot.
Because of its
elegance and realistic
theme this has often
been considered a 3rd
century work, but the
balance and gravity
are reminiscent of the
5th century. It is this
eclectic character
which makes the
statue interesting,
but difficult to date.
The work, which was
either a study or an
ex voto figure
commissioned by an
athlete, was to have
an enduring impact,
many replicas of it
being made both in
classical times and
during the
Renaissance.

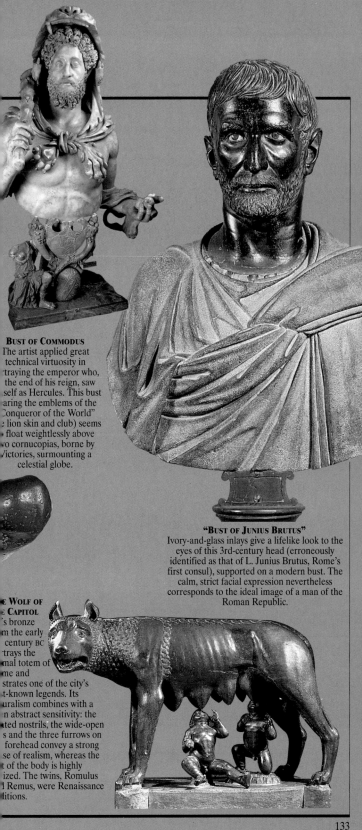

BUST OF COMMODUS
The artist applied great
technical virtuosity in
[por]traying the emperor who,
[at] the end of his reign, saw
[him]self as Hercules. This bust
[we]aring the emblems of the
["Conqueror of the World"
[the] lion skin and club) seems
[to] float weightlessly above
[tw]o cornucopias, borne by
[V]ictories, surmounting a
celestial globe.

"BUST OF JUNIUS BRUTUS"
Ivory-and-glass inlays give a lifelike look to the
eyes of this 3rd-century head (erroneously
identified as that of L. Junius Brutus, Rome's
first consul), supported on a modern bust. The
calm, strict facial expression nevertheless
corresponds to the ideal image of a man of the
Roman Republic.

**[TH]E WOLF OF
[TH]E CAPITOL
[Thi]s bronze
[fro]m the early
[5th] century BC
[por]trays the
[ani]mal totem of
[Rom]e and
[illu]strates one of the city's
[bes]t-known legends. Its
[nat]uralism combines with a
[cert]ain abstract sensitivity: the
[dila]ted nostrils, the wide-open
[eye]s and the three furrows on
[the] forehead convey a strong
[sen]se of realism, whereas the
[res]t of the body is highly
[styl]ized. The twins, Romulus
[and] Remus, were Renaissance
[add]itions.

133

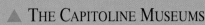

"THE TRIUMPH OF BACCHUS"
Among the works painted by Pietro da Cortona around 1620 for his patron, the Marchese Sacchetti, this is probably the o most clearly influenced by Titian's *Bacchanals* – a ser of paintings that da Cortona had admire when they were acquired by Cardin Ludovisi.

"THE DYING GAUL"
Hellenistic art was prone to the representation of certain ethnic types, such as the Galatian warriors with rough features and thick bushy hair that the sculptors of Pergamon, in Asia Minor, excelled in depicting. This wounded Gaul, with his poignant expression, corresponds exactly to the dominant style of the 3rd century BC. The statue was discovered in the gardens of Villa Ludovisi.

"THE CAPITOLINE VENUS"
This figure of a goddess surprised while bathing, from the 2nd century AD, is one of the many works derived from the famous *Aphrodite of Cnidus* sculpted by Praxiteles in the 4th century BC.

"ST JOHN THE BAPTIST"
Caravaggio probably painted this work between 1600 and 1603. Leonardo da Vinci had already portrayed John the Baptist as a disturbing adolescent in his painting that now hangs in the Louvre, but Caravaggio here removes every religious aspect from the theme. It is no doubt one of the works he painted using a live model in a dark studio lit only by a lamp hanging from the ceiling.

"DOVES DRINKING"
This mosaic panel ▲ *397* from Hadrian's villa is a copy of a motif from a famous mosaic by Sosias of Pergamon. It reveals how persistent the taste for Hellenistic art was in ancient Rome.

THE ORIGINS OF ANCIENT ROME ✪

The Forum, which evolved over twelve centuries of Roman civilization, is a maze of romantic ruins. The best time to explore them is in the early morning (entry, on the Via Salaria Vecchia, is free), ending on the Palatine Hill, the cradle of Rome, for a view over the Eternal City.

The formation of the Forum valley was due to the erosion of bank of volcanic tufa by a stream named the Velabrum, which meandered between the Palatine and Capitoline hills toward the Tiber. Used as a necropolis in the Iron Age (10th to 9th century BC), this marshy area was drained at the beginning of the rule of the Etruscan kings, when Tarquinius Priscus is said to have channeled the waters of the Velabrum in order to implement a series of public works, the most important being the city's huge sewer, the *cloaca maxima* ● 69. Rome then began to develop on this site, which remained its political, administrative and religious center until the end of the Republican period. During the Middle Ages, when the population

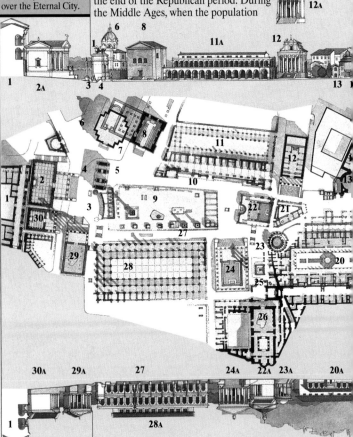

"… the Forum became a cattle market and came to be known by the vile name of *Campo Vaccino*, which it retained up to the time of the excavations ordered by Napoleon."

Stendhal,
Promenades dans Rome

gradually settled in the Campus Martius, the Forum – although strewn with debris – came to be used as grazing land for cattle and acquired the name of *Campo Vaccino* ("the cattle field"). It was not until the 19th century that archeologists began to unearth the half-buried ruins, digging sometimes as deep as 65 feet.

BASILICA AEMILIA

This ancient basilica was a large covered space, divided into aisles, that provided shelter during the rainy season for the

> "The Forum, grey and desolate, in its ruined state. Only dust. Not a patch of grass, only a few blades sprouting between the paving stones of the Via Sacra."
>
> Emile Zola

orum's principal activities: legal, political and economic. ater, Christian churches were built according to this design. he basilica was founded by the censors Marcus Aemilius epidus and Marcus Fulvius Nobilior. After restorations nded by the Aemilii family, under Augustus it was given the rm we see today. On the eastern side there is a dedication Augustus' grandson, which reads "Lucius Caesar, prince of uth". The basilica was burned down in 410 AD, but was restored, for the last time,

1. **Tabularium**
2. **Temple of Concord**
2a. **Reconstruction**
3. **Imperial Rostra**
4. **Arch of Septimius Severus**
5. **Lapis Niger**
6. **Church of Santi Luca e Martina**
7. **Comitium**
8. **Curia**
9. **Main square of Forum**
10. **Via Sacra**
11. **Basilica Aemilia**
11a. **Reconstruction**
12. **Temple of Antoninus and Faustina/Church of San Lorenzo**
13. **Temple of Romulus**
14. **Church of Santi Cosma e Damiano**
15. **Basilica of Maxentius**
15a. **Reconstruction**
16. **Church of Santa Francesca Romana**
17. **Temple of Venus and Rome**
17a. **Reconstruction (elevation)**
17b. **Reconstruction (cross-section)**
18. **Arch of Titus**
19. **Republican buildings**
19a. **Reconstruction**
20. **House of the Vestals**
20a. **Reconstruction**
21. **Regia**
22. **Temple of the Divine Julius**
23. **Temple of Vesta**
23a. **Reconstruction**
24. **Temple of the Dioscuri**
15a. **Reconstruction**
25. **Fountain of Juturna**
26. **Church of Santa Maria Antiqua**
27. **Columns of Diocletian**
28. **Basilica Julia**
28a. **Reconstruction**
29. **Temple of Saturn**
30. **Temple of Vespasian and Titus**
30a. **Reconstruction**

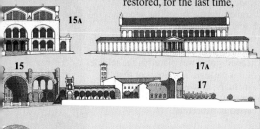

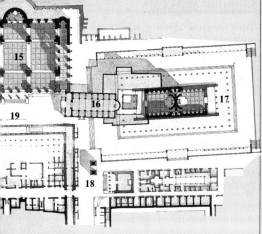

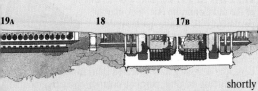

shortly afterward; in various aces in the interior some of the paving stones still display gns of the fire. On the side facing the square the building d a monumental façade with two superimposed orders of xteen arches supported by pilasters. Behind the portico ere were the *tabernae* ("shops") used by bankers. The inner ace, which measures approximately 230 x 100 feet, was vided into four aisles by "African" marble columns that pported the roof. Where the entrance used to stand, one n see a bas-relief illustrating the origins of Rome, which corated the basilica in the 1st century BC.

THE CURIA

Slabs of marble and stucco decorated the main façade of Julius Caesar's Curia, which replaced the Curia Hostilia, destroyed by fire in 52 BC.

THE BAS-RELIEFS OF THE CURIA

The incomplete relief on the left shows the cancellation of fiscal debts. The citizens' records were burned

in the Emperor's presence. The relief on the right (above) shows the institution of the *alimenta*, whereby the interest from agricultural loans to landowners was distributed to poor children. These scenes are set in the Forum and so provide a rare contemporary image of it.

Near the steps of the basilica, to the west, there is a circular marble base which is all that remains of the SANCTUARY OF VENUS CLOACINA, built over the Forum's opening to the *cloaca maxima* ● *69* ▲ *136*. In the Argiletum (the street that separates the basilica and the Curia) stood the famous little TEMPLE OF JANUS, one of the oldest Roman deities, whose two-headed statue was placed in the middle of this passage. The doors of this sanctuary, of which nothing remains, were left open at times of war and closed in peacetime.

COMITIUM AND CURIA

THE COMITIUM. Mirroring Republican institutional principles ● *34*, the Comitium provided circular step-seating for the people who gathered to hear the speeches of legislators. They spoke from a platform known as the Rostra which, in commemoration of the naval victory at Antium (338 BC), was decorated with the bronze figureheads (*rostra*) seized from the vanquished fleet. On the opposite side of the Comitium was the Curia, one of the Senate's meeting places. With the end of the Republic, when electoral meetings were moved to the Campus Martius and Caesar's construction work began, this group of buildings became gradually less important. Between 54 and 44 BC the old Curia Hostilia and Rostra were destroyed.

THE LAPIS NIGER. The only visible remains of the old Comitium is a black marble pavement with a white marble border. The Roman author Festus mentions the *niger lapis ad Comitio* ("the black stone of the Comitium") a a funerary place, associated with the death of Romulus. Dig beneath the paving have revealed ruins from the 6th century BC, including an altar, part of a column, and a fragment of stone with an archaic Latin inscription in boustrophedonic script (running alternately from left to right and from right t left), which appears to have been the ritual and sacrificial rules of a sanctuary dedicated to Vulcan.

THE CURIA. The Senate could hold meetings in any temple, but its official seat was the Curia. The large brick building between the Argiletum and the Comitium is the Curia Julia built by Julius Caesar in order to replace the old one and als to suit the design of his own forum, which Augustus inaugurated in 29 BC. Its present appearance is due to restorations carried out by Diocletian after a fire in 283 AD.

The two bronze panels that were removed to make the main doors of the Lateran Basilica ▲ 198 in the 17th century date from this period, as does the marble paving. Transformed into the Church of Sant'Adriano during the 7th century, the Curia was once again restored in 1930. Its dimensions (approximately 70 feet high, 60 feet wide and 90 feet long) correspond to the proportions recommended by Vitruvius ● 94, the famous architect of the Augustan period. The grandiose interior has a flat ceiling (today's wooden structure is modern). On the left and right there are three low, wide steps on which seats for three to six hundred senators were arranged. Between the two doors at the back there is a large podium, from which the assemblies were directed. Its base was probably adorned with a statue of Victory, placed there by Octavian before he became the Emperor Augustus. The two bas-reliefs illustrating Trajan's Imperial munificence were found in the middle of the Forum; they date from the early 2nd century AD.

AT THE FOOT OF THE CAPITOL

THE ARCH OF SEPTIMIUS SEVERUS. Built in 203 AD, this arch is nearly 70 feet high. On both sides identical monumental inscriptions dedicate it to the Emperor Septimius Severus and his son Caracalla; the fourth line, which was erased and rewritten, gave the name of Septimius' other son, Geta, assassinated by his brother after their father's death. The bases of the columns illustrate the salient events of two victorious campaigns in the Middle East, including Roman soldiers carrying off Parthian prisoners.

SEPTIMIUS SEVERUS (193–211 AD) Born in Africa, he married a Syrian noblewoman, Julia Domna. They had two sons, Caracalla and Geta.

SEPTIMIUS' ARCH
Of the numerous bas-reliefs that feature on this arch, two splendid panels over the minor arches record the most memorable moments from Septimius' Parthian expeditions: the Roman army departs, the Emperor speaks, enemy cities are captured...
In the center of the major arch stands Mars, surrounded by winged Victories with the four seasons at their feet.

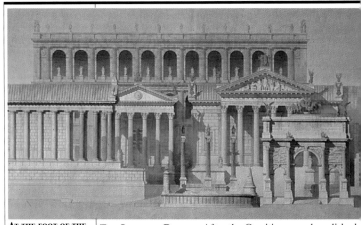

AT THE FOOT OF THE CAPITOL
The achievement of this magnificent reconstruction made between 1865 and 1866 was its appreciation of the spatial relationship between the monuments, virtually stacked together, with the Arch of Septimius Severus and the temples of Concord, Vespasian and Saturn dominated by the massive Tabularium.

THE IMPERIAL ROSTRA. After the Comitium was demolished ▲ *138*, new semicircular Rostra were built at the northwest end of the Forum and inaugurated by Mark Antony between 45 and 44 BC, not long before Julius Caesar's death. A rectilinear structure was later added by Augustus, no doubt in an attempt to obliterate the memory of his former rival and of the purges of 43 AD during which the heads of those executed, including Cicero's, were displayed there. At the end of the Rostra that is nearest to the arch there is a circular brick base known as the *umbilicus urbis* ("the navel of the city"), which symbolized the center of Rome. At the other end of the hemicycle are the remains of the *milliarium aureum*, a small monument erected by Augustus to mark the ideal point of convergence of the Imperial highways and to measure distances from Rome.

TEMPLE OF SATURN. Erected in the earliest Republican times around 497 BC, this temple served as Rome's state treasury and records office (*aerarium*). It was completely rebuilt in 42 BC at Munatius Plancus' request, and was again restored after being damaged in Carinus' fire in 283 AD. The anniversary of the temple's dedication was accompanied by the unbridled merrymaking of the Saturnalia, around December 17. On this date, which marked the end of the solar year, social roles were inverted and slaves were served by their masters.

PORTICO OF THE DEI CONSENTES. In 183 the remains of a portico with columns were discovered in front of an edifice consisting of eight rooms built in brick. It was probably part of the monument that housed the gilded statues of the *dei consentes*. These deities, six male and six female, may date back to the twelve gods that the Etruscans believed Jupiter consulted. Alternatively they may have been the Roman version of the Greek *dodekatheon*: Jupiter, Neptune, Mars, Apollo, Vulcan, Mercury, Juno, Minerva, Diana, Venus, Vesta and Ceres.

THE TEMPLE OF VESPASIAN AND TITUS. This temple dedicated to Vespasian and the Divine Titus (it was customary to worship emperors as gods after they died) was restored under Septimius Severus and Caracalla. Its façade had six columns. All that remains are three marble Corinthian columns supporting a fragment of the architrave, on which the inscription [R]estituer[unt] and a bas-relief showing instruments of sacrifice can be seen. The temple was faced with white marble.

THE TEMPLE OF CONCORD. Founded by Camillus in 367 BC to commemorate the end of the struggle between the plebeians and the patricians, under the Republic this temple was frequently used for meetings of the Senate. Between 7 BC and 10 AD it was restored by Tiberius thanks to booty plundered from the Germans. It contained many works of art, and in imperial times became a sort of museum.

THE CENTRAL PART OF THE FORUM

PHOCAS' COLUMN AND THE LACUS CURTIUS. The paving of the Forum we see today is dated by a large, partially restored inscription near Phocas' Column that reads: *L. Naevius Surdinus pr[aetor]* (9 BC). This column, which stands on a stepped pedestal in front of the Rostra, was dedicated to the Byzantine Emperor Phocas in 608 AD and was the last commemorative monument to be built in the Forum. Slightly to the east is a circular base with a central opening known as the Lacus Curtius. This has given rise to several legends and was originally considered to be the place where the Sabine chief Mettus Curtius was swallowed up, together with his horse, during the legendary Sabine-Roman conflict. Although the original bas-relief on Greek marble illustrating the story is now in the Capitoline Museum, a cast of it can be seen.

BASILICA JULIA ● 65. Between Vicus Jugarius and Vicus Tuscus foundation stones and fragments of columns show the position of the Basilica Julia, built by Julius Caesar and Augustus on the site of the Basilica Sempronia (founded by the father of the Gracchi in 170 BC). Although Diocletian had it restored in the 3rd century, the repeated sacking of Rome left almost nothing of this ancient building. Even the brick pillars we see today are 19th-century reconstructions.

THE TABULARIUM
At the end of the Forum one can still see this enormous tufa substructure, surmounted by a gallery of arches. An underground passage connects it to the Capitoline Museums.

CASTOR AND POLLUX
The *equites* (knights) regarded the Dioscuri as their patrons and regularly celebrated their feast on July 15.

Cicero delivered his fourth tirade against Catilina in the Temple of Concord in 63 BC.

The Temple of the Dioscuri.

The Fountain of Juturna
The nymph Juturna was famous for her beauty. To show his love for her, Jupiter

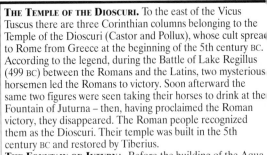

The Temple of the Dioscuri. To the east of the Vicus Tuscus there are three Corinthian columns belonging to the Temple of the Dioscuri (Castor and Pollux), whose cult spread to Rome from Greece at the beginning of the 5th century BC. According to the legend, during the Battle of Lake Regillus (499 BC) between the Romans and the Latins, two mysterious horsemen led the Romans to victory. Soon afterward the same two figures were seen taking their horses to drink at the Fountain of Juturna – then, having proclaimed the Roman victory, they disappeared. The Roman people recognized them as the Dioscuri. Their temple was built in the 5th century BC and restored by Tiberius.

The Fountain of Juturna. Before the building of the Aqua Appia, Rome's first aqueduct, the Roman population drew water from the Tiber, wells and a few rare springs. The most important of these was at the foot of the Palatine Hill. It was deified as Juturna, the sister of the Dioscuri, who like all water goddesses was believed to have healing properties. At the center of its square marble-faced basin stood a rectangular pedestal, which supported the statue of the Dioscuri found lying in pieces in the basin. The sculptured group can now be seen in the Forum's antiquarium. Not far away is a small temple dedicated to Juturna. Behind the fountain was the *statio aquarum* (the "aqueduct office"), which was transferred to the Campus Martius in 328 AD.

The Oratory of the Forty Martyrs. This room, dating back to Trajan's times, was transformed into an oratory by the addition of an apse. On the rear wall a fresco, probably painted in the 8th century AD, portrays the martyrdom of forty Christian soldiers during Diocletian's persecutions at the end of the 3rd century.

Domitian's buildings and the Church of Santa Maria Antiqua. An important group of buildings stands to the south of the Fountain of Juturna: a portico facing the Forum, shops on the Vicus Tuscus,

granted her immortality and gave her power over the springs of Latium. Virgil cast her as the "divine sister of Turnus", the enemy of Aeneas, and describes her role in the conflict between them. Another legend makes her the wife of Janus and mother of Fontus, the god of springs.

and a large brick hall originally covered by a vault. To the east, other rooms adjoin a covered ramp leading to the Imperial palaces of the Palatine. This complex was long thought to have been a monumental porch belonging to the palaces, but it is more likely to have been the Athenaeum, a sort of university founded by Hadrian. The Church of Santa Maria Antiqua was built here in the 6th century; its wall paintings dating from the 7th–9th century, applied in different layers, are a unique source of information on Rome in the early Middle Ages. The oldest paintings to be seen date from the period of Pope John VII (705–7), who resided in the Imperial palace. To the south of this church are the remains of the Horrea Agrippiana, grain stores built by Agrippa, Augustus' friend and son-in-law. The Church of San Teodoro is also in this area, although its entrance is just outside the Forum.

TEMPLE OF THE DIVINE JULIUS AND THE ARCH OF AUGUSTUS.
After Caesar's assassination in Pompey's Curia ▲ 248, his body was brought to the Forum and cremated. A column with the inscription *Parenti patriae* ("To the father of the nation") and a temple, dedicated by Augustus in 29 BC, were erected on this spot. This was the first posthumous deification in Rome, but all that has survived of the temple are parts of the podium and of the tribune built in front of it to display the figureheads of Anthony and Cleopatra's fleet, defeated by Octavian at Actium in 31 BC. Beside the temple lie the scant remains of the ARCH OF AUGUSTUS. This had three openings and is almost certainly the monument built by the Senate in 29 BC to commemorate the victory at Actium.

THE REGIA. The construction of the "Royal house" is attributed to Numa Pompilius ● 26, the second king of Rome, who is said to have used it as his residence. It included the House of the Vestals and the building reserved for the *rex sacrorum*, a title which in early Republican times conferred the priestly attributes of the ancient kings. Later it became the residence of the *pontifex maximus*, Rome's

show Christ and the saints. Only a few fragments of the right aisle's murals can still be seen. They include a niche with a *Virgin and Child*, and the apse with a *Crucifixion* above and *Christ Giving His Blessing* below; on his right is Pope Paul I (757–67).
San Teodoro.

143

TEMPLE OF ANTONINUS AND FAUSTINA
The temple's transformation into a church saved it from destruction. Its fine façade, with steps and cipollino columns, has been preserved. The *cella*'s magnificent frieze, featuring griffins and ornate candelabra (see top of facing page), recalls the temple's funerary vocation.

highest priestly functionary. After a fire and two reconstructions in the early years of the Republic, it acquired the appearance it was to keep throughout Imperial times.

THE TEMPLE OF VESTA AND THE HOUSE OF THE VESTALS ★.
The temple of the goddess Vesta stands in front of the Regia. This sanctuary and the House of the Vestals were designed as a single unit, the Atrium Vestae. A substitute for the royal hearth (perceived as symbolizing all others and representing the permanence of the State), the Temple of Vesta housed the city's sacred fire. Tending this fire was originally the task of the king's daughters, but under the Republic the duty was conferred upon six specialized priestesses known as Vestals. They had to be from patrician families and were selected for this function at the age of six. They were obliged to keep their virginity throughout the time of their priesthood, which lasted for thirty years. The penalty for breaking this vow was to be buried alive in the Campus Sceleratus on the Quirinal Hill (their accomplice merely suffered flagellation in the Comitium ▲ *138*). The temple also housed the "pledges" of the permanence of Rome's universal empire said to have been brought from Troy by Aeneas. The most important of these was the Palladium, an archaic effigy of Minerva reputed to preserve the city that possessed it. The present ruins of the temple, entirely made of brick, date from the end of the 2nd century, as do those of the House of the Vestals. This was a vast building several floors high, with rooms overlooking a rectangular courtyard, itself adorned with three basins and surrounded by statues of the greatest Vestals.

THE OTHER SIDE OF THE VIA SACRA

The Via Sacra was the Forum's most ancient thoroughfare, and its most prestigious. The triumphal parades of victorious generals used it to reach the Temple of Jupiter on the Capitol.

TEMPLE OF ROMULUS. This small domed temple was dedicated to Maxentius' son Romulus ▲ *329*, who died and was deified in 309 AD. Later it was used as the vestibule to the Church of Santi Cosma e Damiano ▲ *168*. The temple was originally erected at street level, but archeological digs in the 19th century exposed its foundations.

TEMPLE OF ANTONINUS AND FAUSTINA ★. This large temple, transformed into the Church of San Lorenzo in Miranda in the Middle Ages, is easily identifiable due to the monumental inscription on its architrave. In 141 AD Antoninus Pius erected it in memory of his wife, Faustina, who had died and been deified that same year. His own name was added to the dedication when he died in 161 AD.

THE ARCHAIC NECROPOLIS. In 1902, to the right of the temple, the remains of a necropolis were discovered, with forty-one Iron Age tombs. The oldest type consisted of a circular pit enclosing tomb furniture and an urn containing cremated remains. Shaped like a hut, the urn was quite a realistic representation of an Iron Age dwelling ▲ *148*. The later tombs were for the burial of bodies. Objects found in the necropolis are displayed in the Antiquarium of the Forum ▲ *147*.

BASILICA OF MAXENTIUS AND CONSTANTINE ● 64. This was one of the most grandiose monuments in Imperial Rome. Begun under Maxentius in 308 AD and completed under Constantine in 312, it covered nearly 65,000 square feet. The barrel vaulting of the huge central nave, 115 feet high, was supported by three immense cross-vaults resting on eight piers. These formed adjacent transepts covering the two lower side aisles, each in turn divided into three great vaulted arches. The roofing was made of gilded bronze tiles, which were reused in the 7th century for the roof of St Peter's. The central transept to the north, which still exists, ended with an apse and was the Emperor's law court. A magnificent entrance with a portico supported on four porphyry columns opened to the south, providing access from the Via Sacra up a central flight of steps. The interior decoration of the basilica consisted of multicolored marble inlays on the walls and floors, gilded stucco coffering on the ceilings, marble and porphyry columns against the walls, and numerous statues that have now disappeared. During the Renaissance the basilica of Maxentius served as a model for many architects, including Bramante in his plans for the new St Peter's.

A view from the Forum (below), and the paving stones of the Via Sacra.

THE BASILICA OF MAXENTIUS
Known for a long time as the Temple of Peace, this ruin was identified by the archeologist Nibby at the start of the 19th century when it was

freed of the rubble that partly covered it. Only one wing is still standing; the rest of the building was probably destroyed by an earthquake, perhaps the one in 1349 that damaged the Coliseum ▲ *170* and the Torre dei Conti ▲ *168*.

HOUSE OF LIVIA AND AUGUSTUS
1. TEMPLE OF APOLLO
2. LIBRARY
   DOMUS TIBERIANA
3. CALIGULA'S EXTENSIONS
4. CRYPTOPORTICUS

THE ARCH OF TITUS ★. Probably erected by Domitian, this arch ▲ *147* owes its partial preservation to having been incorporated into the medieval fortifications built by the Frangipane family and to its restoration in 1821. On the east side one can read the original inscription: "The Senate and the Roman People to the Divine Titus Vespasian Augustus, son of the Divine Vespasian." The allusion to Titus' divinity

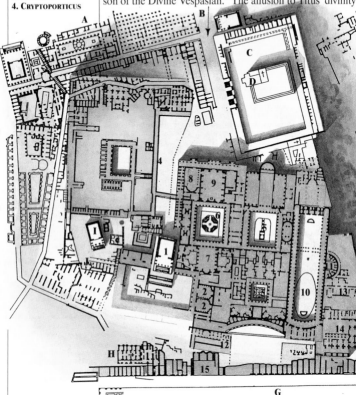

PALACE OF DOMITIAN
5. PERISTYLE OF DOMUS AUGUSTANA
6. PERISTYLE OF DOMUS FLAVIA
7. COENATIO JOVIS
8. BASILICA
9. AULA REGIA
10. DOMITIAN'S STADIUM
11. TRIBUNE
12. PAEDAGOGIUM
    SEVERIAN BUILDINGS
13. BATHS
14. DOMUS SEVERIANA
15. DOMUS PRAECONUM

means that he was already dead when the arch was built. The bas-relief in the center of the arch shows Titus being carried off to heaven on the back of an eagle. The small relief of the frieze on the eastern side illustrates the victory of Vespasian and Titus (who was his eldest son) over the Jews in 71 AD.

THE TEMPLE OF VENUS AND ROME. This was originally the si of the gigantic statue of Nero that stood in front of the *atriu* of the Domus Aurea ▲ *174*. The Emperor Hadrian had to u twenty-four elephants to move this bronze colossus ▲ *171* to its pedestal beside the Coliseum before he could build the temple. Hadrian himself is supposed to have designed this inspired edifice; however, it is said to have displeased a leading architect, Apollodorus of Damascus, to such an exte that his outspoken criticisms cost him his life. Dedicated in 135 AD, the temple consisted of two symmetrical *cellae*, back to back, divided by a central wall, so that "Rome" faced the Forum and Venus faced the Coliseum. The idea of attributir divinity to a city was inspired by a Hellenistic practice alread current in Rome since the 2nd century BC.

FORUM F. SEPTIZODIUM
CLIVUS PALATINUS SEVERIANUM
RANCE G. CIRCUS MAXIMUS
TEMPLE OF H. CHURCH OF
LIOGABALUS SANT'ANASTASIA
SAN SEBASTIANO I. TEMPLE OF CYBELE
URCH J. ARCHAIC HUTS
AQUA CLAUDIA • ARCHAIC CISTERNS

HE ANTIQUARIUM OF THE FORUM. In the setting of the
rmer Convent of Santa Francesca Romana one can see the
ost important archeological finds from the Forum, which
clude objects from the archaic necropolis ▲ 145 and
agments of a marble relief from the Basilica Aemilia ▲ 136
lustrating the myths concerning the origins of Rome.

"Before Jupiter was
born the Arcadians
already lived in their
land, and this people
must be older than
the moon."
Ovid

HE PALATINE ★

ith its lawns and umbrella pines, the Palatine is still one of
the most enchanting parts of the city.

THE CRADLE OF ROME. Its central position made this hill
the most obvious spot for human settlement.According to
legend it was settled at a very early date by a Greek
colony from Pallantion, in Arcadia, led by their king,
Evander. In the *Aeneid* Virgil mentions the
Arcadians that Hercules and later Aeneas are said
to have met in this place. During the Republic
the hill became the residential quarter of
Rome's ruling classes. Augustus' decision to
live on the Palatine was of great importance
for its future: after him all the emperors
chose to reside here, including Tiberius
(whose palace was enlarged by Caligula
and Domitian), Nero, the Flavians (who
built the Domus Flavia and Domus
Augustana) and Septimius Severus.
Consequently the name Palatium
(Palatine) came to mean the palace as
well as the hill. During the Middle Ages
the Frangipane family established their
fortified dwelling here as a refuge for the
popes. In the 16th century Vignola built
the Farnese family sumptuous gardens
(part of which have survived), adorned
with fountains, aviaries and works of art.
It was thanks to this great family that the
first excavations of Domitian's palace
were undertaken in the 18th century,
before those financed by Napoleon III.

MYTHS AND CULTS. The Feast of the Palilia was held on April
1, the anniversary of the city's foundation. The other
mportant feast on the Palatine was the Lupercalia, when
here was a procession from the *lupercal*, the
ve on the Tiber side of the hill where
ccording to tradition the she-wolf suckled
omulus and Remus, the legendary founders of
ome. It also involved a purification and fertility
tual in which *luperci* (wolf priests) raced
ound the hill, clad in the skins of the goats
ey had sacrificed. As they ran, they wielded
reds of the sacrificed animals, which were
pposed to bring fertility to the land and to
nyone they touched, especially women. Several
her cults originated and flourished on the
alatine, including those of Apollo and Cybele.
roceed up the Clivus Palatinus to the eastern
orner of the hill, passing the Farnese Gardens
n your right.)

THE ARCH OF TITUS
Two large marble bas-
reliefs inside the arch
illustrate scenes from
Titus' triumphal
parade. The one to
the south shows a
procession about to
pass through the
Triumphal Gate; the
items carried include
the seven-branched
candelabra and silver
trumpets plundered
from the Temple in
Jerusalem. In the
relief to the north
Titus is shown
advancing in his four-
horse chariot,
preceded by the
lictors. The goddess
Rome holds the
horses by their bridles
while Victory crowns
the Emperor;
allegorical figures
representing the
Senate and the
Roman people follow
behind.

AROUND THE HOUSE OF LIVIA

THE HOUSE OF ROMULUS. This is where Romulus said to have lived, in a hut near the spot where Augustus later chose to build his own house. In 1948 excavations revealed traces of Iron Age dwellings: three hut bases carved in the tufa the hill and protected by a small drainage trench. Between these sites and Livia's house two archaic water cisterns were found, one of them particularly well preserved.

A funerary urn in the shape of an archaic hut. The three hut bases unearthed in 1948 belonged to dwellings of this type; the largest measures 16 feet on its longest side. Wooden posts, which supported the walls and roof, stood in post holes like the ones that can still be seen.

THE TEMPLE OF THE MAGNA MATER. One of the most significant events in the religious crisis that accompanied the Second Punic War against Hannibal was the adoption in 204 BC of the cult of Cybele, the Great Mother. The center of her cult was at Pessinus, in northern Asia Minor, where her image, an amorphous black stone (possibly a meteorite), was said to have fallen from heaven. Its introduction to Rome was due to the consultation of the Sibylline books, a compilation of Greek and Etruscan oracles and prophecies related to the cult of Apollo and brought to Rome by Tarquinius Superbus. The temple was only completed in 191 BC. Its remains are to be seen between the site of the archaic huts and the *tabernae* of the Domus Tiberiana, where there is a statue of the goddess (right).

THE TRANSPORTATION OF THE GODDESS CYBELE
The sacred image of Cybele (the black stone) was brought to Rome by sea. During the feast days of the goddess (the Ludi Megalenses), held once a year around April 4, many plays were performed. It was on such occasions that some of the best works of Plautus and Terence were produced.

THE HOUSE OF LIVIA. To the east of the statue of Cybele is a group of houses dating from the end of the Republic. One of these is probably the part of Augustus' house reserved for his wife, Livia. It was excavated by Pietro Rosa in the middle of the 19th century under Napoleon III's patronage. A sloping corridor leads into a rectangular patio enclosed by pillars. The *tablinum* and two adjacent rooms have very fine "second style" wall paintings dating from around 30 BC. In front of the entrance a painting portraying Polyphemus and Galatea has now almost completely faded. In another room one of the walls is soberly decorated with a festoon of fruit and foliage, while above it scenes of life in Egypt are depicted against a yellow background. All the rooms of the house were paved with simple black-and-white mosaics.

THE HOUSE OF LIVIA ★
The right wall of the *tablinum* is the best preserved. The painted surface is divided into three sections by Corinthian columns. The central panel of the mural portrays Io, watched over by Argos, who has just been freed by Mercury. It is probably a copy of a famous painting by Nikias.

THE HOUSE OF AUGUSTUS. The historian Suetonius states that Augustus purchased the house of the orator Hortensius in 36 AD and later added many other buildings. The smaller

The walls of the Temple of Apollo were adorned with painted terracotta panels. The subtle use of color is characteristic of the Augustan period.

...ms to the west appear to have been the living quarters, ...le the apartments to the east that surround the large ...tral hall were most probably used for official functions.

TEMPLE OF APOLLO. This was believed to be the Temple ...Jupiter Victor until it was definitively identified in 1956. All ...t remains are the stone base of the temple, traces of its ...ble pavement and fragments of Corinthian capitals. ...cording to tradition, Augustus is said to have had the ...ple built within the precinct of his house between 36 and ...BC. The Emperor regarded Apollo – the god of order, ...t and youth – as his personal protector, attributing his ...ory over Mark Antony in 31 BC to him. This faith in the ...eek god was further exemplified by his staging of the ...ular Games in 17 BC and by the sumptuous decoration ...his temple, which was entirely built of Luni marble. ...ree Greek sculptors, Scopas, Kephisodotos and ...notheos, were commissioned to make the statues of the ...ies Apollo, Diana and Leto. It was in the base of the ...tue of Apollo that the Sibylline books were later deposited, ...served until then in the Temple of Jupiter Capitolinus. ...is relocation had the effect of making Augustus' own home ...ually the religious center of the city, a notion that was ...ther reinforced when the Emperor had a statue and ...ur of Vesta transferred there as well.

DOMUS TIBERIANA. The first Imperial palace to be ...ceived as such from the time of its construction was ...t of Tiberius, the successor of Augustus. It extended ...r the area between the Temple of Cybele and the ...pes leading down to the Forum. In the 16th century this ...tion of the Palatine was turned into the Farnese gardens. ...e area so far excavated includes eighteen rooms on the ...th side, an oval basin (which may have been a fish tank) ...d the long cryptoporticus, an underground gallery where ...e can see the remains of murals, fragments of mosaic ...ements and part of a stucco ceiling with Cupids, the ...ginal of which is now in the Palatine's antiquarium ... *151*. To the right, a later wing of this gallery leads to the ...mus Augustana ▲ *150*. Caligula enlarged the palace in ... direction of the Forum, and Domitian had it rebuilt.

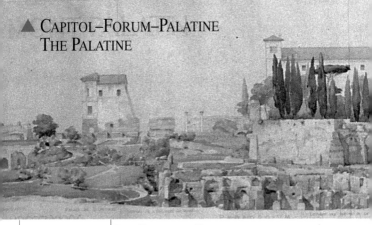

The Palace of Domitian

Palaces gradually replaced the older buildings on the western slopes of the Palatine, transforming the appearance of the hill.

Domus Flavia. Until the end of the Empire, this palace was the official residence of the emperors. Its construction, directed by the architect Rabirius, started at the beginning of Domitian's reign and was only completed in 92 AD. At the center of the Domus Flavia an enormous rectangular peristyle surrounds a great octagonal fountain. Sumptuous rooms open onto it from all sides. To the north is the Aula Regia (throne room), given this name by 18th-century archeologists because of its impressive size. This was where the Emperor gave public audiences. Gigantic statues in colored marble stood in the niches. The apse was where the Emperor appeared with great majesty in the role of *dominus et deus*, as Domitian was the first to want to be called. To the west of the *aula* is the basilica, a slightly smaller rectangular hall with a nave and two aisles culminating in a deep apse, which was probably the Emperor's council chamber. A smaller room to the east is arbitrarily referred to as the *lararium*. Beneath it was discovered the most interesting Republican house in Rome, the House of the Griffins (so called because of a stucco decoration featuring two griffins) dating from the late 2nd century BC. Finally, to the south of the peristyle there is a large hall that still has most of its rich marble pavement, which was raised on a *hypocaustum* so that it could be heated. This was no doubt the grandiose dining hall known as the Coenatio Jovis.

The House of the Griffins ★
The most interesting paintings (c. 100 BC) found here are now in the Antiquarium of the Palatine ▲ *151*, together with those from the Aula Isiaca (a house discovered under the basilica).

The Septizodium, which was destroyed by Sixtus V.

The Domus Augustana. This was the emperors' private residence. The northern end was built around a large peristyle adorned by an ornamental basin; in the center of this, on a high podium, was a little temple that could be reached by means of a bridge. On the south side the ground floor (which is much lower than the rest of the palace) is laid out around a square courtyard that opened via a huge exedra onto the Circus Maximus ▲ *177*. The upper floor, which is badly preserved and over-restored, is of complex design and includes rooms of a more modest size.

Reconstruction of the palace's façade overlooking the Circus Maximus (left). A watercolor of it painted in 1886 (above).

Part of the basilica of the Domus Flavia.

THE STADIUM. This edifice in the shape of a circus, surrounded by a portico on two levels, is the third section of Domitian's palace. Probably used both as a garden and riding track, it may have been the Hippodromus Palatii referred to in the *Acts of the Martyrs* as the place where St Sebastian was killed. Installations of this kind, which included a huge central tribune, were a feature of the large private villas of this period.

THE DOMUS SEVERIANA. This modern name is incorrectly applied to Septimius Severus' enlargement of the Domus Augustana at the end of the 2nd century AD. All that is left of this building are the bare brick substructures that give the Palatine its most striking appearance. Baths were located in the space between this building and the exedra of the stadium. Their water was supplied by a branch of the Aqua Claudia that spanned the gap between the Coelian and the Palatine by means of massive arches (partially preserved). The part of the Palatine facing the Via Appia was adorned with the SEPTIZODIUM (see foot of facing page), a monumental nymphaeum designed, according to Septimius Severus' biographer, to impress travelers arriving from Africa.

HELIOGABALUS (218–22AD)
High priest of a sun-god cult, he came to power at the age of fourteen but was soon deposed and murdered because of his cruelty.

THE ANTIQUARIUM OF THE PALATINE. Situated in the former convent of the Sisters of the Visitation, this museum contains archeological remains from the Palatine Hill, including materials from the archaic huts ▲ *148* and paintings from Republican and Imperial buildings.

CHURCHES ON THE PALATINE AND THE TEMPLE OF HELIOGABALUS. The whole eastern sector of the Palatine consists of massive artificial terracing designed to support a single building, probably of the period of Domitian's adjacent palace. In the center is the beautiful CHURCH OF SAN SEBASTIANO. Since the 11th century it has belonged to the Benedictine Order, although its present appearance dates from the 17th century. South of this church are the remains of a temple that could be the one the emperor Heliogabalus erected to the god El-Gabal, with the aim of persuading Rome to adopt the oriental custom of deifying living sovereigns. At the very end of the Via San Bonaventura stands the little church of the same name, founded in 1677.

S.P.Q.R: SENATUS POPULUSQUE ROMANUS
This time-honored abbreviation stands for "The
Senate and the Roman People". The Roman po
Giuseppe Belli ● 43 interpreted it as: *Solo i pre*
qui regnano ("only priests rule here").

From the Forum Holitorium to the Coliseum

154 The Forum Holitorium and
Forum Boarium
157 The Circus Flaminius area
160 Piazza Venezia
162 The Imperial Forums
167 From Trajan's Markets to
the Coliseum
170 The Coliseum
174 The Domus Aurea

One day

◆ E B2-C2-C3

1. SANTA MARIA IN COSMEDIN
2. TEMPLE OF HERCULES VICTOR
3. TEMPLE OF PORTUNUS
4. ARCH OF JANUS
5. SAN GIORGIO IN VELABRO
6. AREA SACRA DI SANT'OMOBONO
7. SAN NICOLA IN CARCERE
8. THEATER OF MARCELLUS
9. SANTA MARIA IN CAMPITELLI
10. SANT'ANGELO IN PESCHERIA
11. PORTICO OF OCTAVIA
12. SANTA FRANCESCA IN TOR DE' SPECCHI
13. PALAZZO DI VENEZIA
14. BASILICA DI SAN MARCO
15. VICTOR EMMANUEL II MONUMENT

THE FORUM HOLITORIUM AND FORUM BOARIUM

The plain between the Tiber and the group of hills closest to the river (the Capitol, the Palatine and the Aventine) was of vital importance from Rome's earliest days. Two of the main routes of communication for central Italy crossed in this spot: the Tiber, which was navigable from the sea and the north-south route linking Etruria to Campania, which had an easy ford just downstream from Isola Tiberina ▲ 352. Rome's first wooden bridge, the Pons Sublicius, was built here in the 7th century BC. The commercial port of the town, the Portus Tiberinus, occupied the area between the temple dedicated to Portunus (the guardian deity of the port) and a monumental square that became the fruit and vegetable market, the Forum Holitorium (where San Nicola in Carcere stands today). This forum extended from the slopes of the Capitol to the Tiber and was served by the Vicus Jugarius (probably the street of the yoke makers) which was one of the town's main streets. Another road

...om the Roman Forum was the Vicus Tuscus (its name no ...ubt came from the Etruscan merchants based there); this ...irted the Palatine and led to the cattle market, the Forum ...arium, which is now the Piazza Bocca della Verità.

...NTA MARIA IN COSMEDIN. This church was founded in the ...h century on the ruins of the *statio annonae*, the food-...stribution center of classical Rome. Enlarged by Pope ...drian I in the 8th century, it was given to the Greek ...mmunity who lived near the ...ber, in a district called the ...pa Grecae. From that ...ne the church was ...own as Santa ...Maria in

Cosmedin, after the name of a quarter in Constantinople. Beneath the portico is the famous BOCCA DELLA VERITÀ ● 47 ("the mouth of truth"), an ...cient drain covering adorned with the face of the sea god ...ceanus; if any liar was rash enough to place his hand inside ...gaping mouth, the jaws were said to snap it off.

...roughout its history this church was repeatedly restored ...d redecorated, especially in the 12th and 13th centuries. ...oteworthy features include the portico, the elegant ...omanesque campanile, the *schola cantorum* (choir), the rich ...osmatesque ● 76 pavement and decorations, and the Gothic ...ldacchino over the high altar. In the sacristy there is a ...gment of 8th-century mosaic from the original St Peter's ...silica. The block of tufa from which the tiny crypt was ...ollowed out is thought to be the remains of an altar from the ...orum Boarium dedicated to Hercules (in honor of his victory ...er the giant Cacus, who stole his cattle). At the end of the ...th century, the architect Giovanni Battista Giovenale gave ...e church its excessively medieval appearance.

...E TEMPLES OF FORTUNA VIRILIS AND VESTA. The national ...gistry office (*anagrafe*) of modern times is built on the site ...the Portus Tiberinus, the ancient river port to the south of ...e Forum Holitorium. Next to it stands the rectangular ...mple of Portunus (god of ports), better known as the

Temple of Fortuna Virilis, founded in the 5th or 3rd century BC. Over the ages the present building, which dates from the 1st century BC, has undergone a series of restorations. Built of tufa and travertine, both temples were covered with stucco decorations. The circular temple farther to the south, close to the Tiber, is the oldest marble edifice to have survived in Rome. Although long known as the Temple of Vesta, it was in fact dedicated to Hercules Victor.

16. IMPERIAL FORUMS
17. TRAJAN'S COLUMN
18. TORRE DELLE MILIZIE
19. HOUSE OF THE KNIGHTS OF RHODES
20. TORRE DE' CONTI
21. SANTI COSMA E DAMIANO
22. SANTA FRANCESCA ROMANA
23. ARCH OF CONSTANTINE
24. COLISEUM
25. DOMUS AUREA
26. BATHS OF TRAJAN

The house of the Crescenzi ● *72* (above).

TEMPLE OF APOLLO SOSIANO
The decoration of the pediment portrayed Amazons fighting in the presence of Athena. These Greek sculptures from the middle of the 5th century BC are now in the Capitoline Museums.

SAN GIORGIO IN VELABRO. This church was built in the 7th century in an area marked by an important Byzantine presence. Restored several times over th centuries, it finally recovered its mediev appearance (11th-century ciborium and 12th-century portico and campanile). Th portico, destroyed by a bomb in 1993, ha been the object of new restoration work.

ARCO DEGLI ARGENTARI. According to th 204 AD inscription the monumental arch (or gate) next to the Church of San Giorgio in Velabro was dedicated to the Emperor Septimius Severus and his family by the guild of moneychangers (*argentarii*) and cattle dealers. On the inner walls a relief shows Caracalla making a libation on a portable altar. O the other side Septimius and his wife, Julia Domna, can be seen in the act of making a sacrifice.

THE ARCH OF JANUS. Close to the Arco degli Argentarii stands the Arco di Giano, said to have been built by Constantius II in the 4th century. As it straddled a busy road, it was given the name of Janus (one of the oldest Roman divinities), who had two faces and was the guardian of gates and thoroughfares. Close to the arch, a gate in the railings leads to a well-preserved section o the *cloaca maxima* ● *69*. (Take Via di San Giovanni Decollato, where the 16th-century church of this name, with frescoes by Salviati, belonged to a confraternity that offered assistance to those who were sentenced to death. Then turn left into Vico Jugario.)

THE AREA SACRA DI SANT'OMOBONO. Near the small church of Sant'Omobono is a site that has provided exceptionally important historical evidence of the Etruscan presence here in archaic times. This sacred precinct includes two small temples, dedicated to Fortuna and Mater Matuta (Dawn), which according to an ancient tradition were founded by King Servius Tullius (579–534 BC). Archeological finds have fully confirmed this chronology and have also made it possible to date their destruction to the end of the 6th century BC. It seems that Etruscan temples were purposely demolished at the time of the expulsion of the kings, prior to the establishment of the Republic in 509 BC. (Cross the Via del Teatro Marcello.)

SAN NICOLA IN CARCERE. This church owes its name to a prison

arcere) that existed in this spot in the 8th century. The
present church, erected on the site of a former shrine by Pope
Honorius II in 1128 and flanked by a medieval bell tower, was
radically rebuilt by Giacomo della Porta, who was also
responsible for its façade (1599). The doorway on the right side
is a rare example of 15th-century Gothic architecture in Rome.
The columns separating the three naves all come from ancient
temples. The *confessio* (the tomb of a confessor of the faith) is
decorated with a cycle of frescoes depicting *The Baptism of
Christ*. These paintings, which date from the beginning of the
14th century, are now in the Vatican Pinacoteca ▲ *215*. Three
important Republican temples, dedicated to Janus, Spes
(Hope) and Juno Sospita (the "helper"), occupied the site
where the church now stands. It is built on a section of the
central temple, vestiges of which are preserved in the crypt.
Several columns from the other two temples are still visible,
freestanding or embedded within the church walls.

THE CIRCUS FLAMINIUS AREA

Today nothing is left of the circus built in 221 BC by the
"leader" of the people, Caius Flaminius Nepos, which
extended along the Tiber to the south of the Campus Martius.
Triumphal processions to the Capitol started from here.
Consequently, especially at the end of the
Republic, the neighboring district
became the center of intense building
activity (the construction of temples
and porticos) by victorious generals.
THE THEATER OF MARCELLUS. This
theater was begun by Caesar and
completed by Augustus. The choice of
site was determined by the proximity
of the Temple of Apollo, in whose
honor plays were performed. It was
officially dedicated in 13 or 11 BC in
the name of Marcellus,
Augustus' nephew,
son-in-law and heir
designate, who died
prematurely.

Reconstruction of the
steps and tunnels of
the Theater of
Marcellus by
Vaudoyer, who was
awarded the Prix de
Rome in 1783.

**THE THEATER OF
MARCELLUS**
Like many ancient
monuments, the
theater was fortified
in the Middle Ages
and thus saved from
destruction. In the
16th century the
Savelli family
commissioned the
Sienese architect
Baldassare Peruzzi to
build the palace
which now occupies
the upper part; it was
rebuilt by the Orsini
in the 18th century.

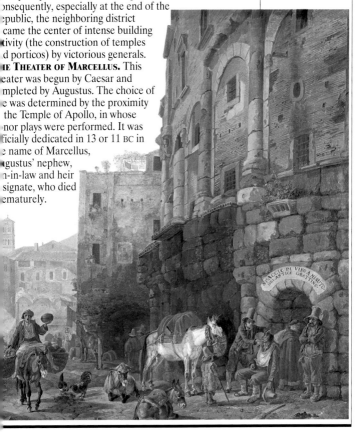

The three columns of the Temple of Apollo Sosianus.

PORTICO OF OCTAVIA
The ruins visible today (the propylaea, part of the portico, five Corinthian columns and the inscription on the architrave) date from the restoration undertaken by Septimius Severus, after a fire in 191 AD during the reign of the Emperor Commodus.

It had previously been used for the Century Games of 17 BC, festivities traditionally held every hundred years to mark the beginning of a new era. This theater was the largest in Rome after that of Pompey ▲ *248*, with a capacity of about 15,000 spectators, and there is no doubt that it inspired the architecture of the Coliseum. One can still see part of the first and second (Doric and Ionic) tiers, while the third (Corinthian) tier has almost entirely disappeared. It was replaced by the Orsini palace. Practically nothing remains of the stage; it was demolished in the 4th century and served as marble quarry, providing building material for the Pons Cestius ▲ *353*. In the 1930's the buildings that jostled against the theater were removed and it was restored.

THE TEMPLES OF APOLLO SOSIANUS AND BELLONA. The first of these temples was built on the site of a sacred grove, where a healing spirit was venerated after an epidemic of plague; it thus came to be dedicated, in 431 BC, to Apollo Medicus. It was the only important building to be erected during this time of crisis. In 34 BC it was completely rebuilt by a certain Caius Sosius. On the podium three magnificent columns remain, surmounted by a frieze of bucranes (ox skulls) and olive-leaf garlands. To the east of it the base of the TEMPLE OF BELLONA, the Latin goddess of war, has been identified. It was begun in 296 BC by Appius Claudius Caecus, who in 312 had commissioned the building of the Via Appia ▲ *318*. The Senate frequently met in these two temples, especially to decide whether or not to grant a Triumph to victorious generals. During the Empire such meetings took place in the Temple of Mars Ultor in Augustus' Forum ▲ *163*. (Take Via del Portico d'Ottavia, to the right of the Theater of Marcellus).

THE PORTICO OF OCTAVIA. Of the great porticos that lined the northern side of the Circus Flaminius, this is the only one that can still be seen. Inspired by Hellenistic architecture, these large squares flanked by colonnades were intended for State religious and political ceremonies. They also served as areas for walking. The Portico of Octavia stands on the site of that of Metellus

46 BC), which included two temples. One was dedicated
Juno Regina; the other, the first Roman building to be
[to]tally made of marble, to Jupiter Stator. Under Augustus,
[be]tween 27 and 23 BC, the portico was restored and officially
[de]dicated to Octavia, the sister of the emperor Augustus,
[to]gether with two libraries, Greek and Latin, which were
[in]stalled in the complex. The Senate sometimes met in the
[cu]ria adjoining the temples. Thirty-four of the numerous
[st]atues that decorated these buildings were made of bronze,
[am]ong them Alexander and his officers at the time of the
[ba]ttle of the Granicus River (against the Persians in 334 BC)
[an]d Cornelia, the mother of the Gracchi, typifying the ideal
[R]oman woman.

[SA]NT'ANGELO IN PESCHERIA. In 755 Pope Stephen III
[fo]unded this small church built into the ruins of the Portico of
[O]ctavia. The church owes its name to the fish market which
[w]as held in the portico during the Middle Ages. Inside the
[ch]urch, in the left nave, is a fresco of *The
[Vir]gin Enthroned between Angels* by Benozzo
[G]ozzoli. (Take the Via della Tribuna di
[Ca]mpitelli.)

[SA]NTA MARIA IN CAMPITELLI. This church was
[bu]ilt in 1663 to house the enamel icon known
[as] the *Madonna del Portico* (11th century), a
[mi]raculous image of the Virgin much revered
[by] the Romans, who attributed the end of a
[pla]gue epidemic to her intervention. The
[arc]hitects Carlo Rainaldi and Vicenzo de'
[R]ossi combined a building in the shape of a
[Gr]eek cross with a square choir surmounted by
[a d]ome, producing a theatrical effect through
[the]ir use of columns. (Take Via del Teatro
[M]arcello, on the left).

[M]ONASTERY OF TOR DE' SPECCHI. The
[me]dieval tower called the Tor de' Specchi
[(T]ower of Mirrors) because of the decoration

[of] its windows, gave its name to the monastery founded by
[Sa]nta Francesca Romana in 1443 ▲ 169. The chapel and
[ref]ectory, which are decorated with a lovely sequence of
[15]th-century frescoes, can be visited, as well as the saint's cell.
[Ta]ke Via d'Aracoeli on the left, then Via della Tribuna di Tor
[de'] Specchi).

[PI]AZZA MARGANA. This lovely little piazza is enchanting, with
[its] harmonious palazzi and houses from the 15th and 16th
[ce]nturies, its irregular shape, and the charm of its uneven
[co]bblestones. It still contains part of the fortified medieval
[to]wer of the Margani, the door of which is decorated with
[pilla]rs and a lintel made from fragments of a classical capitol.
[O]n the right at the end of the piazza, two alleyways lead to
[Pia]zza Venezia).

PORTICO OF OCTAVIA
This drawing by Felix
Duban, a
pensionnaire of the
French Academy in
Rome in 1827 ▲ 315,
shows the
monumental entrance
of the portico,
flanked by columns.
Behind are the two
older temples,
reconstructed with a
few anachronisms.
Traces of the Temple
of Juno Regina (on
the left) survive in the
cellars of the
medieval houses at
No. 5 and No. 28 Via

Sant'Angelo in
Pescheria. The
Temple of Jupiter
Stator (on the right)
was built by the
Greek architect
Hermodorus of
Salamis in the 2nd
century BC.

CLEOPATRA'S RIVAL
Octavia was the sister
of Octavian (the
future Emperor
Augustus). She was
married twice, the
second time to Mark
Antony in 40 BC, and
for a while managed
to keep the peace
between her husband
and her brother.
Antony repudiated
her eight years after
their marriage and
left her for Cleopatra.

PIAZZA VENEZIA

The layout and buildings of Piazza Venezia as they appear today are largely the product of the late 19th century and the Mussolini period: the Victor Emmanuel II Monument, the

A SYMBOLIC SITE
To build the Vittoriano, the remains of the *arx* ▲ *128* on the Capitol and a sizable part of medieval Rome had to be damaged or destroyed. On the right, just after the Museo del Risorgimento, some ancient and medieval ruins can still be seen. On the other side, the Tomb of Publicius Bibulus, from the Republican era, marks the end of the Servian Wall at the start of the Via Flaminia.

Assicurazioni Generali di Venezia building, the two avenues converging from the Imperial Forums and the Theater of Marcellus, and even the arrangement of Piazza Aracoeli. It one of the city's principal junctions. The popular Via del Corso ▲ *308* begins here and, in a straight line, links Piazza Venezia with the Piazza del Popolo ▲ *306*.

THE VICTOR EMMANUEL II MONUMENT ● *91*. This monument was built, between 1885 to 1911, to honor the memory of the first King of Italy, Victor Emmanuel II. It was the subject of ceaseless controversy, embracing town planning, art and politics. Criticized right from the start for its blinding "Nordic" whiteness, then threatened by Mussolini (who at first wanted to demolish it, then decided to use it for mass demonstrations) it was given a series of denigrating nicknames (such as "the typewriter", "the greatest public lavatory in Italy" and "the wedding cake") before finally being acquitted by a jury of architects, art historians, journalists and politicians. In commemoration of the king death in 1878, Giuseppe Sacconi was accorded the dubious honor in 1885 of conceiving "an equestrian statue with, eventually, an architectural background" When the "Vittoriano" was inaugurated, unfinished, in 1911, a banquet for ten people was held in the belly of the horse of the equestrian statue. The *quadrigae* (two-wheeled chariots drawn by four horses) and t *Altare della Patria* (Altar of the Fatherland), which was eventually to house the tomb of the Unknow Soldier, were later additions. The finest artists of the day worked on the monument's decorations; and Sacconi, who died of exhaustion, was succeeded by a trio of architects composed of Gaetano Koch, Manfredo Manfredi and Pio Piacentini. The two allegorical groups of gilded

VICTOR EMMANUEL II
(1829–78)
With the help of the French, he freed his country from Austrian domination, and with the help of Cavour, achieved the unification of Italy.

toration work on the Vittoriano
urrently in progress. Two glass
ators (due to run from June
7) will permit access to the top
he 197-foot-high monument
its breathtaking view.

onze at the foot of the
irway portray
ought and *Action*.
o great fountains
me it: *The*
rrhenian Sea and
e Adriatic. Above
e fountains, from
t to right, are
rble sculptures:
ength, Concord,
crifice and *Law.*
n the first level
e *Altare della*
tria, the work of
e sculptor Angelo
nelli, shows the
umphal Processions
Work and *Love for the Fatherland*, which converge toward
e statue of the goddess Rome. Finally, crowning it all, is the
lossal equestrian statue of Victor Emmanuel, in bronze that
s originally gilded, sculpted by Enrico Chiaradia. The
rtico is dominated by statues representing the regions of
ly. Adding the finishing touches to this powerful tribute to
e united nation, two gigantic bronze *quadrigae*, driven by
nged Victories symbolizing *Freedom* and *Italian Unity*, rise
ove the *propylaea* (porticos). Inside the monument are the
USEO CENTRALE DEL RISORGIMENTO, devoted to the history
the country's unification, and the MUSEO DELLE BANDIERE
ag Museum) devoted to Italian military history.

LAZZO DELLE ASSICURAZIONI GENERALI DI VENEZIA.
esigned by Guido Cirilli to counterbalance Palazzo Venezia,
s neo-Renaissance palace was built between 1902 and 1906
the site of Palazzo Torlonia, which was demolished when
e square was revamped. Its façade is decorated with a 16th-
ntury winged lion, the symbol of the Serenissima (Venice).

LAZZO VENEZIA. Pietro Barbo decided to build this palace
en he became titular cardinal of San Marco in 1451; and in
54, when he became Pope Paul II, he resolved that his
sidence should reflect the importance of his office. After his
ath, work on it continued until the 16th century. Pius IV
nted part of the palazzo to the Venetian ambassadors, who
ided there from 1564 to 1797, and it was then that the
ilding acquired its present name. In 1806, by order of
poleon I, it became the headquarters of the
ench administration. The building
erited its powerful corner tower and
nelations from the medieval
tresses, but the mullioned windows
marble on the *piano nobile*, the
at doorway on Piazza Venezia,
elegant courtyard and the
coration of the rooms all display
finesse of the Renaissance. A
SEUM now occupies the apartments of
ul II and part of the PALAZZETTO
NEZIA (built by the same Pope at the foot of
tower, but moved to the rear of the palace in 1911 to
prove the landscaping of the new square). Its collection

Part of a Garibaldi
uniform in the Museo
Centrale del
Risorgimento.

PALAZZO VENEZIA
Mussolini's offices
were in the palace
from 1929 to 1943.
He used to stand on
the balcony
overlooking the
piazza in order to
harangue the crowd
below.

The courtyard of
Palazzo Venezia.

▲ FROM THE FORUM HOLITORIUM TO THE COLISEUM

1. Trajan's Column
2. Trajan's Markets
3. Caesar's Forum
4. Augustus' Forum
5. Nerva's Forum
6. Temple of Peace

THE "RECONCILIATION" Priests filing past Mussolini at the head of a parade of Fascist youth organizations in the Imperial Forums.

Julius Caesar.

includes tapestries, ceramics, weapon works in silver and gold, sculptures and numerous paintings. The most remarkable rooms in the palace are the Sala Regia, where the ambassado met before being received in audienc by the Pope; the Sala del Concistoric where the cardinals used to meet; an the Sala del Mappamondo, in which Mussolini installed his study. On Piazza San Marco is a figure of a woman, known as Madama Lucrezia perhaps originally from the neighboring Temple of Isis, that became one of the famous talking statues of Rome ● 47.

BASILICA DI SAN MARCO. This church was founded in 336 by Pope Mark, who dedicated it to the evangelist. In the 9th century it was rebuilt by Gregory IV, and in the 12th century a campanile was added. It underwent further modifications when Pope Paul II included it in the new Palazzo di Venezia The outer portico with elegant arcades and the Loggia of th Benediction, which date from this period, form one of the city's most successful Renaissance façades. The interior, designed as a traditional basilica with three naves, has survived, as has part of the Cosmatesque paving ● 76. But th beautiful coffered ceiling decorated with the coat of arms o Paul II was added in the 15th century, and the stucco decoration and paintings in the central nave date from the 18th century. These illustrate the story of St Abdon and St Sennen, two Persian martyrs venerated in the Middle Age whose relics are preserved in the crypt, together with those the basilica's founder. The large mosaic with a gold background in the apse dates from the 19th century and was inspired by the one in the Church of Santi Cosma e Damian

THE IMPERIAL FORUMS

At the end of the Republic it was realized that the Forum was not large enough to meet the needs of the capital of an immense empire. Julius Caesar therefore initiated what was originally supposed to be a mere

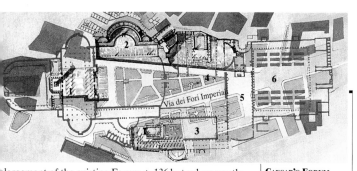

largement of the existing Forum ▲ *136* but subsequently
came the development of the first of the Imperial Forums.
ugustus, the Flavians and Trajan all added new monumental
uares, thus creating a vast public complex stretching from
e slopes of the Quirinal to the Velia. Into it the ideological,
ministrative, legal and commercial activities of the city
erflowed and were eventually concentrated. The dissolution
the Roman Empire led to the abandonment of these
uares, and during the Middle Ages they were gradually
ried. Much of the area was only rediscovered in the 20th
ntury, when on Mussolini's orders the medieval quarter was
molished to make room for the new Via dell'Impero (now
e Via dei Fori Imperiali), linking the northern and southern
rts of the city. The Fascist parades designed to exalt the
discovered grandeur of the Empire took place on this broad
enue which leads from Piazza Venezia to the Coliseum.

AESAR'S FORUM. In 54 BC Cicero wrote to his friend Atticus
ying that he had agreed on Caesar's behalf to acquire the
nd required to build a new forum. To do this it was
cessary to move the Curia and the Comitium ▲ *138*, to
molish the existing dwellings, and to spend the colossal sum
sixty million sesterces for the land alone. In 48 BC, on the
ttlefield of Pharsalus, Caesar vowed to build a temple to
nus (from whom he and the rest of the Julia family claimed
scent through Aeneas) if she would grant him victory over
mpey. This is why he built the magnificent SHRINE TO
ENUS GENITRIX (Venus the Mother), dedicated in 46 BC,
part of his Forum. The purpose of this act of piety is quite
ar: if Caesar's guardian goddess was to be exalted then so
as the dictator himself. The temple was rebuilt several times
fore being reinaugurated in May of 113 AD, on the same
y as Trajan's Column. In July 1999, tombs dating from the
h century BC were uncovered, proving
yond doubt that the area had been
habited long before Rome's official
undation date (753 BC).

CAESAR'S FORUM
This took the form of
an elongated triangle
(about 524 feet in
length), surrounded
by a double portico of
columns under which
there were shops (still
visible today on the
Clivus Argentarius).
The forum was
dominated by an
equestrian statue of
the dictator.

**THE TEMPLE OF
MARS ULTOR**
From Augustus'
Forum a majestic
stairway flanked by
fountains led up to
the temple, which had
a tufa podium faced
with Carrara marble.
The façade featured
eight gigantic
Corinthian columns;
of the eight others
that supported the
sides, three are still
standing. Statues of
Venus, Mars and the
Divine Julius stood in
an apse at the end of
the *cella*.

AUGUSTUS
The Emperor
is shown here as
a pontiff (his head
covered with a fold
of his toga, in
accordance with the
custom of priests in
the act of sacrificing).
He assumed the title
of *pontifex maximus* –
a title inherited by
the popes – which
made him head of
the Roman religion
for life and gave his
power a legitimate
and sacred basis.

THE "FORMA URBIS"
This great marble
town plan, vital for
our topographical
knowledge of ancient
Rome, is kept in
Palazzo Braschi
▲ *279*. Its area was
over 2,500 square
feet. Only a tenth of
it has been found.

Two giant Corinthian
columns (known as
Colonnacce) in
Nerva's Forum,
guarded by Minerva.

AUGUSTUS' FORUM. The second of the Imperial Forums,
with its TEMPLE OF MARS ULTOR (Mars the Avenger), was
created by Augustus after a vow made before the Battle
of Philippi (42 BC) to avenge Julius Caesar, who was his
adoptive father. It was intended that the new square would
provide more space, as the previous forums had been badly
overcrowded, but it served above all to glorify the Emperor
in his military and triumphal roles. To separate it from the
popular neighborhood of ill repute known as the Suburra
and to protect it against the frequent fires, Augustus had
a monumental wall built in great blocks of *peperino* (a type
of tufa) at the back of the square. Statues of historical
personages decorated the lateral porticos, and at the end
niches twice the size of the others held effigies of Aeneas,
Romulus and their descendants. A statue of Augustus
standing in a *quadriga* was placed at the center of the temple.
VESPASIAN'S FORUM AND TEMPLE OF PEACE. This complex
was built by Vespasian between 71 and 75 AD to celebrate
his victory over the Jews. The Temple of Peace contained
the great marble plan of the town, the *Forma Urbis*,
established under Septimius Severus, and items from
the Temple of Jerusalem, including the seven-branched
candelabra and silver trumpets shown
on the Arch of Titus ▲ *146*.

FORVM·DE
·NERVA·

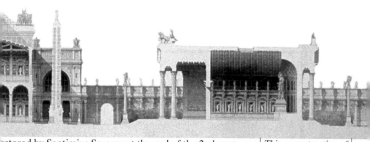

restored by Septimius Severus at the end of the 2nd century
following a serious fire, the temple was damaged again in the
6th century – so badly that, according to the Byzantine
historian Procopius, it had to be abandoned during the
following century. Nevertheless, vestiges of two rooms are still
visible. Of the first, only a brick wall remains, situated
between the Basilica of Maxentius ▲ 145 and the entrance of
the Church of Santi Cosma e Damiano. The *Forma Urbis* was
found in fragments at the foot of this wall in 1552, and holes
for the iron clamps that supported the
marble slabs of the plan can still be seen.
The best-preserved part of the complex,
which is on the other side of the wall, within
the church, undoubtedly formed part of one
of the libraries of the Forum of Peace.

**NERVA'S FORUM (THE FORUM
TRANSITORIUM).** Although construction of
this long, narrow forum was begun and
virtually completed by Domitian, it was
inaugurated, after his death, by the
Emperor Nerva in 97 AD. Because it linked
the existing forums and the Temple of
Peace, it came to be known as the Forum
Transitorium ("the forum in between").
The end was dominated by a temple
dedicated to Minerva; but Pope Paul V, who
used marble from it to build the Fontana Paola in the 17th
century ▲ 364, was responsible for its almost total
destruction. Two columns and the back wall of the lateral
portico remain on the Via Cavour. A figure of Minerva
appears on the attic, while the frieze, which illustrates
feminine crafts, portrays the myth of Arachne, the young
Lydian girl who was turned into a spider by Athena (the
Greek counterpart of Minerva) for daring to compete with
the goddess in the arts of weaving and embroidery.

TRAJAN'S FORUM. This is the last, the greatest and the best
preserved of the Imperial Forums. Created by Trajan with
booty plundered from the Dacians (a people who lived in
what is now Rumania), it was built between 107 and 113 AD
according to designs by Apollodorus of Damascus, the most
famous architect of the age. He achieved some engineering
miracles, leveling the high ridge that linked the Capitol to the
Quirinal – as the inscription on the base of Trajan's Column
records – and moving almost 30,000,000 cubic feet of soil to
gain space to build the imposing monuments. The entrance
is from Augustus' Forum, through a triumphal arch; this led
to a monumental square, in the center of which stood a
gilded-bronze equestrian statue of the Emperor. As in
Augustus' Forum, the porticos on each side opened out into
semicircular exedras; the attic of the porticos was decorated
with statues of Dacian prisoners, alternating with shields
adorned by portraits. At the end of the square was the

This reconstruction of
Trajan's Forum shows
(from left to the
right): the triumphal
arch, the portico,
Basilica Ulpia (in the
center), Trajan's
Column, the libraries
and the temple.

BASILICA ULPIA ● 65
The medieval Torre
delle Milizie and the
remains of Trajan's
Markets can be seen
rising behind the
ruins of the grandiose
basilica that
dominated Trajan's
Forum.

A GREAT GENERAL
After his wars against
the Dacians (one of a
series of conquests),
Trajan (98–117 AD)
attacked the
Parthians, a people of
Iranian origin; forced
to retreat, he died on
the way back to
Rome.

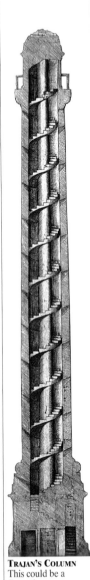

TRAJAN'S COLUMN
This could be a figurative transcription of Trajan's *Commentarii*, a narrative record of his wars against the Dacians (101–6 AD). The spiral of reliefs on the shaft (about 130 feet tall) resembles the form of a papyrus scroll.

BASILICA ULPIA (Trajan's family name), the largest basilica ever built in Rome, and beyond it stood a pair of libraries, Greek and Latin, on either side of the famous marble colum Finally, on the death and deification of the Emperor, a temple to Trajan and his wife, Plotina, was added. Through many activities (the promulgation of laws, the distribution o money to the people, schools, etc.) this forum became one c the main political and administrative centers of the city. Moreover, it formed a complex of such monumental beauty that, according to the historian Ammianus Marcellinus, whe the Emperor Constantius II visited Rome for the first time, 357 AD, he was dazzled by "this monument unique under the heavens and admirable even in the eyes of the gods".

TRAJAN'S COLUMN. The libraries of Trajan's Forum were adorned with terraces from which the painted bas-reliefs of Trajan's Column could be seen perfectly. It consisted of seventeen drums of blue marble from Luni on a cubic base with bas-reliefs showing trophies of Dacian weapons. An inner staircase wound to the top, lit by forty-five loopholes almost invisible from outside. Above the entrance is an inscription framed by two Victories: it states that the colum

rpose was to indicate the "height of the hill, which was
...moved to make room for such large monuments". The
...lumn also served as a resting place for the Emperor,
...ose ashes, contained in a gold urn, were placed in the
...se. The bas-reliefs that relate the story of his victories
...er the Dacians unfold in a spiral 656 feet long. They are
...exceptional historical record and a masterpiece of
...ulpture. From the crossing of the Danube (at the bottom)
...the deportation of the Dacian population that ended the
...r (at the top), each successive stage of the conflict is
...picted: the pitching of camps, speeches rallying the
...ops, battles, assaults, beheadings, and the native
...ieftains' submission to the Emperor. Erected in Trajan's
...nor, the monument portrays him no less than sixty times.
...der Sixtus V, the Emperor's statue, which crowned the
...lumn, was replaced by a statue of St Peter made by
...acomo della Porta.

NTA MARIA DI LORETO. This church, to the left of the
...lumn, was built by Bramante and Antonio da Sangallo the
...unger. Inside are frescoes by Pomarancio (second chapel
...the right), François Duquesnoy's statue of *St Susanna*
...530) and two angels by Maderno. (To the right of the
...URCH OF THE SANTISSIMO NOME DI MARIA, built between
...36 and 1738, a flight of steps leads to Trajan's Markets).

...OM TRAJAN'S MARKETS TO THE COLISEUM

...E MARKETS. Between Trajan's Forum and the lower
...pes of the Quirinal, the architect Apollodorus of
...mascus arranged a complex of utilitarian buildings which,
...er their discovery, were given the name of Trajan's
...arkets. The semicircular brick façade
...ludes three superimposed rows of shops.
...e third level opens onto a rather well
...eserved ancient street, Via Biberatica
...ght), from which a flight of steps leads
...a monumental hall (now the entrance
...the markets) that served as the center
...the complex. Occupying two floors,
...h small shops and perhaps also offices,
...was covered by a huge vault, with six
...ersecting arches supported on massive
...vertine consoles. The complex was
...obably used both for storing the
...ormous quantities of foodstuffs managed
...the State, especially for free distribution
...the plebs, and also for retail purposes.
...l kinds of foodstuffs were sold, including
...ne, oil and saltwater fish kept in tanks.
...e Trajan's Markets, host to contemporary
...hibitions, will soon house the Museo dei
...ri (due to open in 2007).

**AN APOSTLE
FOR AN EMPEROR**
The bronze statue of
St Peter was placed
on top of Trajan's
Column on
December 4, 1587.
Half a cannon from
Castel Sant'Angelo,
three doors (from
Sant'Agnese, the
Scala Santa and
St Peter's) and part
of a pilaster from
the Pantheon were
melted down to make
the statue.

TORRE DE' CONTI
Called Turris Major or Turris Urbis, this was Rome's tallest tower. Like the Torre delle Milizie, it consists of three superimposed sections that become gradually narrower.

The campanile of Santa Francesca Romana.

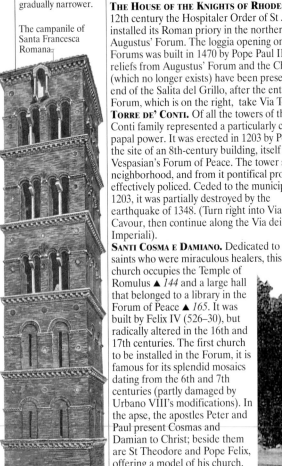

TORRE DELLE MILIZIE ● 73. From the 11th to the 14th centuries the urban dwellings of the aristocracy – both the feudal nobility and the city's elite – tended to take the form of fortified complexes with tall towers. "Roma turrita" boasted more than three hundred towers, many of which still exist, including those of the Arcioni, Capocci, Frangipane, Annibaldi, Margani and Orsini families (the latter near Campo de' Fiori), the Torre del Grillo and the Torre Millina. Built in the 12th to 13th centuries on the ruins of Trajan's Markets, then in the possession of the Arcioni, the Torre delle Milizie was shortened after an earthquake in the 14th century and crenelations were added. Later it belonged to the Annibaldi and then the Caetani, great Roman families who vied for control of the town in the Middle Ages. (Take the Salita del Grillo, on the right.)

THE HOUSE OF THE KNIGHTS OF RHODES. At the end of the 12th century the Hospitaler Order of St John of Jerusalem installed its Roman priory in the northern hemicycle of Augustus' Forum. The loggia opening onto the Imperial Forums was built in 1470 by Pope Paul II. Sculptures and bas-reliefs from Augustus' Forum and the Church of San Basilio (which no longer exists) have been preserved here. (At the end of the Salita del Grillo, after the entrance to Augustus' Forum, which is on the right, take Via Tor de' Conti.)

TORRE DE' CONTI. Of all the towers of the nobles, that of the Conti family represented a particularly clear manifestation of papal power. It was erected in 1203 by Pope Innocent II on the site of an 8th-century building, itself built on the exedra of Vespasian's Forum of Peace. The tower stood guard over the neighborhood, and from it pontifical processions could be effectively policed. Ceded to the municipality in 1203, it was partially destroyed by the earthquake of 1348. (Turn right into Via Cavour, then continue along the Via dei Fori Imperiali.)

SANTI COSMA E DAMIANO. Dedicated to two saints who were miraculous healers, this church occupies the Temple of Romulus ▲ 144 and a large hall that belonged to a library in the Forum of Peace ▲ 165. It was built by Felix IV (526–30), but radically altered in the 16th and 17th centuries. The first church to be installed in the Forum, it is famous for its splendid mosaics dating from the 6th and 7th centuries (partly damaged by Urbano VIII's modifications). In the apse, the apostles Peter and Paul present Cosmas and Damian to Christ; beside them are St Theodore and Pope Felix, offering a model of his church. The chancel arch shows the

Lamb of God between seven candelabra, four angels and the symbols of the evangelists John and Luke.

SANTA FRANCESCA ROMANA. Founded in the mid 10th century in part of the Temple of Venus and Rome ▲ *146*, this was at first called Santa Maria Nova, to distinguish it from Santa Maria Antiqua ▲ *142*, which had had to be abandoned because of flooding. The church acquired its present name in 1608 after the canonization of Francesca Buzzi dei Ponziani, who founded the Congregation of Oblates in 1421. The saint's remains are preserved in the crypt. The Romanesque campanile, decorated with ceramic cups and disks of porphyry, is one of the most beautiful in Rome. The apse is decorated with a 12th-century mosaic showing the Virgin and Child enthroned between four saints: Peter, Andrew, James and John. In the right branch of the transept are the paving stones on which St Peter is said to have knelt to pray to God to stop Simon Magus in full flight; according to tradition, the sorcerer then crashed to his death not far from the church.

THE ARCH OF CONSTANTINE. One of the largest triumphal arches to have survived, this was built to commemorate Constantine's Triumph, celebrated after his victory over Maxentius' troops at the Ponte Milvio ▲ *377* in 312 AD. This imposing edifice is unusual in that it consists of sculptures and decorations taken from other monuments. By this time Rome had probably relinquished her role as capital of the Empire to Constantinople; as a result sculptors, masons and other craftsmen who had relied on Imperial commissions found it hard to earn a living.

A MASTERPIECE OF FRESHNESS AND NATURALISM
This 6th-century mosaic, in the apse of Santi Cosma e Damiano, shows St Peter and St Paul presenting St Cosmas and St Damian to Christ. St Theodore (far right), and Pope Felix IV on the far left, offer Christ a model of the church.

MONUMENTAL MAPS
Mussolini had five huge stone maps hung near the Coliseum to demonstrate the extraordinary expansion of Rome since her origins. Only the four maps tracing Rome's development in antiquity now remain.

THE META SUDANS
A cone-like fountain (below) stood near the arch, dating from c. 80 AD. Although it was demolished in 1936 to make room for Fascist parades, its base was unearthed in the 1980's.

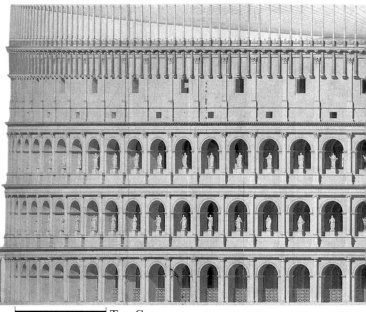

THE COLISEUM ✪
The largest
amphitheater in the
Roman world, whose
façade contains over
300 tons of iron, is
both the emblem of
Roman antiquity in
the Eternal City and
the symbol of Rome
throughout the world.
For those who are
interested in
archeology a pass also
buys admittance to
the Palatine.

THE COLISEUM

THE FIRST STONE AMPHITHEATER. Gladiatorial combats were
originally held in the Forum, where temporary step seating
was erected and rented to spectators. It was only in the time
of Augustus that these combats disappeared from the city
center and moved toward the Campus Martius. In 29 BC
Statilius Taurus built the first permanent amphitheater there
and when this burned down in 64 AD Nero replaced it with
a wooden one. It was not until nearly ten years later that
an amphitheater worthy of the Empire's capital was built,
designed to gratify the people's appetite for entertainment.
The most beautiful amphitheater of the Roman world was
thus built, on the site of the artificial lake with which Nero
had embellished his villa, the Domus Aurea ▲ 174. Begun
in the early years of Vespasian's reign (from 72 AD), it was
completed by his son, Titus. During its inauguration in 80 AD
which lasted for a hundred days, five thousand wild animals
were slaughtered. The last time the Coliseum is known to
have been used was in the reign of Theodoric, in 523 AD.

Although it is not certain that Christians
were martyred there, in the 18th century
a Way of the Cross was set up around the
arena in their honor, where the Pope still
prays every year at Easter. The Coliseum's
consecration to the Christian martyrs put
an end to the pillaging of its marble and
travertine, which had been going on since
the Middle Ages.
ITS FUNCTIONAL ORGANIZATION. The
elliptical amphitheater has a diameter of
approximately 620 feet in its widest section
and 490 feet in its narrowest. The façade is
about 165 feet high. At the top, a row of
consoles served to support the vast *velarium*
a linen awning which unfolded over the
building to protect the spectators from
the sun. This was the special task of a

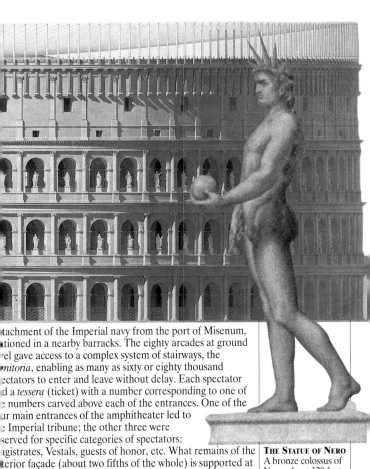

tachment of the Imperial navy from the port of Misenum,
tioned in a nearby barracks. The eighty arcades at ground
el gave access to a complex system of stairways, the
nitoria, enabling as many as sixty or eighty thousand
ectators to enter and leave without delay. Each spectator
d a *tessera* (ticket) with a number corresponding to one of
e numbers carved above each of the entrances. One of the
ur main entrances of the amphitheater led to
e Imperial tribune; the other three were
served for specific categories of spectators:
agistrates, Vestals, guests of honor, etc. What remains of the
terior façade (about two fifths of the whole) is supported at
ch end by two huge walls built in the time of Pius VII.
E LAYOUT OF THE AMPHITHEATER. The interior of the
liseum, most of which has collapsed, can only give a vague
pression of what it must have been like originally. The
bterranean passages of the arena were once covered with a
ovable wooden floor that concealed the services
dispensable for the games: machinery, cages for the wild
imals, weapons, and so on. The thirty deep niches in the
rrounding wall were probably equipped with a system of
lleys for raising animals and gladiators to the level of the
ena. Huge swiveling panels of tufa, equipped with a system
rollers and hinges and moved by counterweights, made it
ssible to raise all kinds of scenery to the center of the
ena, including artificial landscapes with hills and forests for
e *venationes* (hunting contests). The arena's stepped
ating, the *cavea*, was divided into five sectors; the places
re allocated, and access depended on the specifically
termined social class to which the spectators belonged.
cording to the historian Suetonius, the Emperor Augustus
located the first row to the senators, special places to
arried plebeians, and others to adolescent boys still clad in
e *toga praetexta*. He specified that women should occupy the
pper rows. Between Via Labicana and Via San Giovanni in
terano the remains are still visible of the LUDUS MAGNUS,
e main barracks of the gladiators, which were linked directly
the subterranean passages of the Coliseum by a tunnel.

THE STATUE OF NERO
A bronze colossus of
Nero, about 120 feet
tall, stood beside the
Coliseum. The name
Colosseo, first used in
the Middle Ages,
came from the
proximity of this
colossal statue.

SUBTERRANEAN LIFE
The arena's
underground
passages are lit by the
openings made for
hoisting machinery.

The emperors continually strove to make themselves popular with the plebians. They resorted to the distribution of grain and money, the construction of public baths and, above all, the organization of games. Normally three kinds of building were used for the games: the theater, the circus and the amphitheater, where gladiators fought and wild beasts were hunted in exorbitantly costly shows designed to exalt the splendor of the reign.

In the 1st century, the helmets had visors.

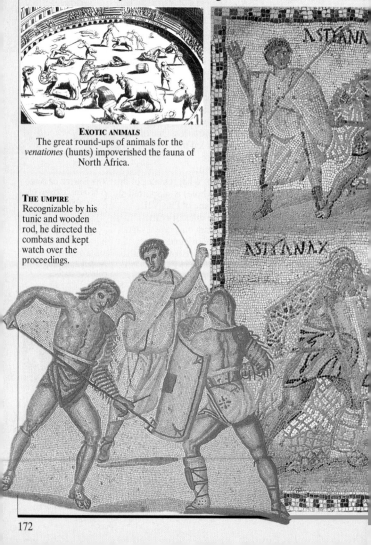

EXOTIC ANIMALS
The great round-ups of animals for the *venationes* (hunts) impoverished the fauna of North Africa.

THE UMPIRE
Recognizable by his tunic and wooden rod, he directed the combats and kept watch over the proceedings.

PROTECTIVE ARMOR

The armor of a gladiator (arm guards and greaves) was designed to protect the parts of the body where the slightest wound might seriously handicap the fighter.

THE GREETING OF THE GLADIATORS
The games opened with a sumptuous procession. The gladiators entered the arena by the *Porta Triumphalis,* behind the magistrates and editors. The pathetic sentence uttered as they stood before Claudius' Imperial tribune became traditional: "Hail Caesar! Those who are about to die greet you!"

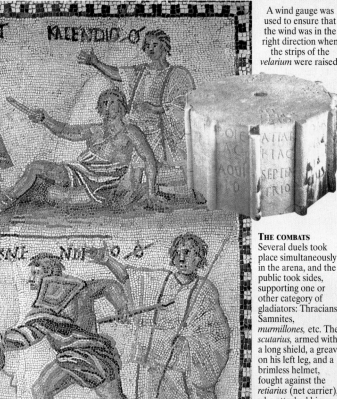

A wind gauge was used to ensure that the wind was in the right direction when the strips of the *velarium* were raised.

THE COMBATS
Several duels took place simultaneously in the arena, and the public took sides, supporting one or other category of gladiators: Thracians, Samnites, *murmillones,* etc. The *scutarius,* armed with a long shield, a greave on his left leg, and a brimless helmet, fought against the *retiarius* (net carrier), who attacked him with the help of a net attached to his belt, a trident and a dagger. The *retiarius* wore only a wide shoulder guard, covering the base of his neck, ankle guards, and a brassard protecting his left arm.

173

The Domus Aurea is currently closed for restoration work. While this work is being carried out (du[...] be completed by the end of 2010), the site should remain open to the public.

THE DOMUS AUREA (THE GOLDEN HOUSE)

THE VILLA OF THE SUN. When the terrible fire of 64 AD destroyed his first palace, Nero replaced it with a much larg[...] building, the Domus Aurea. The architects Severus and Cel[...] were commissioned to build it, and its decoration was entrusted to a certain Fabullus (or Famulus). This complex, adorned with statues from many parts of Greece and Asia Minor, was surrounded by an enormous park. The astronomical orientation of the building confirms the ancie[...] descriptions, all of which state that it symbolized the sun. Indeed everything about it was intended to recall the sun, with which Nero identified – as witness his colossal statue ▲ *171*, the great round hall which pivoted on itself followin[...] the revolving heavens, and the ubiquitous profusion of gold[...]
THE DISCOVERY OF THE "GROTESQUES". At the start of the 15th century laborers working on the hill found subterranea[...] passages decorated with frescoes: these were part of Nero's palace, which had been covered over in the 2nd century by Trajan's baths. These tunnels came to be known as "grotto[...] and their decoration of arabesques and mythological scenes[...] as "grotesques". Renaissance artists were inspired by them, especially Raphael in his celebrated loggias in the Vatican ▲ *228*. The splendid rectangular nymphaeum to the east of the vast courtyard still retains part of these decorations: a mosaic medallion shows Polyphemus, the Cyclops, acceptin[...] goblet of wine from Ulysses.

THE BATHS OF TRAJAN

Trajan's baths, partially built on the ruins of the Domus Au[...] after the fire of 104 AD, were the work of Apollodorus of Damascus ▲ *165*. A demonstration of Imperial generosity t[...] the plebs of the city, they were Rome's first great Imperial baths ● *68*. In 1997 a remarkable fresco (dating from the tu[...] of the 2nd century AD) was placed in the cryptoporticus (see above, left). It represents a view of a city, crossed by a river and bristling with towers, which has been identified as Arle[...] A major mosaic depicting a beautiful hunting scene was als[...] discovered in the baths. The remains of a nymphaeum and [...] library can still be seen in the Parco Oppio. On the other si[...] of the Via delle Terme di Traiano stand the baths' monumental cisterns, the "Seven Halls", divided into nine communicating chambers.

Circus Maximus and the Aventine

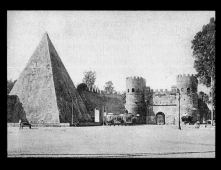

177 Circus Maximus
179 The Aventine
182 The Little Aventine
182 Porta San Paolo
184 Monte Testaccio

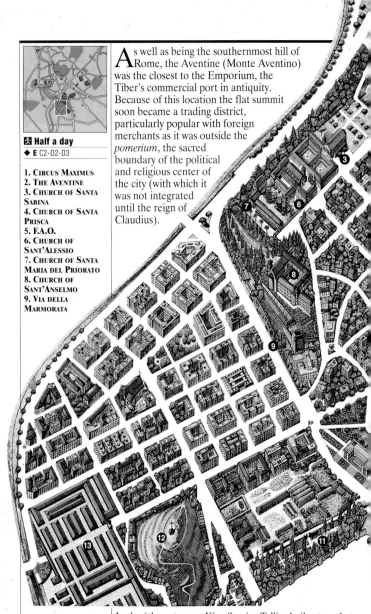

⏳ Half a day

◆ **E** C2-D2-D3

1. CIRCUS MAXIMUS
2. THE AVENTINE
3. CHURCH OF SANTA SABINA
4. CHURCH OF SANTA PRISCA
5. F.A.O.
6. CHURCH OF SANT'ALESSIO
7. CHURCH OF SANTA MARIA DEL PRIORATO
8. CHURCH OF SANT'ANSELMO
9. VIA DELLA MARMORATA

A s well as being the southernmost hill of Rome, the Aventine (Monte Aventino) was the closest to the Emporium, the Tiber's commercial port in antiquity. Because of this location the flat summit soon became a trading district, particularly popular with foreign merchants as it was outside the *pomerium*, the sacred boundary of the political and religious center of the city (with which it was not integrated until the reign of Claudius).

10. PYRAMID OF CESTIUS
11. PROTESTANT CEMETERY
12. TESTACCIO
13. THE SLAUGHTER-HOUSE

In the 6th century BC King Servius Tullius built a temple to Diana on the Aventine which became the official shrine of the Latins. Later, the history of the hill was to illustrate the continuing influence of these early episodes. During the first part of the 5th century a heterogeneous group of craftsmen, shopkeepers and small landowners – all excluded from the privileges of the patrician ruling class – moved to the Aventine and the common people of Rome as a whole came to be known as the plebs. Under the pressure of mounting financial, military and political problems at the beginning of the Republic, the plebs threatened to secede and form an independent state by "retreating" to the Aventine, or alternatively to the Mons Sac on the other side of the Aniene River. Following a fierce struggle leading to a number of plebeian victories

The Aventine.

FORCED MARRIAGES
Rome lacked women and her population risked dying out. Romulus therefore dreamed up a trap for his neighbors, the Sabines, and invited them to a feast along with their daughters. During the banquet, at a sign from Romulus, his companions threw themselves on the Sabine women and carried them off. This episode, at the root of the war between the two peoples, inspired numerous artists; the French painter Jacques-Louis David's picture of the scene, painted in 1799, is one of the most famous.

(notably the election of special magistrates known as the Tribunes of the People), the legal equality of all citizens was finally recognized in the 4th century. After this period the Aventine became a proverbial place of "retreat", and in modern times a group of anti-Fascist members of parliament established themselves there in 1924 to protest against the assassination of Giacomo Matteotti. Under the Empire the poorest inhabitants moved toward the southern plain, near the Emporium, and to Trastevere on the right bank of the Tiber. As a result, the Aventine gradually lost its popular, commercial character and was transformed into a wealthy, aristocratic neighborhood. That is why when Alaric's Goths stormed Rome 410 AD they burned and looted the houses on the Aventine.

CIRCUS MAXIMUS

The construction of Rome's first circus for chariot races, in the valley between the Palatine and the Aventine, was attributed by Livy to Tarquin the Elder (7th century BC), although traditionally Romulus was supposed to have organized the first races here on the occasion of the feast that ended with the rape of the Sabine women.

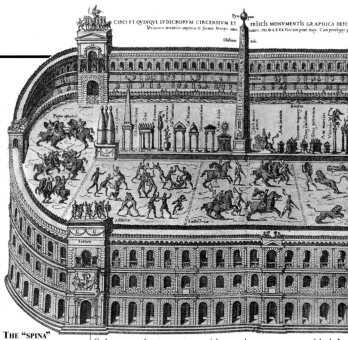

THE "SPINA"
On the *spina*, as well as two obelisks and the seven eggs and seven dolphins that served to mark the laps, there were various small buildings and shrines.

Subsequently stone steps with wooden seats were added. In BC Julius Caesar had the circus enlarged substantially, but the most important event was the erection on the *spina* – the low low central wall that linked the two turning posts – of the obelisk of Ramses II, brought from Heliolopolis by Augustus (in 1589 it was moved to Piazza del Popolo ▲ *306*). Much later Constantius II added a second obelisk, that of Tutmoses III, from Thebes (also removed by Sixtus V in 158 to be re-erected in Piazza San Giovanni in Laterano ▲ *196*). The circus was nearly 2,000 feet long and was said to have a capacity of more than 300,000 spectators. Substantial remain are to be seen at the curved end on the Palatine side; they correspond to the middle of the *cavea* (steps) and date from the time of Hadrian (117–38 AD).

THE GAMES. Caesar organized a mock battle with a thousand infantry, six hundred horsemen and forty elephants. The *spina*, which the *quadrigae* (two-wheeled chariots drawn by four horses) had to circle counterclockwise seven times, was just over 1,100 feet long. The most important races took pla during the Ludi Romani (Roman Games), from September to 18. The four *factiones* (teams) of charioteers, Albata, Russata, Prasina and Veneta, with their white, red, green an blue colors, eventually developed the characteristics of full-blown political parties. The last races in the Circus Maximus were held in 549, during the reign of Totila.

AT THE FOOT OF THE AVENTINE. In line with the Circus Maximus, silhouetted against the sky are the buildings of the F.A.O. (Food and Agriculture Organization of the United Nations), inaugurated in 1951, and the obelisk of Axum (4th century AD) transported from the Ethiopian city to Rome in 1937. THE STATUE OF GIUSEPPE MAZZINI (1805–72) that adorns the Piazzale Ugo La Malfa has had an eventful histo The Freemason sculptor Ettore Ferrari was commissioned t make it in 1890, but because of Mazzini's militant republicanism and controversial political image it was not inaugurated until 1949. (Return to the Tiber, turn left,

THE AVENTINE

In the morning, from the banks of the Tiber climb up the Clivo di Rocca Savella to discover the quiet, secret oasis of the Aventine. Public and monastic gardens afford a peaceful retreat where you can enjoy the beautiful view over the Circus Maximus and the Palatine. (Cross the Parco Savello and take Via di Santa Sabina to the right.)

SANTA SABINA. If tradition is to be believed, this church was built on the site of the house of Sabina, a noblewoman who was converted to Christianity by one of her slaves and died during Hadrian's persecutions. According to another source the saint's body was transferred here from Umbria, where Sabina is supposed to have suffered martyrdom under Vespasian. The church was founded by Peter of Illyria during the pontificate Celestine I (422–32), on the foundations of two small temples and a 3rd–4th century house. The great biography of the popes, the *Liber Pontificalis*, testifies that the work was continued during the pontificate of Sixtus III (432–40). A portico and baptistery, today no longer standing, completed the basilica. Restorations were carried out in the 8th and 9th centuries; then in the following century Albericus, a Roman aristocrat of Frankish origins and rival of Pope John X, integrated the building within the fortifications he had built on the Aventine. It was here, in 1222, that St Dominic presented Pope Honorius III with the rule of the Order of Preachers (the church still belongs to the Dominicans). Several chapels were added later, slightly changing the original building. In 1914, a radical restoration eliminated the chapels, thus returning the apse area to its original state. The doors of carved cedar date from the 5th century, and are a superb and rare example of the iconographic themes of the age. Inside, above the entrance, a mosaic dating from the same period shows two women symbolizing the Church of the Gentiles (New Testament) and the Church of the Circumcision (Old Testament). These figures frame an inscription commemorating the church's construction by Peter of Illyria and Pope Celestine. Set into the paving of the central nave one can see, amongst others, the unusual mosaic-decorated tombstone of Muñoz

PARCO SAVELLO ★ (Giardino degli Aranci). Bordered by the crenelations and turrets of the fortress built by the Savelli family in the 13th century, this charming garden planted with orange trees, roses, pines and cypresses overlooks the Tiber and is one of the most pleasant spots from which to view Rome.

THE DOORS OF SANTA SABINA
Of the three original doors, only two remain. One of these 5th-century carved cedarwood doors, which is unusually well preserved, illustrates the parallel between Christ, Moses, and Elijah expressed by St Augustine.

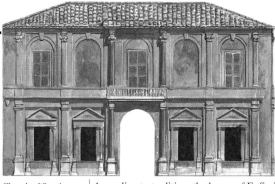

Church of Santi Bonifacio e Alessio.

Fresco in the Basilica of San Clemente ▲ *193* depicting the story of St Alexis (right).

THE ORDER OF THE KNIGHTS OF MALTA
This is a religious order of the Roman Catholic Church and a Catholic order of knighthood. It is governed by an elected Grand Master; he bears the titles of Eminence and Highness, and is recognized internationally as a Head of State, due the honors of a sovereign.

de Zamora, General Master of the Dominicans, who died in 1300. Both the bell tower and the cloister of the monastery date from the 13th century.

SANTI BONIFACIO E ALESSIO.
According to tradition, the house of Eufimianus, the father of Alexis, stood on this site. Converted to Christianity, Alexis fled on the eve of his wedding and spent seventeen years as a pilgrim in the East. After returning to Rome, he presented himself as a slave in the house of his parents, who did not recognize him, and died beneath the steps of his paternal home, having entrusted the story of his life to Pope Clement so that he could reveal it to his father. St Alexis' story was very popular in the Middle Ages; in the 17th century it was set to music by Stefano Landi with a libretto by Cardinal Rospigliosi; and it also appears in the frescoes of San Clemente ▲ *193*. Before the 10th century a church dedicated to St Boniface existed where Sant'Alessio now stands. In 977 it was given to Archbishop Serge of Damascus, who founded a Greek monastery on this spot. Both the Emperor Otto III and Adalbertus, Bishop of Prague, stayed here several times around the year 1000. In 1216 Pope Honorius III rebuilt the church; its structure was further modified in 1750, except for the elegant 13th-century bell tower. In the Romanesque crypt relics of St Thomas à Becket are preserved together with the column to which, according to tradition, St Sebastian was bound.

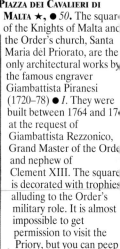

PIAZZA DEI CAVALIERI DI MALTA ★, ● *50*. The square of the Knights of Malta and the Order's church, Santa Maria del Priorato, are the only architectural works by the famous engraver Giambattista Piranesi (1720–78) ● *I*. They were built between 1764 and 1766 at the request of Giambattista Rezzonico, Grand Master of the Order and nephew of Clement XIII. The square is decorated with trophies alluding to the Order's military role. It is almost impossible to get permission to visit the Priory, but you can peep

rough the keyhole (though you may have to join a line of
urists waiting to do so) and discover the vast dome of St
eter's in this miniature frame. The church's façade can be
en from Trastevere; it is punctuated by twin pilasters around
giant oculus and has a neoclassical character. (Take Via di
anta Sabina; turn right into Via Sant'Alberto Magno; then,
hen you reach Largo Arrigo VII, take Via di Santa Prisca).

ANTA PRISCA. This is the oldest place of Christian worship on
e Aventine. The church was built on the site of a Roman
ouse, important remains of which can be seen on the lower
vels. Tradition identifies the house as belonging to St Prisca,
e daughter of Aquila and Priscilla, who offered hospitality
St Peter. Baptized at thirteen, Prisca was condemned under
e Emperor Claudius to be devoured alive by lions;
iraculously saved, she was then decapitated. An early
urch was built here during the 4th to 5th centuries and
stored at various times in the 8th and 9th centuries.
amaged during the sack of Rome in 1084, it was successfully
paired under the pontificate of Pascal II. But at the
eginning of the 15th century the building had to be radically
stored after being partially destroyed by a fire. The Baroque
çade (1660) by Carlo Lombardi is particularly noteworthy.
the apse 17th-century frescoes illustrate the story of the
artyrdom of St Prisca, and the *Baptism of St Prisca*, painted
ound 1600 by Passignano, can be seen above the altar. A
ght of steps from the church's right nave leads to the
ithraeum.

ITHRAEUM OF SANTA PRISCA. Excavations of the church
egun in 1944 revealed, next to the crypt, a richly decorated
ithraeum (shrine for the worship of Mithras), which
ccupies the rooms of an older house, perhaps that of
cinius Sura, a friend of Trajan. From the marks on the
ricks, this building can be dated to about 95 AD. Beyond the
ymphaeum (small grotto) there is now a small museum
ontaining items found during the excavation. In the two
ches at the entrance were statues of the genii, or guardian
irits, of fertility and sterility, Cautes and Cautopathes, of
hich only the former has survived. The niche in the back wall
unique in Rome: in addition to the usual figure of Mithras
lling the bull, there is also a recumbent Saturn whose body
made of amphorae covered in stucco. Paintings covering the
alls above the seats where the faithful used to sit
rtray two processions. The one on the right
ustrates the seven degrees of
itiation into the cult: *Corax*
row), *Nymphus* (spouse),
iles (soldier), *Leo* (lion),
rses (the Persian),
eliodromus and Pater
ather), while the one on the
t shows the *leones* (lions)
proaching Mithras and the Sun,
clining ready for a banquet.
Return to the Via di Santa
isca, cross Viale
ventino, and from
azza Albania take Via
San Saba. You are now
the Little Aventine.)

When decorating the
stelae of the Piazza
dei Cavalieri di
Malta, Piranesi was
inspired by the
military iconography
of the Order and the
emblems of the
Rezzonico family (a
crenelated tower and
a two-headed eagle).
He took his designs
from antiquity.

THE WORSHIP OF MITHRAS

In the 2nd century AD
worship of the
Persian god Mithras
took root in Italy and
in the ports and
garrison towns of the
Roman Empire,
where it competed
with Christianity
before sinking into
oblivion at the end of
the 4th century. A
religion of light,
offering its initiates
the guarantee of
salvation in the
afterlife, Mithraism
involved an elaborate
rite focusing on the
sacrifice of the bull,
which symbolized the
victory of
life over
evil.

THE LITTLE AVENTINE

At the time of the Roman Empire the Little Aventine, a low summit separated from the rest of the hill by a depression, was a district inhabited by aristocrats whose luxurious homes spread below. Although these were later destroyed to make room for the Baths of Caracalla ▲ *319*, excavations have brought to light some magnificent remains, notably of a large Imperial house, preserved today in the Hospice of Santa Margherita.

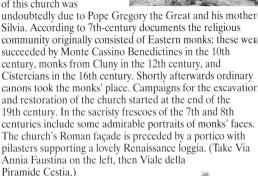

SAN SABA. The foundation of this church was undoubtedly due to Pope Gregory the Great and his mother Silvia. According to 7th-century documents the religious community originally consisted of Eastern monks; these were succeeded by Monte Cassino Benedictines in the 10th century, monks from Cluny in the 12th century, and Cistercians in the 16th century. Shortly afterwards ordinary canons took the monks' place. Campaigns for the excavation and restoration of the church started at the end of the 19th century. In the sacristy frescoes of the 7th and 8th centuries include some admirable portraits of monks' faces. The church's Roman façade is preceded by a portico with pilasters supporting a lovely Renaissance loggia. (Take Via Annia Faustina on the left, then Viale della Piramide Cestia.)

PORTA SAN PAOLO

PYRAMID OF CAIUS CESTIUS. Included in the Aurelian walls, the pyramid of Caius Cestius (possibly the Roman citizen of that name who was a praetor in 44 BC) has been known since the Middle Ages as the *Meta Remi*, the tomb of Remus. Like the *Meta Romuli*, just outside the Vatican (close to today's Via della Conciliazione), the Pyramid

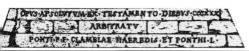

a funeral monument, as is clear from the inscription
both sides. On the eastern side an inscription in
aller characters states that in accordance with the terms
his will the building was completed in less than 333 days.
n the west side is a small door leading to the funeral
amber (not open to the public). The walls are painted with
ch decorations of the third style, now mostly faded. Nearby,
u can see the ancient road that started at one of the gates in
e Aurelian Wall.

IE PROTESTANT CEMETERY. At the foot of the Pyramid of
estius lies the Protestant Cemetery, known as the cemetery
the Acattolici, the first granted by the popes to non-
atholic foreigners. Colonies of cats have become regular
sitors of the illustrious dead, who include the poet Shelley,
owned in the Gulf of La Spezia in 1822, John Keats and his
end the painter Joseph Severn, Goethe's son Julius, and
ore recently Antonio Gramsci, one of the founders of the
alian Communist Party.

DRTA SAN PAOLO. Set within the Aurelian Wall ▲ 323 next
the Pyramid of Caius Cestius is the Porta di San Paolo,
e ancient Porta Ostiense from which the Via Ostia led to
ome's seaport. Together with the Porta Appia, it is the best
eserved of the gates of ancient Rome. Originally it had
o entrances framed by semicircular towers. At the time
Maxentius, in the 4th century AD, two crenelated walls
ere added, with a double gate which also had two arches
travertine marble; during the time of Honorius the two
terior arches were reduced to one. It was through the Porta
stiensis that Totila's Goths entered Rome in 594 BC. Today
houses a museum where models of Ostia and the ports
ilt by Claudius and Trajan are exhibited, along with casts of
liefs and inscriptions evoking the Via Ostia and its wayside
monuments. An annexe of the Capitoline Museums
▲ 132 has been opened near the old Montemartini
power station (Via Ostense).

JOHN KEATS
The English poet
John Keats (1795–
1821) came to Rome
hoping to recover
from tuberculosis, a
disease that had
already carried off of
his mother and his
brother. But he died

three months later.
The poet himself
dictated the epitaph
on his tomb: "Here
lies one whose name
was writ in water."

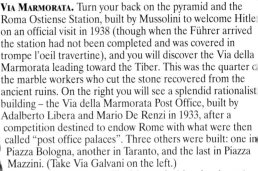

A slaughterhouse worker during the 19th century.

VIA MARMORATA. Turn your back on the pyramid and the Roma Ostiense Station, built by Mussolini to welcome Hitler on an official visit in 1938 (though when the Führer arrived the station had not been completed and was covered in trompe l'oeil travertine), and you will discover the Via della Marmorata leading toward the Tiber. This was the quarter of the marble workers who cut the stone recovered from the ancient ruins. On the right you will see a splendid rationalist building – the Via della Marmorata Post Office, built by Adalberto Libera and Mario De Renzi in 1933, after a competition destined to endow Rome with what were then called "post office palaces". Three others were built: one in Piazza Bologna, another in Taranto, and the last in Piazza Mazzini. (Take Via Galvani on the left.)

THE SLAUGHTERHOUSE. The Mattatoio (slaughterhouse) was built by G. Ersoch between 1888 and 1891 to replace the old buildings on the Via Flaminia ▲ 238. The monumental gate is crowned by a slaughtered bull, a remarkable realist sculpture. The Mattatoio fell into disuse in the 1980s, but it now houses the annexe of the MACRO, Rome's Contemporary Art Museum ▲ 381. In the surrounding neighborhood you can sample traditional Roman dishes featuring offal.

MONTE TESTACCIO

THE MOUNT OF SHARDS. The artificial hill in ancient times called *Mons Testaceus* is about 165 feet high; it has a circumference of just over half a mile, and a surface area of nearly 8 square miles. As its name indicates, it is in fact a heap of debris – the remains of the amphorae that contained products imported by Rome. These came mainly from the trading establishments on the Aventine and from the Emporium, the ancient commercial port on the nearby Tiber. The upper part of the "hill" consists almost entirely of amphorae that held oil from Spain, dating from 140 AD.

THE NEIGHBORHOOD. After the Unification of Italy it was decided to turn the Monte Testaccio area into a neighborhood of craftsmen and workmen. Building was begun in 1883, but was not finished until 1907 after the creation of the Institute for Popular Housing in 1903 put an end to a period of frenetic real-estate speculation. Today it is a lively neighborhood, with the colorful market of PIAZZA SANTA MARIA LIBERATRICE in its midst. The church of the same name was built in 1908, in Roman Byzantine style, replacing the Baroque church in the Forum demolished in 1899 for the restoration of Santa Maria Antiqua ▲ 142. (A little over a mile from the Porta Ostiensis is San Paolo fuori le Mura ▲ 382.)

THE AMPHORAE Because of their inscriptions (maker's mark, exporter's name, dates of inspection, etc.), some of the amphorae of Monte Testaccio have provided valuable evidence of the economy at the end of the Republic and under the Empire.

The Coelian Hill

187   San Gregorio Magno

188   Clivus Scauri

190   Santa Maria in Domnica

191   Santo Stefano Rotondo

192   Santi Quattro Coronati

193   San Clemente

196   The Lateran

200   Santa Croce in Gerusalemme

🏛 **One day**

◆ **E** D3-D4 **G** C2-D1-D2

1. TEMPLE OF
CLAUDIUS
2. BASILICA OF SANTI
GIOVANNI E PAOLO
3. SAN GREGORIO
MAGNO
4. VILLA CELIMONTANA
5. ARCH OF DOLABELLA
6. SANTA MARIA IN
DOMNICA
7. SANTO STEFANO
ROTONDO
8. SANTI QUATTRO
CORONATI
9. SAN CLEMENTE
10. BASILICA OF SAN
GIOVANNI IN LATERANO
11. SCALA SANTA

The Coelian Hill
(Monte Celio),
a strip of high
ground which
stretches as far as the
Coliseum, was included within
the walls of Rome in the 7th century BC. At the end of the
Republic and during the Empire it became partly residential.
Its luxurious villas included those of Mamurra (Julius
Caesar's officer made notorious by Catullus' epigrams) and
those of the Lateranus and Symmachus families. Yet the area
also retained a popular character. After the great fire that
destroyed the city under Nero, apartment blocks (*insulae*)
were built on these slopes, particularly around the base of the
Temple of Claudius. Recent excavations have revealed their
remains. Another feature of this hill was the presence of
several barracks, including those of the 5th cohort of the
vigiles (city guards ▲ 356) near Santa Maria in Domnica, the
two barracks of the *equites singulares* (the Emperor's mounted
guards) and the Castra Peregrina
(around the Church of Santo Stefano
Rotondo), where soldiers from
outside Rome were posted for
special duties such as policing and
mail service. From the end of
antiquity the construction of
important religious buildings gave
this area a new profile. At its

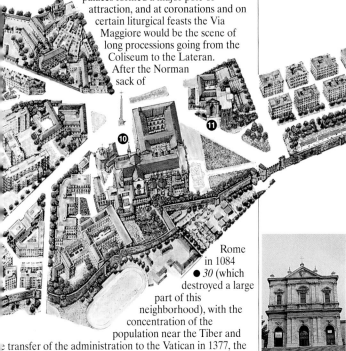

stern extremity San Giovanni in Laterano and the pontifical palaces formed a major pole of attraction, and at coronations and on certain liturgical feasts the Via Maggiore would be the scene of long processions going from the Coliseum to the Lateran. After the Norman sack of

Rome in 1084 ● *30* (which destroyed a large part of this neighborhood), with the concentration of the population near the Tiber and

e transfer of the administration to the Vatican in 1377, the ea became depopulated – to such an extent that the city thorities granted major privileges to the inhabitants of Via aggiore. However, such measures had very little effect. The elian Hill and the neighboring areas remained virtually inhabited, and were planted with vines and orchards up to e end of the 19th century. In fact, the landscape of the part ing the Palatine has hardly changed: the Camaldolesi, who ve lived in the monastery since 1573, still grow their getables on the slopes of the hill, and grass sprouts between e *sanpietrini* (cobblestones) of the Clivus Scauri.

N GREGORIO MAGNO

e monastery of San Gregorio was founded in the 6th ntury by Gregory the Great on the site of his own family me. It was enlarged several times during the Middle Ages, t the buildings that can be seen today were for the most rt erected by the chitect

The monumental façade of San Gregorio Magno, with its imposing flight of steps and atrium, both designed by Soria, dominates the entrance to the Via di San Gregorio. This ancient road lined with pine trees was the Via Triumphalis, where triumphal processions used to take place.

x

187

**1. CASTRENSE
AMPHITHEATER
2. SANTA CROCE IN
GERUSALEMME**

Giambattista Soria (1629–33) under the direction of Cardinal Scipione Borghese. The church's interior was remodeled between 1725 and 1734 by Francesco Ferrari. At the top of the nave, to the left, the Salviati chapel contains a very early fresco portraying the Virgin Mary which, according to tradition, is supposed to have spoken to St Gregory. To the left of the church stand three small chapels that were rebuilt at the beginning of the 17th century. Santa Silvia (on the right) is dedicated to St Gregory's mother. Sant'Andrea (in the center) probably stands on the site of St Gregory's original oratory; it contains two notable frescoes, the one by Domenichino, the other by Guido Reni, both painted in 160 In the third chapel, Santa Barbara, there is a table where, a legend has it, an angel sat among the poor to whom St Gregory was offering a meal.

CLIVUS SCAURI

The campanile and medieval buttresses of the Basilica of Santi Giovanni e Paolo.

The street that climbs from San Gregorio to San Giovanni i built over an ancient Roman street, and in some respects st looks like one. Along it the remains of several Imperial dwellings, which have survived at a relatively high level abov ground, are linked by medieval arches. (At the end of the Clivus, after passing under the arches of the medieval buttresses, you will come to the Church of Santi Giovanni e Paolo.)

SANTI GIOVANNI E PAOLO. With its red-brick architecture, th high windowless walls of the monastery and the tall Romanesque campanile built on the remains of the Temple Claudius, the Piazza dei Santi Giovanni e Paolo is as silent and desolate as those painted by de Chirico. Dedicated to S John and St Paul, two of Constantine's soldiers martyred under Julian the Apostate in 362, the basilica was built abov their house in the 5th century. It was damaged during the sack of Rome in 1084 Emperor Henry IV ● *30*, then partly rebuil between 1099 and 1118, when the campani was erected. The narthex is of a slightly lat period. Restoration work in the 1950's restored the exterior to its medieval appearance, but the interior retains its 18th century decorations.

THE HOUSE OF ST JOHN AND ST PAUL. This can be reached by a small staircase to the right of the choir. It is a moving testimonia to how Christianity took root in heathen so mythological scenes appear alongside symbols of the new religion. At the end of the 19th century two large multistoried Imperial dwellings were unearthed beneath the church. Originally they were separated a small courtyard, which was later

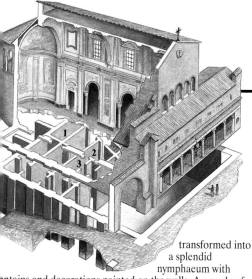

transformed into a splendid nymphaeum with

...ntains and decorations painted on the walls. A parade of ...ids riding sea serpents can still be seen on the right. But ... most remarkable element is a large fresco on one of the ...lls depicting Proserpina returning from Hades. From the ...rt of the nymphaeum you reach the ground-floor rooms, ...ich lead to the Clivus Scauri (1). On a well-preserved vault ... be seen a fresco in twelve sections showing male figures ...rrying scrolls, and pairs of sheep. A praying figure painted ...one of the lunettes gives evidence of the Christian ...racter of the house at that time. At the top of a small ...ircase is the "confessio", a sort of alcove entirely decorated ...h frescoes from the second half of the 4th century, ...icting scenes of martyrdom (arrests, decapitation, and ...eral violence); these describe the passions of ...n and Paul and also those of Crispus, ...pinianus and Benedicta, who were all ...cuted under Julian the Apostate and ...ose bodies were buried in this house.

...E TEMPLE OF CLAUDIUS. At the western ...of the Coelian Hill, overlooking the ...atine, stand the remains of a ...ple dedicated to the Emperor ...udius, who was deified by his ...e Agrippina soon after his ...th in 54 AD. The temple was ...t on top of the ruins of a ...angular building. The ...tern wall, which can ...seen between the ...panile and the ...nastery of Santi ...vanni e Paolo, belongs ...he oldest part of the ...nument. To the east, ...supporting walls ...t run along ...Via Claudia ...n toward the ...seum were ...t by Nero as a ...ne for the ...numental gardens ...he Domus Aurea ...74.

THE HOUSE OF THE SAINTS JOHN AND PAUL

This is painted with remarkable decorations on a white background showing youths supporting green bowers in which there are peacocks and other large birds. The vault is adorned with cupids and birds rampaging in the foliage. Later decorations, which probably date from the 4th century AD, are to be seen in rooms (2) and (3).

CLAUDIUS

The Emperor Claudius (41–54 AD) was often ridiculed, but he was in fact a scholar and a great administrator. As a soldier he pursued Augustus' policies and succeeded in conquering Britain. But this man who stammered and walked with a limp had the misfortune of marrying first Messalina, notorious for her debauchery, and then Agrippina, who had him assassinated to ensure her son Nero's succession to the throne.

189

SANTA MARIA IN DOMNICA

THE ARCH OF DOLABELLA AND THE AREA AROUND SANTA MARIA IN DOMNICA. From Piazza Santi Giovanni e Paolo, the Via San Paolo della Croce rises between high walls, along the side of the Villa Celimontana, toward a travertine arch supporting Nero's aqueduct. The attic bears an inscription (10 AD) giving the names of the consuls Publius Cornelius Dolabella and Caius Junius Silanus. This arch was no doubt originally the Porta Caelimontana, one of the gates in the Republican walls rebuilt by Augustus. It opens onto a very typical Roman scene. To the left is the isolated brick silhouette of a pilaster from Claudius' aqueduct; behind the trees in the background stands the round Church of Santo Stefano; and in the center is the NAVICELLA, a marble ship on a base plate bearing the insignia of Pope Leo X (1513). It has since been transformed into a fountain. A portico built in the same period by Sansovino gives access to Santa Maria in Domnica.

SANTA MARIA IN DOMNICA. No mention of this church can be found earlier than the time of Pope Leo III (795–816), but its foundation, on the remains of the barracks of the 5th cohort of *vigiles* ▲ *356*, probably goes back to the 7th century. The present building dates from the pontificate of Pascal I (817–24), as do the beautiful mosaics in the apse: the chancel arch portrays the Savior seated on the vault of heaven between two angels, while below this the apostles are shown being led by Peter and Paul, Moses and Elijah. At the back of the apse there is a hieratic Byzantine image of the *Virgin and Child* seated in the midst of a crowd of angels, while the Pope (distinguished by the square nimbus of the living) humbly touches her foot. To the left of the church, a monumental door opens onto the Villa Celimontana.

VILLA CELIMONTANA. On sunny days this villa's magnificent trees are an invitation to walk in their shade among the flowers and fountains. The park, which is now open to the public, has been in existence since the 15th century. It was later the garden of the Villa Mattei ▲ *369*, which had been conceived as a pleasure palace and adorned with ancient sculptures collected by its owners. The *casino* was built between 1581 and 1586 by Jacopo del Duca, and an obelisk was erected in the garden. This had previously stood on the Capitol and was given in 1584 to Prince Mattei by the Senate of Rome in gratitude for his good works. Between the 16th and the 19th centuries the villa was open to the public one day a year: during the pilgrimage to the Seven Churches ▲ *381*, rehabilitated by St Philip

The aqueduct built by Nero (54–68 AD) started at Porta Maggiore and brought water to the Palatine Hill.

"The park [of the Villa Celimontana], almost unique in its variety and fantasy among Roman parks, follows the folds of the Coelian Hill, on the ridge of which it stands."

Gabriel Fauré

"VIRGIN AND CHILD" With its vivid colors and iconographic freedom, which combines the Hellenistic and Byzantine styles, this mosaic is one of the finest Carolingian works in Rome.

Pope Leo X had his name and his coat of arms carved on the Navicella fountain.

ri in 1552, the faithful would come to the villa for rest and
reshment. In 1856 the estate was inherited by a Bavarian
on. It was confiscated by the Italian State in 1918 as an
emy asset", and was then given to the city of Rome in
25. Today the villa is the headquarters of the Italian
ographical Society.

N STEFANO ROTONDO ● 74

e first circular church to be built in Rome. Founded by
pe Simplicius (468–83), it was modeled on the Holy
pulcher in Jerusalem. The masonry and the capitals
corated with crosses show that it is not an ancient
monument that was reused. Work continued through the 6th
tury under John I and Felix IV. Pope Innocent II
30–43) added the entrance portico and the three internal
nsverse arches. On the walls erected to close the openings
he external arches Gregory XIII (1572–85) had frescoes
nted portraying scenes of martyrdom; these have survived
e above). (From the Largo della Sanità Militare go into the
zza, then right along Via Celimontana as far as Via dei
ti Quattro Coronati.)

MARTYROLOGY
In Santo Stefano
Rotondo there are
thirty-two frescoes by
Pomarancio showing
the martyrdom of
saints, and several by
Antonio Tempesta
(*The Life of St
Stephen*, *The
Massacre of the*

Innocents and *The
Madonna of Seven
Sorrows*).

**A MONUMENTAL
SANCTUARY**
Originally Santo
Stefano Rotondo had
two concentric
circular galleries,
separated by two
series of columns.
When the sanctuary
was restored in 1453
the outer gallery was
destroyed because it
was in danger of
collapsing. The
diameter of the
building was thus
considerably reduced.
In 1658 excavations
revealed the presence
of a mithraeum (2nd
to 3rd century AD)
beneath the church,
as well as remains of
the Castra Peregrina
barracks ▲ *186*.

SANTI QUATTRO CORONATI

This church was first mentioned in 595, but its foundation goes back to the 4th century. After being renovated by Leo (847–55) and then badly damaged when Rome was sacked i 1084 ● *30*, it was restored under Pascal II (1099–1118), though the side naves were eliminated and its length considerably reduced. The magnificent paving of the centra nave also dates from this period. In 16 Cardinal Millini had the mosaics of the apse destroyed and replaced by fresco by Giovanni da San Giovanni. These illustrate the story of the saints to who the church is dedicated, the four soldi Severo, Severiano, Carpoforo and Vittorino, who were martyred under Diocletian for refusing to worship Aesculapius. In 1912 and 1957 excavations revealed some of the origi structures, including the columns and crypt of the Carolingian church. The monastery, which was known to have existed in the time of Leo IV, was transformed into an impregnable fort in the 13th century. In fact, during the Middle Ages the complex was used as bastion for the defense of the Lateran Palace ▲ *197* and as a refuge for the popes.

THE CHAPEL OF SAN SILVESTRO. The f courtyard leads to the Chapel of San Silvestro, which is preceded by a room adorned with a calendar painted in the 13th century. The chapel was decorated with a beautiful cy of frescoes in 1246 portraying the legend of Constantine. Having become a leper, the Emperor dreams of Peter and Paul; he then sends messengers to Pope Sylvester I, in a

reat on Mount Soracte; the Pope obliges the Emperor to ⟨ven⟩erate images of the apostles and cures him of leprosy by ⟨bap⟩tizing him; finally the Emperor receives the Pope as ⟨sov⟩ereign of Rome. Beyond the naive and picturesque nature ⟨of⟩ their images, these frescoes are of great historical interest: ⟨the⟩y assert the supremacy of the papacy over civil authority, ⟨whi⟩ch at a certain period of the Middle Ages was a highly ⟨con⟩troversial issue. The second courtyard leads to the present ⟨chu⟩rch, where there are 14th-century frescoes on the walls of ⟨the⟩ lateral naves; the left nave leads to the early-13th-century ⟨clo⟩ister, which in turn leads to the 9th-century Chapel of ⟨San⟩ta Barbara.

⟨SA⟩N CLEMENTE ★

⟨TH⟩E BASILICA OF SAN CLEMENTE. This basilica dedicated to ⟨the⟩ third successor of St Peter, Pope Clement I (88–97), was ⟨fou⟩nded before 385 on the site of existing Roman buildings. ⟨Co⟩uncils were held in it in 417 and 499, and it was restored in ⟨the⟩ 8th and 9th centuries before being destroyed during the ⟨sac⟩k of 1084 ● 30. Consequently Pascal II (1099–1118), who ⟨ha⟩d been titular cardinal of San Clemente before becoming ⟨Pop⟩e, commissioned the construction of a new basilica on the ⟨site⟩ of the old one. Carlo Stefano Fontana made modifications ⟨to i⟩t between 1713 and 1719. The paleo-Christian basilica was ⟨onl⟩y discovered in 1857–60 during excavation works.

THE UPPER CHURCH. Externally this has retained its medieval features, with a vestibule, a porch and an atrium. Inside, it is modeled on the lower church, but on a reduced scale. The 12th-century Schola Cantorum in the middle of the central nave is partly made of elements from the earlier church. The ciborium is 6th century, and the paschal candelabra 12th century. The apse is adorned with a splendid 12th-century mosaic, *The Triumph of the Cross*. To the right of the ⟨ma⟩in entrance, the chapel dedicated to St Catherine is ⟨dec⟩orated with frescoes by Masolino da Panicale.

⟨TH⟩E LOWER CHURCH. Through the sacristy one descends to a ⟨virt⟩ual picture gallery. The narthex has splendid 11th-century ⟨fre⟩scoes depicting the miracle of St Clement and ⟨the⟩ transfer of his body from the Vatican to San ⟨Cle⟩mente (above). In the nave there are frescoes ⟨of⟩ *The Assumption* (9th century) and *The ⟨Leg⟩end of St Alexis* ▲ 180. Another 11th-⟨cen⟩tury fresco cycle offers an ⟨amu⟩sing version of the pursuit of ⟨St⟩ Clement by the heathen ⟨pre⟩fect of Rome, Sisinnius: his ⟨ser⟩vants, blinded by God, bind a ⟨col⟩umn, mistaking it for the ⟨Pop⟩e, and try to carry it off. The ⟨ba⟩d expressions the Prefect uses ⟨to e⟩ncourage his men, inscribed ⟨on⟩ the wall as in a cartoon strip, ⟨are⟩ the earliest known examples of ⟨the⟩ vernacular ● 42.

Beneath the Crucifixion, two deer representing all those who aspire to baptism drink from a stream springing from the cross.

At San Clemente the layers of history can be seen in the ground itself. This 13th-century church with its Baroque façade was built on top of a paleo-Christian church, which in turn stands on ancient Roman buildings. Few other sites provide such a graphic illustration of the great historical palimpsest that is one of Rome's chief attractions.

The paleo-Christian basilica was decorated with numerous frescoes. This fragment from the northern aisle is thought to have been part of a *Last Judgment*.

THE MIRACLE OF ST CLEMENT
According to the legend, St Clement was thrown into the Black Sea with an anchor tied to his feet. During the annual procession of Christians at this site, a child was lost and engulfed by waves but the following year, the child was found safe and sound.

Mithras ▲ *181* was born from a stone like a spark from a flint. That is the symbolism of the statue of the god in the niche at the back of the mithraeum.

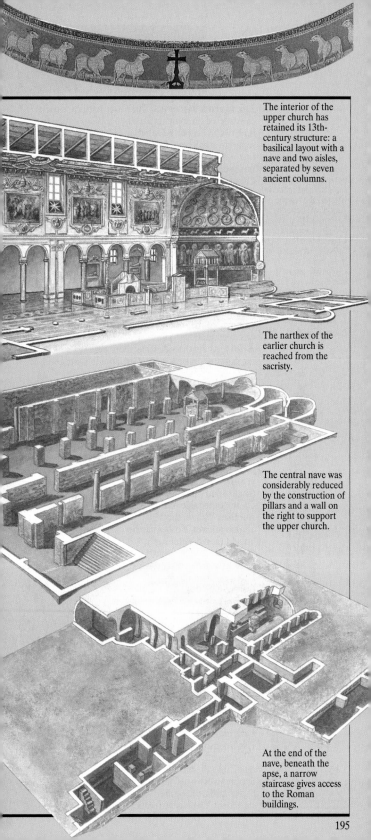

The interior of the upper church has retained its 13th-century structure: a basilical layout with a nave and two aisles, separated by seven ancient columns.

The narthex of the earlier church is reached from the sacristy.

The central nave was considerably reduced by the construction of pillars and a wall on the right to support the upper church.

At the end of the nave, beneath the apse, a narrow staircase gives access to the Roman buildings.

▲ THE COELIAN HILL

THE PINK GRANITE OBELISK
This is the tallest and most ancient of Rome's obelisks (it is over 150 feet high, including the pedestal). Erected in the 15th century BC in front of the temple of Amon in Thebes by Tutmoses III, it was brought to Rome by Constantius II in 357 AD and placed on the *spina* of the Circus Maximus. It was discovered there in 1586. A year later Sixtus V got Domenico Fontana to re-erect it in the Lateran piazza.

THE EARLIER BUILDINGS. The lower basilica is itself constructed on some important buildings dating from the time of the Emperor Domitian (81–96 AD). These were two separate structures, separated by a very narrow corridor. Th first housed the Imperial mint, which had been transferred this spot during the Flavian period from its original site on Capitoline Hill. Its identification was made possible by the discovery near San Clemente of a series of inscriptions dedicated to several gods, including Apollo, Hercules and Fortuna. The second edifice, located to the west of the chur and also built at the time of Domitian, was entirely made of brick. Originally the central courtyard was covered by a vau with skylights. The exact purpose of the building is still unknown but it was certainly public, as the presence of the mithraeum confirms.

THE MITHRAEUM. Its construction dates from the end of the 2nd or beginning of the 3rd century AD, a particularly propitious time for the spread of oriental cults in the city. T entrance to the room would have had doors, and the ceiling was decorated with stars (an allusion to Mithraic cosmology ▲ *181*). Along the side walls there are the usual benches fo the faithful. (Take Via San Giovanni in Laterano.)

THE LATERAN

This is a very different part of Rome – a monumental Rome with its huge basilica dominating the vast unattractive piazz The square was the meeting place of Rome's Communists i the days when leaders such as Togliatti and Berlinguer drew huge crowds. At one time the inhabitants of Rome used to gather here on June 23, the eve of the Feast of St John, to s at long tables, eating *lumache* (snails) and sipping white wine. On the other side of the Aurelian Wall, in the Via Sannio market, clothes can be bought incredibly cheaply.

ORIGINS. After his victory over Maxentius in 312 AD and the Edict of Milan in 313, Constantine donated the basilica as an *ex voto* offering to the African pope Melchiades, together with a *domus ecclesiae*, which became the Lateran Palace. This remained the official residence of the popes until their return from Avignon in 1377. The estate had been an Imperial possession ever since Nero confiscated it from the Laterani family for their part in Piso's conspiracy in 65 AD; subsequently, in 197, it was made into the barracks of Septimius Severus' mounted bodyguards, the *equites singulares*. The basilica, which

E MITHRAEUM (LEFT)
the front of the altar Mithras is
wn slaying the bull. The sides
pict the guardian *genii* Cautes and
utopathes, with torch raised or
ered.

originally dedicated to the Savior, was inaugurated in
7. Recent excavations have revealed a few frescoes
m the Laterani residence, some remains from the
racks and several walls from the original basilica.

E EXTENSION OF THE PALACE. During the 5th
tury the popes began to enlarge the *patriarchium*
e core of the patriarchal palace) and erected
ldings to meet the requirements of a
tralized administration. However,
y never succeeded in making the
teran the real center of Rome.
ter, in order to receive
arlemagne after crowning him
peror in St Peter's on Christmas day
), Pope Leo III added a *triclinium*
anqueting hall) sumptuously decorated with
saics. In the 11th and 12th centuries, with the
ction of dwellings for the prelates and Curia staff
und the basilica and palace, the Lateran assumed the
pearance of a small town. But the fires of 1308 and 1361,
nbined with the absence of the popes throughout most of
14th century, led to such a degeneration of the palace that
en Gregory XI returned to Rome in 1377 he preferred to
e up residence in the Vatican – which had the advantage of
ing easier to defend, due to the proximity of the Tiber and
stel Sant'Angelo. After restorations commissioned by
rtin V (1417–31), Leo X (1513–21) and Paul IV (1555–9),
tus V (1585–90) entrusted the architect Domenico Fontana
h the complete restructuring of the palace. The
riarchium was demolished, and only the Chapel of San
renzo in Palatio, the Scala Santa and the remains of Leo

The Feast of St John
in Piazza San
Giovanni in Laterano.

197

THE NAVE
The theatrical appearance of the Lateran Basilica's central nave is due to the gigantic pilasters that frame an alternating series of vaulted arches and pillars, each containing a gray marble alcove flanked by green marble columns from the original basilica. In each alcove stands a colossal statue of one of the twelve apostles, dating from the early 18th century.

III's *triclinium* were spared. The Lateran Palace is the headquarters of the Vicariate of Rome, and it was here that the famous Lateran Treaty, or "Concordat", between the Holy See and Mussolini was signed on February 11, 1929.

THE LATERAN BASILICA. The basilica is still considered "*Omnium urbis et orbi ecclesiarum mater et caput*", the mother and head of all the churches of the city and the world. Not surprisingly, it bears traces of the endless rebuilding it has undergone. The entrance, as in all the major basilicas, consist of a portico with a balcony for pontifical blessings, traditionally given here on the Feast of the Ascension. In 17 Alessandro Galilei built the façade surmounted – or crushed as critics said at the time – by fifteen colossal statues. The statue of Constantine beneath the porch came from the Imperial baths on the Quirinal Hill. As in St Peter's, of the five doors, the one on the far right, the Holy Door, is opene only in Holy Years ● *52*. The ancient panels of the central door came from the Curia in the Forum ▲ *138*. The appearance of the nave and the two aisles on either side, the same in number as in the original basilica, has changed hard at all since Borromini redesigned the interior between 1646 and 1649. The central nave has a 16th-century carved-wood ceiling, while the lower aisles are adorned with stucco decorations. The entire transept was painted with frescoes at the end of the 16th century under the direction of Cavaliere d'Arpino. In the transept crossing, a 14th-century Gothic tabernacle stands on the altar at which only the Pope celebrates Mass. Althou it was modified in 1851 under Pius IX, contains fragments of the altar on whi the first popes of Rome, from St Peter St Sylvester, officiated. In the choir an the apse, which were rebuilt and redecorated in 1884 under Leo XIII, remains of the older mosaic decorations by Jacopo Torriti (13th century) have al been incorporated. Through the left transept one can reach the splendid 13th-century cloister. The right transept provid access to the side of the piazza, which is dominated by the portico and loggia designed by Domenico Fontana in 1586, Sixtus V's urban replanning having made this side entrance facing the city into the basilica's main entrance. A statue of Henry IV of France by Nicolas Cordier (1608) stands under the portico. This ruler was particularly generous with gifts to the chapter; as a result, all subsequent French heads of state have been made honorary canons of the Lateran Basilica.

THE BAPTISTERY OF SAN GIOVANNI IN FONTE. Built under Constantine and restructured in the 5th century, the baptistery was remodeled under Urban VIII in 1637 and again by Borromini for Alexander VII. Its octagonal interio accentuated by four symmetrical chapels, exalts the sacrame of baptism. The drum of the cupola displays scenes from the life of St John the Baptist by Andrea Sacchi, while frescoes his pupils illustrate the conversion of Constantine. The

THE LATERAN TREATY
▲ *202*
The "Treaty of Conciliation", that gave birth to the Vatican State rehabilitated Catholics in Italian political life after a hiatus of fifty-nine years. Being "extraterritorial", the Lateran is part of the Vatican State.

The cloister of the basilica is the work of the Vassalletto family.

The statues crowning the basilica's façade portray Christ, St John the Evangelist, St John the Baptist and the Fathers of the Church.

...saics in the chapels dedicated to St ...n the Evangelist (5th century) and St ...nanzio (7th century) afford proof of ... building's age. The font (in the ...ter) is a huge green basalt urn ...ginally used for the total ...mersion of those being baptized; it is ...rounded by eight porphyry columns ...d has a bronze cover made between ...77 and 1678.

...E SCALA SANTA AND SANCTA ...NCTORUM. The steps of the Scala Santa ... said to be the ones on which Christ stood ...Pontius Pilate's palace during his trial, and ...Helena is supposed to have brought them to ...me. Pilgrims climb these twenty-eight steps ...their knees as an act of veneration. Sixtus V ...d them erected as a stairway to the private ...apel of the popes, San Lorenzo in Palatio. This ...apel, which was part of the medieval palace, ...es its other name, the Sancta Sanctorum ...Holy of Holies"), to the precious relics it ...ntains. The most famous of these is an ...*eiropoieton*, an image of Christ "not made by ...man hands", which Innocent III (1198–1216) ...d covered with silver leaf. (Proceed along ...le Carlo Felice.)

THE CASTRENSE AMPHITHEATER

The amphitheater owes its survival to its incorporatation into the Aurelian Wall, although only one of

its three levels is well preserved. The name comes from the late Latin *castrum*, meaning "Imperial palace".

CIRCUS VARIANUS

This circus derives its name from the family of the Emperor Heliogabalus, the Varii. It was discovered at the northern end of the Sessorium, running parallel to Claudius' aqueduct and the Aurelian Wall. On the *spina* was placed the obelisk that must have adorned the tomb of Hadrian's favorite, Antinous, on the Pincio. To the north in the former barracks of the grenadiers are further remains, most notably the back wall of a vast apse dating from the time of Constantine.

Santa Croce in Gerusalemme (right).

SANTA CROCE IN GERUSALEMME

The most important ancient remains in this area – the Castrense Amphitheater, the Baths of Helena, the Circus Varianus and the hall converted to create Santa Croce in Gerusalemme – were all part of a single Imperial villa, the Sessorium, begun by Septimius Severus and completed by Heliogabalus in the 3rd century AD. The Baths of Helena were covered over by the construction work for the Via Felice instigated by Sixtus V ● 61.

BASILICA OF SANTA CROCE IN GERUSALEMME. Tradition has it that Santa Croce, one of the major basilicas, was built by Constantine in 320 AD to house the relics brought back from Jerusalem by his mother, St Helena. After frequent restorations in the Middle Ages, it was almost completely rebuilt in 1743 by Domenico Gregorini. Behind its convex façade there is an unusual oval atrium with an elliptical ambulatory (pictured on the left). The ancient columns separating the nave from the two aisles alternate with Baroque pillars. The whole of the interior is adorned with stucco decorations. The frescoes on the main vault of the church and the walls of the choir were painted by Corrado Giaquinto in 1745. The choir vault still has its late-15th-century decorations. The mid-18th-century *baldacchino* rests on the columns of the original medieval ciborium. The underground chapel of St Helena, below the nave, is adorned with a splendid 15th-century mosaic designed by Melozzo da Forlì.

THE CHAPEL OF THE RELICS. Of all the churches in Rome, Santa Croce has one of the richest collections of relics. A special chapel was therefore built for them in 1930. A staircase to the left of the choir leads to this chapel, where one can see three pieces of the True Cross, one of its nails, a

fragment of the INRI ("Jesus of Nazareth, King of the Jews") inscription, two thorns from Christ's crown of thorns, a piece of the sponge that was held up to him, one of the silver pieces paid to Judas, St Thomas's finger which touched the wounds of Christ and the crossbar from the Good Thief's cross. The paving stones are said to have been laid on a substantial amount of earth from Golgotha.

The Vatican

209 St Peter's Basilica
210 The greatest church in Christendom
214 Inside the Vatican
218 The Sistine Chapel
222 The Raphael Rooms
224 The Vatican Museums
232 The Borgo and Via della Conciliazione
233 Castel Sant'Angelo
236 Prati

▲ The Vatican

⚎ One day

◆ D A2-A3-A4

1. **Piazza San Pietro**
2. **St Peter's Basilica**
3. **Sistine Chapel**
4. **Cortile del Belvedere**
5. **Cortile della Pigna**
6. **Entrance to the Vatican Museums**
7. **Pinacoteca (Vatican Picture Gallery)**
8. **Casina di Pio IV**
9. **Vatican Library**
10. **Palazzo del Governatorato**
11. **Vatican Radio**
12. **Vatican Station**
13. **Papal Audience Hall**
14. **Passetto**
15. **Via della Conciliazione**
16. **Castel Sant'Angelo ✪**
17. **Palazzo di Giustizia**

A STATE WITHIN A CITY ✪

Vatican City may be Europe's smallest state, covering less than one fifth of a square mile, and having 282 permanent residents, plus 110 Swiss Guards, but it is also the most visited: 6 million pilgrims and tourists pass through its gates every year. Neither ticket nor pass is necessary to enter St Peter's Basilica and the museums (you may have to return several times, as opening times are unreliable). Those wishing to visit Vatican City should contact the Ufficio Informazioni Pellegrini e Turisti (in St Peter's Square) to book a guide (one visit per day, except Wednesdays and public holidays).

The Vatican City is the smallest State in Euro (less than one fifth of a square mile). Its boun were fixed on February 11, 1929, by the Later Treaty, which recognized the Pope's sovereign over his territory. The treaty also gave extraterritorial status to a number of building including the three other great patriarchal bas of Rome (San Giovanni in Laterano, San Pao fuori le Mura and Santa Maria Maggiore), as as the papal villa of Castel Gandolfo and the Palazzo della Cancelleria.

St Peter's keys
The coat of arms of the popes includes the tiara (the triple papal crown: father of kings and princes, king and rector of the world, and vicar of Christ) and the keys of the Kingdom of Heaven, entrusted by Jesus to St Peter.

The Swiss Guards
The institution of the Swiss Guards (officially the *Cohors pedestris Helvetorium a sacra custodia Pontificis*) goes back to Julius II. In 1505 the pontiff obtained a personal guard composed of two hundred Swiss soldiers. This guard was to receive a tragic baptism of fire on May 6, 1527,

during the Sac Rome ● *36*, an went on to pro value and loya the Pope many times. Each yea May 6 a sumpt ceremony commemorates combat and the of fidelity. The design of their uniform, which remained unch for 450 years, i often wrongly attributed to Michelangelo.

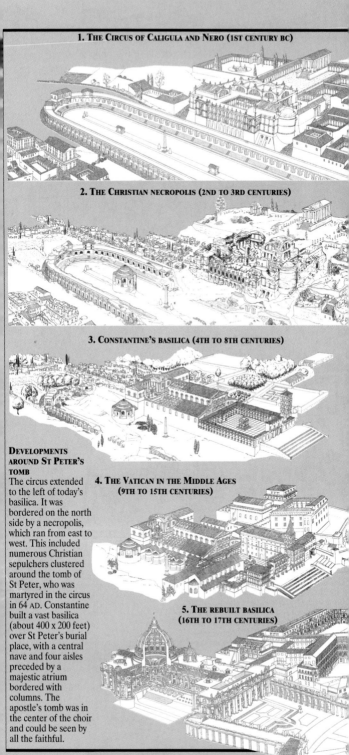

1. The Circus of Caligula and Nero (1st century BC)

2. The Christian necropolis (2nd to 3rd centuries)

3. Constantine's basilica (4th to 8th centuries)

Developments around St Peter's tomb

The circus extended to the left of today's basilica. It was bordered on the north side by a necropolis, which ran from east to west. This included numerous Christian sepulchers clustered around the tomb of St Peter, who was martyred in the circus in 64 AD. Constantine built a vast basilica (about 400 x 200 feet) over St Peter's burial place, with a central nave and four aisles preceded by a majestic atrium bordered with columns. The apostle's tomb was in the center of the choir and could be seen by all the faithful.

4. The Vatican in the Middle Ages (9th to 15th centuries)

5. The rebuilt basilica (16th to 17th centuries)

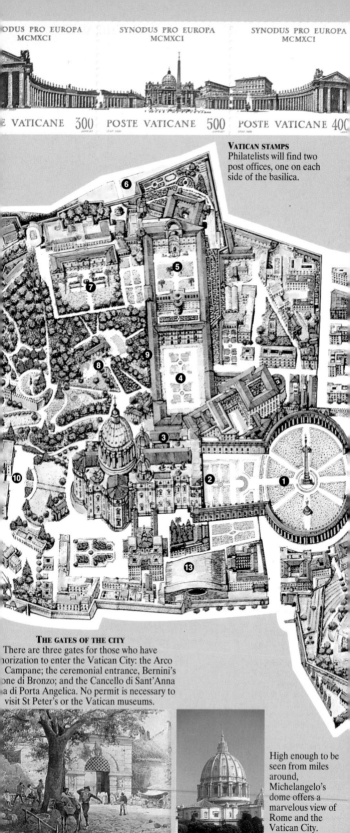

ODUS PRO EUROPA
MCMXCI

SYNODUS PRO EUROPA
MCMXCI

SYNODUS PRO EUROPA
MCMXCI

E VATICANE 300   POSTE VATICANE 500   POSTE VATICANE 40C

VATICAN STAMPS
Philatelists will find two
post offices, one on each
side of the basilica.

THE GATES OF THE CITY
There are three gates for those who have
horization to enter the Vatican City: the Arco
Campane; the ceremonial entrance, Bernini's
one di Bronzo; and the Cancello di Sant'Anna
a di Porta Angelica. No permit is necessary to
visit St Peter's or the Vatican museums.

High enough to be
seen from miles
around,
Michelangelo's
dome offers a
marvelous view of
Rome and the
Vatican City.

The Vatican State has its own diplomats, citizens, police force, army and legal system; it mints its own money and has most forms of communication at its disposal, including a railway station, post offices, television, radio and newspapers. The daily Italian-language paper *L'Osservatore Romano*, founded in 1861, is printed in the Vatican City and contains a section that is the official mouthpiece of the Holy See; there are also weekly editions in several languages and a popular illustrated weekly edition, *L'Osservatore della Domenica*.

L'OSSERVATORE ROMANO

GIORNALE QUOTIDIANO   POLITICO RELIGIOSO

UNICUIQUE SUUM   NON PRAEVALEBUNT

CITTÀ DEL VATICANO

⑮

⑯

THE PASSETTO
This is a fortified passageway linking the Vatican to the Castel Sant'Angelo.

THE WALLS
After the Saracens sacked the Vatican in 846, Leo IV had the first fortifications built; these were subsequently extended many times. The bastions of the time of Nicholas V (1447–55) mark the present-day limits of the city.

Sixtus IV erected the Vatican's first purpose-built library, to house a collection of 2,527 volumes. Although more than 400 manuscripts were lost during the Sack of Rome in 1527, the increasing number of books led Sixtus V to organize a new library, still in use today.

THE LIBRARY
Nicholas V possessed 824 Latin manuscripts, which he wished to keep in a library open to scholars.

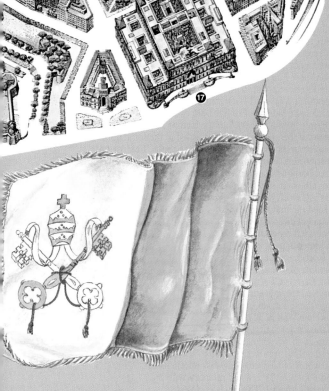

THE VATICAN FLAG
The Church's banner originally featured the figure of St Peter on a red background. Pope Innocent III replaced the figure with symbolic keys surmounted by a white cross; and Boniface VIII opted for a red silk standard spangled with gold stars. The flag remained unchanged until 1824, when Leo XII gave it the colors it has today, yellow and white; the keys have been crowned by the papal tiara ever since.

> The great age of building reached its climax with Bernini's magnificent colonnades, which made the Piazza San Pietro the most theatrical square in the world.

The Ager Vaticanus (the plain between the Tiber and the Vatican Hill) was originally an unhealthy marshland area which, like other low-lying parts of the city, was often subject to terrible flooding by the river. For a long time it was sparsely populated, as the nucleus of the town was concentrated on the left bank of the Tiber.

AROUND ST PETER'S TOMB. In the days when the gardens of Domitian and Agrippina extended over this suburban area it was crossed by several roads, lined with a long procession of tombs. The gardens are thought to have included the circuses of Caligula and Nero, where many of the early Christian martyrs died. This was one of the most important buildings in the area, along with Trajan's *naumachia* and Hadrian's mausoleum ▲ 233. Nevertheless, it appears to have been privately owned, like the Circus of Maxentius ▲ 328, and to have formed part of Agrippina's villa. St Peter was buried in the vicinity of the circus, and it was the presence of the apostle's tomb that influenced the area's development. After his conversion to Christianity Constantine built a basilica over the tomb with an access route from the Pons Aelius (the ancient forerunner of the Ponte Sant'Angelo ▲ 239), and houses soon sprang up along the road. A century later the first monasteries appeared around the shrine, and Pope Symmachus (498–514) constructed the embryo of an episcopal residence. From the 8th century the flood of pilgrims from Northern Europe coming to pray at the tombs of the apostles and martyrs led to the foundation of hospices to house them, such as the Scholae Francorum, Frisonorum, Saxonum and Langobardorum. The neighborhood experienced a fresh bout of growth under the influence of the Carolingians. At the request of Pépin le Bref, King of the Franks, Pope Stephen II turned the mausoleum of Theodosius into a chapel dedicated to St Petronilla, a Roman virgin venerated especially by the Franks; Charlemagne had an imperial palace built in 781, during his second visit to Rome; and Leo III (795–816) commissioned the building of a new papal residence.

THE LEONINE CITY. The Vatican neighborhood survived the ravages of the Goths and Vandals, even though it was located outside the Aurelian Wall ▲ 323, and the imposing mass of the Castel Sant'Angelo ▲ 233 was its only protection. So when, in 846, the basilica and neighboring area were sacked by the Saracens the whole of Christendom was apprehensive and Pope Leo IV erected ramparts with the help of Lothair I. The newly enclosed quarter became known as the Leonine City, a name it retained throughout the Middle Ages – before becoming the Borgo in 1586, when it was integrated into the municipal administrative system. In the 12th century the popes embarked on a vast building project, but it was not until their return from Avignon in 1377 that they and the Curia left the Lateran ▲ 196 to definitively settle in the Vatican.

St Peter's tomb.

THE BORGO
At the end of the 15 century the ramparts were reinforced, and access to the basilica and palace was improved. A road named the Borgo Nuovo was created between the Borgo Santo Spirito and th Borgo Vecchio. At t stage the building of the basilica was started, and after the Sack of Rome in 152 ● 36 the new fortifications of the area were begun. Th major building perio ended a century and half later, when Bernini erected his magnificent colonnades.

Statue of St Peter.

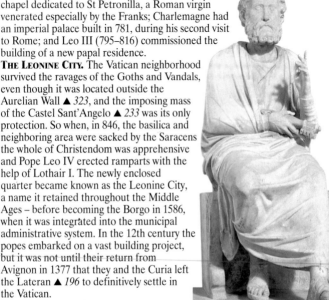

ST PETER'S BASILICA

A NEW SHRINE. Resplendent with magnificent art treasures and precious metalwork, Constantine's ancient basilica, which survived for over a thousand years, threatened to collapse on the return of the popes from Avignon. Repairs and modifications proved insufficient, and Julius II (1503–13) invited amante to design a new church. The demolition and ilding work began in 1506, and was to last for a century and half. Despite the multitude of architects who succeeded one other, often modifying the work of their predecessors, the w basilica turned out to be extraordinarily coherent as a ole.

VAL PLANS. Wanting, as he put it, "to perch the Pantheon top of Constantine's basilica", Bramante planned a urch in the form of a Greek cross crowned by a dome; and s to Bramante that the four central piers and arches pporting the dome are due. After his death in 1514, his ccessors, Raphael, Giuliano da Sangallo, Baldassare ruzzi and Antonio da Sangallo, put forward different ans in the shape of either a Greek or a Latin cross. ichelangelo, who took charge in 1546, opted for the Greek oss and conceived a new dome. Only the drum had been ished at the time of his ath, but the dome was mpleted in accordance with e plans and model that he t. However, the Latin cross s the plan that prevailed. rtly so that the shrine uld be able to hold a eater number of the faithful d partly for aesthetic asons, Paul V (1605–21) ked Carlo Maderno to ngthen the nave by three ys, a modification which d at least one irksome sult: the dome would no nger be visible to the visitor nding at the entrance of e church.

CONTROVERSIAL FAÇADE. Paul V also commissioned aderno to build the façade. The work lasted from 1607 1614 and failed to meet with unanimous approval: it was long in relation to its height and clearly revealed two ries surmounted by an attic, which seemed better suited a palace than a church. Bernini returned to the idea of in towers, which in Maderno's scheme were to have rmounted the exterior bays but had not yet been built. t opinion was so opposed to these towers that they were lled down during the pontificate of Innocent X (1644–55). ladier finally suggested incorporating the two great clocks ible today.

the north date from the 2nd century AD, those to the south from the 3rd century. To the west, where the Christian tombs are concentrated, there is a small rectangular space: this is the site of the tomb identified as that of St Peter. To understand early Christianity it is essential to visit this initially pagan but later Christian necropolis, which was used from the 1st to the 4th centuries, up to the building of Constantine's basilica.

The central nave of Constantine's basilica (above).

▲ THE VATICAN

THE OBELISK
When Domenico
Fontana erected the
obelisk from Nero's
circus in front of the
basilica, Sixtus V
ordered that if

anyone engaged in
the delicate operation
spoke they would be
condemned to death.
Realizing the ropes
were about to snap, a
man yelled "Dampen
the ropes!" – which
was done at once,
enabling the
operation to be
completed
successfully. The
Pope pardoned the
man who had dared
to break the silence
and also rewarded
him.

One of the proposed
plans for the façade
of St Peter's (center).

**MICHELANGELO'S
DOME**
The dome of St
Peter's dominates the
city and could once
be seen from many
miles away. It rests on
a drum pierced by
windows surmounted
by alternating curved
and triangular
pediments and
separated by twin
columns. Its
dimensions are so
vast that there is
room for several
people at a time
inside the ball above
the lantern.

PIAZZA SAN PIETRO ★. In 1626 Urban VIII commissioned
Bernini to continue the work, especially the restructuring of
the façade. Then, after falling from favor under Innocent X
he was brought back by Alexander VII (1655–67) to design
the new square in front of the basilica. Maderno's façade
needed to be given greater breadth; the irregular buildings
surrounding the square had to be hidden; the obelisk set up
the square in 1586 had to be taken into account; and it was
also necessary to enable a larger crowd to see the Pope duri
the "Urbi et Orbi" blessing ● 52. Bernini's solution was to
design a *piazza* in the form of an ellipse, bordered by a
quadruple colonnade forming a portico wide enough to let
carriages pass. The foci of the ellipse are indicated by marb
disks on each side of the two fountains: standing on either o
these disks you can see only one row of columns, instead
of four. Two wings link the colonnades to the
basilica: the one on the right ends at the Scala
Regia ● 85, the one on the left at the Arco
delle Campane.

THE GREATEST CHURCH IN CHRISTENDOM

THE ENTRANCE PORTICO. Beneath
Maderno's portico stand Bernini's
Constantine (1669), at the back on
the right, and *Charlemagne* by

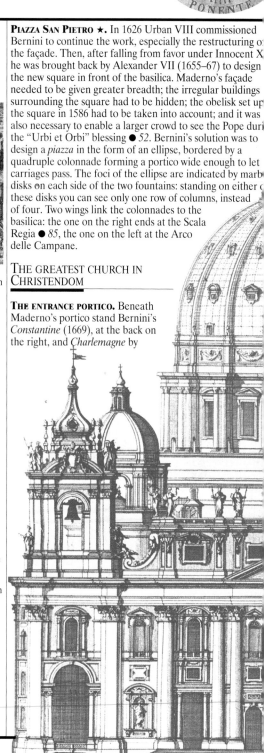

rnacchini (1725) on the left. Thus the first of the Roman
mperors to adopt Christianity and the first Holy Roman
mperor – the secular arms of spiritual power – seem to take
e shrine under their symbolic protection. Access to the
rine is by five doors. The door on the extreme right, the
oly Door ● *52*, is opened only at the beginning of a Holy
ar, which occurs every 25 years. The central door dates
om the 15th century; it was created by Antonio Averulino
d is from Constantine's basilica. Another remnant from it
n be seen if you turn your back to the doorway: the mosaic
the tympanum above the central entrance overlooking the
iazza is a fragment of the *Navicella* mosaic, showing Christ
alking on the water, made for Constantine's shrine.

HE NAVE. Although St Peter's Basilica is the largest
Christian basilica, its immensity is not apparent at first
sight due to its balanced proportions and the
monumental size of all the works of art it
contains. The statues of the principal founders
of the monastic orders, enthroned in tall
niches all along the main nave, are
colossal; these were left to the initiative
of each order and set up as they were
completed (the oldest ones are closest
to the choir). In addition, since the
basilica was conceived to emphasize
the eternal nature of the Church,
fragile materials were eliminated.

THE DOOR OF DEATH
Of the basilica's five
doors, the one on the
left was made by the
sculptor Giacomo
Manzù (1963).
Commissioned by
John XXIII, with
whom he had a close
friendship, it depicts
the descent from the
Cross and the death
of Mary. The
background features
the Pope welcoming
bishops and cardinals
to the second Vatican
Council.

A stoup for holy
water at the entrance
of the nave.

**THE SCALE OF THE
BUILDING**
Cherubs taller than
any visitor, a
baldacchino higher
than the Palazzo
Farnese – these give
an idea of the vast
scale of the building.
In addition, to
indicate the
exceptional length of
the nave (over 600
feet), the lengths of
some of the largest
Christian churches
are inscribed in
gilded bronze on the
paving.

Bernini's gloria.

MICHELANGELO'S "PIETÀ"
Cardinal Jean Bilhères de Lagraulas commissioned Michelangelo to make this group during the sculptor's second stay in Rome. The contract stipulated it should be "the most beautiful work in marble that exists in Rome to this day". It is said that one night, irritated at hearing the statue attributed to another artist, Michelangelo crept into St Peter's to engrave his name on the Virgin's mantle. It is the only sculpture he signed. The marks of suffering such as the stigmata on Jesus' body are reduced to the barest essentials, and the virgin seems as young as her son. These effects are due to the sculptor's quest for ideal beauty.

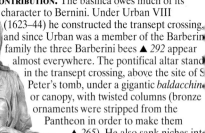

From the end of the 17th century the pictures which decorated it (many of the originals are now kept in Santa Maria degli Angeli) were translated into mosaic. Also, a number of celebrated paintings from other churches in Rome were brought to the Vatican, including *The Transfiguration* by Raphael ▲ *228* and *The Last Communion of St Jerome* by Domenichino ▲ *231*, both now in the Pinacoteca.

BERNINI'S CONTRIBUTION. The basilica owes much of its character to Bernini. Under Urban VIII (1623–44) he constructed the transept crossing, and since Urban was a member of the Barberini family the three Barberini bees ▲ *292* appear almost everywhere. The pontifical altar stands in the transept crossing, above the site of St Peter's tomb, under a gigantic *baldacchino* or canopy, with twisted columns (bronze ornaments were stripped from the Pantheon in order to make them ▲ *265*). He also sank niches into the pillars supporting the dome, where he placed statues of four saints, each corresponding to the most precious relics preserved in the basilica. Thirty years later Alexander VII commissioned him to create the apse. For it Bernini made the *Catedra Petri* (St Peter's Chair), a sort of huge

Tu es Petrus et super hanc petram aedificabo ecclesiam
meam et tibi dabo claves regni caelorum.
("You are Peter and on this rock I shall build my Church and
I shall give you the keys to the Kingdom of Heaven.")

THE CUPOLA ▲ 262
So that the
proportions might be
as harmonious inside
as outside, the
architect fitted one
dome into another.
The steps to the top
are built in the space
between them.

SAINTS AND RELICS
The four saints whose
statues Bernini set
into the pillars
supporting the dome
are those whose relics
are preserved in the
rooms just above.
Shown below are *St
Andrew*, with his X-
shaped cross, by
François Duquesnoy
and *St Longinus*, with
the lance that pierced
Christ's side, by
Bernini himself.

iquary throne in bronze supported by statues of four
octors of the Church, enclosing the remains of a wooden
air believed to be the original episcopal chair of St Peter.
oove it is an enormous gloria: a multitude of gilded bronze
gelic figures, clouds and rays frame a window in which the
ve of the Holy Spirit is surrounded by a shining halo.
rnini also designed the tomb of Urban VIII – balanced, at
back of the apse, by that of Paul III (1534–49) by
glielmo Della Porta – and the grandiose monument of
exander VII (on the left after the transept). The latter
ows the Pope, in prayer, being called by Death, who holds a
lden hourglass (the door beneath the monument is
eniously incorporated in the composition). Both of these
mbs were to have a powerful influence on Bernini's
cessors.

IMAGE TO SCULPTURE. Works from the period before the
construction of the church judged worthy to adorn it were
. Among them are the tomb of Innocent VIII by
Ilaiuolo (second pillar on the left), which dates from 1498,
d the medieval statue of St Peter (by the right-hand pier in
nt of the *baldacchino*) whose foot has been worn away by
kisses of the faithful. Maria Clementina Sobieska – wife of
nes Stuart (the Old Pretender), claimant to the throne of
gland – has a monument sculpted by Filippo Barigiono in
39, between the first and second pillar on the left; just
yond it is a memorial to the last Stuarts by Canova.
posite, between the second and third pillar on the right, is
tomb of Gregory XIII (who introduced the Gregorian
endar in 1582), which was rebuilt between 1715 and 1721.
e several others, it dates from long after the pontiff's

Giuseppe Momo's
helicoidal staircase leading
to the Vatican Museums.

**THE CASINA OF
PIUS IV**
This delightful pair of
charmingly decorated
buildings situated in
the Vatican gardens
was designed by the
Mannerist architect
Pirro Ligorio for
Pope Pius IV
(1559–65) to replace
the Belvedere, the
papal villa which had
gradually evolved into
a palace. Today these
two buildings, which
can easily be visited,
are the headquarters
of the Pontifical
Science Academy.
(Above, detail from
the pediment of the
Casina).

Fresco in the Vatican
Library showing
Domenico Fontana
presenting the plans
of the library to
Sixtus V.

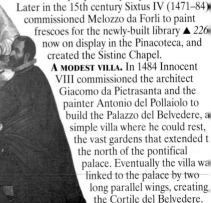

death – and is in fact closer in time to Canova's famous
monument to Clement XIII in the arch beyond the right
transept. It is also worth looking at the monument designed
by Bernini – in 1630 at the request of Urban VIII – in honor
of Countess Matilda of Tuscany, who defended Pope
Gregory VII against the Emperor Henry IV in the 11th
century and bequeathed her property to the Holy See. Near
is the monument designed by Carlo Fontana between 1696
and 1702 to Queen Christina of Sweden, who like Maria
Sobieska died in Rome exiled for converting to Catholicism.
Finally, close to the entrance and protected by a plate-glass
screen is the basilica's most precious statue: Michelangelo's
Pietà ▲ *212*, sculpted for the Jubilee in 1500.

FROM THE GROTTOES TO THE DOME. If time allows, visit the
Treasury, to inspect the Vatican's collection of religious and
historical treasures, and descend to the grottoes where, as
well as remains of Constantine's basilica, you can see the
tombs of numerous popes, including that of John Paul II
(1978–2005). The ascent to the inside of the dome should no
be missed – nor to the balcony surrounding the lantern, for
the amazing panoramic view of Rome.

INSIDE THE VATICAN

THE MEDIEVAL CENTER. During the Middle Ages, until the
return of the popes from Avignon, the Lateran Palace ▲ *197*
was the official papal residence. However, near the basilica
there were two other papal buildings: one to the south built
by Pope Symmachus in the 5th century, and one to the north
dating from the 9th century. Since these were in danger of
falling into ruin, Eugene III (1145–53) constructed a new
fortified residence, to the north of St Peter's, with a tower th
is still standing in the Cortile dei Pappagalli. This became th
core of the Vatican Palace: Nicholas III (1277–80) and his
successors were to transform this fortress into a luxurious
dwelling, gradually adding new wings.

FROM FORTRESS TO PALACE. The aggrandizement of the
Vatican began in earnest under Nicholas V (1447–55). The
Pope chose Fra Angelico to decorate his oratory in the
Innocent III Tower; and Piero della Francesca to
decorate his *stanze* (rooms) with frescoes, which
were eventually replaced by Raphael's ▲ *222*.
Later in the 15th century Sixtus IV (1471–84)
commissioned Melozzo da Forli to paint
frescoes for the newly-built library ▲ *226*
now on display in the Pinacoteca, and
created the Sistine Chapel.

A MODEST VILLA. In 1484 Innocent
VIII commissioned the architect
Giacomo da Pietrasanta and the
painter Antonio del Pollaiolo to
build the Palazzo del Belvedere, a
simple villa where he could rest,
the vast gardens that extended t
the north of the pontifical
palace. Eventually the villa wa
linked to the palace by two
long parallel wings, creating
the Cortile del Belvedere.

lius II (1503–13) wanted Bramante to build these, but he
ly completed the east wing. The west wing was built under
us IV (1560–65) by Pirro Ligorio.

HE GREAT PROJECTS OF THE 16TH CENTURY. Under Paul III,
ntonio da Sangallo restored the palace's oldest wing and
modeled the Pauline Chapel and the Sala Regia. Sixtus V
mmissioned Domenico Fontana to build the Biblioteca
brary) wing (1587–90). This divided the Cortile del
lvedere, forming a new courtyard
own as the Cortile della Pigna. In
dition, he erected an imposing group
buildings to the east of the former
edieval palace, thereby creating the
rtile San Damaso (1589).

HREE CENTURIES OF DECORATION.
nder the Renaissance popes the period
embellishment began. Alexander VI
rgia had his apartments decorated by
nturicchio. Julius II commissioned
ichelangelo to paint the ceiling of the
stine Chapel ▲ 218 (1508–12), and
aphael to redecorate the *stanze* (rooms)
222. Raphael only finished this work
der Leo X, who commissioned him to
corate the Loggias ▲ 218 as well.
nder Paul III, Michelangelo painted
e Last Judgment in the Sistine Chapel,
well as two frescoes in the Pauline
apel. During the 16th and 17th
nturies a whole range of other artists
rther exalted the glory of the popes, embellishing above all
e Sala Regia and the Sala Ducale. In fact the decoration
rk continued until the 19th century.

HE MUSEUM ERA. From the late 16th century until 1870 the
lazzo del Quirinale ▲ 297 became the pontifical residence,
the Vatican underwent few modifications for 250 years.
part from the Scala Regia ● 85, a stairway added by Bernini
the 17th century, most of the changes were associated with
e creation of the various museums and took place during
e late 18th or early 19th century. Under Clement XIV and
us VI the Palazzo del Belvedere was converted into a
useum, the Museo Pio-Clementino. Pius VII (1800–23) built
e Braccio Nuovo (New Wing) as an extension to the
hiaramonti sculpture gallery. He also had the *Aldobrandini*
arriage brought to the Vatican, an Augustan fresco based
a Greek fresco from the 4th century BC.

HE 20TH CENTURY. The restructuring work started
ain after the signing of the Lateran Treaty. Functional
ildings were not the only ones to be erected. Pius XI
mmissioned Giuseppe Momo to construct a
onumental staircase and Luca Beltrami to design the
nacoteca where an outstanding collection of paintings
d a number of important tapestries are on view.

XPLORING THE VATICAN. Only parts of the
atican are open to visitors, and fall into two
tegories, namely the rooms, galleries and
apels prized for their decoration (such as the
stine Chapel) and the museums grouped
ound the Cortile del Belvedere.

Above, from left to
right: the Palazzo del
Governatorato, the
Vatican station, and
the Apostolic Palace.

The Vatican Gardens.

The corridor leading
to the Sala Regia; and
the hall's magnificent
decorations.

Head of Augustus as
a young man (his
hairstyle was adapted
to suit Baroque
taste). This stands in
the Cortile della
Pigna, so called
because of the large
bronze pine cone
there.

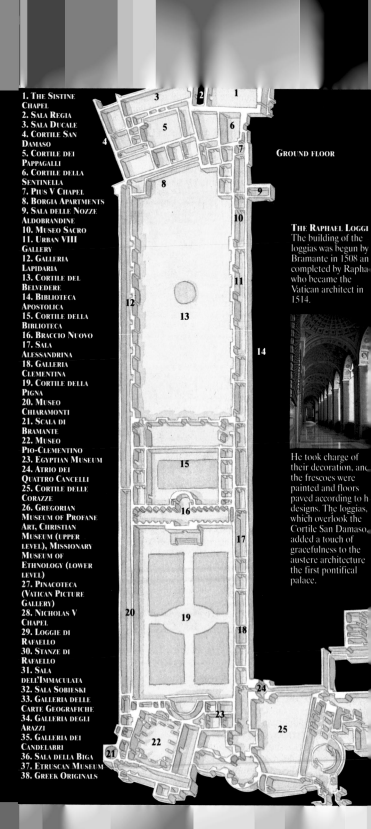

1. THE SISTINE CHAPEL
2. SALA REGIA
3. SALA DUCALE
4. CORTILE SAN DAMASO
5. CORTILE DEI PAPPAGALLI
6. CORTILE DELLA SENTINELLA
7. PIUS V CHAPEL
8. BORGIA APARTMENTS
9. SALA DELLE NOZZE ALDOBRANDINE
10. MUSEO SACRO
11. URBAN VIII GALLERY
12. GALLERIA LAPIDARIA
13. CORTILE DEL BELVEDERE
14. BIBLIOTECA APOSTOLICA
15. CORTILE DELLA BIBLIOTECA
16. BRACCIO NUOVO
17. SALA ALESSANDRINA
18. GALLERIA CLEMENTINA
19. CORTILE DELLA PIGNA
20. MUSEO CHIARAMONTI
21. SCALA DI BRAMANTE
22. MUSEO PIO-CLEMENTINO
23. EGYPTIAN MUSEUM
24. ATRIO DEI QUATTRO CANCELLI
25. CORTILE DELLE CORAZZE
26. GREGORIAN MUSEUM OF PROFANE ART, CHRISTIAN MUSEUM (UPPER LEVEL), MISSIONARY MUSEUM OF ETHNOLOGY (LOWER LEVEL)
27. PINACOTECA (VATICAN PICTURE GALLERY)
28. NICHOLAS V CHAPEL
29. LOGGIE DI RAFAELLO
30. STANZE DI RAFAELLO
31. SALA DELL'IMMACULATA
32. SALA SOBIESKI
33. GALLERIA DELLE CARTE GEOGRAFICHE
34. GALLERIA DEGLI ARAZZI
35. GALLERIA DEI CANDELABRI
36. SALA DELLA BIGA
37. ETRUSCAN MUSEUM
38. GREEK ORIGINALS

GROUND FLOOR

THE RAPHAEL LOGGI

The building of the loggias was begun by Bramante in 1508 and completed by Rapha who became the Vatican architect in 1514.

He took charge of their decoration, and the frescoes were painted and floors paved according to h designs. The loggias, which overlook the Cortile San Damaso, added a touch of gracefulness to the austere architecture the first pontifical palace.

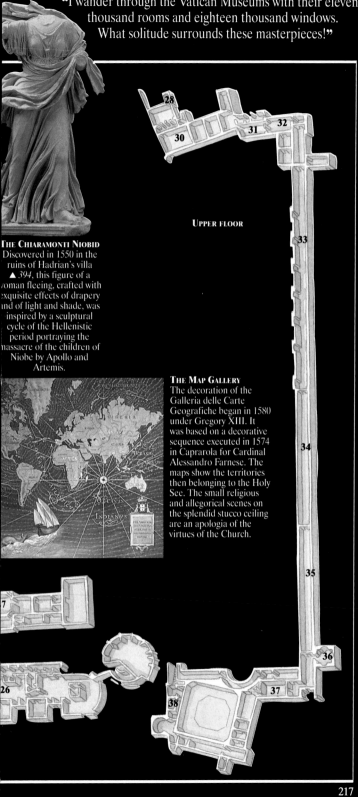

"I wander through the Vatican Museums with their eleven
thousand rooms and eighteen thousand windows.
What solitude surrounds these masterpieces!"

UPPER FLOOR

THE CHIARAMONTI NIOBID
Discovered in 1550 in the
ruins of Hadrian's villa
▲ *394*, this figure of a
woman fleeing, crafted with
exquisite effects of drapery
and of light and shade, was
inspired by a sculptural
cycle of the Hellenistic
period portraying the
massacre of the children of
Niobe by Apollo and
Artemis.

THE MAP GALLERY
The decoration of the
Galleria delle Carte
Geografiche began in 1580
under Gregory XIII. It
was based on a decorative
sequence executed in 1574
in Caprarola for Cardinal
Alessandro Farnese. The
maps show the territories
then belonging to the Holy
See. The small religious
and allegorical scenes on
the splendid stucco ceiling
are an apologia of the
virtues of the Church.

Julius II, who had brought Michelangelo Rome to work on his tomb, commissioned him to paint frescoes on the ceiling of the Sistine Chapel, perhaps at Bramante suggestion.

The scenes on the ceiling develop the theme of the Creation and the Fall of Man. In the center are the three events which made Christ's coming necessary: the Creation of Man, the Creation of Woman, and Original Sin. All around are signs of the forthcoming redemption, in the form of prophets and sibyls who either announced the coming of the Virgin and of Christ or prefigured his life – such as Jonah, who emerged after three days in the belly of the whale (Christ rose on the third day). The four pendentives are painted with scenes narrating the salvation of the Jewish people, which heralded that of humanity: Judith and Holofernes, David and Goliath, the Brazen Serpent, and the punishment of Haman at Esther's request. The lunettes portray the ancestors of Christ. Seated nudes with garlands and festoons surround the scenes of Genesis, supporting *trompe l'oeil* bronze medallions depicting scenes from the Old Testament.

etween 1508 and 512 Michelangelo as to cover the ntire ceiling (over ,000 square feet) ith more than three undred figures. efore starting work, e had all the reparations made by is assistants erased nd the scaffolding made to ensure that e could paint the whole vault single-handedly, without leaving any gaps. He began by painting the frescoes near the door, progressing toward the altar – which explains the more formal style of *The Life of Noah*.

Recent restoration has revived the work's brilliance, which is typical of true fresco painting since the pigments are absorbed by the fresh mortar.

"He brought the blessing of light to the painting, which sufficed to illuminate a world plunged in darkness for centuries."

Vasari

espite the disputable grace of e *ignudi* (nudes), pinions differ as to the eaning Michelangelo tended to give them. s can be seen, he used e chapel's strong chitectural amework to provide a ructure that would ite the work as a hole.

"MOSES AND THE DAUGHTERS OF JETHRO"
When the construction of the Sistine Chapel had been completed, Sixtus IV commissioned various Tuscan and Umbrian painters to decorate the walls with frescoes that would establish a parallel between the life of Moses and that of Jesus. Botticelli painted the events of Moses' early life.

The story runs from right to left. Moses kills an Egyptian (bottom right-hand corner) and takes refuge with the Midianites; he meets Jethro's daughters and puts to flight the shepherds who are preventing them from watering their flock; Jehovah appears to Moses (top left-hand corner) and he leaves Egypt with the Jews (bottom left). In Proust's *Un amour de Swann* Swann falls in love with Odette because of her resemblance to the figure of Zipporah, a daughter of Jethro (see detail, left): "He admired her large eyes, her delicate face which hinted at an imperfect skin, the marvelous strands of hair that clung to her tired cheeks."

"THE LAST JUDGMENT"
Michelangelo's *The Last Judgment* (1536–41) was the last of the chapel's decorations to be carried out. It was planned just after the Sack of Rome (1527) ● *36*. As well as reflecting the anxiety of the Romans, still recovering from the shock, it reveals the personal anguish of the defender of the Florentine Republic. The fresco aroused indignation. Aretino commented that it was more suitable for public baths or a brothel, and El Greco suggested replacing it with a work that was "more modest and more decent". The swathed draperies (*braghe*) were added by Daniele da Volterra in the 16th century, for the sake of decency.

On his arrival in Rome in 1508 Raphael was put in charge of decorating the apartments of Julius II. He began with the Stanza della Segnatura, where he illustrated the main spheres of knowledge: theology (*Disputation Concerning the Holy Sacrament*), philosophy (*The School of Athens*), poetry (*Parnassus*) and law (*Gregory IX Approving the Decretals and Trebonianus Presenting the Pandects to Justinian*). He then painted scenes glorifying the Church (in the Heliodorus Room) and *The Fire of the Borgo*. Giulio Romano painted the Hall of Constantine after Raphael's designs.

In *The Expulsion of Heliodorus from the Temple*, the Syrian general sent to sack the Temple in Jerusalem is seen being beaten to death by angels, a sign that God protects the Church from the demands of temporal powers. (Detail above: a witness to the miracle).

This fresco shows Apollo, in the company of nine Muses, inspiring the greatest ancient and modern poets (including Dante in profile, upper left). In the detail reproduced here Erato (the Muse of lyrical and erotic poetry) is sitting surrounded by Melpomene (Tragedy, holding the mask), Terpsichore (Dance) and Urania (Astronomy). Vasari said that these Muses "so incredibly beautiful and divinely expressive, exhale grace and life".

"THE SCHOOL OF ATHENS"

This work, painted between 1510 and 1511, is a synthetic representation of ancient wisdom, the precursor of Christianity. The main philosophers of antiquity are gathered in a vast building, reminiscent of Bramante's conception of St Peter's. Plato stands in the center, holding his *Timaeus* dialogue (which discusses the nature of divinity) and pointing to the heavens, while Aristotle, carrying the manuscript of his *Ethics* (concerned with human behavior), points to the earth. The statues of Apollo and Minerva represent Harmony and Wisdom. Raphael gave the various philosophers the faces of his contemporaries and included himself on the extreme right, together with his master, Perugino.

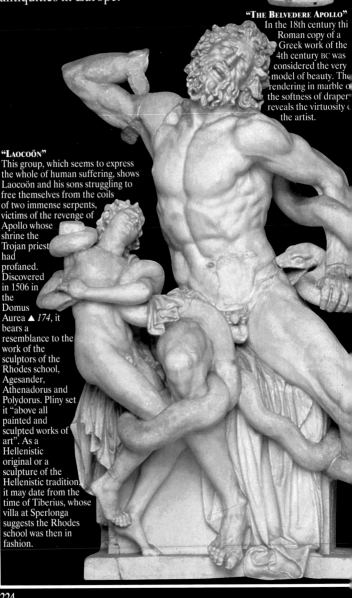

The original nucleus of the Vatican collection – a group of classical sculptures including Apollo, Laocoön and Ariadne – was added to by Julius II (1503–13) and placed in the Octagonal Courtyard. During the 16th century it evolved into one of the most renowned collections of antiquities in Europe.

"THE BELVEDERE APOLLO"
In the 18th century this Roman copy of a Greek work of the 4th century BC was considered the very model of beauty. The rendering in marble of the softness of drapery reveals the virtuosity of the artist.

"LAOCOÖN"
This group, which seems to express the whole of human suffering, shows Laocoön and his sons struggling to free themselves from the coils of two immense serpents, victims of the revenge of Apollo whose shrine the Trojan priest had profaned. Discovered in 1506 in the Domus Aurea ▲ 174, it bears a resemblance to the work of the sculptors of the Rhodes school, Agesander, Athenadorus and Polydorus. Pliny set it "above all painted and sculpted works of art". As a Hellenistic original or a sculpture of the Hellenistic tradition, it may date from the time of Tiberius, whose villa at Sperlonga suggests the Rhodes school was then in fashion.

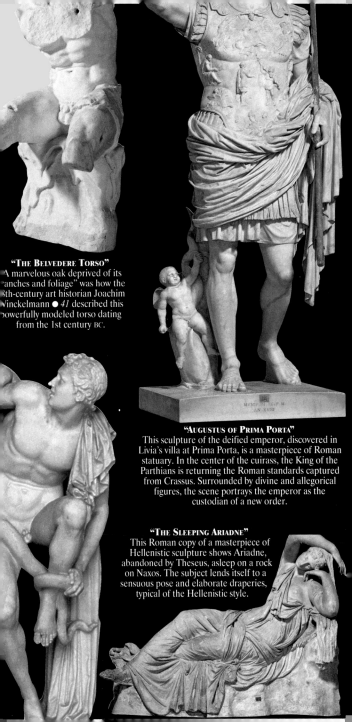

"The Belvedere Torso"

A marvelous oak deprived of its branches and foliage" was how the 18th-century art historian Joachim Winckelmann ● *41* described this powerfully modeled torso dating from the 1st century BC.

"Augustus of Prima Porta"

This sculpture of the deified emperor, discovered in Livia's villa at Prima Porta, is a masterpiece of Roman statuary. In the center of the cuirass, the King of the Parthians is returning the Roman standards captured from Crassus. Surrounded by divine and allegorical figures, the scene portrays the emperor as the custodian of a new order.

"The Sleeping Ariadne"

This Roman copy of a masterpiece of Hellenistic sculpture shows Ariadne, abandoned by Theseus, asleep on a rock on Naxos. The subject lends itself to a sensuous pose and elaborate draperies, typical of the Hellenistic style.

"VIRGIN AND CHILD"

This tondo (round picture), a shape much used at the end of the 15th century, is the work of Pinturicchio (c. 1454–1513), a painter who received numerous commissions from Sixtus IV and Innocent VII, as well as Alexander VI for whom he decorated the Borgia Apartments. Consequently many of his works are to be found in Rome. Vasari judged this artist severely: "Bernadino embellished his paintings with gold so as to satisfy those with bad taste by lavishing greater brilliance and effect on them – the last word in vulgarity in painting." Nevertheless, in this picture there is an undeniable desire to infuse life into the two holy figures encircled by angels: the Virgin smiles and the infant Jesus is totally absorbed in his reading.

"ANGEL MUSICIAN"

This was part of a fresco of *The Ascension* by Melozzo da Forli (1438–95) that decorated the apse of the Basilica dei Santi Apostoli ▲ *300* until 1711. The halo was gilded and the sky painted with a color made from lapis lazuli.

"SIXTUS IV APPOINTING PLATINA PREFECT OF THE VATICAN LIBRARY"

This fresco by Melozzo da Forli originally decorated the Vatican Library. Sixtus IV's nephew, the future Julius II, stands before the Pope with the humanist Bartolomeo Sacchi, known as Platina.

"ST LAWRENCE ORDAINED DEACON BY ST SIXTUS"

This belongs to the cycle of frescoes Nicholas V asked Fra Angelico to paint for his chapel (c. 1450). The painter here combines contemporary Florentine discoveries in the rendering of three-dimensional space with the "subtlety" of gentle Gothic coloring.

The loggias and rooms decorated by Raphael (1483–1520) in the Vatican are among his greatest works. In addition, three key pictures that mark his development as a painter are preserved in the Pinacoteca.

"THE MADONNA DI FOLIGNO"

This work was commissioned around 1512 by Sigismondo dei Conti as an *ex voto* offering. It portrays the Virgin and Child surrounded by St Francis, St John the Baptist and St Jerome, who is introducing the donor of the painting. It is one of the most important works painted by Raphael in the graceful style of his early days in Rome.

"THE TRANSFIGURATION"

The last picture Raphael painted was commissioned by Cardinal Giulio de Medici. The upper part (reproduced here) portrays the divine miracle. Christ rises in a supernatural light, with Moses and Elijah beside him, while three terror-stricken apostles avert their eyes. The lower part shows the other disciples unable to perform a miracle: in the absence of their master, they are seen to be incapable of healing a boy possessed by the devil. By revealing its strong luminous contrasts a recent restoration has retrieved the narrative power of this work, unanimously recognized as a masterpiece of universal art.

THE RAPHAEL LOGGIAS

(These can only be visited by special permission.) They were decorated by Raphael's pupils, following the designs of the master, then Superintendent of Antiquities.

Each of the thirteen bays contains four Old Testament scenes, while the walls and arches are embellished with grotesques inspired by the decorations of the Domus Aurea ▲ *174*, discovered in 1506.

e scenes reproduced here show *The
pulsion from Paradise*, *Isaac Blessing Jacob*,
Parting of the Red Sea and *The Building of
Ark*. These works, frequently reproduced
ngravings, constitute what has been called

"Raphael's Bible". European painting and
decorative arts have drawn from it so often
for Old Testament subjects that most
representations are ultimately derived from it.

"DESCENT FROM THE CROSS"
Painted between 1602 and 1604 for the Oratorians, this picture originally hung in the Chiesa Nuova ▲ *281*. In 1797 it was requisitioned by the

French, despite the discredit in which Caravaggio was held during the 18th century. Its dramatic force derives from the contrast between the pale body of Christ and the shadows

enveloping the holy women and St John. The emphatic gesture of Mary Magdalene stresses the pain which Nicodemus' expression invites us to share. The dark background

heightens the picture's relief. For the body of Christ, Caravaggio came nearer than usual to the classical ideal by choosing a rather beautiful body whose musculature he wished to emphasize

icularly rich collecti...
...es. This was the perio...
...g reached its peak in...
...contains a number...
...ous churches,...
...by the French and...
...n 1815.

THE "PIETÀ"

Pietro Berrettini (1596–1669), known as Pietro da Cortona, was the favorite painter of Pope Urban VIII, who in the 1640's commissioned him to decorate his oratory in the Vatican. The *Pietà* he painted there is much less dramatic than Caravaggio's. The delicate colors show his interest in Venetian painting, and the figures are elegant and graceful.

The Virgin between St Thomas and St Jerome (1625) dates from Guido Reni's mature period, when he sought to soften the contours and colors in his work. (Detail)

"THE LAST COMMUNION OF ST JEROME"

For the past two centuries this picture by omenichino (1614) has been acknowledged a masterpiece of expressive art. The saint is nown admitting his extreme weakness and witnessing his trust in the resurrection.

The Borgo before and after it was gutted.

THE BORGO AND VIA DELLA CONCILIAZIONE

Going down the Via della Conciliazione from St Peter's, on the right you come to Palazzo Cesi (1575), at No. 51, and then Palazzo Serristori (1555), the former Tuscan Embassy. On the same side, at No. 33, is the Palazzo dei Penitenzieri (15th century), built by Baccio Pontelli at the request of Cardinal della Rovere. Opposite is Palazzo Torlonia, followed by Santa Maria in Traspontina (1566–1637).

THE AVENUE OF RECONCILIATION. Formerly, after a long walk through narrow, twisting streets the visitor suddenly emerge at Piazza San Pietro. Its "great theater of colonnades", obel and fountains provided a violent contrast to the surrounding Borgo. Now, after the construction of the Via della Conciliazione – which provides advance preparation for the aesthetic shock from a distance – the effect of surprise, so typical of the Baroque, has vanished. As its name suggests, this broad straight avenue symbolizes the reconciliation of t Holy See and the Italian State, sanctioned by the Lateran Treaty ▲ *198*, *202*. Its construction caused a tremendous upheaval in the old quarters between Piazza San Pietro and Castel Sant'Angelo.

AN OLD IDEA. This was to become perhaps the most famous the demolition operations that marked the urban developments of the Fascist period in Rome and in other cities, and it was strongly criticized. Yet the idea was not nev As long ago as the 15th century Nicholas V had asked Leon

ttista Alberti (1406–72) to rebuild the whole area. His
ans included the demolition of a long row of houses that
tended from the fortress to Piazza San Pietro, forming the
ina ("backbone") of the Borgo. The idea was proposed
ain in the 16th century under Sixtus V and revived in the
th and 19th centuries, but nothing came of it.
UNTING THE COSTS. The operation, which was promoted by
ussolini himself, was entrusted to the architects Piacentini

A view of the Borgo
in the 19th century,
painted by Roesler
(left).

and Spaccarelli. On October 28,
1936, the Duce struck the first
blow with a pickaxe, and
buildings were torn down at
breakneck speed. However, the
reconstruction was not
completed until 1950, and the
toll was heavy. Although several
buildings remained, a large
number were destroyed
(including the churches of
San Giacomo a Scossacavalli,
San Michele Arcangelo and
Santa Maria delle Grazie) or
reconstructed elsewhere. The

lazzo Alicorni was partially rebuilt inside the Palazzo del
overnatore; the house of Leo X's surgeon, Giacomo di
rtolomeo da Brescia, was moved to No. 14 Via Rusticucci;
d the 18th-century Church of the Annunziata was re-
ected on the north bank of the Tiber.

ASTEL SANT'ANGELO

is building has had a checkered history. Originally a
nastic tomb, it was converted into a fortress, then became a
ble dwelling and finally a papal residence; between times it
rved as a barracks, a prison and a museum.
DRIAN'S MAUSOLEUM. Hadrian (117–38 AD) built a tomb in
omizia's gardens that was to become the dynastic sepulcher
the Antonines. Work started in 123 but was only completed
139, after Hadrian's death. The Pons Aelius (the
edecessor of the Ponte Sant'Angelo ▲ *239*),
uugurated in 134, linked the monument to the
ampo Marzio.
HE SEPULCHRAL CHAMBER. The present entrance
hich is about 10 feet above the level of the
cient one) leads via a short corridor to a square
ll. The semicircular niche hollowed out in
e back wall was probably intended to
ntain a statue of Hadrian. On the right
a spiral ramp leading to the *cella*
(ortuary chamber), the heart of
e monument. In this square
om, which was originally
:ed with marble, the
nerary urns of Emperor
drian and his wife, Sabina,

**HADRIAN'S
MAUSOLEUM**
As far as is known,
the mausoleum was
made as follows. On a
square base, a little
less than 300 feet
long, stood a gigantic
rotunda faced with
marble. On this was a
mound of earth that
served as a podium
for an enormous
bronze sculpture of a
quadriga (four-horse
chariot) driven by
Emperor Hadrian.
Numerous efforts
were made in the
17th century to
produce a satisfactory
reconstruction of the
building, and the
French architect
Vaudremer
(1829–1914) also had
a go at tackling the
problem. While at the
Villa Medici ▲ *315*, in
1857 he presented a
comprehensive
project for restoring
the mausoleum,
including plans,
section and
façade (detail
below).

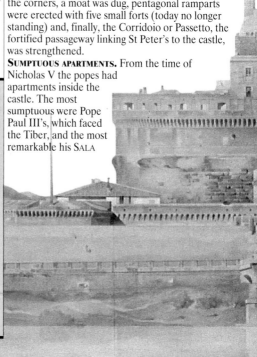

THE PASSETTO
(above) This originally formed part of Leo IV's ramparts. Nicholas III converted it into a fortified passageway linking Castel Sant'Angelo to the Vatican.

Fireworks at the Castel Sant'Angelo.

THE PRISON OF CASTEL SANT'ANGELO
Until 1870 the lower part of the castle was a prison. The dungeons, which had a terrifying reputation, held captive such personalities as the Cenci ▲ 254, the philosopher Giordano Bruno ▲ 249, Count Cagliostro ● 47, and the goldsmith and sculptor Benvenuto Cellini ● 36.

CASTEL SANT'ANGELO, FROM IMPERIAL MAUSOLEUM TO PAPAL RESIDENCE ✪
At dusk this imposing building is bathed in shimmering colors, providing an orange-red background to the contorted outlines of the ten angels on the bridge designed by Michelangelo. After visiting the papal apartments and the collections of arms and armor and ancient artefacts, take a well-earned break at the bar on the top floor, from which there is a splendid view over the Campo Marzio, St Peter's and the Janiculum.

were kept, together with those of the Antonine emperors and Septimius Severus (193–211).

FROM A MAUSOLEUM TO A FORTRESS. Around 270 the ancient sepulcher became an advanced bastion of the Aurelian Wall ▲ 323; it was then strengthened by the Emperor Honorius in 403 AD. In 537 the building resisted the siege of the Ostrogoths under Witigis, but shortly afterward fell into the hands of Totila who, concentrating on new fortifications, made it into a citadel. As a powerful fortress, the building served as a prison from the 10th century and also as a refuge. Gregory VII fled there in the 11th century when Rome was taken by the Emperor Henry IV; the demagogue Cola di Rienzo sought shelter there in the 14th century; and much later, in 1527, this was where Clement VII withstood the six-month siege of the troops of Charles V ● 36. Moreover, since Castel Sant'Angelo was Rome's most important fortified area, anyone who held it had virtually the whole town at his mercy. Consequently, its history reflected the city's turbulent internal conflicts. Between the 10th and 11th centuries it passed into the hands of the most powerful noble families before suffering a massive attack by the Roman people, who made up their minds to demolish it in 1379.

FORTIFICATIONS AND MODIFICATIONS. Under Nicholas III the castle became papal property. Most of the alterations to the building carried out between the pontificates of Nicholas V (1447–55) and Urban VII (1623–44) had a military purpose. Access to the subterranean galleries was blocked, two towers were built at the entrance and four bastions at the corners, a moat was dug, pentagonal ramparts were erected with five small forts (today no longer standing) and, finally, the Corridoio or Passetto, the fortified passageway linking St Peter's to the castle, was strengthened.

SUMPTUOUS APARTMENTS. From the time of Nicholas V the popes had apartments inside the castle. The most sumptuous were Pope Paul III's, which faced the Tiber, and the most remarkable his SALA

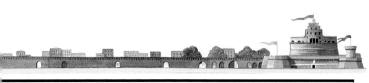

AOLINA, or Council Hall, with its parallel frescoes showing e lives of St Paul and Alexander the Great (Paul III's own ame being Alessandro Farnese). Perin del Vaga was put in arge of painting these frescoes, as well as those of the amera del Perseo and the Camera di Amore e Psiche. The pe's apartments communicate, via a little vestibule ttributed to Antonio da Sangallo the Younger) followed by few steps, with Julius II's lovely loggia and colonnade, built Bramante, facing Ponte Sant'Angelo. It balances Paul III's ggia (1543) – overlooking the garden and the Passetto – hich can be reached by the circular external corridor.

ENEATH THE ARCHANGEL MICHAEL. The castle's central airway will take you to the upper terrace, dominated by Verschaffelt's colossal bronze angel (cast by Giardoni in 1752). This replaced a marble angel by Raffaello da Montelupo (1544), now in another part of the castle (in the Cortile del Angelo). These two statues recall a miracle that happened under Pope Gregory the Great. The legend claims that in 590 the Archangel Michael appeared on the summit of the building brandishing his sword before all the people in procession, who were praying for a plague to end.

A cross-section of Hadrian's mausoleum.

Between 608 and 615 Hadrian's funerary

chamber was converted into a shrine dedicated to St Michael. In 852 the Sepulchrum Hadriani became the Castellum Sancti Angeli.

PRATI

A PIEDMONTESE NEIGHBORHOOD. The Prati quarter, behind the Vatican, is in many ways a typically Piedmontese neighborhood. It was planned in 1870, with a view to housing the innumerable employees of the newly formed Italian State who came from Turin. Its construction gave rise to a flurry of property speculation, the agricultural land being bought for a song by a consortium of bankers who resold it, making huge profits. Rows of apartment buildings line the roads, which are laid out to an octagonal plan. Although Prati is adjacent to the Vatican, the new quarter seems to ignore it, since the dome of St Peter's cannot be seen from its

streets (one wonders if this was by chance, in view of the papacy's resistance to the unitarian forces ● *33*). All the apartment blocks are built to the same design: large courtyards planted with palm trees, huge apartments with dark corridors. Ettore Scola's film *The Family* (1987) gives a good impression of these interiors.

PALAZZO DI GIUSTIZIA (PALACE OF JUSTICE). This stands at the end of the neighborhood facing the Renaissance town. Erected by Guglielmo Calderini between 1889 and 1911, the vast neo-Baroque building cost 40 million lire, instead of the estimated 8 million; it was discovered that it was built on unstable marshy ground, and the affair became a scandal. The outside is adorned with statues of Italian lawmakers and surmounted by a bronze *quadriga*, the work of Ettore Ximenes. Frescoes by Cesare Maccari decorate the interior.

NEIGHBORING BUILDINGS. THE CASA DEI MUTILATI, on the left, is a fine example of the architecture of the Mussolini period, built in 1928 by Marcello Piacentini. Its decoration is based entirely on the theme of war, glorifying condottieri and other soldiers. Within, the Aula Magna and chapel are decorated with mosaics and frescoes (*The Sentinel, The Combatant, The Departure, The Assault* and *The Return of the Soldier*). On the other side of the Palazzo della Giustizia is the neo-Gothic Church of the Sacred Heart (1890) – as well as the astonishing Museum of Souls in Purgatory, containing a collection of objects that are supposed to bear the imprints of the hands of the deceased.

From Ponte Sant'
Angelo to the Ghetto

238 The Campus Martius in
    antiquity
239 Ponte Sant'Angelo
240 Via Giulia
244 Palazzo Farnese
246 The area around
    Palazzo Spada
247 Around Campo de' Fiori
250 The Area Sacra dell'
    Argentina
252 The Ghetto

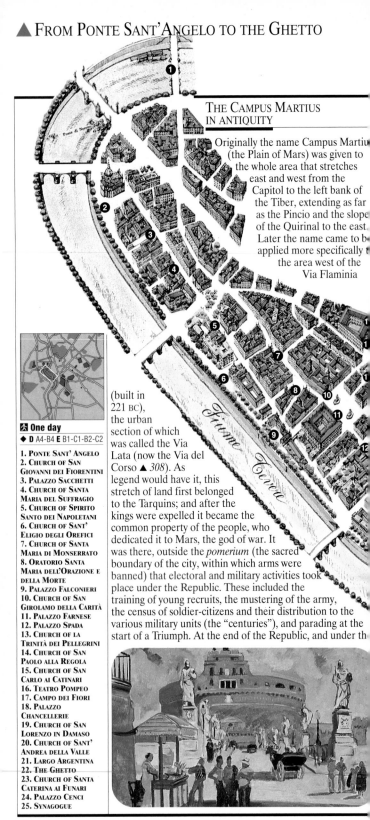

The Campus Martius
in Antiquity

Originally the name Campus Martius (the Plain of Mars) was given to the whole area that stretches east and west from the Capitol to the left bank of the Tiber, extending as far as the Pincio and the slopes of the Quirinal to the east. Later the name came to be applied more specifically to the area west of the Via Flaminia (built in 221 BC), the urban section of which was called the Via Lata (now the Via del Corso ▲ 308). As legend would have it, this stretch of land first belonged to the Tarquins; and after the kings were expelled it became the common property of the people, who dedicated it to Mars, the god of war. It was there, outside the *pomerium* (the sacred boundary of the city, within which arms were banned) that electoral and military activities took place under the Republic. These included the training of young recruits, the mustering of the army, the census of soldier-citizens and their distribution to the various military units (the "centuries"), and parading at the start of a Triumph. At the end of the Republic, and under th

🏃 One day

◆ **D** A4-B4 **E** B1-C1-B2-C2

1. PONTE SANT' ANGELO
2. CHURCH OF SAN GIOVANNI DEI FIORENTINI
3. PALAZZO SACCHETTI
4. CHURCH OF SANTA MARIA DEL SUFFRAGIO
5. CHURCH OF SPIRITO SANTO DEI NAPOLETANI
6. CHURCH OF SANT' ELIGIO DEGLI OREFICI
7. CHURCH OF SANTA MARIA DI MONSERRATO
8. ORATORIO SANTA MARIA DELL'ORAZIONE E DELLA MORTE
9. PALAZZO FALCONIERI
10. CHURCH OF SAN GIROLAMO DELLA CARITÀ
11. PALAZZO FARNESE
12. PALAZZO SPADA
13. CHURCH OF LA TRINITÀ DEI PELLEGRINI
14. CHURCH OF SAN PAOLO ALLA REGOLA
15. CHURCH OF SAN CARLO AI CATINARI
16. TEATRO POMPEO
17. CAMPO DEI FIORI
18. PALAZZO CHANCELLERIE
19. CHURCH OF SAN LORENZO IN DAMASO
20. CHURCH OF SANT' ANDREA DELLA VALLE
21. LARGO ARGENTINA
22. THE GHETTO
23. CHURCH OF SANTA CATERINA AI FUNARI
24. PALAZZO CENCI
25. SYNAGOGUE

...pire, with the withdrawal of the plebs from political life
...e Campus Martius was opened up to popular entertainment
...d leisure activities (theaters, amphitheaters, and public
...ths). It also became a venue for Imperial celebrations.
...E PHASES OF ITS DEVELOPMENT. Today the urban layout of
...tiquity is recognizable, even if certain buildings have not
...vived. The group of ruins known as the Area Sacra del
...rgo Argentina provides a complete range of temples from
...e end of the 4th to the beginning of the 1st century BC. In
...2nd century BC most of the building developments took
...ce around the Circus Flaminius. Later Pompey built a
...jor complex on the central part of the Campus Martius,
...luding a huge portico and a theater; and Augustus erected
... altar to peace (the Ara Pacis Augustae) and his own
...usoleum. After the great fire that devastated the area in
... AD a new intensive phase of construction began, including
...e Odeon ▲ 276 and stadium (now Piazza Navona ▲ 276)
...lt by Domitian. The remains of vast public buildings of this
...riod have been discovered beneath the Palazzo Farnese,
among them remarkable mosaics of *desultores*
(acrobats on horseback). In the
following century
Hadrian and the
Antonines completed
the urbanization of the
area. In 273

THE OCTOBER HORSE
On October 15 the
ancient Romans used
to hold a chariot race
at the end of which
the right-hand horse
of the winning chariot
was sacrificed near
the altar of Mars.
This ritual marked
the close of the
military year, which
had begun the
previous March with
ceremonies such as
the ritual dance of
the Salians (the war
priests), purification
of the horses, and the
sacrifice of a pig, a
sheep, and a bull
known as the
suovetaurilia.

...relian
...gan his great
...mple of the Sun on the east
...e of the Via Lata, probably on the
...ot that is now Piazza San Silvestro.

...NTE SANT'ANGELO

...king Castel Sant'Angelo to the Campus Martius, this
...dge was for a long time the only one to the north of the
...nte Sisto ▲ 363. It had been built in the 2nd century to
...ate an impressive approach to Hadrian's mausoleum
...233. As this was the preferred route of processions to

"THE VIA CRUCIS"
In September 1667, Clement IX, then Pope for two months, began payments to his old friend Bernini for "eight statues of white marble". The drama of the Passion was chosen as the theme: each angel was to bear an instrument of the martyrdom of Christ, such as the nails and cross. Later the number was increased to ten.

St Peter's, two chapels were added at the end of the bridge and used as firing posts for crossbow snipers during the siege of the fortress in 1527. Three years later Clement VII had them destroyed, replacing them with statues of St Paul and St Peter by Lorenzetto and Paolo Taccone respectively. Between 1667 and 1669 Clement IX added ten statues of angels, made by pupils of Bernini after drawings by the master. The approach to the bridge on the Campus Martius side was radically modified when, at the end of the 19th century, the Lungotevere embankments were built and the Corso Vittorio Emanuele was put through. Two streets lead from the bridge which once served as main routes within the Campo Marzio (as the area is now called): the Via del Banco di Santo Spirito and Via Paola, which crosses the Via Giulia in front of San Giovanni dei Fiorentini.

VIA GIULIA

JULIUS II'S STREET. At the beginning of the 16th century Pope Julius II replaced the maze of streets that led from the Capitol to the Vatican with a long straight thoroughfare to which he gave his name. It long served as Rome's main street apart for a brief interval around 1655 when Innocent X had the state prison moved to No. 52. Its entire length is dotted with palazzi and churches, making one of Rome's most attractive streets to walk along.

A NEIGHBORHOOD OF CONTRASTS. For centuries this aristocratic street has been adjacent to a colorful and noisy neighborhood bustling with tradesmen and travelers. The Via del Pellegrino was created by Sixtus IV to funnel pilgrims toward St Peter's, and the followers of St Philip Neri could be seen wending their way along Via di Monserrato to make their devotions at the Seven Churches ▲ 381. The area was also a meeting place for visitors from out of town. The Spaniards had their national church in Via di Monserrato; from 1362 the English had a hospice there (which became the Venerable English College) at No. 45; and the Bolognese, the Sienese, and the Neapolitans had churches in the Via Giulia. All these visitors could stay in the countless inns, ranging from

In the 19th century Emile Zola wrote evocatively of this "fine old quarter fallen into the silence, into the emptiness of abandonment, invaded by a kind of softness and clerical discretion".

ble *alberghi* to humble *locande*, in and around Campo de' ori, where they could visit the print shops and booksellers ng-established in the area. It was an area for crafts of all nds – among them *baullari* (trunk makers), *capellari* atters), *giubbonari* (tailors) and *chiavari* (locksmiths) – and any of these traditions still survive. Trunks are still sold in a dei Baullari; and Via dei Giubbonari has as many clothes ops as houses. In Campo de' Fiori the daily market still ays an important role, even if many different languages are be heard there. A small bookshop that stays open till idnight helps to keep culture alive in e Campo.

SAN GIOVANNI DEI FIORENTINI. The Via ulia was once the main center of the uscan colony in Rome, which is why this urch came to be dedicated to John the aptist, the patron saint of Florence, and as commissioned by a Medici, Leo X. ut of the schemes presented in tender r this contract, which included designs Michelangelo, Peruzzi, and Raphael, e Pope chose Jacopo Sansovino's. owever, his original plans were greatly odified by his successors, among them ntonio Sangallo the Younger (1520), iacomo Della Porta (from 1583 to 02) and Carlo Maderno, who started ork on the project in 1602 and mpleted it in 1620. The church, which s three naves, is in the form of a Latin oss and is surmounted by a cupola. Its çade, by Alessandro Galilei, was not

SAN GIOVANNI DEI FIORENTINI
Originally Michelangelo was invited to design the dome, but again it was Carlo Maderno who actually built it (1614).

Palazzo Sacchetti seen from the Tiber.

KING DAVID'S GLORY
The Mannerist Francesco Salviati (1509–63) was one the most able decorative painters of his generation. His frescoes in Palazzo Sacchetti brilliantly illustrate the epic vein characteristic of the major compositions of the 16th century. The detail reproduced here is from one of the frescoes portraying episodes in the life of David, the shepherd, musician, poet and King of Israel, whose life as a warrior, wanderer and lover inspired many artists.

built until 1734. At the request of Prince Falconieri, Borromini designed the high altar. Among the important figures buried here are the two architects Maderno (1556–1629) and Borromini (1599–1667). Of the many paintings in the church, the works in the St Jerome chapel (third on the right) are of particular interest, as is the large canvas by Salvator Rosa depicting *The Martyrdom of St Cosmas and St Damian* (1669), which hangs in the right transept. (Walk up the Via Giulia to the Palazzo Sacchetti which is No. 66.)

PALAZZO SACCHETTI. Cardinal Giovanni Ricci di Montepulciano had this palace built by Nanni di Baccio Bigio on the site of the house where the architect Antonio Sangallo the Younger (1483–1546) had lived. In the 17th century the palazzo was bought by the Sacchetti, a Florentine family that had been living in Rome since the previous century. This is one of the street's most remarkable buildings, with its long façade adorned with decorated windows and a balcony over the main door. Between 1553 and 1554 Francesco Salviati decorated the hall of the piano nobile known as the Map Room or Cardinal's Audience Hall.

ALONG THE VIA GIULIA. A little further along on the right stands Santa Maria del Suffragio, built in 1662–80 by Carlo Rainaldi (1611–91). In the next street on the right (Via del Gonfalone) you will find the Oratorio di SANTA LUCIA DEL GONFALONE, used today as a concert hall for chamber music. It is decorated with an ensemble of frescoes on the theme of the Passion by a variety of late-16th-century artists.

SPIRITO SANTO DEI NAPOLETANI. Continuing along the Via Giulia, you will pass the national church of the Neapolitans. Rebuilt by Carlo Fontana

between 1701 and 1709, it was radically transformed in the mid 19th century by Antonio Cipolla, who designed the façade. The last sovereigns of the Two Sicilies, King Francesco II and Queen Maria Sofia, are buried here. (Continue along Via Giulia, turn right into Via Sant'Eligio).

SANT'ELIGIO DEGLI OREFICI. This building was erected by Raphael in 1509 for the goldsmiths' guild, St Eligius being the patron saint of goldsmiths and blacksmiths. The façade and the frescoes and painting behind the high altar date from the 17th century. (Return to the Spirito Santo [de]i Napoletani and take the street facing the church; this [le]ads to a small piazza.)

[P]ALAZZO RICCI. The piazza is dominated by the façade of [P]alazzo Ricci. Traces of the grisaille frescoes painted in the [m]iddle of the 16th century by Polidoro da Caravaggio and [M]aturino da Firenze can still be seen on the façade. (Turn [ri]ght into Via di Monserrato.)

[S]ANTA MARIA IN MONSERRATO. This church, begun by [A]ntonio Sangallo the Younger in 1518, has been the national [ch]urch of Spaniards in Rome since 1875. Its façade, built by [Fr]ancesco da Volterra, is adorned with a relief showing the [V]irgin and Child sawing a mountain, an allusion to the [C]atalan shrine of Monserrat. The painting of *San Diego* in the [fir]st chapel on the right is attributed to Annibale Caracci; the [ch]apel also contains the mortal remains of Pope [A]lexander VI and of King Alfonso XIII of Spain, [w]ho died in exile in 1941. On the altar of the [th]ird chapel on the left stands a beautiful statue [of] St James by Jacopo Sansovino. (Cross the [pi]azza di Santa Caterina della Rota.)

[S]AN GIROLAMO DELLA CARITÀ. Once famous for [D]omenichino's painting of *The Last [C]ommunion of St Jerome* above the high altar – [re]moved by the French in 1797 and now in the [pi]cture gallery of the Vatican (a copy has [re]placed it) – this church was redesigned by [D]omenico Castelli in the mid 17th century. Two [ch]apels are of particular interest. The first on [th]e right, the SPADA CHAPEL, was long attributed [to] Borromini but was designed by Virgilio [Sp]ada, perhaps under the master's guidance. [M]edallions portraying previous members of the [Sp]ada family adorn the walls of yellow-and-[br]own marble. The balustrade is formed by two [kn]eeling angels with removable wings holding a marble drape. [Th]e other is the elegant ANTAMORO CHAPEL, to the left of the [hi]gh altar, which is the only work in Rome of the architect [Fi]lippo Juvarra (1678–1736). (Return to the Via Giulia.)

"FINESTRE INGINOCCHIATE"
A particularly fine feature of the Palazzo Sacchetti is its "kneeling" ground-floor windows: the frame of each window is supported on consoles.

The façade of Santa Maria in Monserrato.

The *Last Communion of St Jerome* ▲ 231 by Domenichino, now in the Vatican picture gallery.

Fontana del Mascherone.

PALAZZO FARNESE
A pair of large twin fountains enliven the piazza. The water runs into Egyptian granite basins brought here from the Baths of Caracalla, surmounted by what are often taken to be *fleur-de-lys*. The flowers are in fact irises, the emblem of the Farnese family.

FAMOUS FRESCOES
After studying Michelangelo's frescoes in the Sistine Chapel, Annibale Carracci (1560–1609), youngest and most brilliant artist of the Carracci family, painted the vaulted ceiling of the great gallery of Palazzo Farnese. Within a framework of *trompe l'oeil* architectural effects, these Baroque frescoes brought mythology to life in joyfully exuberant style.

PALAZZO FALCONIERI. Orazio Falconieri, who had bought two adjacent palazzi, asked Borromini to unite them. The façade on the Via Giulia is composed around two doorways framed in rustic bossage; at the back an ample loggia overlooks the Tiber. At each end of the façade there are two tall pilasters supporting falcons' heads on female busts, the vivid emblem of the originally Tuscan Falconieri family.

SANTA MARIA DELL'ORAZIONE E MORTE. This oratory belonging to the confraternity of the "buona morte", which ensured Christian funerals to the poor of Rome, was rebuilt according to plans by Ferdinando Fuga between 1733 and 1737. Its curved façade with pilasters and columns alternating on two levels is clearly influenced by Borromini and the high cupola is a fine achievement. The small skulls used as a decorative motif throughout, particularly over the main door, recall the purpose of this pious confraternity. The building supports a bridge over the Via Giulia to the gardens of Palazzo Farnese. Another bridge was originally to span the Tiber and connect the Palazzo with the Farnesina ▲ *360*; however, Michelangelo's plans for linking the two palaces were never carried out. Farther down the street is the FONTANA DEL MASCHERONE, built of ancient marble remains which takes its name from the mask that decorates it. (Take the Via del Mascherone opposite the fountain.)

PALAZZO FARNESE

PIAZZA FARNESE. Somewhat severe in appearance today, the piazza (formerly also known as Piazza del Duca) was at one time animated by frequent celebrations and spectacles, including bullfights. Due to the influence of Renato Niccolini a member of the municipal council who organized the first *estate romana* ("Roman summer") at the end of the 1970's, it has recovered its past glory.

THE CONSTRUCTION OF THE PALACE. The Palazzo Farnese is the largest of Rome's patrician palaces. Originally planned by Antonio Sangallo the Younger in 1517 for Cardinal Alessandro Farnese, the project was vastly amplified in 1534

en the latter became Pope, taking the name of Paul III. In 46, following Sangallo's death, Michelangelo was entrusted h its continuation. He was responsible for the design of the cond floor, the cornice and the two upper orders of columns the courtyard. After Michelangelo's death in 1564, acomo della Porta completed the building, erecting the ade and the splendid loggia that overlooks the Via Giulia. the 18th century the palace was inherited by the Bourbons Naples. Today it houses the French Embassy and the gnificent library of the Ecole française de Rome, a earch institute for archeologists and historians. The man nickname for the palace is *il dado* ("the dice").

ARCHITECTURE. Some of the materials used for the building re from ancient ruins: the travertine marble that frames the ndows is said to have come from the Coliseum. The façade Piazza Farnese is quite austere. Composed of thirteen ys, it is devoid of decoration save for the window frames d the bossage of the main entrance, which is surmounted by oggia. The courtyard, which used to contain the Farnese lection of ancient statuary, is particularly elegant. The ee orders of classical columns (Doric, Ionic and rinthian) are superimposed in a rhythmic ccession of windows and open arches. The ade on the garden side of the building oes this use of the three orders. ide the palace the most outstanding tures are the Salotto Dipinto corated with frescoes by Francesco viati and Taddeo Zuccari; the Sala le Guardie, which is dominated

The imposing main entrance of Palazzo Farnese.

The *Triumph of Bacchus and Ariadne*, the central fresco by Annibale Carracci in the gallery of Palazzo Farnese.

PALAZZO SPADA
The façade of Palazzo Spada has niches enclosing eight stucco statues of the great men of ancient Rome, among them Marcellus and Caesar (shown above). The walls of the courtyard are decorated with mythological figures such as Venus, Mars, and Pluto.

BORROMINI'S PERSPECTIVE ★
The impression of depth in this corridor, less than 30 feet long, is mainly achieved by the use of diminishing columns placed ever closer together. The perspective effect, which contracts and extends the space deceptively, gives the illusion of a depth of over 120 feet. The actual height of the seemingly tall statue at the end of the corridor, including the pedestal, is less than that of an average person.

The fountain in front of the Monte di Pietà.

by a copy of the statue of Ercole Farnese ▲ *320* (the original is in Naples); and above all the Galleria, with its superb frescoes depicting the loves of the gods and goddesses painted by Annibale Carracci, with the help of his brother Agostino, between 1597 and 1604. (Take Via dei Venti.)

THE AREA AROUND PALAZZO SPADA ● 8

Cross the minute Piazza della Quercia, where an evergreen oak lends a note of rusticity, and you will come to the front of Palazzo Spada. Its façade, in full splendor after restoration work, is festooned with statues, medallions, garlands, and other decorative moldings by Giulio Mazzoni, providing a startling contrast to Palazzo Farnese.

PALAZZO SPADA. Built for Cardinal Girolamo Capo di Ferro between 1548 and 1550, but modified for the Spada family in the 17th century, this palace has been the seat of the Council of State since 1927. On the left as one enters the courtyard one can view the astonishing *trompe l'oeil* perspective devised by Borromini. The Galleria Spada, one of the most important collections of 17th century paintings in Rome, can also be visited. It contains works by Guercino, Honthorst, Reni and Valentin, among others. A remarkable statue of Pompey stands in the Sala Grande. (Turn right as you come out of the palace.)

SANTISSIMA TRINITÀ DEI PELLEGRINI. The celebration of the Jubilee every fifty years attracted crowds of pilgrims to Rome and hostels were created in almost every part of the city. This church was built near one of the hostels between 1603 and 1616. The rendered brick façade, designed by Francesco De Sanctis, was added in 1723. Above the high altar there is Guido Reni's *Holy Trinity* (1625) painted to look like a relief.

SAN PAOLO ALLA REGOLA. According to tradition this church was built on the site of the house where St Paul stayed while in Rome. Its plan, in the shape of a Greek cross, and façade were designed in the 18th century by Giacomo Cioli and Giuseppe Sardi. (Continue through Piazza San Paolo alla Regola and Piazza San Salvatore to the Monte di Pietà.)

MONTE DI PIETÀ. This institution was founded by Pope Paul II to provide Romans with pawnbroking facilities. The financial system of the Pontifical States being largely based upon the fiduciary issue of currency, the Monte di Pietà acquired economic importance in modern times. The present building, erected in the 17th and 18th centuries, was completed by Nicola Salvi (1697–1751), the architect of the Fontana di Trevi ▲ 298. The chapel was decorated in a remarkable Baroque style during the first half of the 18th century. (Take Via dei Specchi, then the first turning on the left.)

AROUND CAMPO DE' FIORI

SAN CARLO AI CATINARI. This church belonging to the Barnabites (who took their name from San Barnaba, their original church, in Milan) was built between 1612 and 1620 according to plans by Rosato Rosati. The façade is the work of Giambattista Soria. The interior is rich in ancient marbles and is surmounted by a fine dome with stucco decorations. On the pendentives paintings by Domenichino illustrate the four cardinal virtues; and above the high altar, which is

adorned with ancient columns, hangs Pietro da Cortona's *St Charles Borromeo during the Procession of the Holy Nail* (1650).

VIA DE' GIUBBONARI. This bustling street is famous for the variety of its shops, and the little restaurant in the Largo dei Librari which serves *filetti di baccalà* (cod in batter), with white wine from the Castelli. (Take the second turning on the right, Via dei Chiavari. The houses in the first street to the left Via di Grotta Pinta stand on the site of Pompey's theater ▲ 248.)

CHARLES BORROMEO
Born in 1538 in Arona, he was raised to the rank of cardinal in 1560 and named archbishop of Milan by his uncle Pius IV. He died in 1584 and was canonized in 1610. The Church of San Carlo ai Catinari was dedicated to him in 1611, and Guido Reni painted this portrait of him in 1636.

THE "CATINARI"
The church received its name because of the presence of makers of wooden bowls (*catini*) in the neighborhood. Today there are still a number of craftsmen in the surrounding streets who ply the traditional trades of the area.

This painting of *The Annunciation* in San Carlo ai Catinari, with its remarkable luminosity and chiaroscuro effects, is one of Giovanni Lanfranco's finest works. The face of the Virgin is illuminated by the light of the Holy Spirit.

The Via di Grotta Pinta is a remarkable example of urban continuity: its houses follow the outline of the *cavea* of the Theater of Pompey. Sections of its walls can be seen in the cellars of several of the buildings.

CAMPO DEI FIORI, APPEALING TO ALL THE SENSES ✪
At dawn, Monday to Saturday, fresh fruit and vegetables, flowers, meat and delicacies are set out on the colorful stalls of Rome's most picturesque market. In the early evening the square comes to life again as people meet up at the *Vineria Reggio* or the *Taverna del Campo* to enjoy a glass of white wine from the Castelli Romani region.

POMPEY'S THEATER AND PORTICOS. In 61 BC work began on Rome's first permanent theater. Until then there had only been wooden stages because it was feared that lasting constructions would encourage people to attend entertainments ▲ *172* too often. Heartened by the particularly sumptuous Triumph he received upon his return

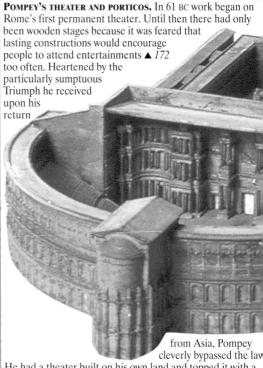

from Asia, Pompey cleverly bypassed the law. He had a theater built on his own land and topped it with a temple dedicated to Venus Victrix (the goddess of victory), so he could claim that the hemisphere of seats was an immense flight of steps leading to the temple! The complex, designed to enhance the creator's image, conferred on him the status of a Hellenistic monarch. The theater, which could hold 18,000 spectators, was inaugurated in 55 BC with literary and musical events, and with hunts lasting several days. One hundred lions, twenty elephants and a number of lynxes were massacred during the festivities. Behind the stage a portico of massive dimensions had been erected. It was adorned with numerous statues of women, and at the end of it was a large exedra which became the Curia (meeting place) of the Senate; this was where Julius Caesar was assassinated. Inside the Curia, diametrically opposite the temple of Venus Victrix, there was a statue of Pompey holding a globe in his hand. Today, remains of the Curia can be seen in the Area Sacra dell' Argentina ▲ *250*.

CAMPO DE' FIORI. This piazza owes its name to the fields full of flowers which were here before the erection of buildings in the 15th century. It soon became the site of inns, bookshops and the colorful market still held here

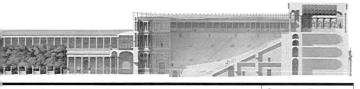

very morning except Sunday. The piazza was also used for executions, and it is was in the Campo de' Fiori that the philosopher Giordano Bruno was burnt at the stake for heresy by the Inquisition on February 17, 1600. (At the far end of the Campo, turn right into Piazza della Cancelleria.)

PALAZZO DELLA CANCELLERIA. Built at the end of the 15th and beginning of the 16th century for Cardinal Raffaele Riario, this palace was traditionally attributed to Bramante (1444–1514); however, it now seems probable that he only contributed to the design of the magnificent courtyard. Leo X confiscated the palace from Cardinal Riario for hatching a plot against him, which is how it became the residence of prelates and served as the *cancelleria* (chancellery) for the drafting pontifical acts. Today it still enjoys the extraterritorial ivileges granted to the Vatican under the Lateran greement ● *33*, ▲ *198*. The long, elegant travertine façade is ven rhythm by a series of pilasters (the main doorway was signed by Vignola). Under Paul III, in 1546 Vasari corated the Sala Grande with frescoes showing scenes lating to the Pope's life. It came to be known as the "hall of e hundred days", referring to the time it took Vasari to mplete the work. "It shows!" is reputed to have been ichelangelo's comment on it. The granite columns of the urtyard came from the original church of San Lorenzo in amaso, which stood here; excavations beneath the ving have revealed the remains of this 4th-century silica.

N LORENZO IN DAMASO. On the right of the façade the Palazzo della Cancelleria there is a door, also signed by Vignola, which is the entrance of the esent church of San Lorenzo in Damaso. Retaining e form of a basilica, with three naves, this church s rebuilt as part of the palace at Cardinal Riaro's quest. Its decoration was modified several times in e course of the 17th and the 19th centuries. (Turn ht into the Corso Vittorio Emanuele.)

E BARRACCO MUSEUM. The small Renaissance lazzo known as the Farnesina ai Baullari, built in 23 by Sangallo the Younger but with a late-19th-ntury façade by Enrico Gui, houses a museum of cient sculpture bequeathed by Senator Giovanni rracco to the city of Rome in 1902. This collection has yptian, Assyrian, Etruscan and Roman sculptures, d is one of the few in Rome that includes Greek

GIORDANO BRUNO
The unveiling of his statue in 1889 gave rise to confrontations between Republicans and supporters of the Pope.

LILIES AND IRISES
French lilies feature on the façade of the Barracco Museum because the building was constructed in the 16th century for Thomas Le Roy, a Breton prelate and emissary of Francis I. The similarity between *fleur-de-lys* and blue irises, part of the Farnese arms gave rise to the name *Piccola Farnesina* by which this building is known.

Head of a priest, or possibly of Caesar, Barracco Museum.

249

"THE CHURCH OF TOSCA"
In one of the chapels of Sant'Andrea della Valle is where Puccini set the first act of *Tosca*; the action takes place in this area, from the Palazzo Farnese to Castel Sant'Angelo, where the tragic story ends. In July 1992 a live television production of the opera was made using the locations indicated by Puccini, each scene being performed at the time of day specified in the libretto.

THE DOME OF SANT'ANDREA
Maderno and other great artists of the 17th century contributed to the decoration of the church. Borromini designed the capitals and the lantern; Lanfranco and Domenichino painted the interior.

originals. Part of the garden of a Roman house dating from 60 AD can be visited in the foundations of the palace. (Continue along the Corso Vittorio Emanuele.)

SANT'ANDREA DELLA VALLE ★. As fine an achievement as the Gesù ▲ *257*, this church has the highest dome in Rome after St Peter's ▲ *210, 213*. Both the dome and the façade were designed by Carlo Maderno, although the façade was completed by Rainaldi and Fontana between 1662 and 1664. It is the church of the mother house of the Theatine Order, founded in 1524 by St Gaetano di Thiene. Construction began in 1591, the design being the outcome of a compromise between the plans of the architect chosen by the Order, Fr Francesco Grimaldi, and those of Giacomo della Porta, who was a protégé of the project's main financial backer, Cardinal Gesualdo. The relative nudity of the nave contrasts with the lavish decorations of the transepts and the apse. The church's frescoes are representative of two different trends. In the cupola Lanfranco painted a trompe l'oeil fresco of the *Assumption of the Virgin Mary* (1625–8), covering the inside of the dome completely. Domenichino, in his frescoes of the Evangelists in the four pendentives and his *Scenes from the Life of St Andrew* in the coffers of the vault over the choir, demonstrates a preference for line and idealized form. The three frescoes in the choir by Mattia Preti depicting *The Martyrdom of St Andrew* were painted in 1650. Among the tombs the ones of the Piccolomini popes, Pius II and Pius III, on either side of the nave are the most notable; these were moved here from St Peter's in 1614.

THE AREA SACRA DELL' ARGENTINA

This group of ruins, below street level, includes four temples from the time of the Republic that, because of uncertain identification, are referred to by the first four letters of the alphabet. Remains of Pompey's Curia ▲ *248* can also be seen here.

TEMPLE C. Built at the beginning of the 3rd century BC, this was probably dedicated to Feronia, the goddess of springs and forests. Her cult was introduced in Rome around 290 BC.

TEMPLE A. This is believed to be the temple dedicated to the water nymph Juturna ▲ *142* erected by Caius Lutatius Catulus after his victory over Carthage in 241 AD. A church c

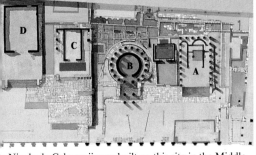

Largo Argentina.

n Nicola de Calcarariis was built on this site in the Middle
es, of which two apses with traces of frescoes survive. East
the temple there are the remains of Pompey's
ecatostylon, an immense portico with a hundred columns.

MPLE D. This temple was probably the one erected by
arcus Aemilius Lepidus following his naval victory over
ng Antiochus in 179 BC.

MPLE B. Fragments of a colossal female statue made of
eek marble were discovered beside this circular temple.
ese fragments can now be seen in the Museo del Palazzo
i Conservatori (Braccio Nuovo) ▲ *132* and are almost
rtainly the remains of the statue of the deity worshiped in
e temple. The building is thought to be the *Aedes Fortunae
uisce Diei* ("temple of today's good fortune") erected in
2 BC by Catulus, colleague of Marius, after their victory at
rcelia over the Cimbri, one of the Teutonic tribes that were
reatening northern Italy. A visual presentation in the Torre
pito explains the layout of the archeological complex.

ORTICUS MINUCIA FRUMENTARIA. To the east of Largo di
rre Argentina in ancient times there was an enclosed space
thin a building called the Villa Publica. This was where
e census of the Roman population, as well as other
ministrative activities, took place. Claudius demolished
e buildings here and replaced them with a large square
rrounded by porticos known as the Porticus Minucia
umentaria, used for the
stribution of free wheat
the people of Rome. In
e center stood a temple
the Republican period,
obably the Temple of the
mphs. Two of its
rinthian columns can be
en in the Via delle
otteghe Oscure, where
ey were discovered
ring excavations in 1938.

ATRO ARGENTINA. In
16 this public theater,
ich replaced the former

vate theater of a ducal family, the Sforza-Cesarini, was
esented the premiere of Rossini's *The Barber of Seville*.
l the great Italian opera composers subsequently had
eir works produced at the Teatro Argentina. (Between
rgo di Torre Argentina and the Tiber is the area that was
ce the Ghetto.)

The Ghetto

"The roaring lion"
This relief on the house of Caius Manilius, in the Via del Portico d'Ottavia, shows a lion (the symbol of Rome) seizing a deer.

The Jews of Rome. Jews are known to have settled in Rome as early as the 1st century BC, and there was such a strong Jewish presence in Trastevere during the Empire that this quarter was described as "the fortress of Roman Judaism". Later, Jews also settled in other parts of the city, such as the Campus Martius, the Suburra and the Aventine; and the Pons Fabricius ▲ 175 came to be known as the Pons Judaeorum (the bridge of the Jews). Nevertheless, the main synagogues remained in Trastevere, and under the city's bylaws of 1363 the Jewish population had to bury their dead near the church of San Francesco a Ripa ▲ 354. Due to the concentration of Jewish inhabitants in this area, by 1309 it had already come to be called the Contrada Iudaeorum (the Jewish quarter). At this time Jews were not excluded from mingling with the Christian community; however, they were forced to indicate their religious background by their clothing, and their ability to practice their religion in public depended on the varying goodwill of the different popes. With the exodus of Jews from Spain and Portugal in 1492 and 1498, the community expanded further: Pope Alexander VI (1492–1503) welcomed nine thousand of them in Rome against payment in gold.

The creation of the Ghetto. When Pope Paul IV (1555–9), who had previously been the Grand Inquisitor of the Kingdom of Naples, issued the bull *Cum nimis absurdium* proclaiming the creation of the

hetto, the Jewish
ommunity – which had
radually moved to the left
ank of the Tiber during the
3th century – was confined
ithin the boundaries of the
ant'Angelo district. Several
ousand people were thus
orced to live in an area of
arely 2.5 acres. From Piazza
iudea (today an anonymou
art of the Piazza delle
inque Scole that was
reviously called Via del
rogresso) the boundary ran
arallel to Via del Portico d'Ottavia and then veered right
oward the Tiber at the Via della Pescheria. Sixtus V enlarged
e Ghetto to include the banks of the river, where the poorest
milies settled. In this area when the Tiber was in spate water
ached the third floor of the houses, and the Jewish
ommunity was forced to pay 100 scudi per stonemason to
onstruct an embankment. At sunset the gates of the Ghetto
Piazza Pescheria and Piazza Giudea were closed.

UNFETTERING THE GHETTO. After a final enlargement in 1823
nder Leo XII, the walls were at last demolished in 1848; and
1883 the Ghetto was officially abolished by law. Today the
hetto area lacks any architectural unity. The history of its
rmented past is evident from the number of neglected
ouses and derelict sites left by reckless demolition. But it has
ot lost its character, and it is fascinating to explore Via del
ortico d'Ottavia, where Roman inscriptions set in the walls
medieval houses vie with the signs of kosher food shops
d those of *trattorie* offering delicious *carciofi alla giudia*
eep-fried artichokes that look like golden sunflowers).

VIA DELLE BOTTEGHE OSCURE AND THE MATTEI PALACES. The
ia delle Botteghe Oscure owes its name ("the street of dark
orkshops") to the existence in the Middle Ages of
orkshops with special ovens used to
duce ancient marble to lime for the
roduction of building materials. Taking
ia Paganica, which crosses it, you will
me to the Mattei *insediamento,* a
uster of buildings owned by the Mattei
mily. To the left are the PALAZZO
AETANI, built in 1564 for Alessandro
attei, and PALAZZO MATTEI DI
AGANICA built in 1541 for Ludovico
attei. The remains of the theater of
albus, the smallest of the theaters of the
ampus Martius, were found in the
llars of the latter. The theater was built
32 BC; behind the stage a large portico,
e Crypta Balbi, has also been found. It
now one of the four seats of the
ational Roman Museum ▲ *336.*

PIAZZA MATTEI. A little further on, the
nterpiece of Piazza Mattei is the
elightful FONTANA DELLE TARTARUGHE
ortoise Fountain) built between 1541

THE ROUND-UP OF 1943
On October 16, 1943, the Ghetto was the victim of a huge round-up of Jews. The German officer in charge forced the residents to pay a ransom of 110 pounds of gold per person. Although this sum was collected, the Nazis surrounded the Ghetto and deported all the Jews who were there. *La Storia* by Elsa Morante and Carlo Lizzani's film *L'oro di Roma* (1961) are both based on this tragic event.

A kosher shop in the Ghetto.

Alessandro Mattei.

and 1584 by Taddeo Landi, possibly to a design by Giacomo Della Porta. It faces the PALAZZO COSTAGU (No. 10), which is famous for its frescoes by some of the greatest artists, including Guercino an the Zuccari. The third Mattei palace, on the left in Via de' Funari, is the PALAZZO MATTEI di Giove, built Carlo Maderno in 1611, which distinguished by its monumenta size and the wealth of its decoratio The remains of one of the finest collections of ancient marble statua can be seen in the two courtyards. This building now houses the Italia Center for American Studies and the Library of Modern History The entrance is on Via Caet (to the left). This was the street where on May 9, 1978, halfw between what was th **the headquarters of th** Italian Communist Part (in Via delle Botteghe Oscure) and the headquarters of the Christian Democrats (in Piazza del Gesù), the body of the Christian Democrat leader Aldo Moro was found after his assassinatio by the Red Brigades.

The Fontana delle Tartarughe (Tortoise Fountain), one of the most famous and elegant in Rome.

THE CENCI
At the end of the 16th century Francesco Cenci, the head of this powerful Roman family, tried to abuse his daughter Beatrice. With her stepmother and her brothers, she murdered him on September 9, 1598. They were executed the following year in front of the Ponte Sant'Angelo.

SANTA CATERINA DEI FUNARI. This church was founded in the 12th century and rebuilt between 1560 and 1564; the façade, by Guidetto Guidetti, is a fine example of Renaissance architecture. The name of the church refers to the rope makers (*funari*) that formerly worked in the neighborhood. (Return to Piazza Mattei and, skirting Palazzo Costaguti, walk downhill toward the Tiber.)

PALAZZO CENCI BOLOGNETTI. The knoll on which the palac was built is formed by the ruins of the Circus Flaminius. The edifice has four wings, and its main façade and the family chapel (San Tommaso ai Cenci, founded in the 12th century) face onto a small square. This chapel was rebuilt and embellished in 1575 by Francesco Cenci in order to hold the future sepulcher of his children Beatrice and Giacomo. (Take Via Catalana.)

THE SYNAGOGUE. After the walls of the Ghetto were torn down a new synagogue was built, by the architects Costa and Armanni, and inaugurated in 1904. It is a massive building in travertine marble, with an aluminium dome in Assyrian-Babylonian style that is clearly visible from the Aventine. Next door to it is the Jewish Museum.

The Campo Marzio
from the Gesù
to Palazzo Madama

257 The Church of the Gesù

258 Palazzo Doria Pamphilj

260 Santa Maria in via Lata

260 Around the Piazza della Minerva

261 Sant'Ignazio

262 The Domes of Rome

264 The Pantheon

267 Piazza Colonna

269 Montecitorio

270 San Luigi dei Francesi

🕙 **One day**

◆ **F** B2-C1-C2-C3

1. CHURCH OF THE GESÙ
2. PALAZZO DORIA-
PAMPHILI
3. FONTANELLA
DEL FACCHINO
4. CHURCH OF
SANT'IGNAZIO
5. CHURCH OF SANTA
MARIA SOPRA MINERVA
6. PANTHEON ✪
7. PALAZZO DELLA
SAPIENZA AND CHURCH
OF SANT'IVO
8. PALAZZO MADAMA
9. CHURCH OF SAN LUIGI
DEI FRANCESI
10. CHURCH OF SANTA
MARIA MADDALENA
11. CHURCH OF SANTA
MARIA IN CAMPO MARZIO
12. PALAZZO DI
MONTECITORIO
13. COLUMN OF MARCUS-
AURELIUS
14. PALAZZO CHIGI
15. GALERIA COLONNA

G iven the presence of monuments such as the Pantheon, Baroque churches like the Gesù and Sant'Ignazio, and buildings such as the Palazzo di Montecitorio and the Palazzo Chigi, you might expect this neighborhood to be fossilized by its very grandeur. Admittedly it is no longer the popular area it once was, and it's a long time since farm laborers in search of work assembled around the Fontana della Rotonda. But the narrow, winding streets are full of surprises: the enormous marble foot of a Roman colossus; the Bernini elephant and, scattered throughout the district, hidden courtyards and little piazzas like the ones in provincial towns.

THE CAMPO MARZIO IN THE MIDDLE AGES

CHURCHES. In the early Middle Ages the Campo Marzio area was not at all densely inhabited. Only three titular churches had been built there: San Marco, San Lorenzo in Damaso and San Lorenzo in Lucina. The wars against the Goths in the first half of the 6th century and then the Lombard sieges had catastrophically reduced the population and radically changed its distribution within the Aurelian Wall. Settlements began to appear in the Forum and the Campo Marzio in this period. In 609 Boniface IV, with the assent of the Emperor Phocas, turned the Pantheon into the Church of Santa Maria dei

artiri. Churches then multiplied in the area bounded by the
⋯er, the Quirinal and the Capitoline.
⋯TTLEMENT. While settlements remained scarce in the 10th
⋯ 11th centuries, they subsequently developed along the
⋯nks of the Tiber and in the vicinity of several dynamic
⋯urches and monasteries. In the northern part of the Campo
⋯arzio property-development projects were started in the
⋯th and 13th centuries under the auspices of the monasteries
⋯ San Silvestro in Capite, Santa Maria della Concezione in
⋯mpo Marzio and others in the area. The result of these
⋯al-estate operations was the creation of new neighborhoods
⋯th a regular urban landscape and a modest and
⋯mogeneous social fabric. They contrasted with the older
⋯ban areas at the center of the Campo Marzio, where the
⋯wers and palaces of the nobles stood out prominently,
⋯minating the humbler houses of their retainers.

⋯E CHURCH OF THE GESÙ ● 78, 81

⋯UNTER-REFORMATION ARCHITECTURE. From 1540 the
⋯suits had only had a small church, which they were eager to
⋯uild in a way that would symbolize the spread of the most
⋯namic Order of the Counter-Reformation. Cardinal
⋯essandro Farnese, who decided to fund the project,
⋯posed his choice of architect, Vignola, and work began in
⋯68. After Vignola's death in 1573, Giacomo della Porta
⋯signed the façade, which is adorned with pilasters; its broad
⋯lutes disguise the difference of width between the two
⋯els. The ribbed cupola, designed by Vignola and completed
⋯ della Porta, is a relatively low one – at least by the
⋯ndards of that time. When completed in 1582, the church
⋯s a sober building: the ceiling of the only nave was bare,
⋯d the pilasters were not of rich marble but of travertine. In
⋯ side chapels, late Mannerist painters such as Pomarancio,
⋯derico Zuccaro and Francesco Bassano left their mark.

**THE ALTAR OF
ST IGNATIUS**
The statue of
St Ignatius of Loyola
by Pierre Legros was
melted down by Pius
VI to help pay for the
Napoleonic wars.
It was remade in
Canova's workshop in
1814, soon after order
was reestablished.

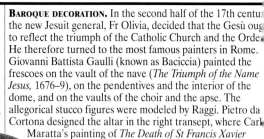

BAROQUE DECORATION. In the second half of the 17th centu
the new Jesuit general, Fr Olivia, decided that the Gesù oug
to reflect the triumph of the Catholic Church and the Orde
He therefore turned to the most famous painters in Rome.
Giovanni Battista Gaulli (known as Baciccia) painted the
frescoes on the vault of the nave (*The Triumph of the Name
Jesus*, 1676–9), on the pendentives and the interior of the
dome, and on the vaults of the choir and the apse. The
allegorical stucco figures were modeled by Raggi. Pietro da
Cortona designed the altar in the right transept, where Carl
Maratta's painting of *The Death of St Francis Xavier*
(1679) was hung.

THE TRIUMPH OF ST IGNATIUS. Artists who were
members of the Society were also called upon;
and one of the most remarkable of them, Fr
Andrea Pozzo, designed the monumental alt
dedicated to St Ignatius of Loyola in the left
transept of the church. This altar is the riche
in Rome. It shows the apparition of the Trin
to St Ignatius, with the Eternal Father and
Christ enthroned on a gigantic block of lapis
lazuli. The saint's monumental figure, cover
with silver, gilded bronze and lapis lazuli, wa
executed by Pierre Legros. On either side of
the tomb, two allegorical groups represent t
Jesuits' mission: the struggle against heresy
(*The Triumph of Faith over Heresy*, by Legros
on the right) and evangelization (*The Trium
of Faith over Idolatry*, by Giovanni Théodon
on the left). In addition to a history of the Order's foundati
there is an extraordinary corridor in *trompe l'oeil* by Fr Pozz
as well as frescoes by Jacques Courtois, nicknamed "il
Borgognone" (the Burgundian), which should not be misse
On the square in front of the church is the PALAZZO CENCI-
BOLOGNETTI (1737), the headquarters of the Italian Popula
Party. (Take the Via del Plebiscito, then turn left into Via
della Gatta.)

THE COLLEGIO ROMANO. Its building began in 1582,
and it remained the first great Jesuit college until 1870.
Fr Athanasius Kircher, one of the Order's most famous
scholars, lived here from 1635 to 1680 and amassed a
collection of curiosities. In 1875, when Rome became the
capital of Italy, the Biblioteca Vittorio Emanuele II was
housed in this building, since many of the books came from
the Jesuits' collection. Now it has been transferred to Castro
Pretorio, near the Stazione Termini. In future the palace wi
house the Ministero dei Beni e delle Attività Culturali, which
manages the Italian cultural and environmental heritage.

THE PERFECT ILLUSION
In this *trompe l'oeil*
corridor Fr Pozzo
used ingenious tricks
of perspective to
create fantastic spacial
effects that are as
pleasing as they are
astonishing.

PALAZZO DORIA PAMPHILJ

THE PALACE. Opposite the
Collegio Romano is the vast
Doria Pamphilj palace, built
in several stages by its various
owners. It was acquired by the
family of Pope Julius II in the
16th century and then
purchased by Cardinal Pietro

The *Flight into Egypt*, one of the four lunettes Annibale Carracci painted for Palazzo Aldobrandini.

Salome with the Head of John the Baptist is one of Titian's early works, but its richness of color and his treatment of light reveal the artist's mastery. Claude Lorrain's *Landscape with Dancers* (bottom) is also an undisputed masterpiece: it demonstrates his virtuosity in rendering the interplay of light and shade, with its subtle passage from the limpid blue of the sky to the deep shadows of the woods.

dobrandini, the nephew of Pope Clement VIII, in 1601. 1647 it was inherited by the nephew of Innocent X, millo Pamphilj, who enlarged the important Aldobrandini d Pamphilj art collections. Between 1731 and 1734 Gabriele lvassori built the façade facing the Corso and completed e upper loggia overlooking the courtyard to house the lleries. Then in about 1740 Paolo Ameli added the façade the Via del Plebiscito. The branch of the Doria Pamphilj nily that inherited the palace in 1760 still owns it today.

E PICTURE GALLERY. Some of the most important pieces in e collection were part of the Aldobrandini bequest, such the celebrated *Aldobrandini Lunettes*. These historical dscapes with biblical scenes, painted by Annibale Carracci d Albani, were originally in the palace chapel, as re Titian's *Salome with the Head of John the Baptist* d Parmigianino's *The Nativity*. The works acquired the Pamphili in the 17th century include lázquez's portrait of Pope Innocent X, ravaggio's *Mary Magdalene* and *Rest on the ght into Egypt*, the magnificent paintings of the ilogna school, and much of the rich collection landscapes (especially those by Claude Lorrain). e Doria Pamphilj enriched the collection with ctures by Bronzino, primitives and tapestries. he gallery's entrance is in Piazza del llegio Romano. It is also possible to visit e private apartments.)

One of the plaques on the walls of Santa Maria sopra Minerva recording the flood levels of the Tiber.

Michelangelo's *Christ Bearing the Cross* (1514) in Santa Maria sopra Minerva has the classical beauty of an Apollo reclining nonchalantly against the cross. The prudish bronze drape was a later addition.

Santa Maria in Via Lata

Returning from the Piazza del Collegio Romano to the Cor on the left is the picturesque FONTANELLA DEL FACCHINO – small fountain featuring a water carrier in 16th-century costume, who became one of Rome's "talking statues" ● 46 thanks to a supposed resemblance to Martin Luther. Facing the fountain is the Church of Santa Maria in Via Lata. This ancient church was rebuilt several times before its appearan was transformed in the 17th century. Bernini designed the high altar and the choir between 1636 and 1643; Cosimo Fanzago redecorated the nave with marble inlays; and Pietr da Cortona created its graceful façade between 1658 and 1662. The two superimposed colonnades standing out again the vestibule create contrasting effects of light and shadow, and distinguish it from the numerous façades with integrate columns. This was the parish church of the Bonaparte fami many of whose members are buried here. On a lower level vestiges of the paleo-Christian church and early frescoes ca be seen, the most beautiful of which is *The Seven Sleepers of Ephesus,* dating from the 7th century.

Around the Piazza della Minerva

Via Pie di Marmo. This narrow street owes its name to the gigantic marble foot of a Roman statue firmly planted o the corner of Via Santo Stefano del Cacco. It probably came from the ancient Temple of Isis and Serapis (tod the Church of Santo Stefano del Cacco, built in the Middle Ages and restored in the 18th century). The small obelisks to be seen in the area also came from the Temple of Isis: one stands in the Piazza della Rotonda, another in Piazza della Minerva.

The Church of Santa Maria sopra Minerva. O its façade there are marks dating from the 16th and 17th centuries indicating the level of the various floods of the Tiber: the water rose to 65 feet in this neighborhood, which is one of the lowest areas in Rome. Founded in the 8th century on the site of an ancient temple of Minerva, the church belongs to the Dominicans. It was rebuilt around 1280 and i the only church in Rome with pointed Gothic arches. In the mid 19th century, in order to resto its Gothic character, the vault was painted and t pillars were faced with imitation marble. St Catherine, the fiery Sienese who did not hesitate admonish the Pope at the time of the great debate of the Avignon schism, died in Rome. Her relics ar preserved in the sarcophagus under the high altar. F reputation was so widespread that many popes wish to be buried beside her and she eventually became patron saint of Italy. Filippino Lippi was summoned from Florence at the end of the 15th century to decorate the Carafa chapel (in the right transept). Michelangelo's *Christ Bearing the Cross* (1519–20) stands in front of the left pillar in the choir. Finally, Dominican painter Fra Angelico from the monastery San Marco in Florence, who died in 1455, has a movingly simple tombstone placed in a dark

Bernini's elephant (1667) supporting the obelisk in Piazza della Minerva; so small that it was called "il pulcin' della Minerva" (Minerva's baby).

...ssageway on the left of the choir. (Leave the church by the ...rridor to the left of the choir and take Via Beato Angelico; ...en turn left and proceed along Via di Sant'Ignazio to Piazza ...Sant'Ignazio, which is off it, at the end, on the right.)

...NT'IGNAZIO

...E PIAZZA. This piazza is like a stage set placed at the foot of ...e towering façade of the Church of Sant'Ignazio. The ...nception of the piazza, designed by Filippo Raguzzini in ...27–8, is one of the most successful and most original in ...me. The symmetrical streets opening into it are concealed ...the façades of the houses, creating the effect of "wings" as ...a theater stage. In one of these streets, the Via dei Burrò, ...e French set up their administrative headquarters during ...e Napoleonic occupation – its name is a corruption of ...ureaux".

...E CHURCH ● 79. The façade of Sant'Ignazio is on two ...els like that of the Gesù, to achieve similar effects; it has ...nerally been attributed to Algardi but may have been the ...rk of Orazio Grassi, the church's architect. Due to lack of ...nds to build a cupola as initially intended, Fr Andrea Pozzo, ...master in the theories of perspective, painted an altar in ...mpe l'oeil (1684–5) ● 82 . He went on to paint the frescoes ...the choir and those covering the entire vault of the nave, ...mpleting them in 1694; *The Triumph of St Ignatius* and *The ...der's Expansion in the Four Parts of the World* are ...presented as an optical illusion, the ...lls of the church extended by false ...umns as if opening onto the ...y. A disk of yellow marble ...in the middle of the ...or of the nave marks ...e spot on which to ...nd in order to get ...e full benefit of the ...rspective and ...mpe l'oeil effects. ...e right transept is ...orned with a ...nptuous altar ...dicated to Luigi ...nzaga, again ...signed by Fr Pozzo, ...h a high relief ...lpted by Pierre Legros; ...the left transept Filippo ...le built the altar of the

SANT'IGNAZIO
"Go forth and give light to the world." The ceiling illustrates St Ignatius' words. "The Father's light, through the Son, descends upon Ignatius and thus illuminates all the known continents."

The famous *trompe l'oeil* cupola in Sant'Ignazio.

ST PETER'S ▲ 210
The elliptical sixteen-ribbed dome is flooded with blue and gold light.

SAN LUIGI DEI FRANCESI ▲ 270
A rim of shadow beneath the lantern sets sinuous forms of the sculptures.

SANT'ANDREA DELLA VALLE ▲ 250
The sixteen windows in the drum and the lantern illuminate Carlo Maderno's cupola.

SANT'IVO ▲ 272
An exercise in architectural virtuosity, re in the dome's purity and fluidity of fo

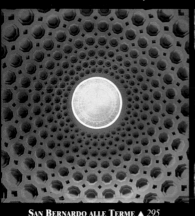

SAN BERNARDO ALLE TERME ▲ 295
The only illumination is a shaft of light provided by the single central oculus.

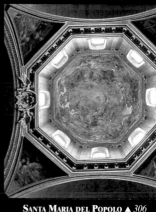

SANTA MARIA DEL POPOLO ▲ 306
An explosion of *trompe l'oeil* framed by plain, rigorous octagon.

the Renaissance model of a cupola – as conceived by Brunelleschi, then Bramante, Antonio di Sangallo the Younger and finally Michelangelo – was a spherical dome with convergent ribbing resting on a drum and surmounted by a lantern. This eventually gave way to the variations of the Mannerist architects, who replaced the sphere with an ellipse, got rid of the lantern, and used frescoes for effect.

SAN ROCCO
The amazing use of color in the pendentives contrasts with the dark cupola.

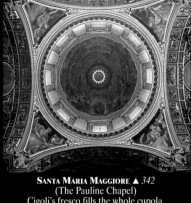

SANTA MARIA MAGGIORE ▲ *342*
(The Pauline Chapel)
Cigoli's fresco fills the whole cupola.

SANTA MARIA IN CAMPITELLI ▲ *159*
An exercise in sobriety, with its monochrome uniformity and even lighting.

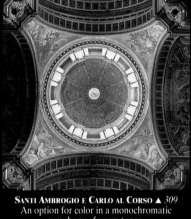

SANTI AMBROGIO E CARLO AL CORSO ▲ *309*
An option for color in a monochromatic symphony of warm tones.

SAN CARLO AI CATINARI ▲ *247*
Diminishing coffers and pictorial foreshortenings enhance the cupola's depth.

SANTA MARIA DELLA VITTORIA ▲ *294*
The architecture is little more than support for an orgy of Baroque painting and stucco decoration.

·M·AGRIPPA·L·FCOS·TERTIVM·FECI·

The Emperor Hadrian had these words inscribed on the architrave: *M(arcus) Agrippa L(ucii) f(ilius) c(on)s(ul) tertium fecit* ("Marcus Agrippa, son of Lucius, third time consul, made [this temple]"). Below, an inscription in smaller lettering refers to restoration work in 202 AD under Septimus Severus and Caracalla.

DONKEY'S EARS
This is how Pasquino described the two bell turrets that Bernini added to the façade of the Pantheon in the 17th century. They were removed in 1883.

Annunciation in 1750. (On leaving the church, turn left into Via del Seminario, which will take you to Piazza della Rotonda.)

THE PANTHEON ★ ● 7

PIAZZA DELLA ROTONDA. The square in which the Pantheon is set was created under Clement XI (1700–21) and involved the demolition of several buildings. At the same time Giacomo della Porta's fountain (1578) was drastically modified: it was given a pedestal decorated with dolphins and the Pope's coat of arms, and an obelisk was added which, like the one in Piazza della Minerva, came from the neighboring Temple of Isis.

AGRIPPA'S TEMPLE. The plan of the Pantheon combines the pronaos (porch) of a temple with a rotunda of the kind found in Roman baths ● 68. A brilliant composite of geometrical forms and contrasting features, its architecture was intended to reflect the terrestrial and cosmic order. This is the best preserved building of ancient Rome – thanks to the Byzantine Emperor Phocas' donation of it to Pope Boniface IV and its transformation into a church, which received the name of Santa Maria dei Martiri (St Mary of the Martyrs) in 609 AD. It was originally built in 27 to 25 BC by Agrippa, who wanted to dedicate it to Augustus, his father-in-law and friend. When Augustus declined the honor, it was dedicated to the major deities venerated by the families of Claudius and Julius Caesar (Mars, Venus and the divine Julius himself) instead. The building was then rectangular and faced south. What we see today dates from the early years of Hadrian's reign, between 118 and 125 AD. The pediment was adorned with a crowned eagle, as witness the sockets. The great portico is supported by eight monolithic granite columns with white marble capitals and bases.

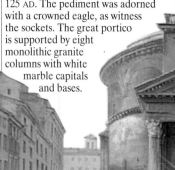

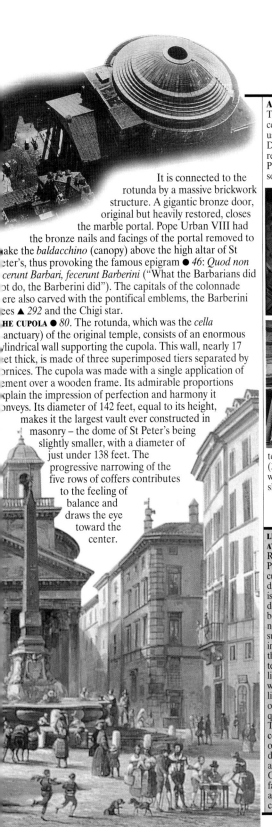

It is connected to the rotunda by a massive brickwork structure. A gigantic bronze door, original but heavily restored, closes the marble portal. Pope Urban VIII had the bronze nails and facings of the portal removed to make the *baldacchino* (canopy) above the high altar of St Peter's, thus provoking the famous epigram ● 46: *Quod non fecerunt Barbari, fecerunt Barberini* ("What the Barbarians did not do, the Barberini did"). The capitals of the colonnade were also carved with the pontifical emblems, the Barberini bees ▲ 292 and the Chigi star.

THE CUPOLA ● 80. The rotunda, which was the *cella* (sanctuary) of the original temple, consists of an enormous cylindrical wall supporting the cupola. This wall, nearly 17 feet thick, is made of three superimposed tiers separated by cornices. The cupola was made with a single application of cement over a wooden frame. Its admirable proportions explain the impression of perfection and harmony it conveys. Its diameter of 142 feet, equal to its height, makes it the largest vault ever constructed in masonry – the dome of St Peter's being slightly smaller, with a diameter of just under 138 feet. The progressive narrowing of the five rows of coffers contributes to the feeling of balance and draws the eye toward the center.

265

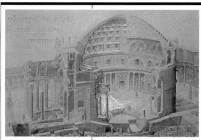

THE PORTICO OF THE ARGONAUTS
Along the left side of the Pantheon is the back wall of the portico that separated Agrippa's temple from the Saepta, a large square used for electoral meetings under the Republic (under the Empire it became a center for entertainment). A reconstruction of the portico is shown above.

THE NICHES
These were originally decorated with statues of the gods and are now chapels. Beneath the third aedicule on the left is the tomb of Raphael (1483–1520), inscribed with the famous epitaph composed by Cardinal Bembo: *Ille hic est Raffaello Sanzio, timuit quo sospite vinci rerum magna parens et moriente mori.* (Alexander Pope, who borrowed the couplet for another epitaph, translated it as "Living, great nature feared he might outvie Her works; and dying, fears herself to die.") Other artists buried here include Giovanni da Udine, Perin del Vaga, Annibale Carracci, Taddeo Zuccari and Baldassare Peruzzi, as well as two kings of Italy, Vittorio Emanuele II and Umberto I.

THE NICHES. Opposite the door is the main niche, over which there is an arch. Its two fine columns are made of *pavonazzetto*, a beautiful violet-veined marble from Synnada in Asia Minor. The other niches – three on either side, alternating from rectangular to circular in shape – are fronted with monolithic columns made of a Tunisian marble known as *giallo antico*. This use of marbles, which was so important in classical architecture, is carried through in the paving of the floor, where geometrical patterns alternate, and also in the shrines (*aedicoli*) between the niches. Columns of red porphyry, *giallo antico* and granite support either triangular or rounded tympanums. Their alternation is said to have served as a model for many renaissance façades, especially that of Palazzo Farnese ▲ 24

THE BASILICA OF NEPTUNE AND BATHS OF AGRIPPA. Behind the Pantheon, along the Via della Palombella, there are columns, a brick wall and a marble frieze which includes dolphins and tridents. These are all that is left of a basilica dedicated to Neptune, erected by Agrippa and rebuilt by Hadrian. A little further on, near the Corso Vittorio

Emanuele, is the site of Rome's most
ancient baths, inaugurated in 19 BC
with an artificial lake, the Stagnum
Agrippae. Both were fed by the Aqua
Virgo.

THE TEMPLE OF MATIDIA. Hadrian
is surely the only man in the
world to have deified his mother-in-law
and to have dedicated a temple to her.
Situated close to the present-day Piazza
Capranica, it can be reached by the Via
degli Orfani. A truncated column from it
can be seen in the alley called the Vicolo
della Spada d'Orlando. (Take Via de' Pastini
to the Piazza di Pietra.)

THE TEMPLE OF HADRIAN. After Hadrian's
death his son, Antoninus Pius, erected a
temple in his honor, which was dedicated in
145 AD. Eleven white-marble columns, now
imprisoned within the northern wall of the
Borsa (STOCK-EXCHANGE BUILDING) on the
Piazza di Pietra, testify to the grandeur of
the temple. Reliefs from it portraying
allegorical figures, alternating with trophies,
are preserved in the courtyard of the Palazzo
dei Conservatori and in the National
Museum of Naples. (Walk through to the
Piazza Colonna, which is nearby.)

PIAZZA COLONNA

The urbanization of this section of the
Campo Marzio began under the Antonines
in the 2nd century.

THE COLUMN OF MARCUS AURELIUS. In the
center of the square rises the column of
Marcus Aurelius. Just over 83 feet tall, it was
made between 193 AD (the year of the
emperor's death) and 196 AD. The lower
part of the column commemorates his
victories over the Germanic tribes on the
Danube frontier, and the upper part his
success against the Sarmatians (in the area
between the Volga and the Vistula rivers).
Its base, originally nearly 30 feet taller, was
decorated with festoons and reliefs showing
victories and scenes of barbarians being
forced to submit: these were destroyed in
1589 by Sixtus V. The column itself has
twenty complete rings of reliefs, rather
fewer than its model, Trajan's column ▲ 166.
With its simplification and violent
contrasts, it heralds the eminently
dramatic 3rd-century style. The facial
expressions, for example, are quite
remarkable – especially those of the
terror-stricken or desperately
beseeching barbarians, the soldiers and
the emperor-philosopher, who is most

The Temple of
Hadrian.

The Bocconi ● *90*
department store
(now Rinascente)
opened in Piazza
Colonna in 1885.
With its metal and
glass structure the
building was
influenced by the
stores that had
sprung up in other
European capitals,
such as La Belle
Jardinière and Le
Printemps in Paris.

**THE COLUMN OF
MARCUS AURELIUS**
Inside the column a
spiral staircase with
190 steps leads to the
top, where the
Emperor's statue
originally stood.
In 1589, at Sixtus V's
request, Domenico
Fontana replaced it
with a statue of
St Paul.

THE CAMPO MARZIO
FROM THE GESÙ TO PALAZZO MADAMA

LEGIONARIES CROSSING A RIVER (THE EMPEROR IS TALKING TO TWO OFFICERS).

AUXILIARY TROOPS PROTECTING THE ARMY ON THE MARCH.

BATTLE SCENE, WITH LEGIONARIES MASSACRING BARBARIANS.

Drawings of the reliefs made by Giovanni Guerra when the column was restored in 1589.

THE COLUMN OF ANTONINUS PIUS
The reliefs on the base depict the apotheosis of the Emperor and his wife Faustina, being carried to heaven by a winged *genius*. On the two smaller sides there are equestrian parades.

frequently sculpted face on, no doubt to make him appear more majestic. Ranuccio Bianchi Bandinelli, a specialist in Roman art, emphasizes the artistic originality of the image of Marcus Aurelius: "Among the scenes of death and destruction, the face of the emperor in person emerges … deeply marked by anguish, exhaustion and age. He must have been about 54 years old: this is certainly not the face of a triumphant conqueror exalted by his victories but that of a man who was 'a total stranger to the habits of the rich' (*The Meditations of Marcus Aurelius*, I, 3), a genuine, suffering lay saint." (The fountain to the right of the column is by Giacomo della Porta. Palazzo Chigi faces it on one side of the square; opposite, on the other side of the Corso, is the Galleria Colonna.)

PALAZZO CHIGI. Carlo Maderno and Felice della Greca both had a hand in the construction of this stark palazzo of the Counter-Reformation period. Building began in 1580 but it was not completed until 1630. The Baroque courtyard is decorated with stucco motifs and a fountain bearing the Chigi arms. The palazzo, acquired by the State in 1917, was the headquarters of the Ministry of Foreign

fairs before it became the seat of the Presidenza del
[Co]nsiglio dei Ministri (Prime Minister's office).

[GA]LLERIA COLONNA. When the Palazzo Boncompagni
[Pi]ombino was demolished by the Municipality of Rome in
[18]89 there were lengthy discussions about what should be
[do]ne with the site. In the end it was decided to build a large
[co]vered gallery which could also house the headquarters of
[th]e Istituto Romano dei Beni Stabili. The gallery was
[in]augurated in 1922. Nearby, on Largo Chigi, the Bocconi
[de]partment store (now Rinascente), completed in 1885–7,
[i]s one of the first buildings in Rome to use modern
[ma]terials (metal and glass) while retaining a Neo-Renaissance
[sty]le. Its architect, Giulio De Angelis, was one of the principal
[ex]ponents of the Roman eclectic trend. (Cross the Corso and
[th]e Piazza Colonna again to get to Piazza di Montecitorio.)

The pictures above
show Palazzo di
Montecitorio (left and
center) and Piazza
Colonna with Palazzo
Chigi (right).

[M]ONTECITORIO

[PIA]ZZA DI MONTECITORIO. Under the Antonines the site
[oc]cupied by the Palazzo di Montecitorio (which houses the
[Ita]lian Chamber of Deputies) was used for the emperors'
[cre]mation ceremonies; the remains of the *ustrina* (logs) found
[he]re can be seen in the National Roman Museum. In 1703 the
[ba]se of Antoninus Pius' column, now in the Cortile della
[Pig]na at the Vatican, was
[al]so discovered here. Other
[fra]gments of the huge
[gra]nite column were used
[in] restoring and stabilizing
[th]e obelisk of Psammetichus
[II] (6th century BC), which
[wa]s erected in the middle of
[th]e piazza in 1792.
[Tra]nsported from Heliopolis
[to] Rome in 10 BC, the
[ob]elisk was originally set up
[in] the Campus Martius by
[Au]gustus to serve as the
[gno]mon (pointer) of an
[en]ormous sundial. It was
[un]earthed in 1748 between
[th]e Piazza del Parlamento
[an]d San Lorenzo in Lucina.

[PA]LAZZO DI MONTECITORIO.
[Th]is building has two very
[dif]ferent aspects: the
[ori]ginal façade by Bernini
[an]d a 20th-century Art
[No]uveau façade (on the
[Pia]zza del Parlamento) by
[Er]nesto Basile. The lovely,
[har]monious Baroque façade
[wa]s begun in 1650 under
[Po]pe Innocent X, who
[wa]nted to build a palace for the Ludovisi. After being held up
[un]til 1694 the project was completed by Carlo Fontana, and
[In]nocent XII decided to install the Tribunals (the Curia
[In]ocenziana) there. When the Piedmontese entered Rome
[in] 1870, they were faced with the problem of finding a suitable

**PALAZZO DI
MONTECITORIO**
Its two façades
contrast in every way.
Whereas Bernini's is
fluid and grandiose,
the façade added by
Ernesto Basile has a
rather cold and stolid
appearance.

269

The colorful market held in Piazza delle Coppelle presents an irresistible invitation to stop and browse.

The Church of Santa Maria in Campo Marzio.

site for the new parliament. In the end it was decided to use the great courtyard to accommodate the Chamber of Deputies, enclosing it with a glass roof. However, it soon became necessary to enlarge the building. Basile's design for the extension is a fine example of the style known as *floreale* (floral) in Italy because of decorative motifs inspired by exuberant vegetation. Flanking the entrance on the Piazza del Parlamento are two statues by Domenico Trentacoste (1911). The semicircular Chamber, entirely paneled in oak, is decorated with an allegorical frieze on canvas (1908–12) by Giulio Aristide Sartorio, portraying Italian civilization, the virtues of the Italian people and the most significant episodes of the nation's history. There is also a bas-relief by Davide Calandra celebrating the glory of the House of Savoy. (To reach the Church of Santa Maria in Campo Marzio, take Via Ufficio del Vicario, where you will find the *gelateria* Giolitti, which sells some of the best ice cream in Rome.)

SANTA MARIA IN CAMPO MARZIO. This church has existed since the 7th century, but it was rebuilt between 1670 and 1685 by Giovanni Antonio de Rossi. From the street nothing but the walls of the convent can be seen, repainted in their original color, a very pale blue. Restorers have been returning to the pale colors which were used for painting façades in Rome before the 19th century. The church's portico opens onto a pretty courtyard, and its graceful cupola has a flattened, oval shape. (From here you can make a detour through the picturesque Piazza delle Coppelle, and stop at the fashionable Hemingway bar; then follow Via delle Coppelle and turn right into Via della Maddalena.)

SANTA MARIA MADDALENA. This 14th-century church was rebuilt in the 17th century by Carlo Fontana. But the façade, a combination of Baroque and Rococco surmounted by a circular pediment, was added in 1735 by Giuseppe Sardi who was greatly influenced by Borromini. The interior has the same sense of movement combined with sumptuous decorations: the organ loft is astonishing – with its gilded woodcarvings, statues and cherubs – and the sacristy is one of the most beautiful in Rome. (Continue to Piazza della Rotonda and turn right into Via Giustiniani, which leads to San Luigi dei Francesi.)

THE SANTA CECILIA CHAPEL. In the Church of San Luigi dei Francesi Domenichino painted a cycle of frescoes based on the saint's legendary life. The *Glory of Cecilia* is shown here.

SAN LUIGI DEI FRANCESI

This is a particularly French neighborhood. Next to San Luigi dei Francesi, which is the French national church, are the

One of the salamanders (the emblem of Francis I) that adorn the façade of San Luigi dei Francesi.

A REVOLUTIONARY USE OF LIGHT
Caravaggio's three masterpieces painted for the Contarelli chapel (1599–1602) mark a major turning point in his style. The realism of his interpretation of the biblical scene is enhanced by his expressive use of light sources, which highlight important elements of the composition. In addition, the *chiaroscuro* (contrast between light and shadow) contributes greatly to the dramatic tension of the scene.

ench bookshop and the Catholic ench Cultural Center.

ᴀɴ Luɪɢɪ ᴅᴇɪ Fʀᴀɴᴄᴇsɪ ★.
odifications to this small church quired by the French colony in 1478 te back to the reign of Francis I. At at time the intention was to create a cular building; some reused gments from it can still be seen, such the salamanders (the emblems of ancis I) that feature on the lower part of the façade. owever, the plans were subsequently altered and, after a riety of architects had succeeded one another throughout e 16th century, the church was finally completed around 89. The austere façade is probably the work of Domenico ntana. The interior was redecorated under Dérizet's ection between 1756 and 1764. Neither Natoire's painting *The Apotheosis of St Louis* (1756) on the vault nor the great sumption* (1580) by Bassano above the main altar manage alleviate the church's rather frigid grandeur. But in the last apel on the left (the CONTARELLI CHAPEL), just before the ɡh altar, there are three pictures that are among the most autiful examples of Caravaggio's work in Rome: *The lling of St Matthew* (on the left), the *Martyrdom of St ttthew* (on the right) and *St Matthew and the Angel* (over the ar). Also outstanding are the frescoes of the *Life of Santa*

At many street corners, small shrines with votive figures await the devotions of passing Romans.

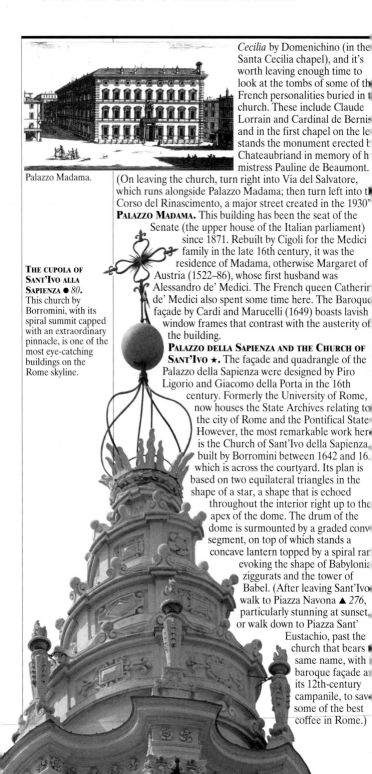

Palazzo Madama.

**THE CUPOLA OF
SANT'IVO ALLA
SAPIENZA ● 80.**
This church by
Borromini, with its
spiral summit capped
with an extraordinary
pinnacle, is one of the
most eye-catching
buildings on the
Rome skyline.

Cecilia by Domenichino (in the
Santa Cecilia chapel), and it's
worth leaving enough time to
look at the tombs of some of th
French personalities buried in t
church. These include Claude
Lorrain and Cardinal de Berni
and in the first chapel on the le
stands the monument erected b
Chateaubriand in memory of h
mistress Pauline de Beaumont.
(On leaving the church, turn right into Via del Salvatore,
which runs alongside Palazzo Madama; then turn left into t
Corso del Rinascimento, a major street created in the 1930
PALAZZO MADAMA. This building has been the seat of the
Senate (the upper house of the Italian parliament)
since 1871. Rebuilt by Cigoli for the Medici
family in the late 16th century, it was the
residence of Madama, otherwise Margaret of
Austria (1522–86), whose first husband was
Alessandro de' Medici. The French queen Catherir
de' Medici also spent some time here. The Baroque
façade by Cardi and Marucelli (1649) boasts lavish
window frames that contrast with the austerity of
the building.
**PALAZZO DELLA SAPIENZA AND THE CHURCH OF
SANT'IVO ★.** The façade and quadrangle of the
Palazzo della Sapienza were designed by Piro
Ligorio and Giacomo della Porta in the 16th
century. Formerly the University of Rome,
now houses the State Archives relating to
the city of Rome and the Pontifical State
However, the most remarkable work her
is the Church of Sant'Ivo della Sapienza
built by Borromini between 1642 and 16
which is across the courtyard. Its plan is
based on two equilateral triangles in the
shape of a star, a shape that is echoed
throughout the interior right up to the
apex of the dome. The drum of the
dome is surmounted by a graded conv
segment, on top of which stands a
concave lantern topped by a spiral ran
evoking the shape of Babyloni
ziggurats and the tower of
Babel. (After leaving Sant'Ivo
walk to Piazza Navona ▲ 276,
particularly stunning at sunset
or walk down to Piazza Sant'
Eustachio, past the
church that bears
same name, with
baroque façade a
its 12th-century
campanile, to sav
some of the best
coffee in Rome.)

Around
Piazza Navona

275 Piazza Navona
279 Around San Pantaleo
280 Santa Maria della Pace
281 Chiesa Nuova
283 Via dei Coronari
283 Around Piazza Tor di
     Sanguigna

Via dei Coronari

"We came to stay at the Bear, where we remained the following day too; on the second day of December we rented rooms in a Spaniard's house, opposite Santa Lucia della Tinta [Via di Monte Brianzo]. We were quite comfortably accommodated with three fine rooms, a hall, a pantry, a stable and a kitchen, all for twenty Ecus a month: for which our host also cooked and provided fire wood for the stove. Lodgings are generally furnished a little better than in Paris, and the more costly lodgings are upholstered with gilded leather. ... M. de Montaigne was peeved to find so many French people in town that he hardly found anyone in the streets who failed to greet him in his own tongue."

Montaigne,
Journal de voyage

THE CAMPO MARZIO DURING THE RENAISSANCE

Between the pontificates of Martin V (1417–31) and Paul III (1534–49) the Campo Marzio underwent major transformations and acquired more or less the appearance it has today. During the Renaissance this area became the true heart of Rome, with about four fifths of the city's entire population settled in it (an estimated forty thousand inhabitants in 1527).

POPES AS TOWN PLANNERS. In this period the occasional isolated attempts to improve the appearance of the city that had characterized the first half of the 15th century, as exemplified by Eugenius IV's restoration of the Pantheon ▲ 264, were replaced by a policy of town planning based on two priorities: to ensure adequate conditions for the movement of traffic through the city, especially in the direction of the Vatican, and to improve the network of streets. At first these measures mostly affected the streets leading to Ponte Sant'Angelo ▲ 239: for example, the old Via Recta (now Via dei Coronari) was widened by Sixtus IV (1471–84) and began to be lined with majestic palazzi decorated with grisaille frescoes. Then in the early 16th century Julius II (1503–13) had the Via Giulia built ▲ 240 to link the Ponte Sisto (recently constructed by Sixtus IV) to San Giovanni dei Fiorentini ▲ 241. Palazzi and churches, such as Palazzo Sacchetti and San Biaggio della Pagnotta, began to appear along this long, straight thoroughfare. However, urban restructuring was not limited to the area leading to St Peter's which was then under construction: Pope Paul II (1464–71), who built what was later to be known as Palazzo Venezia ▲ 161, widened and straightened the Via del Corso ▲ 308. In order to facilitate entry into the city, Leo X (1513–21), whose work was continued by Clement VII and Paul III, had the Piazza del Popolo enlarged ▲ 306, new streets built, and old ones modernized (including Via Leonina and eventually Via di Ripetta, Via del Babuino and Via Flaminia ▲ 308). The network of side streets was affected by less ambitious but no less important measures. Since the medieval streets were cluttered with porticos, external stairways and all sorts of other architectural protuberances that hindered traffic, efforts to eliminate such obstructions began during the pontificate of Sixtus IV. With the paving of the city's streets and squares, gradually the medieval town disappeared.

A NEW COMMERCIAL CENTER. Other measures focused on converting the Campo Marzio into the commercial center of

Map of Rome, showing the city as it was in 1637.

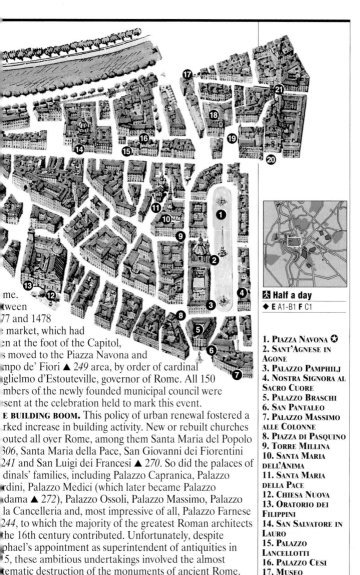

me.
tween
77 and 1478
e market, which had
en at the foot of the Capitol,
s moved to the Piazza Navona and
mpo de' Fiori ▲ 249 area, by order of cardinal
glielmo d'Estouteville, governor of Rome. All 150
mbers of the newly founded municipal council were
sent at the celebration held to mark this event.
E BUILDING BOOM. This policy of urban renewal fostered a
rked increase in building activity. New or rebuilt churches
outed all over Rome, among them Santa Maria del Popolo
306, Santa Maria della Pace, San Giovanni dei Fiorentini
241 and San Luigi dei Francesi ▲ 270. So did the palaces of
dinals' families, including Palazzo Capranica, Palazzo
rdini, Palazzo Medici (which later became Palazzo
dama ▲ 272), Palazzo Ossoli, Palazzo Massimo, Palazzo
la Cancelleria and, most impressive of all, Palazzo Farnese
244, to which the majority of the greatest Roman architects
he 16th century contributed. Unfortunately, despite
phael's appointment as superintendent of antiquities in
5, these ambitious undertakings involved the almost
ematic destruction of the monuments of ancient Rome.

AZZA NAVONA ★

BAROQUE MASTERPIECE.** This piazza, which displays the
ius of such masters of the Baroque as Bernini and
rromini, is one of the finest in papal Rome. Its harmony
l colors, combined with its elegance, give it a charm that is
anced by the surprising contrast of architecturally sober
ses alternating with a number of monumental buildings.
E HEART OF THE CITY. Of all Rome's piazzas, this *isola*
onale (pedestrian precinct) is the one where the liveliness
Roman life is most tangible. It has long been a meeting
ce for the inhabitants of Rome. In the past, in addition to

⚲ Half a day
◆ **E** A1-B1 **F** C1

1. PIAZZA NAVONA ✪
2. SANT'AGNESE IN AGONE
3. PALAZZO PAMPHILJ
4. NOSTRA SIGNORA AL SACRO CUORE
5. PALAZZO BRASCHI
6. SAN PANTALEO
7. PALAZZO MASSIMO ALLE COLONNE
8. PIAZZA DI PASQUINO
9. TORRE MILLINA
10. SANTA MARIA DELL'ANIMA
11. SANTA MARIA DELLA PACE
12. CHIESA NUOVA
13. ORATORIO DEI FILIPPINI
14. SAN SALVATORE IN LAURO
15. PALAZZO LANCELLOTTI
16. PALAZZO CESI
17. MUSEO NAPOLEONICO
18. PALAZZO ALTEMPS
19. SANT'APOLLINARE
20. SANT'AGOSTINO
21. SANT'ANTONIO DEI PORTOGHESI

CIRCVS

the market, processions and spectacles were held here – including *naumachiae*, or mock naval battles. Today life in the piazza revolves around the open-air cafés and the seasonal fairs. Of these, the most popular is the one held in December and early January where toys and crib figures are sold. Its theme is the Feast of Epiphany as well as Christmas, so *la Befana* (the Epiphany witch, who is roughly the Italian equivalent of Father Christmas) features prominently. In the summer the piazza provides a continuous festival of painters, caricaturists, fortune-tellers and buskers.

DOMITIAN'S STADIUM. Piazza Navona is a perfect example of urban continuity in Rome ● *60*. It covers exactly the area occupied by the track of Rome's first stadium (built by Domitian between 81 and 96 AD) and retains the stadium's oblong shape with a rounded north end. The buildings surrounding the piazza are built on top of the *cavea*, the stepped stone seating, designed to accommodate thirty thousand spectators. Beside the stadium – which was devoted to athletic events – Domitian built an odeon, or auditorium for musical competitions. These contests took place during the Certamen Capitolinum, the games instituted by Domitian in 86 AD . The stadium was known as the Circus Agonalis (competition arena), which became corrupted to "n'Agona" and eventually "Navona".

PONTIFICAL AGGRANDIZEMENT. Soon after being elected Pope, Innocent X (1644–55) decided to embellish the piazza in honor of his family, the Pamphilj, just as Urban VIII had revamped part of the Quirinal hill to glorify the Barberini family ▲ *290*. With this in

...ind, he had his family's palace and the ...urch of Sant'Agnese in Agone rebuilt, ...dered the restoration of the two ...untains that Gregory XIII (1572–85) ...d installed at either end of the piazza, ...d commissioned the colossal Fontana ...ei Quattro Fiumi in the center.

THE ENCHANTMENT OF WATER ★. The ...ree fountains, fed by the Aqua Virgo ...queduct ▲ 298, are the main decorative ...ements of the piazza. The most ...markable of these, the FONTANA DEI ...UMI (1651), is an expression of Bernini's ...ost consummate artistry. Innocent X ...anted a monument that would form a ...nterpiece for this elongated space but ...t disrupt its unity. An obelisk from the ...rcus of Maxentius ▲ 328 was erected ...er a rocky grotto, from which a lion and ...horse are to be seen emerging. The ...eroglyphics give an official version of ...omitian's coming to power in 81 AD.

...he fountain is all the more impressive because the obelisk ...pears to be resting on an open cavity; in this Bernini ...hieved a remarkable tour de force that gives it a sense of ...eightlessness. The large figures reclining precariously on the ...cks above the glistening water represent the main rivers of ...e four continents: the Danube, the River Plate, the Ganges ...d the Nile (with a veiled head to indicate that its sources ...re still unknown at that time). All around the monument, ...d also on the tip of the obelisk, the Pope had his family crest ...ulpted: a dove holding an olive branch. The other two ...untains, the basins of which were made in the 16th ...ntury to designs by Giacomo Della Porta, only took ... their present appearance in the 19th century.

Their light-colored stone illuminates the piazza. At the southern end, the figure of an Ethiopian hunting a dolphin that dominates the Fontana del Moro is a copy of a statue designed by Bernini. The surrounding

AN IRONIC GESTURE?
The figure of the River Plate has its hand raised with the palm toward the Church of Sant' Agnese in what Romans say is a gesture of fear – lest the building, by Bernini's rival, Borromini, should collapse on top of it.

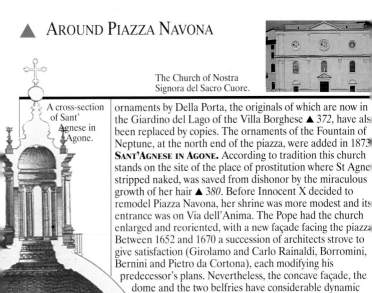

The Church of Nostra
Signora del Sacro Cuore.

A cross-section of Sant' Agnese in Agone.

ornaments by Della Porta, the originals of which are now in the Giardino del Lago of the Villa Borghese ▲ 372, have also been replaced by copies. The ornaments of the Fountain of Neptune, at the north end of the piazza, were added in 1873.

SANT'AGNESE IN AGONE. According to tradition this church stands on the site of the place of prostitution where St Agnes, stripped naked, was saved from dishonor by the miraculous growth of her hair ▲ 380. Before Innocent X decided to remodel Piazza Navona, her shrine was more modest and its entrance was on Via dell'Anima. The Pope had the church enlarged and reoriented, with a new façade facing the piazza. Between 1652 and 1670 a succession of architects strove to give satisfaction (Girolamo and Carlo Rainaldi, Borromini, Bernini and Pietro da Cortona), each modifying his predecessor's plans. Nevertheless, the concave façade, the dome and the two belfries have considerable dynamic unity, being for the most part the work of Borromini. Movement and unity are also primary aesthetic features of the interior. Indeed, although Girolamo Rainaldi's Greek-cross design was retained, the structure of the church is typical of Borromini. The frescoes in the pendentives were painted by Baciccia at Bernini's request, while those in the cupola are by Ciro Ferri, a pupil of Pietro da Cortona. Among other notable features are the marble altars and, above the door, the austere tomb of Innocent X designed by Giambattista Maini in 1729.

PALAZZO PAMPHILJ. Now the Brazilian embassy, this palazzo extends south from the church on the western side of the piazza. Its reconstruction, which began in 1646, was entrusted to Girolamo Rainaldi at the behest of the sovereign pontiff. When Borromini was later called upon to replace Rainaldi, the new plans he presented were mostly rejected, and he was only allowed to decorate the Great Hall and design the Gallery. The latter, which was decorated in 1650 by Pietro da Cortona with a magnificent fresco on the theme of the *Aeneid*, runs the entire length of the building from the point where the palace joins the Church of Sant'Agnese.

NOSTRA SIGNORA DEL SACRO CUORE. This church faces Palazzo Pamphilj across Piazza Navona. The façade overlooking the piazza dates from the period of Alexander VI (1492–1503); it was called the San Giacomo degli Spagnoli and was Spain's national church in Rome. The part facing the Sapienza, on Corso del Rinascimento, is older.

e church was restored several times, notably by Antonio
ngallo the Younger in the 16th century. It has been
decorated in its original colors – as have several
ghboring buildings, which have fine *trompe l'oeil* windows.
LAZZO BRASCHI. The building on the southwest corner of
zza Navona was the last of the palaces built in Rome for
the family of a pope. Begun in 1792 by
Cosimo Morelli for the nephews of Pius VI,
in 1871 it was sold to the State and for a
while served as the Ministry of the
Interior. In 1930 the Fascist Federation
of Rome took it over, then in 1949 it was
given to the city and became the MUSEO
DI ROMA. Sculptures, paintings, drawings,
prints and other items illustrate the
history of Rome from the Middle Ages.
The collection includes works by
Canova and a charming series of
views of Rome by Ippolito Caffi.

ROUND SAN PANTALEO

N PANTALEO. Founded in the 12th century and dedicated to
patron saint of doctors, this church (in the Piazza di San
ntaleo, just beyond Palazzo Braschi) was rebuilt in the 17th
tury by Giovanni Antonio de Rossi. Behind the splendid
ade by Valadier (1806) it has a surprisingly rich interior.
e particularly fine high altar is by Carlo Mureno (1713–64).
LAZZO MASSIMO ALLE COLONNE. To the south of Piazza
vona the Via della Posta Vecchia leads to the back of the
azzo Massimo complex. A column from Domitian's odeon
s placed here as a monument, in front of one of the few
saille frescoes to have survived on a domestic building.
ese frescoes, attributed to the school of Daniele da
lterra, earned this building the name "Palazzo Istoriato"
e illustrated palace). The main façade of the Palazzo
ssimo, on the Corso Vittorio Emanuele, is a masterpiece
Mannerist architecture. Designed by Baldassarre Peruzzi, it
oes the curve of the *cavea* (stone seats) of Domitian's
on, on which it stands. Peruzzi rebuilt the palace for the
ssimi (one of the oldest Roman families) between 1532
1 1536, following the sack of Rome in 1527 ● *36*.
AZZA DI PASQUINO. To the west of the southern end of
zza Navona is an ancient copy of a Hellenistic statue from
rgamon, part of a group representing Menelaus carrying
body of Patroclus. Known as Pasquino ● *46*, "he" presides
over a small piazza, once known
as the Piazza dei Librari because
of the publishers, printers and
booksellers established there.
The first guide to Rome in a
eign language (German) was published here by a certain
urizio Bona. (Take Via Santa Maria dell'Anima.)
RRE MILLINA. At the top of this tower, built in the Middle
es, one can see the birds that were the emblem of the
elfs, the political faction which supported the Pope; their
als, the Ghibellines, supported the Emperor. The rivalry
ween the two factions, which was particularly ardent in
rence, soon spread to other medieval cities.

Palazzo Pamphilj
(above left).

A *tartufo* (chocolate
ice cream) from the
Tre Scalini is a must
(above right).

Pope Innocent X
(left).

**THE MIRACLE OF
MARCH 16**
On the second floor
of the Palazzo
Massimo the room
where St Philip Neri
resuscitated Paolo,
the son of Fabrizio

Massimo, on March
16, 1584, is now a
chapel. On the
anniversary of the
miracle the palazzo is
open to the public,
and continuous
Masses are celebrated
in the chapel.

"PASQUINO"
This statue, which
Bernini greatly
admired, has long
been one of the most
loquacious of Rome's
talking statues ● *46*.

The façade of Santa Maria della Pace.

SANTA MARIA DELL'ANIMA. (The entrance is in Piazza della Pace.) The national church of the Germans; also of the Flemish and the Dutch in the 16th century, when it was rebuilt (1500–23). The high Renaissance façade, attributed to Giuliano da Sangallo, is adorned with carved doors which are the work of Andrea Sansovino. Inside, its three naves inspired by German church architecture are unusual in Rome. The church contains many funerary monuments dating from the 16th to the 19th century. The imposing tomb by Peruzzi in the choir is that of Hadrian VI (1522–3), the last non-Italian pope before John Paul II. Over the high altar

there is a remarkable painting of *The Holy Family with Saints* by Giulio Romano. On the other side of Via dell'Anima is SAN NICOLA, the national church of Lorraine, decorated with frescoes by Corrado Giaquinto (1731).

SANTA MARIA DELLA PACE

THE SIBYLS
The four Sibyls (of Cumae, Persia, Phrygia and Tibur) show the influence of Michelangelo's Sistine Chapel ▲ *218*. This composition flows with an extraordinary variety of rhythms, like a festoon along the curve of the arch.

THE CHURCH OF SANTA MARIA DELLA PACE ★. The elegant façade dominates the Piazza della Pace, a delightful setting for it designed by Pietro da Cortona during the pontificate of Alexander VII (1655–67). The first major reconstruction of this sanctuary was undertaken (possibly by Baccio Pontelli) at the behest of Sixtus IV. The work began in 1482 – the Pope chose the name "della Pace" to celebrate the peace he hoped to restore in Italy – and was finished under Julius II (1503–13). In the 17th century, under Alexander VII, the church was rebuilt again by Pietro da Cortona, who created present façade. While a series of Corinthian columns give rhythm to the upper part, beneath it a circular portico supported by Doric columns projects into the piazza. Inside,

short rectangular nave is followed by an octagonal central body possibly designed by Bramante. The first chapel on the right, the CHIGI CHAPEL, contains Raphael's famous *Sibyl* fresco commissioned by Agostino Chigi ▲ *360*; facing it is the PONZETI CHAPEL decorated with fine frescoes by Baldassare Peruzzi. To the left the

short rectangular nave followed by an octagonal central
[bod]y, possibly designed by Bramante. The first chapel on the
[righ]t, the CHIGI CHAPEL, contains Raphael's famous *Sibyls*
[fre]sco commissioned by Agostino Chigi ▲ *360*; facing it is the
[PO]NZETTI CHAPEL decorated with fine frescoes by Baldassare
[Per]uzzi. To the left there is a passage leading to the sacristy
[and] then to the CLOISTER (1500–4). It was Bramante's first
[wor]k in Rome; he determined the proportions so as to ensure
[rem]arkable effects of light and shade. (Take Via della Pace to
[the] junction with Via Tor Millina – where there are two cafés
[that] are among the liveliest in Rome in the evening – then
[con]tinue into Via del Parione and turn right at the end.)

[PALAZZO] DEL GOVERNO VECCHIO. No.39 is the PALAZZO DEL
[GO]VERNO VECCHIO (Old Government Palace), built between
[147]3 and 1477, which became the official residence of the
[Go]vernor of Rome in 1624. It acquired its present name when
[the] government was moved to Palazzo Madama by Pope
[Ben]edict XIV (1740–58). The building is now in disrepair and
[loo]ks rather shabby but this street is full of charm, with
[num]erous antique and junk shops and an excellent wine bar.
[Tu]rn left into the Via della Chiesa Nuova.)

[CH]IESA NUOVA ★

[PIA]ZZA DELLA CHIESA NUOVA. Until the Corso Vittorio
[Em]anuele was built, this small piazza was the only open space
[in f]ront of the church. The fountain (called the FONTANA
[DEL]LA TERRINA because of its curious shape, resembling a
[cov]ered soup tureen) was originally in the center of the
[Ca]mpo de' Fiori ▲ *249*, on the spot where the statue of
[Gio]rdano Bruno now stands. The two adjacent façades
[ove]rlooking the piazza belong to Santa Maria in Vallicella –
[kno]wn as the Chiesa Nuova (the New Church) – and the
[Ora]torio dei Filippini (the Oratory of St Philip Neri).

The cloister of Santa
Maria dell'Anima
(above left); Piazza
della Pace (center);
and the Fontana della
Terrina.

**THE ORATORIAN
CONFEDERATION**
This was founded by
the Florentine saint
Philip Neri in 1561.
Gaining great
popularity in Rome, it
soon became the
figurehead of the
Counter-Reformation
and was officially

approved by Gregory
XIII in 1575. Its
priests gathered
together to meditate
and listen to sacred
music. They created a
new musical genre:
the oratorio.

[Gr]egory
[XII]I gave the
[chu]rch of Santa
[Ma]ria in Vallicella to St
[Phi]lip Neri's Oratorian
[Co]nfederation, who
[com]missioned its rebuilding in
[157]5. The reconstruction was
[ent]rusted first to Matteo da Città
[di C]astello and then to Martino
[Lo]nghi the Elder. Originally
[con]ceived as a single-naved church, it

A detail from the church of San

Salvatore in Lauro.

THE LIBRARY OF THE ORATORIO
Inside the Oratorio a majestic staircase designed by Borromini leads to the magnificent Biblioteca Vallicelliana, also the work of Borromini. Together with the Biblioteca Angelica (to the right of Sant'Agostino) it was one of the first libraries in Rome to be open to the public.

was widened and aisles were added. The façade by Fausto Rughesi was completed in 1605.

THE INTERIOR. At the time of the Counter-Reformation the interior was very plain, but it was subsequently given rich Baroque decorations. Federico Barocci provided *The Visitation* (fourth chapel on the left) and *The Presentation in the Temple* (in the left transept); and Caravaggio supplied a *Descent from the Cross* ▲ *230*, which was later moved to the Vatican and replaced by a copy (second chapel on the right). The choir has three masterpieces by the young Rubens; the one in the center is composed around an ancient image of the Virgin with miraculous properties. The splendid frescoes in the apse, the cupola and the nave were all painted by Pietro da Cortona between 1650 and 1665; the one in the nave "supported" by *putti* (cherubs) portrays a miracle that is supposed to have taken place during the construction of the church when, in response to St Philip Neri's prayers, the Virgin stopped some scaffolding from collapsing.

THE ORATORIO DEI FILIPPINI. In 1637 the Oratorians invited architects to tender plans for the construction of an oratory specifically for choral services. Borromini was selected, work went ahead fast and the building was consecrated three years later. The façade contrasts with the more conventional one of the Chiesa Nuova and is built in brick, in accordance with the wishes of the Oratorians. It is full of movement thanks to Borromini's use of curves: although its entire surface is slightly concave, the central bay is convex on the first floor, with a concave niche on the floor above. The pediment is all curvilinear, and the windows are ornate. Because the façade is unrelated to what is behind it, the central door is not the main entrance. (Take Via dei Filippini, alongside the oratory.)

AROUND THE CHIESA NUOVA. Borromini gave a finishing touch to his work by erecting a graceful clock tower (1647–9) in what came to be known as the Piazza del Orologio, at the back of the oratory.
(Continue into Via degli Orsini, then turn left into Via di Panico.)

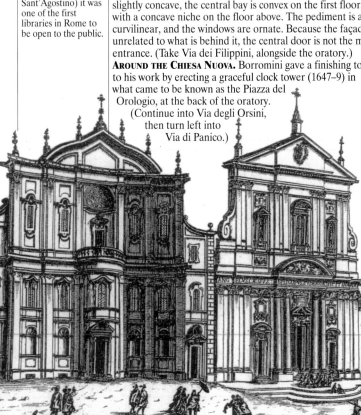

The turret of Borromini's clock tower in Piazza del Orologio is surmounted by a metal structure supporting a star that has 24 points.

e nearby PALAZZO TAVERNA was
lt in the 15th century on the ruins
the Orsini fortress, which
minated the whole area as far as
Tiber. The courtyard is an
azing mixture of styles – ranging
m Renaissance decorations and a
e-17th-century fountain to
edieval" façades rebuilt in the
h century.

A DEI CORONARI ★

tique shops are now scattered on
her side of this long, straight
eet where vendors of *corone*
saries) once vied for the custom
pilgrims approaching St Peter's.
N SALVATORE IN LAURO. After
ing destroyed by fire in 1591, this
dieval church was rebuilt to plans

Via dei Coronari.

Ottaviano Mascherino. Its neoclassical façade designed by
glielmetti in 1862 is adorned with a relief by Rinaldo
naldi, *The Flight of the Sacred House of Nazareth to Loreto*.
e nave, in the form of a Latin cross with travertine
rinthian columns standing clear of the walls, recalls
ladio's Venetian churches. In the third chapel on the right
ere is a remarkably fine *Adoration of the Magi*, one of Pietro
Cortona's first altar paintings (c. 1628). The transept and
choir were added by Ludovico Rusconi Sassi in the 18th
ntury. The ancient monastery beside the church has an
gant Renaissance cloister. The back wall of the refectory is
corated with a large fresco portraying *The Wedding at Cana*
Francesco Salviati. (Return to Via dei Coronari and
cover the charming little Piazzetta di San Simeone, with a
ntain by Giacomo Della Porta erected in 1589. Then turn
t into Via Lancellotti.)

LAZZO LANCELLOTTI. This palazzo was begun by Francesco
Volterra and finished by Carlo Maderno. The *portone*,
med with columns and dominated by a balcony, was
signed by Domenichino, who for the first and only time in
life tried his hand at architecture. Its sumptuous courtyard
ull of stuccos and marbles. The main rooms are decorated
h frescoes by Agostino Tassi and Guercino. (Proceed along
a della Maschera d'Oro.)

ROUND PIAZZA TOR DI SANGUIGNA

PALAZZO CESI. This
16th-century palazzo
(No. 21 Via della
Maschera d'Oro), which
now houses the Military
Supreme Court, has its
entrance at No. 2 Via
degli Acquasparta. In
1603, when it was the
home of Prince Federico
Cesi, the Accademia dei

ALBERGO E LOCANDA DELL'ORSO

THE "TORRE DELLA SCIMMIA"
A monkey is said to have carried off an infant but due to the Virgin's intervention deposited the child on the spot where an effigy of the Madonna now stands. Nathaniel Hawthorne used this story in *The Marble Faun* (1860).

"ISAIAH"
According to Vasari, Raphael was influenced by Michelangelo, whose work on the ceiling of the Sistine Chapel had been shown to him, secretly, by Bramante. The prophets on the other pillars were painted by Gagliardi in 1856.

Lincei ▲ 362 held their first meetings here and Galileo staye for a while as the prince's guest. Although its grisaille fresco decorations have disappeared, those of the Palazzo Milesi ar quite well preserved. (Go down Via Arco di Parma toward Via Tordinona. Now tucked away behind a high wall, this wa once a lively street where one of Rome's most famous theaters was situated from 1670 until 1889; Verdi's operas *Il Trovatore* and *Un Ballo in Maschera* had their premieres at th theater in 1853 and 1859. Return to Via degli Acquasparta t reach the Museo Napoleonico, in Piazza di Ponte Umberto ▶

THE MUSEO NAPOLEONICO. This 16th-century palazzo was bought in 1820 by the Primoli family. In 1909 Count Giuseppe Primoli, the son of Pietro Primoli and Charlotte Bonaparte, had it restored by Raffaele Ojetti, who adapted the building due to the upheavals caused by the construction of the Ponte Umberto I and the creation of Via Zanardelli. The rebuilt palazzo houses a museum devoted to the history of the First and Second Napoleonic Empires, the Primoli Foundation for the promotion of Franco-Italian cultural relations, and the Praz museum of decorative arts. It includes a library of French works and Pietro Primoli's collection of late 19th to early 20th-century photographs. (Take Via dei Soldati.)

PALAZZO ALTEMPS. Begun at the beginning of the 15th centu for Girolamo Riario, this palazzo was rebuilt two centuries later by Martino Longhi the Elder, when it was acquired by the Altemps family. Since 1997 it has acquired the Ludovisi collection, an annexe of the National Roman Museum ▲ 33 which contains numerous ancient Roman works of art collected by Cardinal Ludovisi in the 17th century.

VIA DELL'ORSO. During the Middle Ages and the Renaissance this area was renowned for its inns. The only one left today is the HOSTARIA DELL'ORSO, which counted Rabelais, Montaigne and Goethe among its guests.

SANT'ANTONIO DEI PORTOGHESI. Its façade, together with the neighboring Palazzo Scapucci and the Torre della Scimmia, form a picturesque group The national church of the Portuguese dates from the 15th century, though rebuilt two centuries later. The two superimposed orders of columns of the façade (1631 designed by Martino Longhi the Younger, are linked by male mythical figures rather than the usual simple volutes. Its interior is resplendent with gold, stucco decorations and marbles. The first chapel on the right contains the funerary monument of Alessandro de Souza, sculpted b Canova between 1806 and 180 Facing the church is the AUGUSTINIAN MONASTERY. (Cross Via dell'Orso and take Via dei Pianellari.)

THE "MADONNA OF
THE PILGRIMS" ★
In Caravaggio's
masterpiece painted
between 1603 and
1605 (also known as
*The Madonna of
Loreto*) the sculptural
beauty of the Virgin
is heightened by the
tenderness of her
silent dialogue with
her humble admirers.
The contrast between
Mary, who is
portrayed as a Roman
patrician, and the
poverty of the two
praying peasants is
particularly striking.

THE MADONNA DEL
PARTO ★
This splendid statue,
which stands against
the inner wall of the
façade of
Sant'Agostino, is by
Jacopo Sansovino
(1521). In 1982 *The
Virgin and Child with
St Anne* (1512) by his
mentor Andrea
Sansovino, from
whom he took his
name, was returned
to its original
position, in the niche
of the third pillar on
the right. This
sculpture was
particularly admired
by Vasari: "The older
woman's expression
betrays great natural
gaiety, the Virgin's
beauty is divine, and
the charming child
Jesus is of unmatched
perfection."

NT'AGOSTINO ★. This church, dedicated to St Augustine of
ppo, was completed in 1483; the architects were Giacomo
Pietrasanta and Sebastiano Fiorentino. Its monumental
aracter is reinforced by the broad flight of steps preceding
e dignified façade. The interior is divided into three naves
pillars; these once had niches, which were filled in by Luigi
nvitelli when the church was restored in 1760. To the left,
ove the third pillar, is one of Raphael's most famous
scoes, *The Prophet Isaiah* (1512); the first chapel contains
e of Caravaggio's masterpieces, *Madonna of the Pilgrims*.
e whole transept on the same side, dedicated by the
mphilj family to St Thomas of Villanova, was decorated by
ovanni Maria Baratta between 1660 and 1669. The first
apel to the left of the high altar is decorated with frescoes
Lanfranco; the second, which contains the tomb of St
ugustine's mother, St Monica, is attributed to Isaia da Pisa
5th century). In the center a fine Byzantine Madonna is set
o the high altar by Torriani, which is surmounted by two
gels (1628) based on designs by Bernini. Finally, the right
nsept contains a splendid reredos by Guercino.

NT'APOLLINARE. This group of buildings was given to the
suits by Gregory XIII in 1574. In it they installed the
rman College, or seminary. The church was rebuilt
tween 1742 and 1748 by Ferdinando
ga. He designed it to include two
ces of worship: a square narthex
estibule) for the general public and a
ve for the members of the college. The
th-century Madonna presiding over the
ple narthex was discovered in the 17th
ntury. The ceiling of the nave depicts
e glorification of St Apollinaris; the
h marble altar, copied from a painting
Graziani (1748), is dedicated to the

nt. In the third chapel on the right there is a fine statue of
Francis Xavier by Pierre Legros.

The façade of
Sant'Apollinare.

"Here and there one sees a fine orange ocher that has retained a warm glow, a serene density, beneath its slowly acquired patina."

Valéry Larbaud, *Aux couleurs de Rome*

The Quirinal

290   The Barberini District
292   Galleria Nazionale d'Arte
       Antica
294   Around Quattro Fontane
297   The Quirinal
298   Fontana di Trevi
301   Piazza San Silvestro
302   From the Via Veneto to the
       Porta Pinciana

☒ One day

◆ **E** A2-A3-B2-B3

**1. CHURCH OF SAN
SILVESTRO IN CAPITE
2. CHURCH OF SAN
CLAUDIO DE'
BORGOGNONI
3. CHURCH OF SANTA
MARIA IN VIA
4. INSTITUTO DELLA
CALCOGRAFIA
5. ACCADEMIA DI
SAN LUCA
6. FONTANA DI
TREVI ✪
7. GALLERIA SCIARRA
8. CHURCH OF
SAN MARCELLO AL
CORSO
9. PALAZZO
ODESCALCHI
10. BASILICAE DI
SANTI APOSTOLI
11. PALAZZO
COLONNA
12. CHURCH OF
SAN SILVESTRO
13. PALAZZO
DELLE QUIRINALE
14. CHURCH OF
SANT'ANDREA
AL QUIRINALE
15. CHURCH OF SAN
CARLO ALLE QUATTRO
FONTANE
16. PIAZZA DELLE
QUATTRO FONTANE
17. PALAZZO
BARBERINI
18. CHURCH OF
SAN BERNARDO ALLE
TERME
19. CHURCH OF
SANTA SUSANNA
20. ACQUA FELICE
21. CHURCH OF
SANTA MARIA DELLA
VITTORIA
22. CHURCH OF
SANTA MARIA DELLA
CONCEZIONE
23. MUNICIPAL
GALLERY OF MODERN
AND CONTEMPORARY
ART**

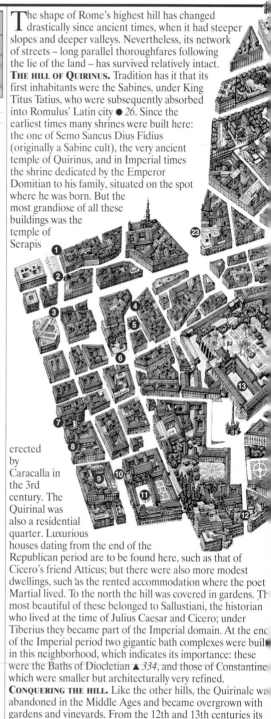

The shape of Rome's highest hill has changed drastically since ancient times, when it had steeper slopes and deeper valleys. Nevertheless, its network of streets – long parallel thoroughfares following the lie of the land – has survived relatively intact.
THE HILL OF QUIRINUS. Tradition has it that its first inhabitants were the Sabines, under King Titus Tatius, who were subsequently absorbed into Romulus' Latin city ● *26*. Since the earliest times many shrines were built here: the one of Semo Sancus Dius Fidius (originally a Sabine cult), the very ancient temple of Quirinus, and in Imperial times the shrine dedicated by the Emperor Domitian to his family, situated on the spot where he was born. But the most grandiose of all these buildings was the temple of Serapis erected by Caracalla in the 3rd century. The Quirinal was also a residential quarter. Luxurious houses dating from the end of the Republican period are to be found here, such as that of Cicero's friend Atticus; but there were also more modest dwellings, such as the rented accommodation where the poet Martial lived. To the north the hill was covered in gardens. Th most beautiful of these belonged to Sallustiani, the historian who lived at the time of Julius Caesar and Cicero; under Tiberius they became part of the Imperial domain. At the end of the Imperial period two gigantic bath complexes were built in this neighborhood, which indicates its importance: these were the Baths of Diocletian ▲ *334*, and those of Constantine which were smaller but architecturally very refined.
CONQUERING THE HILL. Like the other hills, the Quirinale wa abandoned in the Middle Ages and became overgrown with gardens and vineyards. From the 12th and 13th centuries its

QUIRINUS
Like Mars and
Jupiter this ancient
Sabine deity had
warlike attributes,
such as the lance, and
was for this reason
often mistaken for
Mars or Romulus.

THE DIOSCURI
Castor and Pollux,
the Dioscuri ("the
sons of Zeus") ▲ 142,
were the offspring of
Zeus and Leda, the
wife of Tyndareus.
They are also the
brothers of
Clytemnestra (wife of
Agamemnon) and of
the beautiful Helen
of Troy. Their
gigantic statues
originate from the
Baths of Constantine,
which were located
near the current
Piazza del Quirinale,
whose fountain they
now decorate.

slopes
began to
be
inhabited
again, starting
with the area
around Trajan's
Forum on one side and
the Rio de' Trevi on the
other. In the middle of the 16th
century its summit was still a
relatively remote spot with country
villas and cottages. It was at this time, in
1560, that Pius IV had the spacious Via Pia
constructed (later renamed Via del Quirinale and
then Via XX Settembre); and in 1585 Sixtus V had the
Via Felice (now Via Sistina-Via delle Quattro Fontane-Via
e'Pretis) put through to link the Pincio and Santa Maria
aggiore. In order to encourage building along the two
ads, the Quattro Fontane crossroads was created at their
tersection and one of the branches of the Aqua Felice
295, the aqueduct built by Claudius, was rehabilitated to
pply water primarily to this area. In the meantime, the
ilding of the Palazzo del Quirinale as the summer
sidence of the popes began. In the 17th century the
rberini established themselves to the northwest of
e Quattro Fontane crossroads, while the
utheastern slopes remained in the hands of the
suits. After the unification of Italy, in 1871
e summer palace of the popes became a royal
sidence; and later, after the proclamation of
e Republic, in 1947 it became the
esidential palace. From the end
the 19th century various
nistries were
tablished in the
cinity.

289

THE BARBERINI DISTRICT

Horse-drawn carriages parked in the Piazza Barberini in 1933.

"THE TRIUMPH OF DIVINE PROVIDENCE"
The ceiling of the principal salon of the Palazzo Barberini is thought to have the largest fresco ever painted for a non-ecclesiastical building. The three bees, the crest of the Barberini, are magnified to gigantic proportions.

MUNICIPAL GALLERY OF MODERN AND CONTEMPORARY ART.
A collection of works acquired since the Universal Exhibition of 1883 are held in the Carmelite convent, San Giuseppe a Capo le Case. The great names of 19th- and 20th-century Italian art are well represented here. Works dating from 1950 are exhibited in the ancient buildings of the Birra Peroni ▲ *381*.

PIAZZA BARBERINI. Today large modern buildings provide the background to this piazza, which is at the junction of the Via del Tritone and the Via Vittorio Veneto. The character of the area has totally changed since the 17th century and it is hard to imagine just how rural and picturesque a place it was then. Artists frequented its *osterie*, and many of them lived and worked in the area. Their presence lives on in the names of some of the streets: Via degli Artisti, Via dei Modelli, etc. As for the piazza itself, in 1625 its name changed from Piazza Grimani to Piazza Barberini when this great Roman family purchased a villa with grounds stretching from the square to Via Pia. The family of Urban VIII contributed relatively little to the area, apart from the Fontana del Tritone (sculpted for the pontiff by Bernini) and nearby, at the foot of the Via Veneto, the Fontana delle Api (the Bee Fountain) also by Bernini. (Continue up the Via Veneto.)

SANTA MARIA DELLA CONCEZIONE. The Barberini were, however, rather ostentatious in the way they put their mark

on this church, which they wished to have under their protection. When Antonio Barberini, a Capuchin friar and Urban VIII's younger brother, became cardinal, he decided to rebuild the church of his Order; the Pope granted him a subsidy. From then on, many of the great figures of the time, including the Emperor Ferdinand II, sought to sponsor the decoration of the side chapels – so much so that the Capuchins had to make repeated appeals or their church not to be too richly decorated. While the ope seized this opportunity to refuse all help, it did not revent him and his brother from calling upon some of he greatest painters of the time for the altar paintings. he crypt is definitely worth a visit: it is decorated, in aroque taste, with the bones of some four thousand apuchin friars. (Cross Piazza Barberini and take the ia delle Quattro Fontane.)

ALAZZO BARBERINI. The overall plan was entrusted to the rchitect Carlo Maderno, who had to incorporate a palace hat stood on the land bought by the Barberini in 1625. asting aside the traditional scheme for Roman palaces (built around a square courtyard), he finally adopted that of the villa (a central edifice flanked by two wings). The work, which began in 1627, was continued after Maderno's death in 1629 by Bernini, who retained his predecessor's principal assistant, Francesco Borromini. Bernini designed the façade on the garden side of the building, including the main entrance, and the square staircase in the left wing, which leads to the gallery. Borromini was responsible for the oval staircase in the right wing, as well as the *trompe l'oeil* windows on the second floor ● 87. Inside, most of the rooms of the *piano nobile* have painted ceilings – notably by Andrea Camassei and Andrea Sacchi, including his *Divine Wisdom*, painted between 1629 and 1633. However, the most remarkable of all is the ceiling in the principal salon, painted between 1633 and 1639 by Pietro da Cortona. Its allegorical theme was provided by Francesco Bracciolini, a protégé of Urban VIII and his brother's secretary. In the center Divine Providence triumphs over Time and assigns the Barberini emblem to Immortality, while the lateral scenes portray the virtues of Urban VIII and the achievements of his pontificate. Nowhere else in Rome does a painting so shamelessly exalt a pope and his family.

"ST MICHAEL TRAMPLING ON THE DEVIL"
Great painters of the Bologna school such as Guido Reni, whose famous *St Michael Trampling on the Devil* (first chapel on the right) is pictured here, Lanfranco (second chapel on the right) and Domenichino (third chapel) made their contribution to the Capuchin church, as did painters of the younger generation like Pietro da Cortona (first chapel on the right) and Andrea Sacchi (fifth chapel on the right).

THE CRYPT OF THE CAPUCHIN CHURCH
It took no fewer than three hundred journeys with full cartloads to gather the bones that adorn the crypt of Santa Maria della Concezione.

The Barberini family emblem.

To the very rare items remaining from the Barberini collection have been added works from other private collections and State acquisitions and legacies. Thus the museum is able to show paintings by such Italian masters as Filippo Lippi, Lorenzo Lotto, Andrea del Sarto, Perugino, Bronzino and Caravaggio together with works by foreign artists like Quentin Metsys, Holbein and Nicholas Poussin.

Since it became the property of the State in 1949, the Palazzo Barberini has housed the Galleria Nazionale di Arte Antica, created at the end of the 19th century. This museum, which is one of the most important in Rome, takes up practically the whole of the palace's piano nobile. In these rooms one finds works by many of the great Italian and foreign painters of the 13th to the 18th century. The floor above, which was redecorated between 1750 and 1770, offers a fine setting for the collection of 18th-century paintings.

"LA FORNARINA"
This painting, long considered to be the most precious work in the Barberini collection, was purchased by the State when the collection was dispersed. It is commonly thought to be a portrait of La Fornarina, the mistress with whom Raphael was said by Vasari to have indulged in the pleasures of love to such an extent that it caused his death. However, the attribution to Raphael is now disputed.

Reaching Rome around 1591 Caravaggio (1573–1610) worked under the patronage of Cardinal del Monte. He left Rome in 1606.

"Portrait of Stefano Colonna"
By Agnolo di Cosimo, known as "Il Bronzino"
(1503–72). The column on the left is a reference
to Colonna's name; its base bears the date 1546,
the year in which the portrait was painted.

"Madonna and Child"
his work by Filippo Lippi is an elaborate
xercise in perspective. It dates from 1437,
a period when Lippi was under Flemish
influence.

**UDITH BEHEADING
OLOFERNES"** is painting by ravaggio belongs the period of his transition from naturalism (when his compositions were simple and his tones lighter) to his later manner, characterized by violent contrasts and chiaroscuro.

293

QUATTRO FONTANE
The crossroads seen from two different viewpoints. The statues of the 16th-century fountains represent the Nile and the Tiber (on the north side) and Juno and Diana (on the south side). From here one can see the Porta Pia as well as the obelisk in Piazza

della Trinità dei Monti ▲ *314* and those on the Quirinal and the Esquiline.

"THE ECSTASY OF ST TERESA OF AVILA"
● *84* (center)
"Bernini, who in St Peter's seemed to me ridiculous, has in this work found a modern form of sculpture, entirely based on expression. To achieve it, he has allowed daylight to suffuse this pale, delicate face with a luminosity that is like an inner flame – so that, through the transfigured, palpitating marble, we see the soul flooded with joy and rapture, shining like a lamp."
Hyppolite Taine,
Voyage en Italie

AROUND QUATTRO FONTANE

QUATTRO FONTANE. This crossroads – designed toward the end of the 16th century at the intersection of the new streets put through under Pius IV and Sixtus V (then called Via Pia and Via Felice) – was constructed with shorn-off corners so to open up the view. In each of the corners a fountain with a statue was built, to be supplied with water from the recently rehabilitated Aqua Felice aqueduct ▲ *295*. (Follow the Via XX Settembre as far as Piazza San Bernardo.)

SANTA SUSANNA. In 1589 a shrine dating from the 4th century was turned into a parish church to cater to the newly developed area on the top of the Quirinal hill. It was refurbished for this purpose by Carlo Maderno, who added the choir, the main altar, the confessio, the sculpted wood ceilings and the original façade. This church represents an important step in the development of a new architectural language that was to mark the 17th century: while the walls remain rectilinear, the portal is given relief by being framed in closely grouped columns. Today Santa Susanna is the parish church of American Catholics in Rome.

SANTA MARIA DELLA VITTORIA. This church is also the work of Carlo Maderno, except for the façade built a few years later by Giambattista Soria, who designed it to complement that of Santa Susanna. The originally very sober interior was enriched during the 17th and 18th centuries with frescoes, stuccos, jasper and marble. It contains some important works, such as the *Holy Trinity* (third chapel on the left), and three paintings by Domenichino (second chapel on the right). But the most striking is the CORNARO CHAPEL, designed and executed by Bernini in 1646. Architecture,

inting and sculpture play equal parts in enhancing the
amatic effect and illustrate the master's fundamental
inciple: the fusion of the arts. The central theme is St
resa's vision: "God let me see an angel in bodily form on
y left … He was not tall, but he was very beautiful; his
owing face showed that he belonged to the order of the
avenly hierarchy in which the angels seem to be
candescent … In his left hand he held a gold javelin, the
on point of which gave off a flame. He
ddenly pierced my heart to its deepest
ers … Then he left me encumbered
th the love of God. The pain was so
vid that it made me groan, but the
eetness that came with it was so great
at I would not have wanted the pain
moved…." The members of the
ornaro family are portrayed on the side
alls on either side of the altar. The
rved antependium conceals a window

THE FONTANA DEL MOSÈ
This fountain has
three large niches
separated by
columns. The
sculptural ensemble
develops the theme of
the Israelites in the

at Bernini made to bathe the ecstatic scene in diffused light.
ONTANA DEL MOSÈ. The fountain facing the church was built
 Domenico Fontana at the request of Sixtus V. The Pope
d inherited Gregory XIII's project and persevered in having
e Claudian aqueduct restored to bring water from the
ban hills to the highest parts of the city. Thanks to these
orks (1585–9), also entrusted to Domenico Fontana, an
tra five million gallons of water were made available to the
habitants of Rome. The monumental fountain in front of

wilderness, led by
Moses (whose
gigantic figure by
Prospero da Brescia
stands in the center
niche) and Joshua.

Santa Maria della Vittoria was its
point of arrival; the water was then
distributed to the other fountains
on the Quirinal and toward the
Campidoglio. Both the aqueduct
and the fountain were called Felice,
the Christian name of the Pope.

SAN BERNARDO ALLE TERME. This
church was built between 1598
and 1600 on the site of one of
the rotundas dispersed along
the outer walls of the Baths of
Diocletian. Its cupola, inspired by
the Pantheon's ● 70, ▲ 265, was
covered with plaster moldings
during the 19th century.

**SAN CARLO ALLE QUATTRO
FONTANE.** This church and its
neighbor, Sant'Andrea al
Quirinale, magnificently
illustrate the two main schools
of Roman baroque. In 1634
Borromini received what was
probably his first commission from the
Spanish discalced Trinitarians, who
wanted a monastery, a cloister and a
church. By means of ingenious planning, the
architect resolved the problems posed by the
confined area and the irregular shape of the
land. He erected a building said to be small
enough to fit inside one of the pillars supporting

**THE CUPOLA OF
SAN BERNARDO
ALLE TERME** ▲ 262
The coffers of this
cupola, which has a
diameter of 50 feet,
diminish in size
toward the center,
where there is a large
circular window.

SAN CARLO ALLE QUATTRO FONTANE
The lines of the central bay are inverted in the two registers of the façade. From being convex in the lower register, above the curving cornice, they become concave like the lateral bays. The façade is crowned by a large oval medallion supported by two angels, which breaks the horizontal line of the entablature.

the dome of St Peter's. The façade, which was completed in 1685, long after the architect's death, relies on the interplay of concave and convex lines to give a monumental character to the structure as a whole. The interior, which is oval in shape and decorated with white stuccos, is composed of three distinct superimposed zones. At the base, powerful columns punctuate the undulations of the walls, which are a succession of curves and countercurves; above this there is a link zone, surmounted finally by an elliptical dome ● *81* resting on a strong ring whose deep coffers, by diminishing in size toward the summit, accentuate the illusion of height. Light penetrates abundantly through the ample lantern and through skylights in some of the coffers. As a result, the dome seems to be floating weightlessly above the heavy shapes of the area in which visitors can move about.

SANT'ANDREA AL QUIRINALE ● *79*. In 1658 Bernini was asked to build a church for the novices of the Society of Jesus. He too, being faced with a restricted area, chose an elliptical shape and placed the main altar and the entrance on the shortest diameter. On the front of the building two quarter circles of wall prolong and enhance the narrow façade (pictured above, on the right). Inside the building the eye surveys an uninterrupted series of gigantic pilasters until it comes to rest on the recess of the altar, which is a concave echo of the portal's projection. The dark multicolored marbles of the church contrast with the white-and-gilt moldings of the cupola ● *81*. The light, which penetrates through the windows placed between the ribs of the dome and through the lantern, illuminates the central space evenly but leaves the side chapels in shadow. It is said that this great river of Borromini considered this to be his most successful work and, as he grew old, found pleasure in coming to sit and contemplate it. Through the sacristy one reaches the upper floor of the convent where St Stanislas Kotska lived (a Pole who came to Rome as a Jesuit novice and had a vision of the Virgin Mary). A statue of the saint on his deathbed by Pierre Legros (1703) provides a remarkable example of Baroque illusionism in its use of colored marbles.

THE CUPOLA OF SAN CARLO ALLE QUATTRO FONTANE ● *81*
The coffering takes the form of alternating crosses, octagons and hexagons. Yet this busy pattern retains geometric purity and achieves a certain beehive effect.

The Piazza del Quirinale painted by Van Wittel.

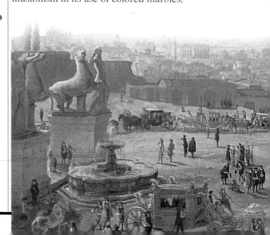

Piazza del Quirinale
seen from the air.

THE QUIRINAL

PIAZZA DEL QUIRINALE. The piazza was built over several centuries. In the 16th century Sixtus V had the two statues of the Dioscuri and their horses erected in the center – which is why the square is also known as Piazza Montecavallo – moving them from the 4th-century Baths of Constantine. In the early 17th century the square was leveled. In 1783 Pius VI added the obelisk, brought from the Mausoleum of Augustus ▲ *143*; and in 1813 the fountain was completed with the addition of the basin, which came from near the temple of the Dioscuri in the Forum, where it had been used as a drinking trough for cattle. With its various components, the fountain illustrates an essential feature of Roman art: the reuse of ancient materials or architectural elements in new constructions. As a finishing touch, in 1886 the balustrade on the west side of the piazza was added, from which there is a magnificent view over the city, stretched out at the bottom of the hill with St Peter's in the distance.

PALAZZO DEL QUIRINALE. Originally the popes' summer residence, then a papal palace, this building was a royal palace between 1870 and 1944. When the Republic was proclaimed it became the official residence of the President. Construction began in the late 16th century under Gregory XIII and was completed under Clement XII (1730–40); many Roman architects of the Counter-Reformation and Baroque period made some contribution to it, and Bernini built the Loggia of the Benedictions over the main entrance. The palace was gradually surrounded by annexes, among them the PALAZZO DELLA CONSULTA, on the north side of the piazza. Built between 1732 and 1734 by Ferdinando Fuga, it now houses Italy's constitutional court. (Take Via XXIV Maggio.)

THE STABLES The stables were built on the site of the Temple of Serapis by Alessandro Specchi and completed by Ferdinando Fuga in the late 18th century. Since their recent restoration, they have been used for temporary exhibitions. (Take Via XXIV Maggio.)

The Corazzieri (presidential guards) in the hall of honor of the Palazzo del Quirinale

Pictured on the left is the elegant helicoidal staircase designed by Ottaviano Mascherino for Gregory XIII. With its pairs of polished-marble columns, it is one of the finest architectural elements in the Palazzo del Quirinale.

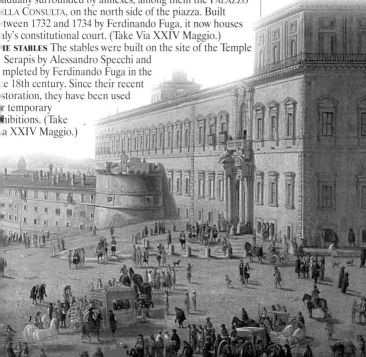

The aqueduct built by Agrippa in 19 BC to sup
water for his baths was given the name Aqua
Virgo, as the location of the spring feeding it ▼
supposed to have been revealed to some Rom
soldiers by a virgin. This bas-relief on the Fon
di Trevi illustrates the legend.

VIA XXIV MAGGIO. Immediately on the
left is the side entrance of the Palazzo Rospiglio
built between 1611 and 1616 for Cardinal Scipion
Borghese. Its gardens boast the Casino Pallavicini
(open to the public the first day of each month), wh
has a famous fresco by Guido Reni, *Aurora* (1614). O
the other side of the street an imposing balustrade ma
the entrance to the gardens of the Palazzo Colonna ▲ 2
Michelangelo is reputed to have frequented them in orde
to meet his great friend the poetess Vittoria Colonna, who
last breath he witnessed. One can still see there a few
remains of Caracalla's temple of Serapis.

SAN SILVESTRO AL QUIRINALE. This richly decorate
church (1524) is concealed behind a 19th-century
façade. (Return toward the Piazza del Quirinale and
down the Via della Dataria, designed by Paul V as the
official access to the papal residence, then take the
second street on the right, Via San Vicenzo.)

FONTANA DI TREVI

THE WISHING FOUNTAIN. At the bottom of the stree
backed by the façade of the Palazzo Poli, which
houses the temporary exhibitions and collections o
the Istituto Nazionale per la Grafica, looms the mo
stunning of the fountains of Rome: the central figu
the Ocean (by Pietro Bracci) dominates sea horses
guided by Tritons, while in the niches on either side
are the figures of Abundance and Health, by Filipp
della Valle. Bernini was originally commissioned by
Urban VIII to construct a monumental fountain, b
the project was abandoned after the Pope's death. Almost a
century later, Nicola Salvi built this ensemble on the site of
one of Rome's earliest fountains designed to receive the wa
of the Aqua Virgo. The bliss of returning to the Eternal Ci
is guaranteed to all foreigners who, with their back turned,
throw a coin over their shoulder into the fountain. Also in
square is the church of Santi Vincenzo e Anastasio. Cardin
Mazarin, who financed the work, commissioned the ornate
Baroque façade (1641–50) from Martino Longhi the Youn
RIONE TREVI. The neighborhood around the fountain
provides one of the most picturesque parts of Rome. This
area, once densely populated, remained of the liveliest
sections of the city throughout the Middle Ages and the
Renaissance. In the 16th century its narrow streets were fill
with craftsmen's workshops which attracted many foreigne
and some craftsmen chose to live here. Later, demolition
works did not detract from its inherent charm. Whether yo
take the Via della Panetteria or the Via del Lavatore, whic
has an open market every morning, you will find that this is
still a lively neighborhood. (Take the
Via della Stamperia to the right of
the fountain.)
ACCADEMIA NAZIONALE DI SAN LUCA.
In 1934 this academy, founded in
1577, moved into the ancient
building once known as Palazzo
Vaini, which was renamed the
Palazzo Carpegna in the 17th

**THE FONTANA DI TREVI
AND THE WATERS OF
FORTUNE** ✪
In a scene of Fellini's
La Dolce Vita the
voluptuous Anita
Ekberg bathes in
the Fontana di Trevi
before Mastroianni's
astonished gaze.
This has become an
unforgettable moment
in Italian cinema.
You may not be able
to do the same – the
fountains of Rome are
not public baths! – but
with your back to the
powerful Neptune, toss
a small coin into the
water; this, so it is said,
will guarantee your
return to the Eternal
City. But do not even
think of diving in after
the coins that glisten
from the bottom of the
fountain: they belong to
the city council, which
hands out this manna
(around 100 € per
week) to the municipal
street cleaners.

Aurora by Guido Reni, of which the 18th-century French President de Brosses said: "Nothing is better conceived, so graceful, so light, nor better drawn; it is an 'incanto' (a delight)."

century when it was modified by Borromini. The original purpose of this institution, which brought together famous painters, was to provide an apprenticeship and theoretical training for young painters so as to control the production and distribution of art in keeping with the strict rules of the Counter-Reformation. In the 17th century it was truly dictatorial: no artist could have a studio in Rome without its authorization. Its picture gallery, containing collections made up of gifts from its members and from various popes, includes works by Raphael, Titian, Bronzino, Poussin and Panini.

CALCOGRAFIA NAZIONALE (6 Via della Stamperia). This museum of engravings has one of the best collections of its kind in the world – comprising more than 23,000 items, including 16th-century plates by De Rossi, and a complete set of Piranesi's engravings. (Walk back along the Via San Vincenzo. Then take its continuation, the Via dei Lucchesi, to Piazza della Pilotta – from the Spanish *pelota*, a ball, but today it is the realm of study rather than ball games. Here you will find two great Jesuit institutions: the BIBLICUM, with its remarkable orientalist library, and the GREGORIANA, the largest Catholic university in Rome. Take Via della Pilotta.)

PALAZZO COLONNA AND ITS GALLERY. You will emerge behind the Palazzo Colonna, which is linked to its terraced gardens by four bridges over the road. (The entrance is in Piazza dei Santi Apostoli, on the far side of the palace from Via della Pilotta.) Originally

ACCADEMIA NAZIONALE DI SAN LUCA. The name originates in the Christian tradition that attributes the talent of painting to St Luke.

St Luke Painting the Virgin Mary by Raphael.

The Fontana di Trevi.

THE GREAT HALL OF THE PALAZZO COLONNA
Its sumptuous decoration was designed by
Antonio del Grande in the mid 17th century
and completed under the supervision of
Girolamo Fontana after del Grande's death.

Peasant Eating Beans
by Annibale Carracci
(1560–1609), one of
the paintings in the
Galleria Colonna.

The Basilica of Santi
Apostoli.

built between 1417 and 1431
by Pope Martin V, a member
of the Colonna family, the
building was restructured
several times before the 18th
century. Worthy of note is the
Salone della Colonna Bellica:
after the red column it
contains, the family emblem,
its ceiling is decorated with a
fresco glorifying Marcantonio
Colonna, the commander of
the papal fleet at the battle of
Lepanto (1571). The picture
gallery contains a magnificent
collection, largely put
together by Lorenzo Onofrio Colonna under the guidance of
the painter Carlo Maratta. In the 19th century it was enlarged
with the acquisition of paintings by primitives and Renaissance
masters. Both the palace and the gallery still belong to this
ancient Roman family. (Return to Piazza dei Santi Apostoli,
where the Waxwork Museum can be found.)

BASILICA DEI SANTI APOSTOLI. To avoid the risk of it falling
into ruins, despite restoration work carried out in the
Renaissance, the original 6th-century basilica was almost
completely rebuilt between 1701 and 1714 by Carlo Fontana
and his son Francesco. It was then given a neoclassical façade
designed by Valadier in 1827. The portico at the front dates
from the 15th century. This work by Baccio Pontelli (1450–9)
was enclosed with railings in the 17th century by Carlo
Rainaldi, who also added the balustrade and the statues of
the apostles. The interior is decorated with gilt plasterwork,
stuccos and frescoes in the taste of 18th-century Rome. On
the vault Christ is portrayed receiving the saints of the
Franciscan Order (Baciccia, 1707). At the very end of the left

ve stands the tomb of Clement
IV, the first monument Canova
ulpted in Rome (1789).

ALAZZO ODESCALCHI (facing the
asilica dei Santi Apostoli). The
çade, designed by Bernini in 1664
r Alexander VII's nephew Flavio
nigi, was a model for a number of
aroque palaces. Bernini broke with
e tradition of building palace
çades without vertical articulation:
ile the ground floor serves as a foundation, on the upper
ories gigantic pilasters divide the seven bays of the central
dy of the building, which is framed by two wings set further
ck. The balance of this façade was destroyed when in 1745,
the request of the owner, Prince Odescalchi, Nicola Salvi
larged the palace, doubling the width of the central body
d building a second door for the sake of symmetry. A small
tour can be made up a narrow alleyway to the Chapel of the
adonna del Archetto, built by Virginio Vespignani. In the
me street is one of Rome's few well-known *birrerie* (beer
llars). (Return to the Via dei Santi Apostoli and proceed to
e Corso.)

N MARCELLO AL CORSO. Although founded in the 4th
ntury, this church was rebuilt after a fire in 1519. It was
signed by Jacopo Sansovino and has a Baroque façade by
rlo Fontana (1682–86). Parts of the interior, including the
ffered ceiling, go back to the 16th century. The tombs of
rdinal Giovanni Michiel and Bishop Antonio Orso, to the
t of the entrance, are the work of Jacopo Sansovino. The
rd, fourth and fifth chapels on the left are decorated with
scoes by Francesco Salviati, Perin del Vaga and Federico
ccaro respectively. The fourth chapel on the right contains
5th-century crucifix which used to be carried in penitential
ocessions. (On leaving the church, take the first street on
e right, Via dell'Umiltà.)

LLERIA SCIARRA ● 90 . A fine example of Roman
ecticism, this gallery , which links Via Minghetti and Via
ll'Umiltà, was built in 1885–6 by Giulio De Angelis. (Go
ough the gallery.)

PIAZZA SAN SILVESTRO

Three churches are in or close to this piazza,
which has changed considerably over the past
two centuries.

SANTA MARIA IN VIA. The first, which
stands on the corner of Via del Tritone,
belongs to the Servite Order. It was
rebuilt by Francesco da Volterra in the late 16th
century on the site of a medieval shrine, to plans
by Giacomo Della Porta. The upper section of
the façade is attributed to Carlo Rainaldi
(1670). Inside, the third chapel on the right has
an *Annunciation* by Cavaliere d'Arpino (1596).

SAN ANDREA E CLAUDIO DEI BORGOGNONI.
This church, rebuilt by Antoine Derizet
between 1728 and 1729, had been the church of
the Burgundians of the Franche-Comté.

GALLERIA SCIARRA
This modern (late
19th century)
structure has very
pretty Pompeian-style
decorations painted
by Giuseppe Cellini.
Among other
inscriptions, on the
right is this verse
from Virgil's fourth
Eclogue: *Incipe, parve
puer, risu cognoscere
matrem* ("Little boy,
learn to greet your
mother with a
smile").

The Via della Pilotta,
which leads to the
gardens of Palazzo
Colonna.

**THE MIRACLE OF
SANTA MARIA IN VIA**
A miracle is said to
be at the origin of this
church's foundation.
An image of the
Virgin painted on a
tile fell into a well,
which overflowed, so
that the image
emerged from the
well. Many faithful
still come here to
drink the well's water
and venerate the
"Madonna del Pozzo"
(the Madonna of the
Well).

SAN SILVESTRO IN CAPITE
This church was constructed on the ruins of the Temple of the Sun built by Aurelian. The name "in Capite" refers to the head of St John the Baptist, which has been preserved here as a relic for centuries.

SAN SILVESTRO IN CAPITE. Both the atrium in front of the church and the bell tower date from the 13th century, but the main part of the building was begun in the 16th century by Francesco da Volterra and finished by Carlo Maderno. The façade was erected by Domenico de Rossi who, with his brother Mattia, redecorated the interior at the end of the 17th century. Don't omit to look at the fresco in the nave by Giacinto Brandi (1623–91), as well as the Pomarancio frescoes in the transept crossing (1605). In 1890 Pope Leo XIII gave San Silvestro in Capite to the English Catholics in Rome as their parish church. The former convent buildings next to it now house Rome's central post office.

FROM THE VIA VENETO TO THE PORTA PINCIANA

The Via Vittorio Veneto has been used as a set for numerous films, and especially in the 1960's show-business personalities used to frequent the terraces of its famous bars, cafés and luxury hotels. Going up the Via Veneto, you enter the Ludovisi neighborhood, named after the beautiful villa that once stood here; its grounds were sold and divided into building lots in the 1880's. Leaving to your right the former Ministry of Corporations (now the Ministry of Industry and Trade) – built in 1932, during the Fascist period by Marcello Piacentini and Giuseppe Vaccaro – you will pass in front of the Banca Nazionale del Lavoro, also built by Piacentini (1036), and will then come to the Palazzo Boncompagni-Piombino (1886–90), which is now the American Embassy. It is also known as the Palazzo Margherita, because it became the residence of Queen Margherita after the assassination of Umberto I in 1900. This building was erected between 1886 and

Paparazzo, the photographer in Fellini's *La Dolce Vita* (played by Walter Santesso), in a night of follies on the Via Veneto.

1890, its architect, Gaetano Koch was inspired by the Palazzo Farnese. If you walk back down the Via Veneto then take Via Bissolati, you will come to Largo Santa Susanna and the Geological Museum built by Raffaele Canevari in 1873. The façade shows the influence of the iron-and-glass construction of the Industrial Revolution.

Il Tridente

306 Piazza del Popolo

308 Via del Corso

309 The Mausoleum of Augustus

310 The Ara Pacis Augustae

313 Piazza di Spagna

314 Trinità dei Monti

315 The Villa Medici

316 The Pincio

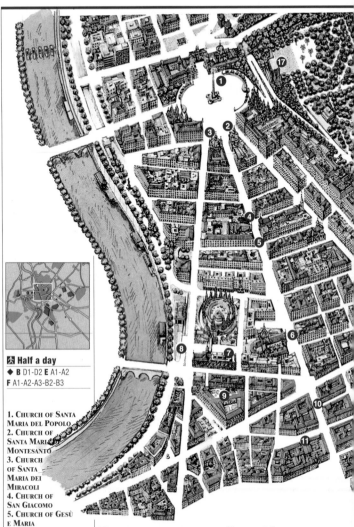

🕐 **Half a day**
◆ **B** D1-D2 **E** A1-A2
F A1-A2-A3-B2-B3

1. CHURCH OF SANTA
MARIA DEL POPOLO
2. CHURCH OF
SANTA MARIA DI
MONTESANTO
3. CHURCH
OF SANTA
MARIA DEI
MIRACOLI
4. CHURCH OF
SAN GIACOMO
5. CHURCH OF GESÙ
E MARIA
6. CHURCH OF SANTI
AMBROGIO E CARLO
AL CORSO
7. MAUSOLEUM OF
AUGUSTUS
8. ARA PACIS AUGUSTAE
9. PALAZZO BORGHESE
10. PALAZZO RUSPOLI
11. CHURCH OF SAN
LORENZO IN LUCINA
12. PIAZZA DI SPAGNA
13. PALAZZO DI
PROPAGANDA FIDE
14. CHURCH OF
SANT'ANDREA DELLE
FRATTE
15. TRINITÀ DEI
MONTI ✪
16. VILLA MEDICI
17. THE PINCIO

THE MODERNIZATION OF CAMPO MARZIO

The cosmopolitan atmosphere of modern Rome is evident
throughout most of this quarter, which is pleasant for
strolling, a shopper's paradise and full of luxury hotels. Yet
until the middle of the 20th century, it was still the scene of
such typically Roman events as the races of barb horses dow
the Via del Corso and the Easter Monday fireworks on the
Pincio. Begun in 1851 and continued until just after the end
World War II, these firework displays marked the anniversa
of the signing of the Statuto Albertini ▲ *100*. In fact, after th
French occupation the neighborhood underwent radical
changes for a period of 150 years. The Piazza del Popolo
(1809–14) and the gardens of the Pincio (1818) were the firs
to be transformed. Then, as the area around Piazza di Spagn
was attracting an increasing number of tourists, more hotels

ere built there. Old houses were either replaced by new buildings, or restructured. By the time of Pius IX (1846–78) any of the ancient buildings in the area had been converted including Palazzo Lepri in Via Condotti and Palazzo Nuñez orlonia in Via Bocca di Leone), and new ones such as the otel Inghilterra (1842) had gone up. In the mid 19th entury, Pietro Camporese built the Academy of Fine Arts on e site of the Palazzo Camerale in Via di Ripetta. The area had always been on the route of pilgrims and other visitors coming into Rome along the Via Flaminia. The construction of Stazione Termini ▲ *338* in the 1860's prompted the humbler hoteliers (*locandieri*) to move to the Esquiline; the Campo Marzio became the preserve of the more affluent. In addition, the government established there the headquarters of institutions such as the Ministry of Public Works and the new Parliament in Piazza Montecitorio ▲ *269*; and in 1878 Malvezzi adapted a former convent in Piazza San Silvestro to house the Postal Ministry. The imposing architecture of the Galleria Colonna ▲ *269* and the Rinascente ▲ *267* department store add to the impression of architectural modernity. The Ponte Cavour was built to link the Campo Marzio with the new residential area of Prati ▲ *236* on the opposite bank – demolishing in the process the Porto di Ripetta that occupied the site where the Marine Ministry now stands. Another bridge, the Ponte Margherita, was also built. This led to odification of the area between the Corso and the Via di ipetta. Other main streets, such as Via Tomacelli and Largo oldoni, were widened. Finally, in 1934, the revamping of the Mausoleum of Augustus totally transformed the area around ; to perpetuate the ethos of Imperial Rome, the Fascist egime decided to glorify the memory of Augustus.

"What a strange thing the natural history of Rome is, in its modern growth!… The dream of Rome the Capital [that has existed] since 1860. And everything has been sacrificed to this necessary but fatal patriotic idea. The struggle against nature, the town that people wanted to restore in spite of the physical obstacles. The lead weight of Antiquity…. And the surge of enthusiasm in the pride of its conception. Intoxication, followed by total collapse when the truth became apparent: an enormous town built for a population that does not exist, the capital of dreams wrecked by the real town with its lack of communications, its deadly belt of sterile land, its dead river. Pride has dreamed of things that reality cannot achieve. What an astonishing and interesting case, what a page in the natural history of a town!" Zola, *Rome*

The churches of Santa Maria dei Miracoli and Santa Maria di Montesanto guarding the entrance to the Via del Corso.

Bust of Giuseppe
Valadier (1762–1839).

A ROYAL ARRIVAL
In 1655 Rome gave a
triumphal welcome to
Queen Christina of
Sweden, whose
conversion to
Catholicism was,
according to Pope
Alexander VII, the
"Church's revenge for
the humiliation of
Westphalia". Her
entry into the city was
celebrated with
extraordinary
splendor, including
illuminations and the
enhancement of the
Porta del Popolo. The
Queen rode her horse
down the Corso
before proceeding to
St Peter's.

PIAZZA DEL POPOLO

PORTA DEL POPOLO. This triumphal arch offers a theatrical
entrance to the city; one of the gateways in the Aurelian Wall
it corresponds to the ancient Porta Flaminia. The inscription
engraved on the attic (upper section) is Rome's welcoming
greeting to visitors: *Felici faustoque ingressui MDCLV* ("For a
happy and blessed entrance, 1655"). It was inscribed for the
visit of Queen Christina of Sweden ▲ *362*, and Bernini was
commissioned to design a new inner façade to give the queen
an appropriate welcome. At the center of the piazza stands
the Egyptian obelisk of Ramses II, which Sixtus V got
Domenico Fontana to move from the Circus Maximus ▲ *177*
in 1589. The fountains and lions were added by Valadier in
1823, during the pontificate of Leo XII.

VALADIER'S DESIGN. To cope with the influx of pilgrims and
other travelers, Giuseppe Valadier was commissioned by the
Prefect of Tournon, who represented France during the
Napoleonic occupation, to review the layout of the piazza.
This work, which was the first of its kind in Rome not to rely
on convicts for labor, was executed between 1816 and 1824.
The architect's plans had to take into account the existing
buildings, such as the churches of Santa Maria del Popolo,
Santa Maria di Montesanto (1662–79) and Santa Maria dei
Miracoli (1675–81), and also, of course, the obelisk, the Porta
Flaminia and the Via del Corso. He built the Pincio ramp as a
solution to the problem of the difference of level between the
piazza and the hill. To appreciate the character of the piazza,
visit one of the two famous rival cafés in the square, Rosati
and Canova.

SANTA MARIA DEL POPOLO ★, ● *79*. Silhouetted against the
pines of the Pincio, the church nestles under the Aurelian
Wall (nicknamed the *Muro Torto*, or "twisting wall", because
of its tortuous outline). The Renaissance façade of the church
rises above a flight of steps. After its reconstruction by Baccio
Pontelli and Andrea Bregno under Sixtus IV
in the 15th century, the church
was embellished by
Rome's leading

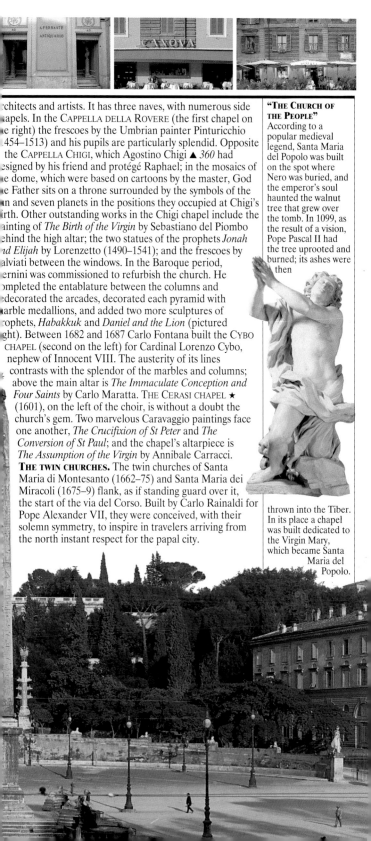

chitects and artists. It has three naves, with numerous side apels. In the CAPPELLA DELLA ROVERE (the first chapel on e right) the frescoes by the Umbrian painter Pinturicchio 454–1513) and his pupils are particularly splendid. Opposite the CAPPELLA CHIGI, which Agostino Chigi ▲ *360* had esigned by his friend and protégé Raphael; in the mosaics of e dome, which were based on cartoons by the master, God e Father sits on a throne surrounded by the symbols of the un and seven planets in the positions they occupied at Chigi's rth. Other outstanding works in the Chigi chapel include the ainting of *The Birth of the Virgin* by Sebastiano del Piombo ehind the high altar; the two statues of the prophets *Jonah nd Elijah* by Lorenzetto (1490–1541); and the frescoes by alviati between the windows. In the Baroque period, ernini was commissioned to refurbish the church. He ompleted the entablature between the columns and edecorated the arcades, decorated each pyramid with arble medallions, and added two more sculptures of rophets, *Habakkuk* and *Daniel and the Lion* (pictured ght). Between 1682 and 1687 Carlo Fontana built the CYBO CHAPEL (second on the left) for Cardinal Lorenzo Cybo, nephew of Innocent VIII. The austerity of its lines contrasts with the splendor of the marbles and columns; above the main altar is *The Immaculate Conception and Four Saints* by Carlo Maratta. THE CERASI CHAPEL ★ (1601), on the left of the choir, is without a doubt the church's gem. Two marvelous Caravaggio paintings face one another, *The Crucifixion of St Peter* and *The Conversion of St Paul*; and the chapel's altarpiece is *The Assumption of the Virgin* by Annibale Carracci.
THE TWIN CHURCHES. The twin churches of Santa Maria di Montesanto (1662–75) and Santa Maria dei Miracoli (1675–9) flank, as if standing guard over it, the start of the via del Corso. Built by Carlo Rainaldi for Pope Alexander VII, they were conceived, with their solemn symmetry, to inspire in travelers arriving from the north instant respect for the papal city.

"THE CHURCH OF THE PEOPLE"
According to a popular medieval legend, Santa Maria del Popolo was built on the spot where Nero was buried, and the emperor's soul haunted the walnut tree that grew over the tomb. In 1099, as the result of a vision, Pope Pascal II had the tree uprooted and burned; its ashes were then thrown into the Tiber. In its place a chapel was built dedicated to the Virgin Mary, which became Santa Maria del Popolo.

▲ Il Tridente

The Silenus.

THE MAIN STREETS. The neighborhood is called "Il Tridente" because of the three streets that fan out, like the prongs of a trident, from Piazza del Popolo. The left-hand prong is the Via del Babuino; along it a variety of antique shops runs all the way to Piazza di Spagna. The street owes its name to an unprepossessing statue of Silenus which now adorns a fountain near the Church of Sant'Atanasio: Romans found the sculpture so ugly that they likened it to a *babuino* (baboon). Parallel to Via del Babuino runs Via Margutta, which has a street fair in June and October where painters exhibit their work. The right-hand prong of the trident is the VIA DI RIPETTA, which used to lead to the old port of Rome (the Porto di Ripetta, which no longer exists today, although many prints and pictures of it have survived). The trident's central prong is the VIA DEL CORSO.

VIA DEL CORSO

THE STREET OF ALEXANDER VII. According to Stendhal, "Via del Corso is perhaps the most beautiful street in the Universe". However, it gets very crowded, particularly at the end of the afternoon. Absolutely straight, and rather narrow in comparison with the wide streets built in the 19th century and the time of Mussolini, it is now lined with clothes shops. It follows the course of the ancient Via Flaminia, then continues for more than a mile between two rows of palazzi and churches before ending at Piazza Venezia. Pope Alexander VII (1655–67) realigned it by demolishing all the buildings in its way and obliged the owners of the remaining palazzi to build new façades. It was nicknamed the "Corso" because of the numerous races (*corse*) that took place there during the Carnival period: human races (for children, old men and Jews), animal races (for donkeys and buffaloes)

The art fairs held in the Via Margutta enable painters, both from the district and the rest of the city, to make themselves known to the general public.

...d, above all, races for barb horses, which attracted the ...ggest crowds. Spectators lined the windows of the palazzi ...which were decked out with flags) in order to watch the ...xtravagant processions, parades and masquerades. Writers ...n the Grand Tour, including Goethe and Dickens ● 113, ...ere greatly impressed by the festivities. During the 18th and ...9th centuries elegant ladies liked to be seen driving along the ...ia del Corso in their carriages. Today its first section is a ...edestrian precinct. It would be interesting to see inside the ...alazzi, but they are closed to visitors. Among these such ...scinating buildings as Palazzo Rondinini, with its courtyard ...ll of antiquities; Palazzo Fiano, which housed a small ...uppet theater in the 19th century; and (toward Piazza ...enezia) Palazzo Mancini – the seat of the French Academy ...om 1725 to 1803 – and Palazzo Bonaparte, which was the ...esidence of Letizia, mother of Napoleon I. Sadly the many ...afés, which from the 18th century onward made this area a ...enter of literary and artistic life, have passed into history and ...e bar of the Hotel Plaza, an immense haven of peace that ...ill retains its *fin-de-siècle* decor, is now completely deserted.

THE CHURCHES OF SAN GIACOMO AND GESU E MARIA. SAN ...IACOMO is located just after the long façade of PALAZZO SAN ...EVERINO. The first church in Rome to ...ave an elliptical design, it was built at ...he end of the 15th century by Francesco ...a Volterra and Carlo Maderno. Facing ..., near the Goethe Museum (No. 18), is ...e CHURCH OF GESU E MARIA (1633); ...e lovely façade (1672–5), one of the few ...n Rome to be based on the Palladian ...odel, was designed by Carlo Rainaldi. ...he lavish interior is decorated with ...ulticolored marble and Sicilian jasper. ...ceiling painted by Giacinto Brandi ...akes it a real Baroque theater.

"Via del Corso...is about 3,500 paces long and is lined with tall buildings, most of which are sumptuous. Its width is not proportionate to its length or to the height of the buildings. Pavements for pedestrians take up six to eight feet on either side. In many

THE CHURCH OF SANTI AMBROGIO E ...ARLO AL CORSO. The "national" church ...f the Lombards (right) was initially ...edicated to St Ambrose, the patron ...aint of Milan. However, it was rebuilt in ...onor of St Charles Borromeo ▲ 247 ...who had been Archbishop of Milan) ...ollowing his canonization in 1610. Its ...edieval plan, designed by Onorio and ...Martino Longhi, is particularly unusual in Rome because of ...e ambulatory which circles the choir. In 1668 Pietro da ...ortona added its elegant dome, one of the largest in the city ...fter that of St Peter's ▲ 210. (Take Via Canova, on the right, ...o the Lungotevere in Augusta.)

places the space left for carriages is no more than twelve to fourteen feet wide, and it is easy to calculate that this is only just enough to accommodate three moving vehicles side by side, at the very most."

Goethe,
Travels in Italy

THE MAUSOLEUM OF AUGUSTUS

THE EGYPTIAN FASHION. On his return from Alexandria in 29 ...D after defeating Mark Antony and conquering Egypt, ...ctavian (who became the Emperor Augustus) had a ...randiose tomb built in the Campus Martius. It was obviously ...nspired by the Mausoleum of Alexander in Alexandria, and ...vas conceived as a dynastic monument. Excavations between ...936 and 1938 cleared a space in the midst of the cypresses,

RES · GESTAE · DIVI · AVGVST

and a circular building with a diameter of about 285 feet was discovered, consisting of a series of concentric walls. The two obelisks that stood before the south-facing door of the building now adorn the Piazza del Quirinale and the Piazza dell'Esquilino.

THE MAUSOLEUM'S INTERIOR. A passage rings the circular burial chamber, which has several niches. These originally held the tombs. In the center, the tomb of Augustus lay exactly beneath the bronze statue of the Emperor that crowned the building. The first to be buried there was Augustus' nephew Marcellus ▲ *157*, who died in 23 BC. His inscription and that of his mother Octavia are engraved on the same block of marble. In the Middle Ages the mausoleum fell into disuse and the Colonna family transformed it into a fortress; in 1780 it was an arena for bull races; and in the 19th century it served as a concert hall known as the Augusteo.

The Mausoleum of Augustus.

THE "RES GESTAE"
This summary of Augustus' achievements is engraved on bronze tablets hung on two pilasters on either side of the entrance to the Mausoleum. One of the ancient copies of this has been found engraved on the entrance walls of the Temple of Rome and Augustus in Ankara. A modern copy can be seen on the façade of the pavilion protecting the Ara Pacis.

Detail of the procession (on the north side of the Altar of Peace).

THE ARA PACIS AUGUSTAE

THE ALTAR OF PEACE. This monument (originally further south, in the vicinity of the Via Flaminia) was dedicated in 9 BC, on January 30, to celebrate the peace established by Augustus after his victories in Gaul and Spain. Fragments of it were unearthed as far back as the 16th century. In 1938–9 it was restored to celebrate the 2,000th anniversary of Augustus' inauguration as Emperor and was encased in a monstrous cement-and-glass cage to protect it from the weather. Designed by the American architect Richard Meier a new glass and travertine structure has been protecting the Altar of Peace since April 2006. However, its resolutely contemporary style has caused a great deal of controversy.

A MASTERPIECE OF ROMAN SCULPTURE ★. The marble walls enclosing the altar are very richly sculpted. The lower part is identical on all four sides, with an intricate tracery of acanthus leaves branching out from a single stem at the center of each panel. The upper part is more varied, the panels beside the doorways being ornamented with reliefs representing mythological and allegorical scenes. One of them (unfortunately badly damaged) is of the Lupercalium, the grotto where the she-wolf is supposed to have suckled Romulus and Remus ● *26*. The other relief on the same side shows Aeneas preparing to sacrifice the sow with thirty piglets which, in his prophetic dream, indicated the place where the city of Rome would be built. On the opposite side, Earth is represented in the form of a buxom woman with her two children (pictured opposite on the right). Two

f-naked female figures symbolize the
er elements: Water riding on a sea
nster, and Air on a swan. Most of the
ht-hand panel is missing, but it is
ught to have featured a figure
sonifying the triumph of Rome. On the
er sides are historical scenes. The relief
that nearest to the Via di Ripetta side is
best preserved. It shows portraits of the
st important members of the Imperial
iily filing past in strict hierarchical order:
gustus, Agrippa, Livia (the wife of Augustus),
erius, Drusus the Elder and Caius Caesar can
be recognized. The reliefs convey the political
ssage as well as the artistic skills of the new
ime; legend, history and religion combine to
or the name of Augustus and glorify the peace
ablished by the power of Rome. (Continue along Via di
oetta, until just after Via dell'Arancio.)

OM PIAZZA BORGHESE TO LARGO GOLDONI

AZZO BORGHESE. This palace was acquired in 1604 by
rdinal Camillo Borghese, the future Pope Paul V, who
ered it to his brothers in 1605, the year of his election.
ended as a symbol of the power and glory of the pontifical
iily in the very heart of Rome, it was begun in 1560 by
rtino Longhi and Flaminio Ponzio, and Ponzio designed
beautiful courtyard. Around 1670 the palace was
ensively remodeled by Carlo Rainaldi, who rebuilt the
ade facing the piazza and redesigned the gardens. Its
gular shape has earned it the nickname of the *cembalo
e harpsichord")*. If you are interested in second-hand
ks and engravings, visit the stalls in Largo della Fontanella
Borghese. (Take the Via della Fontanella di
rghese to return to the Corso.)

Stalls selling
engravings in the
Largo della
Fontanella di
Borghese.

**THE PALAZZO
BORGHESE**
This palace has one
of the most successful
and best preserved of
Rome's Baroque
gardens; its inner
courtyard, a truly
peaceful haven, is
rich with statues,
garlands, *putti*
(cherubs) and
fountains.

Caffé Greco

A.D. 1760
Roma, via Condotti 86

THE CAFFÈ GRECO (No. 85 Via Condotti) The oldest (1760) and for a long time the most prestigious of Rome's cafés is traditionally the haunt of the beau monde and has always been a very cosmopolitan spot. Illustrious clients have included Stendhal, Goethe, D'Annunzio, Berlioz, Modigliani and Toscanini.

PALAZZO RUSPOLI. This building overlooking Largo Goldoni originally belonged to a rich Florentine family, th Rucellai. Around 1556 they commissioned Bartolommeo Ammannati, architect of the courtyard of the Palazzo Pitti in Florence, to buil a residence for them in Rome; they the invited another Florentine, Jacopo Zucchi, to decorate it with a cycle of allegorical frescoes. The ground floor now occupied by the Memmo Foundation, which organizes interesting exhibitions there (t entrance is at No. 418A Via del Corso). (Take the Via di Leoncino to reach Piazza San Lorenzo in Lucina.)

SAN LORENZO IN LUCINA. According to tradition this church was founded during the pontificate of Sixtus III (432–40) on the site of the house of Lucina, a rich Roman matron who bought the remains of martyrs so she could give them a decent burial. Pope Pascal II had it rebuilt at the beginning the 12th century, and the portico and bell tower have surviv from that period. In 1650, the whole building was restored and side chapels added. Of these, the lovely FONSECA CHAPE (the fourth on the right) by Bernini is particularly striking. The church also contains the tomb of the French painte Nicolas Poussin (1594–1665), which Chateaubriand had made 1830. In the fifth chapel o the left are the canvases of Simon Vouet's Caravaggio period. Guido Reni's luminou yet somber Crucifixion adorns the high altar. (Walk back to the Corso and take Via Condotti, which is opposite Palazzo Ruspoli.)

Palazzo di
Propaganda Fide.

COLLEGIVM
VRBANVM
DE PROPAGANDA
FIDE

IAZZA DI SPAGNA

NE OF THE DELIGHTS OF ROME. People never cease to be
duced and surprised by Piazza di Spagna. Today this area,
rtly owned by the Spanish (the embassy) and the French
rinità dei Monti), is swarming with luxury boutiques. It
nsists of two irregular triangular piazzas that interconnect.
e Piazza di Spagna owes its name to the first permanent
nbassy to be established in Rome, the PALAZZO DI
AGNA. Built by Antonio del Grande in 1647
tween Via Borgognona and Via Frattina, it is still
e headquarters of the Spanish Embassy to the
oly See. It was a favorite refuge for artists in
e 17th century (Claude Lorrain, Poussin and
n Laer all stayed there). For a brief rest one
ght prefer BABINGTON'S TEA-ROOMS with
eir utterly Victorian charm to Rome's first
cDonald's, which has opened on the square
ch to the disgust of the Romans. At the foot
the Spanish Steps is the CASINA ROSSA (No. 26
azza di Spagna), the house where the poet Keats
d in 1821 ▲ 183. It houses a small museum
dicated to him, as well as to Shelley and Byron.
No. 31 is the Palazzetto dei Borgognoni where the
etaphysical" painter de Chirico lived.

LAZZO DI PROPAGANDA FIDE. This palace, on the right of
e piazza, is the headquarters of the congregation founded
Gregory XV in 1626 for the training of young missionaries,
d is Vatican property. It was remodeled first by Bernini,
o designed the façade on the piazza, then after 1646 by his
eat rival Borromini who built the small internal church, the
RATORIO DEI RE MAGI. In front of the college is the
LUMN OF THE DOGMA OF THE IMMACULATE CONCEPTION,
e last great Roman monument to be commissioned before
e Unity of Italy ● 33. Designed by Luigi Poletti, it consists
an ancient column with a statue of the Virgin Mary erected
ring the pontificate of Pius IX, after the proclamation of
e Dogma in 1854. Ever since, on December 8, the
niversary of this event, the Pope blesses the crowd that has
cked there to celebrate the Feast of the Immaculate
nception. (Continue to Via di Capo le Case.)

NT'ANDREA DELLE FRATTE. This church once stood amid
rural surroundings, hence the name "*delle Fratte*"
(of the thickets). If the chronicles can be
trusted, a building dedicated to St
Andrew already existed around
1370. When it became a parish church
in the 16th century the shrine was
entrusted to the Minims, who set
about rebuilding it in 1604. However,
once the nave had been completed,
in 1622 the work was interrupted
due to lack of funds, and only
continued thirty years later under
Borromini's direction. The elegant
bell tower (each level of which is
stylistically different) has a special
charm, as does the undulating shape of the
dome. (Return to Piazza di Spagna.)

**FEAST OF THE
IMMACULATE
CONCEPTION**
Every year on
December
8 the

Pope visits Piazza di
Spagna and hands
firemen a garland of
flowers with which
they crown the statue
of the Virgin at the
top of the column.
The faithful then
heap masses of
flowers around the
base.

The Casina Rossa
and the Church of
San Lorenzo in
Lucina.

313

THE STEPS OF TRINITÀ DEI MONTI
At the foot of the Spanish Steps the eagles of Pope Innocent VIII's coat of arms shoulder the French fleurs-de-lys

(a reminder of the diplomatic wrangling between the Holy See and France that preceded their construction).

TRINITÀ DEI MONTI, THE FINEST THEATER SET IN ROME ✪
The Trinità dei Monti is one of the liveliest and most colorful areas of the city. The best time to see it is in May, during the Azalea Festival, when hundreds of fuchsia-colored flowers bedeck the balustrades and the 137 steps of this grand Baroque stairway – or in July when the great Italian couturiers present their fall and winter collections. It is also from the Via Condotti, temple of luxury shopping, that the best view of the stairway can be enjoyed.

TRINITÀ DEI MONTI

FONTANA DELLA BARCACCIA (FOUNTAIN OF THE BOAT). At the foot of the steps is an unusual fountain resembling a half-submerged boat, which – like the Navicella on Monte Celio ▲ *190* – was probably based on one of the fountains of antiquity. Urban VIII decided to have it made in 1629 and channeled the Aqua Virgo ▲ *298* to it. It is not known whether it was designed by Bernini or by his father, Pietro.

A MAJESTIC FLIGHT OF STEPS. The transformation of Piazza di Spagna was completed in the 18th century with the building of a *scalinata* (flight of steps), creating a succession of terraces up to the Church of Trinità dei Monti. The project was financed by King Louis XV of France. His predecessor, Louis XIV, had wanted to build a flight of steps dominated by his own equestrian statue, but the pontiffs opposed this idea. As a result, the project was not begun until 1723 (during the pontificate of Innocent XIII) when the architect Francesco De Sanctis obtained permission to build the steps. The Spanish Steps are at their most charming in the spring, when they are covered with flowering azaleas. Today they are a meeting place for young people, street vendors, caricaturists and, above all, tourists.

TRINITÀ DEI MONTI. This church was founded by the French in 1502 at the request of Louis XII and was entrusted to the Minims. A double flight of steps by Domenico Fontana (15 leads to Giacomo Della Porta's soaring façade with twin bell towers. Inside, the SECOND CHAPEL ON THE LEFT contains one of the most famous frescoes in Rome, the *Descent from the Cross* (1541) by Daniele da Volterra, thought to have been executed according to a preparatory sketch by Michelangelo. THE CONVENT next door belongs to the Dames du Sacré-Coeur (Sisters of the Sacred Heart). The PIAZZA TRINITÀ DEI MONTI, at the center of which stands an obelisk found in the gardens of Sallust ▲ *288*, marks the end of the street formerly called the Via Felice; this extends all the way to Santa Maria Maggiore ▲ *342*, after crossing the Quirinal, the Viminal and the Esquiline. At the same end of the piazza is the Via Gregoriana; here stands the curious 16th-century PALAZZETTO ZUCCARI, built for the Mannerist painter, Federico Zuccari, member of the Accademia di San Luca ▲ *299*. Its door and windows are framed by the gaping mouths of monsters. Here David painted *The Oath of the Horatii* (1784). Today it is the headquarters of the German Institute for Art History and the Hertziana Library. (Walk back through the piazza and take the Viale della Trinità dei Monti, which climbs toward the Pincio. (Follow the wall

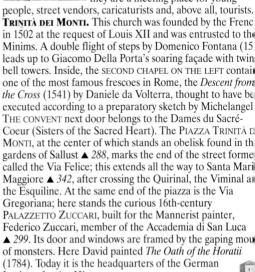

ongside the Convent of the Dames du Sacré-Coeur and the rdens of the Villa Medici until you come to the villa itself.)

HE VILLA MEDICI

RENAISSANCE VILLA. In 1564, at the request of Nanni di ıccio Bigio, Annibale Lippi totally transformed a building the site of the gardens of Lucullus (the military mmander famous for his hedonism and extravagance), ıich extended over this area in the 1st ntury BC. It then passed into the nds of the Medici family. Like many man villas built in the 16th and 17th nturies, it has a severe, unadorned, nost military façade facing the city, ile the façade that overlooks the garden incorporates a gia and is much less austere and more ornate. Integrated the wall facing the garden are bas-reliefs, some of which ne from the Ara Pacis Augustae ▲ *310* – reflecting the thusiasm of the great Roman and Florentine families of end of the 16th century for collecting antiquities.

ITALIAN-STYLE GARDEN. Although it has been ıstically rearranged, the villa's park still retains some the features typical of Renaissance Italian gardens: ıged walks, arbors, alcoves, secret gardens, and ıntains, all decorated with statues. At the back, king onto the Muro Torto ▲ *306*, is the *studiolo* ıdy) of Ferdinando di Medici, totally restored in e 1980's; some 16th-century Mannerist frescoes ere discovered here, as well as a magnificent viary. Between the Villa Medici and the rinità dei Monti, recent excavations have evealed the site of a gigantic curved ymphaeum built by Valerius Asiaticus, who ıwned a villa here during the reign of Claudius.

THE FRENCH ACADEMY. The Académie de France à Rome was founded in 1666 by Louis XIV to enable young artists to be imbued with classical art, and was moved to the Villa Medici in 1804 by a decree of Napoleon. (Continue along the Viale della Trinità dei Monti.)

From left to right: Via Gregoriana and views of the Villa Medici.

BERLIOZ IN ROME
In 1830 Berlioz won the Grand Prix de Rome, which entitled him to a period of residence at the Villa Medici. In his *memoirs* - probably with a touch of romantic exaggeration - he recounts how, climbing the Spanish Steps to reach the Villa Medici, he had to whip out his knife to fend off pickpockets who wanted to rob him of his purse.

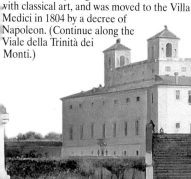

THE PINCIO ★

The Pincio Gardens, which overlook Piazza del Popolo, are a magical place to wander in. In the 4th century the land belonged to the Pinci family. The promenade, designed by Giuseppe Valadier and opened to the public 1828, affords one of the loveliest views of Rome. With its broad walks shaded by parasol pines, palm trees and oaks was an immediate success both with Romans and with artis and foreigners who lived in the Eternal City. The avenues and walks of the Pincio conformed to the contemporary tas for a disciplined and urbanized "nature" and for "belvedere (places from which to admire the view); they were also idea suited to the fashionable practice of "promenading". On fo or in carriages, Roman high society met there regularly, an travelers, diarists and writers – such as Stendhal, Gide and D'Annunzio – celebrated the Pincio's charms.

"The Pincio Gardens are not buried like the Tuileries Gardens, they dominate 80 or 100 feet of the Tiber and the surrounding countryside. The view from them is superb. In winter, at about two o'clock, one often sees the young ladies of Rome getting out of their carriages and walking on foot; it is their Bois de Boulogne."
Stendhal, *Promenades dans Rome*

THE CASINA VALADIER. This enchanting small villa stands in the Viale Mickiewicz. You can sample a *granita di caffè* here while admiring the view. It was planned as a restaurant in 1813, and looks like a garden pavilion built in the finest 18th-century taste. Nevertheless, it fell into disfavor for a time before becoming fashionable in 1922.

THE COMMEMORATIVE MONUMENTS. An array of busts ador the walks of the Pincio, placed there to honor great Italians from the days of ancient Rome. In addition to statues of me such as Metastasio, Canova and Titian, there is a memorial commemorating the Battle of Legnano (the victory, in 1176 of the first Lombard League against the Holy Roman Emp ▲ *100*); dedicated to the municipalities of Italy, it was erecte in 1911. A little further on are monuments to Raphael (183 and Enrico Toti (1922), a *bersagliere* (light-infantryman) wh after losing a leg participated in the fighting in 1916, supporting himself with his crutch. At the center of the avenue named the Viale dell'Obelisco stands the obelisk erected by the Emperor Hadrian to commemorate his favorite, Antinous, which was moved here in 1822.

Monument to Enrico Toti.

MONUMENT TO THE CAIROLI BROTHERS
Close to the point where the Viale della Trinità dei Monti meets Viale Gabriele D'Annunzio stands this memorial, built by Ercole Rosa in 1883, to Enrico and Giovanni Cairoli, victims of the fighting in the Villa Glori in 1867 at the time of Garibaldi's ill-fated march on Rome ● *33*.

Via Appia Antica

319 The Baths of Caracalla

322 Park of the Scipios

323 The Aurelian Wall

324 The Catacombs

326 The Basilica and Catacombs
of San Sebastiano

328 The Villa and Circus of
Maxentius

330 The Tomb of Cecilia Metella

▲ VIA APPIA ANTICA

1. BATHS OF CARACALLA
2. SANTI NEREO E ACHILLEO
3. SAN SISTO VECCHIO
4. SAN CESAREO
5. SAN GIOVANNI A PORTA LATINA

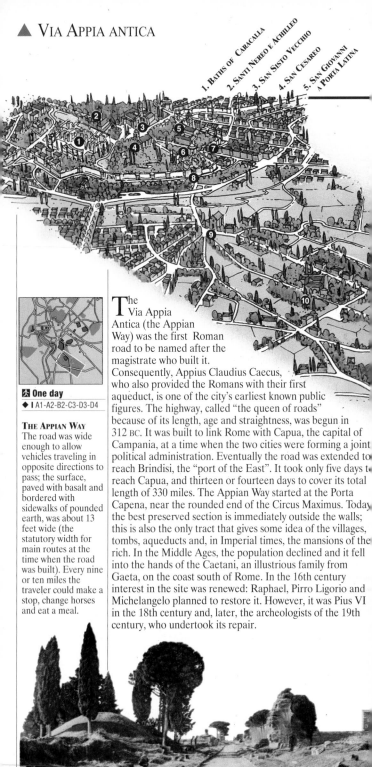

☷ One day

◆ I A1-A2-B2-C3-D3-D4

THE APPIAN WAY
The road was wide enough to allow vehicles traveling in opposite directions to pass; the surface, paved with basalt and bordered with sidewalks of pounded earth, was about 13 feet wide (the statutory width for main routes at the time when the road was built). Every nine or ten miles the traveler could make a stop, change horses and eat a meal.

The Via Appia Antica (the Appian Way) was the first Roman road to be named after the magistrate who built it. Consequently, Appius Claudius Caecus, who also provided the Romans with their first aqueduct, is one of the city's earliest known public figures. The highway, called "the queen of roads" because of its length, age and straightness, was begun in 312 BC. It was built to link Rome with Capua, the capital of Campania, at a time when the two cities were forming a joint political administration. Eventually the road was extended to reach Brindisi, the "port of the East". It took only five days to reach Capua, and thirteen or fourteen days to cover its total length of 330 miles. The Appian Way started at the Porta Capena, near the rounded end of the Circus Maximus. Today the best preserved section is immediately outside the walls; this is also the only tract that gives some idea of the villages, tombs, aqueducts and, in Imperial times, the mansions of the rich. In the Middle Ages, the population declined and it fell into the hands of the Caetani, an illustrious family from Gaeta, on the coast south of Rome. In the 16th century interest in the site was renewed: Raphael, Pirro Ligorio and Michelangelo planned to restore it. However, it was Pius VI in the 18th century and, later, the archeologists of the 19th century, who undertook its repair.

ROADSIDE TOMBS. Since the earliest times the common custom was to bury the dead outside the *pomerium*, the sacred walls of the city. The first few miles of Roman roads were therefore usually flanked by necropolises, distinguished by social status and diversity of funeral rites. Indeed burial and cremation were practiced concurrently, one or the other prevailing according to the fashion. Under the Republic cremation was prevalent so they constructed columbariums (buildings housing thousands of funerary urns) and altars with the ashes of the deceased.

Conversely, in the Imperial times

The Via Appia.

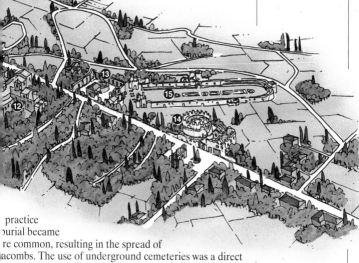

practice of burial became more common, resulting in the spread of catacombs. The use of underground cemeteries was a direct response to the practice of burial, since interment required more space than cremation. From the 4th century the catacombs became almost exclusively Christian, following the conversion of the Roman people.

THE BATHS OF CARACALLA

ROMAN BATHS. From the end of the Republic the Romans frequented public baths, not just for reasons of hygiene and exercise but also for entertainment. The activities offered by the baths and their increasingly important social role led the emperors to build ever larger establishments, accommodating more bathers (the Baths of Caracalla had a capacity of nearly 2000). Progressively, areas for sport were introduced, auditoriums for music, lecture theaters, libraries, gardens, fountains, and porticos to protect walkers from rain and from the sun. At the same time, the architecture and decoration of these buildings became more sophisticated, richer in mosaics, stucco decorations, colonnades, paintings and sculptures. Eventually premises of a monumental size became indispensable because of the large service staff that was necessary (cloakroom attendants, masseurs, those responsible for depilation, doctors, etc.) and the hordes of entertainers that the bathers came to expect (ranging from itinerant

THE BATHS OF CARACALLA
On either side of the portico there was a huge *exedra* enclosing a *palestra* (gymnasium). At the rear a sort of half stadium concealed the enormous water tanks, each with a capacity of about 20 million gallons.

CARACALLA (188–217) Given access to power in 198 AD by his father Septimius Severus, Caracalla became Emperor in 211. He continued his father's initiatives, and his edict of 212 granting Roman citizenship to all inhabitants of the Empire marked the fruition of the policy of "Romanization". He also pursued an ambitious foreign policy, and was assassinated during a campaign against Parthia.

The *Ercole Farnese* ▲ *245*. This statue of Hercules was found in the Baths of Caracalla.

salesmen to musicians, mimics, readers and orators). Thus, unlike the Greek gymnasiums, which were limited to the education and physical development of young men, the Roman baths were places for social encounters and leisure activities, where sport and culture combined in forming, as the poet Juvenal put it, *mens sana in corpore sano* ("a healthy mind in a healthy body"). The baths were open to everyone until sunset; and it was only from the time of Hadrian (117–38 AD) that the sexes were segregated. Today the Baths of Caracalla are still used for cultural purposes: in summer there are open-air performances of opera and ballet.

THE BATHER'S RITUAL. The Baths of Caracalla (Terme di Caracalla), also known as the Thermae Antoninianae, are the most magnificent and best preserved of all the Imperial baths. Built between 212 and 216 AD, they form an almost perfect square covering 27 acres and are surrounded by a wall erected later by Heliogabalus ▲ *151* and Alexander Severus. The arrangement of the central block, which was reserved for sports, is traditional. Access was through the four gates on

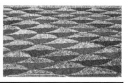

the northeast façade. Each of the vestibules led to a square room, probably the dressing rooms (*apodyteria*), then to one of the two gymnasiums (*palestrae*). Indeed this is where the bather's ritual program began, with intense gymnastic exercises intended to warm up the muscles and induce heavy breathing. After that the body was scraped and oiled, then in the following rooms submitted to contrasting treatments of hot and cold: first dry sweating in the *laconium*, then a hot bath (immersion or aspersion) in the *caldarium*, a great circular room with a diameter of about 110 feet, covered by a vast dome; from here the bather passed into the temperate hall, the *tepidarium*, to accustom the body before plunging into the cold waters of the *frigidarium* (probably only partly roofed), which contained cold baths and a swimming pool (*natatio*). Between the last two rooms was the basilica, a large covered hall that served as a general relaxation room. Other rooms, between this central hall and the dressing rooms, were for massage and medical consultations; there were terraces that served as solariums; and there were also latrines. Finally, the service quarters necessary for the operation of the baths were housed in the basement, which consisted of a vast network of underground rooms and passages. In one of these passages (near the great northwest exedra), a *mithraeum* has been discovered ▲ *181* that is the largest known in Rome. (At the exit of the baths, turn right.)

SANTI NEREO E ACHILLEO. According to tradition, when Peter was escaping from the Mamertine prison ▲ *131* it was at this spot that the bandage (*fasciola*) wrapped around the sores caused by his chains dropped from his leg. A church, called the Titulus Fasciolae, is known to have existed here as early as 377. It was first enlarged around 800, during the pontificate of Leo III, and the very beautiful mosaic on the chancel arch has survived from that time. During the 15th century the church was almost entirely rebuilt; it was then decorated by Cardinal Baronius, who commissioned the frescoes in 1597.

SAN SISTO VECCHIO. This very ancient foundation was restored by Pope Innocent III (1198–1216), who gave it to Dominic so he could found the first monastery for his order in Rome. Both the church and the monastic buildings were restructured by Filippo Raguzzini between 1724 and 1730, under the patronage of Benedict XIII. Remains of the medieval church are visible in the cloister; the Romanesque bell tower dates from the restoration of Innocent III.

The rich decorations of the Columbarium of Pomponius Hylas. Part of this room was hollowed out of the rock.

THE TOMB OF THE SCIPIOS
Almost nothing is left of the original northwest-facing façade, nor of the foundations carved into the rock and covered by frescoes.

THE SARCOPHAGUS OF SCIPIO BARBATUS
The inscription on the coffin praises the merits of the conqueror of the Samnites and Etruscans: "Lucius Cornelius Scipio Barbatus, son of Cnaeus, a brave and wise man; he was a consul in your country and an aedile (magistrate responsible for buildings and public works). He took Taurasia and Cisauna in Samnium and subdued Lucania, from which he took hostages." (The original sarcophagus and the funerary inscriptions found here are now in the Vatican Museums.)

PARK OF THE SCIPIOS

SAN CESAREO. This churc was erected in the 15th century on top of a ruine building (possibly baths) dating from the 2nd century AD. Just below th paved floor of the church a black-and-white mosaic with marine motifs has survived from this earlier building. Inside, the splendid mosaics of *The Eternal Father* in the apse and *The Annunciation* on the chancel arch were executed to designs by Cavaliere d'Arpino, who painted the frescoes on the upper part of the walls of the nave.

THE TOMB OF THE SCIPIOS. In 1780, in the basement of a private property, several rooms containing sarcophagi were discovered, of which the oldest dated from the beginning of the 3rd century BC. This was the sepulcher of a great Roman family, the Scipios, most famous for having defeated Hanniba in 202 BC. This celebrated discovery taught archeologists tha the Romans were already familiar with burial rites at the tim of the Republic. The actual entrance to the tomb is on the V di Porta San Sebastiano. Hollowed out of a natural mound o tufa, it is made up of six intersecting galleries. At the back of the central gallery is a copy of the oldest tomb of all, that of Lucius Cornelius Scipio Barbatus, consul in 298 BC; and to t left of the central passage you can see the remains of the original sarcophagus of Lucius' son, who was consul in 259 B

THE COLUMBARIUM OF POMPONIUS HYLAS. On request the caretaker will take visitors to see a small, extremely well-preserved underground columbarium dating from the early years of the Empire. Situated just across the park wedged between the Via di Porta San Sebastiano and the Via di Port Latina, it is reached by a flight of steps that has survived fro

e same period. Opposite the last few steps there is a niche
corated with a mosaic inscription showing two names:
1[aeus] *Pomponius Hylas* and *Pomponia Vitalis* (left). The
ctangular room, part of which is hollowed out of the rock, is
autifully decorated with stuccos and paintings almost
tirely from the time of Nero. During the 19th century three
her columbariums were discovered close by, in the Vigna
odini (now privately owned).

RATORIO SAN GIOVANNI IN OLEO. This small octagonal
apel erected in 1509 by the French prelate Benoît Adam
ands on the spot where, according to tradition, St John
nerged unharmed from the cauldron of boiling oil into
hich he had been flung; after this episode the Evangelist was
iled to Patmos. Benoît Adam had his coat of arms engraved
ove the door, with his motto: "Au plaisir de Dieu". The
apel was restored in 1658 by Borromini, then again in 1716
der Clement XI.

AN GIOVANNI A PORTA LATINA ● 74. This church was
unded by Pope Gelasius I (492–6) and built according to an
iental design. In the 11th century it housed a community of
iests who practiced poverty and obedience. Animated by
tense zeal, they were at the root of the Gregorian reform
30 led by Popes Gregory VI and Gregory VII. In recent
nes the church has recovered its medieval appearance. A
ortico with five arches supported by four graceful marble-
id-granite columns precedes the façade, which is flanked by
a elegant six-story campanile. The central nave is decorated
ith an important cycle of 12th-century frescoes depicting
enes from the Old and New Testaments.

HE AURELIAN WALL

ORTA LATINA. The Emperor Aurelian (270–5) undertook to
ve Rome new walls as a protection against barbarian
vasions. All of the masons' guilds in Rome were called to
ork on them. Building began in 271 and was completed by
e time of Aurelian's death. The ramparts, nearly 12 miles
long, about 13 feet wide and
fortified every 100 feet
with a square tower,
originally constituted
a fairly modest
defense system. They
were therefore
improved several times,
especially between 401
and 402, so as to withstand
attacks from the Goths. The
height of the wall was raised;
the exposed walkway for the
sentries was replaced by a
covered gallery with
windows, above which a
second passageway was
built, fortified with
crenelations; and the
towers, also reinforced,
virtually became
independent fortresses.

THE AURELIAN WALL
From the Porta San
Sebastiano, which
houses a museum
devoted to the history
of the Aurelian Wall,
you can follow part of
the sentries' beat.
The construction of
the wall followed a
strategic line that
encompassed the
seven hills of Rome
and incorporated
many monumental
buildings, including
the Castrense
Amphitheater ▲ 200,
the Castra Praetoria
▲ 335 and the
Pyramid of Caius
Cestius ▲ 182. Thus
one tenth of the
ramparts consisted of
pre-existing buildings.

PORTA LATINA
The Porta Latina was
doubly secure. As
well as its two internal
gates, there was a
portcullis on the
outside that could be
lowered to instantly
block access. In the
upper part five arched
windows lit the room
used for operating the
portcullis; these were
probably blocked
during the war against
the Goths.

323

PORTA SAN SEBASTIANO
An interesting figure is engraved on the left gatepost. It represents the Archangel Gabriel and is accompanied by an inscription in curious medieval Latin commemorating the Roman victory over Robert d'Anjou, King of Naples, on

September 29, 1327.

One of the milestones on the first section of the Appian Way.

AN UNUSUAL RESTAURANT
You can eat in a columbarium! Since the end of the 19th century there has been a restaurant in the Columbarium of the Freedmen of Augustus (on the left, after the junction with the Via Appia Pignatelli).

The section between the Porta Appia and the Porta Latina i one of the best preserved parts of the wall. The façade of the Porta Latina, faced in travertine, more or less retains its original appearance but the size of the gate was reduced whe it was restored in the 5th century, and the tower on the left i medieval. (Take the Via di Porta San Sebastiano.)

PORTA SAN SEBASTIANO. Just after the ARCH OF DRUSUS – originally part of the aqueduct feeding the baths of Caracall – you will come to the Porta San Sebastiano (in ancient time called the Porta Appia), which marks the beginning of the first stretch of the Appian Way outside the city walls. The most monumental of the gates in the Aurelian Wall, it was rebuilt five times. Originally the road was spanned by twin arches between two round towers. Duri its final reconstruction the towers were enlarged and reinforced, and the intermediate section was raised one sto Like the Porta Latina, it could be secure with double doors and a portcullis.

CLIVUS MARTIS. About 350 feet from th gate, on the right is a column marking t position of the first milestone of the Via Appia (the original milestone is in the Piazza del Campidoglio ▲ 129). A little farther on, to the left, is a TEMPLE TO MARS – hence the nam Clivus Martis ("Ascent of Mars") given to this section of the Via Appia. Remains of several tombs from different ages are visible just before the railway bridge. The road then dips and crosses the Almone, the stream where in ancient times every year on March 27 the statue of the goddess Cybele ▲ 415 wa ritually washed, after being carried in procession to this spot. On the right-hand side, just before the crossroads with the Via Ardeatina, an ancient hostelry conceals a large tomb generally identified as that of Titus Flavius Abascantus, Domitian's powerful freed slave, who had it built for his wife Priscilla. Opposite this tomb, the small church known as DOMINE QUO VADIS ("Lord, whither goest thou?") indicates the spot where Jesus is said to have appeared to St Peter as l was fleeing the persecutions of Nero's reign. To the apostle's question, Jesus replied, "To Rome, to be crucified a second time," which Peter understood as an indication that he should return to Rome to suffer martyrdom. Visitors to the church are shown a replica of the stone that was miraculously impressed with Christ's footprints (the original is in the Church of San Sebastiano ▲ 327).

THE CATACOMBS

UNDERGROUND CEMETERIES. The vast labyrinth of the catacombs was formed from simple hypogeums (vaults) which were eventually linked by passages. At first these underground cemeteries were private, but later they were managed by funeral associations as the practice of burial in the Roman world gradually became more widespread among pagans, Jews and Christians. People were buried in the catacombs until the 6th century AD, but very soon these cemeteries also became places of

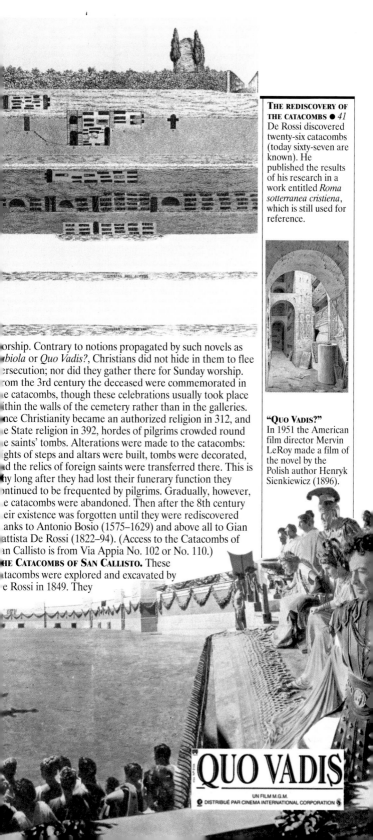

De Rossi discovered twenty-six catacombs (today sixty-seven are known). He published the results of his research in a work entitled *Roma sotterranea cristiena*, which is still used for reference.

"QUO VADIS?"
In 1951 the American film director Mervin LeRoy made a film of the novel by the Polish author Henryk Sienkiewicz (1896).

...orship. Contrary to notions propagated by such novels as *...biola* or *Quo Vadis?*, Christians did not hide in them to flee ...rsecution; nor did they gather there for Sunday worship. ...rom the 3rd century the deceased were commemorated in ...e catacombs, though these celebrations usually took place ...ithin the walls of the cemetery rather than in the galleries. ...nce Christianity became an authorized religion in 312, and ...e State religion in 392, hordes of pilgrims crowded round ...e saints' tombs. Alterations were made to the catacombs: ...ghts of steps and altars were built, tombs were decorated, ...d the relics of foreign saints were transferred there. This is ...hy long after they had lost their funerary function they ...ontinued to be frequented by pilgrims. Gradually, however, ...e catacombs were abandoned. Then after the 8th century ...eir existence was forgotten until they were rediscovered ...anks to Antonio Bosio (1575–1629) and above all to Gian ...attista De Rossi (1822–94). (Access to the Catacombs of ...an Callisto is from Via Appia No. 102 or No. 110.)

...HE CATACOMBS OF SAN CALLISTO. These ...tacombs were explored and excavated by ...e Rossi in 1849. They

QUO VADIS
UN FILM M.G.M.
DISTRIBUÉ PAR CINEMA INTERNATIONAL CORPORATION

Chi-Rho monogram (the first two letters of Christ's name in Greek). A symbolic praying figure (far right).

The good shepherd, one of the numerous Christian symbols that can be seen on the walls of the catacombs.

are the largest of the Christian burial complexes and were widely used from the 3rd century; at the same time it also became customary for the popes to be buried there. Calixtus to whom they owe their name, administered these catacombs while he was a deacon and enlarged them after he became Pope in 217. In places they were developed on four levels, and their galleries extend for more than 12 miles. Like many Christian catacombs, they are the result of the 4th-century unification of several earlier nucleuses. The oldest part, the Crypt of Lucina, beside the Via Appia, probably dates from the end of the 2nd century AD. This section is itself composed of two parts, certainly linked at the time of the burial of Pope Cornelius in 253. ZONE I, through which the catacombs are reached, was constructed later. Visitors first enter a *cella trichora* (room with three apses), which originally housed the bodies of Pope Zephyrinus (who died in 217) and the martyr Tarsicius. This *cella* became an underground basilica in honor of Sixtus II, who was martyred with four deacons in the cemetery during Valerian's persecutions in 258. Steps then lead to a vestibule with walls covered in graffiti, which opens on to the CRYPT OF THE POPES, discovered in 1854, where four niches for the sarcophagi may be seen and six *loculi* ("niches for bodies") on each side. It is thought that at least fourteen popes were buried in San Callisto, and it is certain from the inscriptions that five of them reposed in this crypt: namely Pontian (230–5), Anterus (235–6), Fabian (236–50), Lucius I (253–4) and Eutychian (275–83). De Rossi believed that the crypt known as the CRYPT OF ST CECILIA contained her tomb, but this opinion is now rejected. The learned archeologist thought he recognized the figures of

The Catacombs of San Callisto.

Cecilia, Pope Urban and Christ in the Byzantine frescoes, which were in fact too badly damaged to allow identification. The niche which according to this tradition was destined to contain St Cecilia's sarcophagus now contains a copy of her effigy by Stefano Maderno (the original is in the Church of Santa Cecilia in Trastevere ▲ *353*). Other sections of the catacombs that can be visited include the five *cubicula* ("funeral chambers") known as the Crypt of the Sacraments, which are adorned with 3rd-century frescoes, and the Crypt of Pope Eusebius, who died in 310.

IXΘYC

The fish, a symbol of Christ.

THE BASILICA AND CATACOMBS OF SAN SEBASTIANO

This complex is located just after the crossroads between the Via Appia and the Via delle Sette Chiese. The latter acquired its name from the custom revived in the 16th century of making a pilgrimage to the seven most important churches of Rome ▲ *381*, including San Sebastiano.

THE BASILICA. This basilica-cemetery built in the time of

The catechumen struggling with the serpent.

onstantine was originally dedicated to the apostles Peter and
aul. Its shape resembled that of a circus, with three naves
parated by masonry pillars surmounted by brick arches. In
e 17th century Cardinal Scipio Borghese had it rebuilt, and
e edifice was reduced to a single nave. Above the tomb of St
ebastian, whose veneration had overshadowed that of the
o apostles after the 9th century, a new chapel was built (the
rst on the left) in which a statue of the martyr was placed,
ased on a model by Bernini. The altar now in the Chapel of
elics (the first on the right) once stood in the center of the
asilica, above the Triclia (see below) where the apostles were
enerated. It also contains some venerable relics, including
e famous stone supposed to bear the impression of Christ's
otprints ▲ *324*. From the apse, where the ambulatory has
en transformed into a museum, one reaches the PLATONIA,
richly decorated tomb at the back of the basilica that
ntains the relics of St Quirinus, Bishop of Pannonia.
HE CATACOMBS. Throughout the period of late antiquity this
emetery was simply referred to by the expression *ad
tacumbas*, from the Greek *kata kymbas* ("near the caves",
hich may possibly have referred to the
eighboring stone quarries). Subsequently the
ame was used for all necropolises of this type.
ere the sepulchers of pagans and Christians lie
de by side, as they do in almost all the
tacombs. The first of the four levels of
lleries has been virtually destroyed. The
RYPT OF SAN SEBASTIANO, the first site visited,
longer contains the martyr's remains, as they
ere removed in the 9th century. Next to be
en are the three pagan hypogeums, which
ere columbariums ▲ *319* before becoming
urial places. Magnificently preserved, they
ve stucco decorations and frescoes combining
agan motifs (such as the Gorgon's head) with
hristian ones (the miracle of the demoniac of
erasa), some of them as early as the 1st or 2nd
entury AD. The inscription reveals that Marcus
laudius Hermes was the owner of the tomb on

The frescoes in the
Catacombs of
Priscilla (on the Via
Salaria) and
Commodilla (on the
Via Ostiense).

The first and last
letters of the word
"martyr".

The Catacombs of
San Sebastiano.

Several of the
buildings of the
Triopius of Herodes
Atticus have survived
destruction. These
include a temple
which in the 9th
century became the
Church of
Sant'Urbano alla
Caffarella (below);
and the Nymphaeum
of Egeria, a sort of
water castle, richly
decorated and
adorned with a
fountain, that has

never ceased to
intrigue travelers and
artists.

The Circus of
Maxentius.

the right. One then passes into the MEMORIA APOSTOLORUM,
an irregular room remarkable for its red-painted walls
covered with about a hundred graffiti, dating from the 3rd
and 4th centuries, in honor of the apostles Peter and Paul.
This room, known as the Triclia, was formerly an open space
where funeral banquets were celebrated in honor of the
apostles. No convincing archeological argument has yet made
it possible to choose between two interpretations that have
puzzled generations of scholars. Were the bodies of the two
apostles buried *ad catacumbas* just after their martyrdom,
then transferred from the catacombs at a much later date? Or
were they merely temporarily buried here at the time of
Valerian's persecution in 258? Either way, the Constantinian
basilica was built around the Memoria Apostolorum, which
was painstakingly preserved as a place of veneration.

THE VILLA AND CIRCUS OF MAXENTIUS

Between the second and third milestones of the Via Appia, on
the left, is a complex built by the Emperor Maxentius, whose
brief reign lasted from 307 to 312 AD. It included three main
buildings: a palatial villa, a circus and a mausoleum.
THE CIRCUS OF MAXENTIUS. This building is the most intact
part of the complex, and the two great towers at the western
end attract instant attention. Some 1,700 feet long, it had a
capacity of at least 10,000 spectators. A long corridor linking
the Imperial palace with the circus and the mausoleum gave
the Emperor direct access to his box, located above the
finishing post. On the south side was a box for the magistrate
who oversaw the games. The chariot teams started from
twelve *carceres* (stalls) at the western end of the circus. The
archway that served as the main entrance was at the center of
these stalls, which were flanked by the two towers. On the east
side stood another great arch (the triumphal entrance), where
in 1825 fragments of a dedication to Maxentius' son Romulus
were found, making it possible to identify the monument. As
in other circuses, the *spina* ▲ *177–9* around which the chariots
raced was surmounted by a variety of ornamental features,

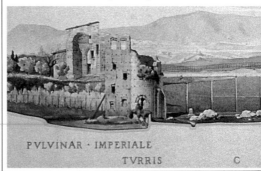

PVLVINAR · IMPERIALE
TVRRIS

cluding fountains and, in the middle, an obelisk. This was
ｏmitian's obelisk, perhaps taken from the Campus Martius;
 1650 Pope Innocent X had it moved to Piazza Navona
 276 to crown Bernini's Fontana dei Quattro Fiumi.

ＡUSOLEUM OF ROMULUS. Maxentius' son Romulus, who
ｅｄ in 309, was certainly buried here, but this was probably a
ｒnastic tomb intended for the whole family. The mausoleum
ｅlf, which stands in the middle of a grandiose quadriportico
ｏur-sided portico) facing the Via Appia, is a circular
ｉlding, about 100 feet in diameter, with a projecting
ｏnaos (porch) similar to that of the Pantheon ▲ 264.
ｒrounding it are numerous monumental tombs of the 4th
ｎtury. Originally there were two floors, of which only the
ｗer one remains, partly buried and half hidden by a modern
ｒmhouse; niches for sarcophagi were hollowed out in the
ｌl. The upper floor has almost entirely disappeared, but it
ｓ probably devoted to the funerary cult of Maxentius' son
ｄ would have been covered by a vast dome.

ﾋ TRIOPIUS OF HERODES ATTICUS AND
ＬＬA OF MAXENTIUS. Herodes Atticus
ｓ a very rich Greek from Athens. A
ｆted public speaker, he became the
ｔor of the children of the Emperor
ｎtoninus Pius (138–61) and married
ｎnia Regilla, a Roman aristocrat who
ｗned a villa on the Appian Way. When
ｓ young wife died suddenly, her family
ｃused Herodes of murdering her. After
ｓ acquittal he dedicated his land to the

ｄs of the underworld and to the funerary cult of his wife. A
ｍple was also built here in honor of the goddess Demeter
ｄ Antoninus Pius' wife Faustina. The whole heritage was
ｎamed "Triopius", from the name of the Thessalonian
ｉopas whose cult in Cnides, in Asia, was associated with that
 Demeter. Later, Maxentius' villa was built on this site;
ｒdly anything remains of it, but the few ruins that have
ｒvived, particularly those of the great reception hall, give an
ｅa of the sumptuousness of the villa.

RIVMPHALIS · TRIBVNAL · IVDICVM
· PRIMA PORTA · LIBITINENSIS
Ｅ Ｒ Ｅ Ｓ TVRRIS

At the entrance remains of tombs on the Via Appia excavated in 1836 are set into the walls.

EASTERN INFLUENCES
The form of the Tomb of Cecilia Metella is similar to that of the Mausoleum of Augustus ▲ *309* and other tombs from the same period found in Italy. These buildings provide evidence of the evolution of funerary architecture both in Rome and elsewhere in Italy, and indicate the progressive diffusion of new ideological models influenced by Asian and Hellenistic traditions.

THE TOMB OF CECILIA METELLA

After the Maxentius complex, the Via Appia rises steeply toward a massive tomb (on the left). This is the best known and best preserved of the mausoleums beside the road. Its dedication states that it was the tomb of Cecilia Metella, the daughter of Quintus Metellus Creticus (consul in 69 BC) and wife of Crassus (probably the son of the fabulously wealthy contemporary of Caesar and Pompey). The building consists of a circular tower, about 95 feet in diameter and 36 feet high, set on a square cement base that has been stripped of its facing. It leans against the ruins of a fortress built in the 12th century by the Caetani, who used it as a dungeon. The marble frieze is decorated with a relief featuring garlands of flowers, weapons and

bucranes (ox skulls); because of the *bucranes* the locality became known as Capo di Bove. Inside the castle (to the right of the entrance) there is a display of fragments of inscription and decorations from tombs on the Via Appia. From here a narrow corridor leads to the funeral chamber, the upper part of which consisted of an enormous cone faced with bricks.

ROMANTIC RUINS. Opposite the mausoleum, on the other side of the road, stands the small church of SAN NICOLA A CAPO DI BOVE built by the Caetani family. This section of the Appian Way has been considerably damaged, and the villas and numerous tombs with which it was lined are now barely identifiable ruins. But if you are traveling by car, go as far as the fifth milestone; near it (on the right) are three tumulus-shaped tombs. In the 19th century it was believed that these were the TOMBS OF THE HORATII AND THE CURIATII who died in the famous duel which ended the war between Rome and Alba Longa. A little further on (on the left) you will come to the picturesque ruins of the VILLA DEI QUINTILI (2nd century AD), part of a huge estate that belonged to one of the great aristocratic families of ancient Rome. The four Quintilii brothers came to an untimely end: under the pretext that they were plotting against him, the Emperor Commodus (180–92) had them assassinated and confiscated their villa, which he wanted for himself.

From the baths of Diocletian to San Pietro in Vincoli

333 Piazza della Repubblica

336 National Roman Museum

338 Stazione Termini

339 Via Giovanni Giolitti

339 Porta Maggiore

340 Piazza Vittorio Emanuele II

342 Basilica of Santa Maria Maggiore

344 Santa Pudenziana and Santa Prassede

346 Basilica of San Pietro in Vincoli

347 Toward the Via Nazionale

▲ FROM THE BATHS OF DIOCLETIAN TO SAN PIETRO IN VINCOLI

🚶 **One day**

◆ **E** A3-A4-B3-B4-C3
G B1-B2

1. PIAZZA DELLA REPUBBLICA
2. BATHS OF DIOCLETIEN AND CHURCH OF SANTA MARIA DEGLI ANGELI

3. MUSEO DELLE TERME
4. STAZIONI TERMINI
5. CHURCH OF SANTA BIBIANA
6. TEMPLE OF MINERVA MEDICA
7. PIAZZA VITTORIO EMANUELE II
8. THE TROPHIES OF MARIUS
9. BASILICA DI SANTA MARIA MAGGIORE
10. CHURCH OF SANTA PRASSEDE
11. CHURCH OF SAN MARTINO AI MONTI
12. CHURCH OF SAN PIETRO IN VINCOLI
13. VIA NAZIONALE
14. ÉGLISE SANTA PUDENZIANA

The northern part of Rome underwent a fresh bout of town planning activity in the mid 15th century and again at the time of Sixtus V (1585–90) who concentrated on the reorganization and repopulation of the upper part of the town. Here he moved the cattle market that had traditionally been held on the grounds of the Abbey of Farfà and installed workshops for silk production in his own villa (the Villa Peretti, now vanished), planning to divert water there from the Aniene River. A network of streets was woven around Santa Maria Maggiore, the starting point for pilgrimages to the basilicas outside the walls ▲ 380 and to San Giovanni in Laterano ▲ 198. The district retained its new features until the 1850's, when Rome's main station was built.

FUNCTIONAL TOWN PLANNING. In modernizing Rome, Pius IX (1846–78) respected the grand design of Sixtus V's plans. The first of the new arterial roads was Via Nazionale, built in 186_ in accordance with the directions of Msgr de Merode, who had acquired part of the area included in the project. After 1870 and the arrival of the Piedmontese ● 33, who wanted to make "modern Rome" the capital of a united Italy, the government had to decide on the location of the future ministries, and the Ministry of Finance was built along Via XX Settembre. The 1871 general urban plan also provided for the construction of dwellings in the Esquiline, Castro Pretori_ and Viminale areas. This was an incentive for particularly aggressive property speculation around Piazza Vittorio Emanuele, Santa Maria Maggiore and Porta San Lorenzo. The whole district between the station and the Piazza Vittori_

manuele was built at the turn of the 20th century, and Via Nazionale was lined with apartment blocks. This planned neighborhood consists of a grid of monotonous, uniform ocher buildings, mostly four or five stories high. However, some examples of finer architecture remain: notably the Piazza della Repubblica, the Bernich Aquarium, and the Church of Sant'Antonio da Padova built by Luca Carimini (1884–87).

The Piazza della Repubblica and details of the Fountain of the Naiads.

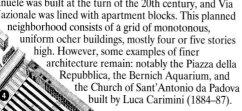

❹

❺

❽

❼

PIAZZA DELLA REPUBBLICA

❻

THE LAYOUT OF THE SQUARE. This important architectural ensemble (also known as Piazza Esedra) and the Via Nazionale, which runs into it, mark the transition between ancient and modern Rome. Gaetano Koch, who was given the task of designing the square in 1887, built large neoclassical semicircular palaces with porticos echoing the curve of the exedra of the Baths of Diocletian. In the center, Mario Rutelli sculpted the Fountain of the

"I do not want the famous Rome, I want the present-day Rome with its clashing modernism amidst its antiquity, with its humble people and its bourgeois."

Émile Zola,
Rome

Piazza della Repubblica (or Piazza Esedra as it was then and still is commonly called) at the beginning of the 20th century. Stazione Termini can be seen in the background, preceding its reconstruction just before World War II.

▲ FROM THE BATHS OF DIOCLETIAN TO SAN PIETRO IN VINCOLI

ST BRUNO
(c. 1030–1101)
This statue of the saint who founded the Carthusian order is in the passage leading to the transept of the Church of Santa Maria degli Angeli. It is the work of the sculptor Jean-Antoine Houdon (1741–1828), who was a "pensionnaire" (art scholar) at the French

Academy's Villa Medici ▲ *315*, from 1766 to 1768.

1. CHURCH OF SANTA BIBIANA
2. TEMPLE OF MINERVA MEDICA
3. PORTA MAGGIORE

THE SUNDIAL OF SANTA MARIA DEGLI ANGELI
This sundial in the floor of the transept was used to regulate the clocks of Rome from 1702 to 1846.

Naiads (1901), which created a furor, the nudity of the lovely bathers outraging local sensibilities. Finally passions cooled, and the central group alone was altered: the marine deity Glaucus now grasps a dolphin.

THE BATHS OF DIOCLETIAN
(Terme di Diocleziano). On his return from Africa in the autumn of 298 AD, the Emperor Maximian undertook the building of a sumptuous complex of baths, designed to enable some three thousand people at a time to engage in a variety of sports and cultural activities. The baths were only completed after the abdication, on May 1, 305, of Maximian and his co-emperor Diocletian. Surrounded by a wall, the complex covered an area measuring about 1,230 x 1,200 feet (the central building alone measured approximately 820 feet x 590 feet). It was constructed according to the usual plan ● 68, ▲ *319*: a large central hall, a *caldarium-tepidarium-natatio* complex along the minor axis, and gymnasiums on either side of the major axis. These central structures are the best preserved, but important vestiges of the outer walls are still standing; some sections of the baths now form part of the National Roman Museum. The façade of the Facoltà di Magistero stands on the site of the northwestern façade of the ancient buildings. On the west corner, toward Via Cernaia, the great octagonal hall (transformed in 1928 into a planetarium and then a movie theater) has since 1991 housed a display of ancient sculptures from various baths in the city. One of the rotundas at the corners of the external walls is now the Church of San Bernardo alle Terme ▲ *295*.

SANTA MARIA DEGLI ANGELI. Responding to the vow of a Sicilian priest who had a vision of a cloud of angels flying round the Baths of Diocletian, in 1561 Pope Pius IV commissioned Michelangelo to build a church here dedicated to the angels and to the Christian martyrs who, according to tradition, had been forced to build the baths. One of the well-preserved apses of the *caldarium* forms the church's entrance (as seen in the picture at the foot of the page). Through it you enters a small circular room with two great square exedras, flanked by the tombs of the painters Salvator Rosa (1615–73) and Carlo Maratta (1625–1713); this is the former *tepidarium*.

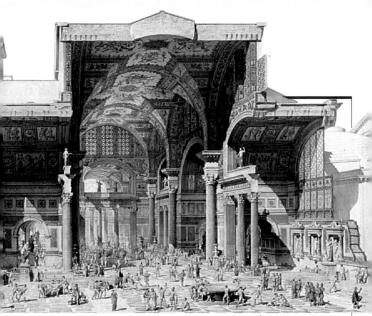

he visitor finally reaches the main body of the church,
hich occupies what was the central hall of the baths. Despite
e modifications introduced by Michelangelo and then by
nvitelli in 1749, the church retains the vast proportions
the ancient building. Its vaults, as well as the eight immense
lumns of red granite, also belong to the original building.
igantic paintings – many of which come from St Peter's
212, where they were replaced with mosaics – decorate
e walls of the transept and the choir. The most remarkable
these paintings are the *Fall of Simon the Magician* by
mpeo Batoni (1755), the *Martyrdom of St Sebastian* by
menichino (1629) and the *Baptism of Jesus* by Carlo
aratta (c. 1697). (Turn left.)

USEUM OF THE BATHS. This used to house the National
oman Museum ▲ *336,* whose works have been transferred
the Palazzo Massimo ▲ *338* and the Palazzo Altemps
284. It now houses archaeological works from the Baths
Diocletian and other large public buildings such as the
mple of Aurelian. There is in addition an epigraphical
ction, some which boasts 10,000 inscriptions. A section
voted to the prehistory of the Eternal City is open to
e public on the first floor of the cloister. (Turn into Via
aeta).

ASTRO PRETORIO (Praetorian barracks). Between 21
d 23 AD the Emperor Tiberius built a huge barracks
mplex on the northwest boundary of the town for
e Praetorian cohorts (the permanent guard for the
nperor, originally created by Augustus), who until that
ne had been billeted in different parts of Rome. The
aetorian guard used the area between the barracks
d the Servian Wall for training. As well as containing
e guards' dwellings, the barracks included various
nctional buildings: the commander's headquarters,
e treasury, the armory, a hospital and granaries (*horrea*),
c. The perfectly preserved wall of the building is visible
the northeast of Stazione Termini, between Viale Castro
etorio and Viale del Policlinico. The main national library,
e Biblioteca Vittorio Emanuele II, built between 1965
d 1975, now occupies part of the site. (Walk back toward
e station, taking the Via San Martino della Battaglia and
a Solferino.)

As the inscription at
the entrance of the
National Roman
Museum indicates, it
was necessary to
demolish numerous
buildings in order to
make room for the
Baths of Diocletian.
It took an army of
workmen eight years
to build the gigantic
baths complex –
including, according
to medieval tradition,
40,000 Christians.

**MUSEUM OF THE
BATHS**
It is pleasant to walk
in the Great Cloister
and the old garden of
the Baths, which
include archeological
remains, sarcophagi
and ancient
inscriptions.

Established in 1889 in the Carthusian convent
house the archeological finds of the period, the
National Roman Museum is one of the mc
important museums in the world as regards t
art of antiquity. Archeological collections are
displayed in four different locations: the Baths
of Diocletian, the Palazzo Massimo, the Palaz
Altemps and the Crypta Balbi. Its treasures
include the famous collection gathered in the
17th century by Cardinal Ludovisi and exhibite
at the Palazzo Altemps, together with the thro

"THE MAIDEN OF ANZIO"

This young girl is standing, with her head slightly bowed, holding a tray. Her tunic, which is slipping off one shoulder, is gathered at the waist. The vivacity, the freshness and the grace expressed in the motion of the body and the position of her head, freed from classical conventions, date this as a 3rd century BC work.

THE PORTONACCIO SARCOPHAGUS

In the center a Roman general, whose expression is clearly depicted, spurs his horse against the enemy; all around him Roman soldiers with helmets and breastplates are triumphing over barbarians, shown in pathetic attitudes. This theme of the fray, rendered here with splendid relief work, was frequently used in the iconographic repertoire of the Roman sarcophagus workshops in the 2nd century AD.

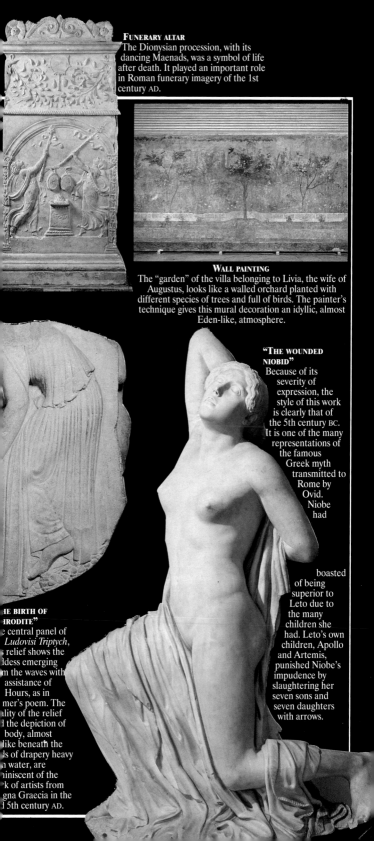

FUNERARY ALTAR
The Dionysian procession, with its dancing Maenads, was a symbol of life after death. It played an important role in Roman funerary imagery of the 1st century AD.

WALL PAINTING
The "garden" of the villa belonging to Livia, the wife of Augustus, looks like a walled orchard planted with different species of trees and full of birds. The painter's technique gives this mural decoration an idyllic, almost Eden-like, atmosphere.

"THE WOUNDED NIOBID"
Because of its severity of expression, the style of this work is clearly that of the 5th century BC. It is one of the many representations of the famous Greek myth transmitted to Rome by Ovid. Niobe had boasted of being superior to Leto due to the many children she had. Leto's own children, Apollo and Artemis, punished Niobe's impudence by slaughtering her seven sons and seven daughters with arrows.

IE BIRTH OF IRODITE"
e central panel of *Ludovisi Triptych*, relief shows the dess emerging m the waves with assistance of Hours, as in mer's poem. The lity of the relief l the depiction of body, almost like beneath the ls of drapery heavy n water, are niniscent of the k of artists from gna Graecia in the l 5th century AD.

STAZIONE TERMINI

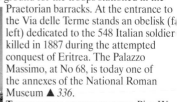

PIAZZA DEI CINQUECENTO. This square served in the 19th century as a parade ground for the troops stationed in the Praetorian barracks. At the entrance to the Via delle Terme stands an obelisk (far left) dedicated to the 548 Italian soldier killed in 1887 during the attempted conquest of Eritrea. The Palazzo Massimo, at No 68, is today one of the annexes of the National Roman Museum ▲ 336.

The Bernich Aquarium (below right).

ROME'S STATION
The name Stazione Termini was chosen for the station because of the baths (*terme*) nearby.

THE HISTORY OF THE STATION. Pius IX developed the railways in the Pontifical States. About 1857 the idea was put forward of combining the arrivals and departures, previously divided. The site for the new station was chosen in 1860, but the design of architect Salvatore Bianchi was not accepted until 1867: a building flanked by two wings, with alternating Tuscan, Ionic and Corinthian columns concealing a metal structure. Following the creation of the State Railways, from 1905 proposals were put forward for the general restructuring of Stazione Termini. The Universal Exhibition of 1942 ▲ 386 contributed a new impetus, and in 1938 the old station was partially replaced with buildings designed by Angiolo Mazzoni del Grande. In 1967 the refurbishment was completed with the impressive structure housing the main hall, ticket offices and restaurant. Thus the present station combine the architecture of the Fascist period and that of the 1960's. (Follow the via Giovanni Giolitti, then take Via Cattaneo as far as Piazza Fanti.)

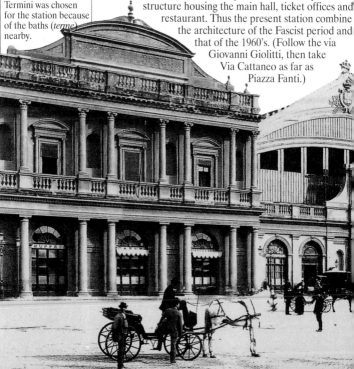

Via Giovanni Giolitti

THE BERNICH AQUARIUM. Between the station and Piazza Vittorio Emanuele II, one can now visit a very pretty but long neglected building put up between 1885 and 1887. Designed as the municipal aquarium, it combines travertine marble and [ca]st iron in an extremely original setting entirely focused on [th]e marine environment. It now contains the House of [Ar]chitecture, which hosts conferences and exhibitions. [(F]ollow Via Rattazi to return to Via Giovanni Giolitti.)

[SA]NTA BIBIANA. Now practically nestling against the [rai]lway track, this small 5th-century basilica was [ori]ginally located in the heart of the country. In [16]24 the bodies of St Bibiana, her parents and her [sis]ter were exhumed from under the main altar; [sub]sequently Urban VIII decided to rebuild the [chu]rch. Bernini designed the façade as well as [the] main altar, which he crowned with his first [gre]at religious sculpture. The saint's left hand [ho]lds carefully worked folds of drapery which [giv]e life and movement to the statue. Above the [col]onnade in the nave, frescoes representing [Bib]iana's life were painted by Agostino Ciampelli [(on] the right) and Pietro da Cortona (on the left). [Th]is was Cortona's first major work, and [hen]ceforth Urban VIII involved these two painters in [all] the important artistic enterprises of his pontificate.

[TE]MPLE OF MINERVA MEDICA. This large decagonal hall, [wh]ich once had a circular dome, was originally part of the [Ga]rdens of Licinius. It dates from the 4th century AD and was [na]med after a statue of Minerva found close by, now [pre]served in the Vatican.

[PO]RTA MAGGIORE

[CL]AUDIUS' AQUEDUCT. The Porta Maggiore, a magnificent [arc]hway in travertine marble, was formed from arches [bel]onging to two aqueducts, the Aqua Claudia and the Anio Novus, begun by Caligula in 38 AD and completed by Claudius fourteen years later. It only became a true gateway when it was included in the Aurelian Wall ▲ *323*. In the 5th century Honorius added an external bastion, the demolition of which in 1838 led to the discovery of the tomb of Eurysaces. On the upper part of the structure one can read the inscriptions, repeated on both sides, of Claudius and also of Vespasian and Titus, who restored the arch in 71 and 81 AD respectively.

THE TOMB OF EURYSACES. This tomb was built around 30 BC

The station in 1866.

TEMPLE OF MINERVA MEDICA
The bold architecture of the temple inspired many Renaissance buildings. Today, bordered by railway tracks and ugly apartment blocks, it has lost much of the charm that Stendhal found in it.

PORTA MAGGIORE
The tall attic (upper section) with three superimposed bands corresponds to the conduits of the two aqueducts. The monument was built using the so-called "unfinished" technique typical of the time of Claudius, which merely hinted at many of the architectural elements.

for Marcus Vergilius Eurysaces, a baker who supplied bread to the army, and his wife Atistia, as the inscriptions recall. I location between the Via Labicana and the Via Prenestina determined its curious trapezoidal design. The cylindrical architectural elements are evocative of the receptacles in which dough was kneaded, and the relief shows the various phases of breadmaking (above). All the decorative motifs of the tomb are designed to exalt the profession of this freed slave who lined his pockets during the civil wars.

THE UNDERGROUND BASILICA OF PORTA MAGGIORE. This intriguing building (closed to the public) was discovered by chance in April 1917. Its function is not known for certain: may have been a tomb, a funeral basilica, a nymphaeum, or neo-Pythagorean temple. It comprises a large hall (about 40 30 feet), preceded by a square vestibule divided into three naves; the central one ends in an apse All the walls are covered with stucco decorations, but the vault and the apse are the most interesting elements; the former consists of three sections featuring mythological and realistic scenes, masks and other decorative elements that are arranged in an evident attempt at symmetry. In the apse one can see Sappho who, pushed by a cupid, is flinging herself into the sea from the cliff of Leucas; under the gaze of Apollo, she is welcomed by a triton and Leucothea, who is raising h veil. The decoration is rich in mysterious metaphysical and symboli meanings which are not yet fully understood. (Take the Via Porta Maggiore, then Via Principe Eugenio.)

The tomb of Eurysaces.

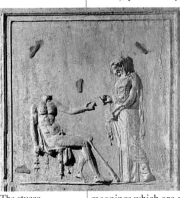

The stucco decorations of the vault of the underground basilica.

PIAZZA VITTORIO EMANUELE II

AN ANIMATED CENTER. In building the Esquiline neighborhood, the first large urban project in Italy's new capital ● 33, the vast square dedicated to King Victor Emmanuel II formed the focal point for the streets leading from San Giovanni in Laterano, Santa Croce in Gerusalem and Porta Maggiore. Its porticos, completed in 1882 and 18 reflect the influence of Piedmontese architecture, as Tu

THE ARCH OF GALLIENUS
(Take Via Merulana, then Via San Vito.) Completely rebuilt by Augustus, this is one of the gateways in the oldest of the city walls; it was originally called the Porta Esquilina. The inscription of Marcus Aurelius Victor to the Emperor Gallienus and his wife Salonina, engraved on the cornice bordering the attic, is a later addition.

Piazza Vittorio Emanuele II in the last century.

as the first capital of the new kingdom; and at its center is
e of Rome's most picturesque markets. In the gardens
ere is a fountain by Mario Rutelli, a mass of tritons,
lphins and octopuses originally designed to adorn the
untain of the Naiads in Piazza della Repubblica ▲ *334*. This
arine cluster has earned the fountain the nickname of *fritto
isto* ("fish fry")!

HE TROPHIES OF MARIUS. The monumental brick structure
the northwest corner of the gardens was, in Renaissance
nes, named "I Trofei di Mario" due to the two 1st-century
arble reliefs that adorned it before they were moved to the
lustrade of the Capitol ▲ *334*. It is in fact the remains of a
assive fountain dating from the time
Alexander Severus (3rd century
). which crowned the water tower
the Aqua Julia. Nearby stands
e intriguing Porta Magica,
scribed with an alchemist's
rmula for making gold. (Turn
ft into Via Leopardi.)

**HE AUDITORIUM OF
IAECENAS.** This was certainly
irt of the house of Maecenas,
ugustus' famous minister who
as a patron of many writers
id poets. An apsidal hall, partly
iderground and completely
ructured in *opus reticulatum*,
may have been designed for
iblic readings of literary
orks by authors such as
orace or Virgil, who both
ved in the neighborhood.
here are six deep rectangular
ches on either side of the
ill, with sumptuous bucolic
ecorations. The exedra has
ven narrow steps, above which
ere are five niches decorated with
irden scenes; under them runs a
ieze with a black background
owing hunting scenes, which are a
ntinuation of the
ecorations in the main
irt of the hall. (Take
ia Merulana.)

TROPHIES OF MARIUS
There is no doubt
that the fountain
resembled the
proposed restoration
shown on the left; a
monumental façade
with a central niche
flanked by two open
arches. These held
the two trophies
portraying the
weapons of the
"barbarians" (the
Chatti and the
Dacians) conquered
by Domitian in 89 AD.

TROPHÉE VVLGAIREMENT APPELÉ DE MARIVS
TROVVÉ SVR LES RVINES DV CHATEAV DE L'EAV IVLES

PIAZZA DELL'ESQUILINO AND PIAZZA SANTA MARIA MAGGIORE
The Basilica of Santa Maria Maggiore is framed by two squares on which the popes left their mark. To match the obelisk in the Piazza dell'Esquilino, Paul V had the fluted marble column from the Basilica of Maxentius ▲ 145 erected in the Piazza Santa Maria Maggiore. Carlo Maderno set it on a pedestal and crowned it with a statue of the Virgin.

BASILICA OF SANTA MARIA MAGGIORE ★

CHURCH OF MANY NAMES. The Virgin Mary herself is supposed to have shown Pope Liberius (352–66) where this church was to be built by causing snow to fall on the top of the Esquiline on August 5, 356. The church is therefore also known as the Liberian Basilica, but it was built by St Sixtus I (432–40) immediately after the maternity of Mary had been defined at the Council of Ephesus (431). Dedicated to the Virgin Mary, the fourth patriarchal basilica was subsequently given the name of Santa Maria ad Praesepe ("St Mary of the Crib") because of a shrine dedicated to the holy crib situated under the altar of the Sixtus V chapel.

THE FAÇADE. On the Piazza di Santa Maria Maggiore the basilica has a baroque façade enhanced by a loggia, designed by Ferdinando Fuga for Pope Benedict XIV in the mid 18th century. Returning from Avignon in 1377, Gregory XI had the CAMPANILE (bell tower) built; approximately 245 feet high, it still the tallest in Rome. Under the 12th-century PORTICO, restored by Gregory XIII for the Holy Year of 1575, there is bronze statue of Philip IV of Spain, the benefactor of the basilica. To the left of the portico a flight of stairs leads to the loggia, where one can admire the fine mosaics with which Filippo Rusuti adorned the original façade at the end of the 13th century. From here the Pope used to bestow his benediction "Urbi et Orbi" upon the crowds.

PAPAL MODIFICATIONS. Despite the numerous alterations introduced by various popes over the centuries, the general appearance of the basilica's interior is still quite similar to

at it
riginally was.
orty Ionic
olumns, of
hich 36 are
arble
onoliths,
ivide the inner
ace into three
ves of majestic proportions. In the 9th century Pascal I
idertook the restoration of the choir and Benedict III
habilitated the baptistery. The beautiful paving that Eugene
I had made by the Cosmati (1145–53) was, however,
dically rearranged when Ferdinando Fuga was
mmissioned to restore the basilica in the 18th century. But
e most important modifications were carried out under
icholas IV (1288–92), who had a transept and a new apse
signed. Rodrigo Borgia, the future Pope Alexander VI
492–1503), commissioned Giuliano da Sangallo to make the
lendid coffered ceiling with the Borgia arms. The fact that
ornamental roses are some 3 feet in diameter gives an idea
the building's dimensions. This ceiling is said to have been
ded with the first gold brought from the New World.
HE MOSAICS ★. Thirty-six panels of 5th-century mosaics
ong the central nave above the architrave illustrate scenes
om the Old Testament; they are
nong the earliest Christian mosaics
Rome. Those on the chancel arch,
nich date from the same period and
splay Byzantine influence, show
enes of the birth and childhood of
sus above representations of the
wns of Jerusalem and Bethlehem (below). They proclaim
e glory of the Virgin, who is dressed as an Oriental empress.
ne mosaics in the apse, which complete the series in the
ive in a blaze of color, are by Jacopo Torriti (1295), a pupil
Cavallini. They consist in part of 5th-century elements (the
liage and the Jordan, for example) and consecrate the
umph of Mary: between the windows episodes of her life
nfold, and in the arched vault above the apse is Torriti's
asterpiece The Coronation of the Virgin (above).
HE CHAPELS. Two domed chapels stand on either side of the
confessio. On the right is
the richly ornamented
SISTINE CHAPEL, which
Sixtus V commissioned
Domenico Fontana to build
in 1586. It was adorned with
marbles from the
Septizodium ▲ 150 and
decorated with frescoes.
Fontana also designed the
monumental tombs of Sixtus V
and Pius V, each decorated with
five bas-reliefs. When Paul V
asked Flaminio Ponzio to build
the PAULINE CHAPEL to the same
design, Ponzio also used the
form of the Greek cross and for

**"THE CORONATION
OF THE VIRGIN"**
In Torriti's
masterpiece, Christ
and the Virgin are
seated on a precious
throne; the Son is
crowning his Mother.
To the right, in the
midst of a procession
of angels and saints
are St Francis and St
Anthony, the
Franciscan saints, as
well as the Order's
former general, Pope
Nicholas IV, kneeling
beside Cardinal
Giacomo Colonna.
In the episode of the
Dormition, the artist
and his assistant are
shown kneeling at the
feet of Our Lady.

THE PAULINE CHAPEL
Between 1611 and
1615 most painters in
Rome worked on the
decorations of this
chapel. One finds the
older generation –
Cigoli (The Virgin
Mary and the Apostles,
in the dome) and
Cavaliere d'Arpino
(Prophets and Sibyls,
in the pendentives of
the dome and
Apparition of the
Virgin and St John,
above the altar) – as
well as younger artists
such as Lanfranco
and Guido Reni, who
painted the figures of
saints above the
tombs.

FROM THE BATHS OF DIOCLETIAN TO SAN PIETRO

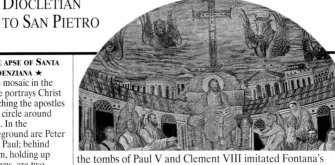

THE APSE OF SANTA PUDENZIANA ★
The mosaic in the apse portrays Christ teaching the apostles in a circle around him. In the foreground are Peter and Paul; behind them, holding up crowns, are two women personifying the Church of the Circumcision and the Church of the Gentiles. A portico closes off the scene, beyond which the roofs of a town, no doubt Jerusalem, are visible. In the sky, on each side of a cross encrusted with precious stones, are the four evangelists in their symbolic forms of the eagle, the bull, the lion and the angel.

Santa Pudenziana: the bell tower, the doorway, and a detail of the façade.

the tombs of Paul V and Clement VIII imitated Fontana's arrangement.

PIAZZA DELL'ESQUILINO. Sixtus V transformed this square and re-erected there one of the obelisks that had stood outside the entrance to the Mausoleum of Augustus ▲ *309*. When the twin cupolas of the chapels of Santa Maria Maggiore were completed, it became apparent that they needed to be integrated with the basilica as a whole. Eventually Clement X (1670–76) entrusted the building of the apsidal end to Carlo Rainaldi, and the basilica now appears in its full glory at the top of his magnificent tiers of steps leading from the Piazza dell'Esquilino. (Turn left into Via Urbana.)

SANTA PUDENZIANA AND SANTA PRASSEDE

A HOLY FAMILY. According to tradition, St Peter was given hospitality by a senator named Pudens who had two daughters, Pudentiana and Praxedes, and two sons, Novatus and Timothy. The latter was probably St Paul's companion. After the death of her parents and husband, Pudentiana is said to have turned her house in Vicus Patricius (now the Via Urbana) into a church. A few years later, after the death of Pudentiana and Praxedes, Pope Pius I (1402–55) is reputed to have built two churches, one in Vicus Patricius dedicated to St Pudentiana and the other dedicated to St Praxedes.

SANTA PUDENZIANA. Excavations below the church have revealed a Roman house over which baths were built in the 2nd century. Although the church itself dates back to the 4th century, a variety of modifications radically altered the appearance of this paleo-Christian building. The bell tower was added at the end of the 12th century, and the lovely doorway in the 16th century (using much older materials); then in 1588 Francesco da Volterra was entrusted with a major refurbishment of the church and the building of an elliptical dome. Santa Pudenziana is best known for the mosaic in the apse (although it suffered some damage during the restoration work of the 16th and early 17th centuries); dating from the end of the 4th or beginning of the 5th century, it is one of the earliest Christian mosaics in Rome. The CAETANI CHAPEL in the left nave – perhaps the first place of worship in Pudens' home – is one of the richest in Rome, embellished with marble and stucco decorations. (Return to Piazza Santa Maria Maggiore and Via di Santa Prassede.)

The mosaics in the apse (left).

SANTA PRASSEDE
Mosaic of the Heavenly City on the chancel arch (above).

THE CHAPEL OF ST ZENO
The door is flanked by two columns – the one of granite, the other of black porphyry – and surmounted by mosaics showing the Virgin and Child between St Praxedes and St Pudentiana. On the vault of the chapel, four angels are bearing the Savior's image. The walls are decorated with figures of saints in the heavenly paradise (Praxedes, Pudentiana and Agnes are on the left; Andrew, James and John on the right).

ʌNTA PRASSEDE ★. There is no archeological evidence of a ʌurch here before 489, and the earliest restorations date ɔm the pontificate of Pope Hadrian I (772–95). The present ɯilding dates from the time of St Pascal I (817–24), who ʟbuilt the church completely, changing its orientation and ɯding a monastery. The splendor of its Carolingian mosaics ɯve earned it renown, especially those in the choir and in the ʌapel of St Zeno. The mosaics in the apse, similar to those ʟ the Church of Santi Cosma e Damiano ▲ 168, show the ʌvior surrounded by six people: to the right, St Peter, St ɯdentiana and St Zeno, or perhaps St Cyriaca; to the ʟt, St Paul, St Praxedes and Pope Pascal I ʟlding a model of the church. Two palm ɯes (the two Testaments) frame the ɯmposition; a phoenix, the symbol of ɯ Resurrection, perches on the one ʌ the left. Above, twelve sheep ɯpresenting the Apostles converge ɯward the mystical Lamb. On the ʌancel arch, the elect proceed ɯward the heavenly Jerusalem, ɯere Christ is flanked by two ɯgels. Part of the mosaic had to ɯ sacrificed in order to sink ɯches into the piers of the arch: ɯ Charles Borromeo intended ɯem to house the martyrs' relics. ɯe CHAPEL OF ST ZENO ★ opens ʌf the right-hand nave. It was ɯilt by Pascal I in honor of his ɯother Theodora, who was buried ɯere. The chapel, in the form of a ɯuare, is entirely covered with ɯsaics; a matching chapel ɯdicated to St John the Baptist ɯs planned for the opposite

PIAZZA SAN PIETRO IN VINCOLI. This watercolor by Roesler shows the medieval tower of the Margini, which was converted into a bell tower for the national church of the Calabrians, San Francesco di Paola.

A "TRAGEDY" The construction of the tomb of Julius II took nearly forty years; Michelangelo described it as a "tragedy".

The Salita Borgia, which leads to the Basilica of San Pietro in Vincoli, is lined with medieval houses.

nave. (Take Via di San Martino ai Monti.)

BASILICA OF SAN MARTINO AI MONTI. Pope Silvester I (314–35) had established an oratory in the house of a priest called Equitius, and a later pope, St Symmachus (498–514), built a basilica there dedicated to St Martin of Tours. From 1636 to 1663 it was radically transformed by Pietro da Cortona. Gaspard Dughet, Poussin's brother-in-law, subsequently painted the lateral naves with frescoes in which the countryside of the Roman Campagna features prominently. Behind the basilica, in the Piazza di San Martino ai Monti, are two crenelated medieval towers, much restored, that belonged to the families Graziani (on the left) and Capocci; both towers were built with bricks from the Baths of Trajan ▲ *174*. (Take Via delle Sette Sale, in front of the church on the right.)

BASILICA OF SAN PIETRO IN VINCOLI

ST PETER'S CHAINS. The basilica owes its name (St Peter in Chains) to the precious relic it guards: the links of the chains used to fetter St Peter during his imprisonment in Jerusalem and in Rome. According to tradition, when the two chains were brought together, they were miraculously united. Preserved in the confessio, they are the object of veneration of pilgrims.

ADDITIONS OVER THE CENTURIES. The original basilica, dedicated to the Apostles and built over a 3rd-century house, first saw the light during the 4th century; it was rebuilt and consecrated under Sixtus III in 439. Cardinal Giuliano della Rovere, the future Julius II, completely transformed the church between 1471 and 1503, and it was further modified in the 18th century. Entered via a portico with five arches, the church is built to the plan of a basilica. The interior is divided by twenty ancient marble columns, and on the ceiling there is a beautiful fresco painted by the Genoese artist Giovanni Battista Parodi in 1706. Of particular note, among the church's numerous works of art are the paleo-Christian sarcophagus in the crypt, paintings by Guercino and Domenichino, a Byzantine mosaic showing a bearded St Sebastian, and the tomb of Nicholas of Cusa (a philosopher and the church's titular cardinal from 1448 until his death in 1464). **THE TOMB OF JULIUS II.** Located at the end of the right nave, this work by Michelangelo, although very

ferent from its grandiose initial conception, eclipses all the her riches of the church. In 1505, intent on commissioning a lendid mausoleum, Pope Julius II summoned the sculptor om Florence. The monument, intended for St Peter's, would ve included more than forty statues. Interrupted by a arrel between the artist and the Pope, then by the coration of the Sistine Chapel in the Vatican, e substantially reduced project was continued in 13 after the Pope's death. It was at this moment at Michelangelo sculpted the two slaves now in e Louvre and the famous *Moses*, the only work on the tomb for which he alone was responsible. Work was again suspended in 1516, since the new pontiff, Leo X, preferred to make Michelangelo work for his family, the Medici. It was not until between 1542 and 1545 that the monument was finally completed. The master entrusted the main part of the work to his pupils, especially Raffaello da Montelupo. However, he himself was largely responsible for the two female figures next to *Moses* representing Jacob's wives, *Rachel* (on the left) and *Leah* (on the right), which evoke the Contemplative Life and the Active Life respectively. The statue of the Pope and those of the sibyl and the prophet and the Virgin and Child were successfully executed in accordance with his designs. (From Via Cavour, go up the Via dei Serpenti, which leads into Piazza Madonna dei Monti. The church there dates from 1580 and is one of the masterpieces of Giacomo della Porta.)

TOWARD THE VIA NAZIONALE

VIA PANISPERNA. This street, at right angles to the Via dei Serpenti, was created by Sixtus V (1585–90) to link Santa Maria Maggiore with the center of Rome. Situated in the ancient Suburra neighborhood, its construction resulted in the modernization of the surrounding area. In front of the Church of SAN LORENZO IN PANISPERNA – known to have existed in the 9th century and rebuilt during the 17th to 18th centuries – stands the residence of the Portuguese ambassador, the PALAZZO CIMARRA. Work on it began in 1736, and it became famous for the banquets held there. In this same street, the

AN ANCIENT DISTRICT
It is well worth taking a stroll through the Monti district, one of the few quarters (*rioni*) that has succeeded in keeping its lively character relatively unchanged. In particular, explore Via Baccina, Via dei Serpenti and Via degli Zingari, the streets trodden by the beggar pilgrim Benoît Labre (1748–83) during the last six years of his life. "A spectacle that edifies some and shocks others", wrote Cardinal de Bernis. The holy man is buried in the Madonna dei Monti church.

THE DISAPPEARANCE OF ETTORE MAJORANA
Ettore Majorana was one of the most brilliant physicians of his time. Probably tormented by the disastrous potential

of his discoveries, in 1938 he announced that he intended to commit suicide and vanished without trace. The famous author Leonardo Sciascia wrote an account of his disappearance, *La Scomparsa di Majorana*, that reads like a thriller.

▲ FROM THE BATHS OF DIOCLETIAN TO SAN PIETRO IN VINCOLI

SAN PAOLO ENTRO LE MURA
The alternating bands of red brick and travertine marble, together with the elegant bell tower, are proof of the desire to give this Episcopal church "an Italian character".

"EST, EST, EST". In the Middle Ages a German prelate traveled through Italy preceded by a servant who had been told to sample the local wines. "Est," the servant said when the wine was good. When he arrived in Monte-fiascone, near Lake Bolsena, the white wine was so delicious that in his enthusiasm he exclaimed "Est, est, est!" The wine took its name from this anecdote, as did the popular pizzeria in the Via Genova.

scientists Enrico Fermi and Ettore Majorana from the scien faculty of Rome perfected the fission of uranium in the 1930's. (Return to the Via dei Serpenti.)

VIA NAZIONALE. Begun under Pius IX, this became the main thoroughfare of Piedmontese Rome. On the left is the great neo-Renaissance palace of the BANK OF ITALY, built betwee 1887 and 1902 by Gaetano Koch. Opposite one can see the cast-iron and reinforced-cement structure of the former MAGAZZINI ROVATTI (now the Renault building) erected around 1900, notable for the innovative treatment of the

windows and display areas. Together wi the PICCOLO ELISEO, these buildings are the most outstanding examples of Liber (Art Nouveau) architecture in Rome. On the same side of the street, after the Umberto I Tunnel, is the vast PALAZZO DELLE ESPOSIZIONI built by Pio Piacent between 1878 and 1882. This building excited considerable controversy at the time of its construction: its windowless façade, massive size and style, consider "not at all Italian", were all furiously criticized. Inside, large open areas separated by columns give it a neoclassical character. This building provides the "cultural space" that had been lacking in Rome. Along with temporary exhibition it has a cinematheque and, on the top floor, in pleasant surroundings, a cheap and welcoming cafeteria. On the corner of Via Napoli stands the American Episcopalian Church of SAN PAOLO ENTRO LE MURA (St Paul's within the Walls). Built in 1873, it was the first non-Catholic place of worship to be erected in Rome after the fall of the Papal State. The work of George Edmund Street, a gifted Victoria architect, is also the only example in Italy of the English Art

and Crafts style. The mosaics in the apse and the choir, mad in Murano, are by the pre-Raphaelite painter Sir Edward Burne-Jones, and the ceramics decorating the internal walls by William Morris. The HOTEL QUIRINALE, built in 1874, is linked by an underground passage to the Opera (above). Verdi stayed here for the Rome premiere of his opera Falsta in 1893. The apartments close to the Piazza della Repubblic are the oldest in the Via Nazionale, dating from the time of the real-estate operation undertaken by Msgr de Merode in 1864 to 1870. Built in a flaky, poor-quality white stone, they surprised Pius IX: when he visited the building site, he asked if the apartments were made of ricotta.

Trastevere

352 Isola Tiberina

353 Ripagrande

357 Basilica of Santa Maria
     in Trastevere

359 Via della Lungara

360 The Farnesina

362 Palazzo Corsini

363 Ponte Sisto

363 The Janiculum

From early times Trastevere
(which means "across the
Tiber") was primarily a
working-class quarter. In
the 2nd and 3rd
centuries it was the
main center for
communities
belonging
to

🗓 **One day**

◆ **D** B3-B4-C3-C4-D3-D4
E C1-D1

1. ISOLA TIBERINA
2. PALAZZO AND TOUR ANGUILLARA
3. CHURCH OF SAN CRISOGONO
4. BASILICA OF SANTA CECILIA
5. CHURCH OF THE MADONNA DELL'ORTO
6. OSPEDALE SAN MICHELE
7. PORTA PORTESE
8. CHURCH OF SAN FRANCESCO A RIPA
9. SYRIAN SANCTUARY OF THE JANICULUM
10. EXCUBITORIUM
11. BASILICA OF SANTA MARIA IN TRASTEVERE
12. CHURCH OF SAN PIETRO IN MONTORIO
13. ACQUA PAOLA
14. JANICULE
15. CHURCH OF SANTA MARIA DEI SETTE DOLORI
16. CHURCH OF SANTA MARIA DELLA SCALA
17. PORTA SETTIMIANA
18. PIAZZA TRILUSSA
19. PONTE SISTO
20. PALAZZO CORSINI
21. FARNESINA
22. MONASTERY OF SANT'ONOFRIO

oriental religions ● *252*. The early presence of Christians in this area led to the foundation of three titular churches in the 4th century: Santa Maria in Trastevere, San Crisogono and Santa Cecilia. After the period of decline following the great invasions and repeated sacking of the city ● *30*, the population was concentrated around these buildings.

EXPANSION. From the 10th and 11th centuries, like the rest o the city, the neighborhood experienced rapid expansion, marked by the development of the new river port known as Ripagrande or the Ripa Romea. Then in the middle of the 13th century Trastevere was integrated into the administrativ system of the city of Rome, which brought the number of Rome's districts or *rioni* up to thirteen. A few noble families

cluding the Stefaneschi, Papareschi and Alberteschi) lived the area, but of their homes only those belonging to the nguillara and the Mattei have survived from that period oth heavily restored). When the papacy returned from vignon, for a little while Trastevere became the seat of the udium Urbis university. At that time, there were only two ints of communication with the left bank of the Tiber: la Tiberina (Tiber island) and from 1475 the Ponte Sisto, nich was intended to give pilgrims access to St Peter's.

CESS ROUTES. Until the 14th century no great town planning initiatives affected this district, its population being concentrated close to the Tiber.

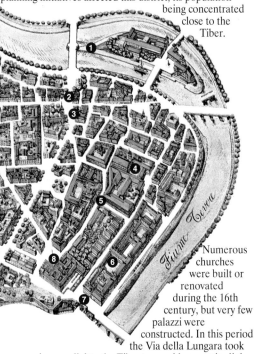

Fiume Tevere

Numerous churches were built or renovated during the 16th century, but very few palazzi were constructed. In this period the Via della Lungara took

ape, running parallel to the Tiber to provide an easier link th the Borgo (the *rione* of St Peter's ▲ *232*). But it was not til the 19th century that the main avenues were built: the ale di Trastevere running through the middle of the district, d the Lungotevere skirting the river.

LIVELY QUARTER. Trastevere remained a predominantly rking-class area until the 1960's, when it increasingly came be seen as a neighborhood of restaurants and nightlife. But the morning it retrieves some of its traditional character, d the *vicoli* (small streets) around Santa Maria in astevere offer a glimpse of the daily life of the past. The ue spirit of the district is revealed in the month of July

THE TRASTEVERE, CENTER OF NIGHTLIFE ✪
Having attracted travelers and artists since antiquity, the Trastevere is Rome's bohemian quarter par excellence. Today it is frequented most especially by night owls, rivaling the Via Veneto ▲ *302*, capital of *la dolce vita*, and the Piazza Navona ▲ *276* in the number of establishments that stay open until the early hours. It has lost much of its original character after housing speculation in the 1960s drove out the craftsmen, the small local shops and the ordinary working people. However, something of its old spirit returns in July during the Festa de Noantri ("our own feast"), when restaurant tables invade the sidewalks and processions, concerts, theatrical performances and firework displays fill the small squares and narrow streets.

THE TRASTEVERINI
With their own dialect, the people of Trastevere had always considered themselves the descendants of the ancient Romans. The quarter was frequently a source of uprisings; consequently the popes distrusted the Trasteverini. In 1849 this was the area that continued to defend the short-lived Republic of Rome to the very end.

SAN BARTOLOMEO ALL'ISOLA
Only the Romanesque campanile of the old church remains. A well with beautiful medieval statues stands beside the presbytery. The church was completely rebuilt in 1624 by Martino Longhi the Younger but still retains the columns of the pagan temple.

PONTE ROTTO
At the southern tip of the island is the Ponte Rotto (the "broken bridge"). This is all that remains of the Pons Aemilius (2nd century BC), which was rebuilt several times before it finally collapsed in the 15th century. The point of the island is formed by a ship's prow sculpted in travertine in reference to the story of Aesculapius – part of a marble wall that once encircled the island to make it look even more like a ship.

The Tiber.

during the *Festa de' Noantri* ("our own feast") ● *44*. On summer nights in the back streets behind Via Garibaldi it is common to see people bringing chairs out into the street for convivial improvised meal with neighbors.

ISOLA TIBERINA

THE ORIGIN OF THE ISLAND. According to legend the island in the Tiber was formed when the people flung the wheat harvest of the Campus Martius (which at that time belonged to the Etruscan kings) into the river after the expulsion of Tarquinius Superbus from Rome in the 4th century BC. Another legend has it that in order to end a plague some Romans went to Epidaurus in Greece to fetch Aesculapius, the god of medicine, and brought back a sacred serpent symbolizing the god. The serpent swam ashore to the island, the shape of which is said to be identical to that of the ship. In 293 BC a temple to Aesculapius was built here; its ruins lie beneath the Church of San Bartolomeo all'Isola, erected in the 10th century by the German Emperor Otto III. Until the 19th century this was the church of the millers' corporation, who used to celebrate their feast on the island on December
A SPARSELY POPULATED ISLAND. The Isola Tiberina was barely inhabited until the Middle Ages, when the Pierleoni and Caetani families settled there. A tower that formed part of

heir fortifications remains standing at the head of the Ponte
abricio. In the 17th century, especially during the plague of
656, it was used as a place of quarantine for plague victims in
rder to limit epidemics in the city. The island's medical
ocation has remained; even today the Fatebenefratelli
ospital covers almost all of it. The Baroque interior of the
ttle church of San Giovanni Calibita should not be missed.

BRIDGES OVER THE TIBER. Two bridges span the Tiber from
he island. The one, the Ponte Fabricio, links the island with
he Campo Marzio; on it is an inscription giving the name of
s builder (Lucius Fabricius, son of Caius) four times over
nd the date 62 BC. The two four-headed busts of Janus
raming the entrance on the Campo Marzio side have earned
. the popular nickname of Ponte dei Quattro Capi ("Bridge
f the Four Heads"). The other bridge, the Ponte Cestio, built
 the 1st century BC as a link with Trastevere, was partly
emolished in 1888 and rebuilt in 1892.

The Ponte Rotto
(above left) and the
Church of Santa
Cecilia.

RIPAGRANDE

THE PORT OF RIPAGRANDE. Sadly this was destroyed when the
ungotevere embankments were built at the
nd of the 19th century. The river now flows
etween high walls (*muraglioni*) and it is not
ossible to imagine how colorful and busy it
nce was. Barges arriving from Ostia used
 be hauled from the right bank of the
iber by men or buffaloes, which explains
he presence near Porta Portese of an area
alled the *bufalara*. The port was also known
s the Ripa Romea (the "bank for pilgrims
oing to Rome") because pilgrims bound
or St Peter's used to alight there.

Medieval buildings in
the vicinity of Santa
Cecilia.

PIAZZA IN PISCINULA. The piazza's appearance today dates
rom the end of the 19th century when the palazzo facing
alazzo Mattei was demolished. Some rather questionable
estorations have attempted to recreate a medieval Roman
iazza. There are theories that Palazzo Mattei dates back to
he time of Gregory IX (1227–41), or even to the time of
nnocent II (1130–43) and the Papareschi family; but as it
ow stands it doesn't go back further than the 14th or 15th
entury. SAN BENEDETTO IN PISCINULA is the smallest
omanesque basilica in the city and boasts a fine bell tower, a
3th-century fresco of *St Benedict* in the porch and a splendid
osmatesque ● 76 paving in the nave. In the area around the
quare there are many fine medieval features to be seen, such
s the beautiful porches of some of the houses (in Vicolo
ell'Atleta, for instance) or the little church of Santa Maria in
apella, which you come to after taking Via Anicia and
assing SAN GIOVANNI BATTISTA DEI GENOVESI, which has a
5th-century cloister attributed to Baccio Pontelli.

**THE MARTYRDOM OF
SANTA CECILIA**
On her wedding night
Cecilia, a devout
Christian, revealed to
her husband Valerian
that her purity was
protected by an angel
and that he would be
able to see it if he
converted. Valerian
agreed to be baptized
on the Via Appia,
and was able to see
the angel. Their faith
was discovered and
they were both
martyred. When their
remains were
unearthed in 1600,
Stefano Maderno was
commissioned to
make a statue of the
saint in the exact
position her body was
found in.

The church of the Madonna dell'Orto.

"THE BLESSED LODOVICA ALBERTONI"
As in Santa Maria della Vittoria ▲ *294*, in the Church of San Francesco a Ripa Bernini paid careful attention to lighting effects. An indirect light heightens the movement of the copiously draped agonizing figure. Her body rests on a mattress of multicolored marble fringed with gilded bronze. Above the statue a painting by Baciccia (*The Virgin and Child with St Anne*, 1675) reveals the nature of the blessed visionary's apparition.

BASILICA OF SANTA CECILIA. Set aside from the bustle of Piazza dei Mercanti (where the restaurant D meo Patacca aims to provide tourists with the atmosphere of a traditional tavern) and protected by a quadrangle planted with a rose garden, Santa Cecilia offers a haven of silence. It is believed to have been built on the remains of the house of Cecilia and her husband Valerian, and after their martyrdom it became a titular church. As a shrine already documented in the 4th century, it was restored during the pontificate of Pascal I (817–24), who commissioned the mosaics in the apse and donated a precious ciborium.
A monastery dedicated to these holy martyrs was founded next to the church (this was rebuilt by Pascal II in 1100). At the end of the 13th century a rich French prelate, Cardinal Cholet, entrusted Pietro Cavallini with the task of decorating the church with frescoes. His amazing *Last Judgment* (a detail of which is shown on the right) was discovered during restorations in 1900 and can be seen today on the first floor, where it is jealously guarded by the Benedictine oblates. Also, Arnolfo di Cambio was commissioned to build a new ciborium in the church choir (1293), which is one of the finest works by this artist in Rome. The church was radically modified several times, most significantly in 1600. A corridor to the right of the entrance leads to the *caldarium* from which Santa Cecilia is supposed to have emerged unscathed after being tortured by suffocation. Beneath the church, as well as the crypt containing Cecilia's and Valerian's sarcophagi, one can see important remains of Roman buildings from different periods of antiquity, including pavements, baths, columns and inscriptions. (Take Via di San Michele, on the right, then turn into Via della Madonna dell'Orto.)
SANTA MARIA DELL'ORTO. This church was founded in 1492 by the corporation of market gardeners. Its façade, built between 1566 and 1579, was probably designed by Vignola. But its most remarkable features are inside, where an exuberant profusion of garlands, wreaths, flowers and fruit makes a sumptuous display of Baroque decoration. These stuccos, dating from the 18th century, were donated by the local guild (*università*), which included gardeners (*ortolani*), millers (*molinari*) and fruit, poultry and pasta vendors (*fruttaroli*, *pollari* and *vermicellari*). The high altar by Giacomo dell'

...rta has a superb image of the Virgin Mary. (Take Via ...nicia, on the right.)

...N FRANCESCO A RIPA. This church is built on the site of the ...n Biagio Hospice, where St Francis is supposed to have ...ayed, and it still belongs to the Franciscan Order. ...emodeled by Mattia De Rossi around 1682, it contains many ...pulchers dating from the 17th and 18th centuries. In the ...rst chapel on the left there is a splendid *Birth of the Virgin* by ...mon Vouet, painted between 1618 and 1620 and clearly ...fluenced by Caravaggio. Three chapels farther on, you will ...d *The Blessed Lodovica Albertoni* (1671–5), one of Bernini's

...st and greatest sculptures. The funerary monuments here ...ing to mind an item mentioned by Stendhal in his *...hroniques italiennes*: a Roman princess was reported to have ...d a midnight Requiem Mass celebrated here for the lover ...e was about to have killed. Skirting the church and taking ...a Ascianghi, you will come to the PIAZZA DI PORTA PORTESE ...n ancient times the arsenal of Rome stood near here). On ...nday mornings the city's famous flea market takes place in ...is piazza and in the neighboring streets. From the corner ...e SAN MICHELE A RIPA GRANDE complex, which has a ...çade more than 1,000 feet long, stretches back along the ...ber embankment. This gigantic building was erected at the ...d of the 17th century as a home for the poor, then became ...n institution for juvenile delinquents. After undergoing ...ther lengthy restoration works (begun in 1972), it now ...ouses a variety of departments belonging to the Ministero dei ...eni e delle Attività Culturali (the ministry responsible for ...aly's cultural and environmental heritage). It contains two ...agnificent courtyards, the first unfortunately disfigured by a ...odern staircase. (Return to Viale Trastevere and take Viale ...lorioso and Via Dandolo to No. 47.)

...HE SYRIAN TEMPLE ON THE JANICULUM. From the end of the ...epublic the commercial area on the Tiber attracted many ...aders and freed slaves of oriental origin. It is therefore not ...rprising that on both sides of the river traces have been found of religions originating in Anatolia (the cult of Cybele), Egypt and Syria. These include inscriptions confirming that a close link existed between slave traders and the goddess of Syria. The

PORTA PORTESE
Rome's famous flea market has been used as a location for many films. In *Bicycle Thieves* (Vittorio de Sica, 1948) the hero takes his son to Porta Portese in the hope of finding his stolen bicycle. In *Mamma Roma* (Pier Paolo Pasolini, 1962) the son of the prostitute Mamma Roma (played by Anna Magnani ● *43*) goes there to try to sell a record he has just stolen from his mother.

The long façade of San Michele.

AN INTRIGUING ROOM
In the Syrian temple on the Janiculum there is an octagonal room with an apse at the end of it. In a cavity beneath the triangular altar a bronze statuette was found, portraying a human figure entwined in a serpent's coils – probably the Egyptian deity Osiris.

355

"A COMMON NEIGHBORHOOD"
"This is a fiercely common neighborhood, shunned and isolated on the right bank of the Tiber, where

people work in the tobacco factory and the factories that make wicks and candles for the city's hundreds of churches.... The warehouses over smoke-filled doorways or open stables expose both the traders and their merchandise to the light of day and the air of the street ... stalls, industry and labor in their natural state fill the small squares beneath the flapping of the washing hanging from every window..."
This was how the Goncourt brothers described Trastevere in the 19th century.

temple in Trastevere, discovered in 1906, proves the continuity from the 1st century AD of a Syrian cult, probably dedicated to Hadad (Heliopolis' equivalent of Jupiter), Atargatis (the Syrian goddess most widely worshiped in Rome) and Simios (the equivalent of Mercury). The sanctuary is made up of three parts: a rectangular central courtyard (the entrance), a room to the east containing a triangular altar; and a basilica, on the west side, preceded by a sort of atrium. (Go back down Via Dandolo to Piazza San Cosimato.)

PIAZZA DI SAN COSIMATO. The Benedictine monastery facing the piazza passed into the hands of the Franciscans in the 13th century and is now a hospital. It has two cloisters, one Romanesque and the other dating from the 15th century. (Return to the Viale di Trastevere.)

VIALE DI TRASTEVERE. This wide avenue, originally named Viale del Re, was built between 1880 and 1890 to link Ponte Garibaldi to Stazione Trastevere. Few buildings along it are modern, save for the TOBACCO FACTORY (1863) designed by Antonio Sarti.

THE EXCUBITORIUM. On the corner of Via di Monte Fiore and Via della VIIª Coorte is the entrance of the Excubitorium, a building dating from Imperial times that was the guardhouse of the seventh cohort of the *vigiles* (city guards). This private house, which was turned into a barracks toward the end of the 2nd century AD, provides a valuable insight into the activities of the *vigiles*. These units were formed under Augustus in 6 B and served as a police force for the city as well as a fire brigade.

SAN CRISOGONO. The present building was erected in the 12th century on top of a paleo-Christian church, but on a much greater scale, with three wide naves separated by 22 ancient columns. The campanile (bell tower) dates from 1125; the mosaics attributed to Pietro Cavallini and the Cosmatesque paving ● 76 are 13th century. The rest of the building was restored by Giambattista Soria in 1620. Bernini designed the CHAPEL OF THE BLESSED SACRAMENT. From the sacristy you can go down to the church beneath, the Titulus Chrysogonus, built in the 5th century to house the tomb of the holy martyr beheaded in the time of Diocletian. This sanctuary with a single nave was restored and decorated with frescoes during the pontificate of Gregory III (731–41). The *Scenes from the Life of St Benedict* were added in the 10th century. (Walk across Piazza Sonnino.)

THE ANGUILLARA PALAZZO AND TOWER. The name of the Anguillara family, already famous in the 11th and 12th centuries, came from their feudal domain near Lake

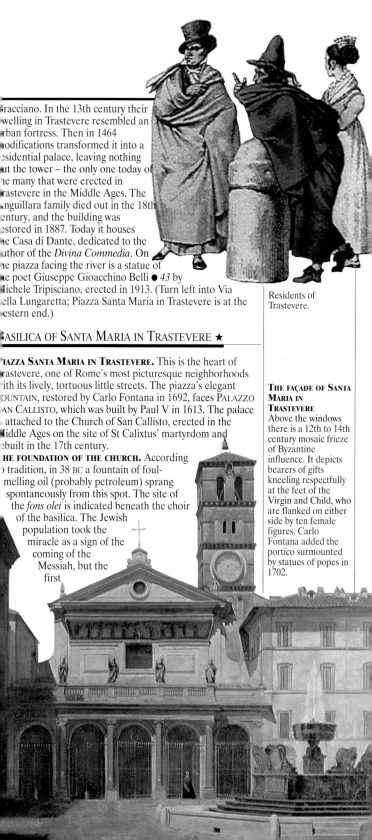

racciano. In the 13th century their dwelling in Trastevere resembled an urban fortress. Then in 1464 modifications transformed it into a residential palace, leaving nothing but the tower – the only one today of the many that were erected in Trastevere in the Middle Ages. The Anguillara family died out in the 18th century, and the building was restored in 1887. Today it houses the Casa di Dante, dedicated to the author of the *Divina Commedia*. On the piazza facing the river is a statue of the poet Giuseppe Gioacchino Belli ● *43* by Michele Tripisciano, erected in 1913. (Turn left into Via della Lungaretta; Piazza Santa Maria in Trastevere is at the western end.)

Residents of Trastevere.

BASILICA OF SANTA MARIA IN TRASTEVERE ★

PIAZZA SANTA MARIA IN TRASTEVERE. This is the heart of Trastevere, one of Rome's most picturesque neighborhoods with its lively, tortuous little streets. The piazza's elegant FOUNTAIN, restored by Carlo Fontana in 1692, faces PALAZZO SAN CALLISTO, which was built by Paul V in 1613. The palace is attached to the Church of San Callisto, erected in the Middle Ages on the site of St Calixtus' martyrdom and rebuilt in the 17th century.

THE FOUNDATION OF THE CHURCH. According to tradition, in 38 BC a fountain of foul-smelling oil (probably petroleum) sprang spontaneously from this spot. The site of the *fons olei* is indicated beneath the choir of the basilica. The Jewish population took the miracle as a sign of the coming of the Messiah, but the first

THE FAÇADE OF SANTA MARIA IN TRASTEVERE
Above the windows there is a 12th to 14th century mosaic frieze of Byzantine influence. It depicts bearers of gifts kneeling respectfully at the feet of the Virgin and Child, who are flanked on either side by ten female figures. Carlo Fontana added the portico surmounted by statues of popes in 1702.

This depiction of the
last episode of Mary's
life is one of the six
mosaics by Pietro
Cavallini in the choir
of Santa Maria in
Trastevere; the
others are *The Birth
of the Virgin, The
Annunciation, The
Birth of Jesus, The
Adoration of the Magi,*
and *The Presentation
in the Temple.* To the
left, St Paul is weeping
at Mary's feet; at the
right, together with
the Apostles and
some bishops, is
St Peter, with the
Roman pallium and
the censer, while
kneeling beside the
deceased is St John.
In the middle,
between two angels,
is the Redeemer
bearing Mary's soul.
Cavallini's use of lines
in this composition
was an innovation
in Byzantine
iconography.

The mosaic in the
choir shows Innocent
II offering the church
to the
virgin.

Christian shrine commemorating it was not established until
the 3rd century. The existence of the shrine led to friction
between the Christians and the local innkeepers. The
Emperor Alexander Severus was asked to intervene and is
said to have sided with the former, preferring the building to
be occupied by an unconventional sect rather than by
drunkards. The official biography of the popes, the *Liber
pontificalis*, gives a different version, stating that Calixtus
(who was Pope from 217 to 222) invited the faithful to a Mas
in a domestic church (*titulus*) which was later converted into
a basilica. Between 772 and 795 Hadrian I added the lateral
naves. Then Gregory IV (827–44) made extensive changes.
As well as having the choir raised, the altar covered with a
ciborium, and a crypt made to accommodate the relics of
Saints Calixtus, Calepodius and Cornelius, he had a chapel
to the Holy Crib built (in imitation of Santa Maria Maggiore
▲ *342*) and added a monastery to serve the basilica.
INNOCENT II'S BASILICA. In the 12th century Innocent II
(who belonged to one of the great Trastevere families, the
Papareschi) further modified the building, adding the transe
and decorating the apse with splendid mosaics. Most of the
materials came from the baths of Caracalla ▲ *319*. The new

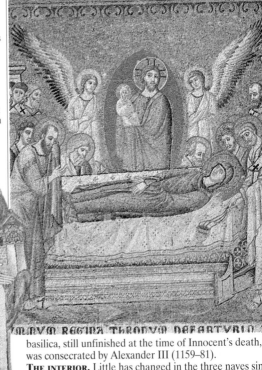

basilica, still unfinished at the time of Innocent's death,
was consecrated by Alexander III (1159–81).
THE INTERIOR. Little has changed in the three naves sinc
the time of Innocent II. The ceiling was designed by
Domenichino, who also painted *The Assumption of the
Virgin* in the center. The handsome Cosmatesque
paving ● *76* was restored in 1870. To the left of
the apse, the ALTEMPS CHAPEL (1584) was probabl

Achille Pinelli

the first Counter-Reformation chapel to be dedicated to an ancient cult of the Virgin.

MOSAICS OF THE CHOIR ★. These mosaics show traces of Byzantine influence, but belong to the Roman tradition. Those on the chancel arch portray the prophets Isaiah and Jeremiah, the symbols of the four evangelists, the seven candelabra of the Apocalypse, and the cross with the Alpha and the Omega. In the apse one sees Christ and the Virgin enthroned (above); to the left are St Calixtus, St Lawrence and Pope Innocent II donating the church to the Virgin; to the right are the saints Peter, Cornelius, Julius and Calepodius; below, two rows of sheep are shown emerging from Jerusalem and Bethlehem and converging toward the Lamb of God. These 12th-century mosaics mark a renewal in the devotion to the Virgin, and the theme of the coronation of the Virgin was to recur a century later in Jacopo Torriti's masterpiece in Santa Maria Maggiore ▲ 342. Lower down is one of the finest works of Pietro Cavallini: six episodes from the life of St Mary (1291). The artist makes an astonishing use of color, treating the mosaic as if it were a fresco. (Follow Via della Paglia, on the left as you come out of the basilica, until you reach Piazza Sant'Egidio, where you will find the 17th-century Church of Sant'Egidio and the Museo del Folklore e dei Poeti Romaneschi. Then take Via della Scala.)

SANTA MARIA DELLA SCALA. This church, which belongs to the Discalced Carmelites, was built by Francesco da Volterra. Although the Superiors of the Order refused *The Death of the Virgin* painted for them by Caravaggio, many of his pupils' works found their place in this church. They include *The Decapitation of St John the Baptist* by Honthorst in the first chapel on the right, and *The Death of the Virgin* by Carlo Saraceni in the second chapel on the left. The monastery's pharmacy has retained its 17th-century furnishings and decoration. (Take the Via Santa Dorotea.)

VIA DELLA LUNGARA

PORTA SETTIMIANA. This triumphal arch was built by Septimius Severus as an entrance to one of his villas; but in the 6th century it was incorporated, as a gateway, into the Aurelian Wall. Its present appearance dates from the modifications to the city made by Alexander VI (1498).

VIA DELLA LUNGARA. This long, straight road was constructed during the pontificate of Pope Julius II. Before the building of the Tiber embankments it was the only road linking

MUSEO DI ROMA IN TRASTEVERE
This small museum is dedicated to the life, customs and traditions of Rome in the 18th and 19th centuries. It is in five sections: the Carnival, aspects of daily life, the watercolors of Franz Ettore Roesler, the Artists' Festival in Cervara and firework displays. As well as engravings of the Piè di Marmo, the Bocca della Verità and Pasquino, there is a reconstruction of the poet Trilussa's study, containing paintings, photographs, documents and other possessions, and manuscripts of some of his poems. (This museum is fascinating, but by no means a substitute for the Museo delle Arte e Tradizioni Popolari in EUR ▲ 387.)

ACHILLE PINELLI (1809–41) The son of the painter Bartolomeo Pinelli (1781–1835), Achille began painting at an early age. His best-known works are two hundred watercolors of the churches of Rome, including one of Santa Maria della Scala, above. They are now in the Museo di Roma.

● 8

Trastevere to the Vatican. Along it are the Farnesina, the Palazzo Corsini and the Regina Coeli (Queen of Heaven) prison.

THE FARNESINA

AGOSTINO CHIGI'S VILLA. In 1509 this banker, who was the financier of Pope Julius II and Pope Leo X, commissioned Baldassare Peruzzi to build a sumptuous "country villa" with gardens stretching to the Tiber. Dubbed "il Magnifico" and known for his refined taste, this patron of the arts and man of letters even founded a printing press for the publication of classical texts. Not surprisingly, when it came to decorating the apartments of his villa, Chigi called upon the greatest artists of his time, among them Raphael, who was his friend and protégé. The paintings and frescoes of the young artist and his associates make this residence one of the gems of the Renaissance. After Chigi's death in 1520 the villa was abandoned, and in 1527 it was plundered and overrun by Charles V's troops ● 36. It acquired the name Farnesina when it was purchased by Alessandro Farnese around 1580. With the construction of the Lungotevere embankments at the end of the 19th century, part of its gardens were destroyed (revealing remains of an ancient Roman villa) and part of the loggia overlooking the river was demolished. Purchased by the Italian State in 1927, the Farnesina has been the property of the Accademia dei Lincei ▲ 362 since 1944 and now includes the Gabinetto Nazionale delle Stampe (the national collection of prints and drawings).
THE LOGGIA OF PSYCHE. The main entrance to the villa was situated beneath the loggia overlooking the garden, where theatrical performances were often staged. Two orders of columns are surmounted by a terracotta frieze that masks the third-floor windows. The loggia, is decorated with frescoes depicting Cupid and Psyche; these were painted by pupils of Raphael, following cartoons by the master. Giovanni da Udine is the author of the pergola composed of garlands of fruit and flowers that supports the two *trompe l'oeil* tapestries on the ceiling; these show the council of the gods welcoming Psyche on Mount Olympus and the wedding feast of Cupid and Psyche. Painted *putti* above the arches of the loggia and the false windows bear the attributes of the gods, while the lunettes recount the main episodes of Psyche's story.
THE LOGGIA OF GALATEA. To the right of the loggia of Psyche is the Galatea Room, named after Raphael's fresco *The Triumph of Galatea*; the artist is reputed to have used no models for it apart from ideal beauty as he conceived it.

When Ettore Roesler Franz painted this watercolor in 1880, the Farnesina's loggia overlooking the Tiber still existed. It was demolished between 1884 and 1886 during the construction of the Lungotevere embankments.

...ruzzi painted the ...iling with ...ythological ...escoes showing the ...nstellations of the ...diac in their ...sition at the time ... Agostino Chigi's ...rth. The lunettes ...e decorated with ...escoes based on ...vid's *...etamorphoses* by ...ebastiano del ...ombo, who also painted the fresco on the wall of ...lyphemus, the Cyclops, pining for the nymph Galatea.

...HE SALA DELLE PROSPETTIVE. Also known as the "room of ...e columns", this vast room on the *piano nobile* is famous for ... imposing *trompe l'oeil* frescoes by Peruzzi. The artist's ...tention was to create the illusion of an open loggia offering ...ews over the Roman countryside and the city's monuments. ... is recognized as one of the masterpieces of the early 16th ...ntury. Peruzzi's virtuosity makes this a pictorial *tour de force* ... the Roman Baroque style. The floor pattern extends into ...e illusory loggia, and the painted scenery is organized ...ound the focal point of the doorway through which you ...ter the room.

...HE SALA DI ALESSANDRO. For his bedroom Chigi ...mmissioned Giovanni Antonio dei Bazzi, known ... Il Sodoma, to adorn the main wall with a fresco ...picting the marriage of Alexander the Great ... Roxana. Painted around 1513, this is based ... an ancient model by Aetion that no longer ...isted but of which the Greek writer Lucian ...d provided a description. The wall on

A TROMPE L'OEIL ROOM
The originality of Baldassare Peruzzi's work in the Sala delle Prospettive lies neither in the decorative elements, such as the landscapes and columns, nor in the taste for *trompe l'oeil* perspectives (which was very widespread at the time), but in his ingenious use of traditional motifs to achieve the perfect optical illusion of making the walls of the room "disappear".

"THE TRIUMPH OF GALATEA"
Standing on an ethereal chariot drawn by dolphins, Galatea is no longer the cold figure of the Hellenistic and Roman traditions, but has entered the limpid world of the Muses of Parnassus. In this fresco the formal vitality of the figures is derived from the clarity of Raphael's classicism.

361

the right portrays the family of Darius submitting to Alexander. Finally, to the left of the entrance is a fresco of inferior quality showing Alexander taming Bucephalus.

PALAZZO CORSINI

Facing the Farnesina across Via della Lungara, Palazzo Corsini replaced the Palazzo Riario, the residence of Queen Christina of Sweden from 1662 until her death in 1689. It wa built between 1736 and 1758 by Ferdinando Fuga for Cardin. Neri Corsini, a nephew of Clement XII. The original conception was much more ambitious than what was built. The long façade is articulated around a central body with three portals leading into three galleries. The middle entran

THE ACCADEMIA DEI LINCEI. Founded in 1603 by Federico Cesi and of which Galileo was an eminent member, this society brought together scholars who wished to "read the great book of the true and universal world, to visit its different parts, and to learn to observe and experiment". They chose as their symbol the lynx (*lince*), known for the sharpness of its eyesight.

"VENUS AND ADONIS" By casting a pale light over the whole scene Giuseppe Ribera abandoned the chiaroscuro that was such a prominent feature of his earlier work.

"REBECCA AT THE WELL" In this composition Carlo Maratta (1625-1713) strove to capture Raphael's manner of painting draped figures and Annibale Carracci's gift for portraying facial character.

was designed to allow vehicles to reach the courtyard and gardens, while the other two lea to two staircases that meet on the *piano nob* This building is now th headquarters of the Accademia dei Lincei. **GALLERIA CORSINI.** Th main floor now houses part of the collection o the Galleria Nazionale d'Arte Antica, the remainder being in Palazzo Barberini ▲ 29 Among the most

The Orto Botanico contains a rich variety of Mediterranean trees and plants.

tstanding works are Caravaggio's *St John the Baptist*;
lome Bearing the Head of John the Baptist, attributed to
uido Reni; paintings by the Bologna school and the school
Caravaggio; and a number of Neapolitan Baroque works,
cluding Salvator Rosa's *Prometheus*.

ⁱᴇ Orto Botanico. The botanical garden belonging to the
niversity of Rome was originally the park of Palazzo Corsini.
covers an area of nearly 30 acres and boasts a splendid
ircase with a waterfall. (Go back along Via della Lungara
d turn left into Via Santa Dorotea.)

ᴏɴᴛᴇ Sisto

ᴇ ʜᴏᴍᴇ ᴏꜰ La Fornarina. The house at No. 20 Via Santa
Dorotea (now the Romolo restaurant) is supposed to have been the bakery owned by the father of Raphael's mistress, La Fornarina, traditionally identified as the subject of the famous portrait in Palazzo Barberini ▲ 292. It is said that in order to accelerate work on the Farnesina, Agostino Chigi allowed the painter to have her live with him on the premises. (Walk to the end of Via Santa Dorotea.)
Piazza Trilussa. This piazza bears the name of the Trastevere poet Carlo Alberto Salustri (1871–1950), known as Trilussa. When alterations were made to the piazza during the construction of the Tiber embankments at the end of the 19th century, the fountain commissioned by Paul V from Giovanni Fontana and Giovanni Vasanzio in 1613 was moved here from the end of the Via Giulia. This fountain was designed to distribute the water supplied by the Aqua Paola aqueduct ▲ 364.
Ponte Sisto. This bridge, which

ks Trastevere to the left bank of the Tiber, was built in 1475
der Sixtus IV to replace an ancient Roman bridge which
d been destroyed ▲ 364. Widened in the 19th century, it is
w closed to motor vehicles. The middle of the bridge
ords splendid views: of the dome of St Peter's; of the
entine hill and the Aqua Paola, dominated by the
niculum. (Go back along Via Santa Dorotea, past the
urch of Santa Dorotea, which is in the shape of a Greek
oss; built in 1475, it was remodeled in the 18th century.
en take Via Garibaldi.)

ʜᴇ Janiculum

e name Gianicolo, or Janiculum, is derived from the cult of
e god Janus. The hill still bears traces of the fierce fighting
at took place here between French troops and the
pporters of the Republic of Rome in 1849 ● 33. The Via

The Trastevere poets
The two great bards of Trastevere are Giuseppe Gioachino Belli (whose statue stands near the river in the piazza that bears his name ▲ 357) and Trilussa, to whom the monument in Piazza Trilussa was erected in 1954. Because Belli wrote his sonnets in *Romanesco* (Roman dialect 142–3), he has regrettably not achieved the fame he deserves. And yet the epic and tragic dimensions of his satire and the lucid, sarcastic irony with which he describes the pontifical Rome of the 19th century make him a truly great writer. Trilussa, whose writing is easier and less caustic, gives a vivid picture of the lives of the "little" people of Rome.

The Ponte Sisto fountain.

VIEW OF ROME FROM THE JANICULUM
From left to right Sant'Andrea della Valle, the Gesù, Santa Maria Maggiore, San Carlo ai Catinari and the monument to Victor Emmanuel.

The Fontana Paola.

Garibaldi used to be called Via delle Fornaci because of th brick factories beside it. It leads to the most beautiful panoramic view of the city, which according to one French 18th-century diarist, de Brosses, was in itself sufficient to justify "the journey to Italy".

BOSCO PARRASIO. To the right of Via Garibaldi there is a p leading to what was once the seat of the Arcadia academy, founded in 1690. With its aim of "exterminating bad taste" and of refining poetry, Arcadia exerted a profound influen on Italian literature. In 1926 it became the Italian Academ Literature.

SANTA MARIA DEI SETTE DOLORI. Built between 1643 and 1667 according to a design by Borromini ● 80, this church characterized externally by simple brickwork in an interpla of curves and countercurves. Inside, the 19th-century decoration detracts from the rhythm and balance of Borromini's architecture. (Continue up Via Garibaldi.)

SAN PIETRO IN MONTORIO. This church provides a splendid point from which to view the city, which unti the end of the 19th century was clearly divided in two distinct parts: ancient Rome on the right an modern Rome on the left. The church's austere façade was built at the end of the 15th century w funds provided by the Spanish sovereigns Ferdinand of Aragon and Isabella of Castile. Attached to the church is a convent which is n largely occupied by the Spanish Academy. The church contains many 16th-century works of ar including Sebastiano del Piombo's famous fres *The Flagellation*, based on a drawi by Michelangelo. Bernini worked the RAYMONDI CHAPEL and the fourth chapel on the left has lunettes painted by David de Haen as well as a *Descent from the Cross* by Dirk van Babu In the middle of a cloister to the right of the church, on the spot where St Peter is supposed to have been crucified, stands one of the most elegant buildings of the Renaissance, Bramante's TEMPIETTO (1502).

THE FONTANA PAOLA. This fountain was built by Flaminio Ponzio and Giovanni Fontana to receive the waters of Trajan's ancient aqueduct, rehabilitated by Paul V to supply water to Trastevere, the Via Giulia area and the Vatican. Its three arches, modeled on t Aqua Felice fountain ▲ 295, stand in front of a charming garden. (The street to the left after the fountain leads to th PORTA SAN PANCRAZIO, rebuilt in 1854.)

THE TEMPIETTO
Bramante's small circular temple (right) is believed to have been the first Renaissance monument inspired by the architecture of ancient Rome. Modeled on the Sibyl's shrine in Tivoli ▲ 392, it was based on early Renaissance research.

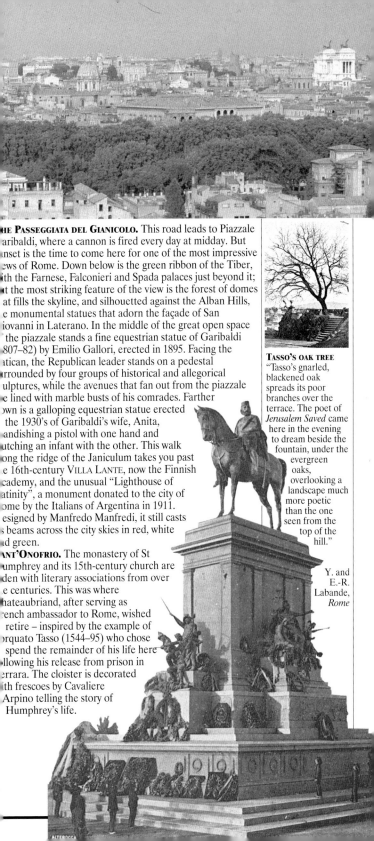

HE PASSEGGIATA DEL GIANICOLO. This road leads to Piazzale aribaldi, where a cannon is fired every day at midday. But nset is the time to come here for one of the most impressive ews of Rome. Down below is the green ribbon of the Tiber, th the Farnese, Falconieri and Spada palaces just beyond it; t the most striking feature of the view is the forest of domes at fills the skyline, and silhouetted against the Alban Hills, e monumental statues that adorn the façade of San iovanni in Laterano. In the middle of the great open space the piazzale stands a fine equestrian statue of Garibaldi 807–82) by Emilio Gallori, erected in 1895. Facing the atican, the Republican leader stands on a pedestal rrounded by four groups of historical and allegorical ulptures, while the avenues that fan out from the piazzale e lined with marble busts of his comrades. Farther wn is a galloping equestrian statue erected the 1930's of Garibaldi's wife, Anita, andishing a pistol with one hand and utching an infant with the other. This walk ong the ridge of the Janiculum takes you past e 16th-century VILLA LANTE, now the Finnish cademy, and the unusual "Lighthouse of atinity", a monument donated to the city of ome by the Italians of Argentina in 1911. esigned by Manfredo Manfredi, it still casts beams across the city skies in red, white d green.

NT'ONOFRIO. The monastery of St umphrey and its 15th-century church are den with literary associations from over e centuries. This was where hateaubriand, after serving as ench ambassador to Rome, wished retire – inspired by the example of orquato Tasso (1544–95) who chose spend the remainder of his life here llowing his release from prison in errara. The cloister is decorated th frescoes by Cavaliere Arpino telling the story of Humphrey's life.

TASSO'S OAK TREE
"Tasso's gnarled, blackened oak spreads its poor branches over the terrace. The poet of *Jerusalem Saved* came here in the evening to dream beside the fountain, under the evergreen oaks, overlooking a landscape much more poetic than the one seen from the top of the hill."

Y. and E.-R. Labande, *Rome*

As monuments in piazzas or discreet ornaments in courtyards and on street corners, fountains abound in every part of Rome.

From Villa Giulia
to the Foro Italico

370 Villa Giulia

372 Villa Borghese

376 Galeria Nazionale
   d'Arte Moderna

377 Monte Mario

377 The Foro Italico

THE CASINO DEI QUATTRO VENTI
(Villa Doria Pamphilj)
When Giambattista Pamphilj became pope in 1644 (taking the name Innocent X),

he apparently commissioned the sculptor and architect Alessandro Algardi to build the "Casino of the Four Winds". Breaking with the traditional *casino* design (with two wings), this one was built according to an almost cubelike plan. While there are some slight projections on the main façade, the other façades display a greater respect for tradition, with the inclusion of classical statues and bas-reliefs. The rooms on the ground floor are decorated with a stucco frieze designed by Algardi.

From the Middle Ages until modern times urban development only really affected the Campus Martius and the low-lying parts of Rome. From the Renaissance, in order to escape the risk of malaria, which was rife in the center of the town throughout the summer from the month of June, the great Roman families had villas built on the outskirts or in the hills. These villas tended to have vast landscaped gardens that included small buildings, the most important of which was the *casino* or "little house". As leisure homes, they also often contained the rich collections of classical antiquities which aristocratic families felt it was both their privilege and their duty to amass. By the second half of the 18th century, villas were being built solely for this purpose. The VILLA ALBANI (now called Villa Torlonia ▲ *381*), built between 1747 and 1767, is an outstanding example of this type of "villa museum", which united a delight in classical art with a love of nature. Cardinal Albani knew how to choose his friends and advisers: he got Anton Raphael Mengs to decorate his house with frescoes and brought in another lover of antiquities, Johann Joachim Winckelmann ● *41*, to be his librarian.

VILLAS THAT HAVE DISAPPEARED. When General Cadorna's troops entered Rome in 1870 ● *33* the city still had a rural appearance. But with the resolve to build a great capital, speculation on real estate reached fever pitch. Villa Peretti-Montalto, where Sixtus V had liked to relax, disappeared; so

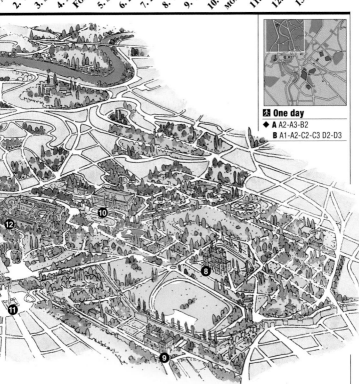

🚶 **One day**

◆ **A** A2-A3-B2

B A1-A2-C2-C3 D2-D3

...udovisi in the northern part of the town (about 2½ acres of ...s grounds remain around the Casino dell'Aurora).

...RCHEOLOGICAL SITES. Other villas were integrated into ...oups of ancient buildings. THE FARNESE AND BARBERINI ...LLAS on the Palatine Hill, built in the 16th and 17th ...nturies respectively, now form part of the archeological site ...ere, their gardens having been destroyed or radically ...odified by the late-19th-century excavations.

...UBLIC PARKS. The grounds of several villas have become ...ublic parks. Thus VILLA MATTEI was completely transformed ... the 19th century and its park relandscaped *all'inglese* to ...ecome the Villa Celimontana ▲ *190*. The VILLA DORIA-...AMPHILI ■ *20*, behind the Janiculum, has one of the largest ...arks in Rome (nearly 455 acres). The undulating terrain lent ...self to cascades, grottoes, a lake, and numerous fountains. ... also has two *casini*, a small one overlooking Via Aurelia, ...hich was used as a residence by the family, and a larger one ...esigned originally for receptions and to house art collections.

...CADEMIES AND MUSEUMS. Several villas have been reused ...ithout being greatly altered – such as the VILLA MEDICI ... *315*, which now houses the French Academy. With its ...çade overlooking the gardens at the back, decorated with ...ntique bas-reliefs, it served as a model for most villas built ... a later date. Several villas in the Pincio area have become ...useums, including VILLA GIULIA and VILLA BORGHESE, and ...e discreet house at No. 20 Via Mancini which houses the ...ans Christian Andersen Museum.

VILLA BORGHESE, A WEALTH OF MUSEUMS ✪

Rome's green lung and an open-air museum, the grounds of the Villa Borghese, now a public park, are a haven of peace where Romans like to stroll, jog, cycle or at dusk simply enjoy one of the most romantic view over the city (from the terrace of the Pincio Gardens, reached via the Church of the Trinità dei Monti or the Piazzale Flaminio). In addition to the Galeria Nazionale d'Arte Moderna, the Villa Giulia and the zoological gardens and museum, the park also contains the Galeria Borghese, which is a fitting showcase for its most illustrious collection. A limited number of tickets are issued per day and booking is compulsory.

In 1551 Pope Julius III asked Vignola and Ammannati to build him a summer villa. The two architects erected a delightful group of Mannerist buildings in the midst of pleasant gardens, which used to stretch as far as the Tiber, enabling the Pope to reach his villa by boat. A portico leads to the famous nymphaeum resembling a three-tiered theater. On the upper levels there are niches with statues, which include figures such as the Arno and the Tiber, while below the Aqua Virgo fountain is decorated with marble caryatids. In 1889 Villa Giulia became Rome's Etruscan Museum.

THE "CISTA FICORONI"
(4th century BC)
An inscription gives the name of the maker of this famous bronze *cista* (casket) as Novius Plautius. The handle on the lid portrays Dionysus between two satyrs; the fine engravings illustrate an episode from the legend of the Argonauts.

URNS AND VASES (5TH TO 4TH CENTURY BC)
Greek terracotta ceramics were highly appreciated and imitated in Etruria, where these two red-figure vases were found. The larger one, showing figures of Amazons, is from Attica; the smaller one, showing Aurora's chariot, was made in Etruria.

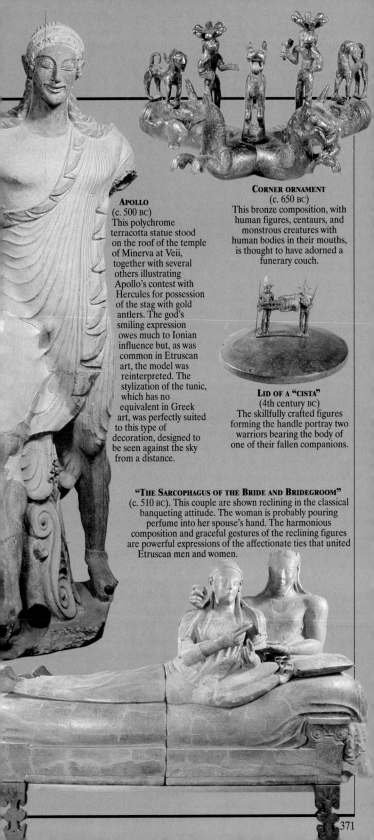

APOLLO
(c. 500 BC)
This polychrome terracotta statue stood on the roof of the temple of Minerva at Veii, together with several others illustrating Apollo's contest with Hercules for possession of the stag with gold antlers. The god's smiling expression owes much to Ionian influence but, as was common in Etruscan art, the model was reinterpreted. The stylization of the tunic, which has no equivalent in Greek art, was perfectly suited to this type of decoration, designed to be seen against the sky from a distance.

CORNER ORNAMENT
(c. 650 BC)
This bronze composition, with human figures, centaurs, and monstrous creatures with human bodies in their mouths, is thought to have adorned a funerary couch.

LID OF A "CISTA"
(4th century BC)
The skillfully crafted figures forming the handle portray two warriors bearing the body of one of their fallen companions.

"THE SARCOPHAGUS OF THE BRIDE AND BRIDEGROOM"
(c. 510 BC). This couple are shown reclining in the classical banqueting attitude. The woman is probably pouring perfume into her spouse's hand. The harmonious composition and graceful gestures of the reclining figures are powerful expressions of the affectionate ties that united Etruscan men and women.

This is one of Rome's largest villas, extending over the Pincio, behind the ramparts of the city. It was created by Cardinal Scipione Borghese, Paul V's nephew, and was sold to the Italian State in 1901. The park, which had already been transformed by the creation of the Giardino del Lago, was subsequently opened to the public. The Casino Borghese, built by Giovanni Vasanzio in 1613–14, has been turned into a museum. A large part of the collections were assembled by Cardinal Borghese.

THE CASINO BORGHESE
The casino was redecorated in 1782 by Prince Marcantonio Borghese, who was forced to sell its finest classical statues to his brother-in-law, Napoleon Bonaparte, in 1807. These are now in the Louvre.

"PAULINE BORGHESE"
This famous work by Canova portrays Pauline Bonaparte as Venus. Napoleon's sister had married Prince Camillo Borghese.

SCIPIONE BORGHESE
The cardinal's passion for work of art made him ruthless in seeking to enlarge his collection. He even imprisoned Cavaliere d'Arpino in 1607 so he could confiscate his collection of paintings, which consisted of about 105 canvases; and he had Domenichino arrested to force him to sell his painting of *Diana the Huntress*, originally commissioned by Cardinal Aldobrandini.

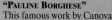

The beauty of its lines lends this sculpture such propriety that the art historian Mario Praz described Canova as an "erotic frigidaire". The work was originally covered with a layer of slightly tinted wax, which made it even more striking by torchlight. Defying the morals of the time, Pauline is said to have posed in the nude for Canova – yet she was indignant when her husband, after their separation, showed the statue to guests.

e park is adorned
th statues that form
eritable bestiary.

"THE RAPE OF PROSERPINA"

In this work intended to be viewed from
all sides, Bernini contrasts the two
bodies twisting in opposite directions.
Pluto's muscular figure is inspired by
Michelangelo's sculptures, but
Proserpina's flesh demonstrates the
artist's concern with rendering nature
rather than seeking to portray "Ideal
Beauty".

"APOLLO AND DAPHNE"

This sculpture by
Bernini portrays the
moment, as described
by Ovid, when
Daphne turned into a
bay tree in order to
escape from Apollo's
embrace. A masterly
use of the marble
heightens the contrast
between the
nymph's
lithe
body
and the
bark
beginning
to cover her and her
hair changing into
branches. On the
pedestal, as well as
Ovid's verses, there is
an inscription by the
future Urban VIII
attempting to
moralize about the
scene, which many
had found too
libertine.

"SACRED AND PROFANE LOVE"

This early work by Titian was painted in 1514 for N. Aurelio, a collector linked to the humanist movement in Venice. It expresses the abstract theme of the "two Venuses": one being the symbol of universal and eternal beauty, while the other symbolizes the progenitive force. But it is the quality of the artist's painting that is striking, rather than the complexity of the theme.

"THE MADONNA OF THE SERPENT"

Painted by Caravaggio in 1605 for the Chapel of Sant'Anna dei Palafrenieri in the Vatican, this picture found its way into the Borghese collection either because it was deemed too irreverent by the Corporation of Palafrenieri, who commissioned it, or because the cardinal exerted the necessary pressure. Under the eye of St Anne (the patron of the Corporation), the Virgin Mary and Jesus are shown crushing the serpent under foot. This was a way of affirming, in opposition to Protestant denials, that Mary actually participated in the salvation of humanity. The very natural appearance of Christ and the portrayal of Mary as a woman of the common people make the fusion of the human and the divine almost tangible. The novelty of such a representation might well have shocked certain people in those days.

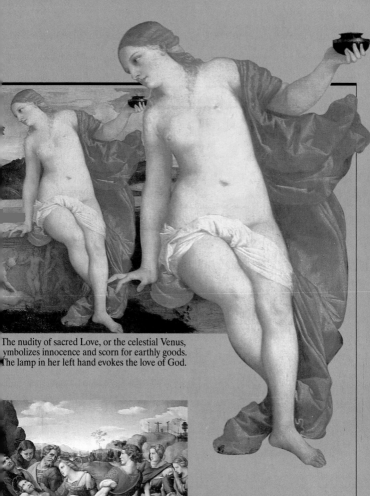

The nudity of sacred Love, or the celestial Venus, symbolizes innocence and scorn for earthly goods. The lamp in her left hand evokes the love of God.

"THE DEPOSITION"

This was one of the last works Raphael painted before he left for Rome. It was commissioned by Atlanta Baglioni of Perugia in memory of her son, who had been murdered a few years previously. Raphael borrowed the composition from a sarcophagus of the classical period and made every effort to convey pathos by a careful study of expressions of grief in the figures portrayed.

"DANAË"

This is one of four erotic paintings Federico II di Gonzaga ordered from Correggio in 1530 as a gift for Charles V. Correggio's graceful style earned him a reputation equal to that of Raphael and Titian. Until the 19th century it was essential for great collections to include an example of his work.

THE PARCO DELLA MUSICA AUDITORIUM

Designed by Renzo Piano, Rome's Auditorium is being erected on some 600,000 square feet of leafy ground, in a park situated between the Villa Glori and the Olympic Village. Reminisce of giant scarabs, its three impressive glass, travertine and lead structures shelter three concert halls set around an open-air amphitheater. Rehearsal and recording rooms, shops and restaurants complement this "City of Music", now a landmark in Roman cultural life.

GALLERIA NAZIONALE D'ARTE MODERNA

THE EXHIBITION OF 1911. To commemorate the fiftieth anniversary of the Unification of Italy, a huge exhibition was organized in the northern part of the city. It included an ethnographic and regional section, set up on the right bank o the Tiber, and an exhibition of fine arts in the Valle Giulia (o the site of the Villa Cartoni, on the left bank). In addition, major archeological discoveries were displayed in the Baths of Diocletian; and celebrations in the honor of Garibaldi, the "Father of the Nation", were held in the Vittoriano ▲ *160*, which was inaugurated at the same time. The two main centers of the exhibition were linked by a new bridge, the Ponte Risorgimento, built in reinforced concrete by the French architect François Hennebique. The numerous foreign pavilions brought together an amazing profusion of architectural styles. The BRITISH PAVILION, designed by Edwin Landseer Lutyens in neoclassical style, was built to last and is now the British Academy of Rome. One of the most interesting pavilions was the Austrian one, devised by Josef Hoffmann, which has a room decorated by Gustav Klimt. This lush green valley has been chosen as the site for many academies and research institutes, including the Belgian, Danish, Dutch, Swedish, Rumanian, and Egyptian academies.

GALLERIA NAZIONALE D'ARTE MODERNA. Another building that remained, the Palazzo delle Belle Arti designed by Cesare Bazzani, became Rome's museum of modern art. The same architect was responsible for landscaping the Valle Giuli with its avenues, shady piazzas, and fountains approached by flights of steps. The gallery contains the most important collections of 19th- and 20th-century Italian paintings and sculptures:

e neoclassical school, the romantics, historical painters, and
course the macchiaioli, the Futurists, "metaphysical"
inters (Giorgio de Chirico), and artists of the Novecento
rdengo Soffici). A museum of the 21st century, the MAXXI,
signed by the Anglo-Iraqi architect Zaha Hadid and devoted
contemporary art since 1968, is being set up in the old
ontello barracks (Via Guido Reni). Temporary exhibitions
e being held in a part of the building open to the public
til the installation has been completed (December 2007).

ONTE MARIO

the north of the Prati area ▲ 236 is the Piazzale Maresciallo
iardino (which can be reached by car or bus). From here
e can go up to the astronomical and meteorological
servatory of Monte Mario and the Astronomy and
opernican Museum (1870). Monte Mario (height 600 feet)
ves its name to Marius, the Roman general and statesman
86–57 BC). In the Middle Ages it was known as Mons Gaudii
Mount of Joy"). Pilgrims arriving by what is now the Via
ionfale caught their first glimpse of the city and of St Peter's
asilica, the object of their journey, from the crest of this hill.
day it offers a fine view over the most modern parts of
ome as well as the northern section of the ancient city.
ONTE MILVIO. Further north the Ponte Milvio spans the
ber, guarding the point where the *Viae* Cassia, Flaminia,
lodia and Veientana converged. Constantine's victory over
laxentius here in 312 AD ● 29 marked the triumph of
hristianity.

HE FORO ITALICO

t the foot of Monte Mario, in the midst of pine trees, extends
e imposing complex of the Foro Italico, originally called the
oro Mussolini. Construction of this huge sports center was
egun during the Fascist period under the direction of the
chitect Enrico del Debbio and ended when the Olympic
tadium was completed in 1953. The regime required stadiums
oth for its gigantic political rallies and as worthy settings for
s "ceremonies" devoted to youth and to sport, aiming to
iltivate a "strong and healthy" youth that would ensure the
physical improvement of the race". In the center of the
uildings stands a marble obelisk dedicated to Mussolini ● 93.

Ponte Milvio.

**THE CULT OF
PHYSICAL EDUCATION**
The Foro Mussolini
was inaugurated on
November 4, 1932, on
the last day of the
celebrations marking
the tenth anniversary
of the March on
Rome. The occasion
was also used to
solemnly celebrate
the large number of
medals won by Italian
athletes at the Los
Angeles Olympics –
the trophies being
perceived as shining
evidence of the
physical superiority of
Fascist youth.

Statues of athletes in
the Stadio dei Marmi.

AN OLD RIVALRY
Rome has two long-established soccer teams which have always been rivals, namely Roma (founded in 1927) and Lazio (1900). The yellow-and-red of the Roma team and the blue-and-white of Lazio meet twice a year for "local Derby" matches.

SUMPTUOUS DECORATIONS
Giulio Romano, Baldassare Peruzzi, Giovanni da Udine, and the Florentine sculptor Baccio Bandinelli were jointly commissioned to decorate Villa Madama. It took the artists four years to complete their work.

STADIO DEI MARMI. The "Marble Stadium" is the highlight of the Foro Mussolini. Designed for twenty thousand spectators, its elegant space is surrounded by sixty statues of athletes modeled on those of antiquity, provided by the provinces of Italy. Two wrestlers, in bronze, adorn the tribune of honor. In front of the obelisk a vast forum, paved with mosaics illustrating the Fascists' punitive missions and the March on Rome, stretches as far as the splendid Fountain of the Sphere, inaugurated in 1934.

THE ACADEMY OF PHYSICAL EDUCATION. This academy was founded in 1928 to enable the regime to train instructors and to develop a national taste for sports. The establishment built by Enrico Del Debbio in 1928 to 1932 has the appearance of a school or barracks; it consists of two symmetrical buildings linked by a loggia adorned with statues of athletes. The use of Pompeian red with white ornamentation is a reference to the Roman Empire and the "gymnasiums" of antiquity. It is now the headquarters of the Italian Olympic Committee (CONI).

STADIO OLIMPICO. Built with the 1960 Rome Olympics in mind, this stadium capable of holding 80,000 spectators was inaugurated in 1953. It was enlarged in 1990 for the soccer World Cup, and on most Sunday afternoons it is overrun by the supercharged *tifosi* (supporters) of Roma or Lazio.

PALAZZO DELLE TERME. The group of buildings on the right, known as the Palazzo delle Terme (1937), houses an indoor swimming pool decorated with mosaics and marble. Part of this complex was turned into a youth hostel. Behind the Foro Italico is the MINISTRY OF FOREIGN AFFAIRS (Affari Esteri). Originally conceived in 1937 as the Lictor's palace, it was only completed and inaugurated in 1956. (Return to the Piazzale Maresciallo Giardino and take Via di Villa Madama.)

VILLA MADAMA. Impressed by Agostino Chigi's residence ▲ *360* and eager to have an even more sumptuous abode built for himself, Cardinal Giulio de' Medici (who later became Pope Clement VII) chose Raphael for this task in 1516. The latter drew up the plans but left the actual construction to Antonio Sangallo the Younger. Like Palazzo Madama ▲ *272*, this villa owes its name to "Madama", alias Margaret of Austria (1522–86), who married first Alessandro de' Medici and then Ottavio Farnese. The villa now belongs to the Italian State and is used for official receptions.

Rome
outside the walls

380 Sant'Agnese and Santa Costanza

381 San Lorenzo fuori le Mura

382 San Paolo fuori le Mura

384 Cinecittà

386 EUR

THE MACRO IS GROWING

New "high-tech" spaces, designed by the French architect Odile Decq, are to be added to the MACRO (Rome's Contemporary Art Museum). As well as new exhibition rooms, the project includes a roof-terrace with a garden which will be open to the public even outside the museum's opening hours. The work is due for completion in 2008.

◪ One day

1. SANTA SABINA,
SANTA COSTANZA
2. EUR
3. SAN PAOLO
4. CINECITTÀ
5. SAN LORENZO

THE HOLY MARTYR
It is said that when Agnes was stripped of her clothes in a brothel, her hair grew miraculously, covering her nakedness; at the same time, an angel brought her a dazzling white garment from heaven. Condemned to being burned alive at the stake, she prayed so fervently that the flames spared her. In order to kill her, the torturer had to plunge a dagger into her throat.

SANT'AGNESE AND SANTA COSTANZA

THE MARTYRDOM OF ST AGNES. Tradition claims that Agnes, who belonged to an aristocratic family, suffered martyrdom in the year 250 when she was barely twelve years old. Her parents buried her in one of their properties on the Via Nomentana, where several catacombs already existed. Their daughter appeared to them surrounded by other young martyrs, with a lamb beside her. This is why every year on the Feast of St Agnes, two live lambs are blessed on the altar of the church of Sant'Agnese fuori le Mura and offered as a tithe to the Lateran Basilica: their wool is used to weave the palliums presented by the Pope to the archbishops of the Catholic Church. St Agnes' burial place became a center for pilgrimages, and Constantia, a daughter of the Emperor Constantine, subsequently bought the surrounding land and built a basilica above the catacomb.

SANT'AGNESE FUORI LE MURA. Rebuilt by Pope Honorius I (625–38) and restored by Hadrian I (772–95), the basilica was extensively modified during the 16th century: the choir was renovated, chapels added, and the new altar crowned with a *ciborium.* The basilica underwent further restoration in the 19th century. The apse was decorated with a splendid 7th-century mosaic, one of the finest examples of Byzantine art in Rome. In the center is the saint, draped like a Byzantine empress, at her feet the instruments of her martyrdom, the fire and the sword; at her side Pope Symmachus and Pope Honorius are shown presenting the church to her. The entrance to the catacombs is in the left nave. Don't miss seeing the mausoleum of Constantia (now the Church of Santa Costanza), which is reached via a path through the garden.

SANTA COSTANZA. Built in the 4th century to receive the sepulcher of Constantia and Helen (who was also a daughter of Constantine), the mausoleum was transformed

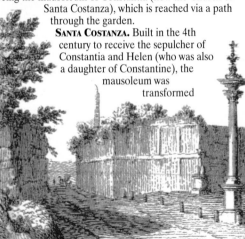

Above, from left to right: the Church of Santa Costanza, Villa Torlonia, and the former premises of the Peroni brewery.

into a baptistery, and, in 1254, it became a church. However, to make matters even more confusing, the church was dedicated to Santa Costanza, a nun, instead of to Constantia. The mausoleum's interior is built with perfect classical proportions according to a concentric design. Twelve pairs of columns support the drum dome, which has twelve openings. An aisle circles this central space, above which is a vault covered with 4th-century mosaics – some of the oldest in Rome to have survived *in situ*. The exquisite floral and geometrical motifs, characteristic of the art of the declining Empire, are splendidly well preserved. (Return by the 36, 37 or 60 bus to the junction of Via Nomentana and Viale Regina Margherita. Then take a 19 or 30 tram for San Lorenzo fuori le Mura; get off at Piazzale del Verano.) If you have time while visiting the basilicas outside the walls, you can explore a part of Rome that is less well known. Turning off the Via Nomentana at the junction with Viale Regina Margherita, you can see the PERONI BREWERY – which now houses Rome's Contemporary Art Museum (MACRO) ▲ *184* – the rich Art Nouveau decorations of the VILLINO XIMENES (Piazza Galeno), or the park of the 19th-century VILLA TORLONIA (open to the public since 1978). Another interesting neighborhood is the area around San Lorenzo fuori le Mura: the streets trodden by little Useppe and his mother in Elsa Morante's *La Storia* are still just the same.

SAN LORENZO FUORI LE MURA

LAWRENCE THE DEACON. The ban on burying the dead within the city led Romans to bury their deceased on the fringes of the town, along the main roads ▲ *319*. Via Tiburtina, like others, was lined with tombs and catacombs. St Lawrence, who was burnt to death on a grid in 258, was buried there and pilgrims soon flocked to the spot.

THE BASILICA. In 330, in order to cope with the increasing flow of pilgrims, Constantine built a basilica over the martyr's tomb; this church (known as the Minor Basilica) was totally rebuilt by Pelagius II in the 6th century. A century earlier, St Sixtus III had erected a second edifice, the basilica dedicated to the Virgin (known as the Major Basilica), which has also been attributed to Pope Hadrian I. Either Honorius III (1216–27) or Hadrian I was responsible for enlarging Pelagius'

THE PILGRIMAGE TO THE SEVEN CHURCHES
This is a very ancient pilgrimage, and numerous engravings illustrate the itinerary leading from St Peter's to Santa Maria Maggiore by way of San Paolo fuori le Mura, San Sebastiano on the Via Appia ▲ *326*, San Giovanni in Laterano ▲ *196*, Santa Croce in Gerusalemme ▲ *200* and San Lorenzo fuori le Mura. The pilgrimage was reinstated in the 16th century by St Philip Neri, who on Shrove Tuesday led an enormous crowd on this pious walk. As the pilgrimage proceeded, people sang, prayed and ate in a festive atmosphere – a spiritual "carnival" that contrasted with the approaching constraints of Lent.

San Lorenzo fuori le Mura.

THE SARCOPHAGUS OF THE GRAPE HARVEST
(5th–6th century)
The name is due to the decorations of vine branches

edifice and combining the two churches by demolishing their respective apses. In the same period Pietro Vassalletto added the portico, where amazing frescoes illustrate the life of St Lawrence and St Stephen. Between 1855 and 1864 Virginio Vespignani restored the basilica and did away with the Baroque additions. San Lorenzo was severely damaged by bombing in July 1943, in common with the rest of the area, but was restored soon after the war. The front section of the church corresponds to the former basilica dedicated to the Virgin and is divided into three naves, while the raised chancel is formed by the 6th-century building. The paved floor – where the imagination of the Cosmati is evident in the sense of color and the variety of the geometrical motifs – spreads its carpet of white marble, porphyry and serpentine the central nave. A 6th-century mosaic on the CHANCEL ARCH which distinctly divides the two churches, portrays Christ in the act of blessing; on the left Pope Pelagius II advances, offering the church to the Lord, who is enthroned on a blue globe. The CIBORIUM (1148), the oldest to have been made by the Roman marble workers, dominates the altar, its simplicity contrasting with the rich colors of the EPISCOPAL THRONE (1254) ● 76. Access the 12th-century cloister is through the sacristy. At the side of the basilica stand a beautiful bell tower (also 12th century behind it stretches the vast Campo Verano cemetery, which has a monumental entrance (1874–8) designed by Vespignani.

THE CITTÀ UNIVERSITARIA. Marcello Piacentini was the architect of the campus of the University of Rome built between 1933 and 1935 to replace the Palazzo della Sapienza, which had long been overcrowded. The university library the Biblioteca Alessandrina, was founded by Pope Alexander VII (1655-67) and inaugurated in 1670. (Turning south, beyond the city walls you will find two of the seven churches of the traditional Rome pilgrimage: San Sebastiano, on the Via Appia ▲ 326, and San Paolo fuori le Mura on the Via Ostiense.)

THE CLOISTER OF SAN PAULO ★ ● 76
This elegant 13th-century construction, partly the work of the Vassalletto family, is enchanting due to the sheer variety of the columns (some studded with gems, some smooth, some twisted), which are encrusted with multicolored marble and mosaics. The frieze, which consists of stylized heads of lions, wolves and monsters, is reminiscent of ancient Etruscan sculpture.

SAN PAOLO FUORI LE MURA ●

THE FIRST BASILICA ● 76. Rome's largest church until the rebuilding of St Peter's in the 16th century, it was built on the site of a small chapel, about a mile from the Aurelian Wall, on the spot where St Paul was supposed to have been buried after his martyrdom in 67 AD . Construction began under Constantine, but the building was enlarged and only completed in 395 under Honorius. During the 13th to 15th centuries it was decorated with mosaics, frescoes and paintings by some of the leading artists of the time.

THE GREAT RESTORATION. On the night of July 15 to 16, 1823 a terrible fire devastated the basilica. Only part of the façade, the chancel arch, the transept and the cloister were saved. After much agonizing the architects called in by Leo XII

(Luigi Poletti in particular) decided to rebuild the basilica, relying on pictures and documentation to make the new church as similar as possible to the old one. An appeal was made to the public to finance the work; and, as well as money, gifts in kind were received, such as the alabaster columns sent by the Viceroy of Egypt and the blocks of malachite sent by Tsar Nicholas I. The restoration lasted for more than a century, and was completed with the building of a huge quadriportico (covered atrium) by Guglielmo Calderini that has a hundred columns (1928). Although the church is grandiose and majestic, its atmosphere is cold.

THE TREASURES INSIDE. The fire spared some of the church's treasures, including fragments of frescoes by Pietro Cavallini (kept in the basilica's museum), the Gothic *ciborium* by Arnolfo da Cambio, the marble candelabra by Nicolò di Angelo and Pietro Vassalletto (in the choir), the original Byzantine door, and the apse mosaic made by Venetian artists commissioned by Honorius III. This shows the Pope prostrate in adoration at the feet of the Redeemer; the pontiff's diminutive size emphasizes his humility. In the Chapel of the Blessed Sacrament (1725) is a 13th-century mosaic representing the Mother of God that was also rescued from the flames; in front of this mosaic St Ignatius founded the Company of Jesus in ✠ 1541.

Perchè l'Italia Fascista diffonda nel mondo più rapida la luce della civiltà di Roma

Roma - Stabilimenti Cinematografici

CINECITTÀ

THE FIRST STONE
On the morning of January 29, 1936, Benito Mussolini laid the foundation stone of the Cinecittà studios and thus launched the megalomaniac project of creating an Italian Hollywood.

Hidden behind high walls, the long studio buildings of Cinecittà extend between the fifth and sixth mile of the Via Tuscolana. Originally designed to produce propaganda for the Fascist regime, these studios have been used for shooting countless films and have enabled many of the great Italian film directors to make their debut. Nowadays, abandoned by the film industry, they are mostly used for making television series and advertisements – and the props from the great productions are being sold off.

> "More than most other doors or thresholds, the gates of Cinecittà are symbolic for me: they marked a turning point in my life."
>
> Federico Fellini

FELLINI'S KINGDOM
Of all the famous Italian film directors, Federico Fellini was the one who made the greatest use of Cinecittà's facilities. After 1960 all his films were studio productions.

"OUR MOST POWERFUL WEAPON"
Cinecittà was inaugurated on April 28, 1937, only 475 days after its construction began. This enormous complex covers an area of approximately 150 acres.

In spite of the regime's intention to use the cinema as a means of propaganda, only 17 of the 279 films shot between April 1937 and July 1943 focused on the war or exalted Fascism. Cinecittà hoped to become a "dream factory", like its American model.

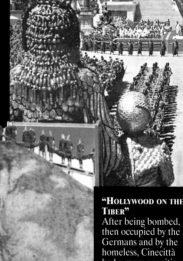

"HOLLYWOOD ON THE TIBER"
After being bombed, then occupied by the Germans and by the homeless, Cinecittà had a more propitious period during the 1950's. The Americans, whose assets had been frozen by the Italian government in 1947, used it to make a number of super-productions (twenty-seven films in fifteen years, including Mankiewicz's *Cleopatra* in 1963).

Benito
Mussolini
(1883–
1945).

**THE GRANDEUR OF
ANTIQUITY**
EUR is a tangible
manifestation of
Mussolini's vision of
the *"Urbs Magna"*, an
Imperial Rome
linking the city of
Augustus with the
megalopolis of il
Duce's dreams.

"The Square
Coliseum".

EUR

The vast wasteland along the Via Cristoforo isolating the
suburb of EUR from Rome is bounded by Via
Laurentina, Via Ostiense and Via del Mare. The layout of
EUR imitates that of a Roman town: the main roads of
the Via Imperiale (today the Via Cristoforo Colombo)
and the Viale Europa cross at right angles.

THE THIRD ROME. Mussolini planned to celebrate the
twentieth anniversary, in 1942, of his March on Rome
with a universal exhibition "open to all the sciences, arts,
and all possible forms of work and activity". A group of
administrative buildings were to be built between Rome
and the sea; the area was initially called E 42 and then
EUR (Esposizione Universale di Roma), and was supposed
to have been the nucleus of a modern urban center – "the
Third Rome" – a visible symbol and apotheosis of Imperial
power. The overall plan was prepared in 1938 by the Roman
architect Marcello Piacentini, who had already created several
of the monumental works most typical of the Fascist period.
Piacentini surrounded himself with a group of architects,
varying philosophies, including Giuseppe Pagano, Luigi
Piccinato, Ettore Rossi and Luigi Vietti. Originally, on little
more than 6 acres, there was to be a Palazzo del Turismo, a
Palazzo degli Italiani all'Estero (for Italians domiciled
abroad), a museum of ancient art, a museum of modern art, a
Palazzo del Cinema and a Palazzo delle Esposizioni, including
exhibition halls devoted to telecommunications and the
economics of cooperatives, etc. But the war put an end to the
work and the buildings were badly damaged first by German
and then by Allied occupation.

THE NEW ADMINISTRATIVE CENTER. When the project
continued in 1951, provision was made for additional
buildings and the decentralization of
administrative offices (some political,
others the headquarters of
big companies,
such as

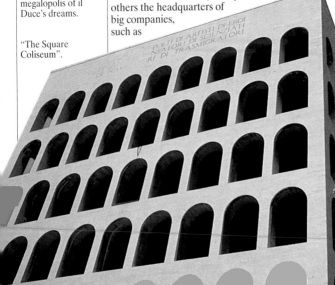

NI and Alitalia) and more useums. Consequently the status of UR changed: conceived as a onumental center, it became an dministrative one. At the same time residential district was developed, aking EUR – now linked to Rome y the Metro – into a satellite town ith shady avenues and vast anoramas.

IAZZALE DELLE NAZIONI UNITÀ. This splanade is flanked by two emicircular buildings with porticos esigned by Giovanni Muzio, Mario aniconi and Giulio Pediconi.

HE PALAZZO DELLA CIVILTÀ DEL AVORO. Without a doubt this uilding (pictured below, left), begun y Giovanni Guerrini, Ernesto Bruno a Padula and Mario Romano in 938, is the most beautiful in EUR. It

as been nicknamed the "Square Coliseum" by the Romans, nd its massive white walls punctuated by six floors of ythmic arcades dominate the Tiber. The statues in each rcade on the ground floor represent the arts and human ctivities; four sculptured groups decorate the monumental tairway. At the opposite end of the Viale della Civiltà del avoro stands the PALAZZO DEI CONGRESSI, designed by the ationalist architect Adalberto Libera (1938). Its cube-shaped entral section projects from behind a vast portico. Both the echnical installations and the general concept of the building re remarkably well thought out.

IAZZA MARCONI. Originally called Piazza Imperiale, this quare was renamed because of the obelisk (1939–59) in iemory of Guglielmo Marconi, inventor of the radio, in the enter, which was intended as the focal point of EUR and of Iussolini's Universal Exhibition. Among the buildings that surround the square is the GRATTACIELO ITALIA, a skyscraper that includes offices and a hotel. To the right stands the PALAZZO DELLE SCIENZE, which now houses the Museo Preistorico ed Etnografico Luigi Pigorini and the Museo dell'Alto Medievo; to the left the MUSEO DELLE ARTI E TRADIZIONI POPOLARI, which displays examples of popular crafts collected at the beginning of the 20th century for the great ethnographic exhibition held in 1911 ▲ 92. Some interesting prehistoric and ethnographic exhibits collected in the 17th century by the Jesuit Athanase Kircher and added to by Luigi Pigorini are on view in the MUSEO PIGORINI, which was founded by Pigorini in 1875. The MUSEO DELL'ALTO MEDIEVO (early Middle Ages), inaugurated in 1967, houses the 4th to 10th century collections formerly in the National Roman Museum ▲ 335.

The buildings of EUR are not unlike the ones that two decades earlier had haunted the canvases of the metaphysical painter Giorgio De Chirico (1888–1978) – such as *The Melancholy of the Politician*, painted in 1913 (above).

ORDER AND GRANDEUR
Fascist architects aimed to impress the "new man" with the values of Mussolini's

regime. A sense of grandeur, order and symmetry was a fundamental part of the image that the regime wished to give of itself.

The Ferris Wheel at Rome's Luna Park, near the Abbazia delle Tre Fontane.

MUSEO DELLA CIVILTÀ ROMANA (Museum of Roman Civilization). The archeological material from the great prewar exhibitions, the 1911 exhibition ▲ 376, and the one devoted to Rome under Augustus in 1937 to 1938, the Mostra Augustea della Romanità, was reassembled in the vast rooms of this museum opened in 1955. Plaster casts of statues and monuments, reconstructions of buildings, reproductions, charts and models illustrate in great detail what life in ancient Rome was like and trace the history and influence of Roman civilization.

VIALE EUROPA On the right at the end of this avenue stands the massive BASILICA DI SANTI PIETRO E PAOLO (1938). On the left is the ARCHIVIO DELLO STATO building, initially intended to house a museum devoted to the armed forces; the original documents of all the laws and decrees of the Italian State since it came into being are kept in the archives here.

VIALE AMERICA Parallel to this avenue is an artificial lake almost three quarters of a mile long, which was supposed to have been spanned by a great arch. The Passeggiata Giappone by the water is bordered by thousands of cherry trees donated by the people of Japan. Also interrupting the Via Cristoforo Colombo is the spectacular PALAZZO DELLO SPORT, built by Marcello Piacentini and Pier Luigi Nervi for the 1960 Olympic Games ● 33, 93.

ABBAZIA DELLE TRE FONTANE This fresh green oasis is locate just off Via Laurentina, the eastern boundary of EUR.

St Paul is supposed to have been martyred here, and it is said that after he was beheaded his head bounced three times, causing three fountains to gush from the ground. Three churches were therefore built on this spot: Santi Vincenzo e Anastasio, Santa Maria Scala Coeli, and San Paolo alle Tre Fontane. Since 1868 the area has belonged to the Trappists, who drained the marshy land and planted eucalyptus trees in order to rid the neighborhood of malaria. The monk make a eucalyptus liqueur, which you can buy at the abbey's shop.

Tivoli and Palestrina

390 Tivoli

391 Via Tiburtina

391 A walk in the town

392 Villa d'Este

394 Villa Adriana

398 Palestrina

399 The Temple of Fortuna

400 The Nile mosaic

402 Around the ancient forum

🔲 20 miles
🕐 One day

History

MEDIEVAL HOUSES
A number of these can still be seen along Via Campitelli, and a fine group stands in Via del Colle. Both the Via del Duomo and the streets leading into it have fully retained their medieval appearance.

THE ANCIENT TIBUR. Tivoli (Latin name: Tibur) occupies a strategic position, being located at the point where the Aniene (the ancient Anio) flows down from the Abruzzi to the valley. It thus controlled the only viable route to Latium from these mountains, which were originally inhabited by the Volsci, Sabine and Samnite tribes. The town's origins are uncertain. According to one legend it was a colony of Alba Longa, while another legend links it with Tiburnus, one of the sons of the Greek hero Amphiaraos. All that is known of its early history is its hostile encounters with Rome: initially in 361 BC, when Tibur seems to have been an ally of the Gauls, and finally during the Latin War, which ended with the total submission of Latium in 338 BC. From that time on, Tivoli's history was identical with Rome's. From the 2nd century AD the Roman aristocracy fell under the spell of the natural beauty of the place, which had become a part of the Roman *campania*, and luxurious villas began to appear amid "the thick bowers of Tibur", as the poet Horace eulogized them.
FROM THE MIDDLE AGES TO TODAY. Having become a prosperous episcopal town and an autonomous commune, Tivoli was often prey to Rome's expansionist policies. It was

not until 1816, however, that it completely lost its autonomy (until 1870), becoming a small town like so many others in the Papal States.

VIA TIBURTINA

Whereas today's Via Tiburtina winds its way to Tivoli through olive groves, the old road, after Ponte Lucano, used to lead straight to the town. It passed close to a large domed circular hall, the Tempio della Tosse (Temple of the Tosse), which was turned into a church in the Middle Ages. Then it ran alongside the sanctuary of Hercules Victor, the god of war, assimilated with Mars, and also the god of commerce. The temple, which contained an oracle, was at the end of an enormous square surrounded by a portico reached by two great stairways on either side; between these rose the steps of a theater. This combination of temple and theater was typical of sanctuaries in central and southern Italy, such as Praeneste ▲ *398*, Petrabondante and the Teatro Pompeo in Rome ▲ *248*.

WALK IN THE TOWN

Starting with Piazza Trento, one can discover numerous medieval houses in the streets of this little town, which is dominated by the Rocca Pia fortress built by Pius II (1458–64).

SANTA MARIA MAGGIORE. This church, founded in the 5th century but rebuilt in the 13th century, has a Romanesque façade and a Gothic portal. Its atrium has a fine 13th-century fresco of *The Virgin and Child*. (Proceed to Piazza del Duomo, part of which is built on the site of the ancient forum.)

THE DUOMO. The cathedral dedicated to St Lawrence was built in 1650. However, its Romanesque campanile dates from the 12th century. Inside, one should see the famous 13th-century sculpture of *The Deposition* in the fourth chapel on the right; and the *Triptych of the Saviour* (12th–14th century) in the third chapel on the left, opened on request.

VILLA GREGORIANA. This was created by Pope Gregory XVI at the beginning of the 19th century. The park extends along both banks of the Aniene, which the pontiff had partly channeled. Go to the belvedere halfway up the great waterfall and you will appreciate the force with which the river roars down this 350-foot cataract.

TEMPLE OF THE SIBYL. Two temples (reached through the La Sibilla restaurant) stand on the edge of the Aniene falls. The rectangular one, the older of the two (2nd century BC), is dedicated to Tiburnus, the legendary founder of the town. The round temple, built in the Corinthian style, is that of the sibyl Albunea. Surrounded by columns and built of great slabs of travertine, it stands on a podium, the steps of which have disappeared. (Go along Via del Colle as far as the CHURCH OF SAN SILVESTRO, which is Romanesque and has very

A CURIOUS AEDICULE
Between the portal and the great rose window of Santa Maria Maggiore there is a small Gothic aedicule.

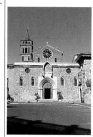

THE TEMPLE OF HERCULES VICTOR
The cult of Hercules Victor, which had a major following in Latium, certainly started in Tibur, reaching Rome by the end of Republican times. The opulence of this temple was so well known that Octavian, the future Augustus, attempted to gain possession of it in 41 BC. Subsequently, the Emperor's cult was linked to this deity.

fine 13th-century frescoes. A little further on is the old entrance of the Villa d'Este. The perspective of the gardens was originally designed to be seen from this spot. Finally, return to Piazza Trento.)

VILLA D'ESTE ●

In 1550 Cardinal Ippolito d'Este was appointed Governor of Tivoli. He immediately took possession of the Governor's palace, located in a former Benedictine monastery which he asked Pirro Ligorio to remodel to his taste. The Villa d'Este' fame, however, is due more to its gardens than to the buildin itself. Each alley, path or avenue reveals a new mossy founta in a carefully landscaped vista: there are supposed to be five hundred fountains altogether. This most famous of Italian-style gardens, which has been widely imitated, reverberates with the sound of so many fountains that it inspired the Romantic composer Franz Liszt to write a piano suite called *Fountains of the Villa d'Este*.

THE LAYOUT OF THE GARDENS. To clear space for the gardens whole area of the town had to be demolished, many inhabitants being forced to sell or face expropriation. Due to the steepness of the terrain, enormous earth-moving works were undertaken in order to create alternating terraces and slopes. In addition, the site had an irregular shape. The overall layout, designed to be seen from the original entranc at the foot of the hill, had to achieve two main purposes: to create the illusion that the villa was centrally placed (it is in fact slightly off-center) and to set it back by visually increasin the depth of the property. The means chosen to achieve this were unusual for the time. A central alley prolonging the loggia, known as the Avenue of Perspectives, was made to intersect with five paths linking the monumental fountains; these were mostly positioned toward th sides to give the effect of an enclosure i relation to the surrounding landscape.

DECAY AND RENEWED SPLENDOR. When the cardinal died, the gardens were unfinished despite the speed with which the project had been implemented, and the work was continued by his descendants. This was followed by a period of decay, when the Habsburgs inherited the property. The contents of the villa were sold and, since the upkeep of the gardens proved too costly, they were left to grow wild, forming the unkempt thickets painted by Fragonard and Hubert Robert in the 18th century. After being confiscated by the Italian State during the First World War, the villa was completely restored and opene to the public in the 1920s. Further restoration work is now being done.

A SOBER AND MAJESTIC BUILDING. The *cortile*, surrounded by a portico and adorned with a fountain took the place of the former cloister of the Benedictine monastery. Passing through it, you come to the Appartamen Vecchio. This apartment is at ground level on the courtyard

IPPOLITO D'ESTE
A favorite retreat of the ancient Romans, Tivoli was bound to appeal to this cardinal who was a patron of the arts, friend of the humanists and avid reader of classical texts. The richest of all the Italian cardinals, after his hopes of becoming pope were dashed he lavished his wealth on the Villa d'Este.

"The green, blue or almost black waters of these vast pools add their tranquil tones to the insistent, impassioned song of the cascades. On all sides, water jets and

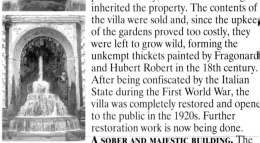

cypresses compete, thrusting skyward in bold rivalry."
Gabriel Fauré

ide but one floor up on the façade overlooking the gardens. The villa has a central living room which opens onto a terrace offering a magnificent view. All the rooms are decorated with 16th-century frescoes and hung with Flemish paintings as well as copies of famous pictures. You then descend to the appartamento Nobile, with ceilings painted by Federico Zuccaro and Girolamo Muziano exalting the glory of the d'Este family and the mythological origins of Tivoli. Its middle room opens onto a loggia (the only decorative feature of an otherwise austere façade), which leads to the gardens.

TOUR OF THE GARDENS. From the first avenue at the foot of the building you come to the Cardinal's Walk, in the center of which there is a loggia echoing that of the palace above. Immediately below this, facing the Avenue of Perspectives, is the Fontana del Bicchierone designed by Bernini. On the third level down you enter the Avenue of a Hundred Fountains (below), at the south end of which stands the Rometta Fountain, created according to a design by Ligorio (1567) and representing ancient Rome in its Tiber setting. Below, the disturbing Fountain of the Dragons, at the center of the avenue that bears its name, emphasizes the perspective with its powerful jet of water. From the level of the fish ponds you can see the gigantic Fontana dell'Organo Idraulico (Water-Organ Fountain) designed by Claude Vernard, which unfortunately no longer plays music. Going still lower, you reach the Rotunda of the Cypresses, the final landmark of the perspective from the loggia. To find the other fountains, all of which have resounding names, explore the smaller paths and alleys; you will also discover the innumerable "grottoes" scattered all over the gardens, like the Grotto of Diana near the villa.

VILLA ADRIANA

This enormous estate created by the Emperor Hadrian (117–138 AD) extends over the slopes of the Tiburtine Hills. Its size (nearly 300 acres), the variety of its architecture and the sheer beauty of the place make it one of Italy's most extraordinary archeological sites.

FROM PLUNDER TO ARCHEOLOGY
The Villa Adriana's fate was the same as that of many other Roman monuments: it was laid waste by the barbarians and became a marble quarry until the 16th century. Then the architect Pirro Ligorio undertook its excavation and drew a map of it. Since then, archeologists have tried their best to reconstruct it and to identify its buildings, most of which were richly decorated.

TRAVEL SOUVENIRS. Hadrian built two of Rome's greatest monuments, his mausoleum ▲ 233 and the Pantheon ▲ 264, but his masterpiece was the Villa Adriana. Thanks to a 6th-century biographer we know that Hadrian, a cultured man and a great traveler, wanted his villa to mirror the famous sites of the Empire – bringing together, as it were, his travel souvenirs. Each part of the estate was thus named after the thing or place it was supposed to represent: the Lyceum, the Academy, the Prytaneum, the Stoa Poikile, Canopus, the Val of Tempe, etc. "And to make sure nothing was omitted, he even included Hades (Hell)."

THE LARGEST ROMAN VILLA. This gigantic complex, which was built during the first ten years of Hadrian's reign and was actually designed by the Emperor himself, consisted of a series of pavilions skillfully placed in a natural setting. As well as the Imperial abode, it included accommodation for the Emperor's retinue and for guests, special housing for slaves and bodyguards, three bath complexes, libraries, a stadium and an esplanade with a swimming pool, all of which were adorned with fountains, ponds and lakes to reflect the harmony of earth and sky. Underground, more than one and a half miles of service tunnels were excavated, some of them wide enough for horse-drawn carriages to pass through. The most important of these converged in the south to form "Hades" – a long trapezium, more than 15 feet wide, formed by four of the tunnels, which may have been nothing more sinister than a "chariot park"!

THE TERRACE OF TEMPE. A model of the villa is on view in a modern structure near the entrance. From there, go due east as far as the terrace overlooking a valley that Hadrian called Tempe after the famous valley in Thessaly, in Greece. Further on, to the right one finds the *hospitalia*. These sleeping quarters with mosaic floors were probably reserved for the Praetorian guards responsible for guarding the entrance to the Imperial palace, which consisted of three courtyards with peristyles.

THE LIBRARY COURTYARD. This was the site of two libraries (Greek and Latin) located on the north side. A set of

Model of Villa Adriana.

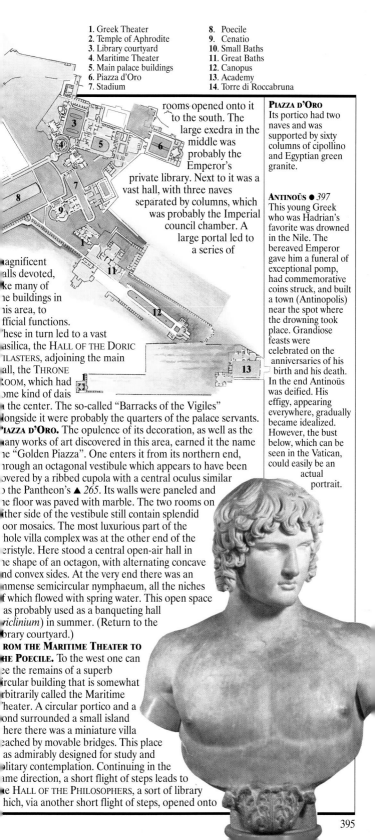

1. Greek Theater
2. Temple of Aphrodite
3. Library courtyard
4. Maritime Theater
5. Main palace buildings
6. Piazza d'Oro
7. Stadium
8. Poecile
9. Cenatio
10. Small Baths
11. Great Baths
12. Canopus
13. Academy
14. Torre di Roccabruna

rooms opened onto it to the south. The large exedra in the middle was probably the Emperor's private library. Next to it was a vast hall, with three naves separated by columns, which was probably the Imperial council chamber. A large portal led to a series of magnificent halls devoted, like many of the buildings in this area, to official functions. These in turn led to a vast basilica, the HALL OF THE DORIC PILASTERS, adjoining the main hall, the THRONE ROOM, which had some kind of dais at the center. The so-called "Barracks of the Vigiles" alongside it were probably the quarters of the palace servants.

PIAZZA D'ORO. The opulence of its decoration, as well as the many works of art discovered in this area, earned it the name the "Golden Piazza". One enters it from its northern end, through an octagonal vestibule which appears to have been covered by a ribbed cupola with a central oculus similar to the Pantheon's ▲ 265. Its walls were paneled and the floor was paved with marble. The two rooms on either side of the vestibule still contain splendid floor mosaics. The most luxurious part of the whole villa complex was at the other end of the peristyle. Here stood a central open-air hall in the shape of an octagon, with alternating concave and convex sides. At the very end there was an immense semicircular nymphaeum, all the niches of which flowed with spring water. This open space was probably used as a banqueting hall (*triclinium*) in summer. (Return to the library courtyard.)

FROM THE MARITIME THEATER TO THE POECILE. To the west one can see the remains of a superb circular building that is somewhat arbitrarily called the Maritime Theater. A circular portico and a pond surrounded a small island where there was a miniature villa reached by movable bridges. This place was admirably designed for study and solitary contemplation. Continuing in the same direction, a short flight of steps leads to the HALL OF THE PHILOSOPHERS, a sort of library which, via another short flight of steps, opened onto

PIAZZA D'ORO
Its portico had two naves and was supported by sixty columns of cipollino and Egyptian green granite.

ANTINOÜS ● 397
This young Greek who was Hadrian's favorite was drowned in the Nile. The bereaved Emperor gave him a funeral of exceptional pomp, had commemorative coins struck, and built a town (Antinopolis) near the spot where the drowning took place. Grandiose feasts were celebrated on the anniversaries of his birth and his death. In the end Antinoüs was deified. His effigy, appearing everywhere, gradually became idealized. However, the bust below, which can be seen in the Vatican, could easily be an actual portrait.

395

COUNT FEDE'S CYPRESSES
In the 18th century Count Fede planted splendid pines and cypresses at Villa Adriana. He also undertook archeological excavations there between 1730 and 1742.

The elegant colonnade at the northern end of Canopus.

the Poecile. This double portico, flanked by a vast rectangular space and measuring more than 750 feet in length, owes its name to the Athenian Stoa Poikile (multicolored portico) on which it was modeled. Its two rows of columns, on either side of a high central wall, were originally covered by a gabled roof. Thanks to the building's clever orientation one could walk along its cool north-facing side in summer and keep to the warm, sheltered south-facing side in the winter. As an inscription discovered in the 18th century testifies, it was prescribed for health-giving walks (*ambulatio*). The square itself has an ornamental garden and a large rectangular pool in the center. Its western end rests on an astonishing substructure consisting of the "Cento Camerelle" (one hundred cells), which probably housed the villa's staff. It currently undergoing restoration. Going south, one reaches a space with three exedras paved in marble. This was a huge dining hall (*cenatio*) used for official banquets. Since it was north-facing, it seems likely that it was designed only for summer use; the Emperor would in any case have done his winter entertaining on the Palatine ▲ *146*. To the east there i a *pinacoteca* (picture gallery) and then a nymphaeum (long thought to have been a stadium), which linked the dining hal to a spacious area where there is a swimming pool and a cryptoporticus. Continuing to the south, one reaches the Small Baths and the Great Baths, which are separated by a courtyard. The fact that they are so close together would seem to indicate that the one complex was for women and the othe for men; moreover, their proximity to the "Cento Camerelle" suggests that they were reserved for the villa's staff.

CANOPUS. South of the baths there is a valley with a long pon surrounded by a splendid colonnade. At the bottom there stands a nymphaeum that is recognizably a temple of Serapis (*Serapeum*). It consists of a semicircular exedra with a ribbed cupola, extended by a long vaulted corridor. This ensemble, which is decorated with fountains and statues, was for a long time believed to be an evocation of the Egyptian town of Canopus, linked to Alexandria by a canal from the Nile and famous for its Temple of Serapis. A more recent interpretation gives it another meaning: the pond is not the canal but the Mediterranean, which explains the presence of Greece (symbolized by copies of the caryatids from the Erechtheion in Athens) and of Asia (represented by copies of two *Amazons* by Phidias that

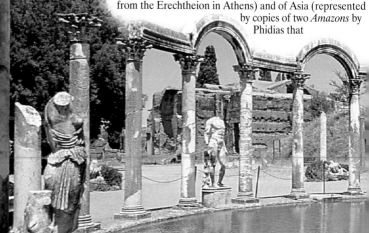

orned the Temple of Artemis in Ephesus and a copy f Praxiteles' renowned *Venus of Cnidus*). The chitectural complex at the bottom of the lake is seen symbolizing Egypt; at least that is what one may educe from the three sculptured groups that ecorated it, the layout of which is reconstructed in e Vatican's Egyptian Museum. Its composition nsisted of Osiris-Apis in the center, Isis-Demeter at e back and, on the walls, several repetitions of ntinoüs ▲ *395*, Hadrian's young favorite who, after s premature death in Egypt in 130 AD, was deified the Emperor. (Allow time to visit the small useum beside Canopus to see the items discovered uring the excavations of the 1950's.)

ORRE DI ROCCABRUNA AND THE ACADEMY. On the ll overlooking the valley of Canopus from the southwest, e can see a number of places of long-standing fame. The rst is the Torre di Roccabruna, an octagonal building with o floors covered by a dome, probably erected as a sort of anoramic observatory. One then reaches the Academy, a st square surrounded by a portico. The best-preserved uildings in this area are the TEMPLE OF APOLLO, a large rcular hall surmounted by a cupola, and to the south the DEON, a small theater of which the stage front remains. The nest works of art discovered in the Villa Adriana came from e Academy, including the *Mosaic of the Doves* ▲ *135*. eturning to the entrance of the archeological site, one can alk down a pleasant avenue lined with cypresses to reach the reek theater and the nymphaeum, nich are at the northern end of e villa.

THE CARYATIDS OF CANOPUS
In the middle the columns are replaced by six caryatids, four of which are copies of those supporting the roof of the Erechtheion, one of the temples of the Acropolis in Athens; the other two are Sileni. The original statues are now in the museum.

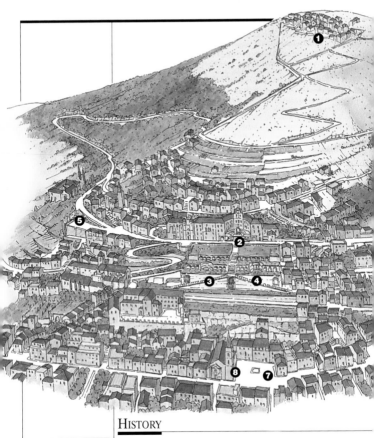

HISTORY

☒ 23 miles
☒ One day

The exedra on the right of the Terrace of the Hemicycles.

A STRATEGIC POSITION. Situated to the east of Rome, near the twenty-fifth milestone on the Via Prenestina, in ancient times Palestrina was called Praeneste. Built on the slopes of Mount Ginestro, the southernmost bastion of the Praenestine Hills, the town overlooks the gorge separating them from the Alban Hills and also dominated the Via Labicana and Via Latina, which lay at the bottom of the valley. This geographical location explains the importance the town acquired from the 7th century BC. Legends abound as to its origins. Some link its foundation to Praenestos, the son of King Latinos; others to Teleganos, the putative son of Ulysses and Circe, or to Caeculus, the son of the god Vulcan.

REBELLION AND SUBMISSION. The earliest references by historians to Praeneste concern its fraught relations with Rome: conquered in 380 BC, it rebelled several times, formed an alliance with the Gauls in 358, and took part in the last Latin War. At the end of the 2nd century BC the town seems to have enjoyed great prosperity – presumably due to its trade with the East – and grandiose constructions, including the shrine to Fortuna, transformed its appearance. In the following century Praeneste sided with Marius, thus earning the hatred of Sulla, who massacred the Praenestines in reprisal. At the beginning of the Empire the town's importance diminished. However, the oracle that had ensured

1. CASTEL SAN PIETRO
2. PALAZZO COLONNA-BARBERINI
3. TERRAZZA DEGLI EMICICLI
4. TERRAZZA DELLA CORTINA
5. BELVEDERE
6. CATHEDRAL
7. PIAZZA REGINA MARGHERITA

ts posterity retained its influence until the 4th century AD.

A COLONNA FIEFDOM. In the Middle Ages a new town was born on the site of the sanctuary. As a fiefdom of the Colonna's, the town was destroyed several times. Finally, in 1630, this great family sold it to Carlo Barberini, Urban VIII's brother.

THE TEMPLE OF FORTUNA

NUMERIUS' DREAM. In a passage recounting the myth of the town's foundation and the sanctuary's vocation, Cicero speaks of a certain Numerio Suffustio who was told in his dreams to go and break a stone in a precise spot. Since the dreams recurred, he decided to obey. The split stone revealed *sortes* ("lots"), oak tablets inscribed with prophetic words. The author added that the spot where the lots were discovered was not far from the place where mothers venerated the statue of the goddess Fortuna and her two children, Jupiter and Juno. At the same time, near the Temple of Fortuna honey flowed from an olive tree and convinced the priests to proclaim that the Praeneste *sortes* were destined for celebrity. Cicero thus clearly distinguished between two very ancient places of worship: the statue of Fortuna associated with the oracle and the temple where the miracle of the olive tree occurred. These firmations are in fact confirmed by the layout of the site, hich consists of a series of superimposed terraces linked by oping ramps and flights of steps that converge at the top.

ORTUNA AND THE "SORTES". The main access was provided y two oblique ramps. Where these two met, in the center, a ight of steps led to the TERRAZZA DEGLI EMICICLI (Terrace f the Hemicycles), named after the two porticoed exedras on ther side of the steps. The better preserved of the two is the ne on the right, which is covered by a coffered vault. The racle was located directly in front, as can be seen from the ase, which probably supported the statue of Fortuna – the atue near which, according to Cicero, the lots were found.

HE UPPER TEMPLE. The steps then lead up to the TERRAZZA EI FORNICI A SEMICOLONNE (Terrace of the Niches with Two olumns) and up another flight to the TERRAZZA DELLA ORTINA (Terrace of the Curtain), which with its colonnade d porticoes constituted the upper sanctuary. The rrace was open on the valley side, but on the ree other sides was closed by a rtico with a double row of rinthian columns. its center as the

A PROSPEROUS TOWN
Items from Praeneste's remarkable princely tombs – such as the bowl shown above – are exhibited as part of the Bernardini, Barberini and Castellani collections in the Villa Giulia ▲ 370 and on the Capitol ▲ 132. They provide ample evidence of the town's prosperity in the 7th century BC.

"THE WELL OF THE SORTES"
Near the base of the statue of Fortuna there is a well covered by a circular aedicule, with columns set on a high podium. This was the shrine of the oracle into which, according to Cicero, a child would descend to choose one of the oracular tablets (*sortes*). The text inscribed on it would then be read out to the faithful waiting in the neighboring exedra.

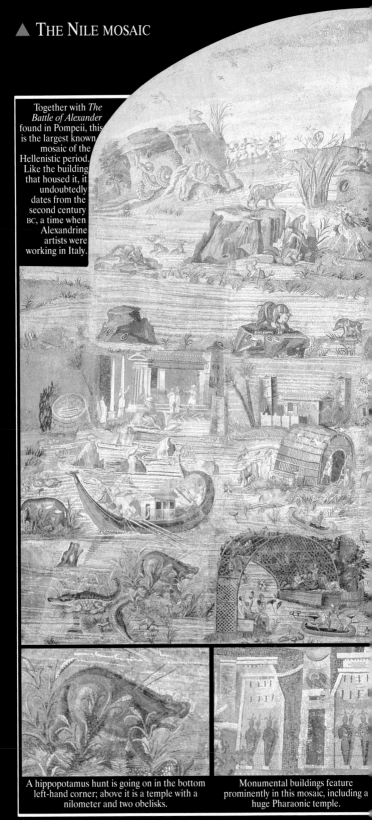

▲ THE NILE MOSAIC

Together with *The Battle of Alexander* found in Pompeii, this is the largest known mosaic of the Hellenistic period. Like the building that housed it, it undoubtedly dates from the second century BC, a time when Alexandrine artists were working in Italy.

A hippopotamus hunt is going on in the bottom left-hand corner; above it is a temple with a nilometer and two obelisks.

Monumental buildings feature prominently in this mosaic, including a huge Pharaonic temple.

The mosaic shows Egypt flooded by the Nile. In the top section the artist created an image of Upper Egypt, with real or imaginary wildlife being pursued by hunters. The names of the animals are given in Greek.

The pictures at the bottom depict the Ptolemies' palace in Alexandria, including a lively scene with soldiers and a priestess.

On the right a warship and a sailing ship symbolize the military and commercial ports. The scene above depicts a religious ceremony.

A statue of the famous composer Giovanni Pier Luigi da Palestrina (1525–94) stands in the main piazza (top). The Church of Sant'Agapito (bottom).

THE ROAD TO CASTEL SAN PIETRO
The tireless historian and traveler Gregorovius (1821–91) tells how on a hot day in August he walked up the rocky path to Castel San Pietro, the small village on the site of the citadel of Praeneste. It was along this same path that Gina Lollobrigida rode her donkey in the film *Pane, Amore e Fantasia*. You don't have to follow in Gregorovius' footsteps, but a car ride to this spot, and beyond to Guadagnolo, the highest village in Lazio, offers panoramic views over mountain landscapes and the **finest natural scenery** in the region.

cavea (semicircular stepped stone seating) of a theater, beneath which ran the portico. A round temple crowned the sanctuary.

THE MUSEUM. Palestrina's Palazzo Colonna-Barberini was converted into a museum in 1953. Some of its treasures are quite remarkable. Room III contains a large 2nd-century Hellenistic marble head, which probably came from the statue of Fortuna, since it was found near the Well of the Sortes ▲ *399*. Also in this room is a fine example of Hellenistic sculpture from Rhodes, a tall female figure in black marble (possibly Isis since black was the color of this goddess). Rooms VIII and IX contain objects such as bronze *cistae* and mirrors, ceramics, and toilet articles made of wood and ivory that were traditionally placed inside sarcophagi and tufa urns with the remains of the deceased. These objects come from the Praeneste necropolis. Finally, in Room XIV there is the famous *Nile Mosaic* ▲ *400*, which originally covered the apse of the great hall in the forum. (One can also visit the citadel of Praeneste, now a small village, Castel San Pietro).

AROUND THE ANCIENT FORUM

FROM PAGAN TEMPLE TO CATHEDRAL. Piazza Regina Margherita, in the middle of the modern town, corresponds to the forum of the ancient Praeneste. The cathedral (above left), built on the site of a temple dating from the 4th century BC, is dedicated to the town's patron, St Agapitus, who was martyred in the amphitheater during Aurelian's persecution in the 3rd century AD.

THE AERA SACRA. Also in the main piazza are the remains of an ancient basilica (on the right). Opposite, at No. 1, is the entrance to the aera sacra which consists of a vast hall with an apse. This has been identified as a shrine to Isis (*Iseum*) because of the famous mosaic (Nile Mosaic ▲ *400*) and the black marble statue, both now in the museum, as well as two obelisks found outside. It is flanked on one side by a natural grotto known as the Antro delle Sorti (Cave of the Sortes), decorated and paved with fine fish-motif mosaic. In the lower part reached through a low-vaulted door there is a small barrel-vaulted room that served as the town's treasury (*aerarium*).

Ostia

405 Porta Romana

406 Hadrian's Quarter

406 The Theater and piazzale delle Corporazioni

408 The corporations' mosaics,

410 Via di Diana

411 Around the Forum

412 Via della Foce

413 The Baths of the Seven Sages

414 Porta Marina

415 Campo della Magna Mater

416 The Ostia area

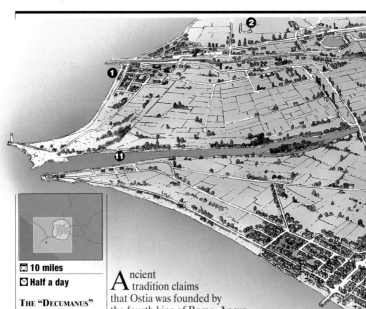

📷 **10 miles**

🕐 **Half a day**

THE "DECUMANUS" AND THE "CARDO"
When the Romans founded a colony, their surveyors established two perpendicular thoroughfares, the *decumanus maximus* (east-west) and *cardo maximus*, which enabled the territory to be divided into a grid of squares or "centuries".

THE DAILY LIFE OF THE "CISIARII"
This mosaic shows details of the carters' life, including a journey, a halt, the animals being harnessed, and even the names of the mules: Pudes, Podagrosus, Barosus …

Ancient tradition claims that Ostia was founded by the fourth king of Rome, Ancus Marcius (640–616 BC). But the oldest part of the town uncovered by archeologists, the *castrum*, was built by the Romans in the 4th century BC to guard the area where the Tiber flows into the sea and the salt marshes at the mouth of the river ("Ostia" comes from the Latin word *ostium*, meaning "mouth"). In the Republican period a town grew up around this small fortified colony, which became a military outpost and above all a port supplying Rome. Here, as in Pozzuoli, food reserves destined for the capital arrived from all over the Empire, especially wheat; these were stored in great warehouses (*horrea*) before being moved to the city on light barges hauled along the banks of the Tiber. A land route, the Via Ostiensis, also linked Ostia to Rome, corresponding to the southernmost stretch of the Via Salaria (the ancient salt route). In the 1st century BC Ostia was the victim of several disasters – including being sacked by Marius' troops in 87 – and was radically modified. Sulla fortified it with great ramparts, and Augustus embarked on a major public works program, which included the forum and the theater. From the reign of Claudius the creation of a new port (later enlarged by Trajan) reduced Ostia's role; the old Roman colony nevertheless remained one of the centers of Rome's supply network, henceforth managed by a special official, the procurator of the *annona.* Between the reigns of Domitian and Hadrian, Ostia acquired the features that are recognizable today: large public buildings, warehouses, and residential quarters characterized by tall brick apartment blocks (*insulae* ● *69*) several stories high. The town had been virtually deserted when, between the 4th and 5th

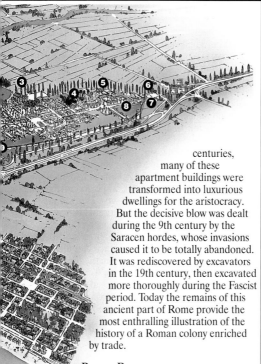

centuries, many of these apartment buildings were transformed into luxurious dwellings for the aristocracy. But the decisive blow was dealt during the 9th century by the Saracen hordes, whose invasions caused it to be totally abandoned. It was rediscovered by excavators in the 19th century, then excavated more thoroughly during the Fascist period. Today the remains of this ancient part of Rome provide the most enthralling illustration of the history of a Roman colony enriched by trade.

PORTA ROMANA

In accordance with the Roman tradition ▲ 319, the Via Ostiensis was lined with tombs, the oldest of which date from the 2nd century BC. It ended at the Porta Romana, the main entrance to Ostia for those arriving from Rome. Set back a little in relation to the walls and flanked by two square towers, this monumental gate has retained traces of its elegant marble decorations due to the restoration works carried out during the reign of the Emperor Domitian. This is where the colony's main road, the *decumanus maximus* (see left), begins. It runs absolutely straight for nearly half a mile and forms the urban tract of the Via Ostiensis; the *cardo maximus* crosses it at right angles.

PIAZZALE DELLA VITTORIA. On the left of the Porta Romana, this vast square of the Imperial age owes its modern name to the winged statue of Minerva Victoria, which was probably part of the gate's ornamentation at the time of Domitian's building work. One of the two inscriptions adorning the gate identifies the man responsible for this restoration as "*P. Clodius Pulcher consul*".

TERME DEI CISIARII. In Republican times a sort of bazaar extended along the right side of the road, which under Hadrian was partially transformed into the Terme dei Cisiarii ("the Baths of the Carters"). The *frigidarium* has retained its superb mosaic (opposite), which mainly portrays scenes from the carters' daily life (even the names of their mules are given). There is no doubt that these baths belonged to a school for this profession.

THE PORTS OF CLAUDIUS AND TRAJAN
Aware of the need to increase Ostia's storage capacity, when he came to power the Emperor Claudius decided to build another harbor to the north of the mouth of the Tiber. Work began in 42 AD and was completed, in the reign of Nero, in 54. However, at the end of the 1st century this basin proved inadequate and began to silt up. Trajan therefore built a new port, while allowing the old one to continue operating. Warehouses (*horrea*) along the wharfs provided storage facilities for newly arrived merchandise.

Minerva as the goddess of victory.

405

An inscription in the Caserma dei Vigili.

THE MITHRAEUM OF THE SEVEN SPHERES Initiates had to pass through seven stages, symbolized by semicircles representing the seven spheres of the planets: on the left, Diana (the Moon), Mercury and Jupiter; on the right, Mars, Venus, Saturn and finally Mithras (the Sun).

THE THEATER As well as being influenced by Greek drama, Roman theater drew on an Italic tradition in which humor was an important element: hence the success of farces, mimes and the comedies of Plautus and Terence. The masks worn by actors inspired the decorative motifs commonly used in Roman theaters.

HADRIAN'S QUARTER

This quarter, which extends to the right from the crossing with the Via dei Vigili, dates entirely from the time of Hadrian. The street was bordered by a magnificent portico sheltering numerous shops.

THE BATHS OF NEPTUNE ★. Ostia had a number of public baths, most of which were richly decorated with mosaics, marble and statues. The name of the Baths of Neptune, whose monumental size can be admired from a terrace overlooking the *decumanus* ▲ *404*, derives from a black-and-white mosaic showing the sea god surging forth on his *quadriga* of sea horses, surrounded by a multitude of Tritons, Nereids and dolphins. In the neighboring hall another mosaic shows Neptune's wife, Amphitrite. The bathing rooms occupy the eastern side of the complex, while opposite a gymnasium bordered by a lovely colonnade served for warming-up exercises ▲ *321*. The cistern was located beneath it.

THE CASERMA DEI VIGILI. Continuing on the left, you will see the entrance to the barracks of the *vigiles* ▲ *356*. A detachment of these soldiers, who acted as night police and firemen, was stationed at Ostia from the time of Claudius. The barracks give onto a large central courtyard surrounded by a covered arcade; this originally had two floors onto which the living quarters opened. At the back is a sanctuary, the *Caesareum*, for the cult of the Emperor. (Return to the *decumanus*.)

THE THEATER AND PIAZZALE DELLE CORPORAZIONI ★

THE THEATER. Like baths, theaters were a salient feature of the scenery of Roman towns. The theater of Ostia, with the adjacent square, forms one of the town's most important architectural groups. It was built by Agrippa and partially restored at the end of the 2nd century by the Emperor Commodus. Its present appearance (mainly tiers of steps and a portico) dates to its radical restoration in 1927. It had a capacity of about three thousand (four thousand after Commodus' restoration). The stage (*orchestra*) has alternating rectangular and curved niches; above are decorative

ements in marble, found during the excavations. On the
cumanus side the steps (*cavea*) were flanked by two circular
untains; one was turned into a Christian chapel dedicated to
Cyriacus, Bishop of Ostia, at the end of the 4th century.
day plays are performed in the theater in summer.

AZZALE DELLE CORPORAZIONI. Unique of its kind, this group
buildings famous for their splendid mosaics has provided
portant documentation on the commercial life of Ostia. It
cludes a huge portico (some 350 x 250 feet), in the center of
nich is a temple probably dedicated to Vulcan. The sides of
e square are divided into sixty rooms, which were clearly the
fices of the corporations of shipowners and merchants who
ad settled in Ostia. The black-and-white mosaics in each of
ese offices, which date from the time of the Severians (early
d century AD), depict scenes featuring navigation and trade.
effect they provide a trade map of the Roman world.
avi[cularii] Narbonenses, one can read on the mosaic in the
fice of "the shipbuilders of Narbonne"; in another,
avicul[arii] et Negotiantes Karalitani ("the shipbuilders and
erchants of Cagliari", in Sardinia); and so on.

HE HOUSE OF APULEIUS. Southwest of the Piazzale delle
orporazioni stands the entrance to a beautiful house
omus) dating from the 2nd century AD. Its structure testifies
the evolution of private Roman architecture: the *atrium* is
longer a simple room open to the sky, and the presence of
lumns heralds the peristyles of later houses ● 69. This
illding is especially remarkable for its rich decoration of
osaics and marble.

HE MITHRAEUM OF THE SEVEN SPHERES. This is one of the
st preserved of the seventeen sanctuaries of the Persian god
ithras discovered in Ostia. The mithraeum has a typical
rangement and decoration. The doorway is off the road, so
at the interior was not visible from outside; within, the
nches along the sides were reserved for initiates; and at the
r end, on a throne, is the image of Mithras slaughtering the
bull. Also of interest are the two
genii bearing torches (Cautes and
Cautopathes), and along the
corridor the seven semicircles
symbolizing the seven degrees of
initiation.

THE WHEAT TRADE
On its arrival in Ostia,
wheat was weighed by
the public authorities
before being
unloaded.

**THE OSTIA
LIGHTHOUSE**
"Claudius created the
port of Ostia by
having two curved
jetties built on the
right and on the left,
as well as a
breakwater in the
deeper water to bar
the entrance; to
anchor this
breakwater more
firmly, they began by
sinking the ship that
had brought the great
obelisk from Egypt,
then built numerous
pillars on top of it to
support a very tall
tower, which like the
lighthouse at
Alexandria was
destined to light up
the ships' paths at
night."

Suetonius
Claudius, XX, 3

One of the numerous representations
of Ostia's lighthouse (below).

The Romans gave pride of place to mosaics,
which they arranged on walls, floors and
ceilings, exploring all the possibilities of
this art form, from purely decorative
motifs and polychrome geometrical
pavings to the most complex figurative
images. The mosaics in Ostia (especially the
2nd-century ones in the Piazzale delle
Corporazioni ▲ 406) are notable for their figurative designs in
black and white, with the outlines of men and animals
silhouetted on the ground like Chinese shadows.

**OIL FROM
MAURETANIA**
Quantities of
foodstuffs arrived a
Ostia from all the
Mediterranean
ports. The amphora
between two palm
trees, symbolizing
the oil trade, bears
the initials M.C.
("Caesar's
Mauretania"),
indicating its place
of origin.

MARINE THEME
Known to be earlier than the others, this mosaic with a Nereid sitting on a sea horse is reminiscent of the mosaics in the Baths of Neptune ▲ *406*. It captures movement with the same artistry, and the same lightness of form.

THE IVORY TRADE
The inscription reads: *sta[tio] Sabratensium*. This refers to the authority in Sabratha, in Libya, that was in charge of the ivory trade. It may also have been responsible for supplying elephants for the Roman arenas.

AFRICAN GAME RESERVE
The boar is part of a mosaic which also shows a deer and an elephant, all animals used for games in the amphitheaters of Rome: hunts (*venationes*), combats between gladiators and animals, and combats between animals.

CUPID WITH A WHIP
In the center a Cupid is riding a dolphin. The two medallions above possibly symbolize Africa. Everything is full of movement: the sea is suggested by parallel lines, and the dolphins' bodies have white lines to emphasize their undulations.

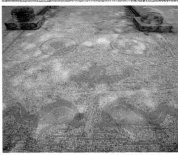

Most of what is known about *insulae* (apartment buildings) is due to the excavations in Ostia. They could have as many as seven or eight floors, but Augustus limited their height to approximately 65 feet. Unlike the *domus* (house), which was built around an *atrium* (inner courtyard), the *insula* faced the street, as shown above.

FOUR REPUBLICAN TEMPLES. To the south of the mithraeum four small temples stood on the same podium, built at the beginning of the 1st century BC by an influential citizen, Publius Lucilius Gamala. They were dedicated to Venus, Fortuna, Ceres and Spes (Hope), goddesses associated with good fortune and therefore patrons of shipping and trade.

AROUND THE "CASTRUM". Great quantities of wheat destined for the capital arrived at the port of Ostia. The grain was temporarily stored in the *horrea* (the remains of a gigantic example can be seen behind the four temples). Ostia also supplied Rome with flour for bread; this is why mills are often found close to the warehouses, like the one situated a little further on, in Via dei Molini. Between the *decumanus* and the Via dei Molini, you come to the gate of the *castrum* (the original heart of the town ▲ 404), built with great blocks of tufa. Excavations on this spot have revealed the level of the road in Republican times. A well-preserved section of the wall of the *castrum* is also visible. (Take Via di Diana.)

VIA DI DIANA ★

CASA DI DIANA. This *insula* with several floors and a projecting balcony was built in the 2nd century AD. It had apartments for rent, but the arrangement of some of the rooms, where light and air are lacking, make it likely that it was also an inn, especially since Ostia was an important port for travelers. On the opposite side of the street one can recognize a *THERMOPOLIUM* (refreshment bar) by its broad marble counter and shelves for the display of dishes; its situation within a stone's throw from the forum must have brought it a roaring trade in ancient times. During the summer clients could eat or drink in a small inner courtyard with a delightful fountain.

CASEGGIATO DEI DIPINTI. This group made up of three apartment

buildings owes its name to the paintings that are found there. The one known as the INSULA DI GIOVE E GANIMEDE is richly decorated with 2nd-century murals. In the main room is the largest wall painting in Ostia, which includes a tableau of Jupiter together with his cupbearer, Ganymede. The INSULA DEI DIPINTI is also decorated with frescoes and has an attractive garden area. A beautiful view of the whole site can be enjoyed from the terrace on the upper floor, opposite the *thermopolium*.

THE MUSEUM. At the end of Via di Diana is a small museum containing works of art found in Ostia. The large marble statue of the eastern god Mithras▲ 406 slaying the bull (in Room III, devoted to oriental cults) and the fine 4th-century marble-inlay wall decoration depicting lions attacking deer are particularly remarkable. Room XII is devoted to paintings from the necropolis of the Isola Sacra ▲ 416. (Take Via del Capitolium to rejoin the *cardo maximus* ▲ 404.)

This sign and the type of construction made it possible to date the *thermopolium* to the 3rd century AD.

VIA DEI MOLINI
One large mill still has its millstones of volcanic rock (below left). In front of it are six shops, which may have sold bread.

CASA DI DIANA
In the courtyard is an image of Diana, the divinity who was the patron of the house that today bears her name. The two rooms on the northeastern side were converted into a mithraeum ▲ 181 at the end of the 2nd century.

AROUND THE FORUM

THE CIVIC CENTER OF OSTIA. It was not until the reign of the Emperor Hadrian that the colony of Ostia was endowed with a monumental square worthy of its commercial and political status. To the north, an imposing brick building with a podium faced in marble replaced the ancient religious buildings. This was the most important temple of the town, the CAPITOLIUM, a place of worship dedicated to the principal gods of the Roman religion. Its façade, which had six columns and was approached by a fine flight of steps, has been entirely stripped of its decorations; but from 19th-century drawings one can get an idea of the geometrical motifs of the marble pavement of the *cella*. Inside, statues adorned the wall niches, and at the back were three rooms where the cult statues were kept. Like all of Rome's forums, Ostia's had a Curia, where the council of *decuriones* sat. However, this monument (to the north of the *decumanus*) looks more like a temple, and its identification is still uncertain. Finally, to the south (on the other side of the *decumanus*) is the BASILICA that housed the law courts. This consists of a large hall with a nave bordered by a colonnade; on its southern side the remains of the podium which was used by the judges can still be seen.

THE FORUM
The buildings must be imagined with their decorations (all removed) made from various marbles, including white Carrara marble and antique yellow from North Africa.

The Temple of Hercules.

THE LATRINES
Beyond the east portico of the forum you enter the Via della Forica (Street of the Latrine). On the left, after a series of shops, two public latrines, for men and for women, have been identified, with the stone seats ranged around the sides and a small basin between the entrances.

Below (from left to right): the latrines; the Temple of Rome and Augustus; a detail of the polychrome pavement in the House of Cupid and Psyche; and the Casa degli Aurighi.

THE TEMPLE OF ROME AND AUGUSTUS. In honor of his adoptive father, Tiberius had one of the most elegant buildings of the colony erected on the south side of the forum opposite the Capitolium. Today the remains of this temple have lost their marble facing, and fragments of its decoration have been left where they were found. The winged statue of *Victory* now fixed against the wall probably stood on the temple rooftop. (Leaving to the south the monumental baths of the forum built in the 2nd century AD and restored in the 4th century, return to the *decumanus* ▲ *404.*)

CASA DEL LARARIO. The *insula* of the shrine of the Lares is an interesting example of a market with shops opening onto it. This shopping center owes its name to the presence of a small shrine consecrated by the shopkeepers to their gods, the Lares. Opposite is the TEMPIO ROTONDO (Round Temple), which was probably dedicated to the cult of the Imperial family. It was originally covered with a dome and had a large rectangular courtyard in front of it. (Go through the western gate of the *castrum.*)

HORREA EPAGATHIANA AND EPAPHRODISIANA. As the marble slab above the entrance indicates, these warehouses of the 2nd century AD belonged to two rich freed slaves named Epagathos and Epaphroditos. The presence of a double door suggests that they contained precious merchandise. Sixteen rooms open onto an inner courtyard surrounded by a portico; the largest one was no doubt used as an office. (Take Via del Foce, toward the *foce* or ancient mouth of the Tiber.)

VIA DELLA FOCE

THE REPUBLICAN SANCTUARY. This sacred area included three temples: the Temple of Aesculapius, the god of medicine, on the north side of the precinct; the one known as the "Temple with the Circular Altar"; and the largest, the Temple of Hercules (about 100 BC), set on a raised podium with an impressive flight of steps leading up to it. Hercules was honored here as a god of war whose oracle had to be consulted by the captains of the military fleet before each expedition. Indeed, a votive relief showing a *haruspex* consulting the oracle was discovered near the building. The idealized statue of Cartilius Poplicola ("friend of the people"), the most important politician in Ostia's history, is another votive monument. (Take Via del Tempio di Ercole.)

THE HOUSE OF CUPID AND PSYCHE. A family of important officials or wealthy merchants lived in this richly decorated house dating from the 4th century AD. Like many others, it was built on an earlier construction consisting of shops. The large hall at the back has magnificent marble decorations and a marble pavement with geometrical motifs. One of the rooms opening onto the passage is adorned with a copy of a sculpture of *Cupid and Psyche* (center);

e original is in the museum ▲ *411*. Going back down Via
lla Foce, you come to the Baths of Buticosus, an interesting
ample of private baths (*balnea*) of the 2nd century AD. As
ell as being smaller, they differed from the public baths in
at they had no *palestra*. However, their fresco and mosaic
corations (pictures of gardens and marine scenes) are no
less refined. (Retrace your steps and
take the Via del Serapide).

THE SERAPEUM ★. Many foreign
cults that were not officially
recognized by the Roman religion
were practiced in the outskirts of
this port town, such as the cult of
the Egyptian god Serapis, who was
identified with Jupiter. The entire
decoration consists of motifs
associated with Egypt, and the
mosaic in the courtyard
features scenes of life on the
Nile. (Return to the Via della
Foce.)

THE BATHS OF THE SEVEN SAGES

The whole block between Via
della Foce and Cardo degli
Aurighi is a magnificent
architectural group, built under
Hadrian and Antoninus Pius. It
includes two apartment
buildings, the Insula del
Serapide and the Insula degli
Aurighi, separated in the
center by the Baths of the
Seven Sages, which were
reserved for the residents'
use. The floor of the main
room of the baths, a large
circular hall (*frigidarium*) originally covered
with a dome, is decorated with
mosaics featuring hunting scenes
and foliage. A small adjacent room
has frescoes showing seven Greek
sages with their names written in
Greek: Solon, Thales, Chilon,
Periander, Bias, Cleobulus and
Pittacus. Each is described with a
piquant Latin epigram: for
example, *Ut bene cacaret ventrem
palpavit Solon* ("To defecate well,
Solon rubbed his stomach"). This
reveals a whole tradition of
humor, of the type that was
representative of Roman
culture, and was particularly
lively in the theater. (Rejoin
the *decumanus* and
proceed toward the west.)

Four views of the
Baths of the Seven
Sages, and the
Serapeum (above).

THE LARES
These were the gods
of the places
frequented by man,
such as homes, fields,
shops and
neighborhoods.

THE IMPERIAL CULT
When an Emperor
died his deification
was entrusted to a
flamen, a priest
appointed for life from
among the city's
eminent personalities.

413

THE SYNAGOGUE
The earliest part of
the building dates
from the 1st century
BC, which could mean
that the development
of the Jewish
community in Ostia
was linked to the
increase of trade after
Claudius built the
port.

AROUND THE INSULA DELLE VOLTE DIPINTE

On the right-hand side of the
decumanus is a CHRISTIAN BASILICA, the
largest Christian building to have survived in Ostia.
Built partly over some preexisting baths, it is an elongated
building with two naves preceded by a kind of vestibule. A
little further on is the TEMPIO DEI FABRI NAVALES, where the
naval smiths worshiped. The imposing "SCHOLA DEL
TRAIANO", facing the temple, was in fact the official seat of
their corporation, the importance of which is obvious in a
town that relied on the sea. (At the crossroads take Cardo
degli Aurighi, then Via delle Volte Dipinte.) Built in
Hadrian's reign, the residential complex known as the INSULA
DELLE VOLTE DIPINTE includes a sequence of rooms opening
onto a long corridor; its name refers to some remarkable 2nd-
century frescoes that have been preserved there. Close by, the
Case a Giardino offered their residents the amenity of a large
garden adorned with six fountains. Two groups of buildings
should be imagined in the middle of the garden, each
consisting of four almost identical houses with a covered
passage between them. The absence of shops suggests the
refined character of these dwellings, and this is confirmed by
a mosaic on one of the fountains that features Nile scenes
with crocodiles and Pygmies. (Take the *decumanus* as far as
the Porta Marina.)

PORTA MARINA

A large suburb developed outside this "Marine Gate", which
formed part of the Republican walls. On the right stands the
DOMUS FULMINATA ("the house struck by lightning"), with an
inscription stating: F[*ulgur*] d[*ium*] c[*onditum*] ("A divine
thunderbolt fell here"). As in the House of Apuleius ▲ 407,
the *atrium* has made way for a peristyle – an inner courtyard
surrounded by columns, which assumed the central function
of the building. A little farther on, in the first street on the
left, is the Tomb of CARTILIUS POPLICOLA ▲ 412, in the shape
of an altar; the upper part is decorated with a naval battle
scene. You can then continue to the SYNAGOGUE, which dates
from the 1st century AD. Discovered in 1961, this is the oldest

**THE TOMB OF
CARTILIUS POPLICOLA**
The frieze of the
tomb (right) shows a
naval battle, no doubt
an episode in the war
against Sextus
Pompeius (c. 39 BC).
The prow of the
trireme on the right is
decorated with a head
of Minerva; on the
left are armed
infantrymen
accompanied by an
unusually tall person.

ynagogue found
n the ancient Roman West.
Returning to the *decumanus*, just after the junction with Via
lel Pomerio, you will come to the MEAT MARKET (*macellum*),
vith shops arranged around an inner courtyard. Access is
hrough a portico and an entrance with columns, where there
re two shops that probably sold fish. (Go back to the *cardo
naximus* ▲ *404.*)

CAMPO DELLA MAGNA MATER

Between the *cardo maximus* ▲ *404* and the Porta Laurentina,
Hadrian created a sacred precinct dedicated to Cybele, the
Phrygian goddess of fertility ▲ *148.* In Ostia this is one of the

The *Horrea* of
Hortensius.

CYBELE AND ATTIS
During the Feast of
the Hilaria the
faithful mutilated
themselves, imitating
the act of Attis, to
become Galli, the
eunuch priests of the
goddess Cybele.

DYERS' WORKSHOP
Four large basins
were used for
washing the wool,
which was then
trampled (above),
squeezed, dyed and
mangled. Wool from
Puglia, Istria and
Padua was dyed in
Ostia before going on
to Rome.

ost widely attested oriental cults. The goddess was
orshiped together with two other divinities: Attis, her male
ompanion, and Bellona, goddess of war. These two divinities
ad a smaller shrine on the south side of the precinct, at the
nd of the long portico that borders it. Eunuch priests called
alli celebrated the cult in the month of March. (Return to
he *cardo,* then take the Semita dei Cippi, an important
ommercial route, and Via della Fortuna Annonaria.) Here
ands one of the richest houses in Ostia. Built on the site of a
ormer *insula,* with its large courtyard framed by a portico, it
typical of the aristocratic dwellings of the 4th century AD. In
e Via degli Augustali there is a 2nd-century *fullonica*
aundry and dyers' workshop). Returning to the *decumanus,*
u will come to a temple that probably belonged to a
orporation of shipwrights and carpenters. From here on, the
ght-hand side of the *decumanus* is occupied by the HORREA
F HORTENSIUS, a string of warehouses dating from the end of
e Republic that opens onto a large courtyard surrounded by
lumns.

THE OSTIA AREA

THE MEDIEVAL VILLAGE. During Imperial times a necropolis sprang up outside Ostia, and it was there that St Aurea, martyred during the reign of Claudius II (268–70), was buried. This led to the development of a suburb that, in the Middle Ages, became the last refuge of the population of Ostia. The castle (above) guarded access to the Tiber, which formerly flowed past this spot. Although the keep was erected by Martin V (1417–31), the rest of the castle was built by Cardinal Giuliano della Rovere (the future Pope Julius II) between 1483 and 1486. The CHURCH OF SANTA AUREA, which stands within the fortified medieval village, over the martyr's tomb, was totally rebuilt in the 15th century. The body of St Augustine's mother, St Monica, who died in Ostia in 387, was interred here before being moved to the Church of Sant'Agostino ▲ *284* in Rome.

THE MODERN TOWN. Ostia Antica gives no hint of the modern town. With its sad grid of apartment buildings, the town survives mainly because of its beaches, to which the Roman crowds flock from May to September. Although the seashore has been badly spoiled by the number of bathing establishments (most of which are *abusivi* – that is, built without the necessary permit from the municipal administration), and despite a frequently polluted sea, Romans still love these beaches with their black volcanic sand. Among the villages on the sea front, Fregene – further to the north and certainly rather more attractive – has taken root in

a landscape that was transformed during the Fascist period when the Maccarese marshes were drained. The very flat land, crisscrossed by canals edged with reeds, is regularly punctuated by farms and small red houses; it is a far cry from Ostia's surroundings, with their lovely pine woods. Fiumicino

(between Ostia and Fregene) is a well-known name because of its vicinity to the huge Leonardo da Vinci airport, built between 1950 and 1957 but totally altered and modernized in the early 1990's. Today a metro line links it to the center of Rome.

Practical information

418   Getting there
420   Staying in Rome from A to Z
428   Hotels
432   Roman cuisine
434   Restaurants
441   Cafés, bars, nightclubs
445   Shopping
447   Useful words and phrases
448   Places to visit
468   Bibliography
472   List of illustrations
480   Glossary
482   Biographical index
491   General index
501   Map section

ADDRESSES

→ UNITED KINGDOM
■ **ITALIAN EMBASSY**
14 Three Kings' Yard
London W1K 4EH
Tel. 020 7312 2200
www.amblondra.
esteri.it

■ **ITALIAN CULTURAL INSTITUTE**
39 Belgrave Square
London SW1X 8HX
Tel. 020 7235 1461
www.iiclondon.
esteri.it

→ UNITED STATES
■ **ITALIAN EMBASSY**
3000 Whitehaven St
NW, Washington,
D.C. 20008
Tel. 202 612 4400
www.ambwashington
dc.esteri.it

■ **ITALIAN CONSULATE**
12400 Wilshire Blvd
Suite 300
Los Angeles,
CA 90025
Tel. 310 820 0622

■ **ITALIAN CONSULATE**
690 Park Avenue
New York, NY 10021
Tel. 212 737 9100
or 212 439 8600

■ **ITALIAN CULTURAL INSTITUTE**
686 Park Avenue
NY 10021 New York
Tel. 212 879 4242
www.iicnewyork.
esteri.it

→ TOURIST OFFICES
■ **ITALIAN GOVERNMENT TOURIST AGENCIES**
www.enit.it
www.italian
tourism.com
– **New York**
630 Fifth Avenue,
Suite 156,
New York, NY 10028
Tel. (212) 245 4822
– **Los Angeles**
Tel. (310) 820 0098
– **Chicago**
Tel. (312) 644 0990

■ **ITALIAN TOURIST OFFICE (UNITED KINGDOM)**
1 Princes St,
London W1B 2AY
Tel. 020 7408 1254
www.italian
board.co.uk

→ ROME ON THE NET
www.comune.roma.it
The official website
of Rome's city
council (in Italian).
www.romaturismo.it
Tourist office website.

Comprehensive,
practical information
about the Eternal
City and cultural
events.
www.vatican.va
The Vatican official
website.
www.atac.roma.it
Information on
transport in Rome
and the surrounding
area (in Italian).

MONEY

→ EXCHANGE
The Italian monetary
unit is the Euro.
€1 = £0.70 or $1.30
(at the time of going
to press).
You can change
money at autotellers,
banks and bureaux
de change, but the
latter charge higher
rates.

→ CREDIT CARDS
Accepted at most
ATMs, and by most
hotels, restaurants
and some stores.

BY AIR

→ FROM THE UK
There are regular
flights from London,
Edinburgh,
Manchester and
other UK cities direct
to Rome. A return
flight from London
can cost as little as
£90. Journey time
2½ hrs.

■ **ALITALIA**
Tel. 0870 544 8259
www.alitalia.com
To Rome Fiumicino
airport.
■ **BRITISH AIRWAYS**
Tel. 0870 850 9 850
www.ba.com

To Rome Fiumicino
airport.
■ **EASYJET**
Tel. 0870 600 0000
www.easyjet.co.uk
To Ciampino airport,
9 miles southeast of
the city.
■ **RYANAIR**
Tel. 0871 246 0000
www.ryanair.com
To Ciampino airport.

→ FROM THE US
There are regular
flights from most
major US cities to
Rome Fiumicino.
– **New York–Rome**
from $500 return;
journey time 11 hrs.
– **Chicago–Rome**
from $650 return;
journey time 14 hrs.
– **Los Angeles–Rome**
from $700 return;
journey time 20 hrs.
■ **ALITALIA**
Tel. 1 800 223 5730
www.alitaliausa.com
■ **AMERICAN AIRLINES**
Tel. 1 800 433 7300
www.aa.com
■ **CONTINENTAL**
Tel. 1 800 252 0280
www.continental.com
■ **DELTA**
Tel 1 800 223 5730
www.delta.com
■ **USEFUL WEBSITES**
www.orbitz.com
www.travelocity.com
www.cheapflights.com

→ TRAVEL DISCOUNTS
Airline fares are less
expensive in winter

than in summer.
The best deals are
usually obtained by
traveling midweek
and staying over the
Saturday night befor
returning. Fares are
much higher over
Easter and
Christmas.

BY CAR

→ DOCUMENTS
Valid driving license
car registration
papers and proof of
insurance. You only
need your license
to drive in Italy, but
an International
Driver's Permit is
recommended.
■ **AMERICAN AA**
Tel. 1 800 564 6222
www.aaa.com
■ **AA (UK)**
Tel. 0870 550 0600
www.theaa.co.uk

→ SPEED LIMITS
80 mph (130 km/h)
on highways, 56 mp
(90 km/h) on nationa
roads and 37 mph
(50 km/h) in towns
or built-up areas.

→ FREEWAY TOLLS
Freeway tolls can
be paid in cash, by
banker's card or
Viacard. Viacards
(€25, €50 and €75)
are available from
Italian service
stations, tollbooths,
certain banks and
tourist offices.
■ **RESCUE SERVICES**
Automobile Club
Italiano (ACI)
Tel. 803 116 (from
a landline)
Tel. 800 116 800
(from cellphone).

BY COACH

→ FROM THE UK
■ **EUROLINES**
Tel 08705 808 080
www.national
express.com

BY TRAIN

→ LONDON–PARIS
Eurostar from
London Waterloo to
Paris-Gare du Nord.

INFORMATION
rostar (London):
l. 08705 186 186
ww.eurostar.com
ail Europe (London):
l. 08708 371 371
ww.raileurope.co.uk
ail Europe (US):
l. 1-800-524-2420
ww.raileurope.com

PARIS–ROME
FROM PARIS-BERCY
y night: nonstop
ily service
eparting at 7.09pm
urney time:
ound 15 hrs).
FROM PARIS-
RE DE LYON
y day: TGV to
lan, then Intercity
Eurostar to Rome
urney time:
pprox. 7 hrs from
aris to Milan, then
other 4 ½ hrs
Rome).
INFORMATION
ww.voyages-
sncf. com
ww.trenitalia.it

FORMALITIES

passport or ID card
recommended
r EU nationals.
on-EU nationals
eed a valid passport
nd should check
th the nearest
alian consulate
r any visa
quirements.
ritten authorization
required for minors
aveling without
eir parents.

HEALTH

MEMBERS OF THE
EUROPEAN UNION
European health
ard has now
placed the old
orm E-111. It is
sued by the Health
uthorities of EU
ountries and
ntitles members
emergency
edical treatment.
pply for it in good
ne.
arning:
e European
ealth Card may
ot be valid for all
rvices. You are

advised to keep all
prescriptions, bills
and receipts.

→ OTHER
COUNTRIES
Non-EU members
must take out
personal medical
insurance. Contact
your travel agent or
insurance broker for
details.

TOUR
OPERATORS

→ IN THE UK
■ **ITALIATOUR**
205 Holland Park
Avenue
London W11
Tel. 020 7371 1114
■ **SWAN HELLENIC**
77 New Oxford St
London WC1A 1PP
Te: 020 7800 2300
Art and architecture
tours of Rome.

→ IN THE US
■ **ITALIATOURS**
P.O. Box 5209
Hoboken, NJ 08030
Tel. 800-283-7262
General tours to Italy.
www.italiatours.com
■ **ESPLANADE TOURS**
581 Boylston St,
Boston, MA 02116
Tel. 617 266 7465
or 800 426 5492
Art and architecture
"Treasure Tours".

STUDENTS

→ CARDS AND
CONCESSIONS
■ **ISIC CARD**
The international
student's card
gives reductions
in museums and
hotels, as well as
air and train tickets.
■ **YOUTH CARD**
Foreign visitors under
26 years who are not
students may join
the Italian CTS:
Centro Turistico
Studentesco e
Giovanile
C.so Vittorio
Emanuele II, 297
Tel. 06 68 72 67.
■ **YOUTH HOSTEL**
ASSOCIATION
UK:
YHA Adventure Shop

14 Southampton St
London WC2
Tel. 0870 770 8868
www.yha.org.uk
US:
www.eurotrip.com/
hostels
Also consult the
international
hostelling website
wwwiyhf.org
The Italian youth
hostel association is
known as AIG. The
minimum age for
access to youth
hostels is 8 years.

TELEPHONE

→ CALLING ROME
FROM THE UK
■ Dial 00 + 39 + the
number you wish
to call.

→ CALLING ROME
FROM THE US
■ Dial 011 39 + the
number you wish
to call.

TIME ZONE

Italy is in one hour
ahead of Greenwich
Mean Time. When it
is noon in Rome, it is
11am in London, and
6am in New York.

WHEN TO GO

In the early fall, so as
to avoid the peak of
the tourist season.
Then, temperatures
are pleasantly warm
and suitable for
sightseeing, and the
light perfect for the
typical ochers and
reds of the buildings.

→ INFORMATION
■ **ACCOMMODATION**
From July through
September, almost
all hotels are fully
booked. You are
therefore strongly
advised to book a
hotel in advance
through the Internet,
a travel agent or
tour operator, or by
contacting Hotel
Reservation, a
central bureau in
touch with 500 hotels
in all price ranges.

TEMPERATURES °F		
	min./max.	
Jan.	41	52
Feb.	43	55
March	45	59
April	50	64
May	56	72
June	63	86
July	68	86
Aug.	63	81
Sep.	55	70
Oct.	48	61
Nov.	48	61
Dec.	43	54

Tel. (39) 06 699 10 00
7am–10pm daily.
Warning:
During the winter
months, remember
to pack warm
clothing. The
temperature rarely
drops below zero,
but it can still feel
chilly.
■ **AVOIDING**
THE CROWDS
Holy Week should
be avoided because
of the vast number
of pilgrims in Rome,
not only around the
Vatican but all over
the city. In August
Rome is deserted
as Romans flee to
escape the heat,
and it also means
that many stores
and restaurants
are shut.

WHAT THINGS
COST

→ CATEGORY
■ **BUDGET**
Hotel: €90–120
Restaurant: €20–25
■ **TYPICAL**
Hotel: €150–200
Restaurant: €25–40
■ **LUXURY**
Hotel: from €300
Restaurant: from €50

→ TYPICAL PRICES
■ One entry to
a museum €2–10
■ One postcard,
with stamp €1.65
■ One espresso
€0.70
■ Breakfast €3
■ One saltimbocca
alla romana €12
■ One tiramisù €2.50
■ One glass of
amaretto €2

◆ STAYING IN ROME FROM A TO Z

Accommodation, airlines, airports, airports to city center

ACCOMMODATION

→ HOTELS

Italy classifies its hotels using the European star system (from 1 to 5) controlled by the APT (Azienda di Promozione per il Turismo).

■ RESERVATIONS
Hotel Reservations
Tel. 06 699 10 00
(7am–10pm)
www.hotelreservation.it
A central reservation agency with 500 hotels in all price ranges. There are two offices at Termini station (platforms 4 and 20), three at Fiumicino airport and one at Ciampino airport. There is no real low season in Rome. It is advisable to book in advance for Holy Week and from July through September.

■ PRICES
Hoteliers are obliged to display their tarifs in each room. In general prices tend to be quite high but they vary according to location and season. In the low season hotels have special (negotiable!) offers for a minimum stay of two nights, or if booking is made on the Internet. The prices given ◆ 428–31 are for one night for two people in a double room, without breakfast.

→ RELIGIOUS ASSOCIATIONS

A good way of lodging in Rome, but men and women are often segregated and the doors are locked at 10pm, or 11pm at the latest.
■ CASA ALLOGGIO SANTA PUDENZIANA
Via Urbana, 158
Tel. 06 488 00 56
For young women.
■ PASTORAL INFORMATION CENTER
Via Santa Giovanna d'Arco, 12

Tel. 06 68 19 24 64
Fax 06 683 23 24
Mon-Fri 10am–12.30pm, 2.30–5pm
centpastrome@
hotmail.com
This center sets up accommodation for tourists in religious institutions.

→ APARTMENTS AND ROOMS IN PRIVATE HOUSES

■ BED & BREAKFAST
Via dell'Umiltà, 48
Tel. 06 67 92 158
www.bedroma.it
■ LATTE E MIELE
Tel. 06 321 17 83
www.sleepinitaly.com
Open Mon.–Fri.
10am–6pm.
Addresses of apartments and B&Bs.

→ YOUTH HOSTELS

■ OSTELLO PER LA GIOVENTÙ
Ostello del Foro Italico
Viale delle Olimpiadi, 61
Tel. 06 323 62 67
Fax 06 324 26 13
■ INFORMATION
Associazione Italiana Alberghi per la Gioventù,
Via Cavour, 44
Tel. 06 487 11 52
Fax 06 488 04 92
www.ostellionline.org

→ APARTMENTS

N FAMILY HOUSE
Via Bixio, 72
Tel. 06 700 07 70
Fax 06 70 49 79 96
info@family-house.it

AIRLINES

→ ALITALIA

Via Bissolati, 11
Tel. 06 6562 21
Open Mon.–Thu.
9am–6pm, Fri.
9am–4.30pm
■ INFORMATION
Tel. 06 22 22
One number for the whole of Italy, available 24 hrs daily

→ BRITISH AIRWAYS

– Information and reservations:
Tel. 199 712 266
Mon.–Fri. 9am–6pm,

Sat. 9am–5pm
– Customer Relations:
Viale Città d'Europa 681, 00144 Rome
Tel. 06 52 49 27 56

AIRPORTS

Rome has two international airports.

→ LEONARDO DA VINCI-FIUMICINO

Via dell'Aeroporto di Fiumicino, 320
Located 17 miles southwest of Rome and 15 miles from the EUR suburb.
■ INFORMATION
Tel. 06 659 51
Daily, 24 hours
■ AIRPORT SERVICES
– Luggage
Tel. 06 65 95 42 52
Open 24 hours daily
– City police
Tel. 06 65 95 40 30
Open daily 7am–2pm
– First aid
Tel. 06 65 95 31 33
Open 24 hours daily
– Lost property
Tel. 06 65 95 35 41
Open Mon.–Fri.
9am–12.30pm,
Thur. 2–3.30pm
■ TOURIST OFFICE
Terminal B
Open daily 8am–7pm
■ CAR RENTAL
Usually open
Mon.–Fri. 8am–8pm;
Sat. 10am–noon
– Avis
Tel. 199 10 01 33
– Europcar
Tel. 06 65 01 08 79
– Hertz
Tel. 06 65 95 41 43
– Maggiore
Tel. 06 65 01 06 78
– Sixt
Tel. 06 65 95 35 47

→ G.B. PASTINE-CIAMPINO AIRPORT

Via Appia Nuova, 1651
Located at the foot of the Castelli Romani, about 9 miles southeast of the city center. Used for charter flights.
■ INFORMATION
Tel. 06 79 49 41
Daily 7am–11pm

■ AIRPORT SERVICES
– City police
Tel. 06 79 49 44 50
– First aid
Tel. 06 79 49 43 36
Open 24 hours daily
– Lost property
Tel. 06 79 34 83 20
– Luggage
Tel. 06 79 49 42 25
Open daily 7am–11pm
■ CAR RENTAL
Usually open
Mon.–Fri. 8am–8pm
Sat. 10am–noon
– Avis
Tel. 06 79 34 01 95
– Europcar
Tel. 06 79 34 03 87
– Hertz
Tel. 06 79 34 00 95
– Maggiore
Tel. 06 79 34 03 68
– Sixt
Tel. 06 79 34 08 38

FROM AIRPORTS TO CITY CENTER

→ FIUMICINO TO ROME CITY CENTE

■ BY BUS
Cotral
(On the international arrivals level.) From Fiumicino to Lepant where you catch the subway line A. Journey time about 90 mins. Service every 40–60 mins, 5.30am–7.10pm. Fare: €3.60. Ticket office located in the terminal (open daily 7am–6.40pm). Night buses run between the airport and Roma Tiburtina Station. Connection with the ferrovia metropolitana FM2 and subway line B. Hourly service, 1.15am–5am. Fare: €
Terravision Shuttle
To Termini station. Journey time about 1½ hrs. Service over 2 hours 8.30am–8.30pm. Fare: €9.
■ BY SUBWAY
Fiumicino-subway EUR Magliana. Connection with line B. Journey time 15 mins. Hourly service 5.57am–11.27pm

420

BY TRAIN
ONARDO EXPRESS
Termini station
stops): journey
me about 30 mins.
rvice every
mins, 6.37am–
.37pm. Fare: €11
RROVIA
ETROPOLITANA (FM1)
Tiburtina station
stops): journey
me about 45 mins.
rvice every
mins (every
mins Sun.)
on.–Fri. 6.57am–
27pm, Sat.–Sun.
57am–11.27pm.
re: €5
BY TAXI
urney time around
mins. Fare: about
40 to Termini
ation (additional
ck-up charge and
pplements for
ggage, nighttime
d public holidays)

CIAMPINO–
OME CITY CENTER
BY BUS + TRAIN
Ciampino station
e A). Journey time:
mins. Service
ery 20 mins.
re: €1. Then train
Rome Termini
ation. Journey
ne: 12 mins,
rvice every
mins.
BY BUS + SUBWAY
otral/Schiaffini
coach brings
u to Anagnina
bway station
e A). It leaves from
e international
rminal. Journey
ne about 15 mins.
rvice every 40
ins, 6am–10.40pm.
re: €1 (tickets
n be bought on
e bus)
BY BUS
chiaffini
rect to Rome
rmini station.
urney time:
5 mins. Service
proximately every
hrs, 10.30am–7pm.
re: €5
erravision Shuttle
cheduled to
nnect with Ryanair
d EasyJet flights.
re: €8 one way

■ BY TAXI
Taxi rank opposite
the arrivals terminal.
The journey time
is around 30 mins.
Fare: around €30

CARROZZE

A tour in a horse-
drawn carriage is
a very pleasant way
of seeing the sights
of the Eternal City.
Before setting off,
check the exact
price per carriage
or per person (about
€50 per hour)

■ DEPARTURE POINTS:
Piazza San Pietro,
in front of the
Coliseum, Piazza
Venezia, Piazza di
Spagna, Fontana
di Trevi, Via Veneto,
Villa Borghese,
Piazza Navona.

CHILDREN

Rome is probably
not the ideal place
for a vacation with
young children.
However, there are
various suitable
entertainments,
including the
botanical gardens
(Orto Botanico),
the zoological park
(Bioparco) and
the Luna Park in
the EUR.

→ CINEMA
Dei Piccoli
Viale della Pineta,15
Tel. 06 855 34 85
Price: €5

→ TRADITIONAL CHRISTMAS CRIBS
(Dec. 20 –Jan.10)
Via Giulia, Santa
Maria in Aracoeli,
San Giacomo al
Corso, Santa Maria in
Via, San Lorenzo in
Lucina, San Marcello,
and Sant'Ignazio.
■ CRIB MUSEUM
Via Tor de' Conti, 31a
Tel. 06 679 61 46

→ CHRISTMAS MARKET/TOY FAIR
Piazza Navona,
in December. On
Jan. 6, Fiera della
Befana (with toys
for the children).

→ EXPLORA, CHILDREN'S MUSEUM
Via Flaminia, 82-86
Tel. 06 361 37 76
The first museum
entirely dedicated to
children aged 1 to
12, who are allowed
to touch things and
to experiment.

CYCLING

Cycling in Rome
is not for the faint-
hearted. The best
districts of the city for
cycling are around
the Villa Borghese,
along the banks
of the Tiber, the
Piazza Navona
and the Pantheon.
On public holidays,
bicycles may be
carried on Line B
of the Metro and on
the Roma–Ostia line.
(€1/bicycle)

→ BICYCLE RENTAL
■ BICI E BACI
Via del Viminale, 5
Tel. 06 482 84 43
■ CYCLÒ
Via Cavour, 80/a
Tel. 06 481 56 69

DRIVING

For car rental,
see "Airports" and
"Trains".
→ ZONA A TRAFFICO LIMITATA (ZTL)
Driving in the historic
center of Rome is
prohibited Mon.–Fri.
6.30am–6pm and
Sat. 2–6pm. Tourists
who need to reach
their hotels by car
must apply for
special authorization
by sending a fax to
the STA, indicating
their license plate
number and the
length of their stay.
■ STA
Tel. 06 57 11 83 33
Fax 06 57 11 82 59
Open Mon.–Fri.
9am–5pm

→ PARKING
In the center of
Rome and in areas
immediately around
the center, there is a
charge for parking.
Parking is free only
on national holidays
and at night. Parking
meters take €0.10,
€0.20, €0.50, €1
and €2 coins,
as well as parking
cards, which are
sold in bars, kiosks
and tobacconists.
■ CAR POUND
– Farnesina
Tel. 06 33 22 05 27
– Cocchieri
Tel. 06 541 16 39
– G.B. Valente
Tel. 06 25 20 96 42

◆ STAYING IN ROME FROM A TO Z

Excursions, fairs, festivals, food and drink, guided tours

The penalty is around €100.

■ **PARKING LOTS**
There are about 35 supervized parking lots in the center of Rome. Charges are around €1–2 per hour.

■ **PARK AND RIDE**
The parcheggi di scambio ("park and ride" parking lots), near subway stations, allow motorists to park their cars and transfer to public transport. The daily charge (around €2) is the best value, but the parking lots are unattended.
– Connecting to subway line A:
Piazza di Spagna–Villa Borghese; Anagnina, Colli Albani–Via Albano; Arco di Travertino; Cinecittà.
– Connecting to subway line B:
Ponte Mammolo; Tiburtina; Garbatella; EUR Magliana; Laurentina.

EXCURSIONS

→ **THE LAKES**
Romantics will enjoy the lakes of the Castelli Romani (Roman castles): Nemi and Albano. Fishing enthusiasts will prefer Lake Bracciano.

→ **THE SEASIDE**
For a simple picnic on the beach, go to Ostia. If you intend to swim, go to Fregene, which is very popular with Romans.
■ **TRAVEL BETWEEN ROME AND OSTIA ANTICA**
Take the subway (line B) to Piramide, then the train (service every 30 mins.).

→ **THE MOUNTAINS**
For walking go to Fiuggi, the spa, and the Ernici hills. For winter skiing, try Terminillo (7,262 feet above sea level). It is the ski resort closest to Rome.

FAIRS

→ **ANTIQUES**
■ **FIERA DELL'ANTIQUARIATO**
Via dei Coronari May, 10am–1pm, 4–11pm

→ **ART**
■ **VIA MARGUTTA**
In the fall and in spring. Paintings.
■ **VIA GIULIA**
Various fairs throughout the year.

→ **CRAFTS**
■ **TEVERE EXPO**
June–July, 6pm–1am, between Ponte Sant'Angelo and Ponte Cavour.

FESTIVALS

→ **RELIGIOUS FEASTS**
■ **MIDNIGHT MASS**
Dec. 24, in most churches.
■ **FEAST OF THE EPIPHANY**
Jan. 6, Piazza Navona.
■ **FEAST OF ST JOSEPH**
March 19, Trionfale area (fritters are cooked and eaten on the streets).
■ **GOOD FRIDAY**
9pm, Stations of the Cross from the Coliseum to the Palatine.
■ **EASTER SUNDAY**
Noon, the Pope's blessing *urbi et orbi*, Piazza San Pietro.
■ **FEAST OF ST JOHN**
June 24, Piazza di Porta San Giovanni (banquet, fireworks, and more).
■ **FEAST OF ST PETER AND ST PAUL**
June 29, St Peter's Basilica.

→ **SECULAR FEASTS**
■ **ANNIVERSARY OF THE FOUNDATION OF ROME**
April 21, Piazza del Campidoglio.
■ **FESTA DEI NOANTRI**
July, "our own feast", the people's festival, in Trastevere.
■ **NEW WINE FESTIVAL**
End of November, Campo dei Fiori.

→ **SUMMER IN ROME** ("Estate Roma")
During the summer numerous cultural events take place in different parts of the city (cinema, theater, dance, art, literature, photography, etc.).
■ **INFORMATION**
www.estateromana. comune.roma.it

→ **"NOTTE BIANCA"**
In September, *l'Estate romana* closes with a "White night", holding shows, exhibitions, sporting activities, etc., in the city.
■ **INFORMATION**
Tel. 06 06 06
www.lanottebianca.it

→ **CINEMA, FESTA INTERNAZIONALE DI ROMA**
This movie festival takes place in October at the Auditorium-Parco della Musica, and includes concerts and lectures.
■ **INFORMATION**
www.romacinema fest.org

FOOD AND DRINK

See also "Roman cuisine" ◆ 432 and Restaurants ◆ 434.

→ **CAFÉS**
You will be spoilt for choice! The atmosphere is unique and the famous Italian espresso justifiably renowned.
■ **THE ART OF DRINKING COFFEE**
caffè ristretto: concentrated
caffè lungo: weaker
caffè macchiato: an espresso with a drop of milk
cappuccino: extra strong coffee with frothy milk
latte macchiato: a shot of coffee in a glass of milk
caffè freddo: iced coffee
caffè corretto: coffee topped with grappa.

GUIDED TOURS

→ **OFFICIAL GUIDES**
■ **SINDACATO NAZIONALE DELLE GUIDE TURISTICHE**
Tel. 06 639 04 09
Open Mon.–Fri. 9am–1pm
www.centroguide roma.org

CENTRO GUIDE CAFT
ia Cavour, 184
el. 06 482 56 98
pen Mon.–Fri.
.30am–1pm,
.30– 6pm;
at. 9.30am– 1pm
ww.cast-turismo.it

ROME BY BUS
BUS 110 OPEN
formation
el. 06 46 95 22 52
epartures: every
5–20 mins, 8.40am–
25pm; duration:
hrs; price: €13.
ightseeing tours
f Rome taking in
e city's major
storic monuments.
ARCHEOBUS
formation
el. 06 46 95 22 52
epartures: every
our, 9.45am–
.45pm; duration:
¾ hrs; price: €8.
ightseeing tour
f the Via Appia
onuments.
ombined
cket: Bus 110 +
rcheobus €20.

HEALTH

EMERGENCIES
MEDICAL ASSISTANCE
Guardia medica)
om–8am
el. 06 58 20 10 30
ITALIAN RED CROSS
MBULANCES
el. 06 55 10
POLICLINICO
MBERTO I
ntipoison center)
el. 06 49 06 63

HOSPITALS
EMERGENCIES)
FATEBENEFRATELLI
a Cassia, 600
el. 06 335 81 or
6 33 58 26 44
SAN GIACOMO
ia Canova, 29
el. 06 362 61 or
6 36 26 63 54
SAN GIOVANNI
ia dell'Amba
radam, 9
el. 06 770 51 or
6 77 05 56 61
POLICLINICO
MBERTO I
iale del
oliclinico, 155
el. 06 499 71 or
6 49 97 95 01

→ **PHARMACIES**
For those open
24 hours see the list
of night pharmacies
published in the
local press or call
06 22 89 41
■ FARMACIA
ARENULA
Via Arenula, 73
Tel. 06 68 80 32 78
■ FARMACIA JUCCI
MARIA CLOTILDE
Piazza dei
Cinquecento, 49–51
Tel. 06 488 00 19
■ FARMACIA PIRAM
Via Nazionale, 228
Tel. 06 488 07 54

INTERNET

Internet cafés have
sprung up around the
city and you should
find one easily.
■ EASYEVERYTHING
CAFÉ
Via Barberini, 2
Daily, 24 hours
www.easyeverything.
com

MAIL

Italian mail boxes
are red. Those in
the Vatican are blue.
The Vatican post
costs the same as
the regular Italian
mail service, but it
has the advantage
of being quicker! Use
the *Posta Prioritaria*
tarif, as the service is
truly faster than the
Ordinario.

→ **POST OFFICES**
■ INFORMATION
Tel. 803 160
www.poste.it
■ MAIN POST OFFICE
Piazza San
Silvestro, 18–20
Open Mon.–Sat.
8am–7pm
■ VATICAN
POST OFFICE
Piazza San Pietro
Open Mon.–Fri.
8.30am–7pm;
Sat. until 6pm.

MARKETS

→ **FOOD MARKETS**
These markets are
often picturesque
and colorful.

They play such an
important part in
Rome that food
stores are relatively
scarce in the historic
city center.
■ CAMPO DEI FIORI
Mon.–Sat.
6am–2pm.
The quality of
the produce and the
sheer beauty of this
market are some
compensation for
rather steep prices.
■ PIAZZA VITTORIO
EMANUELE II
Mon.–Sat.
7am–2pm.
This market has the
lowest prices.

→ **FLOWERS**
■ MERCATO DEI FIORI
Via Triunfale
Tue. 10.30am–1pm.

→ **BROCANTE**
Small *brocantes*
(secondhand goods
and flea markets)
can be found in
many parts of the
city on weekends.
Details are given in
Trovaroma magazine.

→ **BOOKS
AND PRINTS**
■ MERCATO
DELLE STAMPE
Largo della
Fontanella di
Borghese /
Piazza Borghese
Mon.–Sat. 7am–1pm
(times vary according
to the vendors).

→ **FLEA MARKET**
■ MERCATO DI
PORTA PORTESE
Via di Porta Portese
Sun. 6.30am–2pm.
Most business is
done early in the
morning and just
before the market
closes, around
1.30pm.
■ VIA SANNIO
Via Sannio
Mon.–Fri. 8am–1pm;
Sat. 10am–6pm

→ **CLOTHES**
■ MERCATO
DI TESTACCIO
Piazza Testaccio
Mon.–Sat.
7.30am–1.30pm

MEDIA

→ **ROME**
■ DAILY NEWSPAPERS
The main Roman
daily newspapers
are *Il Messaggero*
and *La Repubblica*.
■ FOREIGN
NEWSPAPERS
Available from kiosks
in the city center,
especially those on
the Via Veneto.
■ RADIO
RFI broadcasts on
satellite Astra 1C.
■ TELEVISION
National networks:
Rai Uno, Due and Tre.
The most important
paying channels are
Canale 5, Italia 1
and Rete 4. Thanks
to cable, many
European networks,
as well as CNN
International, can
be received.

→ **VATICAN**
■ PRESS
*L'Osservatore
Romano*
■ RADIO VATICAN
93.3 MHz and
105 MHz FM

MONEY

→ **AUTOTELLERS**
Most banks have
autotellers for use
with credit cards.
Exchange rates
are not always
favorable and your
bank usually also
charges you a cash
withdrawal fee.
In case of difficulties,
contact:
Tel. 800 01 85 48
or 800 81 90 14
AmericanExpress
Tel. 06 72 28 21
For lost or stolen
cards, *see*
"Useful numbers
and addresses",
page 427.

→ **CHANGE**
Money can be
changed in some
travel agents and
at the bureaux de
change in Roma
Termini station, in
Piazza di Spagna
and on Via Veneto.

◆ STAYING IN ROME FROM A TO Z

Museums and heritage sites, music, opening hours

The bureaux de change at the Vatican museums charge no commission, but overall the best exchange rates are to be found in banks.

→ PAYING BY CREDIT CARD
Most restaurants, hotels and shops accept credit cards. Trattorie, small *pensione* or *agriturismi* do not usually have the facilities.

MUSEUMS AND HERITAGE SITES

For information about events, look out for *Trovaroma*, the informative Thursday supplement of *La Repubblica*; *Città aperta*, a weekly publication with a section in English; and *Ente provinciale per il turismo*, a free monthly brochure.

→ CARDS/PASSES
■ CENTRO PRENOTAZIONE SOPRINTENDENZA ARCHEOLOGICA DI ROMA
Tel. 06 39 96 77 00
Information:
Via G. Amendola, 2 (Termini station)
Tel. 06 481 55 76
Open Mon.–Sat. 9am–1pm, 2–5pm
■ ROMA ARCHEOLOGIA CARD
A 7-day card costs €20 and gives entry to the Coliseum, the Palatine, the Baths of Caracalla, the tomb of Cecilia Metella, the Villa dei Quintili and all the sites belonging to the Roman National Museum.
■ ROMA PASS
This three-day card costs €18 and gives free access to all public transport and to two museums, as well as reductions to other sites.
Tel. 06 82 05 91 27

or 06 06 06
ww.romapass.it
→ FREE ENTRY
Entry to churches is free (or almost free). It is a good idea to carry some small change to activate the lighting. Entry to certain military and scientific

museums is also free. Entry to the Vatican museums is free on the last Sun. in the month.
Note:
Reservation is compulsory for the Galleria Borghese (tel. 06 32 810)
Online reservations:
www.ticketeria.it

→ WHAT TO WEAR
Dress soberly when visiting churches: avoid shorts, sleeveless tops and low necklines.

→ PHOTOGRAPHY
Photography is absolutely forbidden in museums. Art galleries do not allow the use of flash. When buying film, bear in mind that prices are usually higher in shops near the major monuments.

MUSIC

→ CLASSICAL
■ AUDITORIUM DE L'ACCADEMIA DI SANTA CECILIA
Via della Concilazione, 4
Tel. 06 32 81 71
www.santacecilia.it
■ AUDITORIUM DEL FORO ITALICO
Piazza Lauro De Bosis, 5
■ AUDITORIUM DEL GONFALONE
Via del Gonfalone, 32/a
Tel. 06 85 30 17 58
(Il Sogno)

■ AUDITORIUM PARCO DELLA MUSICA
Via de Coubertin, 30
Reservations:
Tel. 06 80 12 81
www.auditorium.com
■ TEATRO DELL'OPERA
Piazza B. Gigli, 1
Tel. 06 48 16 02 55
www.operaroma.it
■ RESERVATIONS
Romans are very keen opera-goers. Tickets should be booked several months in advance. Cooperativa Il Sogno
Tel. 06 85 30 17 58

→ SUNG MASS
■ SAN PAOLO FUORI LE MURA:
January 25
■ SAN GIOVANNI IN LATERANO:
June 24
■ ST PETER'S (THE SISTINE CHAPEL CHOIR):
June 29
■ IL GESÙ (TE DEUM):
December 31.

→ CHURCH MUSIC
■ CHOIR OF THE CAPPELLA GIULIA, ST PETER'S
Mass at 10.30am; vespers at 5pm.
■ SANT'APOLLINARE
Sunday morning and on major feast days.

OPENING HOURS

→ BANKS
Open Mon.–Fri. 8.30am–1.30pm, 2.30–4pm (sometimes Sat. am) These times may vary with individual banks.

→ BUREAUX DE CHANGE
Open 9am–1pm, 3.30–7pm

→ MUSEUMS
Most are closed on Monday. The Vatican museums are closed on Sunday, except the last Sunday in the month.

→ RESTAURANTS
Noon–3pm and 8–11pm. Many

lose in August
nd on Sunday.

STORES

am–1pm and
30–7pm. Many
re closed Thursday,
nd food stores
specially can be
osed on Saturday.
fternoon. Most
cores close in
ugust for two weeks
round Assumption.

PUBLIC HOLIDAYS

apodanno:
New Year's Day
(January 1)
a Befana:
Epiphany
(January 6)
unedì dell'Angelo:
Easter Monday
nniversary of the
Liberation (April 25)
esta del lavoro:
Labor Day (May 1)
esta della
epubblica:
Republic Day
(June 2)
erragosto:
Assumption
(August 15)
gnissanti:
All Saints' Day
(November 1)
nmacolata
Concezione:
mmaculate
Conception
(December 8)
atale: Christmas
(December 25)
anto Stefano
(December 26)

PUBLIC TRANSPORTATION

SUBWAY

he Roman subway
Metropolitana),
hich consists of
vo lines intersecting
t Termini station,
the quickest and
heapest means of
aveling around the
ty. Subway stations
re marked by a
hite M on a red
ackground.

LINES

(red): northwest
southeast.
(blue): northeast
southwest.

■ **INFORMATION**
Call free 800 43 17 84
(Italian), 8am–8pm

→ **BUSES AND TRAMS**
The 339 bus routes
and the 6 tramway
lines constitute the
public transport
network ATAC.
A clear map of the
different routes is
available at the
information center.
Stops are marked
by yellow signs,
which also show
the routes, times
and connections.
■ **INFORMATION**
Tel. 06 46 95 20 27
Open Mon.–Fri.
9am–5pm
www.atac.roma.it
Tel. 800 43 17 84
Open Mon.–Sat.
8am–8pm

→ **SCHEDULES**
■ **SUBWAY**
5.30am–11.30pm
(12.30am Sat.)
■ **BUSES**
5.30am–midnight, or
5am–1am, depending
on route.
■ **NIGHT BUSES**
There are about
20 of them, showing
a number followed
by a stylized owl.
■ **TRAMWAY**
5.30am–midnight,
or 5am–1am,
depending on route.

→ **TICKETS**
Metro tickets are sold
in subway stations.
Bus tickets are not
sold on the buses
themselves (except
on night buses); they
must be bought at
subway or train
stations, from ticket
machines at bus
terminals, or from
tobacconists, kiosks,
travel agencies and
some hotels.
Warning:
Ticket machines
do not always give
change and often
do not work.

→ **FARES**
■ **SINGLE TICKET**
Biglietto Integrato

a Tempo (BIT): €1,
valid 75 mins from
time it is stamped
(subway, all buses
and urban trains).
■ **DAY TICKET**
Biglietto Integrato
Giornaliero (BIG):
€4, valid 24 hrs.
■ **TOURIST TICKET**
Biglietto Turistico
Integrato (BTI):
€11, valid three days
and for an unlimited
number of journeys.
■ **WEEKLY TICKET**
Carta Integra
Settimanale (CIS):
€16, valid 7 days.

→ **LOST PROPERTY**
■ **BUSES AND TRAMS**
Tel. 06 581 60 40
Mon, Wed.–Fri.
8.30am–7pm,
Tue. 3–5pm
■ **SUBWAY**
Line A
Tel. 06 487 43 09
Open Mon., Wed.,
Fri. 9.30am–12.30pm
Line B
Tel. 06 57 53 22 64
Open Mon.–Sat.
8am–6pm

ROMAN LIFE

Essentially
Mediterranean!

→ **"PASSEGGIATA"**
The Romans love
going for a stroll late
afternoon in the
parks, down the
streets and around
the squares lively
with cafés. Favorites
are Via del Corso,
Piazza di Spagna
and Campo dei Fiori.

→ **PACE OF LIFE**
Lunch is taken
between 1 and 3pm,
dinner around 9pm.
An afternoon nap is
still the custom in
certain districts.

SCOOTERS

The famous Vespa
of the 1950's – as
ridden by Gregory
Peck and Audrey
Hepburn in Roman
Holiday – or the
motorino (motor-
cycle) is an excellent

way of traveling in
the center, though
renting one is quite
expensive. It is
compulsory to wear
a helmet. Remember
to take your driving
license.

→ **RENTING A BIKE OR SCOOTER**
■ **BICI E BACI**
Via del Viminale, 5
Tel. 06 482 84 43
■ **SCOOT-A-LONG**
Via Cavour 302
Tel. 06 678 02 06

SECURITY

Do not walk around
with a lot of cash
(most hotel rooms
have a safe). Do not
leave valuables in
parked cars. Be
vigilant when using
public transport.
Keep photocopies
of passports and
other documents.

→ **POLICE**
■ **VIGILI URBANI**
(city police)
In blue (in winter)
or white uniform
(in summer).
■ **CARABINIERI**
(police)
In pants with red
braid.
■ **POLIZIA**
(state police)
In blue uniform
and white beret.

SHOPPING

→ **ART AND ANTIQUES**
Most antique shops
and art galleries
are to be found in
Via dei Coronari,
Via Giulia and Via
Monserrato, the
Tridente. Here
prices are high:
many of the pieces
on display come
from Paris or London.

→ **ARTS AND CRAFTS**
Silverwork is one
of the strong points
of Roman arts and
crafts. The best
shops are on the
Piazza Cola di Rienzo.

→ FASHION

The shops with the widest choice of quality clothing will be found in the historic center of the city. The smartest are around the Piazza di Spagna (Via Condotti and Via Borgognona).

■ **SALES**
Sales are usually in January and July.

→ LATE OPENING

■ **DRUGSTORES**
For everything from food to books, perfumes to bread.
– **Termini**
Termini station.
– **Tiburtina**
Tiburtina station

→ OPEN ON SUNDAY

■ **DEPARTMENT STORE**
– **La Rinascente**
Piazza Colonna
Tel. 06 679 76 91
Open 10.30am–8pm.

■ **FOODSTORE**
– **Riposati**
Via delle Muratte, 8
Tel. 06 679 28 66
Open 7am–9pm.

→ RECEIPTS

Make sure you ask for a receipt (*scontrino*) whenever you pay for something. In some cafés you must pay first and then take your receipt to the bar. An inspector (*guardia di finanza*) could ask to see your receipt and you will be fined if you fail to produce it.

SHOWS

→ MOVIES

In Italy, the movies are usually in Italian with no subtitles, except during festivals and in certain cineclubs. A membership card is sometimes required.

■ **SOME ADDRESSES**
– **Azzurro scipioni**
Via degli Scipioni, 82
Tel. 06 39 73 71 61
Experimental and art movies shown in the summer.

– **Nuovo Sacher**
Largo Ascianghi, 6
Tel. 06 581 81 16
– **Quattro Fontane**
Via Quattro Fontane, 23
Tel. 06 474 15 15
■ **PRICE**
About €7 (reductions on Wed.)

→ SON ET LUMIÈRE

Son et lumière shows for groups are regularly given by the city of Rome at the Fori Imperiali.
■ **INFORMATION**
From the tourist office (APT) or from the city hall.

→ THEATER

■ **CLASSIC THEATER**
– **Argentina**
Largo di Torre Argentina, 52
Tel. 06 68 80 46 01
– **Teatro Quirino**
Via M. Minghetti, 1
Tel. 06 679 45 85
– **Teatro Valle**
Via Teatro Valle, 23/a
Tel. 06 686 90 49
■ **CONTEMPORARY THEATER**
– **Politecnico**
Via Tiepolo 13a
Tel. 06 321 98 91
– **Teatro Tordinona**
Via degli Acquasparta, 16
Tel. 06 68 80 58 90
■ **MUSICAL COMEDY**
– **Teatro Olimpico**
Piazza Gentile da Fabriano, 17
Tel. 06 326 59 91
Closed in Aug.
– **Teatro Sistina**
Via Sistina, 129
Tel. 06 420 07 11
■ **POPULAR THEATER AND VARIETY SHOWS**
Salone Margherita
Via Due Macelli, 75
Tel. 06 679 14 39
■ **OPEN-AIR THEATER**
Anfiteatro Quercia del Tasso
Viale Aldo Fabrizi
Information:
Estate romana ◆ 422.
www.estateromana.comune.roma.it

→ RESERVATIONS

Tickets can be bought on the day of the performance.

WHAT SIZE?			
MEN		**WOMEN**	
US/UK: ITALY		US/UK: ITALY	
JACKETS		**JACKETS**	
24/26	42	6/8	34
26/28	44	8/10	36
28/30	46	10/12	38
30/32	50	12/14	40
32/34	54	14/16	42
34/36	56	16/18	44
		18/20	46
PANTS		**SKIRTS AND DRESSES**	
26/28	44	6/8	34
28/30	46	8/10	36
30/32	50	10/12	38
32/34	54	12/14	40
34/36	56	14/16	42
		16/18	44

■ **HELLO TICKETS**
Tel. 800 90 70 80
■ **LISTICKET**
Tel. 199 10 97 83
■ **MESSAGGERIE MUSICALI**
Via del Corso, 473
Tel. 06 68 19 23 49
■ **ORBIS SERVIZI**
Piazza Esquilino, 37
tel. 06 474 47 76

SIZES

See table above.

SPORT

→ FOOTBALL

Two teams and two groups of supporters! Lazio (blue stripe) and Roma (red and yellow stripe).
■ **FIXTURES**
Sunday afternoons at 3pm.
Stadio Olimpico
Viale Foro Italico
Tel. 06 368 51
■ **INFORMATION**
Online tickets
www.listicket.it
Associazione Sportiva Lazio
Via di Santa Cornelia, 1000
Tel. 06 97 60 71 11
Associazione Sportiva Roma
Via Trigoria
Tel. 06 50 19 11

→ INTERNATIONAL EQUESTRIAN EVENT

Villa Borghese, in May.

→ INTERNATIONAL TENNIS TOURNAMENT

Foro Italico, in May.

STREET NUMBERING

There are two types of street numbering:
■ In newer districts, buildings are even-numbered on one side of the street and odd-numbered on the other, with numbering on both sides starting at the same end of the street.
■ In older districts the buildings are numbered all the way along one side of the street and back along the other (with odd and even numbers alternating).

TAXIS

Official taxis are yellow or white. They can be hailed in the street or found at a taxi rank (there are 140). However, with the traffic congestion, a taxi is not the cheapest way of moving around the city.
■ **FARES**
The pick-up charge plus the first 2 miles or

e first 9 minutes €3 (supplement harged on ublic hols).

RADIO TAXI
el. 06 55 51
el. 06 35 70
el. 06 49 94

TELEPHONE

CALLING
HE UK/US
ial 00, then the ountry code 4 for the UK, for the US), then e area code (for K numbers, omit e initial 0), then e phone number.

INTERNATIONAL
IRECTORY ENQUIRIES
el. 12 54

COLLECT CALLS
el. 170

PUBLIC
ELEPHONES
ost are ard-operated. nonecards are vailable from obacconists, ost offices and ome bars. alling centers ffer reduced narges for calls proad.

TIPPING

ervice is always cluded in staurants, but tips re still expected. is usual to leave tip in cafés and tip taxi drivers and otel staff.

TRAINS

INFORMATION
all center
el. 89 20 21
aily 24 hrs

→ **ROMA TERMINI CENTRAL STATION**
Piazza della Crocerossa, 1
Tel. 06 441 01
■ **RESERVATIONS**
Tel. 89 20 21
Daily 24 hrs
■ **STATION FACILITIES**
Bureau de change
Open daily 24 hrs
Left luggage
Tel. 06 47 30 62 75
Open daily 6am–midnight
Tourist information
Tel. 06 487 12 70
Open daily 8am–9pm
Lost property
Via Nicolò Bettoni,1
Tel. 06 581 60 40
Open daily 8.30am–1pm
Hotel reservations
Tel. 06 482 18 88
Open daily 7am–10pm
■ **CAR RENTAL**
Avis
Tel. 06 481 43 73
Open Mon.–Fri. 7am–8pm;
Sat. 8am–6pm;
Sun. 8am–1pm
Hertz
Tel. 06 474 03 89
Open Mon.–Fri. 7am–8pm;
Sat. 8am–6pm;
Sun. 8am–1pm
Maggiore
Tel. 06 488 00 49
Open Mon.–Fri. 7am–8pm;
Sat. 8am–6pm;
Sun. 8am–1pm

→ **ROMA TIBURTINA STATION**
Circonvallazione Nomentana
From Tiburtina to the city center:
Subway line B, or bus.
From Tiburtina to Roma Ostiense station: Ferrovia Metropolitana line FM1 (Orte-Fiumicino).

→ **ROMA OSTIENSE STATION**
Piazzale dei Partigiani
From Tiburtina to the city center:
take subway line B, or bus.

USEFUL NUMBERS AND ADDRESSES

→ **EMERGENCY NUMBERS**
■ **EMERGENZA SANITARIA (ambulance)**
Tel. 118
■ **CARABINIERI (police)**
Tel. 112
■ **POLIZIA (police assistance)**
Tel. 113
■ **POLIZIA MUNICIPALE**
Tel. 06 676 91
■ **POLIZIA STRADALE (highway police)**
Tel. 80 31 16

■ **VIGILI DEL FUOCO (fire department)**
Tel. 115
■ **LOST OR STOLEN CREDIT CARDS**
AmericanExpress
Tel. 06 722 03 48
or 336-393-1111 (US-collect)
Visa
Tel. 800-819-014

→ **TOURIST OFFICES**
■ **NAPT (AZIENDA DI PROMOZIONE TURISTICA)**
Via Parigi, 11
Tel. 06 82 05 91 27
www.romaturismo.it
Branches
– Via Parigi, 5
Tel. 0648 89 92 00
Open Mon–Sat. 9am–7.30pm
– Termini station
Open daily 9am–6pm
– Fiumicino Airport (Terminal B)
Open daily 8am–7pm
■ **CITY OF ROME TOURIST INFORMATION PHONELINE**
Tel. 06 82 05 91 27
■ **INFORMATION FOR THE DISABLED**
Tel. 06 57 17 70 94
www.romapertutti.it
www.romeguide.it/ monum_disabili.htm
■ **CHAMAROMA CALL CENTER**
Tel. 06 06 06 (24 hrs)
Information about public services (in Italian).

→ **EMBASSIES**
■ **BRITISH EMBASSY**
Via XX Settembre, 80
00167 Rome
Tel: 06 42 20 00 01
Emergencies (British nationals):
Tel. 06 4220 2600
Mon.–Fri. 9.15am–12pm (except on public holidays)
www.britain.it
■ **US EMBASSY**
Via Vittorio Veneto, 121
00187 Rome
Tel. 06 46 74 1
U.S. Citizen Services:
Mon.–Fri. 8.30am–12.30pm
www.usembassy.it
http://rome. usembassy.gov

◆ HOTELS

The Vatican, Aventine, Capitol, Palatine, Coliseum

HOTELS
☐ < €75
☐ €75–100
☐ €100–150
☐ > €150

The following hotels are listed by district, then by alphabetical order. The reference given with each hotel (e.g. ◆ F D4) allows it to be located in the map section, starting page 502.

THE VATICAN

Amalia
◆ A D3
Via Germanico, 66
Tel. 06 39 72 33 56
Fax 06 39 72 33 65
www.hotelamalia.com
The rooms in this late-19th-century palazzo with its unmistakable red-and-white façade have been refurbished. The simplest and cheapest are austerely furnished (pale-wood furniture and no-frills bathroom), but, in contrast, the more expensive ones are bigger and more elaborately decorated, with bathrooms worthy of a Hollywood mansion. Before making your choice, ask to visit the rooms, as the difference between the prices of the two types is not excessive. Doubles €150–210, including breakfast.
☐

❏ Bramante
◆ D A3
Vicolo delle Palline, 24-25
Tel. 06 68 80 64 26
Fax 06 68 13 33 39
www.hotel bramante.com
This 16-room hotel in the Borgo Pio, the medieval neighborhood separating Saint Peter's from the Castel Sant'Angelo, is located right next to the walls of the Vatican and was once the home of Domenico Fontana, who worked as an architect for Pope Sixtus V in the late 16th century. Great care has been taken to avoid disrupting the atmosphere in even the tiniest detail, and looking out of the window is like taking a journey back in time. Some rooms boast coffered ceilings and overlook a paved alleyway, while the others are set in the attic and give on to a pretty terrace; all are equally delightful, and to top it all the service is warm and attentive. Rooms €150–220.
☐

Colors
Hotel & Hostel
◆ A D4
Via Boezio, 31
Tel. 06 687 40 30
Fax 06 686 79 47
www.colorshotel.com
The Enjoy Rome agency, which owns Colors, was determined to dispel the preconception that a youth hostel or cheap hotel have to look drab. The doors and walls have been painted in a variety of colors, the rooms have cheerful furniture and the communal areas are spruce and convivial. Furthermore, the service is excellent, and, as an added bonus, English is spoken. Doubles €60–90, including breakfast (with bathroom €80–120), depending on the season, and a 5-bed dorm for €18–25/person. All the rooms are equipped with air conditioning, and a kitchen is available for the use of guests.
☐

Hotel Florida
◆ A D3
Via Cola di Rienzo, 243
Tel. 06 324 18 72
Fax 06 324 18 57
www.hotelflorida roma.it
To the right, the Piazza dell'Unità and the Vatican; opposite, Castroni and Franchi, respectively a top-class grocery and a superb purveyor of hot takeout food… and all this in a bustling street that goes totally unheard in the bedrooms, as they overlook the inner courtyard. The comfort cannot be faulted (bathroom, TV, telephone) but the atmosphere is somewhat impersonal. Doubles with bathroom €90–120, depending on the season.
☐

AVENTINE

Domus Aventina
◆ E D2
Via di S. Prisca,11/b
Tel. 06 574 61 35
Fax 06 57 30 00 44
www.hoteldomus aventina.com
An attractive hotel set in a 17th-century convent next to Santa Prisca, the oldest place of Christian worship in the Aventine. The upper floors are once again occupied by monks. The 26 rooms are spacious and comfortable (TV, modern bathrooms) and look onto the private garden of the church of Santa Prisca. There's nothing austere about it – on the contrary, it's charming and welcoming. Doubles €110–240, depending on the season.
☐

❏ Villa San Pio
◆ E D2
Via Santa Melania, 19
Tel. 06 574 52 31
Fax 06 574 11 12
www.aventino hotels.it
Stay in this hotel and you will feel like a favored guest in one of those elegant Italian country villas. Here the city seems so distant that it is hard to imagine that it is actually bustling all around. This impression is particularly striking at breakfast in the lovely garden, or if one has been lucky enough to get a room on this side of the hotel. Three superb villas house 79 rooms, all with marble bathrooms, elegant furniture and an interior decoration that evokes the peace of the countryside. Doubles €140–220, depending on the season.
☐

CAPITOL, PALATINE
COLISEUM

Antica Locanda
◆ E B3
Via del Boschetto, 84
Tel. 06 48 48 94
Fax 06 487 11 64
www.antica-locanda.com
Rossini, Puccini, Verdi, Vivaldi and Caravaggio are among the honored patrons of the nine rooms in a small hotel that skillfully mines a seam of nostalgia. Each room is different, although they are all comfortable and finely furnished. A further attraction is the romantic terrace, which is ideal for hot or moonlit nights. Doubles €130–210, depending on the season.
☐

Bolivar
◆ F D4 / E B2
Via della Cordonata, 6
Tel. 06 679 16 14 / or 06 699 16 66
Fax 06 679 10 25
www.travel.it/roma/ bolivar

olivar@ludovici
modern, well
ppointed hotel on a
ecluded little square
ear the Forum of
ajan. In a central
cation but away
om the bustle of
e city. The quality
the rooms is
neven (some are
uite luxurious and
pacious, while
thers are more
rdinary), so ask to
ew them if possible
nd check the prices
efore making your
hoice. From €130–
10.
▯

rifo
E B3
a d. Boschetto,144
el. 06 487 13 95
 06 482 75 96
ax 06 474 23 33
ww.hotelgrifo.com
rifo is a clean and
dequate hotel,
mous for the view
om its magnificent
rrace and with
e advantage of
central location,
 a street lined
ith antique shops,
tisans' workshops
d enoteche.
peccable but
npersonal rooms.
oubles €110–250,
reakfast included.
▮

otel Fiori
E B3
a Nazionale, 163
el. 06 679 72 12 /
5 25
ax 06 679 54 33
ww.travel.it/roma/
notelfiori
telfiori@tiscalinet.it
his hotel set in a
ylish palazzo near
e Piazza Venezia
d the historic
enter offers 12
omfortable rooms
at enjoy a view of
e gardens and
ave been capably
furbished with
astel colors and
retty furniture. No
orries about noise
ere: the double
azing is effective,
d so is the air

conditioning. There
is one drawback,
however: the price of
the bridal suite rises
steeply in the high
season (€75–180
with breakfast)
🖬

Nerva
◆ **E B3**
Via Tor de' Conti, 3
Tel. 06 678 18 35
Fax 06 69 92 22 04
www.hotelnerva.com
This small, modern,
stylish hotel is
located in the heart
of one of the last
remaining working
districts of Rome.
The spacious
rooms, light, airy,
soundproofed and
lined with fabric,
are well appointed
and extremely
comfortable.
The best have
original beams
or a mezzanine.
Doubles €130–220,
breakfast included.
🖬

Perugia
◆ **F C3**
Via del Colosseo, 7
Tel. 06 679 72 00
Fax 06 678 46 35
www.hperugia.it
info@hperugia.it
The best thing about
this hotel is its
location in a quiet
street close to the
Coliseum. The
building could do
with a fresh coat of
paint and the
atmosphere is quaint,
but it is one of the
cheapest hotels in
the neighborhood
and rates can be
negotiated in the
low season. Doubles
€90–135, breakfast
included. All the
rooms have air
conditioning.
🖬

▮ HISTORIC CENTER

Abruzzi
◆ **E B1**
Piazza
della Rotonda, 69
Tel. 06 679 20 21
Fax 06 697 880 76

www.hotelabruzzi.it
This hotel promises
unbeatable views, as
its 25 rooms overlook
the Pantheon, one
of Ancient Rome's
most beautiful
monuments. The
Abruzzi is therefore
right in the heart of
the city, with all
advantages and
inconveniences
which that entails.
Travelers in search
of la dolce vita who
are happy to lounge
around in cafés until
late at night will be in
their element here.
Doubles €175–195,
including breakfast.
🖬

Albergo del Sole
◆ **F D1**
Via del Biscione, 76
Tel. 06 68 80 68
73/687 94 46
Fax 06 689 37 87
www.solealbiscione.it
The street-level
entrance hardly looks
promising, but if
you climb the steep
staircase leading
to the reception on
the first floor you
will discover the
hidden charms of
this typically Roman
old building: small
balconies laden with
floors on every floor
and a terrace on the
top, overlooking the
dome of the Church
of Sant'Andrea
della Valle and the
neighboring pink and
ocher roofs. The 58
rooms have all been
renovated (some
more effectively
than others, but the
prettiest have
preserved their
coffered wooden
ceilings). Doubles
€110–150, without
breakfast. Garage.
🖬

Arenula
◆ **E B1-C1**
Via Santa Maria
dei Calderari, 47
(off Via Arenula)
Tel. 06 687 94 54
Fax 06 689 61 88
www.hotel

arenula.com
Set in a 19th-century
palazzo, near the
Ghetto and the
Campo dei Fiori,
this hotel offers
reasonably priced
rooms despite its
location. The 50
rooms are rather
charmless, but with
all that one could
wish for in terms of
comfort. Doubles
€95–125, breakfast
included.
🖬

Pensione Barrett
◆ **F D2**
Largo Torre
Argentina, 47
Tel. 06 686 84 81
Fax 06 689 29 71
This pensione is set
in the heart of the
historic center, near
the remains of the
Area Sacra, but also
close to the new tram
line running toward
the Trastevere. You
have only to cross
the threshold of this
elegant palazzo to
be seduced by its
charm and its warm
atmosphere, further
enhanced by the
greenery and the
paintings on the
walls. The rooms are
simple but functional
(small fridge and
espresso machine,
TV, hydromassage
bathtub). Opt for
those overlooking
the courtyard, as they
are more attractive
and less noisy than
those giving on to
the Largo di Torre
Argentina. Doubles
€115.
🖬

Campo de' Fiori
◆ **F D1**
Via del Biscione, 6
Tel. 06 687 48 86 /
688 068 65
Fax 06 683 090 36
www.hotelcampode
fiori.com
A hotel with 23 clean,
comfortable and
recently renovated
rooms, as well as
16 mini-apartments.
At the top is a

◆ HOTELS

Historic center, Il Tridente, Porta Maggiore,

Termini, Baths of Diocletian

fabulous terrace with deck chairs and 360° panoramic views of Rome. Doubles €150–250, including breakfast. The hotel also lets out 16 well-equipped apartments, which can accommodate 2 to 6 people: €100–230, breakfast and cleaning included.
▣

Navona
◆ F C1
Via dei Sediari, 8
Tel. 06 686 42 03
Fax 06 68 80 38 02
www.hotelnavona.com
info@hotelnavona.com
Located in the heart of the historic center, on the upper floor of an old palazzo, this hotel is among the best in the area. The rooms are quiet (even those that look out onto the street) and attractive. Doubles €125–140, depending on the season.
▣

Pomezia
◆ E B1
Via dei Chiavari, 12/13
Tel./fax 06 686 13 71
hotelpomezia@libero.it
The 25 rooms in this hotel – all with bathroom, air conditioning and telephone – have been refurbished, along with the foyer and the breakfast room. The decor is somewhat gaudy, although its impact is muted by the parquet floors and pale wooden furniture. The main virtues here are comfort and cleanliness, as well as the setting in a pleasant street close to the Campo dei Fiori. Doubles €75–140.
▣

Raphael
◆ F C1
Largo Febo, 2
Tel. 06 68 28 31

Fax 06 687 89 93
www.raphaelhotel.com
The Raphael is tucked just behind Piazza Navona in an ivy-clad building. Some of the rooms have balconies, and those on the upper floors command the best views of the city, along with the rooftop terrace where it is possible to have lunch and dinner. The reception is stuffed with antiques and modern sculpture, while the rooms boast the finest furnishings and marble bathrooms with unusual tiling. Doubles €380–420.
▦

Teatro di Pompeo***
◆ E B1
Largo del Pallaro, 8
Tel. 06 68 7 28 12
Fax 06 6899 055 31
www.hotelteatro
dipompeo.it
Another small hotel in a magical location, the original site of the Theater of Pompei (55 BC), between Piazza Navona and Campo dei Fiori. The vestiges have been preserved and incorporated into the dining room décor. Book well in advance as there are only 12 rooms (six with a view over the square and the others above a small courtyard). Doubles €180–205. Excellent buffet breakfast.
▦

Boccaccio
◆ F B4
Via del Boccaccio, 25
Tel./fax 06 488 59 62
www.hotelboccaccio.
com
Guests in this delightful family pensione, a stone's throw from the Piazza Barberini, find themselves being welcomed

as if they were long-lost relatives. The excellence of the service is matched by the furnishings in the seven rooms overlooking a quite street (or, in one case, an inner patio). Doubles without bathroom €76 (these share two impeccable communal bathrooms), with bathroom €93, breakfast not included.
▣

Hotel Parlamento
◆ F B3
Via delle Convertite, 5
Tel./fax
06 69 92 10 00
www.hotelparla
mento.it
The setting here could hardly be more enticing: a 17th-century palazzo close to the Piazza di Spagna and the chic shopping streets. It has been modernized with taste and almost all the rooms offer a degree of comfort worthy of a three-star hotel. On the top floor, three rooms (two with a jacuzzi) open on to a terrace awash with flowers. Doubles €90–130 with breakfast, €90–160 for those with terrace.
▣

Pensione Panda
◆ F A2/A3
Via della Croce, 35
Tel. 06 678 01 79
Fax 06 69 94 21 51
www.hotelpanda.it
Tourists who want the Spanish Steps close at hand or fancy jogging in the grounds of the Villa Borghese will find no better base than the Panda (at least not for these prices). It offers 20 renovated rooms overlooking a pretty inner courtyard – much quieter than

the Via della Croce, which is very busy in the daytime – and eight that are brand new. Doubles €68 (without bathroom) to €98 (with bathrooms).
▣

🖤 Rome à Volonté
◆ G C2
Via Balilla, 13
Tel. 06 77 59 10 03/
339 789 66 59
Fax 06 77 59 10 03
soleil@romevolonte
.com
www.romevolonte.com
A standard B & B that will delight travelers who are bored with impersonal hotels. One of the hostesses, Frenchwoman Sophie Bénézech, is an offical guide to the city and can suggest dozens of interesting excursions for all ages. There are 10 rooms and 6 apartments (sleeping from 1 to 7 people). From €50–170 a night.
⊡

Hotel Kennedy
◆ E B4
Via Filippo Turati, 62/64
Tel. 06 446 53 73
Fax 06 446 54 17
www.hotelkennedy.net
One of the most reliable hotels in the Esquilin area. It was once an old-fashioned pensione but it has been taken over by a family that has made every effort to turn it into a classy hotel. The rooms were gradually repainted, the bathrooms were refurbished and a gym was installed, so now everything is as good as new. Ask for one of the rooms with a view of the Roman Aquarium and the neighboring park.

Doubles €95–159
(€160 at New Year),
including breakfast.
⬥

Hotel Ercoli
◆ B D4
Via Collina, 48
Tel. 06 474 54 54
Fax 06 474 40 63
www.hotelercoli.com
This comfortable
hotel is slightly
detached from the
usual tourist circuit. It
has recently been
refurbished and
boasts 14 rooms with
dazzling bathrooms.
Doubles €80–115.
⬥

Hotel Galli
◆ G A1
Via Milazzo, 20
Tel. 06 445 68 59
Fax 06 446 85 01
www.albergogalli.com
info@albergogalli.com
The area round the
Termini railroad
station is dotted
with hotels and it
would be easy to
dismiss them all as
products of the
neighborhood's
seedy reputation, but
the Galli stands out
from the bunch.
Spread over two
floors, it offers
comfortable, well-
kept rooms with TV
and air conditioning.
The prices do not
include breakfast, but
here are plenty of
bakeries and cafés in
the vicinity. Doubles
€55–110.
⬥

Papà Germano
◆ E A4
Via Calatafimi, 14/a
Tel. 06 48 69 19/47
88 12 81
Fax 06 47 82 52 02
www.hotelpapa
germano.com
Low prices,
cleanliness and
friendly service: this
formula has served
Papà Germano well
for thirty years. He is
very proud of his
reputation and
displays the covers of
the numerous
guidebooks praising
his establishment like
trophies. Some of the
rooms are slightly
dowdy, despite their
floral wallpaper or
lemon-yellow paint,
but they all have air
conditioning, TV and
telephone, as well as
being spacious,
functional, regularly
refurbished and
invariably spotless.
A breakfast room
and kitchen have
recently been
installed. Internet
connection. Doubles
with bathroom
€75–100, without
bathroom €60-80,
depending on the
season.
⬥

Pensione
Di Rienzo
◆ E B4
Via Principe Amedeo,
79/a
Tel. 06 446 71 31
Fax 06 446 69 80
This is very much a

family affair, with a
hospitable couple
and their daughters
eager to provide
friendly and efficient
service. The 15
rooms are simple but
impeccable and
overlook a quiet patio
bedecked with
flowers. It is
advisable to book in
advance. Doubles
with bathroom
€35–75 (€30–60
without bathroom),
depending on the
season.
⬥

Viminale
◆ E B4
Via Cesare Balbo, 31
Tel. 06 488 19 10 / 80
Fax 06 487 20 18
www.leonardi
hotels.com
The Viminale has
fifty-five spacious
and elegant rooms
with all the comfort
one may wish for,
three terraces (two
on upper levels and
one on the ground-
floor where breakfast
is served in summer)
and an efficient
welcome. €78–232,
depending on the
season.
⬥

TRASTEVERE

Hotel Trastevere
◆ D C4
Via Luciano Manara,
24a/25
Tel. 06 581 47 13
Fax 06 588 10 16

www.hoteltrastevere
.net
info@hoteltrastevere
.net
This hotel offers a
ringside view of the
spectacle that
unfolds every day in
the Piazza San
Cosimato in the
Travestere
neighborhood,
complete with stalls
selling oranges,
small cherry
tomatoes, wild
rocket, cooked
meats and cheese.
The hotel's interior
is slightly
characterless,
although great
pains have been
taken to make the
rooms clean and
comfortable.
Special offer for
families: the double
rooms can be
turned into triples
or quadruples
thanks to bunk
beds that come out
of the closets.
Doubles €103,
triples €130,
quadruples €155,
including breakfast.
⬥

◆ ROMAN CUISINE

List of restaurants ◆ 434

Food is just as much an important part of the Roman experience as antiquities and museums. It has sometimes been claimed that Rome, the cradle of modern civilization, has the most 'popular' cuisine in the world, in the strictest sense of the word – rural, Mediterranean and rooted in a local, peasant tradition, with a preponderance of pasta, on the one hand, and tripe and other offal on the other.

EATING OUT

→ A TYPICAL MEAL
■ *Antipasti:* starters.
■ *Primo:* pasta, soup, risotto, gnocchi.
■ *Secondo:* meat or fish, accompanied by *contorno* (vegetables) or *insalata* (salad), ordered separately.
■ *Formaggio* (cheese), *frutta* (fruit) or *dolci* (dessert).

→ CUSTOMS
■ PANE E COPERTO
The bread and cover charge are added to the bill.
■ SERVIZIO
The service charge (10-15%) is generally supplementary.
■ TIPPING
It is customary to leave a tip (*mancia*) of 5–10%.

→ WHERE TO EAT
In Rome, the difference between the types of restaurants is particularly marked. It should be noted that booking is almost obligatory in restaurants at night and at the weekend; also remember that many are closed in August.
■ FOR A FULL MEAL
A *ristorante* or a *trattoria* (more informal, in both atmosphere and cooking).
■ FOR A CHEAP MEAL
A pizzeria or *spaghetteria*.
A *tavola calda* is a cheaper, down-market version of a *trattoria* (or sometimes the equivalent), where food is sometimes

served at the bar.
■ FOR A LIGHT MEAL
An *enoteca* – some offer hot or cold dishes, others are closer to a delicatessen – a *birreria*, *panineria* (hot sandwiches), *rosticceria* (roast chicken, *supplì*) or a café.
■ FOR MORE
EXOTIC MEALS
Food from other parts of the world is all the rage in Rome. Sushi bars have recently been launched to great success.

→ SNACKS
BETWEEN MEALS
There is no danger of starving in Rome. Almost all the bars serve *tramezzini* (sandwiches), stuffed white pizza or *pizza al taglio* (pizza slices). If you prefer freshly made *panini*, most *alimentari* (grocery stores) are happy to prepare cooked meat or cheese in front of you and put it in a *rosetta* (round bread roll). Delicatessens often have a fast-food service and will heat up *antipasti* or vegetables for you (◆ 446).
■ GLOSSARY
Spuntini: snacks, sold in *rosticcerie* and *friggitorie*.
Pizza bianca: 'white' pizza, with no tomatoes, just oil and salt.
Supplì: rice croquettes fried in oil, filled with meat and mozzarella.
Tramezzini: sandwiches

DRINKS

→ APERITIFS
In fine weather, the evening means aperitivo time and the traditional meeting place for this is the Campo dei Fiori. It may be hard to find a table on the terraces but there are pleasant alternatives nearby, toward the Piazza Navona (Piazza del Fico), Vicolo della Pace, Via della Fossa). Another popular area is the Triangolo delle bevute, the 'Triangle of Drinks', in the historic center, as its alleyways are dotted with bars.

TRADITION AND INFLUENCES

Legend has it that when a Roman Emperor or Pope wanted to hold a banquet, their cooks sought inspiration in the Jewish ghetto or the back streets of the plebeians' quarters. This is not to say that these rulers lacked refinement but their food undoubtedly retained a rustic flavor. These days some trattorias perpetuate ancient traditions, particularly in the Testaccio neighborhood, renowned for Roman specialties based on offal (*rigatoni alla pajata* – with milk calf's intestines, tripe and *coda alla vaccinara* – oxtail).

→ JEWISH FOOD
Best sampled in the old ghetto (near the Portico of Octavia). Pride of place goes to deep-fried dishes such as cod fillet (*filetti di baccalà alla giudea*) and *carciofi alla giudea*, whole artichokes deep-fried in a vat of boiling oil. (Artichokes are superb in Rome: you can also try them *alla romana* – with herbs and oil.)

SPECIALTIES

Abbacchio: roast lamb with mushroom and wine sauce.
Carciofi: artichokes, either deep-fried (*alla giudea*) or with oil and herbs (*alla romana*).
Coda alla vaccinara: oxtail with tomatoes and white wine, topped with a sauce of celery, pine nuts, raisins and bitter chocolate.
Coratella: fried lamb's offal.
Fave al guanciale: sautéed broad beans with onions and ham.
Gran misto di cervelli, ricotta, carciofi e zucchine: dish based on brains, ricotta, artichokes and zucchini.
Pajata: milk calf's intestines in tomato sauce.
Pasta all'amatriciana: pasta with a highly seasoned sauce based on lard, onion and bacon.
Pasta alla carbonara: pasta in an egg-and-bacon sauce.

Pecorino romano: ewe's cheese.

Risotto alla romana: rice, liver, sweetbreads and pecorino cheese.

Saltimbocca alla romana: veal scalope wrapped in a slice of ham and seasoned with sage.

Trippa alla romana: tripe with tomato and mint served with cheese.

PASTA

Nobody knows the exact origin of *pastasciutta*, the dried pasta made from durum wheat semolina – some theories point to Sicily or China – but there is no question that it has flourished on the coasts of southern Italy, where the combination of wind and sun provides perfect conditions for drying. Although pasta drying on an industrial scale is now concentrated in factories in northern Italy, the small-scale production of the south, with its incredible range of shapes and sizes, is still highly prized by connoisseurs and has carved out a niche in the international market.

SOME TYPES OF PASTA

Bucatini: hollow spaghetti.

Fusilli: short spirals.

Linguine: flat spaghetti.

Lumaconi: snail shapes.

Maccheroni: Neapolitan-style long macaroni.

Occhi di lupo: smooth penne.

Orecchiette: in the form of small ears.

Paccheri: short, smooth and rectangular.

Pasta paglia e fieno: colored with spinach and mushrooms.

Penne: short and pointed.

Rigatoni: short and rectangular.

■ **MUSEO NAZIONALE DELLE PASTE ALIMENTARI** Piazza Scanderbeg, 117 Tel. 06 699 11 20 An overview of the history and manufacture of pasta.

TOMATOES

The tomato, known as *pomodoro* or 'golden apple', is ubiquitous, whether in the thick sauces that accompany pasta, as a garnish for pizza or an ingredient in stews.

PIZZAS

Pizzas may be popular all over the world, but you can only eat the 'real' item in Italy. It also comes in a closed version with an egg inside (*calzone*) and as a sweet *pizza dolce*.

CHEESE

In this land of sheep farming, most cheese is made with ewe's milk: *ricotta*, whether fresh for filling ravioli and cakes, or matured and salted for grating over pasta; *pecorino romano*, which is aged for at least eight months before emerging hard with a very strong taste; *burrata* (from Puglia, Apulia and Calabria), a soft, fresh ewe's cheese with a knob of unsalted butter inside. Buffalo's milk is used to make *mozzarella* (a world away from the tasteless balls sold in supermarkets!) and *provola*, either natural or smoked. *Scamorza*, based on a mixture of cow's and goat's milk, is often served grilled.

ICE CREAM

Rome is a paradise for lovers of iced desserts, and an extensive vocabulary has grown up to describe the combinations made with fruit juices and syrups, not to mention the dozens of different flavors available. Ice creams are eaten by people of all ages at any time of day (although only tourists seem to find them appetizing in winter!).

→ GRATTACHECCA This variant of a famous specialty from southern Italy (*granita*) should not be missed. It is a cross between a drink and a dessert, with a base of crushed ice and fruit juice or syrup.

COFFEE

Contrary to received wisdom, Italians do not drink very much coffee, but they do take great pride in knowing how to prepare and appreciate it. How to spot a good capuccino: the cream should be thick and a streaky hazelnut color; the powdered sugar should sink in slowly and the cream should reform once the liquid has been stirred. The coffee market is dominated by three family businesses: Lavazza (the leader), Illy and Segafredo Zanetti.

WINES

White wine rules in the province of Rome! Be sure to try the fresh, dry whites of the Castelli Romani, such as Marino and Frascati from the Alban Hills.

SPIRITS

Grappa, the generic term for brandy, is traditionally consumed after a meal. It changes its form and name according to the region; in Rome, it is known as *sambuca*, which is flavored with aniseed and often served with a coffee bean in the bottom of the glass.

◆ RESTAURANTS

The Vatican

RESTAURANTS
- 🔳 < €20
- 🔳 €20–35
- 🔳 €35–50
- 🔳 > €50

The restaurants are listed by district, then by alphabetical order. The references (e.g. ◆ E B2) allow them to be located in the map section ◆ 501.

VATICAN

Antico Falcone
◆ A C2
Via Trionfale, 60
Tel. 06 39 73 64 04
Open Wed.–Mon.
noon–3.30pm,
7–11.30pm
This palazzetto stands out in an unremarkable modern residential area as a country inn left over from the 16th century. This trattoria is not just a pretty façade, however, as it has also won a well-deserved reputation for its Roman specialties like artichokes alla giudea. To add to the charm, one of the city's most famous grattachecca kiosks stands just opposite the entrance.
🔳

Checchino dal 1887
◆ H A3
Via di Monte Testaccio, 30
Tel. 06 574 38 16
Tel./Fax 06 574 63 18
www.cecchino-dal-1887.com
Open 12.30–3pm,
8pm–midnight.
Closed Sun.–Mon.,
Aug. and at Christmas.
An institution.
For over a century, it has been run in the slaughterhouse area by a family who approach Roman cuisine with the rigor of archeologists, not only with regard to their recipes but also in their careful choice of ingredients and the revival of the culinary styles and cooking methods of times gone by. Classics, such as coda alla vaccinara (braised oxtail) and abbacchio alla cacciatora (braised suckling lamb), were invented here. There's a wonderful wine list: visit the wine cellar dug into the Monte dei Cocci. The remains of amphorae that have built up over the centuries form an artificial hill known as Monte Testaccio. A la carte costs around €40.
🔳

'Da Oio' a Casa Mia
◆ H A3
Via Galvani, 43-45
Tel. 06 578 26 80
Open Mon.–Sat.
12.30–2pm,
7.30pm–midnight
Da Oio – a corruption of 'olio', meaning 'oil' – is a favorite haunt of both fans of AS Roma (the walls are adorned with soccer posters and emblems in the team's colors of orange and dark red) and gourmets, who come here to recapture the flavors of their mother's cooking. Appropriately, Do Oio is a family affair, with the lively and cheerful mistress of the house waiting at the tables, her husband in the kitchen and photos of their children in communion outfits on the walls of the second dining room. The menu features traditional specialties (tonnarelli cacio e pepe, rigatoni alla pajata) and succulent secondi: porchetta di vitella (roast veal stuffed with spices), meatballs, tripe or straccetti (beef sautéed in white wine) accompanied by rocket or puntarelle (chicory hearts).
🔳

Dal Toscano
◆ A D3
Via Germanico, 58/60
Tel. 06 39 72 33 73
Open Tue.–Sun.
12.30–3.15pm,
8–11.30pm.
Closed in Aug.
When it comes to meat, it is difficult to beat this noisy restaurant close to the Vatican in the Prati neighborhood, run by the Bruni family for three generations. As its name implies, it specializes in Tuscan food and the Fiorentina steak is magnificent, as is the simply grilled filet de bœuf. It prepares its French fries either in the traditional finger shape or in large circles – crisp and delicious, as are the fried zucchini flowers. Two separate dining rooms, one with a fireplace and facing the open kitchen. Excellent contorni.
🔳

Osteria dell' Angelo
◆ A D3
Via G. Bettolo, 24
Tel. 06 372 94 70
Open Tue.–Fri.
12.30–2.30pm,
8–11pm; Mon., Sat.
8–11pm. Closed Sun.
The rules are simple: at lunch you choose what you want from a range of Roman specialties on offer; at dinner, the rate is €25 a head, including everything from antipasti to dessert, washed down with house white. Tuna mousse, crostini with sausage and haricot beans, tonnarella cacio e pepe or gnocchi with zucchini and fresh tomatoes are some of the primi choices. Veal with raisins and pinenuts, or oxtail are among the choices for secondi, and there are biscotti with sweet wine for dessert. The interior is like a kind of sporting museum with photos of racing cyclists, Formula 1 drivers, boxers and rugby players.
🔳

Pizzeria Remo
◆ H A3
Piazza Santa Maria Liberatrice, 44
Tel. 06 574 62 70
Open Mon.–Sat.
7pm–1am
The Remo, set in the Testaccio, specializes in Roman pizza – a great deal thinner than the Neapolitan variety. An army of waiters is on hand with a menu listing the ingredients that can be added to or removed from the standard pizzas: so, for example, you could choose an eggplant pizza, but with chicory instead of tomato sauce. For starters, be sure to try the freshly fried suppli (rice croquettes stuffed with meat and mozzarella) or the delicious crostini and bruschette (bread slices with toppings).
🔳

🔳 Trattoria Agustarello
◆ H A3
Via Giovanni Branca, 98/100
Tel. 06 574 65 85
Open Mon.–Sat.
12.30–3pm,
7.30pm–midnight
The locals love this place and it is easy to see why, with the posters and newspaper clippings on the walls singing the praises of Rome's other soccer team, Lazio (almost a provocation in the Testaccio, the heartland of AS Roma). Fans of both teams have no trouble agreeing about the excellence

🔲 The editors' choice

f the food, however: gatoni alla pajata pasta with intestines f milk calf – or, these ays, lamb, since the nplementation of ne European Community's egulations to control ad cow disease), xtail alla vaccinara tew flavored with aisins and pine nuts) nd abbacchio amb) are the house pecialties. Consider ooking in advance.
◼

GECCHINO DAL 1887

Fori Imperiali and the Coliseum more than justifies its good reputation. It has a well-stocked cellar (follow the advice of the staff) and a range of appetizers that perfectly complement the wines: specialties from Calabria, Sardinia and Tuscany (olives, dried tomatoes, cooked meat, cheese), salads, carpaccio and tasty desserts (semifredo with honey, pine nuts and orange sauce). Reckon on spending €15–30.
🔲

AVENTINE

rattoria Augusto
◆ **D** C4

iazza de' Renzi, 15 el. 06 580 37 98 pen Mon.–Fri. 2.30–3pm, 8–11pm; at. 12.30–3pm t first sight, this attoria does not ok out of the rdinary, with its ondescript decor nd two dining rooms at are always acked and noisy. he food is omething special, owever: moderate ortions of rigatoni l'amatriciana or acio e pepe (ewe's heese and pepper), violi stuffed with cotta and spinach, llowed by succulent econdi like roast mb or chicken with otatoes and osemary, baccalà od) on Fri. and tripe n Sat. Finish off with superb tiramisù. attoria-style ooking at its uthentic best.
◼

CAPITOL, PALATINE
COLISEUM

Cavour 313
◆ **E** B3

a Cavour, 313 el. 06 678 54 96 pen daily 2.30–2.30pm, 30-12.30am losed Sun. nchtime in summer his enoteca near the

🔲 Taverna Romana
◆ **E** B3

Via Madonna dei Monti, 79 Tel. 06 474 53 25 Open Mon.–Sat. noon–3pm, 7–11pm Closed in Aug. Many locals consider this to be one of the city's best taverns in this price range, citing the pasta paglia e fieno ('straw and hay', fresh pasta colored with spinach and served with mushrooms or tomato sauce), the secondi, each one better than the next (lamb, veal slices, osso buco, sausage and beans, beef straccetti with rocket) and the owner, whose severe façade conceals a motherly concern. Ask to try her coppiette, raw ham (originally horsemeat) seasoned with fennel and peppers, a recipe

that has now fallen out of fashion.
◼

HISTORIC CENTER

🔲 Boccon Divino
◆ **D** B4

Via del Pavone, 28 Tel. 06 68 13 50 51 Open Mon.–Sat. 8.30pm–midnight Closed in Aug. Design and contemporary art serve as the backdrop for sophisticated but unpretentious food: eggplant ravioli with tomato sauce or seafood ravioli with asparagus cream, followed by straccetti (thinly cut sautéed beef) with herbs or tagliata (sliced beef) flavored with truffles. The success of this restaurant is based on its skilful fusion of traditions and creativity, its menu that changes with the seasons and the high quality of its fresh ingredients.
◼

Boccondivino
◆ **F** B2

Piazza Campo Marzio, 6 Tel. 06 68 30 86 26 Open Mon.–Sat. 1–3pm, 8pm–midnight Closed in Aug. The Boccon Divino is a well-kept secret, virtually inaccessible to the uninitiated. There is no street sign or even a window to hint at the delights on offer at number 28: magnificent primi of linguine with

langoustines and zucchini flowers or schiaffoni (large ravioli) stuffed with octopus or crabmeat and leeks; for secondo, game or fish and, for dessert, a moist torta caprese (almond and chocolate tart), tiramisù or homemade panna cotta. Note that it is essential to book and take a low profile – the owner does everything in his power to avoid attracting tourists!
▣

Cul de Sac
◆ **E** B1

Piazza Pasquino, 73 Tel. 06 68 80 10 94 Open noon–4pm, 6pm–12.30am. The pioneer of Rome's wine bars is always full to bursting but nobody seems to care: just find yourself a small space, allow yourself to be guided through the mind-boggling list of 1,400 wines and nibble on the cheese and cooked meat. As this bar is set on the corner of Piazza Navona, you will obviously not be the only tourist, but the locals will be happy to share your company.
◼

Da Baffetto
◆ **E** B1

Via del Governo Vecchio, 114 Tel. 06 686 16 17 Open 6.30pm–1am
Da Baffetto 2
Piazza del Teatro di Pompeo Campo dei Fiori, 18 Tel. 06 68 21 08 07 Open 10am–3.30pm, 6.30pm–1am Closed Tue. Da Baffetto is one of the most famous Roman pizzerias, a charming, informal place with paper tablecloths and old photographs

◆ RESTAURANTS

Historic center

RESTAURANTS
▪ < €20
▪ €20–35
▪ €35–50
▪ > €50

on the walls, in a pedestrianized street. The pizzas have delicious thin, light, crispy crust and the variety, quality and price justify the long wait for a table. No credit cards. Pizzas from €4. In 2004, the daughter of the chef opened another branch with the same menu, but this one has a terrace, is open at lunchtime (unlike the original Da Baffetto) and you don't have to wait so long for a table.
▪

Da Francesco
◆ E B1
Piazza del Fico, 29
Tel. 06 686 40 09
Open daily 11.50am–2.50pm, 7pm–0.45am
Closed Tue. lunchtime
A classic. Just as the Bar del Fico, across the way, is a hallowed institution on the Triangolo delle bevute ('Triangle of Drinks'), this trattoria is one of the first places where a Roman will take a visitor to eat. The buffet of antipasti is seemingly interminable: artichokes in various forms (marinated, alla romana, alla giudea), zucchini sautéed in balsamic vinegar, eggplants (grilled or marinated in olive oil), mushrooms... The primi and secondi do not offer any startlingly original dishes but everything is prepared with great precision: pasta cacio e pepe (with cheese and pepper), with ragù (tomato and meat sauce), all'amatriciana (with pancetta and tomato sauce), followed by tripe, sausages or grilled chicken. Pizzas are also served at night.
▪

Dal Pompiere
◆ E C-1
Palazzo Cenci
Via Santa Maria dei Calderari, 38
Tel. 06 686 83 77
Open 12.30–3pm, 7.30–11pm. Closed Sun. and Aug.
At the entrance to the old Ghetto, in a wing of the 16th-century Beatrice Cenci palace, a huge staircase leads to Al Pompiere. Very good fried dishes – try the carciofi all Giudìa (fried artichokes); the fritti vegetali (vegetable fritters) are a must for vegetarians. During festivals they serve traditional Roman dishes such as pajata (intestines), coda (tail), tripe and sweetbreads. Desserts include ricotta tart with morello cherries. Friendly staff, some seriously good cooking and a pleasant setting.
▪

Dar Filettaro a Santa Barbara
◆ E B1
Largo dei Librari, 88
Tel. 06 686 40 18
Open Mon.–Sat. 5.30–11.10pm (summer), 5–10.40pm (winter)
Closed in Aug
One of Rome's most popular eateries is hidden away in a pretty little square in the historic center, with a small church tucked between a series of palazzetti that look as thought they could be made of papier mâché. There is no standing on ceremony here, so do as the Romans do and eat your cod fritters with your hands, accompanied by a salad of puntarelle (chicory hearts with garlic-and-anchovy sauce).
▪

Il Convivio Troiani
◆ E A1
Vicolo dei Soldati, 31
Tel. 06 68 80 59 50
or 06 68 69 94 32
www.ilconvivio troiani.com
Open 8–11pm.
Closed Sun.
A jewel in the crown of Italian restaurants, listed in several European gastronomic guides. They rework classic recipes with imagination, using seasonal produce. The wine list can't fail to please, with about 2,500 labels. The setting is smart, with archways and frescos in three pleasant rooms. Gastronomic tasting menu for €95 per person.
⊞

▯ La Casa Bleve
◆ F C1
Via del Teatro Valle, 48/49
Tel. 06 686 59 70
www.casableve.it
Open Tue.–Sat. 10.30am–3pm, 6–8pm (10pm Wed.–Fri.)
Closed in Aug.
This bar near the Senate and the Pantheon has one of the best selections of wine in the city, purchased directly from vineyards. The friendly waiters are eager to share their knowledge and recommend the most appropriate vintage. All the food on offer can be taken out, but the best way to enjoy the wine is by making up your own plate of antipasti to accompany it: involtini (rolls) of Parma ham stuffed with ricotta and dried tomatoes or stracchino (a very creamy cheese) and green asparagus, bresaola (dried beef) and rocket, wild-boar ham, zucchini flowers with Parmesan, smoked salmon or a

selection of formaggi misti (mixed cheeses). Reckon on around €35 for a platter and a glass of wine.
▪

La Rosetta
◆ E A1-B1
Via della Rosetta, 8-9
Tel. 06 686 10 02
or 06 68 30 88 41
www.larosetta.com
Open Mon.–Sat. 12.45–2.30pm, 7.30–10.30pm
In a quiet side street close to the Pantheon, the Rosetta is expensive but it is the place in Rome for fish-lovers. You'll find a warm welcome, extra-fresh produce and an extremely talented chef. Besides seasonal specialties, they serve spaghetti with prawns and zucchini, tonnarelli with seafood, sea bass with ginger and artichokes. The menu changes regularly but prices stay roughly the same. Special gastronomic menu €60 (lunch), €160 (dinner).
⊞

Maccheroni
◆ F B-C1
Piazza delle Coppelle, 44
Tel. 06 68 30 78 95
www.ristorante maccheroni.com
Open 1–3pm, 7.30–11pm
Politicians from the neighboring House of Parliament are known to pop out to lunch in this trattoria, but not only because it is so close at hand – its other virtues include its efficient service and attractive setting, designed in an Italian approximation of American style, with a huge open kitchen, three dining rooms in a row and a small terrace. Not to mention the food: an abundance of

◘ The editors' choice

hoice in both the
opious and tasty
rimi (cacio e pepe,
esto, amatriciana,
arbonara), the
elicious salads
spelt or rocket, pear
nd Parmesan) and
he classic, perfectly
dged secondi.

**steria
r Galletto**
◆ **E** B1
ampo dei Fiori
iazza Farnese, 102
el. 06 686 17 14
pen Mon.–Sat.
2.15–3pm and
.15–11.15pm
he terrace of Ar
alletto, set opposite
e French Embassy
n the Piazza
arnese, is one of
e main reasons for
oming here to eat,
a price barely
gher than that of
good trattoria.
ther good reasons
re the excellent
ntipasti and
rilled meats, as
ell as the friendly
ervice.

perno
E C1
a Monte dei Cenci, 9
el. 06 68 80 66 29
ww.ristorante
perno.it
pen Tue.–Sat.
2.45–2.20pm,
–10.15pm; Sun.
2.45–2.20pm.
osed in Aug.
he journey to
iperno will lead you
one of the small
quares typical of the
hetto, lined with the
ng façades of old
uildings. The Jewish
od is similarly
vathed in nostalgia:
tichokes alla
udea, fritti misti
election of fritters)
d ricotta pie are
e outstanding
ecialties.
npeccable
rvice and
phisticated
ientele in a highly
tractive setting.

Pizzeria Montecarlo
◆ **E** B1
Vicolo dei Savelli, 12
Tel. 06 686 18 77
Open noon–3.30pm,
6.30pm–1am
Closed Mon.
The Montecarlo
is big, lively and
invariably crowded,
with lines of
customers waiting
to be served
(vouching for the
excellence of the
thin, crispy pizzas).
If you are tired of
pizzas, try ordering
fritti or bruschette
(toasted bread with
toppings).
◘

Santa Lucia
◆ **F** C1
Largo Febo, 12
Tel. 06 68 80 24 27
Ouvert noon–3pm,
7–11.30pm
Closed Tue.
This restaurant is very
enticing, thanks to
both its meticulously
designed decor and,
above all, its food
based on Neapolitan
traditions. For
starters, octopus
salad, potatoes,
green beans and
dried tomato, small
broccoli gateaux,
pumpkin and walnut
or a salad of braised
eggplants. If you are
bored with the
eternal Roman primi
of carbonara and
amatriciana, Santa
Lucia will restore
your faith in pasta by
offering homemade
tortellini filled with
ricotta and walnuts,
as well as rigatoni
with eggplant, with
salted ricotta or alla
provola (smoked
cheese). For secondi,
cod all'acqua pazza
(spicy broth), rolls
of veal stuffed with
almonds and dates
or deep-fried fish.
It's expensive though
– reckon on spending
€40 per person.
Delightful terrace in
summer. Booking
recommended.
◘

Trattoria Da Sergio
◆ **E** B1
Vicolo delle Grotte, 27
Tel. 06 686 42 93
Open Mon.–Sat.
12.30–3pm,
6.30pm–midnight
Da Sergio is almost
a caricature of
Roman rusticity,
and its proximity to
the Campo dei Fiori
only emphasizes its
picture-postcard
appearance. The
service is slightly
offhand but there
is a good mix of
locals and tourists.
Spaghetti alla
carbonara, gnocchi
alla romana, tripe
and grilled meat,
all washed down
by regional wines.
◘

**Trattoria
Da Tonino**
◆ **E** B1
Via del Governo
Vecchio, 18/19
Tel. 333 587 07 79
Open Mon.–Sat.
noon–3pm, 7–11pm
Outside on the street,
there is no sign, the
glass doors are
permanently misted
over and the only
indication of Tonino's
activity is a faint whiff
of broccoli; inside,
there are two neon
lights on the ceiling
and a cast of
characters worthy
of a comic strip who
will not give you a
second look. This is
the kind of trattoria
that only an insider
can recommend, as
it would be virtually
impossible to
stumble across it on
your own. The primi
offer hearty fare,
slightly on the greasy
side (carbonara,
amatriciana, rigatoni
with broccoli,
pasta and beans
in minestrone), but
the secondi are
delicious: involtini alla
romana (rolls of beef
stuffed with small
vegetables), roast
lamb with potatoes,
straccetti con rucola

(thin strips of beef
sautéed in white
wine, accompanied
by rocket) or
sausages with lentils.
◘

IL TRIDENTE

Buccone
◆ **B** D1
Via di Ripetta, 19/20
Tel. 06 361 21 54
Open Mon.–Thu.
9am–8.30pm,
Fri.–Sat. 9am–
midnight
Closed 3 weeks
in Aug.
The huge letters
on the sign outside
are unmissable
and almost pull
customers off the
street into this long-
established wine bar.
Inside, the bottles
are stacked from the
floor to the ceiling,
while a few tables
are set in an adjacent
room to sample the
house specialties
along with the wine:
soups, salads, pies
of the day and
delicious antipasti
(ewe's cheese, tuna
roe in honey, stuffed
eggplant).
◘

**Enoteca Antica
di Via della Croce**
◆ **F** A2-A3
Via della Croce, 76b
Tel. 06 679 08 96
Open 11am–1am
Founded in 1726,
this is the oldest wine
bar in Rome. Hidden
away in a very busy
street with no sign
outside, it is on the
corner of the Via
Bocca di Leone.
It can be recognized
by its green door.
Inside is a very old
bar that has slates
with the wines
chalked up on them.
Snacks and meals.
Main dishes cost
€7.50–12.
◘

◘ **Fiaschetteria
Beltramme**
◆ **F** A2
Via della Croce, 39

◆ RESTAURANTS

Il Tridente

RESTAURANTS
■ < €20
■ €20–35
■ €35–50
⊞ > €50

No telephone
www.fiaschetteria
beltramme.com
Open Mon.–Sat.
noon–3pm, 8–11pm
*No frills here! You
may find yourself
sharing a table, you
may be asked to pay
up as soon as you
have swallowed your
last mouthful and it is
almost impossible to
book – but once you
accept these ground
rules, you can be
sure of receiving
simple but excellent
food. The burrata e
pomodorini (a type
of mozzarella stuffed
with cream and small
cherry tomatoes),
traditional primi
(rigatoni all'
amatriciana,
tonnarelli cacio e
pepe) and good
secondi (straccetti
with rocket, breaded
veal escalope, grilled
slices of beef) pack
them in for both
lunch and dinner.*
■

Giuseppe al 59
◆ B D1
Via Angelo Brunetti, 59
Tel. 06 321 90 19
Open Mon.–Sat.
(lunch and dinner).
Closed Sat. lunchtime
June–July
*At the end of a small
street linking the Via
del Corso with the
Tiber, close to the
Piazza del Popolo,
this restaurant honors
the contention that
the best food in Italy
comes from Emilia-
Romagna. The
primi can all be
recommended: the
tasty tortelli (stuffed
with ricotta, pumpkin
or meat) or tagliatelle
alla bolognese are
almost a meal in
their own right when
followed by the
exceptional tiramisù
or zabaglione. The
decoration has been
refurbished. Both
the food and the
service are well
worth a detour.*
■

Gusto
◆ F A2
Piazza Augusto
Imperatore, 9
Tel. 06 322 62 73
www.gusto.it
Restaurant and
pizzeria: open
daily 12.30–3pm,
7.30pm–midnight
Wine bar and store:
open daily 10am–2am
*Those who are not
put off by the formica
tables and blazing
lights in this trattoria
will appreciate the
New York style of the
place, which is just
opposite the
mausoleum of
Augustus. The huge
area has a wine bar in
the rear, a smart
restaurant on the
mezzanine level, a big
pizzeria, a kitchen
utensil shop and a
bookstore. This
'concept restaurant'
is full every night with
thirtysomething
yuppies, romantic
couples, families. It's
calmer at lunchtime,
when you can sit and
read the papers.
Pizzas, fritters and
antipasti are all good.
If you haven't
booked, you can sit
in the comfort of the
bar and discover a
rare Italian red wine
from the slopes of
the Alps.*
■

Margutta
Vegetariano
◆ B D2
Via Margutta, 118
Tel. 06 32 65 05 77
www.ilmargutta.it
Daily 12.30–3.30pm,
7.30–11pm
Closed in Aug.
*Walking along via
Margutta towards the
Piazza di Spagna,
you'll find yourself on
a road lined with art
galleries and
antiquarian
bookstores, before
you reach no. 118.
It is a Roman
institution, one of the
very few vegetarian
restaurants in Rome.
The big white space*

*feels contemporary,
with comfortable
black leather seats.
At lunchtime you can
have a 'green brunch'
(€15, including a
drink) which gives
you a choice of
antipasti (artichokes,
aubergines, sun-
dried tomatoes), of
salads, cheese and a
hot dish such as
ricotta and zucchini
canneloni or polenta
with mushrooms and
cherry tomatoes. For
dessert there might
be fruit salad or tart.
In the evening,
several inventive
specialities are on
offer: wild rice salad
with pomegranate
and Parmesan
shavings; pumpkin
tortelloni with truffle.
Allow €28–40. On
Sundays the 'green
brunch' is self-
service and there is
more to choose from.*
■

Mario
◆ F A3-B3
Via della Vite, 55
Tel. 06 678 38 18
Open Mon.–Sat.
noon–3pm, 7–11pm;
Sun. 7–11pm
Closed in Aug.
*The hunting trophies
by the door
immediately set the
tone here, as Mario
specializes in game
dishes. Although
the country-inn
atmosphere is at
odds with the up-
market surroundings,
it has nevertheless
attracted many
famous names –
and there are press
articles and photos
on display to prove it!
Tuscan charcuteries,
excellent meat and
a top-notch wine list.
Reckon on paying
€35–40.*
■

▢ Matricianella
◆ E A2
Via del Leone, 2/4
Tel. 06 683 21 00
Open Mon.–Sat.
12.30–3pm,

7.30–11pm
*Regular customers
flock here for the
traditional specialties
(bucatini
all'amatriciana,
gnocchi alla romana)
or for the more
delicate seasonal
dishes (risotto with
artichoke and truffles
or zucchini flowers).
The menu has other
delights in store,
however: superb
fritti (lamb's brain or
vegetable fritters)
and succulent meat
dishes: lamb with
artichokes, coda
alla vaccinara (oxtail
with vegetables) and
polpette alla romana
(meat balls). Not to
mention the desserts
pears cooked in
Barolo (wine from
Piemonte), Jewish
ricotta and chocolate
tart or nonna, a pie
with cream and
pine nuts. Formal
but efficient
service, invariably
accompanied by
advice about
choosing wine.*
■

Settimio all'Arancio
◆ F A2
Via dell'Arancio,
50/53
Tel. 06 687 61 19
Open Mon.–Sat.
12.30–3.30pm,
7.30pm–midnight
*It has to be admitted
from the outset that
although Settimio's
primi (pasta and
risotto) are superb,
the secondi
(meat and fish) are
disappointing.
It is not a serious
problem, however,
because you are
unlikely to be very
hungry after a hearty
plate of tonnarelli
(fresh egg pasta
resembling square
spaghetti) with
seafood, pappardelle
(extra-long tagliatelle
with wild-boar
sauce or ravioli filled
with ricotta and
orange zest.*
■

☑ The editors' choice

TERMINI / BATHS OF DIOCLETIAN

gata e Romeo
E B4
a Carlo Alberto, 45
el. 06 446 61 15
pen Mon.–Fri.
-3pm, 7.30–
0.30pm
losed beginning of
an. and in Aug.
ou might not expect
 find one of the
est restaurants in
ome, even in Italy,
ose to the station,
ut you would be
rong. Agata and
omeo Carraccio's
staurant has just 7
bles, offering seats
r 25 clients, and the
ecoration is simple,
ut the menu is sheer
enius. They update
aditional recipes
ich as minestra
arzilla (broccoli or
rate broth), beef or
mb with truffles. For
essert there is a
illefeuille that
ould be renowned
roughout Europe.
n excellent gourmet
enu offering 8
ourses and wine
sts €150.
eservations are
sential given the
ze of the place.

a Franco
Vicoletto
G B2
a dei Falisci, 2
l. 06 495 76 75
uvert 1–3.30pm,
-11.30pm
osed Mon.
you think your
udget precludes
eafood and fish, Da
anco will come to
ur rescue: this is
ur chance to savor
ngoline (small
ockles), octopus
lad, lasagne di
are, pasta e fagioli
n frutti di mare,
illed fish and
eafood (sea bream,
rbot, squid,
ngoustines) or
ed anchovies at
ices more usually
sociated with a
attoria (menus from

€16.5, sample menu
€20–25: 11 dishes in
small portions!). The
motto of the house is
ci pensiamo noi –
'we look after you' –
and it lives up to its
promise. Franco set
up shop here several
years ago in a former
grocery store, having
outgrown his old
restaurant just across
the way. Success
continues to smile
on him, as the
place is invariably
packed with family
gatherings, business
meetings and
dating couples.
Some remains of
19th-century
frescoes can be
seen on the ceiling
and the vaults.
◪

Pizzeria
Formula Uno
◆ **G** B2
Via degli Equi, 13
Tel. 06 445 38 66
Open Mon.–Sat.
6.30pm–12.30am
You need to go to
San Lorenzo to
discover this pizzeria,
so typical that it
seems almost a
caricature, in the
heart of a working-
class neighborhood
and much loved by
fans of AS Roma
soccer club. Even
if you do not share
their sporting
passion, the delicious
pizza is alone worth
the trip.
◪

Tram-Tram
◆ **G** B3
Via dei Reti, 44-46
Tel. 06 49 04 16
Open 12.30–3.30pm,
7.30–11.30pm
Closed Mon.
This restaurant owes
its name to the old
tram line that passes
in front of its doors
on its way across
San Lorenzo. It
contains two dining
rooms that are often
alive with chatter and
laughter, particularly
at weekends, when

it attracts family
groups. The dishes
on the menu come
not only from Rome
itself but also from
other parts of the
Mediterranean:
gnocchetti alla
pescatora (octopus,
squid, mussels,
cockles), crab risotto,
baby lamb, stuffed
swordfish, chicory
and anchovy tarts
and mouthwatering
homemade desserts
(lemon cream,
zabaglione, crostata
– tart with jam).
◪

TRASTEVERE

Alberto Ciarla
◆ **E** C1
Piazza
San Cosimato, 40
Tel. 06 581 86 68
www.albertociarla.com
Open Mon.–Sat.
8.30pm–12.30am
The 1970's decor is
a reminder that the
almost mythical
reputation of this fish
restaurant wasn't
created yesterday.
The pasta e fagiolo
(pasta with beans)
and the rustic platter
are excellent, as are
the calamare and
mussels. For the
secondo, try sea
bass grilled with
aromatic herbs or
seafood. Great wine
list. Gastronomic
tasting menus: €65,
€75 and €85;
traditional menus:
€49.50 and €65.
A la carte: wine not
included. Reservation
advised.
⊞

Da Lucia
◆ **D** C4
Vicolo del
Mattonato, 2/b
Tel. 06 580 36 01
Open 12.30–3pm,
7.30–11pm. Closed
Sun. and in Aug.
Strings of garlic and
copper pans serve as
decoration, and this
simplicity is reflected
in the tasty food:
traditional primi

(gnocchi on Thurs)
and good secondi:
rolled escalopes
alla romana, tripe,
cuttlefish with petits
pois and cod in
guazzetto on Fri
(fried cod
accompanied by
tomato sauce
enriched with
anchovies, raisins
and pine nuts).
◪

Enoteca Ferrara
◆ **D** C4
Via del Moro, 1/a
Tel. 06 58 33 39 20
www.enotecaferrara.it
Open daily 6pm–2am
(winebar), 8–11.30pm
(restaurant)
Although the amazing
selection of both red
and white wines is
the main reason for
coming here, the
small dishes that
accompany the
drinks would alone
be worth a visit.
Apart from the usual
cheese and cooked
meats, the menu
features recipes that
give a new twist to
ingredients often
neglected by today's
culinary trendsetters:
pulses and sprouting
seeds, presented
here with all kinds of
sauces, as well as in
soups, salads and
mousses. Delicious
desserts. Be warned
that eating here is
not cheap (reckon
on €45 without the
wine).
◪

Osteria Gensola
◆ **E** C1
Piazza della
Gensola, 15
Tel. 06 581 63 12
Open 12.30–4pm,
7.30pm–midnight
The Gonsela's
discreet terrace
barely encroaches on
the adjacent Piazza in
Piscinula, where the
atmosphere fulfils
all the romantic
expectations of
Rome. The interior
is somewhat
nondescript but

◆ RESTAURANTS

Trastevere, Tivoli

visitors can be consoled by the Sicilian specialties (marked in red on the menu), which are the main attraction here. Start off with caponata siciliana (ratatouille with charred peppers and eggplants mixed with capers, olives and celery), then follow this with a primo such as linguine with sardines or fusilli with anchovies and peppers, before a delicious secondo like rolled swordfish or breaded anchovies stuffed with raisins. If you have any room left, you can conclude with a cannolo, a pastry filled with ricotta cream, chocolate and candied fruit. Friendly and efficient service.

◼

Pizzeria Panattoni-I Marmi
◆ **E** C1

Viale di Trastevere, 53
Tel. 06 580 09 19
Ouvert 6.30pm–2am
Closed Wed.
This is the Trastevere's counterpart of the highly popular pizzerias on the Piazza Navona. In summer, it is an ideal place to while away the time watching

the trams go by and enjoying a stuffed olive or some potato or rice croquettes before going on to a pizza. Unfortunately, however, there are often too many people to permit such a leisurely pace. Do not be put off by this pizzeria's nickname of l'obitorio, the 'morgue' – it is derived from its white marble tables.

◼

Sabatini
◆ **D** C4

Piazza Santa Maria in Trastevere, 13
Tel. 06 581 20 26
www.sabatini-fratelli.com
Open 12–3pm, 7.30–11.30pm
Tourists are not the only ones to enjoy the Sabatini's terrace stretching out opposite the Church of Santa Maria in the heart of Trastevere, as many locals are regularly drawn here by the Roman specialties (unoriginal but always good) and fish dishes, such as the truly exceptional spaghetti alle vongole (with clams). Such delicacies obviously come at a price, particularly when served in such a strategic location.

◼

▨ Trattoria Da Enzo
◆ **E** C1-2

Via dei Vascellari, 29
Tel. 06 581 83 55
Open Mon.–Sat.
1–3pm, 8–11pm
Closed 2 weeks in Aug.
You should arrive here early with a healthy appetite to take full advantage of this wonderful place, which is always full of regular customers (who may look slightly askance at an intruder). The decor has everything you could expect of a typical Roman trattoria: children's drawings, a calendar and photos of Alberto Sordi on the walls, two neon lights and a fan on the ceiling. The dishes of the day always come in copious portions: classic primi (cacio e pepe, carbonara, arrabbiata, gnocchi on Thurs, homemade cannelloni) and mouthwatering secondi (oxtail, lamb, veal escalopes with lemon). Wash it all down with the house wine, a white from the Castelli Romani, and if you are still hungry, treat yourself to wild strawberries with sugar.

◼

Hotel-Ristorante Adriano

Via di Villa Adriana, 19
Tel. 0774 53 50 28
www.hoteladriano.it
If you do not feel like having a picnic unde the olive trees of Vill Adriana, rest assured that one of the best restaurants in Tivoli awaiting you right next to the entrance to the archeological site. In fine weather, it is possible to have your meal in the garden. Inside, the setting is elegant but restrained (pretty crockery, old furniture) and offers very attentive service. Do not miss the fresh pasta and, if you still have the appetite for a secondo, try the house specialty of leg of lamb with juniper berries. The hotel offers double rooms at €100–115. Restaurant closed Sun evening in the low season.

◼

CAFÉS, BARS, NIGHTCLUBS ◆

ntico Caffè ella Pace
◆ D B4

ia della Pace, 3-7
el. 06 686 12 16
pen Mon. 4pm–
am, Tue.–Sun
.30am–3am
his café is fairly
uiet by day but is
acked at night,
articularly at the
eekend, as this is
place to be seen,
referably with
utting-edge fashion
ccessories and the
test model of cell
hone or Palm
omputer on show.
he drinks are
omewhat expensive
eckon on € 5-6).

ntico Caffè Greco
◆ F A3

ia dei Condotti, 86
el. 06 679 17 00
pen Tue.–Sat.
am–7.30pm
un.–Mon.
0.30am–7pm
rtists, intellectuals
nd heads of state
ave graced the
enches of this café,
hich opened in
760. The paintings
nd photos on the
alls pay homage
● some of these
ustrious customers,
cluding Goethe,
tendhal, Elsa
lorante, Alberto
loravia and Orson
elles. Nowadays,
eir places have
een taken by both
urists and ordinary
omans, appreciative
f the relatively low
rices of the coffee.

Bar del Fico
E B1

azza del Fico, 26-28
el. 06 686 52 05
pen daily 9am–2am
nother of the
nblematic bars in
e Triangolo delle
evute. It is slightly
t apart, in the
adow of the huge
tree at the edge
the little square,
ut it is invaded until

very late by a crowd
of young Romans
and tourists.

Bartaruga
◆ E B1

Piazza Mattei, 9
Tel. 06 689 22 99
Open Mon.–Thu.
5pm–midnight,
Fri.–Sat. 5pm–2am
This bar overlooking
one of the city's
prettiest squares,
in front of the
Turtles Fountain,
is popular with
artists and bohemian
intellectuals – and
it is one of our
favorites too. Red
velvet, subdued
lighting and mirrors
set the tone.

Café Romano–Hotel d'Inghilterra Bar
◆ F A2-A3

Via Bocca di Leone, 14
Tel. 06 69 98 11
www.hotel
dinghilterraroma.it
Cocktails much
appreciated by
Rome's bright young
things. Romantic and
very classy.

▢ Caffè Sant'Eustachio
◆ E B1

Piazza
Sant'Eustachio, 82
Tel. 06 68 80 20 48
Open daily 8.30am–
1am (1.30am Fri.,
2am Sat.)
The gran caffè in this
highly atmospheric
temple of coffee is a
frothy and aromatic
espresso that comes
already sweetened
(unless you specify
'amaro'). If you want
to try repeating the
experience back
home, you can buy
the house coffee
blend. Obviously,
this excellence does
not come cheap:
the gran caffè costs
€2.20 – more
expensive than
elsewhere, but
well worth the
price. Another plus
is the excellent
pastries served at
breakfast time.

Caffè della Scala
◆ D C4

Via della Scala, 4
Tel. 06 580 36 10
Open daily 5pm–2am
This bar tucked away
in a small, quiet street
is a favorite haunt of
night owls. Cocktails,
good wines by the
glass and excellent
beers.

Chiosco Testaccio
◆ H A2-A3

Via Giovanni Branca
(corner of Via
B. Franklin
Open May–Sep. 15
daily noon–1.30am
This kiosk opened
in the 1930's and
has been slightly
modernized over
the years but its
grattachecche have
retained the time-
honored quality that
has made it famous
all over the city.
Noteworthy flavors
include tamarind
and lemon combined
with coconut.

▢ Enoteca Il Goccetto
◆ D B4

Via dei Banchi
Vecchi, 14
Tel. 06 686 42 68
Open Mon.–Sat.
11.30am–2pm,
6.30pm–midnight
Closed in Aug.
You can have a snack
here, or even a light
dinner, but the best
way to appreciate
this enoteca is to
allow the owner to
recommend one of
his wines and savor
it with a few slices
of cheese or olives
on the side. Wine
by the glass at
reasonable prices
(reckon on €10 for a
glass and a snack).

▢ Forno La Renella
◆ D C4

Vicolo del Moro, 15/16
Tel. 06 581 72 65
Open daily 7am–
10pm (Fri.–Sat.
7am–1am)
This is nominally
a bakery, but no
ordinary one, as

evidenced by the
sign informing
customers that
everything is made
with extra-virgin olive
oil and top-quality
ingredients. A few
stools are set along
the bar, allowing you
to observe the cook
preparing pizza slices
with toppings that
include spinach and
sausage, zucchini,
potatoes and onions.
Customers flock here
from far and wide to
buy leavened and
corn bread, cakes
(ciambella alla
ricotta, plain or
with chocolate)
and cookies. As a
result, patience is
sometimes required,
as the line can be
dauntingly long.

Hotel de Russie Bar
◆ B D2

Via del Babuino, 9
Tel. 06 32 88 81
www.roccoforte
hotels.com
Open 10am–1am
You may not be able
to afford a night in
this luxury hotel but
in warm weather you
can make up for it by
enjoying a drink in
the magical gardens
of its bar, lit up by
large candles and
sometimes
complemented
by the sounds of
classical music.

Jonathan's Angels
◆ E B1

Via della Fossa, 16
Tel. 06 689 34 26
Open daily
8om–3.30am
The toilets in this bar-
bazaar with several
cozy spaces are
worth a visit in
themselves: statues,
niches, touches of
Afro-Cuban Santeria
and an old fountain
where you can throw
in a coin and wish
for luck. The bar
itself, with its walls
covered with frescoes
depicting the owner,
attracts a young,
trendy crowd.

🔲 La Buvette
◆ **B** D2/**F** A2
Via Vittoria, 44–47
Tel. 06 679 03 83
Open daily
8am–midnight
The imposing wood trim and leather benches are set off here by warm and efficient service. The cappuccino is one of the best in town (although it comes without the surcharge typical of the other great cafés), with a fragrant, airy foam that stays in place right to the bottom of the cup. The pastries maintain this high standard with cream cakes and small, flaky sfogliatelle as good as any produced in Naples, while the savory delicacies are out of the ordinary (pizza bianca, tramezzini – crustless sandwiches).

La Casa del Tramezzino
◆ **C4/E** C1
Viale di Trastevere, 81
Tel. 06 581 21 18
Open Tue.–Sun.
6am–2am
The Tramezzino offers a kind of Italian-style club sandwich, made with carefully chosen ingredients such as grilled eggplant, smoked mozzarella, gorgonzola, rocket and cooked meats – a good alternative to pizza and pasta.

Le Bain Art Gallery
◆ **E** B2
Via delle Botteghe Oscure, 32–33/a
Tel. 06 686 56 73
Open Mon.–Sat.
12.30–3.30pm,
7.30pm–midnight
(bar around 2am)
Closed Sun.
This bar-restaurant, strikingly decorated in a sophisticated minimalist style, is set in an old 16th-century palazzo. The atmosphere is laid back, with
comfortable sofas ideal for a leisurely aperitif. DJ sessions.

Sisini
◆ **D** C4/**E** C1
Via San Francesco a Ripa, 137
Tel. 06 589 71 10
Open Mon.–Sat.
9am–10pm
Sisini, known in the neighborhood for its pizza al taglio and roast chicken with rosemary, gathers together the inhabitants of the area, workers taking a quick bite on the street outside and a sprinkling of tourists. A good place to stock up for an improvised picnic on the lawn of the Villa Doria-Pamphilj.

🔲 Sora Maria
◆ **A** D2
Corner of Via Trionfale and Via Telesio
Open daily
5pm–2am
This is undoubtedly one of Rome's most popular grattachecce. Its flavors embrace both citric and tropical fruit, with large chunks of fresh fruit thrown in as a bonus.

Taverna del Campo
◆ **E** B1
Campo dei Fiori, 16
Tel. 06 687 44 02
Open daily
8.30am–2am
Closed Mon. in winter and Mon. evening in summer
The focaccia bread (filled with radicchio and gorgonzola, eggplant and mozzarella, smoked ham and mascarpone, cooked meat or vegetables) is popular with workers from the nearby offices, but the staff remains unperturbed by the crowds and is remarkably friendly. Good white wines, from €2 a glass.

🔲 Tazza d'Oro
◆ **E** B2
Via degli Orfani, 84–86
Tel. 06 678 97 92
www.tazzadorocoffee shop.com
The demand for the espresso in the 'Golden Cup' is such that the line to the cashier sometimes almost reaches the Pantheon Square outside. Connoisseurs also come here to buy coffee beans, sold in distinctive bright-red packs adorned with the image of a young female coffee planter. The other attraction – worth crossing the city for – is the delectable coffee granita, with whipped cream on the bottom, crushed coffee-flavored ice in the middle and a dab of cream on the top. Espresso €0.70.

Vineria Reggio
◆ **E** B1
Campo dei Fiori, 15
Tel. 06 68 80 32 68
Open Mon.–Sat.
8am–2am
This has one of the city's busiest terraces, with a stimulating mixture of young and old, and of Romans and tourists. Good wines and snacks accompanied by bread and olives.

Vitti
◆ **E** A2
Piazza San Lorenzo in Lucina, 33
Tel. 06 687 63 04
Open Apr.–Sep.:
daily 7am–1am;
Oct.–end of March:
daily 7am–10pm
Vitti provides an ideal spot to lounge in the shade of a parasol in a small square, out of reach of the dedicated shoppers on the Via del Corso. This bar-pastry shop is well known for its appetizing breakfasts, its rum babas, its Neapolitan sfogliatelle
and its Sicilian cannoli (rolls stuffed with cream and chocolate).

NIGHTCLUBS

Alexanderplatz
◆ **A** D2
Via Ostia, 9
Tel. 06 39 74 21 71
Open daily
9pm–2am
This jazz club has welcomed some of the best musicians from both Italy and the rest of the world. Creative cuisine and good atmosphere. It is advisable to book in advance.

Alpheus
◆ **H** B3
Via del Commercio, 3
Tel. 06 574 78 26
www.alpheus.it
Open Thu.–Sun.
This very well-known club, spread over three floors (jazz and blues, Latin, rock), plays host to one of Rome's most popular party nights: the 'mucca assassina' (the murderous cow'), complete with exuberant drag queens. It is put on by the famous Mario Mieli Circle of Homosexual Culture.

Brancaleone
Via Levanna, 11
Tel. 06 82 00 43 82
www.agathaonline.it
www.brancaleone.it
This former squat in a palazzo remains a standard bearer of Rome's alternative scene. It is a dynamic, independent center that has helped develop multimedia projects mixing genres and developing new idioms. It boasts its own recording studio and cinema, as well as organizing courses in photography, yoga and shiatsu.

a Friday nights it
rts on one of the
liveliest party nights
town, presided
er by Agatha.

ruso
H A3
a di Monte
staccio, 36
l. 06 574 50 19
pen Tue.–Sat.
abaret, bar, disco,
eater and concerts.
e Caruso puts on
e summer Tevere
zz festival on the
nks of the Tiber.

assico Village
H C3
a Libetta, 3
l. 06 57 43 364
ww.classico
illage.com
pen Mon.–Sat.
lecticism is the
atchword in this
ghtclub with three
fferent spaces,
t in an old factory
orld music, house,
ncerts, exhibitions,
c). It attracts a
otley crowd of
ages.

Ex-Magazzini
H B3
a dei Magazzini
enerali, 8 bis
l. 06 575 80 40
ww.exmagazzini.it
pen Tue.–Sun.
his club near
me old food
arehouses offers
mixed program
DJ sessions,
medy and live
usic. Small flea
arket on Sun.

Goa
H C3
a Libetta, 13
l. 06 574 82 77
pen Tue.–Sun.
his is the city's most
shionable night
ub, with top-notch
Js from Italy and
eyond displaying
eir skills in a cozy
tmosphere (dimmed
ghts and candles).

azz Café
F B1
ia Zanardelli, 10-12
l. 06 68 21 01 19 /

06 68 21 55 08
Open daily
8am–2am
Closed first week
in Aug.
*Futuristic sofas,
an atmosphere
evoking New York,
live electro music
in the basement
and a discotheque
upstairs.*

Il Qube
Via di
Portonaccio, 212
Tel. 06 438 54 45
www.qubedisco.com
Open Thu.–Sat.
*This enormous
nightclub is spread
over three levels on
converted industrial
premises. Decadent
atmosphere
guaranteed,
especially at the
Friday-night gay
party (the 'mucca
assassina'), which
invariably draws a
big crowd.*

La Palma
Via G. Mirri, 35
Tel. 06 43 59 90 29
www.lapalmaclub.it
Open Mon.–Sat.
10pm–1am
*This unusual venue
operates as a cultural
association (annual
membership €2)
and presents both big
names and promising
newcomers from the
fields of modern jazz,
world music and
experimental rock.
Most concerts are
free, otherwise
reckon on paying
€10–15.*

**☑ Locanda
Atlantide**
◆ **G** B2
Via dei Lucani, 22/b
Tel. 06 44 70 45 40
www.locandatlantide.it
Open daily
Closed in summer
*A huge multimedia
space that is always
open to new ideas,
active in promoting all
kinds of music,
theater, dance,
photography,
literature and
anything else*

*imbued with a
spirit of adventure…*

Ombre Rosse
◆ **D** C4
Piazza
Sant'Egidio,12
Tel. 06 588 41 55
www.ombrerosse.com
Open daily
7.30am–2am,
Sun. 6pm–2am
*A popular terrace,
jazz concerts
and a varied mix
of customers –
depending on the
time of day, you may
come across locals
having lunch or a
coffee or groups
of high-spirited
party people. Brunch
on Sun. The jazz
concerts generally
take place on Wed
and Sun, Oct–May.*

Piper
◆ **B** B4-C4
Via Tagliamento, 9
Tel. 06 855 53 98
www.piperclub.it
Open Fri.–Sun.
Closed in summer
*This historic nightclub
opened in 1965 but
has managed to stay
abreast of recent
trends. It has been
totally refurbished
in a sophisticated
'ethnic' style and
offers the best of
modern electro
music, as well as
fashion shows,
installations and
concerts.*

Villaggio Globale
◆ **H** A3
Lungotevere
Testaccio, 2
Tel. 06 575 72 33
vglobale@tiscalinet.it
www.ecn.org/villaggio
globale/
*This center
occupying part
of Testaccio's old
abattoirs puts on
theater shows,
movie festivals,
talks and concerts
(electronic, world,
punk, reggae, etc.).
It offers the added
advantages
of a bar, a tea
room, a trattoria,*

*a cosmopolitan
restaurant and even
a small youth hostel.*

Antonini
◆ **A** C3
– Piazza di Spagna,
23
Tel. 06 678 60 27
Open 9am–8.15pm
– Via Sabotino, 21/29
Tel. 06 37 51 78 45
Open daily 7am–9pm
*This gelateria is off
the tourist trail but
attracts plenty of
connoisseurs and
locals from the
area, who relish the
superb montebianco
(meringue, marron-
glacé vermicelli,
whipped cream)
and homemade ice
creams (the melon
flavor is particularly
delicious), eaten
on the spot or
taken out.*

Babington's
◆ **F** A3
Piazza
di Spagna, 23
Tel. 06 678 60 27
Open daily
9am–8.15pm
*This English-style
tearoom offers a
respite from the
noise and intensity of
the city. No displays
of bravura here, just
customers reading
their newspapers
and speaking to
each other in hushed
tones. Babington's
has been going for
over a century now,
soothing visitors
dizzy from a surfeit
of sunshine, chic
stores and Italian
food.*

Caffè Rosati
◆ **B** D1
Piazza del
Popolo, 4-5/a
Tel. 06 322 58 59
Open daily
7.30am–11.30pm
*An elegant café and
ice cream parlor
that remains
fashionable in the
21st century.*

◆ CAFÉS, BARS, NIGHTCLUBS

Gelateria A. Cecere
◆ **F** B3
Via del Lavatore, 84
Tel. 06 679 20 60
Open March–Nov.
daily 10am–2am
*Once you have
thrown all your loose
change over your
head into the Trevi
fountain and wished
for a speedy return
to the Eternal City,
there still remains
one essential ritual
to perform: eating
one of Cecere's
zabaglione ice
creams!*

Giolitti
◆ **F** B2
Via degli Uffici
del Vicario, 40
Tel. 06 699 12 43
www.giolitti.it
Open daily 7am–2am
*The most famous ice
cream parlor in Rome
since 1900. Scoops
of truly scrumptious
ice cream and 100
different flavors.*

Il Palazzo
del Freddo di
Giovanni Fassi
◆ **G** C1-C2

Via Principe
Eugenio, 65-67
Tel. 06 446 47 40
Open Tue.–Sat.
noon–midnight,
Sun. 10am–midnight
*Although this
gelateria has an
enticingly old-
fashioned air, the
iced desserts are
disappointing and
customers are
always unduly
pressed to make
a choice from the
countless flavors
on offer (these
decisions take time!).
The rice-milk ice
cream does justify
a detour, however.*

⚑ San Crispino
◆ **F** B3
Via della
Panetteria, 42
Tel. 06 679 39 24
Open Wed.–Mon.
noon–12.30am
(1.30am Fri.–Sat.)
Branches:
– Via Acaia, 56
(San Giovanni)
*Doubtless, this is
the best ice cream
parlor in Rome.
Always produced*

*with creative flair,
the flavors follow
whatever fruits are
in season. They're
innovative (meringue),
unusual (liquorice-
lemon), basic (their
signature flavor is
crema made with
wild Sardinian honey).
They also do a mean
zabaglione.*

Tre Scalini
◆ **E** B1
Piazza Navona, 28-30
Tel. 06 68 80 19 96
Open daily 9am–1am
Closed in Jan.
*Famous for its ice
creams, especially
the chocolate tartuffo
variety.*

PASTICCERIA

Pasticceria
Il Boccione
◆ **E** B1-C1
Via Portico d'Ottavia,
1 Tel. 06 687 86 37
Open Sun.–Thu.
8am–7.30pm, Fri.
8am–4 or 5pm
*This cake shop in the
heart of the Ghetto
specializes in Jewish
pastries, including a*

*sweet Hebrew pizza
which, it is claimed,
follows the oldest
recipe of its kind in
existence. One thing
is for sure: it is
delicious and richly
flavored (candied
fruit, almonds, pine
nuts). The other
standout is less
sugary: torta alla
ricotta, traditionally
stuffed with Morello
cherries. Also worthy
trying are the cookies
made with cinnamon
and almonds; you can
discreetly dunk these
in the hot tea that is
also served here.*

Bibli
◆ **E** C1
Via dei Fienaroli, 28
Tel. 06 58 14 534
www.bibli.it
Open Mon.
3.30pm–midnight;
Tue.–Sun. 11am–
midnight
A fine bookshop as
well as a café where
you can have
breakfast, and also a
concert venue. The
perfect place to while
away time in the
Trastevere when it is
raining or unbearably
hot outside.

Librerie Feltrinelli
◆ **B** D2
Via del
Babuino, 39-40
www.feltrinelli.it
Mon. 2–7.30pm;
Tue.–Sat. 10am–
1.30pm; Sun. 10 am–
1.30pm, 4–7.30pm
Chain of bookstores
named after a
publisher. Pleasant
atmosphere and well-
stocked, although the
service can be a little
brusque.
Other stores at:
Largo Torre
Argentina, 5/11
Via V. E. Orlando,
84/86

Mel Bookstore
◆ **E** A3-B3
Via Nazionale,
252-255
Tel. 06 488 54 05
www.melbookstore.it
Open Mon.–Sat.
9am–8pm; Sun.
and public hols.
10am–1.30pm,
4–8pm (4.30–8.30pm
in high season)
A very lively store
spread over several
floors.

**Messaggerie
Musicali**
◆ **B** D1-D2
Via del Corso, 472
Tel. 06 68 44 01
www.messaggerie
musicali.it
Open Mon.–Sat.
10am–11pm;
Sun. 10am–8.30pm
Books, CDs,
DVDs, international
newspapers.
Practical, open
until late at night,
up-to-date stock
but unfortunately
not very convivial.

Odradek La Libreria
◆ **D** B4
Via dei Banchi
Vecchi, 57
Tel. 06 683 34 51
www.odradek.it
Open daily
9am–8pm
Closed Sun. in
summer
This militant
bookstore is named
after an adventurous
publishing company
with interests that
range from
philosophy,
epistemology
and communication
sciences to
contemporary
literature, science
fiction, avant-garde
art and the history
of alternative
movements. The
adjacent room is
regularly used for
book presentations
and talks.

RicordiMediaStores
◆ **B** D1-D2
Via del Corso, 506
Tel. 06 36 12 370
Open Mon.–Sat.
9.30am–8pm;
Sun. 10am–8pm
Closed Sun. in Aug.
The musical
equivalent of the
Feltrinelli bookstores,
complete with
listening posts.

Rinascita
◆ **E** B1-B2
Via delle Botteghe
Oscure, 2
Tel. 06 679 74 60/
76 37
Open daily
10am–8pm
Slightly old-
fashioned, but
nevertheless one of
the best bookstores
in Rome. Rinascita
Dischi, just next door,
is famous for its
selection of music.
Well-informed and
attentive staff.

Italy's reputation in
the fashion field is not
without foundation,
as its clothes are
among the most
elegant in the world.
The stores on Via dei
Condotti, near the
Piazza di Spagna,
offers a display of
all the Italian labels
that have become
synonymous with
luxury: Prada, Gucci,
Valentino, Max Mara,
Armani, Alberta
Ferretti, Furla, etc.
However, unless you
are in Rome for the
January or July sales,
or have the benefit of
an unlimited budget,
the prohibitive prices
rule out any spending
spree.

Angelo di Nepi
◆ **A** D3-D4
– Via Cola di Rienzo,
267/a (Prati)
Tel. 06 322 48 00
– Via dei Giubbonari,
28 (Campo dei Fiori)
Tel. 06 689 30 06
– Via Frattina, 2
(Piazza di Spagna)
Tel. 06 678 65 68
www.angelodinepi.com
This label has
really impressed us
on account of its
audacity and ethnic
inspiration, as well
as the quality of its
materials and its end
products. It is a little
pricy, but its clothes
have a character all
their own.

Ethic
◆ **B** D1-D2
– Via del Corso, 85
Tel. 06 36 00 21 91
– Via del
Pantheon, 46-47
Tel. 06 68 80 317
– Piazza
Cairoli, 11-12
Tel. 06 68 30 10 63
www.ethic.it
This firm plays
with textures, cuts
and colors with an
abandon rarely
found in ready-
to-wear clothing.
It has several stores
in Rome.

Fausto Santini
◆ **E** A2
Via Frattina, 120
Tel. 06 678 41 14
www.faustosantini.com
A pair of Italian
shoes is certainly
one thing you should
bring back from your
trip to Rome. Here
you will find last
season's shoes
by Fausto Santini
(Giacomo's son),
on sale all year round
at half the original
price or less. The
new collections are
on sale at Via Frattina,
120. If you do not
find what you're
looking for in this
shop, head for
Sergio Rossi, Piazza
di Spagna (◆ **F** A3)
or the more classic
designs of Bruno
Magli, Via Condotti
(◆ **E** A2-A3).

**Galleria Colonna-
Alberto Sordi**
◆ **E** A2
Piazza Colonna, 31-35
Open daily
10am–10pm
This magnificent
Art-Nouveau
shopping gallery
(1922) reopened in
late 2003, bearing
the name of the
famous actor who
had died earlier
that year. It contains
stores selling clothes
and accessories
at accessible prices,
as well as a huge
Feltrinelli bookstore
and a café in each of
its two passageways.

Ibiz
◆ **E** B1
Via dei Chiavari, 39
Tel. 06 68 30 72 97
A wide range of
leather goods
at reasonable
prices, made in
the workshop next
door: key rings in
the form of a rose,
handbags in original
shapes, belts, big
backpacks and
armchairs. The
craftsmen can be
seen at work in
the morning.

Mandarina Duck
◆ **E** A2
– Via dei
Due Macelli, 59
Tel. 06 67 86 414
– Via Cola di Rienzo
270-272
Tel. 06 689 64 91
This brand is internationally known for its resistant bags in attractive designs. The prices are barely lower than in other European countries, but the sales season offers good bargains.

Castroni
◆ **A** D3-D4
Via Cola
di Rienzo, 196
Tel. 06 687 43 83
www.castronigroup.it
Closed Sun.
The most beautiful grocery store in Rome is a world of its own, impervious to passing fashions. The smell of ground coffee lingers in the air as customers stock up with liquorice from Calabria, Baci Perugina chocolates with a big hazelnut inside, balsamic vinegar, black-truffle cream, dried ceps... More exotic tastes are also catered for: Argentinean corned beef, Japanese ginger pickles and British chutneys.

Franchi
◆ **A** D3-D4
Via Cola
di Rienzo, 204

Tel. 06 687 46 51
www.franchi.it
Open Mon.–Sat.
8.15am–9pm
This cheese and charcuterie store with a hot-food takeout counter rivals its illustrious neighbor, Castroni, in both abundance and exquisite delicacies like salami, buffalo mozzarella and fresh pasta. Whether you eat them on the spot or buy them to enjoy later, they are well worth a detour.

Volpetti
◆ **E** D1
Via Marmorata, 47
Tel. 06 574 23 52
Open Mon.–Sat.
8am–2pm, 5–8.15pm
This institution, over a hundred years old, is at one and the same time a fine grocery store, a charcuterie, a dairy and a catering service. It offers a dazzling array of specialties: artichokes alla romana, braised vegetables, baby mushrooms in balsamic vinegar, cheese, fresh pasta, dried tomatoes, ceps and a good selection of wines.

Porta Portese
◆ **H** A2
Via Portuense,
parallel to Viale
di Trastevere
Open Sun. 5am–8pm
The most famous market in Rome. To say that it resembles

Ali Baba's cave is an understatement: from CDs of the latest international hits to stalls with cooked meats from Calabria, via telephones from the 1970s, designer jeans, plastic gadgets made in Taiwan, Indian jewelry, African craftwork, leather goods, embroidered sheets, sexy underwear and secondhand books (invariably including some about Mussolini and Nero). Bargaining is the order of the day – and so is pickpocketing, so hang on tightly to your bags and be vigilant.

Mercato di Campo dei Fiori
◆ **E** B1
Mon–Sat
7am– 1.30pm
A very colorful flower and vegetable market on one of the city's prettiest squares. Extraordinary smells too. On Tuesdays (10am–1pm, Via Trionfale, 45), the wholesale flower market is also open to the public. There you will find an incredible selection of plants and flowers at very low prices.

Mercato Esquilino
◆ **A** D3
Via Principe Amadeo
Mon–Sat 8am–1pm
A very popular market with alimentari (groceries), spices,

vegetable stalls, and a jovial atmosphere.

AS Roma Store
◆ **E** A2
Piazza Colonna, 360
Tel. 06 678 65 14
www.asromastore.it
AS Roma official store is the place to go for a number 10 shirt with the name of Totti and a badge depicting a she-wolf

Lazio Point
◆ **E** B4
Via Farini, 34-36
Tel. 06 482 66 88
www.sslazio.com
A store selling the kit of Rome's other soccer team, with colors of blue and white.

TAD Concept Store
◆ **B** D2
Via del
Babuino, 155/a
Tel. 06 32 69 51 31
www.taditaly.com
One of the most interesting stores in Rome. Perfume, home furnishings, accessories, shoes: if it's hip, it's on sale here, in this two-story haven of cool design (10,764 square feet). The Tad Café serves breakfast and snacks.

BASICS

es: sì
o: no
oday: oggi
omorrow: domani
esterday: ieri
do not understand:
on capisco
hat time is it? Che
ra è ? / Che ore sono ?

POLITE PHRASES

lease: per favore /
er cortesia
hank you: grazie
hank you very much:
razie mille
xcuse me (asking
ermission to pass):
ermesso
xcuse me (catching
omeone's attention,
rmal): mi scusi
xcuse me (catching
omeone's attention,
formal): scusami
oodbye (informal):
rivederci; (formal:
rivederla
ood morning:
uongiorno
ood evening:
uona sera
ood night:
uona notte

DAYS

he day: il giorno
he night : la notte
he morning:
mattina
he afternoon:
pomeriggio
he evening: la sera
londay: lunedì
uesday: martedì
Vednesday: mercoledì
hursday: giovedì
riday: venerdì
aturday: sabato
unday: domenica

THE MONTHS

anuary: gennaio
ebruary: febbraio
larch: marzo
pril: aprile
lay: maggio
une: giugno
uly: luglio
ugust: agosto
eptember: settembre
ctober: ottobre
lovember: novembre
ecember: dicembre

NUMBERS

ne: uno
vo: due
hree: tre
our: quattro
Five: cinque
Six: sei
Seven: sette
Eight: otto
Nine: nove
Ten: dieci
Eleven: undici
Twelve: dodici
Thirteen: tredici
Fourteen: quattordici
Fifteen: quindici
Sixteen: sedici
Seventeen: diciasette
Eighteen: diciotto
Nineteen: dicianove
Twenty: venti
Twenty-one: ventuno
Twenty-two: ventidue
Thirty: trenta
Forty: quaranta
Fifty: cinquanta
Sixty: sessanta
Seventy: settanta
Eighty: ottanta
Ninety: novanta
One hundred: cento
One thousand: mille

TRAVEL

Luggage: i bagagli
Customs: la dogana
Travel documents:
i documenti
The train: il treno
The station: la stazione
The platform: il binario
The plane: l'aeroplano
The airport: l'aeroporto
The porter: il facchino
The bus/coach:
l'autobus
The stop: la fermata
The car: la macchina
A hired car: una
macchina a noleggio
The taxi: il taxi

ON THE ROAD

The road: la strada
The motorway/
freeway: l'autostrada
Petrol/gas: la benzina
Oil: l'olio
The fault (motor): il
guasto
The tyre: la gomma
To put air in: rigonfiare
The exit: l'uscita

FINDING YOUR WAY

Where is... ? Dove si
trova...?
Is it far/close?
E' lontano/vicino?
On the right: a destra
On the left: a sinistra
Straight ahead: dritto

IN TOWN

The street: la via
The high street: il corso
The side street:
il vicolo
The square: la piazza /
il campo
The city ring road:
il raccordo anulare

VISITING

Opening times: l'orario
Open: aperto
Closed: chiuso
Working days:
i giorni feriali
Sundays and national
holidays: i giorni festivi
The ticket: il biglietto
The church: la chiesa
The palace: il palazzo
The excavations:
gli scavi
The museum: il museo
The gallery: la galleria

FOOD AND DRINK

A coffee: un caffè
A coffee with frothy
milk: un cappuccino
An ice cream:
un gelato
A cake: un dolce
To have lunch: pranzare
To dine: cenare
Place setting:
il coperto
The glass: il bicchiere
The plate/dish: il piatto
Plain tap water: l'acqua
naturale
Mineral water
(usually fizzy):
l'acqua minerale
Wine: il vino
Bottle: la bottiglia
Wine by the carafe:
il vino sfuso
Beer: la birra
Starter: l'antipasto
Meat: la carne
Fish: il pesce
Vegetables:
la verdura, il contorno
Cheese: il formaggio
Fruit: la frutta
The bill: il conto

AT THE HOTEL

I would like a room for
tonight: Vorrei una
camera per questa notte
I would like to book a
room for the… : Vorrei
prenotare una camera
per il...
For one person: per
una persona
For two people: per due
persone
With a double bed: con
letto matrimoniale
With two beds: camera
doppia

With bath: con bagno
With shower: con
la doccia
To order breakfast:
ordinare la prima
colazione

AT THE POST OFFFICE

The mail/post office:
la posta
Postage stamp:
il francobollo
The letter: la lettera
The post card:
la cartolina
The telegram:
il telegramma

HEALTH

The chemist/
pharmacy: la farmacia
The hospital: l'ospedale
Could you please call a
doctor? Mi chiama un
medico, per favore?

SHOPPING

A pair of trousers:
i pantaloni, i calzoni
A shirt: una camicia
A skirt: una gonna
A dress: un vestito
A jacket: una giacca
A coat: un cappotto
A jerkin: un giubbotto
A sweater: un maglione
it is too large/small:
E' troppo grande/ troppo
piccolo
The size: la taglia
Earrings: gli orecchini
A belt: una cintura
Shoes: le scarpe
A tie: una cravatta
A handbag: una borsa
A travel bag:
un borsone / una valigia

USEFUL
EXPRESSIONS

How much does this
cost? Quanto costa? /
Quanto viene?
That is too expensive:
E' troppo caro
Where can I change
some money? Dove
posso cambiare i soldi?
Where can I find ... ?
Dove posso trovare ... ?
What time does this
shop open? A che ora
apre questo negozio?
What time does it
close? A che ora
chiude?

◆ PLACES TO VISIT

Caprarola, Ostia, Palestrina, Rome

The ★ symbol refers to places that deserve to be seen first if time is short.

CAPRAROLA

VILLA CAPRAROLA Palazzo Farnese Tel. 0761 64 60 52	*Open 8.30am–6.45pm.* *Closed Mon.*	● 88

OSTIA

ARCHEOLOGICAL AREA ★ Viale dei Romagnoli, 717 Tel. 06 56 35 80 99	*Dyer's workshop, basilica, Christian basilica, capitolium, Caseggiato dei Dipinti, Caseggiato del Larario, Caserma dei Vigili, Caesareum, curia, Domus Fulminata, Horrea Hortensius, Horrea Epagathiana, Horrea Epaphrodisiana, Serapeion, Insula dei Dipinti, Insula dei Auriges, Meat Market, House of Cupid and Psyche, House of Apuleius, Casa di Diana, Mithraeum of the Seven Spheres, Piazzale delle Corporazioni, Republican Sanctuary, Schola del Traiano, synagogue, Temple of Rome and Augustus, Temple of the Shipwrights and Carpenters, round temple, Republican temples, theater, Baths of Buticocus, Baths of Neptune, Baths of the Seven Sages, Tomb of Cartilius Poplicola.* *Open 8.30am–4pm in winter; 8.30am–6pm in summer. Closed Mon.*	▲ 41
CHURCH OF SANTA AUREA Piazza della Rocca, 13 Tel. 06 565 00 18	*Open 7.30am–noon, 4–6.30pm (4–8pm in summer)*	▲ 41
MUSEO OSTIENSE **(ARCHEOLOGICAL MUSEUM)** Viale dei Romagnoli, 717 Tel. 06 56 35 80 99	*Open 9am–4.30pm in winter; 9am–5.30pm in March; 9am–1.30pm, 2.15–6.30 in summer.*	

PALESTRINA

CATHEDRAL OF SANT'AGAPITO Piazza Regina Margherita Tel. 06 953 44 28	*Open 7am–noon, 4–7pm.*	▲ 402
NATIONAL ARCHEOLOGICAL MUSEUM Palazzo Barberini Piazza della Cortina Tel. 06 953 81 00	*Open 9am–7pm.*	▲ 402
TEMPLE OF FORTUNA Piazza della Cortina	*Open 9am–1pm until 1 hour before sunset.*	▲ 399

ROME

ACADEMY OF FINE ARTS Via di Ripetta, 222 Tel. 06 32 11 09 64	*Open Mon.–Fri. 10am–noon.* *Closed July 15–Sep. 1.*	▲ 305 ◆ F A
ACADEMY OF PHYSICAL EDUCATION Foro Italico Piazzale L. de Bosis 15 Tel. 06 36 73 35 99	*Visits on request (Fax 06 36 73 35 31).*	▲ 378 ◆ A A
ACCADEMIA DI SAN LUCA Palazzo Carpegna Piazza Accademia di San Luca, 77 Tel. 06 679 88 50	*Archives: Mon., Wed. 10am–noon; Tue., Thu. 2–7pm* *Library: Mon.-Fri. 9am–1pm; Tue.,Thu. 9am–1pm, 3–6pm. Museum: closed for restoration.*	▲ 299 ◆ F B
ARA PACIS AUGUSTAE ★ Lungotevere in Augusta Tel. 06 32 11 16 05	*Open 9am–7pm.* *Closed Mon.*	▲ 310 ◆ F A
AREA SACRA DI LARGO ARGENTINA **– TEMPLES A, B, C, D** Via San Nicola de' Cesarini Tel. 06 67 10 38 19	*Closed for building work.*	▲ 256 ◆ E A
– TORRE DEL PAPITO Largo di Torre Argentina	*Not open to the public.*	
ARSENAL PONTIFICIO Via Portuense, 11	*Not open to the public.*	◆ H B
ASTRONOMY AND **COPERNICAN MUSEUM** Viale Parco Mellini, 84 Tel. 06 35 42 21 47	*Closed.*	▲ 377 ◆ A A-E

The symbol ▲ refers to the Itineraries section. The symbol ◆ refers to the Map section.

AUDITORIUM OF MAECENAS Largo Leopardi, 22 Tel. 06 487 32 62	*Open Tue.–Sat. 9am–7pm in summer; 9am–5pm in winter; Sun. and public holidays. 9am–1pm.*	▲ 341 ◆ E B4
AUDITORIUM–PARCO DELLA MUSICA Viale Peitro de Coubertin, 30 Tel. 06 80 24 12 81	*Opening times may vary according to events.*	▲ 376 ◆ B A1
BANCA NAZIONALE DEL LAVORO Via Vittorio Veneto, 119 Tel. 06 470 21	*Visits on request.*	▲ 302 ◆ B D3
BANK OF ITALY Via Nazionale, 91 Tel. 06 479 21	*Not open to the public.*	▲ 348 ◆ F D4
BARRACCO MUSEUM (Farnesina ai Baullari) Corso V. Emmanuele II, 168 Tel. 06 68 80 68 48	*Open 9am–7pm.* *Closed Mon.*	▲ 249 ◆ F D1
BARRACKS OF THE CASTRA PEREGRINA Piazza San Giovanni in Laterano Tel. 06 69 88 49 47	*Excavations of San Giovanni in Laterano: not open to the public.*	▲ 186 ◆ G D1
BARRACKS OF EQUITES SINGULARES Piazza San Giovanni in Laterano	*Excavations of San Giovanni in Laterano: not open to the public.*	▲ 186 ◆ G D1
BARRACKS OF THE 5TH COHORT Church of S. Maria in Dominica Via della Navicella, 10 Tel. 06 77 20 26 85	*Vestiges can be seen in the crypt.*	▲ 186 ◆ E D3
BASILICA OF SAN BENEDETTO IN PISCINULA Piazza in Piscinula, 40 Tel. 06 58 33 16 09	*Open 8am–noon, 4.30–7.30pm.* *Closed Mon.*	▲ 353 ◆ E C1
BASILICA OF SAN CLEMENTE ★ Via San Giovanni in Laterano Tel. 06 70 45 10 18	*Open 9am–12.30pm, 3.30–6.30pm (3–6pm in winter).*	▲ 193 ◆ E C4
BASILICA OF SAN GIOVANNI IN LATERANO ★ Piazza S. Giovanni in Laterano, 4 Tel. 06 69 88 64 33	*Open 7am–6.30pm (basilica);* *7am–noon, 3–6.30pm (baptistry);* *9am–6pm (cloister and museum).*	
BASILICA OF SAN LORENZO FUORI LE MURA Piazzale del Verano, 3 Tel. 06 49 15 11	*Open 7.30am–12.30pm, 3.30–6.30pm (3.30–7.30pm in summer)*	● 76 ▲ 381 ◆ G A3
BASILICA OF SAN MARCO Piazza San Marco, 48 Tel. 06 679 52 05	*Open 8am–noon, 4–7pm.*	▲ 162 ◆ F D3
BASILICA OF SAN PAOLO FUORI LE MURA Via Ostiense, 184 Tel. 06 541 03 41	*Open 7am–7pm in summer; 7am–6.30pm in winter; 9am–1pm, 3–6pm (cloisters); Mon.–Sat. 9am–1pm, 3–6pm (pinacoteca).*	▲ 382 ◆ H D3
BASILICA OF SAN PIETRO ★ Piazza San Pietro, Vatican Tel. 06 69 88 16 62	*Open 7am–7pm (basilica); 8am–6pm (5pm in winter) (tombs of the Popes, treasury, cupula).*	
BASILICA OF SAN PIETRO IN VINCOLI ★ Piazza San Pietro in Vincoli, 4a Tel. 06 488 28 65	*Open 8am–12.30pm, 3–7pm.*	▲ 346 ◆ E C-B3
BASILICA OF SAN SEBASTIANO Via Appia Antica, 136 Tel 06 780 88 47	*Open 8.30am–5pm (6pm in summer).*	▲ 326 ◆ I D4
BASILICA OF SANTA CECILIA IN TRASTEVERE Piazza Santa Cecilia, 22 Tel. 06 589 92 89	*Open 9.30am–12.30pm, 4–6.30pm.*	▲ 353 ◆ E C1
BASILICA OF SANTA CROCE IN GERUSALEMME Piazza S. Croce in Gerusalemme Tel. 06 701 47 69	*Open 7am–1pm, 2–7pm.*	▲ 200 ◆ G C2
BASILICA OF SANTA MARIA IN TRAVESTERE ★ Piazza Santa Maria in Trastevere Tel. 06 581 94 43	*Open 7.30am–7.30pm.*	▲ 357 ◆ D C4

◆ PLACES TO VISIT

BASILICA OF S. MARIA MAGGIORE ★ Piazza Santa Maria Maggiore Tel. 06 48 31 95	*Open 7am–7pm.*	▲ 342 ◆ E B4
BASILICA OF SANTI APOSTOLI Piazza Santa Maria Maggiore Tel. 06 679 40 85	*Open 7am–12pm, 4–7pm.*	▲ 300 ◆ F C3
BATHS OF CARACALLA ★ Via delle Terme di Caracalla, 52 Tel. 06 39 96 77 00	*Open 9am until 1 hour before sunset;* *Mon. 9am–2pm.*	▲ 319 ◆ I A1
BATHS OF DIOCLETIAN ★ Viale E. de Nicola, 78 Tel. 06 39 96 77 00	*Open Tue–Sun. 9am–7.45pm. (See National Roman* *Museum).*	▲ 334 ◆ E A4
BATHS OF TRAJAN Parco del Colle Oppio	*Information: Tel. 06 06 06 (ChiamaRoma).*	▲ 174 ◆ E B2
BERNICH AQUARIUM Piazza Manfredo Fanti, 47 Tel. 06 97 60 45 98	*Houses the House of Architecture. Opening times* *may vary according to exhibitions* *www.casadellarchitettura.it*	▲ 339 ◆ G B1
BIBLICUM **(INSTITUTE OF BIBLICAL STUDIES)** Piazza della Pilotta, 35 Tel. 06 69 52 61	*Guided tours on request (Fax 06 695 26 61 51).* *(Groups only.)*	▲ 299 ◆ F C3
BONCOMPAGNI LUDOVISI MUSEUM **(MUSEO DELLE ARTI DECORATIVE)** Via Boncompagni, 18 Tel. 06 42 82 40 74	*Open 9.30am–7pm.* *Closed Mon.* *Group visits on request.*	◆ B D3–4
BOTANICAL GARDENS **(ORTO BOTANICO)** Largo Cristina di Svezia, 24 Tel. 06 49 91 71 07	*Open Tue.–Sat. 9.30am–5.30pm in winter;* *9.30am–6.30pm in summer.* *Closed Sun.–Mon. and public holidays.*	● 363 ◆ E A2
BRITISH PAVILION Via Gramsci, 61	*British Academy of Rome.* *Visit on request (Tel. 06 326 49 39).*	▲ 376 ◆ B C2
CALCOGRAFIA NAZIONALE Via della Stamperia, 6 Tel. 06 69 98 01	*Visit on request (groups only).*	▲ 299 ◆ F B3
CAPITOL (CAMPIDOGLIO) ★ Piazza del Campidoglio Tel. 06 6 71 01		▲ 128 ◆ E B-C2
CAPITOLINE MUSEUMS ★ **– CENTRALE MONTEMARTINI** Via Ostiense, 106 Tel. 06 574 80 30	*Open Tue.–Sun. 9am–7.45pm.* *Reservation: Tel. 06 82 05 91 27.*	▲ 132, 183 ◆ H A3
– PIAZZA DEL CAMPIDOGLIO, 1 Tel. 06 67 10 24 75	*Open Tue.–Sun 9am–7.45pm.* *Reservations: Tel. 06 82 05 91 27.*	▲ 130 ◆ E B-C2
CASA DEI CRESCENZI Via del Teatro Marcello, 54	*Not open to the public.*	● 72 ◆ E C2
CASA DEI MUTILATI Piazza Adriana, 3	*Group visits only, by appointment (tel. 06 687 53 52).*	▲ 236 ◆ A C2
CASINA DELLE CIVETTE Via Nomentana, 70 Tel. 06 82 05 91 27	*Museum of stained glass. In the Villa Torlonia.* *Open 9am–5pm in winter; 9am–7pm in summer.* *Closed Mon.*	◆ C C2
CASINA ROSSA Piazza di Spagna, 26 Tel. 06 678 42 35	*Keats-Shelley Museum.*	▲ 313 ◆ E A2
CASINA VALADIER Piazza Bucarest Pincio Villa Borghese	*Open 12.30–3pm, 8–11pm.* *Closed Sun. evening and Mon.*	▲ 316 ◆ B C2–3
CASTEL SANT'ANGELO ★ Lungotevere Castello, 50 Tel. 06 681 91 11	*Open 9am–6.30pm.* *Closed on Mon.*	▲ 233 ◆ D A4
CASTRO PRETORIO Viale Castro Pretorio, 105 Tel. 06 498 92 49	*Houses the Biblioteca Vittorio Emanuele II.* *Open Mon.–Fri. 8.30am–7pm; Sat. 8.30am–1.30pm.* *Closed Sun.*	▲ 335 ◆ G A1
CATACOMBS OF SAN CALLISTO Via Appia, 110 Tel. 06 51 30 15 80	*Open 8.30am–noon, 2.30–5pm (5.30 in summer).* *Closed Wed. and in Feb.*	▲ 326 ◆ I D3

CATACOMBS OF SAN SEBASTIANO Via Appia Antica, 136 Tel. 06 785 03 50	*Open 9am–noon, 2–5pm.* *Closed Sun. and Nov. 10–Dec. 10.*	▲ 326 ◆ I D4
CHAPEL OF SAN TOMMASO DEI CENCI Via Monte dei Cenci, 14 Tel. 06 68 30 00 55	*Visits on request.*	▲ 254 ◆ E C1
CHURCH DEI MADONNA DELL'ORTO Via S. Maria dei Calderari, 29 Tel. 06 5 88 32 50	*Open Sun. 9am–noon.*	▲ 354 ◆ E C1
CHURCH OF GESÙ E MARIA Via del Corso, 45 Tel. 06 361 37 17	*Open 8am–12.30pm, 4–7.45pm.*	▲ 309 ◆ E A-B2
CHURCH OF NOSTRA SIGNORA **DEL SACRO CUORE ADDOLORATA** Piazza Navona Tel. 06 684 03 11	*Open Mon.–Sat. 7am–noon, 5–8pm.* *Sun. 9am–1.30pm, 5.30–8pm.* *Closed in Aug.*	▲ 278 ◆ F C1
CHURCH OF SAN BARTOLOMEO Isola Tiberina, 22 Tel. 06 687 79 73	*Open Mon.–Sat. 9am–12.30pm, 3.30–6pm;* *Sun. 10am–1pm.* *Closed in Aug.*	▲ 352 ◆ E C1
CHURCH OF S. BERNARDO ALLE TERME Piazza San Bernardo Tel. 06 4 88 21 22	*Open 6am–12.30pm, 4–7pm;* *Sun. and public holidays 9am–12.30pm, 4–7pm.*	▲ 295 ◆ E A3
CHURCH OF S. BIAGIO DELLA PAGNOTTA Via Giulia, 63 Tel. 06 68 80 48 91	*Open 4.30–9.15pm.*	▲ 274 ◆ D B1
CHURCH OF SAN BONAVENTURA Via San Bonaventura, 7 Tel. 06 678 03 31	*Open 8am–8pm.*	▲ 151 ◆ E C2-3
CHURCH OF SAN CARLO ALCATINARI Piazza Benedetto Cairoli, 117 Tel. 06 68 30 70 70	*Open 7.30am–noon, 4–7pm.*	▲ 247 ◆ F CD1
CHURCH OF SAN CARLO **ALLE QUATRO FONTANE** Via del Quirinale, 23 Tel. 06 488 32 61	*Open Mon.–Sat. 10am–1pm, Sun. 10.30–11am;* *3–7pm in winter.*	▲ 295 ◆ E A3
CHURCH OF SAN CESAREO Via di Porta San Sebastiano, 4 Tel. 06 58 23 01 40	*Visit on request.*	▲ 322 ◆ I A2
CHURCH OF SAN CLAUDIO **DE' BORGOGNONI** Via del Pozzetto, 160 Tel. 06 679 03 10	*Open Mon.–Sat. 7am–1pm, 2–7.45pm;* *7.30–11am, 4.30–7.15pm (July–Aug.);* *Sun. and public hols. 9.30am–12.30pm, 4–7.45pm;* *10.30am–12.30pm, 4.30–7.15pm (July–Aug.)*	▲ 302 ◆ F B3
CHURCH OF SAN CRISOGONO Piazza Sonnino, 44 Tel. 06 581 82 25	*Open Mon.–Sat. 7–11.30am, 4–7.30pm;* *Sun. 8am– 1.15pm, 4–7.30pm.* *Early Christian basilica: Mon.–Sat. 8–11am,* *4.30–7pm; Sun. 9am–1pm, 4.30–7pm.*	▲ 356 ◆ E C1
CHURCH OF SAN FRANCESCO A RIPA Piazza S. Francesco d'Assisi, 88 Tel. 06 581 90 20	*Open 7.30am–noon, 4–7.30pm.*	▲ 354 ◆ E D1
CHURCH OF SAN GIACOMO Via del Corso, 499 Tel. 06 321 94 19	*Open 8am–noon, 4.30–7.15pm.*	▲ 309 ◆ E A-B2
CHURCH OF SAN GIACOMO **DEGLI SPAGNOLI** Via della Lungara, 141 Tel. 06 686 90 17	*Visits on request.*	▲ 275 ◆ D B-C4
CHURCH OF SAN GIORGIO AL VELABRO Via del Velabro, 19 Tel. 06 69 20 45 34	*Open 10am–12.30pm, 4–6.30pm.*	▲ 156 ◆ E C2
CHURCH OF S. GIOVANNI **A PORTA LATINA** Via di Porta Latina, 17 Tel. 06 70 49 17 77	*Open 7am–12.30pm, 3–6.30pm.*	▲ 323 ◆ I A2
CHURCH OF SAN GIOVANNI CALIBITA Isola Tiberina, 39 Tel. 06 683 73 42	*Ospedale Fatebenefratelli. Open Sun. 10am–noon;* *Mon.–Sat. visits on request (tel. 06 683 73 10).*	▲ 353 ◆ E C1
CHURCH OF S. GIOVANNI DEI FIORENTINI Piazza dell'Oro, 1 Tel. 06 68 89 20 59	*Open 7am–1pm, 4–7pm; 7–9am in Aug.,* *Mon.–Fri. 5–7pm.*	▲ 241 ◆ E B1 F A1

◆ PLACES TO VISIT

The ★ symbol refers to places that deserve to be seen first if time is short.

CHURCH OF S. GIOVANNI DEI GENOVESI Via Anicia, 12 Tel. 06 581 24 16	*Sun. 8.30–11am. Closed in Aug.* *Cloister: Tue., Thu. 2–4pm in winter;* *3–6pm in summer.*	▲ 353 ◆ E C1
CHURCH OF S. GIROLAMO DELLA CARITÀ Via di Monserrato, 62/a Tel. 06 687 97 86	*Sun. 10.30am–11.30am.* *Mon.–Sat. visits on request.*	▲ 243 ◆ F D1
CHURCH OF S. GIUSEPPE DEI FALEGNAMI Clivio Argentario, 1 Tel. 06 679 29 02	*Fri. 4–7pm; Sat.–Sun. 10am–7pm.*	▲ 131 ◆ E C2
CHURCH OF SAN GREGORIO MAGNO Piazza San Gregorio al Celio, 1 Tel. 06 700 82 27	*Open 8.30am–12.30pm, 3–6.30pm.*	▲ 187 ◆ E D3
CHURCH OF SAN LORENZO IN DAMASO Piazza della Cancelleria, 1 Tel. 06 69 88 75 21	*Open 7.30am–noon, 4.30–8pm.*	▲ 249 ◆ E B1
CHURCH OF SAN LORENZO IN LUCINA Piazza San Lorenzo, 4 Tel. 06 6 87 14 94	*Open 8am–8pm.*	▲ 312 ◆ E A2 F B2
CHURCH OF SAN LORENZO IN MIRANDA Temple of Antonin and Faustine Roman Forum, Via in Miranda Tel. 06 6 79 21 23	*Open Thu. 10am–noon.*	▲ 145 ◆ E C2-
CHURCH OF SAN LORENZO **IN PANISPERNA** Via Panisperna, 90 Tel. 06 48 36 67	*Open Sat. 4.45–5.45pm; Sun. and public holidays* *9.45–10.45am, 4.45–5.45pm.* *Closed from Aug. 11 until the first Sat. in Sep.*	▲ 347 ◆ E B3
CHURCH OF SAN LUIGI DEI FRANCESI ★ Piazza San Luigi dei Francesi Tel. 06 68 82 71	*Open 8am–noon, 3.30–7pm.* *Closed Thu. afternoon.*	▲ 270- ◆ F C1
CHURCH OF SAN MARCELLO AL CORSO Piazza di San Marcello, 5 Tel. 06 69 93 01	*Open Mon.–Sat. 7.30am–noon; 4–7pm;* *Sun. and public hols. 9am–noon, 4–7pm.*	▲ 301 ◆ F C3
CHURCH OF SAN NICOLA DA BARI Via Passeroni, 1 Tel. 06 568 36 07	*Open 7.30am–8pm;* *Sun. 7.30am–1.30pm, 4–8pm.*	▲ 330 ◆ E B-C
CHURCH OF SAN NICOLA IN CARCERE Via del Teatro Marcello, 46 Tel. 06 68 30 71 98	*Open 10.30am–7pm.*	▲ 156 ◆ E C1
CHURCH OF SAN PANTALEO Piazza San Pantaleo Tel. 06 684 07 41	*Open 9am–noon, 4–7pm.* *Closed in Aug.*	▲ 279 ◆ A A1
CHURCH OF SAN PAOLO ALLA REGOLA Via San Paolo alla Regola, 6 Tel. 06 68 80 24 08	*Closed for restoration.*	▲ 247 ◆ E B1
CHURCH OF SANTI PIETRO E PAOLO Piazzale San Pietro e Paolo, 8 Tel. 06 592 61 66	*Open 7am–noon (12.30pm Sun), 3.30–7pm.*	● 92 ▲ 388
CHURCH OF SAN PIETRO IN MONTORIO Piazza S. Pietro in Montorio, 2 Tel. 06 581 39 40	*Open 8.30am–noon, 3.30–5pm.*	▲ 364 ◆ D C4
CHURCH OF SAN SABA Piazza Bernini, 20 Tel. 06 574 33 52	*Open 8.30am–noon, 4–7.15pm.* *Closed Sun.*	▲ 182 ◆ H A4
CHURCH OF SAN SALVATORE IN LAURO Piazza S. Salvatore in Lauro, 15 Tel. 06 687 51 87	*Open 8.30am–noon, 4–6pm.*	▲ 283 ◆ D A4
CHURCH OF SAN SEBASTIANO **AL PALATINO** Via San Bonaventura, 1 Tel. 06 678 42 36	*Open 9am–noon, 3–6pm.* *Closed Sat.–Sun.*	▲ 151 ◆ E C2-
CHURCH OF SAN SILVESTRO Via 24 Maggio, 10 Tel. 06 679 02 40	*Open Sun. and on feast days 10.30am–noon.*	▲ 298 ◆ F D4
CHURCH OF SAN SILVESTRO IN CAPITE Piazza San Silvestro, 8 Tel. 06 697 71 21	*Open 7am–7pm;* *Sun. and public holidays 9am–5.30pm.*	▲ 302 ◆ F B3
CHURCH OF SAN SISTO VECCHIO Piazzale Numa Pompilio, 8 Tel. 06 77 20 51 74	*Open 9am–11am, 3.30–5.30pm.* *Closed Aug. 1–Sep. 15.*	▲ 321 ◆ E D3-

The symbol ▲ refers to the Itineraries section. The symbol ◆ refers to the Map section.

CHURCH OF SAN TEODORO Via di San Teodoro, 7 Tel. 06 678 66 24	Open 9.30am–12.30pm.	▲ *142* ◆ E C2
CHURCH OF SANT'AGNESE IN AGONE Piazza Navona, 2 Tel. 06 68 19 21 34	Open 9.30am–12.30pm, 4–7pm. Closed Mon.	▲ *278* ◆ F C1
CHURCH OF SANT'AGOSTINO ★ Piazza Sant'Agostino Tel. 06 68 80 19 62	Open 8am–noon, 4–7.30pm.	▲ *284* ◆ F B1
CHURCH OF SANT'ANDREA **AL QUIRINALE** Via del Quirinale, 29 Tel. 06 474 48 72	Open 8.30am–noon, 3.30–7pm.	▲ *296* ◆ E B3
CHURCH OF SANT'ANDREA **DELLA VALLE** Piazza Vidoni, 6 Tel. 06 686 13 39	Open 7.30am–12.30pm, 4.30–7.30pm.	▲ *250* ◆ E B1
CHURCH OF SANT'ANDREA **DELLE FRATTE** Via di Sant'Andrea delle Fratte, 1 Tel. 06 679 31 91	Open 6.30am–12.15pm, 4.30–7.45pm.	▲ *313* ◆ F B3
CHURCH OF SANT'ANGELO **IN PESCHERIA** Via Tribuna di Campitelli, 6 Tel. 06 68 80 18 19	Closed for works.	▲ *159* ◆ E B-C2
CHURCH OF SANT'ANSELMO **ALL'AVENTINO** Piazza Cavalieri di Malta, 5 Tel. 06 579 11	Open 8am–8pm.	▲ *182* ◆ E D1
CHURCH OF SANT' ANTONIO **DEI PORTOGHESI** Via dei Portoghesi, 2 Tel. 06 68 80 24 96	Open 8.30am–1pm, 3–6pm.	▲ *284* ◆ F B1
CHURCH OF SANT'APOLLINARE Piazza Sant'Apollinare Tel. 06 687 52 11	Open 7–10am.	▲ *285* ◆ F B1
CHURCH OF SANT'EGIDIO Piazza di Sant'Egidio, 3a Tel. 06 58 56 61	Headquarters of the order of Sant'Egidio. Not open to the public.	▲ *359* ◆ E C1
CHURCH OF SANT'ELIGIO DEGLI OREFICI Via Sant'Eligio degli Orefici, 8/A Tel. 06 686 82 60	Open Mon.–Fri. 10–11am.	▲ *243* ◆ E B1
CHURCH OF SANT'EUSTACHIO **IN CAMPO MARZIO** Via di Sant'Eustachio, 19 Tel. 06 686 53 34	Open 7–8pm in winter; noon–1pm, 7–8pm in summer.	◆ F C1
CHURCH OF SANT'IGNAZIO Piazza Sant'Ignazio Tel. 06 679 44 06	Open 7.30am–12.15pm, 3–7.15pm.	▲ *261* ◆ F C2
CHURCH OF SANT'IVO ALLA SAPIENZA Corso Rinascimento, 40 Tel. 06 686 49 87	Open Sun. 9am–noon.	▲ *272* ◆ F C1
CHURCH OF SANT'IVO DEI BRETONI Vicolo della Campana, 8 Tel. 06 68 80 38 15	Open 9am–noon, 4–7pm.	◆ E A1
CHURCH OF SANT'OMOBONO Vico Jugario	Visit by permission of the Corporation of Rome (Tel. 06 06 06 ChiamaRoma).	▲ *156* ◆ E C2
CHURCH OF SANT'ONOFRIO Piazza Sant'Onofrio, 7 Tel. 06 686 44 98	Visits on request.	▲ *365* ◆ D B-C3
CHURCH OF SANTA BIBIANA Via Giovanni Giolitti, 154 Tel. 06 446 10 21	Open 8.30–10am, 5.30–6.30pm.	▲ *339* ◆ G B2
CHURCH OF S. CATERINA DEI FUNARI Via dei Funari, 9 Tel. 06 69 88 64 41	Open Mon. 10am–noon; Thu. 2–4pm.	▲ *254* ◆ E C2
CHURCH OF SANTA DOROTEA E **SAN GIOVANNI DELLA MALVA** Via di Santa Dorotea, 23 Tel. 06 580 62 05	Open 7.30–noon, 4–7.30pm.	▲ *363* ◆ D C4

◆ PLACES TO VISIT

CHURCH OF S. FRANCESCA ROMANA Piazza S. Francesca Romana, 4 Tel. 06 679 55 28	*Open 10am–noon, 3–5.30pm.* *Closed on Wed.*	▲ *169* ◆ E C3
CHURCH OF SANTA MARIA ANTIQUA	*See Forum. Information: Soprintendenza* *archeologica: Tel. 06 699 01 10.*	▲ *142,* *334* ◆ E A4
CHURCH OF SANTA MARIA **DEGLI ANGELI E DEI MARTIRI** Piazza della Repubblica Tel. 06 488 08 12	*Open 7am–6.30pm (7.30pm on Sun.).*	
CHURCH OF S. MARIA DEI MIRACOLI Piazza del Popolo Tel. 06 361 02 50	*Open 7am–1pm (8am on Sun.), 2–7.30pm.*	▲ *307* ◆ E A-B2
CHURCH OF S. MARIA **DEI SETTE DOLORI** Via Garibaldi, 27	*Not open to the public.*	▲ *364* ◆ D C4
CHURCH OF S. MARIA DEL POPOLO ★ Piazza del Popolo, 12 Tel. 06 361 08 36	*Open Mon.–Sat. 7am–noon, 4–7pm;* *Sun. 8am–1.20pm, 4.30–7.30pm. On public* *holidays, visits are not permitted during services.*	▲ *306* ◆ B D1
CHURCH OF S. MARIA DEL PRIORATO Piazza dei Cavalieri di Malta, 4	*Visit on request (Tel. 06 67 58 12 34).*	▲ *180* ◆ E D2
CHURCH OF SANTA MARIA DELL'ANIMA Via Santa Maria dell'Anima, 66 Tel. 06 686 41 60	*Open 8am–1pm, 4–6pm.*	▲ *280* ◆ F C1
CHURCH OF S. MARIA **DELLA CONCEZIONE** Via Veneto, 27 Tel. 06 487 11 85	*Open 7am–noon, 3–7pm.*	▲ *290* ◆ F A4
CHURCH OF S. MARIA DELLA PACE ★ Piazza della Pace, 5 Tel. 06 686 11 56	*Open Mon.–Sat. 10am–noon, 4–6pm;* *Sun. 9–11am.*	▲ *280* ◆ F C1
CHURCH OF S. MARIA DELLA SCALA Piazza della Scala, 23 Tel. 06 580 62 33	*Open Mon.–Sat. 9am–noon, 3.30–5.30pm;* *Closed Sun. in summer.*	▲ *359* ◆ E B1
CHURCH OF S. MARIA DELLA VITTORIA Via XX Settembre, 17 Tel. 06 42 74 05 71	*Open Mon.–Sat. 7am–noon, 3–6.30pm;* *Sun. 8am–1pm, 3–6.30pm.*	▲ *294* ◆ E A3
CHURCH OF SANTA MARIA DI LORETO **AL FORO TRAIANO** Piazza Madonna di Loreto, 26 Tel. 06 679 22 35	*Open 4–6pm; weekend 10am–1pm, 4–6.30pm.*	▲ *167* ◆ F D3
CHURCH OF S. MARIA DI MONSERRATO Via Giulia, 151 Tel. 06 688 96 51	*Open 10am–1pm.* *Closed in Aug.*	▲ *243* ◆ D B4
CHURCH OF S. MARIA DI MONTESANTO Via del Babuino, 197 Tel. 06 361 05 94	*Open Mon.–Sat. 4–7pm; Sun. 11am–1pm.* *Closed in Aug.*	▲ *307* ◆ B D1
CHURCH OF SANTA MARIA **IN ARACOELI ★** Piazza del Campidoglio, 4 Tel. 06 679 81 55	*Open 9am–12.30pm, 3–6.30pm;* *4.30–5.30pm in winter.*	▲ *130* ◆ E B2
CHURCH OF S. MARIA IN CAMPITELLI Piazza Campitelli, 9 Tel. 06 68 80 39 78	*Open 7am–12.30pm, 3–7.30pm.*	▲ *159* ◆ E B-C2
CHURCH OF SANTA MARIA IN CAPELLA Via di S. Maria in Cappella, 6	*Closed.*	▲ *353* ◆ E C2
CHURCH OF SANTA MARIA **IN COSMEDIN** Piazza Bocca della Verità, 18 Tel. 06 678 14 19	*Open 10am–5pm.*	▲ *154* ◆ E C2
CHURCH OF S. MARIA IN DOMINICA Via della Navicella, 10 Tel. 06 77 20 26 85	*Open 9am–noon, 3–7pm.*	▲ *190* ◆ E D3
CHURCH OF S. MARIA IN TRASPONTINA Via della Conciliazione, 14 Tel. 06 68 80 64 51	*Open 7am–noon, 4.30–7pm.*	▲ *232* ◆ D A3
CHURCH OF S. MARIA IN VALLICELLA Via del Governo Vecchio, 134 Tel. 06 687 52 89	*Open 8am–noon, 4.30–6.30pm.*	▲ *281* ◆ D B4

CHURCH OF SANTA MARIA IN VIA Largo Chigi Tel. 06 697 67 41	*Open 7.30am–12.30pm, 4–7.45pm;* *Sun. 8.30–10am*	▲ *301* ◆ F B3
CHURCH OF SANTA MARIA IN VIA LATA Via del Corso, 306 Tel. 06 679 61 90	*Open 9.30–11.30am, 5–11pm.*	▲ *260* ◆ F C3
CHURCH OF SANTA MARIA LIBERATRICE Piazza Santa Maria Liberatrice Tel. 06 575 02 94	*Open 6.30am–noon, 4.30–8pm;* *4–7pm in winter.*	▲ *184* ◆ H A3
CHURCH OF S. MARIA MADDALENA Piazza della Maddalena, 53 Tel. 06 89 92 81	*Open 7.45am–noon, 4.45–8pm.*	▲ *270* ◆ F C2
CHURCH OF S. MARIA SOPRA MINERVA Via Beato Angelico, 35 Tel. 06 679 39 26	*Open Mon.–Sat. 7am–7pm;* *Sun. 7am–noon, 3.–7pm.*	▲ *260* ◆ F C2
CHURCH OF SANTA PRASSEDE ★ Via Santa Prassede, 9/a Tel. 06 488 24 56	*Open 7.15am–noon, 4–6pm; 4–6pm in Aug.*	▲ *344* ◆ E B4
CHURCH OF SANTA PRISCA Via di Santa Prisca, 11 Tel. 06 574 37 98	*Open 7am–noon, 4.30–6.30pm.*	▲ *181* ◆ E D2
CHURCH OF SANTA PUDENZIANA AL VIMINALE Via Urbana, 160 Tel. 06 481 46 22	*Open 8am–noon, 3–6pm.*	▲ *344* ◆ E B4
CHURCH OF SANTA SABINA ALL'AVENTINO Piazza Pietro d'Illiria, 1 Tel. 06 574 35 73	*Open 7am–1pm, 3.30–6pm.*	▲ *179* ◆ E D2
CHURCH OF SANTA SUSANNA Via XX Settembre, 14 Tel. 06 42 01 45 54	*Open 9am–noon, 4–7pm.*	▲ *294* ◆ E A3
CHURCH OF SANTI AMBROGIO E CARLO AL CORSO Via del Corso, 437 Tel. 06 682 81 01	*Open 7am–7pm.*	▲ *309* ◆ E A2
CHURCH OF SANTI BONIFACIO E ALESSIO Piazza di Sant'Alessio, 23 Tel. 06 574 34 46	*Open 8.30am–12.30pm, 3.30–5pm.*	▲ *180* ◆ E D2
CHURCH OF SANTI COSMA E DAMIANO IN VIA SACRA ★ Via dei Fori Imperiali, 1 Tel. 06 692 04 41	*Open 9am–1pm, 4–7pm.*	▲ *168* ◆ E C3
CHURCH OF SANTI DOMENICO E SISTO Largo Angelicum, 1 Tel. 06 670 21	*Visit on request.*	▲ *347* ◆ F D4
CHURCH OF SANTI GIOVANNI E PAOLO Piazza dei SS. Giovanni e Paolo, 13 Tel. 06 772 71	*Open 8.30am–noon, 3.30–6pm.*	▲ *188* ◆ E C3
CHURCH OF SANTI LUCA E MARTINA Via della Curia, 2 Tel. 06 679 52 05	*See Roman Forum.* *Visits on request.*	▲ *131* ◆ E B–C2
CHURCH OF SANTI NEREO E ACHILLEO ALLE TERME DI CARACALLA Viale delle terme di Caracalla, 28 Tel. 06 575 79 96	*Visits on request (tel. 06 68 75 289).*	▲ *321* ◆ I A2
CHURCH OF SS. VINCENZO E ANASTASIO Vicolo dei Modelli, 73 Tel. 06 678 30 98	*Open 7.30am–noon, 4–7pm.*	▲ *388* ◆ F C3
CHURCH OF THE SANTISSIMO NOME DI MARIA Via del Foro Traiano, 89 Tel. 06 679 80 13	*Open Mon.–Thu. 4–6pm; Sun. 9.30am–1pm,* *4–6pm.*	▲ *167* ◆ F D3
CHURCH OF SANTO STEFANO DEL CACCO Via Santo Stefano del Cacco, 26 Tel. 06 679 38 60	*Visit on request.*	▲ *260* ◆ F D2

◆ PLACES TO VISIT

The ★ symbol refers to places that deserve to be seen first if time is short.

CHURCH OF SANTO STEFANO ROTONDO Via Santo Stefano Rotondo, 7 Tel. 06 70 49 37 17	*Closed for renovation.*	▲ *191* ◆ E D4
CHURCH OF THE ANNUNZIATA Via del Gonfalone, 34 Tel. 06 68 80 24 01	*In course of restoration.*	▲ *233* ◆ E B1
CHURCH OF THE GESÙ ★ Piazza del Gesù Tel. 06 69 70 01	*Open 7am–12.30pm, 4–7.45pm.*	▲ *257* ◆ E B2
CHURCH OF THE SACRED HEART Lungotevere Prati, 12 Tel. 06 68 80 65 17	*Open 7–10am, 6–7.30pm in summer;* *7–11am, 6.30–7.30pm in winter.* *Sun. 8am–3pm, 4.30–8pm.*	▲ *236* ◆ E A1
CHURCH OF THE SANTI **QUATTRO CORONATI** Via dei Santi Quattro Coronati, 20 Tel. 06 70 47 54 27	*Open 6.15am–1pm, 3–8pm; 10.30–11.45am,* *4.30–5.45pm (cloister and chapel).*	▲ *192* ◆ E C4
CHURCH OF THE SPIRITO SANTO **DEI NAPOLETANI** Via Giulia, 34 Tel. 06 69 88 62 17	*Open Sun. 9.30am–1pm.*	▲ *242* ◆ D B4
CHURCH OF THE TRINITÀ **DEI MONTI ★** Piazza della Trinità dei Monti, 3 Tel. 06 679 41 79	*Open 11am–1pm, 3–7pm.*	▲ *314* ◆ F A3
CHURCH OF THE TRINITÀ DEI **PELLEGRINI AI CATINARI** Via dei Pettinari, 36/A Tel. 06 686 84 51	*Visits on request.*	▲ *246* ◆ E B1
CINETECA NAZIONALE Via Tuscolana, 1524 Tel. 06 72 29 41	*Open Mon.–Fri. 9am–4pm.* *Library 9am–4pm. Closed Sat.–Sun.*	
CIRCUS OF MAXENTIUS Via Appia Antica, 153 Tel. 06 780 13 24	*Open 9am–1pm.* *Closed Mon.*	▲ *328* ◆ I C3-D4
CIRCUS MAXIMUS (CIRCO MASSIMO) Via del Circo Massimo	*Open access.*	▲ *177* ◆ E D1-2
COLISEUM (COLOSSEO) ★ Piazza del Colosseo Tel. 06 39 96 77 00	*Open 9am until one hour before sunset.*	▲ *170* ◆ E C3
COLLEGIO ROMANO Piazza del Collegio Romano	*Not open to the public.*	▲ *258* ◆ F C2
CRIMINOLOGY MUSEUM Via del Gonfalone, 29 Tel. 06 68 30 02 34	*Open Wed, Fri.–Sat. 9am–1pm; Tue. and Thu.* *9am–1pm, 2.30–6pm. Closed Sun. and* *public holidays.*	◆ D B4
DOMINE QUO VADIS (CHURCH) Via Appia Antica, 51 Tel. 06 512 04 41	*Open 7am–12.30pm, 2.30–7pm.*	▲ *324* ◆ I C3
DOMUS AUREA ★ Via della Domus Aurea Parco Oppio Tel. 06 399 67 77 00	*Closed for restoration.*	▲ *174* ◆ E C3-4
EPISCOPALIAN CHURCH OF SAN PAOLO **ENTRO LE MURA** Via Napoli, 58 Tel. 06 47 35 69	*Visits by appointment 9am–6pm (last entry).*	▲ *348* ◆ E A3
ETRUSCAN MUSEUM Piazzale di Villa Giulia,9 Tel. 06 322 65 71	*Open Tue.–Sun. 8.30am–7.30pm;* *Closed Jan. 1, May 1 and Dec. 25.* *Reservations: www.ticketeria.it*	▲ *370* ◆ B C2
EXCUBITORIUM Via della VII Corte, 9	*Visits on request: Tel. 06 06 06 (ChiamaRoma).*	▲ *356* ◆ E C1
FARNESINA ★	*See Villa Farnesina.*	
FORO ITALICO Piazzale L. De Bosis	*Open access.*	▲ *377* ◆ A A3

he symbol ▲ refers to the Itineraries section. The symbol ◆ refers to the Map section.

FRENCH ACADEMY Viale Trinità dei Monti, 1 Tel. 06 676 11	*Visits on request or during events.* *Information: www.villamedici.it*	▲ 315 ◆ F A3
GABINETTO NAZIONALE DEI DISEGNI **E DELLE STAMPE** Via della Lungara, 230 Tel. 06 69 98 01	*Open Mon.–Fri. 9am–1pm;* *Tue, Thu 2.30–4.30 by appointment.* *Closed Sat.–Sun.*	▲ 360 ◆ D B4
GALLERIA / MUSEO BORGHESE ★ Piazzale del Museo Borghese, 5 Tel. 06 841 76 45	*Open Tue.–Sun. 9am–7.30pm. Admission every* *two hours. Reservation compulsory (Tel. 06 32 810)* *or www.ticketeria.it. Closed Jan. 1, Dec. 25.*	▲ 372 ◆ B C3
GALLERIA COLONNA Piazza SS. Apostoli, 66 Tel. 06 678 43 50	*Open Sat. 9am–1pm.* *Closed in Aug.*	▲ 300 ◆ E B2
GALLERIA DELL'ACCADEMIA **DI SAN LUCA** Largo Accademia San Luca, 77 Tel. 06 69 92 43 62	*Closed.*	▲ 299 ◆ F B3
GALLERIA DORIA-PAMPHILJ ★ Piazza del Collegio Romano, 2 Tel. 06 679 73 23	*Open 10am–5pm. Closed Thu.*	▲ 258 ◆ F D-C3
GALLERIA NAZIONALE D'ARTE **ANTICA ★** **– PALAZZO BARBERINI** Via Barberini, 18 Tel. 06 481 45 91	*Open 8.30am–7.30pm. Closed Mon., Jan. 1,* *Dec 25. Reservations: Tel. 06 328 10 or* *www.ticketeria.it*	▲ 291-2 ◆ E A3
– PALAZZO CORSINI Via della Lungara, 10 Tel. 06 68 80 23 23	*Visits Tue.–Fri. at 9.30am, 11am and 12.30pm;* *Sat.–Sun. 8.30am–1.30pm.* *Closed Mon., dec. 25, Jan. 1.* *Reservations (tel. 06 328 10 or www.ticketeria.it).*	▲ 362 ◆ D B-C3
GALLERIA COMUNALE D'ARTE **MODERNA E CONTEMPORANEA** **– CARMELITE CONVENT OF** **SAN GIUSEPPE A CAPO LE CASE** Via Francesco Crispi, 24 Tel. 06 474 28 48	*Closed for building works.*	▲ 376 ◆ F A-B4
GALLERIA NAZIONALE D'ARTE MODERNA Viale delle Belle Arti, 131 Tel. 06 32 29 81	*Open Tue.–Sun. 8.30am–6.40pm.* *Reservations: Tel. 06 32 29 82 21.*	▲ 376 ◆ B C2
GALLERIA SPADA Piazza Capo di Ferro, 13 Tel. 06 687 48 93	*Open Tue.–Sat. 8.30am–7.30pm.* *Closed Jan. 1, Dec. 25.* *Reservations: Tel. 06 683 24 09 or www.ticketeria.it*	▲ 246 ◆ E B1
GALLERIA SCIARRA Via dell'Umiltà		▲ 301 ◆ F C3
GEOLOGICAL MUSEUM Largo di Santa Susanna,13 Tel. 06 49 91 48 25	*Open Tue.–Thu. 10am–1pm, 2–4pm.*	▲ 302 ◆ E A3
GREGORIANA (PONTIFICIA **UNIVERSITÀ GREGORIANA)** Piazza della Pilotta, 4 Tel. 06 670 11	*Visit by arrangement* *Library: open Mon.–Fri. 8.30am–6.30pm;* *Sat. 8.30am–12.30pm. Closed Sun.*	▲ 299 ◆ E A2-3
HANS CHRISTIAN ANDERSEN MUSEUM Via Pasquale S. Mancini, 20 Tel. 06 321 90 89	*Open 9am–7pm. Closed Mon.*	▲ 369 ◆ B C1
HOSTARIA DELL'ORSO Via dell'Orsp, 25	*Not open to the public.*	▲ 284 ◆ F B1
HOTEL QUIRINALE Via Nazionale, 7 Tel. 06 47 07		▲ 348 ◆ E A3
HOTEL INGHILTERRA Via Bocca di Leone, 14 Tel. 06 699 81		▲ 305 ◆ F A2-3
HOTEL PLAZA Via del Corso, 126 Tel. 06 69 92 11 11	*Visits by appointment.*	▲ 309 ◆ E A-B2
HOUSE OF THE KNIGHTS OF RHODES Piazza del Grillo, 1 Tel. 06 678 15 18	*Open 9.30am–1pm, 3.30–6pm. Closed Tue.–Wed.* *Guided tours with archeologist Sat.–Sun.* *Information and reservations: Spazio Libero* *Cooperative, Tel. 06 70 45 45 44.*	▲ 168 ◆ F D4

◆ PLACES TO VISIT

HOUSE OF ST JOHN AND ST PAUL Piazzale Santi Giovanni e Paolo, 13 Tel. 06 77 27 11	*Not open to the public.*	▲ *188* ◆ E C-D3
HOUSE OF GIACOMO DI BARTOLOMEO DA BRESCIA Via Rusticucci, 14	*Open Mon.–Fri. 9am–1pm, 3–6pm;* *Sat. 11am–2pm, 3–6pm. Closed Sun.*	▲ *233* ◆ D A3
KEATS–SHELLEY MEMORIAL HOUSE Piazza di Spagna, 26 Tel. 06 678 42 35	*Open 7am–7pm.*	▲ *313* ◆ E A2
LATERAN BASILICA Piazza S. Giovanni in Laterano, 4 Tel. 06 69 88 64 33	*Headquarters of the Vicariate of Rome* *(Tel. 06 69 38 61 78).* *Open Sat., first Sun. in the month 9am–12.30pm.*	▲ *198* ◆ G D1
LATERAN PALACE Piazza San Giovanni in Laterano	*Open Sun. 8.30am–12.30pm.*	▲ *196* ◆ G D1
MACRO **(MUSEO D'ARTE CONTEMPORANEA)** Tel. 06 67 10 79 00		
– OLD PERONI BREWERY Via Reggio Emilia, 54	*Open Tue.–Sun. and public hols. 9am–6.30pm.*	▲ *381* ◆ C C-D1
– MATTATOIO (OLD SLAUGHTERHOUSES) Piazza Orazio Giustiniani, 4	*Open Tue.–Sun. and public holidays* *4pm–midnight.*	▲ *184* ◆ H A2-3
MAUSOLEUM OF AUGUSTUS ★ Piazza Augusto Imperatore	*Open Sat.–Sun. 10am–1pm.*	▲ *309* ◆ E A1
MAUSOLEUM OF CECILIA METELLA Via Appia Antica, 161 Tel. 06 39 96 77 00	*Reservations: Tel. 06 39 96 77 00.* *Open 9am until one hour before sunset.*	▲ *330* ◆ I D4
MAUSOLEUM OF ROMULUS Via Appia Antica, 153 Tel. 06 780 13 24	*Circus of Maxentius and Mausoleum of Romulus.* *Closed for works.*	▲ *329* ◆ I D4
MEDIEVAL HOUSE IN TRASTEVERE Vicolo dell'Atleta, 14	*Not open to the public.*	● *73* ◆ E C1
MEMMO FOUNDATION Ruspoli Palace, Via del Corso, 418 Tel. 06 683 21 79	*Opening hours may vary according to exhibitions.*	▲ *312* ◆ E A-B2
MINISTRY OF INDUSTRY AND TRADE Via Molise, 2 Tel. 06 47 88 79 28	*Visit by permission: Tel. 06 47 88 79 43* *(ufficio stampa).*	▲ *302* ◆ E A2
MINISTRY OF MAIL Palazzo Malvezzi Piazza San Silvestro Tel. 06 679 84 95	*Headquarters of the mail service.*	◆ E A3
MONASTERY OF SAN COSIMATO Piazza San Cosimato	*To arrange a visit, contact the hospital* *management (Tel. 06 584 41).*	▲ *356* ◆ D C4
MONASTERY OF SAN GREGORIO Piazza Certaldo, 85 Tel. 06 55 26 16 17	*Open 9.30am–12.30pm, 2.30–6.30pm.*	▲ *187* ◆ E D3
MONASTERY OF SANT'ONOFRIO Piazza Sant'Onofrio, 2 Tel. 06 686 44 98	*Visit on request.*	▲ *365* ◆ D B3
MONTE DE PIETA Piazza del Monte di Pietà, 33	*Headquarters of the Bank of Rome:* *Tel. 06 54451 or 06 67078488 (archives).*	▲ *247* ◆ E B1
MONTE MARIO ASTRONOMICAL AND METEOROLOGICAL OBSERVATORY Viale Parco Mellini, 84 Tel. 35 34 70 56	*Maximum of ten people, by appointment.* *Duration of the visit: one hour.*	▲ *377* ◆ A B2
MUSEO CANONICA Viale P. Canonica, 2 Tel. 06 884 22 79	*Open Tue.–Sun. 9am–7pm.* *Closed Jan. 1, May 1, Dec. 25.*	◆ B C2-3
MUSEO CASA DI DANTE Palazzo Anguillara Piazza Sydney Sonnino, 5 Tel. 06 581 20 19	*Library: Mon., Wed., Fri. 4–6pm.*	▲ *357* ◆ E C1

MUSEO CENTRALE DEL RISORGIMENTO Palazzo del Vittoriano Via San Pietro in Carcere Tel. 06 679 35 98	*Open daily 9.30am–6pm.*	▲ *161* ◆ E B2
MUSEO CIVICO DI ZOOLOGIA Via Aldrovandi, 18 Tel. 67 10 92 70	*Open Tue.–Sun. 9am–5pm.*	▲ *369* ◆ B C3
MUSEO DELL'ALTO MEDIOEVO Via Lincoln, 3 Tel. 06 54 22 81 99	*Open Tue.–Sun. 9am–7.30pm.*	▲ *387*
MUSEO DELLA CIVILTÀ ROMANA Piazza G. Agnelli, 10 Tel. 06 592 60 41	*Open Tue.–Sat. 9am–2pm; Sun. 9am–1.30pm.*	▲ *388*
MUSEO DELLA VIA OSTIENSE Piazza di Porta San Paolo, 3 Tel. 06 574 31 93	*Open Wed., Fri., Sat. 9am–1.30pm; Tue., Thu 9am–1.30pm, 2.30–4.30pm; first and second Sun. of the month 9am–1.30pm. Closed Mon.*	▲ *183*
MUSEO DELLE BANDIERE Via dei Fori Imperiali	*Inside the Victor Emmanuel II Monument.* *Open 9.30am–3pm. Closed Mon.* *Tel. 06 47 35 50 02.*	▲ *161* ◆ E B2
MUSEO DELLE CERE Piazza Santi Apostoli, 67 Tel. 06 679 64 82	*Open 9am–8pm.*	◆ F C3
MUSEO DELLE MURA Via di Porta San Sebastiano, 18 Tel. 06 70 47 52 84	*Open Tue.–Sun 9am–2pm.*	◆ I A2
MUSEO DEI CALCHI E DEI GESSI (MUSEO DELL'ARTE CLASSICA) Piazzale Aldo Moro, 5 Tel. 06 49 91 39 60	*University of Rome La Sapienza, Faculty of Literature and Philosophy, Institute of Archeology.* *Open Sun.–Fri. 9.30am–5pm.*	◆ G A2
MUSEO DI GOETHE Via del Corso, 18 Tel. 06 32 65 04 12	*Open 10am–6pm.* *Closed Tue.*	▲ *309* ◆ B D2
MUSEO DI ROMA Palazzo Braschi Piazza San Pantaleo, 10 Tel. 06 67 10 83 46	*Open 10am–6pm. Closed Mon.*	▲ *279* ◆ F C1
MUSEO DI ROMA IN TRASTEVERE (FORMERLY: MUSEO DEL FOLKLORE) Piazza Sant'Egidio, 1b Tel. 06 581 65 63	*Open 10am–7pm. Closed Mon.*	▲ *359* ◆ D C4
MUSEO MARIO PRAZ Via Zanardelli, 1 Tel. 06 686 10 89	*Open Tue.–Sat. 9am–1pm, 2.30–6.30pm.* *Admission every hour. Reservation advised.*	▲ *284* ◆ F B1
MUSEO NAPOLEONICO Piazza di Ponte Umberto I, 1 Tel. 06 68 80 62 86	*Open Tue.–Sun. 9am–7pm;* *Closed Jan. 1, May 1 and Dec. 25.*	▲ *284* ◆ F B1
MUSEO NAZIONALE D'ARTE ORIENTALE Palazzo Brancaccio Via Merulana, 248 Tel. 06 487 44 15	*Open Mon., Wed., Fri. 8.30am–2pm; Tue., Thu., Sun. and public holidays 8.30am– 7.30pm.* *Closed 1st and 3rd Mon. in the month.*	◆ E B-C4
MUSEO NAZIONALE DI CASTEL SANT'ANGELO ★ Lungotevere Castello, 50 Tel. 06 681 91 11	*Open 9am–6.30pm. Closed Mon.*	▲ *233* ◆ D A4
MUSEO NAZIONALE DELLE ARTE E TRADIZIONI POPOLARI Piazza Marconi, 8–10 Tel. 06 592 61 48	*Open Tue.–Sun. 9am–2pm.*	▲ *387*
MUSEO NAZIONALE ROMANO	*See under National Roman Museums*	
MUSEO NUMISMATICO DELLA ZECCA ITALIANA Via XX Settembre, 97 Tel. 06 47 61 33 17	*Ministry of Finance (Treasury).* *Open Tue.–Sat. 9am–12.30pm. Closed public hols and in Aug.*	▲ *333* ◆ E A4
MUSEO PORTA SAN PAOLO Via Raffaele Persichetti, 3 Tel. 06 574 31 93	*Open Mon., Wed., Fri. 9am–1.30pm, 2.30–4.30pm; Tue. and Thu. 2.30–4.30pm.*	▲ *446*

◆ PLACES TO VISIT

The ★ symbol refers to places that deserve to be seen first if time is short.

MUSEO PREISTORICO ED ETNOGRAFICO NAZIONALE L. PIGORINI Piazza Marconi, 14 Tel. 06 54 95 21	*Open Tue.–Fri. 9am–2pm; Sat.–Sun. 9am–8pm. Closed Sun.*	▲ 387
MUSEUM OF MUSICAL INSTRUMENTS Piazza S. Croce in Gerusalemme, 9a Tel. 06 701 47 96	*Open Tue., Thu. 9am–7pm; Wed., Fri., Sat. 9am–2pm; Sun. 9am–1pm.*	◆ G C2
MUSEUM OF SOULS IN PURGATORY Church of the Sacro Cure di Gesù in Prati, Lungotevere Prati, 12 Tel. 06 68 80 65 17	*Open 7.15–10am, 6–7.30pm in summer; 7.15–11am, 4.30–7.30 in winter.*	▲ 236 ◆ E A1
NATIONAL ROMAN MUSEUM ★ Piazza dei Cinquecento, 67	*Reservations: Tel. 06 39 96 77 00 (Mon.–Sat. 9am– 1.30pm, 2.30–5pm).*	▲ 336 ◆ E A4
– AULA OTTAGONA Via G. Romita, 8	*Open Tue.–Sat. 9am–2pm; Sun. and public holidays 9am–1pm.*	
– CRYPTA BALBI Via delle Botteghe Oscure, 31	*Open Tue.–Sun. 9am–7.45pm.*	
– PALAZZO ALTEMPS Piazza di Sant'Apollinare, 44	*Open Tue.–Sun. 9am–7.45pm.*	
– PALAZZO MASSIMO ALLE TERME Largo di Villa Peretti, 1	*Open Tue.–Sun. 9am–7.45pm.*	
– BATHS OF DIOCLETIAN Viale E. De Nicola, 78	*Open Tue.–Sun. 9am–7.45pm.*	
ORATORIO DEI FILIPPINI Palazzo dei Filippini Piazza della Chiesa Nuova, 18 Tel. 06 687 52 89	*Closed for works.*	▲ 282 ◆ E B1
ORATORIO DEL GONFALONE Via del Gonfalone, 32a	*Concert hall (classical music). Reservations: Cooperativa Il Sogno, Tel. 06 85 30 17 58.*	▲ 242 ◆ D B4
ORATORIO DI SAN GIOVANNI IN OLEO Church of San Giovanni in Oleo Via di Porta Latina, 17 Tel. 06 70 49 17 77	*Contact the church authorities.*	▲ 323 ◆ I A2
ORATORIO DI SANTA MARIA DELL'ORAZIONE E DELLA MORTE Church of Santa Maria dell'Orazione e della Morte Lungotevere Tebaldi, 12 Tel. 06 68 80 68 62	*Church: Sun. 4.30–6pm; public holidays 4–6pm.*	▲ 244 ◆ D B4
PALAZZO ALTEMPS ★ Piazza di Sant'Apolinnare, 44 Tel. 06 66 83 37 59	*A branch of the National Roman Museum.*	▲ 284 ◆ E A1
PALAZZO ANGUILLARA Piazza Sonnino	*Not open to the public.*	▲ 356 ◆ E C1
PALAZZO BARBERINI Via delle Quattro Fontane, 13	*Headquarters of the Galleria Nazionale di Arte Antica (Tel. 06 328 10).*	▲ 291 ◆ E A3
PALAZZO BONAPARTE Piazza Venezia, 5	*Not open to the public.*	▲ 309 ◆ F D3
PALAZZO BORGHESE Piazza Borghese	*Not open to the public.*	▲ 311 ◆ F A-B
PALAZZO BRASCHI Piazza San Pantaleo, 10	*Headquarters of the Museo di Roma (Tel. 06 67 10 83 46).*	▲ 279 ◆ F C1
PALAZZO CAETANI Via della Botteghe Oscure, 32	*Not open to the public.*	▲ 253 ◆ F D2
PALAZZO CAPRANICA Piazza Capranica, 101	*Capranica movie theater.*	▲ 275 ◆ F C2
PALAZZO CENCI Piazza Cenci, 56	*Not open to the public.*	▲ 254 ◆ E C1
PALAZZO CENCI-BOLOGNETTI Piazza del Gesù, 46	*Not open to the public.*	▲ 258 ◆ E B2

the symbol ▲ refers to the Itineraries section. The symbol ◆ refers to the Map section.

PALAZZO CESI Via della Conciliazione, 51	Not open to the public.	▲ 232 ◆ D A3-4
PALAZZO CESI Via Acquasparta, 2 Tel. 06 686 91 69	The old Palazzo Gaddi. Headquarters of the military tribunal. Not open to the public.	▲ 283 ◆ E A1
PALAZZO CHIGI Piazza Colonna, 370	The Cabinet Office. Group visits (schools, associations only) by permission (Tel. 06 677 91).	▲ 268 ◆ F B2
PALAZZO CIMARRA Via Panisperna, 197/198	Not open to the public.	▲ 347 ◆ E B3
PALAZZO COLONNA Piazza dei Santi Apostoli, 66 Tel. 06 678 43 50	Visits on request (groups only).	▲ 300 ◆ E B2
PALAZZO CORSETTI Via Monserrato, 22	Not open to the public.	◆ D B4
PALAZZO CORSINI Via della Lungara, 10 Tel. 06 68 80 23 23	Headquarters of the Galleria Nazionale di Arte Antica and of the Accademia Nazionale dei Lincei.	▲ 362 ◆ D B-C4
PALAZZO COSTAGUTI Piazza Mattei, 10	Not open to the public.	▲ 254 ◆ E C2
PALAZZO DE PROPAGANDA FIDE Piazza di Spagna, 48	To visit the Cappella dei Rei Magi, Tel. 06 69 87 92 99.	▲ 305 ◆ F A3
PALAZZO DEI PENITENZIERI Via della Conciliazione, 33 Tel. 06 686 54 35	Hotel Columbus.	▲ 232 ◆ D A3
PALAZZO DEL QUIRINALE ★ Piazza del Quirinale Tel. 06 469 91	Open Sun. 8.30am–noon. Closed public hols. and July–Aug. The gardens are open on June 2.	▲ 297 ◆ F C4
PALAZZO DELLA BORSA Piazza di Pietra	The building incorporates the Temple of Hadrian. Not open to the public.	▲ 267 ◆ F C2
PALAZZO DELLA CANCELLERIA Piazza della Cancelleria Tel. 06 69 88 75 66	Chancellor's Office.	▲ 249 ◆ E B1
PALAZZO DELLA CONSULTA Piazza del Quirinale, 41	Seat of government. Open for special events (Tel. 06 469 81).	▲ 297 ◆ F C4
PALAZZO DELLA SAPIENZA Corso Rinascimento, 40	The Archivio dello Stato building. Visits to part of the building on request (Tel. 06 681 90 81).	▲ 272 ◆ E B1
PALAZZO DELLE ASSICURAZIONI GENERALI DI VENEZIA Piazza Venezia Tel. 06 67 59 71	Visit on request.	▲ 161 ◆ F D3
PALAZZO DELLE SCUDERIE PAPALI Via XXIV Maggio, 16 Tel. 06 39 96 75 00	Open only during exhibitions. Information: www.scuderiequirinale.it	▲ 297 ◆ E A3
PALAZZO DI GIUSTIZIA Piazza Cavour	Not open to the public.	▲ 236 ◆ A C4
PALAZZO DI MONTECITORIO Piazza Montecitorio	Office of the Chamber of Deputies (Tel. 06 676 01). Guided tours on 1st Sun. in the month 10am–6pm.	▲ 272 ◆ F B2
PALAZZO DEL GOVERNO VECCHIO OR PALAZZO NARDINI Via del Governo Vecchio, 39	Not open to the public.	▲ 281 ◆ E B1
PALAZZO DELLA CIVILTÀ DEL LAVORO Quadrato della Concordia, 9	Not open to the public.	◆ D B4 ▲ 387
PALAZZO DELLE EXPOSIZIONI Via Nazionale, 194 Tel. 488 54 65	Closed for renovation works. Information: www.palazzoesposizioni.it	▲ 348 ◆ E B3
PALAZZO DELLE TERME Foro Italico Piazza L. de Bosis	Swimming pool of the Foro Italico.	▲ 378 ◆ A A3
PALAZZO DELLO SPORT (EUR) Via Apollodoro, 10	Concerts and sports events.	▲ 388

◆ PLACES TO VISIT

PALAZZO DI SPAGNA Piazza di Spagna, 57 Tel. 06 679 59 16	*Spanish Embassy.* *Not open to the public.*	▲ 313 ◆ F A3
PALAZZO DORIA-PAMPHILJ ★ Piazza del Collegio Romano, 2 Tel. 06 679 73 23	*Guided tours, maximum of 15 people, of the* *private apartments and conference rooms;* *10.30am, 11am, 11.30am, noon.*	▲ 258 ◆ F D3
PALAZZO FALCONIERI ODESCALCHI Via Giulia, 1	*Hungarian Academy.* *Visits on request (Tel. 06 688 96 71).*	▲ 244 ◆ D B4
PALAZZO FARNESE ★ Piazza Farnese, 67 Tel. 06 68 89 28 18	*French Embassy. Visits Mon. and Thu. at 3pm,* *4pm and 5pm. Book well in advance and bring* *an ID card with you on the day of the visit.* *Exceptional opening July 14 and during the* *"White Night".*	▲ 244 ◆ E B1
PALAZZO FIANO Piazza San Lorenzo in Lucina	*On the corner of Via del Corso.* *Not open to the public.*	▲ 309 ◆ F B2
PALAZZO LANCELLOTTI Via Lancellotti, 18	*Not open to the public.*	▲ 283 ◆ D A4
PALAZZO MADAMA Piazza Madama, 2 Tel. 06 67 06 24 30	*Senate.* *Guided tours on 1st Sat. in the month 10am–6pm.*	▲ 272 ◆ F C1
PALAZZO MANCINI Via del Corso, 270–272	*Head office of the Bank of Sicily.* *Visits Sat. am by reservation (tel. 06 67 14).*	▲ 309 ◆ F A-B2
PALAZZO MARUSCELLI–LEPRI Via dei Condotti, 11	*Not open to the public.*	▲ 305 ◆ E A2
PALAZZO MASSIMO ALLE TERME Largo di Villa Peretti, 1	*A branch of the National Roman Museum.* *Open Tue.–Sun. 9am–7.45pm.* *Reservations: Tel. 06 39 96 77 00.*	◆ E A4
PALAZZO MASSIMO ALLE COLONNE Corso Vittorio Emmanuele II, 141	*Visits on March 16 only, 8am–1pm.*	▲ 279 ◆ F D1
PALAZZO MATTEI Piazza in Piscinula	*Not open to the public.*	▲ 353 ◆ F D2
PALAZZO MATTEI DI GIOVE Via Caetani, 32	*Not open to the public.*	▲ 254 ◆ E B2
PALAZZO MATTEI-PAGANICA Piazza dell'Enciclopedia Italiana 4 Tel. 06 689 81	*Headquarters of the Enciclopedia Italiana.* *Visits on request.*	▲ 253 ◆ E B1-2
PALAZZO MILESI Via della Maschera d'Oro, 7	*Not open to the public.*	▲ 284 ◆ F B1
PALAZZO NUNEZ Via Bocca di Leone, 79	*Not open to the public.*	▲ 269 ◆ F A3
PALAZZO NUOVO **OR OF THE CAPITOLINE MUSEUMS** Piazza del Campidoglio Tel. 06 67 10 24 75	*Open Tue.–Sun. 9am–8pm.*	▲ 132 ◆ E B-C2
PALAZZO ODESCALCHI Piazza dei Santi Apostoli, 81	*Not open to the public.*	▲ 301 ◆ F C3
PALAZZO ORSINI Via di Monte Savello, 31	*Not open to the public.*	▲ 158 ◆ E C2
PALAZZO OSSOLI Piazza della Quercia, 1	*Not open to the public.*	▲ 275 ◆ F C1
PALAZZO PAMPHILJ Piazza Navona, 14 Tel. 06 68 39 81 Fax 06 686 78 58	*Brazilian Embassy.* *Visits by appointment.*	▲ 278 ◆ F C1
PALAZZO PIOMBINO **OR MARGHERITA** Via Veneto, 119A	*United States Embassy.* *Not open to the public.*	▲ 302 ◆ B D3
PALAZZO POLI Piazza dei Crociferi, 53	*Opening times may vary according to exhibitions.* *Information: tel. 06 69 98 02 42.*	▲ 298 ◆ E B2
PALAZZO RICCI Via di Monserrato	*Not open to the public.*	▲ 243 ◆ D B4

PALAZZO RONDININI Via del Corso, 518/519	*Headquarters of the chess club of Rome.* *To visit tel. 06 321 05 43.*	▲ *309* ◆ **B** D1
PALAZZO ROSPIGLIOSI-PALLAVICINI Via 24 Maggio, 43	*Visits once a month; consult the warden.*	▲ *298* ◆ **E** B3
PALAZZO RUSPOLI Via del Corso, 418 Tel. 06 687 47 04	*Fondazione Memmo. Opening times may vary* *according to exhibitions.* *Information: www.fondazionememmo.com*	▲ *312* ◆ **F** A2
PALAZZO SACCHETTI Via Giulia, 66	*Not open to the public.*	▲ *242* ◆ **D** B4
PALAZZO SAN CALLISTO P. Santa Maria in Trastevere, 24	*Not open to the public.*	▲ *357* ◆ **D** C4
PALAZZO SCAPUCCI O DELLA SCIMMIA Via dei Portoghesi, 18	*Not open to the public.*	▲ *284* ◆ **F** B1
PALAZZO SENATORIO Piazza del Campidoglio	*Seat of the city council. Not open to the public.*	▲ *130* ◆ **E** C2
PALAZZO SERRISTORI Via della Conciliazione, 1	*Not open to the public.*	▲ *232* ◆ **D** A3
PALAZZO SPADA Piazza Capo di Ferro, 13 Tel. 06 683 24 09	*Opening times vary.*	▲ *246* ◆ **E** B1
PALAZZO TAVERNA Via Monte Giordano, 36 Tel. 06 683 37 85	*Visits by previous permission.*	▲ *283* ◆ **E** A1
PALAZZO TORLONIA Via della Conciliazione, 30	*Not open to the public.*	▲ *232* ◆ **D** A3
PALAZZO VENEZIA Piazza Venezia, 3 Tel. 06 679 88 65	*Open 9am–7pm. Closed Sun–Mon.*	▲ *161* ◆ **F** D3
PALAZZO DI VENEZIA MUSEUM Piazza Venezia, 3 Via del Plebiscito, 118 Tel. 06 69 99 43 18	*Open Tue.–Sun. 8.30am–7.30pm.*	▲ *161* ◆ **E** B2
PALAZZO ZUCCARI Via Gregoriana, 28	*Seat of the German Institute of the History of Art* *and of the Hertziana Library. Visit on request.*	▲ *314* ◆ **F** A3
PANTHEON ★ Piazza della Rotonda Tel. 06 68 30 02 30	*Open Mon.–Sat. 8.30am–7.30pm; Sun. 9am–6pm;* *public holidays. 9am–1pm.* *Services Sat. 5pm, Sun. 10.30am.*	▲ *264* ◆ **F** C2
PARK OF THE SCIPIOS Via di Porta Latina	*Access from 9am to sunset.*	▲ *322* ◆ **I** A2
PHARMACY OF THE MONASTERY **OF SANTA MARIA DELLA SCALA** Church of S. Maria della Scala, Pza. della Scala, 23 Tel. 06 841 42 09	*Visits by appointment.*	▲ *359* ◆ **D** C4
PINCIO GARDENS ★ Villa Borghese Via G. d'Annunzio	*Open from dawn until sunset.*	▲ *316* ◆ **B** D2
POLLI (DEPARTMENT STORE) Via Nazionale, 183 Tel. 06 474 01 07	*Site of the Eliseo art gallery.*	◆ **E** B3
POST OFFICE Via della Marmorata, 4 Tel. 06 55 49 40	*Open Mon.–Fri. 8.30am–6.30pm;* *Sat. 8.30am–1pm.*	▲ *184* ◆ **H** A3
PROTESTANT CEMETERY Via Caio Cestio, 6	*Open Mon.–Sat. 9am–4.30pm.* *www.protestantcemetery.it*	▲ *183* ◆ **H** A3
RACCOLTA TEATRALE DEL BURCARDO Via del Sudario, 44 Tel. 06 681 94 71	*Open Mon.–Fri. 9am–1.30pm.*	◆ **E** B1
REGINA COELI PRISON Via della Lungara, 29	*The public are not admitted inside the prison.*	▲ *360* ◆ **D** B4
LA RINASCENTE (DEPARTMENT STORE) Piazza Colonna Tel. 06 679 76 91	*The old Bocconi deparment store.*	▲ *305* ◆ **E** A2
ROMA OSTIENSE STATION Via della Marmorata Tel. 06 575 07 32		▲ *184* ◆ **H** B4

◆ PLACES TO VISIT

The ★ symbol refers to places that deserve to be seen first if time is short.

ROMAN FORUM AND PALATINE ★ Piazza S. Maria Nova, 53 or Via dei Fori Imperiali or Via di San Gregorio, 30 Tel. 06 39 96 77 00	*Open 9am until 1 hour before sunset.*	▲ 13(◆ E C2 C3
SAN MICHELE Via di San Michele, 17	*Headquarters of the Ministry of Culture (Tel. 06 584 31).*	▲ 35! ◆ E D
SAN CLEMENTE ARCHEOLOGICAL SITE ★ Piazza San Clemente Tel. 06 70 45 10 18	*Open to the public during cultural events. Open 10am–12.30pm; public holidays 10am–12.30pm, 3–6pm (lower levels).*	▲ 19: ◆ E C
ST PETER'S ★ Piazza San Pietro, Vatican	*See Basilica di San Pietro*	
SOVEREIGN ORDER OF THE NIGHTS OF MALTA Via dei Condotti, 68 Tel. 06 6 75 81	*The order's headquarters are not open to the public.*	● 50 ◆ E A2
STADIO DEI MARMI Foro Italico Viale dello Stadio dei Marmi	*Free access.*	▲ 37{ ◆ A A:
STADIO OLIMPICO Viale Foro Italico	*Free access.*	▲ 37{ ◆ A A:
SYNAGOGUE (AND JEWISH ART MUSEUM) ★ Lungotevere dei Cenci Tel. 06 68 40 06 61	*Museum: Sep.–April, Mon.–Thu. 10am–5pm, Fri. 9.30am–2pm; Sun. 10am–5pm; May–Aug. Mon.–Thu. 10am–7pm, Fri. 9am–2pm. Closed Sat. and on Jewish holidays.*	▲ 25 ◆ E C:
TABULARIUM AND TEMPIO DI VEIO Piazza del Campidoglio Tel. 06 67 10 24 75	*Tabularium open Tue.–Sun. 9am–8pm. Templo di Velo not open to the public.*	● 64 ◆ E B-(
TEATRO ARGENTINA Largo di Torre Argentina, 52 Tel. 06 67 10 60 17/18	*Visits on request (tel. 06 67 10 60 17).*	▲ 25. ◆ F D
TEATRO ARGENTINA MUSEUM Largo di Torre Argentina, 51 Tel. 06 68 40 00 61	*Open Tue.–Fri. 10am–2pm; Sat. 9am–2pm, 3–5pm; Sun. 9am–2pm.*	▲ 25 ◆ D C
TEATRO DELL'OPERA Piazza Gigli, 1 Tel. 06 48 16 01	*Visits by appointment (groups of ten minimum); tel. 06 48 16 02 14.*	◆ E A:
TEATRO DI POMPEI Via di Grottapinta	*Not open to the public.*	▲ 24{ ◆ F D
TEATRO DI MARCELLO Via del Portico d'Ottavia, 29 Tel. 06 57 25 04 10	*Free access.*	▲ 157 ◆ E C
TEATRO ELISEO Via Nazionale, 183/d Tel. 06 474 34 31		▲ 34{ ◆ F C
TEMPLE OF HADRIAN Palazzo della Borsa Piazza di Pietra	*See Palazzo della Borsa.*	▲ 267 ◆ F C
TEMPLE OF HERCULES VICTOR (CIRCULAR TEMPLE) Forum Boario Piazza Bocca della Verità		▲ 15! ◆ E C
TEMPLE OF JUPITER CAPITOLINUS Palazzo Caffarelli Piazza del Campidoglio Tel. 06 67 10 24 75	*Recently renovated. Telephone for opening hours.*	● 70 ◆ E C
TEMPLE OF MINERVA MEDICA Via Giovanni Giolitti (corner of Via Pietro Micca)	*Visit by permission of the Sovrintendenza Archeologica (Tel. 06 679 01 10). Undergoing building work.*	▲ 33! ◆ G D
TEMPLE OF PORTUNUS Forum Boario Piazza Bocca della Verità		▲ 15! ◆ E C:
TERME DI CARACALLA ★ Via delle Terme di Caracalla, 52 Tel. 06 39 96 77 00	*See also Baths of Caracalla. Open 9am–one hour before sunset; Mon. 9am–2pm.*	

e symbol ▲ refers to the Itineraries section. The symbol ◆ refers to the Map section.

ERME DI DIOCLEZIANO ★ 'iale E. de Nicola, 78 Tel. 06 39 96 77 00	*See also Baths of Diocletian and National Roman Museum. Open Tue.–Sun. 9am–7.45pm.*	
OBACCO FACTORY Piazza Mastai, 11	*Currently under renovation.*	▲ *356* ◆ E C1
OMB OF EURYSACES Piazza di Porta Maggiore Tel. 06 67 10 20 70		▲ *339* ◆ G C2
OMB OF THE SCIPIOS **ND COLUMBARIUM** Parco degli Scipioni Via di Porta Latina 06 67 10 38 19	*Closed for works.*	▲ *322* ◆ I A2
ORRE ANGUILLARA Piazza Sonnino Palazzo Anguillara	*Not open to the public.*	▲ *356* ◆ E C1
ORRE BONIFACE IX Piazza del Campidoglio	*Not open to the public.*	▲ *130* ◆ E B-C2
ORRE CENTRALE DE LONGHI Piazza del Campidoglio	*Not open to the public.*	▲ *130* ◆ E B-C2
ORRE DE' CONTI Largo Ricci	*Visits to the underground section only, by permission.*	▲ *168* ◆ E B3
ORRE DEI ANNIBALDI Via degli Annibaldi	*Not open to the public.*	▲ *168* ◆ E C3
ORRE DEI ARCIONI Salita dei Borgia	*Not open to the public.*	▲ *168* ◆ F D4
ORRE DEI CAPOCCI Piazza di San Martino ai Monti	*Not open to the public.*	▲ *168* ◆ E B4
ORRE DEI FRANGIPANI/ **ELA SCIMMIA** Palazzo Scapucci Via dei Portoghesi	*Not open to the public.*	▲ *168* ◆ F D4
ORRE DEI MARGANI Piazza Margana, 49/A	*Not open to the public.*	▲ *159* ◆ F D2
ORRE DEI ORSINI / **ORRE ARPACASA** Campo dei Fiori	*Not open to the public.*	▲ *168* ◆ E B1
ORRE DELLE MILIZIE Via IV Novembre, 94	*Visits by appointment: Tel. 06 69 78 05 32. Works in progress.*	▲ *168* ◆ F D4
ORRE MARTIN V Piazza del Campidoglio	*Not open to the public.*	▲ *130* ◆ E B2
ORRE MILLINA Piazza Navona	*Not open to the public.*	▲ *279* ◆ F C1
ORRE SANTA FRANCESCA **N TOR DE' SPECCHI** Via del Teatro di Marcello Specchi	*Not open to the public.*	▲ *159* ◆ E B-C2
RAJAN'S MARKETS **ND IMPERIAL FORUMS ★** Via IV Novembre, 94 Tel. 06 679 00 48	*Restoration works in progress. Partially open to the public 9am–2pm. Closed Mon. Information and reservations: Tel. 06 69 78 05 32.*	▲ *167* ◆ F D4
ULLANIUM / MAMERTINE PRISON Church of San Giuseppe dei Falegnami Clivo Argentario, 1 Tel. 06 679 29 02	*Open 9am–7pm (March–Sep.); 9am–6pm (Oct.) 9am–5pm (Nov.–Feb.)*	▲ *131* ◆ E C2
NDERGROUND BASILICA OF **PORTA MAGGIORE** Piazza di Porta Maggiore Tel. 06 702 30 64	*Closed for works.*	▲ *340* ◆ G C2
VICTOR EMMANUEL II MONUMENT Piazza Venezia		▲ *160* ◆ F D3
VILLA ALBANI Via Salaria	*Visits on request from the wardens of the Villa Torlonia (tel. 06 686 10 44).*	▲ *368* ◆ B C-D4
VILLA ALDOBRANDINI Via Mazzarino, 11 Tel. 06 678 78 57	*Visits on request.*	◆ F D4

◆ PLACES TO VISIT

Tivoli

The ★ symbol refers to places that deserve to be seen first if time is short.

VILLA BONAPARTE Via Piave, 23 Tel. 06 680 26 26 (St-Louis des Français Center)	*French Embassy near the Holy See.* *Visit by permission (Fax 06 68 02 26 20).*	◆ **B** D4
VILLA BORGHESE (GARDENS) ★	*Access on the Piazzale San Paolo del Brasile,* *Piazzale Flaminio, Via di Porta Pinciana,* *Via Mercadante, Via Aldovrandi, or Viale delle Arti.* *Open all day.*	▲ 372 ◆ **B** C-C3
VILLA CELIMONTANA **(GARDENS)** Piazza della Navicella, 12	*Open from sunrise to sunset.*	▲ 190 ◆ **E** D3
VILLA DEI QUINTILI Via Appia Nuova, 1092	*Reservations: Tel. 06 39 96 77 00.* *Open 9am–one hour before sunset.*	▲ 330
VILLA DORIA-PAMPHILJ **(GARDENS)** Via Aurelia Antica, 183 Tel. 06 39 37 66 16	*Gardens: access on the Via Aurelia Antica, Via San* *Pancrazio, Via della Nocetta or Via Leone XIII.*	▲ 369 ◆ **D** C2
VILLA FARNESINA ★ Via della Lungara, 230 Tel. 06 68 02 72 68	*Open 9am–1pm.* *Closed Sun. and on public holidays.*	▲ 360 ◆ **D** B4
VILLA GIULIA ★ Piazzale di Villa Giulia, 9 Tel. 06 322 65 71	*Houses the Etruscan Museum (see under that entry* *for opening times).*	▲ 370 ◆ **B** C2
VILLA LANTE Via Lisbona, 3	*Finnish Embassy (Tel. 06 85 22 31). Open 9am–noon* *(for formalities).*	▲ 365 ◆ **D** B-C3
VILLA MADAMA Via di Villa Madama	*Visit with prior permission from the Ministry of* *Foreign Affairs.*	▲ 378 ◆ **A** A2
VILLA MEDICI ★ Via della Trinità dei Monti, 1 www.villamedici.it	*French Academy (tel. 06 676 11). Exhibitions, lectures* *and concerts. Guided tour of the gardens Sat.–Sun.* *at 10am and 11.40am.*	▲ 315 ◆ **B** D2
VILLA TORLONIA (GARDENS) Via Nomentana, 70	*Open from sunrise to sunset.*	▲ 381 ◆ **C** C-D2

TIVOLI

CHURCH OF SAN SILVESTRO Via del Colle Tel. 07 74 33 56 27	*Open 8am–12.30pm, 3.30–7pm.*	▲ 391
CHURCH OF SANTA MARIA MAGGIORE Piazza Trento, 2 Tel. 07 74 31 13 29	*Open 7am–noon, 4–7.15pm.*	▲ 391
DUOMO Piazza del Duomo Tel. 0774 31 71 92	*Open 8.30am–noon, 4–6pm.*	▲ 391
TEMPLE OF THE SIBYL Via della Sibilla, 50	*The temple is in the gardens of the restaurant* *La Sibilla (Tel. 0774 433 52 81). Closed Mon.*	▲ 391
VILLA ADRIANA ★ Via di Villa Adriana, 204 Tel 07 74 53 02 03	*Open Jan., Nov.–Dec. 9am–3.30pm;* *Feb. 9am–4.30pm; March 9am–5pm;* *April, Sep. 9am–5.30pm; May–Aug. 9am–6pm.* *Closed Jan. 1, May 1 and Dec. 25.* *Reservations: Tel. 07 74 38 27 33*	▲ 394
VILLA D'ESTE ★ Piazza Trento, 1 Tel. 07 74 31 20 70	*Open Jan., Nov.–Dec. 8.30am–4pm;* *Feb. 8.30am– 4.30pm; March 8.30am–5.15pm;* *Apr. 8.30am–6.30pm; May–Aug. 8.30am–6.45pm;* *Sep. 8.30am–6.15pm; Oct. 8.30am–5.30pm.* *Closed Mon., Jan. 1, May 1 and Dec. 25.*	▲ 392
VILLA GREGORIANA Largo Sant'Angelo Tel. 06 39 96 77 01	*Open March 1–31: Tue.–Sun. 10am–2.30pm;* *April 1–Oct. 15: Tue.–Sun. 10am–6.30pm;* *Oct. 16–Nov. 30: Tue.–Sun. 10am–2.30pm;* *Dec. 1–Feb. 2: reservations compulsory.* *Closed Mon. except when public hol.*	▲ 391

The symbol ▲ refers to the Itineraries section. The symbol ◆ refers to the Map section.

VATICAN		
BASICLICA OF SAN PIETRO (ST PETER'S BASILICA) ★ Piazza San Pietro Tel. 06 69 88 16 62	*Open 7am–7pm (basilica); 8am–6pm (tombs of the popes, treasury, dome). 7am–6pm in winter.*	▲ 209 ◆ D A3
CASINA OF PIUS IV OR PONTIFICAL SCIENCE ACADEMY Piazza del San Uffizio Tel. 06 69 88 31 95	*Not open to the public.*	▲ 214 ◆ D A2
VATICAN GARDENS ★	*Guided tours: Tel. 06 69 88 46 76.*	▲ 214
VATICAN LIBRARY Via di Pora Angelico Tel. 06 69 87 94 02	*Not open to the public.*	▲ 214 ◆ D A2
VATICAN MUSEUMS ★ Viale Vaticano Tel. 06 69 88 33 33 www.vatican.va	*Open Nov.–Feb.: Mon.–Sat. 8.45am–1.45pm; March–Oct.: Mon.–Fri. 8.45am–4.45pm, Sat. 8.45am–2.45pm (final admission 1 hour and 25 mins. before closing time). Open and free admission on the final Sun. of the month 8.45am–1.45pm. Closed Jan. 1 and 6, Feb. 11, Easter Sun. and Mon., May 1 and 20, June 10 and 29, Aug. 15, Nov. 1, Dec. 8, 25 and 26.* *Borgia Apartments, Biblioteca Apostolica, Chapel of Nicolas V, Chapel of Pius V, Pauline Chapel, Sistine Chapel, Galleria Clementina, Galleria dei Candelabri, Map Gallery, Galleria Lapidaria, Galleria degli Arazzi, Urban VIII Gallery, the Raphael Loggias, Museo Chiaramonti, Christian Museum, Belvedere Museum, Egyptian Museum, Etruscan Museum, Gregorian Museum, Museum of Ethnology, Museo Pio-Clementino, Museo Sacro, Pinacoteca, Sala Ducale, Sala Regia, Sala Alessandrina, Sala dell'Immaculata, Sala della Biga, Sala Sobieski, Raphael Rooms.*	▲ 216-31 ◆ D A3

◆ BIBLIOGRAPHY

ESSENTIAL READING

◆ GREGOROVIUS (F.):
History of the City of Rome in the Middle Ages, English tr., London, 1906; reprinted New York, 1967
◆ MASSON (G.):
Companion Guide to Rome, London, 1965
◆ NASH (E.): *Pictorial Dictionary of Ancient Rome,* London, 1966
◆ *Michelin Guide to Rome,* London (many editions)
◆ SHOWERMAN (G.):
Monuments and Men of Ancient Rome, New York, 1935
◆ STORTI (A.):
Rome, A Practical Guide, Venice, 1980
◆ VARRIANO (J.):
Rome, A Literary Companion, London, 1991

GENERAL

◆ ARMELLINI (M.), CECCHILLI (C.): *Le Chiese di Roma dal secolo IV al XIX,* 2 vol., Rome, 1942
◆ *Attraverso l'Italia, Roma,* Touring Club Italiano, Milan, 1986
◆ BENTLEY (J.):
Rome: Architecture, History, Art, London, 1991
◆ CIPRIANI (G.B.):
Architecture of Rome, originally Rome 1835–7, reprinted New York, 1986
◆ *Civiltà del Lazio primitivo* (exhibition catalogue), Rome, 1976
◆ DE TOMMASSO (F.):
Le Cupole di Roma, Rome, 1991
◆ D'ONOFRIO (C.):
Castel Sant'Angelo, Rome, 1972
◆ *Fontana di Trevi,* Fratelli Palombi Editori, Rome, 1992
◆ GALASSI PALUZZI (C.):
Chiese romane, Ente provinciale per il turismo di Roma
◆ *Guida al Quirinale,* Fratelli Palombi Editori, Rome, 1985
◆ HAUSER (E.D.):
Italy, a Cultural Guide, New York, 1981
◆ Hutton (E.):
Rome, London, 1950
◆ LANCIANI (R.):
New Tales of Old Rome, London, 1901
◆ LANCIANI (R.):
Wandering through Ancient Roman Churches, New York, 1924
◆ *Lazio,* Touring Club Italiano, Milan, 1967

◆ MENEN (A.):
Rome Revealed, London, 1960
◆ MORETTI (U.):
Artists in Rome, Tales of the Babuino, (tr. W. Weaner), London and New York, 1958
◆ PARTNER (P.):
The Lands of St. Peter, London, 1972
◆ PEREIRA (A.):
Rome, London, 1990
◆ PIETRANGELI (C.), PERICOLI (C.):
Guide rionali di Roma, Fratelli Palombi Editori, Rome 1971–80
◆ POTTER, (O.M.):
The Colour of Rome, London and Philadelphia, 1909
◆ RAVAGLIOLI (A.):
La Storia in piazza. Breve profilo della storia urbanistica della citta di Roma, Edizioni di "Roma Centro Storico", 1987
◆ RAVAGLIOLI (A.):
Tutta Roma, Rome, 1983
◆ *ROMA,* Touring Club Italiano, Milan, 3 1992
◆ SHARP (M.):
A Guide to the Churches of Rome, Philadelphia, 1966
◆ VENTRIGLIA (U.):
La Geologia della citta di Roma, Rome, 1971
◆ WILLEY (D. and M. C.):
Welcome to Rome, Glasgow, 1981

GENERAL HISTORY

◆ DURUY (V.):
History of Rome and the Roman Peoples, Boston, 1890
◆ GIBBON (E.):
The Decline and Fall of the Roman Empire Alfred A Knopf, New York/Everyman's Library, London, 1994
◆ HIBBERT (C.):
Rome – the Biography of a City, London, 1985
◆ MOMMSEN (T.):
The History of Rome (many editions)

ANCIENT ROME

◆ ASBY (TH.):
The Roman Campagna in Classical Times, E. Benn, London, 1927
◆ BAKER (G.B.):
Twelve Centuries of Rome, 753 BC–AD 476, London, 1936
◆ BALSDON (J.P.V.D.):
Julius Caesar and Rome, Harmondsworth, 1967
◆ BARROW (R.H.):
The Romans, Harmondsworth, 1949
◆ BARTON (I.M.) (ED.):
Roman Public Buildings, Exeter, 1989
◆ COARELLI (F.):

◆ BERTOLOTTI, IOPPOLO, SARTORIO: *La Residenza Imperiale di Massenzio,* Itinerari d'Arte di Cultura, Rome, 1989
◆ BIRLEY (A.):
Marcus Aurelius, London, 1966
◆ BREEM (W.):
Eagle in the Snow: General Maximus and Rome's Last Stand, Weidenfeld and Nicolson, 2003
◆ BORTOLOTTI (L.):
Roma fuori le mura, Laterza, Rome-Bari, 1988
◆ CAPRINO (C.), COLINI (A.M.), GATTI (G.), PALLOTTINO (M.), ROMANELLI (P.):
La Colonna di Marco Aurelio, Rome, 1955
◆ CARCOPINO (J.):
Daily Life in Ancient Rome, Harmondsworth, 1941
◆ CARY (M.):
History of Rome down to the Reign of Constantine, London and New York, 1935
◆ CASTAGNOLI (F.):
Il Campo Marzio nell'antichita, Mem. Acc. Lincei, 7,1, 1946, p.93
◆ CASTAGNOLI (F.):
Il Circo di Nerone in Vaticano, Rendic Pont. Acc. 32, 1959–60, pp. 97 sqq.
◆ CASTAGNOLI (F.):
Topografia e urbanistica di Roma antica, Società Editrice Internazionale, Turin, 1969
◆ CASTAGNOLI (F.), ZOCCA (M.), CECCHELLI (C.), GIOVANNONI (G.):
Topografia e urbanistica di Roma, Bologna, 1958 (Storia di Roma, 22)
◆ COARELLI (F.):
Il Campo Marzio occidentale, storia e topografia, in *Mélanges de l'Ecole française de Rome,* 89, 1977, pp.807 sqq.
◆ COARELLI (F.):
L'"Ara di Domizio Enobarbo" e la Cultura artistica in Roma nell'il secolo a. C., in *Dialogi di Archeologia,* 2, 1968, pp.302 sqq.
◆ COARELLI (P.):
Public Building in Rome between the Second Punic War and Sulla, in *Papers of the British School at Rome,* 45, 1977, pp. 1 sqq.
◆ COARELLI (F.):
Il Complesso pompeiano del Campo Marzio e la sua decorazione scultorea, Rendic. Pont. Acc. 44, 1971–72, pp. 99 sqq
◆ COARELLI (F.):

Il Foro romano, 2 vol., Quasar, 1985
◆ COARELLI (F.):
Il Sepolcro degli Scipion a Roma, Itinerari d'Arte di Cultura, Rome, 1989
◆ COARELLI (F.):
Italia centrale, Laterza, Rome-Bari, 1985
◆ COARELLI (F.):
L'identificazione dell'Are Sacra dell'Argentina, in *Palatino,* 12, 4, 1968, pp. 365 sqq.
◆ COARELLI (F.):
Roma sepolta, Curcio, Rome, 1984
◆ COLINI (A.M.):
Il Campidoglio nell'antichita, in *Capitolium,* 40, 4, 1965 pp. 175 sqq.
◆ COLINI (A.M.), COZZA (L.): *Ludus Magnus,* Rome, 1962
◆ DE ROSSI (G.B.):
La Roma sotterranea cristiana, 3 vol., Rome, 1864–77
◆ DILL (S.):
Roman Society from Nerito Marcus Aurelius, London, 1925
◆ DIXON (S.):
The Roman Family, London and Baltimore, 1992
◆ D'ONOFRIO (C.):
Gli Obelischi di Roma, Rome, 1965
◆ FRANK (T.):
Roman Buildings of the Republic, Rome, 1924
◆ GIULIANI (C.F.):
Domus Flavia: una nuov lettura, in *Römische Mitteilungen,* 84, 1977, pp.91 sqq.
◆ GARDNER (J.F.) and WIEDEMANN (T.):
The Roman Household, A Sourcebook, London, 1991
◆ GRANT (M.):
The World of Rome, London, 1960
◆ GRANT (M.):
The Roman Emperors, 31 BC–476 AD, London
◆ GREENIDGE (A.H.J.):
Roman Public Life, New York, 1901
◆ GREENIDGE (A.H.J.) AND CLAY (A.M.):
Sources for Roman History, Oxford, 1903
◆ GUARDUCCI (M.):
L'Isola Tiberina e la sua tradizione ospitaliera, Rendic. Acc. Lincei, 26, 3–4,1971, pp.26 sqq.
◆ GUIDOLBALDI (F.):
Complesso archeologico di San Clemente. Risultati degli scavi più recenti e nesame dei resti architettonici, Rome, 1978
◆ GUZZO (P.G.):
Antico e archeologia. Scienza e politica delle diverse antichità, Nuova

fa Editoriale, Bologna,
993

HANFMAN (C.M.P.):
*oman Art, A Modern
urvey of the Art of
nperial Rome*, New
ork, 1975

IVERSEN (E.):
belisks in Exile, 1,
openhagen, 1968

JORDAN (H.):
orma Urbis Romae,
erlin, 1874

La Colonna Traiana,
d. Carte segrete,
ome, 1874

*L'Area Sacra di
Omobono*, coll.
a Parola del Passato,
o. 32, 1977, pp. 9 sqq.

LANCIANI (R.):
Antica Roma,
ome, 1970

LANCIANI (R.):
*he Destruction of
ncient Rome*, New
ork, 1899

LANCIANI (R.):
*toria degli scavi di
oma,*
IV, Rome 1902–4
eprinted. 1989–92)

LEWIS (N.) AND
EINHOLD (M.):
*oman Civilization. 1.
he Republic*, New York,
952

LEWIS (N.) AND
EINHOLD (M.):
*oman Civilization. 2.
he Empire*, New York,
955

LIDDEL (H.G.):
*History of Rome,
om the Earliest Times
o the Establishment of
he Empire*, New York,
889

LUGLI (G.):
*a Tecnica edilizia
omana*, Rome, 1957

MATYSZAK (P.)
*he Enemies of Rome:
rom Hannibal to Attila
he Hun* Thames and
ludson, 2004

◆ MEIGGS (R.): *Roman
stia 2*, Oxford, 1973

MOATTI (C.): *The
earch for Ancient
ome*, London and New
ork, 1993

NASH (E.):
*ictorial Dictionary of
ncient Rome*, London,
982

PARKER (J.H.):
he Archaelogy of Rome,
)xford and London,
974

◆ PAVOLINI (C.):
)stia, Laterza,
ome-Bari, 1988

◆ PLATNER (S.B.),
.SBY (TH.):
*Topographical
ictionary of Ancient
ome*, Oxford University
ress, 1929

QUENNEL (P.):
he Colosseum,
ew York, 1971

◆ QUILICI (L.):
*Via Appia da Porta
Capena al Colli Albani*,
Fratelli Palombi Editori,
Rome, 1989

◆ RODRIGUEZ ALMEIDA
(E.): *Aggiornamento
topografico del colli
Oppio, Cispio e Viminale
secondo la Forma Urbis
Marmorea*, Rendic. Pont.
Acc, 48, 1975–6, p.263
sqq. *Roma Antiqua 2.
Grandi edifici pubblici*,
Ed. Carte segrete,
Rome, 1992

◆ SAVAGE (S.M.):
*The Cults of Ancient
Trastevere*, in *Memoirs of
the American Academy
in Rome*, 17, 1940,
pp.26 sqq.

◆ SEAR (F.):
Roman Architecture,
London, 1982

◆ SYME (R.):
The Roman Revolution,
Oxford, 1939

◆ TODD (M.):
The Walls of Rome,
London, 1978

◆ UCELLI (G.):
Le Navi dei Nemi,
Libreria dello Stato,
Rome, 1950

◆ WARD-PERKINS (J.B.):
Roman Architecture,
London, 1979

◆ WILKINSON, (L.P.):
The Roman Experience,
London, 1975

◆ ZANKER (P.):
Forum Augustinum,
Tübingen, 1968

MEDIEVAL ROME

◆ BARBERINI (M.G.):
*I Santi Quattro Coronati
a Roma, Itinerari d'Arte e
di Cultura*, Rome, 1989

◆ BERTOLINI (O.):
*Roma di fronte a
Bisanzio e di Longobardi*,
Bologna, 1941 (Storia di
Roma, 9)

◆ BOYLE (L.):
*Piccola guide di San
Clemente*, Rome, 1976

◆ BRENTANO (R.):
*Rome before Avignon,
a Social History of 13th
century Rome*, London,
1991

◆ BREZZI (P.):
*Roma e l'Imperio
Medioevale, 774–1252*,
Bologna, 1947, in
Storia di Roma, 10

◆ CARDILLI (L.) (ED):
Edicole sacre romane
Fratelli Palombi Editori,
Rome, 1990

◆ DUPRE-THESELDER (E.):
*Roma dal Comune di
Popolo alla Signoria
Pontificio (1252–1377)*,
Bologna, 1952, in *Storia
di Roma*, 11

◆ *Fragmenta picta,
affreschi e mosaici
staccati del Medioevo
romano*, Rome, 1989

◆ HERMANIN (F.):
*L'Arte in Roma dal
secolo VII al XIV*,
Bologna, 1945 (Storia di
Roma, 27)

◆ FROTHINGHAM (A.L.):
*The Monuments of
Christian Rome*, New
York, 1908

◆ GOLZIO (V.), ZANDER
(G.): *Le Chiese di Roma
dal XI al XVI secolo*,
Bologna, 1963 (Roma
cristiana, 4)

◆ HUELSEN (CH.): *Le
Chiese di Roma nel
Medioevo*, Cataloghi Ed.
Appunti, Florence, 1927

◆ KRAUTHEIMER (R.),
CORBETT (S.), FRANKI
(W.), FRAZER (A.K.):
*Corpus basillicarum
christianarum Romae*,
6 vol., Vatican City,
1937–80 (*Monumenti di
antichia cristiana*)

◆ KRAUTHEIMER (R.):
*Rome, Profile of a City,
312–1308*, Princeton,
1980

◆ *Le Fortificazioni
medievali a Roma.
La Torre dei Conti e la
Torre delle Milizie*, Fratelli
Palombi Editori, Rome,
1991

◆ LLEWELLYN (P.):
Rome in the Dark Ages,
New York, 1971

◆ MASSIMI (G.):
*La Chiesa di Santa
Maria in Cosmedin*,
Rome, 1989

◆ MATTHIAE (G.):
*Le Chiese di Roma dal IV
al X secolo*, Bologna,
1962 (Roma cristiana, 3)

◆ MATTHIAE (G.):
*Mosaici medioevali delle
chiese di Roma*, 2 vol.,
Rome, 1967

◆ MATTHIAE (G.):
*Pittura romana del
Medioevo* (prepared for
publication by Andaloro
(M.) and Gandolfo (F.), 2
vol., Rome, 1987–8

◆ OAKESHOTT (N.): *The
Mosaics of Rome from
the Third to the
Fourteenth Century*,
London, 1989

◆ *Roma nel Duecento
l'arte nella Citta dei papi
de Innocenzo III a
Bonifacio VIII*, ed. a cura
di Angela Maria
Romanini, Turin, 1991

◆ WALEY (D.):
*The Papal State in the
Thirteenth Century*,
London, 1969

RENAISSANCE AND
MODERN ROME

◆ ABRAMSON (M.C.):
*Painting in Rome during
the Papacy of Clement
VIII: a Documented
Study*, Garland, London
and New York, 1981

◆ ARGAN (G.):
*L'Architettura barocca in
Italia*, Milan, 1957

◆ BARTONCCINI (F.):
Roma nell'Ottocento,
Bologna, 1985

◆ BELLIBARSALI (I.):
*Conoscere le ville di
Roma e del Lazio*, Rome,
1982

◆ BLUNT (A.):
Guide to Baroque Rome,
London, 1982

◆ BLUNT (A.):
Borromini, London, 1979

◆ BONNEFOY (Y.):
Rome 1630, Paris and
Milan, 1970

◆ BORSI (F.):
Le Bernin, Hazan, Paris,
1984

◆ BRANDI (C.):
*La Prima Architettura
barocca, Pietro da
Cortona, Borromini,
Bernini*, Bari, 1970

◆ BRIGANTI (G.), LAUREATI
(L.), TREZZANI (L.):
*The Bamboccianti.
The Painters of Every
Day Life in Seventeenth-
century Rome*, Rome,
1983

◆ CARACCIOLO (A.):
*Roma capitale dal
Risorgimento alla crisi
dello Stato liberale*,
Rome, 1956

◆ CLARK (A.):
*Studies in Eighteenth
Century's Roman
Baroque*, London, 1982

◆ D'ONOFRIO (C.):
*Renovatio Romae, storia
e urbanistica del
Campidoglio all'EUR*,
Rome, 1973

◆ EATON (C.):
*Rome in the Nineteenth
Century*, London, 1820

◆ ELLING (C.):
*Rome, the Biography of
its Architecture from
Bemini to Thorwaldsen*,
Tübingen, 1975

◆ ENGASS (R.):
*Early Eighteenth Century
Sculpture in Rome*,
Pennsylvania State
University Press, 1976

◆ FREEDBERG (S.L.):
*Painting in Italy 1500-
1600*, 2nd ed, London,
1983

◆ FROMMEL (C.L.):
*Der Römische Palastbau
der Hochrenaissance*,
Tübingen, 1972

◆ HIBBERD (H.):
Carlo Moderno,
London, 1972

◆ HOOK (J.):
The Sack of Rome,
London, 1972

◆ HOWELLS (W.D.):
Roman Holidays, London
and New York, 1908

◆ INSOLERA (I.):
*Roma, Immagini e realtà
dal X al XX secolo*,
Laterza, Rome-Bari,
1985

◆ BIBLIOGRAPHY

◆ KRAUTHEIMER (R.): *Rome, Profile of a City*, Princeton, 1980

◆ *Il Campidoglio e Sisto V*, Ed. Carte segrete, Rome, 1991

◆ KLACZKO (J.): *Rome and the Renaissance*, New York, 1926

◆ KOSTOF (S.): *The Third Rome, 1870–1950*, Berkeley, 1973

◆ *L'Accademia dei Lincei e la Cultura europea nel XVII secolo*, Accademia dei Lincei, Rome, 1991

◆ *L'Accademia nazionale di San Luca*, Rome, 1974

◆ *La Galleria nazionale d'Arte antica*, Fratelli Palombi Editori, Rome, 1988

◆ *L'Arte degli Anni santi Roma, 1300–1875*, Rome, 1984–5

◆ *L'Arte per i papi e per i principi nella campagna romana: grande pittura del 600 et del 700*, Rome, 1990

◆ *La Villa de la Farnésine à Rome*, Ministero per i Beni culturali e ambientali, Rome, 1990

◆ *"La pittura del Cinquecento a Roma e nel Lazio"* in *La Pittura in Italia, Il Cinquecento*, Electa, 1987, Vol. II

◆ LEES-MILNE (J.): *St. Peter's*, London, 1967

◆ MAHON (D.): *Studies in Seicento Art and Theory*, London, 1947

◆ MALLORY (N.A.): *Roman Rococo Architecture from Clement XI to Benedict XIV*, New York, 1977

◆ MONELLI (P.): *Roma 1943*, Turin, 1945

◆ MONTAGU (J.): *Roman Baroque Sculpture*, London and New Haven, 1989

◆ MURRAY (P.): *Architecture of the Italian Renaissance*, London, 1960

◆ ORBAAN (J.A.F.): *Sistine Rome*, London, 1910

◆ PADULA (A.): *Roma e la regione nell'epoca napoleonica*, Rome, 1969

◆ PESCI (U.): *I Primi Anni di Roma capitale*, Florence, 1907

◆ *Piranesi e la veduta del Settecento a Roma*, Artemide Edizioni, Rome, 1989

◆ POLLAK (D.): *Die Kunsttätigkeit unter Urban VIII*, Vienna, 1927–31

◆ POPE-HENNESSY (J.): *Italian High Renaissance and Baroque Sculpture*, Vol. III, 3rd ed., Oxford, 1985

◆ PORTOGHESI (P.): *Rome of the Renaissance*, London, 1972

◆ PORTOGHESI (P.): *Baroque Rome*, London, 1970

◆ *Rome in Early Photographs, the Age of Pius IX, photographs 1846–78*, Copenhagen, Thorwaldsen Museum, 1977

◆ PRATESI (L.): *Via Giulia, Itinerari d'Arte e di Cultura*, Rome, 1989

◆ SAFARIK (E.A.): *Breve guida della galleria Doria Pamphili*, Fratelli Palombi Editori, Rome, 1991

◆ SALERNO (L.): *Pittori di paesaggio del Seicento a Roma*, Rome, 1977–80, 3 vol.

◆ SCHLEIER (E.): *"La pittura a Roma nel Seicento"* in *La Pittura in Italia, Il Seicento*, Electa, 1988, Vol. II

◆ SMITH (G.): *The Casina of Pius IV*, Princeton, 1977

◆ *Specchio di Roma barocca. Una guida inedita del XVII secolo* (presented by Connors (J.) and Rice (L.), Ed. dell'Elefante, Rome, 1991

◆ TITI (F.): *Studio di pittura, scultura et architettura nelle chiese di Roma, 1674–1763*, ed. comparata a cura di Contardo (B.) e Romano (S.), Florence, 1987

◆ TREVELYAN (R.): *Rome '44, the Battle for the Eternal City*, London, 1981

◆ TREVES (P.): *L'Idea di Roma e la Cultura italiana del secolo XIX*, Milan-Naples, 1962

◆ VENUTI (R.): *Descrizione topografica e istorica di Roma moderna*, Rome, 1964, reprinted 1977

◆ VANNELLI (V.): *Economia dell'architecttura in Roma liberale*, Ed. Kappa, Rome, 1979

◆ VOSS (H.): *Die Malerei des Barocks in Rom*, Berlin, undated. (1925)

◆ WATERHOUSE (E.): *Italian Baroque Paintings*, 2nd ed., London, 1976

◆ WITTKOWER (R.): *Art and Architecture of Italy, 1600–1750*, 3rd ed., 1973

◆ WITTKOWER (R.): *Studies in Italian Baroque*, London, 1975

◆ WITTKOWER (R.): *Gianlorenzo Bernini, the Sculptor of Roman Baroque*, 2nd ed., London, 1966

ROME TODAY

◆ ACCASTO (G.), FRATICELLI (V.), NICCOLINI (R.): *L'Architettura di Roma capitale, 1870-1970*, Rome, 1971

◆ *Art et fascisme* (under the direction of Milza (P.) and Roche-Pezard (F.), Complexe, Paris, 1989

◆ BENEVOLO (L.): *Roma oggi*, Laterza, Rome-Bari, 1977

◆ CEDERNA (C.): *Mussolini urbanistia*, Bari, 1983

◆ CHAMBERLAIN (E.R.): *Rome* (Time-Life Books), Amsterdam, 1976

◆ DE GUTTRY (I.): *Guida di Roma moderna dal 1870 ad oggi*, De Luca Ed d'Arte, Rome, 1989

◆ FRIEDMAN (J.): *Inside Rome*, London, 1993

◆ INSOLERA (I.): *Roma moderna*, Turin, 1962

◆ INSOLERA (I.): *Roma, immagini e realta dal X al XX*, Bari, 1980

◆ *L'Architettura del Ventennio a Roma*, Fratelli Palombi Editori, Roma, 1990

◆ *Museo del Folklore. Restauri e nuove acquisizioni*, Multigrafica Editrice, Rome, 1989

◆ QUARONI (L.): *Immagini di Roma*, Bari, 1949

◆ ROSSI (G.A.): *Rome from the Air*, London, 1989

◆ SAN FILIPPO (M.): *La Terza Roma*, Rome, 1993

◆ *The Vatican Collections, The Papacy and Art*, New York, Chicago and San Francisco, 1983

MAPS AND PLANS

◆ CARETTONI (G.), COLINI (A.M.), COZZA (L.), GATTI (G.): *La Pianta marmorea di Roma antica*, Rome, 1960

◆ DE ROSSI (G.B.): *Piante iconografiche e prospettiche di Roma anterio al XVI secolo*, Rome, 1879

◆ FRUTAZ (A.P.): *Le Piante di Roma*, Rome, 1962

◆ LANCIANI (R.): *Forma Urbis Romae*, Quasar, Rome, 1988

◆ LANCIANI (R.): *La Pianta di Roma antica e i Disegni archeologici di Raffaello*, in Rendic. Acc. Lincei, 1895, pp.791–804

◆ RAVAGLIOLI (A.): *Plan monumental et a vol d'oiseau du centre historique de Rome*, 1972

◆ PRESSOUYRE (S.): *Rome au fil du temps, Atlas historique d'urbanisme et d'architecture*, Bologna, 1973

◆ RODRIGUEZ ALMEIDA (E.): *Forma Urbis Marmorea Aggiornamento generale 1980*, Rome, 1980

TRADITIONS AND LIFESTYLE

◆ CECCARELLI (L.): *Letture romane, Antologia di curiosità, personaggi e avvenimenti della città*, Fratelli Palombi Editori, Rome, 1989

◆ GRAF (A.): *Roma nella memoria e nelle immaginazioni del Medioevo*, Turin, 1915

◆ HARE (A.C.): *Walks in Rome*, London, 1887

◆ HUTTON (E.): *Rome*, London, 1909

◆ *I Mobili del Museo di Roma, Stilli, forme, tendenze dal XV al XIX secolo*, Fratelli Palombi Editori, Rome, 1979

◆ LEES-MILNE (J.): *Roman Mornings*, London, 1988

◆ *L'Ordine di Malta ieri e oggi*, Sovrano Militare Ordine Ospedaliero di San Viovanni di Gerusalemme detto di Rodi detto di Malta, Rome, 1992

◆ *La Rome pittoresque. Les aquarelles d'Ettore Roester-Franz*, Plurigraf, Narni-Terni, 1981

◆ *Lo Sport nel mondo antico*, Ed Quasar, Rome, 1987

◆ MORTON (H.V.): *A Traveller in Rome*, London and New York, 1957

◆ NAVAL (M.): *A Roma si racconta che... Leggende, aneddoti, curiosità*, Nuova Editrice Spada, Rome, 1978

COOKERY

◆ *A Taste of Ancient Rome*, I. Gozzini Giacosa (tr. by A. Herklotz), University of Chicago

ess, 1994
*Around the Roman
ble*, P. Fass,
acmillan, 2003
*In a Roman Kitchen:
meless Recipes from
e Eternal City*, J.
ettoja, John Wiley &
ons Inc , 2003
*Roman Cookery:
ncient Recipes for
odern Kitchens*,
 Grant
*Roman Cookery:
ecipes and History
ooking Through the
ges)*, J. Renfre, English
eritage Publications,
004
*Rome, at Home:
e Spirit of La Cucina
omana in Your Own
tchen*, S. Dunaway,
oadway Books, 2004
*Cooking and Dining in
perial Rome*, Apicius
, J. Dommers Vehling),
999

LITERATURE
LATIN WRITERS

DAVENPORT (B.) (ED.):
e Portable Roman
eader*, Harmondsworth,
979
GRANT (M.):
tin Literature,
 Anthology*,
armondsworth, 1978
GRANT (M.) (ED.):
oman Readings*,
armondsworth, 1958
GRANT (M.):
oman Literature*,
armondsworth, 1954
AMMIANUS
ARCELLINUS:
e Later Roman Empire*
 W. Hamilton), London,
86
LIVY:
story of Rome*
any translations)
PLINY THE YOUNGER:
tters* (tr. B. Radice),
enguin 1969
SUETONIUS:
e Twelve Caesars*
 R. Graves),
armondsworth, 1957
TACITUS:
e Histories* (several
nslations)
TACITUS:
e Annals* (several
nslations)

LITERATURE:
LATER WRITERS

BOWEN (E.):
Time in Rome*, London
d New York, 1966
BROWNING (R.):
e Ring and the Book*
any editions)
BYRON (LORD):
hilde Harold*, London
12–17 (many editions)
CELLINI (B):
utobiography*,

(tr John Addington
Symonds), London 1925
◆ CHATEAUBRIAND (F.R.
DE):
Memoirs (tr. R. Baldick),
London, 1961
◆ CLARK (E.):
Rome and a Villa,
Garden City, 1952
◆ CRAWFORD (F.M.):
Ave Roma Immortalis,
New York, 1898
◆ DICKENS (C.):
Pictures from Italy,
London, 1846
◆ DYER (J.):
The Ruins of Rome,
London, 1740
◆ EVELYN (J.):
Diaries (many editions)
◆ GOETHE (J.W. VON):
Italian Journey (tr. W.H.
Auden and E. Mayer),
Alfred A Knopf, New
York/Everyman's Library,
London, 2002
◆ GRAVES (R.):
I Claudius, London, 1934
◆ JAMES (H.):
Daisy Miller, London,
1879
◆ MONTAIGNE (M. DE):
*The Journal of
Montaigne's Travels in
Italy*, London, 1903
◆ MORAVIA (A.):
Roman Tales (tr. A.
Davidson), London, 1956
◆ NIGHTINGALE (F.):
*Florence Nightingale in
Rome. Letters Written in
the Winter of 1847-48*,
Philadelphia, 1981
◆ ROGERS (S.):
Italy, a Poem,
London, 1830
◆ SHAKESPEARE (W.):
Julius Caesar
◆ STENDHAL:
A Roman Journal (tr. H.
Chevalier), London, 1959
◆ STENDHAL:
Rome, Naples, Florence
(tr. R.N. Coe), London,
1959
◆ TAINE (H.):
Italy. Naples and Rome
(tr. J. Durand), London,
1867
◆ TWAIN (M.):
Innocents Abroad,
Hartford, Connecticut,
1869
◆ ZOLA (E.):
Rome (tr. E.A. Vitzetelly),
New York, 1896

FILMOGRAPHY

◆ *Accattone*,
P.P. PASOLINI, 1961
◆ *Bellissima*,
L. VISCONTI, 1951
◆ *The Belly of an
Architect*,
P. GREENAWAY, 1987
◆ *Ben Hur*,
W. WYLER, 1959
◆ *Bicycle Thieves*,
V. DE SICA, 1948
◆ *Cleopatra*, J.L.
MANKIEWICZ, 1963

◆ *La Dolce Vita*, F.
FELLINI, 1960
◆ *The Eclipse*, M.
ANTONIONI, 1962
◆ *The Fall of the Roman
Empire*,
S. BRANSTON, 1964
◆ *Fellini Roma*,
F. FELLINI, 1971
◆ *Fellini-Satyricon*,
F. FELLINI, 1969
◆ *Julius Caesar*,
J.L. MANKIEWICZ, 1953
◆ *Mamma Roma*,
P.P. PASOLINI, 1962
◆ *Nights of Cabiria*,
F. FELLINI, 1957
◆ *Quo Vadis?*
M. LEROY, 1951
◆ *Roman Holiday*,
W. WYLER, 1953
◆ *Roman Spring of Mrs
Stone*, J. QUINTERO,
1961
◆ *Rome, Città aperta*,
R. ROSSELLINI, 1945
◆ *La Storia*,
L. COMENCINI, 1985
◆ *Sunday in August*,
L. EMMER, 1949
◆ *Three Coins in a
Fountain*,
J. NEGULESCO, 1954

ACKNOWLEDGMENTS

Grateful
acknowledgment is
made to the following for
permission to reprint
previously published
material:

◆ CURTIS BROWN LTD:
Excerpt from *The Grand
Tour of William Beckford*,
edited by Elizabeth
Mavor, © 1986 by
Elizabeth Mavor.
Reprinted by permission
of Curtis Brown Ltd.,
London, on behalf of
Elizabeth Mavor.

◆ GREENE & HEATON
LIMITED: Excerpt from
Grand Tour Today, by
William Sansom, © 1968
by William Sansom, The
Hogarth Press, London.
Reprinted by permission
of Greene & Heaton
Limited, London.

◆ SIMON & SCHUSTER,
INC.: Excerpt from *The
Letters of John Cheever*
by Benjamin Cheever,
© 1988 by Benjamin
Cheever. Reprinted by
permission of Simon &
Schuster, Inc.

◆ THAMES & HUDSON
LTD: Diary entries of Oct.
31, 1950, and Nov. 7,
1952, from *The
Passionate Sightseer* by
Bernard Berenson,
© 1960 by Thames &
Hudson Ltd. Reprinted
by permission of Thames
& Hudson Ltd, London.

◆ VIKING PENGUIN:
Excerpt from August,
1906, letter of James
Joyce from *Selected
Letters of James Joyce*
by James Joyce, edited
by Richard Ellmann,
copyright © 1957, 1966,
renewed 1985 by The
Viking Press, Inc.:
copyright © 1966, 1975
by F. Lionel Munro as
Administrator of the
Estate of James Joyce.
Reprinted by permission
of Viking Penguin, a
division of Penguin
Books USA Inc.

◆ LIST OF ILLUSTRATIONS

When the city is not mentioned, it is Rome except in the case of ENSBA, ENIT, Gallimard, musée du Louvre, RMN for which it is Paris; Giraudon for which it is Vanves (France) and TCI (Touring Club Italiano) for which it is Milan.

Alfred A Knopf edition, front cover View from the Pincio, I. Caffi, coll. Noferi, Florence © Scala.
Back cover Basilica de San Pietro & Ponte San Angelo-Morning, the Vatican © Walter Bibikow/Danita Delimont, Agent.
1 Temple of Castor and Pollux, Roman Forum, postcard, all rights reserved. **10-11** Piazza Navona, photo, c. 1857–65, cl. Siegert, Munich. **12** Goats in Trajan's Forum, photo, early 20th century © Alinari-Giraudon. **12–13** Piazza Bocca della Verità, idem. **14** View of the bridge and the Castel Sant'Angelo, photo, early 20th century © Alinari-Giraudon. **16–17** Cl. Guido Prola.
25 Roman she-wolf, Etruscan bronze, 5th century BC, Musei Capitolini © Scala. **26** Foundation rites, bas-relief, Museo della Civiltà Romana © Dagli Orti, Paris. Romulus and Remus, marble bas-relief © AKG, Berlin. Stele dedicated to Romulus, founder of the city, Museo de la Civiltà Romana © Dagli Orti, Paris. Head of Pyrrhus, marble © Ny Carlsberg Glyptotek, Copenhagen
27 Roman noble, marble sculpture, cl. Jean Mazenod in L'Art de l'ancienne Rome © Editions Citadelles & Mazenod, Paris. The Punic Wars, Hannibal in Italy, J. Ripanda, fresco, 1508, Musei Capitolini © Dagli Orti, Paris. Scipio the African, film poster © Archivio S.A.C. Cicero accuses Catilina of conspiracy in the Senate, C. Maccari, fresco, 1859, Palazzo Madama © AKG Berlin.
28 Assassination of Julius Caesar, V. Camuccini, oil on canvas, early 19th century, Museo di Capodimonte, Naples © Pedicini, Naples. The Prima Porta Augustus, detail, marble statue, Braccio Nuovo, Vatican © Scala. Votive shield, marble, 8th century, musée lapidaire d'Art païen, Arles © Dagli Orti, Paris. **28–29** Romans, watercolored litho © de Selva Tapabor, Paris. **29** Rome besieged by the Goths, manuscript De civitate dei © Bibl. nat., Paris. Romulus Augustulus, coin, idem. **30** St Gregory I the Great, detail, in Registrum Gregori, c. 984 © Stadtbibliothek, Trier. Charlemagne crowning his son in Rome, manuscript © Bibl. nat., Paris. **31** Pope Gregory XI returning to Rome from Avignon, detail, B.D. Giovanni, fresco, early 16th century, Museo delle Pie Disposizioni, Sienna © Scala. Portrait of Cola di Rienzo, engraving © Bibl. nat., Paris. Portrait of Jules II, Morace, engraving, idem. The Sack of Rome, anon. Flemish, oil on canvas, private coll., Paris. **32** Portrait of Sixtus V, detail, attributed to F. Bellini, oil on canvas, coll. Guy de Aldecuat, Paris. Pope Pius IX on the Dedia Gestatoria, water color © photo A.D. P.C./Artphot. **33** Portrait de Garibaldi, P. Palizzi, oil on canvas, late 19th century, Museo del Risorgimento © Scala. Idem, detail, Italian flag. Mussolini enters Rome, October 1922, photo © L de Selva Tapabor, Paris. John XXIII © ENIT. **34** Provoco, Republican coin © Bibl. nat., Paris. Haruspex, drawing, after a funeral altar, Galleria degli Uffizi, Florence. **34–5** Relief of Domitius Ahenobarbus, c. 100 BC, musée du Louvre © RMN. **35** Marcus Aurelius making a sacrifice, bas-relief, Palazzo dei Conservatori, Musei Capitolini © Scala. Voting scene, coin, Gens Licinia period © Bibl. nat., Paris. The Tetrarchs, porphyry, Basilico di San Marco, Venice © Scala. **36** Standard bearer, Urs Graf. wood engraving, 1527 © Öffentlich Kunst Sammlung, Basel. Clement VII and Charles V, Vasari's studio, oil on canvas, Palazzo Vecchio, Florence © Scala.
36–7 Death of the Constable of Bourbon in Rome, engraving, 1527 © Bibl. nat., Paris. **37** Siege of the Castel Sant'Angelo, engraving, 1527 © idem. Signature of the Constable of Bourbon, all rights reserved. **38–39** 8th General Assembly of the Synod of Bishops, cl. Nusca Antonello © Gamma. **39** The religions in Un an à Rome, J-B. A. Thomas, watercolor © Bibl. nat., Paris. **40** Nero's Golden House, Laocoön Room, G. Ghedanne, watercolor, musée des Beaux-Arts, Rouen © Dagli Orti,

Paris. **40–41** Working on the Pincio in Rome, litho after a drawing by Pinelli © Pierre Pinon, Maisons-Alfort.
41 Institut de correspondance archéologique, 19th century engraving, German Archeological Institute © Ikona. Portrait of Johann Joachim Winckelmann, oil on canvas, Kunsthaus, Zurich © Ikona. Visit to the catacombs by Pius IX, De Rossi, litho © Explorer. Mussolini: the first blow with the pickaxe, Via dei Fori Imperiali, photo © all rights reserved. **42** Detail of a program of the Jovinelli Theater, Ceccarius coll. © Bibl. naz., Rome. Latin inscription, cl. M. Marzot. Dante, engraving © Bibl. nat., Paris. **43** Signature of Cola di Rienzo, all rights reserved. Portrait of G. G. Belli, Ceccarius coll. © Bibl. naz., Rome. Roma, città aperta, Aldo Fabrizi, film poster © Archivio S.A.C. **44** Vicolo dei Chiodaroli, street sign, cl. M. Marzot. Typical Trastevere figure, coll. Ceccarius © Bibl. naz., Rome. Via Capocciotto nel Ghetto, oil on canvas, Muse di Roma, cl. C. Bernoni. **I** Frontispiece of Prima parte d' architetture e prospettive, G. B. Piranesi, 18th century engraving, private coll. **II** Portrait of G. B. Piranesi, frontispiece of Opere varie, 1750, idem. Second frontispiece of Vedute di Roma, 18th century, idem. **III** Trajan's Column, idem. **IV–V** Circus Maximus, idem. **VI–VII** Via Appia, idem. **VIII–IX** Campo Vaccino (Roman Forum), idem. **X–XI** The Coliseum, idem. **XII–XIII** The Isola Tiberina, idem. **XIV** Numerals, cl. M. Marzot, The Arch of Titus, Piranesi, engraving, Bibl. nat., Paris. Front of the pedestal of Trajan's column, C.Percier, wash, ENSBA. **XV** Base of the obelisk, Piazza di San Giovanni in Laterano, N. Van Delft, engraving, all rights reserved. Ancient inscription in Roma Sotterranea. De Rossi © Bibl. nat., Paris. **XVI** The coats of arms of the Popes, all rights reserved. **45** Roman peasant woman, pensive. E. Herbert, oil on canvas, musée Hébert, Paris © RMN. **46** Monumental statue known as Marforio, sculpture in the round, Musei Capitolini © Alinari-Giraudon. Il Pasquino, engraving © Bibl. nat., Paris. **46–7** The Bocca della Verità, cl. M. Marzot. **47** Cagliostro and Lorenza, fan, 1786, musée Carnavalet © Giraudon. Madama Lucrezia, marble bust, cl. A. Idini. **48** Figures for Il Carnevale romano, Goethe's description. G. M. Kraus, after J.G. Schütz, watercolored engraving on wood, 1788–9 © Goethe-Museum, Düsseldorf. **48–9** October Festival outside the walls of Rome, W. Marstrand, oil on canvas, 1839 © Thorsvaldsens Museum, Copenhagen. **49** Feas of St Joseph, A. Pinelli, watercolor, 1852, Museo di Roma, cl. B. Brizzi. Moccoletti in Via del Corso, detail, 1833, idem. Spring festival at Trinità dei Monti, cl. S. Bottani. **50** Cross of the Order of Malta, all rights reserved. The Knight of Malta, H. Baldung Grien, oil on canvas, early 16th century, Nouvelle Résidence, Bamberg © Giraudon. Siege of Rhodes by the Turks, Latin manuscript 60067 © Bibl. nat., Paris. **51** Series of postage stamps, Poste magistrali, Sovrano Militare Ordine di Malta. The Grand Master receiving the standa of the Order from John the Baptist, gold coin, © Sovereign Military Order of Malta. Profile of Fra Andre Bertie, idem. Baptism of Jesus, idem. Lourdes Grotto and Basilica, idem. **52** Papal tiara, watercolor, coll. Luigi Ceccarelli. Opening of the Holy Door, engraving, in L'Illustration, cl. Gallimard. **52–3** Papal blessing, Piazza San Pietro, I. Caffi, oil on canvas, Museo di Roma © Scala. **53** Julius II on the Sedia Gestatoria, detail, Raphael, fresco, Stanza di Eliodoro, Musei di Vaticano © Scala. **54** Stages of restoration of the equestrian statue of Marcus Aurelius, bronze ©.C.R. **55** Stratigraphical section, cl. S. Pelizzoli. Erosion of the stone due to pollution, cl. E. Scalfari/AGF. Restoration of a statue in situ, cl. Adam, detail from The Creation of Man. Michelangelo, fresco before restoration, Sistine Chapel ceiling © Scala. Idem, after restoration © Musei Vaticani/photo P. Zigrossi-A. Bracchetti. **56–7** Preparatic of carciofi alla romana, cl. Gallimard, La Cuisinère, W. Campi, oil on canvas, Galleria Doria-Pamphili © Scala. **58** Chasuble, cl. N. Pacarel. Typical products, cl. Gallimard. **60** Mime, engraving in La Vie des Grecs et

LIST OF ILLUSTRATIONS ◆

des Romains © all rights reserved. Map of Rome, anon., oil on canvas, Palazzo Ducale, Mantua, 1538 © Scala. Obelisk of San Giovanni in Laterano, engraving, all rights reserved. **65** Basilica of Maxentius, transversal section, P.-M. Gauthier, watercolor 1899 © ENSBA. **66** Circus games in the Coliseum, G. Lauro, engraving, all rights reserved **66–7** The Coliseum, after restoration. L.-J.Duc, 1830–1 © ENSBA. **67** Circus of Maxentius. A. Recoura, watercolor, 1899, idem. Pompey's Theater, V. Baltard, watercolor, 1837, idem. **70** The Trophies of Marius, A.-M.Garnaud, wash, 1821, idem. The Arch of Constantine, G. Lauro, engraving, all rights reserved. **70–1** The Temple of Venus and Rome, L. Vaudoyer, watercolor, 1830, idem. **83** The Steps of the Pontifical Chapel, G. B. Falda, engraving, all rights reserved. **84–5** Vault of St Ignazio A. Pozzo, fresco © Scala. Details, idem. Façade of the Cancelleria, P. Letarouilly, engraving, all rights reserved, colored by Tony Cobb. **87** Façade of Palazzo Spada, overall view and detail, Pl Letarouilly, engraving, all rights reserved., colored by C. Quiec. **88–9** Cortile del Belvedere, Perin del Vaga, fresco, Castel Sant'Angelo © Scala. **90** Galleria Sciarra, fresco, cl. G. Berengo Gardin © TCI. **95** Casino de Raphaël à Rome, J. D. A. Ingres, oil on wood, c. 1807 © Musée des arts décoratifs de la Ville-de-Paris/L. Sully-Jaulmes. **96** Gallery of views of modern Rome, idem. G. P. Pannini, oil on canvas, 1759, musée du Louvre, © RMN. **96–7** Gallery of views of ancient Rome, idem. Self-portrait of Pannini, drawing © British Museum, London. **98** Goethe in the country, J. H. Wilhelm Tischbein, 1787, Städelsches Kunstinstitut © AKG, Berlin. **98–9** View of the French Academy in Rome, G. Moreau, wash, musée Gustave Moreau © RMN. The Pyramid of Cestius, J. W. von Goethe, wash © AKG, Berlin. **100–1** View of the Coliseum from the Farnese gardens, J.-B. Corot, oil on canvas, c. 1826, musée du Louvre © RMN. Villa Borghese, G. Balla, oil on canvas, Galleria d'Arte Moderna © Scala. **101** Corot's signature, all rights reserved: Portrait of Corot by Nadar © Bibl. nat., Paris. **102–3** View from the Pincio, I. Caffi, coll. Noferi, Florence © Scala. **104** View of Castel Sant'angelo, V. Brayer, watercolor, private coll. © Giraudon/A. D. A. G P. **105** Alaric takes Rome, F. Chauneau, Engraving © Bibl. nat., Paris. **106** Roman temple, H. Robert, etching, idem. **107** Mausoleum of Augustus, details, G. B. Piranesi, engraving, idem. Mausoleum of Augustus, G. B. Piranesi, engraving, idem. Column of Phocas, Rossini, engraving, 1819, idem. **108–9** Map of Rome, engraving, 16th century, idem. **110–11** Detail of the frontispiece of Monumenti antichi inediti, Guattani, engraving by Mochetti, idem. **112** Leo XII in his pontifical robes, watercolored litho, coll. L. Ceccarelli. **113** Portraits of popes, all rights reserved The start of the barb horse race, Piazza del Popolo, B. Pinelli, litho © Bibl. Nat. Paris. **114** Trastevere personnage. coll. Ceccarius © Bibl. naz., Rome. **115** The Tiber, photo © ENIT. **116–17** Forum Boarium, engraving, P. Gall © Bibl. nat., Paris. **117** Announcement of the gladiatorial games in Pompeii, engraving in La Vie des Grecs et des Romains, all rights reserved. Horse race in Circus Maximus, postcard, private coll. **118** A. Curver, photo, all rights reserved. J. Gracq, photo © Lapi Viollet, Paris. Nizon, cl. C. Seiler © Ed. J. Chambon. **118–19** Fountain of the Four Rivers, engraving Bibl. nat., Paris. **119** Study for the elephant Piazza Minerva, Bernini, drawing, idem. **120** Biblioteca nazionale © ENIT. **121** The Pincio Hill in the morning, H. Caffi, oil on canvas, Ca'Pesaro © Scala. **122** View from the Janiculum © ENIT. Via della Conciliazione, cl. W. Louvet. The EUR, cl. N. Pascarel. **123** The Tiber, cl. idem. The Coliseum, cl. W. Louvet, Neptune Fountain, cl. S. Grandadan. **124** Trastevere café, cl. N. Pascarel. Metro sign, cl. idem. Religious at the Vatican, cl. W. Louvet. **125** Market, cl. N. Pascarel. Flower seller in the Campo de' Fiori, cl. S. Grandadan. Roman policemen, cl. W. Louvet. **126** Via Appia Antica, cl. N. Pascarel. Façade of a house, cl. W. Louvet. Ecclesiastical clothes shop, cl. N. Pascarel. **127** Map of ancient Rome. A. Brambilla, engraving, 1582 © Bibl. nat., Paris. **128** Roman Forum,

cl. W. Louvet. Criminal flung from the Tarpeian Rock, R. Della Porta, manuscript Romuleon © Bibl. nat., Paris. **128–9** Triumph, G. Lauro, engraving, all rights reserved. **130** One of the Dioscuri on the Capitol Hill, cl. S. Bottani. Statue of Marcus Aurelius, detail, G. P. Pannini, oil on canvas, 18th century, Galleria Nazionale dell'Arte Antica, Palazzo Corsini © Scala. **130–1** View of the Capitol, early 19th century photo © Brogi-Giraudon. **131** Piazza del Campidoglio by night © ENIT. Bas-relief of saints Peter and Paul, Mamertine Prison, cl. M. Marzot. Fragments of the colossus of Constantine, Cortile Palazzo dei Conservatori, cl. S. Grandadan and N. Pascarel. Santo Bambino of the Aracoeli, print, all rights reserved. **132** Head of Constantine, fragment of the colossus, 312–15, Musei Capitolini © Scala. Young girl with a dove, Greek stele, archaic period, idem. Boy with a thorn, bronze, 1st century BC, idem. **133** Bust of Commodus as Hercules, marble, idem. Capitoline Brutus, bronze head, idem. Roman she-wolf, Etruscan bronze, 5th century BC, idem. **134** Triumph of Bacchus, P. da Cortona, oil on canvas, idem. **134–135** Dying Gaul, marble, idem. St John the Baptist, Caravaggio, oil on canvas, inacoteca, idem. **135** Capitoline Venus, marble, idem. Dove mosaic, idem. **138** The Curia, photo © ICCD. Roman senator, sculpture, 3rd century BC © Nimattalah/Artephot, Paris. **139** Triumph, reconstruction from the arch of Septimius Severus, litho, all rights reserved. Effigy of Septimius Severus, coin © Bibl. nat., Paris. Arch of Septimius Severus, litho, all rights reserved **140** The Tabularium, restored state, C. Moyaux, watercolor, 1865 © ENSBA. Column of the Temple of Vespasian, photo © ENIT. **141** The Tabularium, present state, C. Moyaux, watercolor, 1865 © ENSBA. Statue on the Capitol, cl. W. Louvet. Temple of Concord, bronze coin of the time of Caligula © Bibl. nat., Paris. **142** Temple of the Dioscuri, cl. A. Idini. View of the Fountain of Juturna © Scala. **143** Christ on the Cross, fresco, Santa Maria Antiqua © Scala. Saint, idem. San Teodoro, A. Pinelli, watercolor, 1834, Museo di Roma, cl. B. Brizzi. **144** Statue of a Vestal cl. A. Idini. View of the temple of Antoninus and Faustina © Magnum, Paris. Idem, cl W. Louvet. **144–145** Basilica of Constantine, J. J. Haffner, watercolor, 1921 © ENSBA. **145** Capital and frieze of the Temple of Antoninus and Faustina, Desgodetz, engraving, in Les édifices de Rome © Bibl. nat. Paris. View of the Temple of Antoninus and Faustina, cl. W. Louvet. Paving stones in the Forum, cl. M. Marzot. **146–147** Arch of Titus, photo, early 20th century © Alinari-Giraudon. **148** Funerary urn in the shape of an archaic hut, terracotta, Forum Antiquarium © Scala. Headless statue of Cybele, Palatine © Scala. Io guarded by Argos, whom Mercury has just set free and garlands, details of fresco, House of Livia © Scala. **149** Apollo and Artemis, decoration on a sacred pillar, terracotta from the Temple of Apollo, Palatine Antiquarium © Werner Forman Archive, London. Terracotta plaque, probably from the Temple of Apollo on the Palatine, today in the Palatine Antiquarium, 28 BC © TCI. **150** Griffins, from the House of Griffins, © Scala. Septidozium, S. Dupérac, engraving, all rights reserved. **150–151** Palace of the Caesars, J.-A. A Deglane, watercolor, 1886 © ENSBA. **151** Reconstruction, idem. Ruins of the Basilica Flavia © Scala. Head of Heliogabalus, sculpture, 3rd century, Musei Capitoline © Scala. **152** Collection of S.P.Q.R. signs, cl. M. Marzot. **153** View of the Coliseum, A. Matveiev, oil on canvas, early 18th century, Tret'kov Gallery, Moscow © Scala. **154–155** Church of Santa Maria in Cosmedin and Temple of Vesta, postcard, all rights reserved. **155** Bocca della Verità, cl. M. Marzot. **156** Interior of St Giorgio in Velabro, idem. Casa dei Crescenzi and Money Changers' Arch, cl. A. Idini. Mounted Amazon, detail of pediment of Temple of Apollo Sosiano © Barbara Malter. **156–157** Rome scene in front of the Theater of Marcellus, H.Bürkerl, oil on canvas © Kunstmuseum, Düsseldorf. **157** Section of Theater of Marcellus, A.L.T. Vaudoyer, watercolor, 1786 © ENSBA. **158** The three columns of the Temple of Apollo, cl. A. Idini. The Portico of Octavia, photo, early 20th century © Alinari-Giraudon. **159** *Portico of Octavia,* reconstruction of façade, F. Duban, watercolor, 1827 © ENSBA. *Old houses by the Portico of Octavia,* F. Roesler, oil on canvas, 19th century, Museo di Roma, cl. C. Bernoni. Piazza Margana, cl. M. Marzot. **161** Jacket of Garibaldi's uniform, Museo Centrale del Risorgimento © Scala. Mussolini declares war on France from the balcony of the Palazzo di Venezia, photo © Roger-Viollet, Paris. Horses of St Mark's in the courtyard of Palazzo di Venezia, coll Ceccarius © Bibl. naz., Rome. **162** Parade on Via dell'Impero, photo © Roger-Viollet, Paris. *Julius Caesar,* engraving, all rights reserved. **162–163** *The Forum of Augustus,* reconstruction, F.-J. T. Uchard, watercolor, 1869 © ENSBA. **163** Study for the base and the capitol of the Temple of Mars the Avenger, L. Noguet, Indian-ink drawing, 1869 © ENSBA. **164** *Augustus as pontiff,* marble, cl. Jean Mazenod, in *L'Art de l'ancienne Rome* © Éditions Citadelles & Mazenod, Paris. Temple of Minerva, photo © Siegert coll., Munich. *Forum of Nerva,* detail, inscription, L. Noguet, 1869, watercolor © ENSBA. **164–165** *Trajan's Forum,* reconstruction, *idem.* **165** View of the Basilica Ulpia, Trajan's Forum © Scala. Image of Trajan, coin © Bibl. nat., Paris. **166** *Section of Trajan's Column,* engraving © ICCD. Trajan's Column, A. Idini, colored photo, 1921 © musée Albert-Kahn-Dépt. des Hauts-de-Seine. **167** Details of Trajan's Column, bas-reliefs, cl. M. Marzot. *Main side of the pedestal of Trajan's Column,* C. Percier, Indian ink and wash © ENSBA. *Statue of St Peter on Trajan's Column,* engraving, all rights reserved. View from the steps of Trajan's Market © Scala. **168** The Torre dei Conti Tower, Piazza Venezia, photo, Ceccarius coll. © Bibl. naz., Rome. The Torre dei Milizie, cl. M. Marzot. *The campanile of Santa Francesca Romana,* litho, all rights reserved. **168–169** Arch of Constantine and the Meta Sudans, photo, c. 1873, Piantanida-Sartori coll. **169** Vault of the apse, Santi Cosma e Damiano, mosaic © Scala. The extension of Rome in the time of Trajan, geographical map © Scala. **170** *The interior of the Coliseum,* C. W. Eckersburg, oil on canvas, 19th century © Thorvaldsens Museum, Copenhagen. **170–171** The Coliseum, reconstruction, J. Duc, atercolor, 1830–1 © ENSBA. **171** *Golden Colossus of Nero,* reconstruction, detail, E.-G-Coquart, watercolor, 1863, *idem.* Underground passages beneath the Coliseum Nimatallah/Artephot, Paris. **172** Gladiator's helmet, bronze, 1st century AD, Museo Archeologico, Naples © Dagli Orti, Paris. *Circus games,* G. Lauro, engraving, all rights reserved. *Gladiators' combat,* mosaic, musée de Nennig cl. Musée archéologique, Lattes. **172–173** *Amphitheater scene,* mosaic, 4th century AD, Archeological Museum, Madrid © Nimatallah/Artephot, Paris. **173** Gladiator's greave, gladiator's arm guard, and retiarius' shoulder guard, bronze, 1st century AD, musée du Louvre © RMN. *Ave Caesar, morituri te salutant,* J.-L. Gérôme, oil on canvas, 19th century © Yale University Art Gallery, New Haven. Base of an anemometer, marble, Vatican Museums © IGDA, Milan. **174** Compartment of coffered ceiling decorated with grotesques from the Domus Aurea, in *Dessins de peintures antiques,* S. Bartoli, 17th century, Bibl. nat., Paris. *Trajan's Baths,* engraving, *idem.* **175** The Pyramid of Cestius, postcard, private coll. **177** View of the Aventine, cl. J.-L. Malroux. *The Sabine women interrupt the fighting between the Romans and the Sabine men,* L. David, oil on canvas, musée du Louvre © RMN **178** *The Four Factiones of the Augurs,* mosaic, Museo Terme Diocleziano © Scala. **178–9** *Circus Maximus,* engraving, Bibl. nat., Paris © Giraudon. **179** Door of Santa Sabina, detail, wood © Scala. *Santa Sabina,* A. Pinelli, watercolor, 19th century, Museo di Roma, cl. B. Brizzi. **180** *The Legend of St Alexis,* fresco, San Clemente © Scala. *Alof de Wignacourt, Grand Master of the Order of Malta,* Caravaggio, oil on canvas, musée du Louvre © RMN. **181** Emblem of the Order of Malta, detail of a stamp, all rights reserved. Drawing for stelae on the Piazza dei

Cavalieri di Malta © Pierpont Morgan Library, New York. *Mithras sacrificing the bull,* high relief, 1st–3rd century AD musée du Louvre © Lauros-Giraudon. **182** Street on the Aventine, cl. J.-L. Malroux. *San Saba Church,* F. Roesler, oil on canvas, Museo di Roma, cl. C. Bernoni. **182–3** *The Pyramid and the Protestant Cemetery, idem.* **183** Dedication on the Pyramid of Cestius, engraving all rights reserved. The tomb of John Keats, cl. A. Idini. **184** Bull, on the door of the slaughterhouse, cl. A. Idini. A slaughterhouse employee photo, Primoli Foundation © O. Savio. The Amphora Fountain, cl. M. Marzot. View of Testaccio, cl. A. Idini. **185** Basilica of San Giov anni in Laterano, Charpentier, litho, all rights reserved. **186–7** *The Celio,* engraving © Bibl. nat., Paris. **187** Details of the façade of San Gregorio Magno, high reliefs, cl. M. Marzot. Façade of San Gregorio Magno, cl. Gallimard. **188** Campanile of SS. Giovanni e Paolo, cl. Gallimard. View of the apse of SS. Giovanni e Paolo © Scala. **189** Statue of Claudius as Jupiter, Museo Pio-Clementino, Vatican © Scala. **190** Park of Villa Celimontana, cl. A. Idini. The Dolabella Arch, *idem. Madonna and Child,* apse mosaic, Santa Maria in Domnica © Scala. **190–1** *Interior of Santo Stefano Rotondo,* F.-M. Granet, oil on canvas, cl. B. Terlay © musée Granet, Palais de Malte, Aix-en Provence. **191** Navicella fountain, cl. M. Marzot. *Martyrs,* Pomarancio, fresco, Santo Stefano Rotondo, 16th century © A. de Luca. Interior of Santo Stefano Rotondo, cl. A. Idini. **192** *Santi Quattro Coronati,* A. Pinelli, watercolor, Museo di Roma, cl. B. Brizzi. Santi Quattro Coronati , cl. A. Idini Basin for ablutions, cloister of Santi Quattro Coronati, cl. M. Marzot. **193** *Triumph of the Cross,* apse mosaic of San Clemente © Scala. *St Catherine freed by angels,* Masolino, fresco, *idem.* **194** Fragment of a fresco, probably a *Last Judgement,* nave of San Clemente © Scala. Statue of Mithras, San Clemente © Scala. **195** Lambs, frieze of apse vault, mosaic, *idem. © idem.* **196** Altar of Mithra, *idem. © idem. Obelisk of San Giovanni in Laterano,* engraving © Bibl. nat., Paris. **196–7** *Feast of St John,* J.-B. A. Thomas, watercolored litho © Bibl. nat., Paris. **197** Angels transporting the San Giovanni obelisk, detail *idem.* **198** Façade of San Giovanni in Laterano, photo © Alinari. Interior of the Basilica of San Giovanni in Laterano, G.-B. Piranesi, engraving © Bibl. nat., Paris. Mussolini signing the Lateran Treaty, photo © Roger-Viollet, Paris. **199** Cosmatesque mosaics, cloister of San Giovanni in Laterano, litho, all rights reserved. View of the cloister, San Giovanni in Laterano, *idem.* Statue on the summit of San Giovanni in Laterano, cl. A. Idini. **200** The Castrense Amphitheater, cl. A. Idini. Grenadiers' Barracks, *idem.* Interior of Santa Croce in Gerusalemme, *idem.* Façade of Santa Croce in Gerusalemme, © ENIT. **201** *Papal Blessing on San Pietro,* I. Caffi, Museo di Roma © Scala. **202** Swiss Guard, postcard, private coll. **203** *Porta Angelica,* F. Roesler, watercolor, Museo di Roma, cl. C. Bernoni. The dome of St Peter's, cl. M. Marzot. **204** *L'Osservatore Romano,* newspaper name, all rights reserved. Passetto, cl. F. Marzi. Leonine Wall, cl. *idem.* **205** Latin Bible 614, folio 219 verso, ill. Ghirlandaio, Bibl. Vaticane, cl. F. Marzi. Papal apartments, cl. F. Marzi. **206** St Peter's tomb, cl. F. Marzi Statue of St Peter, Grotte Vaticane © Scala. **207** *The Creation of Man,* Michelangelo, fresco, Sistine Chapel © Musei Vaticani. **209** *Constantine's Basilica,* Tassoli, fresco, Grotte Vaticane, 16th century © Scala. Mausoleum of Aelius Thyrannus, Necropoli del Vaticano, cl. Marzi-Morselli. **210** *Ponente,* marble paving stone, Piazza San Pietro, cl. Marci-Morselli. *Obelisk, Piazza San Pietro,* engraving, © Bibl. nat., Paris. **210–11** *Project for the façade of St Peter's,* engraving © Electa, Milan. **211** Cardinals in St Peter's, cl. Marzi-Morselli. Nuns, Piazza San Pietro, cl. W. Louvet. The Door of Death, cl. F. Marzi. Holy water stoup in St Peter's, cl. Marzi-Morselli. **212** *Gloria,* Bernini, cl. Marezi-Morselli. *Pietà,* Michelangelo, marble, St Peter's © Scala. **212–13** *Cardinal Melchior de Polignac visiting St Peter's*

LIST OF ILLUSTRATIONS ◆

Basilica in Rome, G. P. Pannini, musée du Louvre © RMN. **213** View of the dome of St Peter's, cl. Marzi-Morselli. *St Longinus*, Bernini, marble, cl. Marzi-Morselli. St Veronica, *idem*. **214** Spiral staircase to entrance of Vatican Museums, cl. A. de Luca. Pediment of Casina of Pius IV, bas-relief, cl. F. Marzi. *Domenico Fontana presenting his project for the Vatican library to Sixtus V*, P. Facchetti, fresco, Sistine Hall © Bibl. del Vaticano. **215** Palazzo del Governatorato, Vatican Station, Palazzo Apostolico, Vatican Gardens, corridor leading to the Sala Regia and interior of the Sala Regia, cl. Marzi-Morselli. Colossal head, Cortile della Pigna, sculpture © ENSBA. **216** Vatican Loggias, cl. F. Marzi. **217** The Chiaramonti Niobid, after a 4th-century Greek original, Museo Pio Clementino © Scala. *Geographical map*, fresco, Galleria delle Carte Geografiche, Musei Vaticani, cl. F. Marzi. **218** *The Delphic Sibyl*, Michelangelo, fresco, detail of the Sistine Chapel vault, photo A. Bracchetti © Musei Vaticani. **218–19** Overall view of the Sistine Chapel vault, Michelangelo, fresco, photo A. Bracchetti/P. Zigrossi © *idem*. **219** Adam, detail of *The Creation of Man*, *idem*. *Ignudo*, next to the scene of Noah's Flood, *idem*. **220** Scenes of the life of Moses, *Moses and Jethro's daughters*, S. Botticelli, fresco, late 15th century, Sistine Chapel, Vatican © Scala. **221** *The Last Judgement, the Damned and Christ Triumphant*, Michelangelo, 1537–41, *idem*. **222** The *Expulsion of Heliodorus from the Temple*, detail, Raphael and his pupils, fresco, Stanza d'Eliodoro, Vatican © Scala. **222–3** *The School of Athens*, Raphael, fresco, Stanza della Segnatura, *idem*. **223** *Erato, surrounded by Polyhymnia, Melpomene, Terpsichore and Urania*, Stanza della Segnatura, *idem*. **224** *Belvedere Apollo*, marble, Museo Pio Clementino, statue © ENSBA. **224–5** The *Laocoön*, *idem*. **225** The *Belvedere Torso*, *idem*. *Augustus of Prima Porta*, marble, Braccio Nuovo, Vatican © Scala. The *Sleeping Ariadne*, marble, Museo Pio-Clementino, *idem*. **226** *Angel Musician*, M. da Forlì, fragment of a fresco, c. 1480, cl. S. Grandadan. *Sixtus IV appointing Platina Prefect of the Vatican Library*, M. da Forlì, c. 1475–7, fresco, Pinacoteca Vaticana © Scala. **226–7** *Madonna and Child*, Pinturicchio, fresco, Sala dei Santi, Appartamento Borgia, Vatican © Scala. **227** *St Lawrence ordained deacon by St Sixtus*, Fra Angelico, fresco, Capella di Niccolò V © Scala. **228** *Portrait of Raphael*, engraving, © Bibl. nat., Paris. *The Transfiguration*, Raphael, oil on canvas, Pinacoteca Vaticano © Scala. *The Expulsion of Adam and Eve from Paradise*, Raphael, fresco, Loggie di Raffaello © Scala. *Isaac blessing Jacob*, *idem*. **229** *The Madonna of Foligno*, Raphael, oil on canvas, Pinacoteca Vaticano © Scala. *The Crossing of the Red Sea*, Raphael © Scala. *The construction of Noah's Ark*, *idem*. **230** *Descent from the Cross*, Caravaggio, oil on canvas, 1604, Pinacoteca Vaticano © Scala. **231** *Pietà*, P. da Cortona, fresco, Cappella di Urbano VIII © Scala. *The Last Communion of St Jerome*, Domenichino, oil on canvas, 1614 Pinacoteca Vaticana © Scala. *St Thomas*, detail of *the Virgin between St Thomas and St Jerome*, G. Reni, oil on canvas, 1625–30, Pinacoteca Vaticana © Scala. **232** Piazza San Pietro, photo, early 20th century Alinari-Giraudon. Piazza San Pietro, cl. W. Louvet. **233** Shield with blazon and details of façades in the Borgo, cl. M. Marzot. Monk, Piazza San Pietro, cl. W. Louvet. *Via del Campanile in the Borgo*, F. Roesler, oil on canvas, 19th century, Museo di Roma, cl. C. Bernoni. *Reconstruction of Hadrian's Mausoleum*, E. Vaudremer, watercolor, 1857 © ENSBA. **234** *Firework display at the Castel Sant'Angelo*, J. Wright of Derby, oil on canvas © Birmingham Art Gallery. **234–5** *Hadrian's Mausoleum, Castel Sant'Angelo*, E. Vaudremer, watercolor, 1857 © ENSBA. **235** *Idem*, longitudinal section. *Angel*, R. da Montelupo, marble, Cortile del Angelo © ENIT. **236** *Palazzo di Giustizia*, F. Roesler, oil on canvas, Museo di Roma, cl. C. Bernoni. View of Prati, photo © Primoli Foundation. **237** Ponte Sant'Angelo, photo © ENIT. **238** *The bridge and the Castel Sant'Angelo*, V. Brayer, watercolor © Giraudon/ A.D.A.G.P. **239** Ponte

Sant'Angelo, cl. A.Idini. Fragment of a double sacrifice to the god Mars, marble relief, musée du Louvre © RMN. **240** Ponte Sant'Angelo, cl. Malroux. Angel on the Ponte Sant'Angelo, Bernini, marble, cl. A. Idini. **241** *Tribune of the Church of San Giovanni dei Fiorentini*, G. cl. J.-L. Malroux.Van Wittle, oil on canvas, private coll. © Scala. Dome of San Giovanni dei Fiorentini, cl. A. Idini. Sculpture, San Giovanni dei Fiorentini, cl. J. L. Malroux. Via Giulia, cl. M. Marzot. **242** *The story of David*, F. Salviati, Palazzo Sacchetti © Scala. *Church of the Spirito Santo dei Napoletani*, A. Pinelli, watercolor, c. 1835 Museo di Roma, cl. B. Brizzi. **242–3** *Palazzo Sacchetti*, M. Corneille, wash on cardboard, T. Ashby coll. © Biblioteca Vaticana. **243** Window of Palazzo Sacchetti, cl. A. Idini. Façade of Santa Maria di Monserrato, cl. A. Idini. *The Last Communion of St Jerome*, Domenichino, oil on canvas, 1614 Pinacoteca Vaticana © Scala. **244** Fountain of the Mascherone, cl. M. Marzot. Piazza Farnese, cl. *idem*. **244–5** *Triumph of Bacchus and Ariadne*, Annibale Carracci, fresco, Palazzo Farnese © Scala. **245** Palazzo Farnese, G. B. Piranesi, engraving © ENIT. Façade on the courtyard of Palazzo Farnese, cl. A. Idini. *Venus and Anchises*, detail, Annibale Carracci, fresco, Palazzo Farnese © Scala. **246** Façade of Palazzo Spada, cl. A. Idini. *Trompe l'oeil* gallery, Palazza Spada, F. Borromini © Scala. Monte di Pietà, fountain, cl. Gallimard. **247** *Portrait of St Charles Borromeo*, engraving © Bibl. nat., Paris. Via dei Giubbonari, cl. M. Marzot. *The Annunciation*, L. Lanfranco, oil on canvas, San Carlo ai Catinari © Scala **248** Via di Grotta Pinta, cl. A. Idini. Campo de' Fiori, cl. *idem*. *Idem*., cl. M. Marzot. *Idem*., cl. J.-L. Malroux. **248–9** *Pompey's Theater*, V. Baltard, watercolor, 1837 © ENSBA. Model of Pompey's Theater © O. Greppi/Amis du plan de Rome, Université de Caen. **249** *Portrait of Giordano Bruno*, engraving © Bibl. nat., Paris. Head of Caesar or a priest, Museo Barracco © Scala. **250** Sant'Andrea della Valle, cl. J.-L. Malroux. **251** Temple A, Largo Argentina, cl. A. Idini. Temple B, *idem*. Temple C, *idem*. Porticus Minucia Frumentaria, *idem*. *Music Festival in Teatro Argentina*, G. P. Pannini, oil on canvas, 1747, musée du Louvre J RMN. **252** *Roaring lion*, façade of Caio Manilio house, cl. M. Marzot. Portico Ottavia and the fish market, Charpentier, watercolored litho, all rights reserved. **253** Jewish shop, photo, Centro di Documentazione Ebraico ontemporaneo, Rome, all rights reserved. Via Botteghe Oscure, cl. M. Marzot. Ghetto street, cl. A. Idini. *Portrait of Alessandro Mattei*, engraving © Bibl. nat., Paris. **254** Tortoise Fountain, cl. J.-L. Malroux. *Portrait of Beatrice Cenci*, G. Reni, oil on canvas, Galleria Nazionale di Arte Antica © Scala. The Synagogue, cl. A. Idini. **255** *The Pantheon*, I Caffi, oil on canvas, Ca Pesaro, Venice. **257** *St Ignatius of Loyola*, anon., oil on canvas, Duques del Infantino, Madrid © Artephot/Oronoz, Paris. *Urban VIII in the Gesù*, A. Sacchi, oil on canvas, Galeria Nazionale d'Arte Antica © Scala. **258** Altar of St Ignatius of Loyola, Gesù © Scala. Passage of the Camerette di Sant'Ignazio, A. Pozzo © Scala. Palazzo Doria-Pamphili, cl. A. Idini. **259** *The Flight into Egypt*, Annibale Carracci, oil on canvas, Palazzo Doria-Pamphili © Scala. *Salome*, Titian, idem. *Countryside with dancers*, C. Lorrain, *idem*. **260** The marble foot, cl. A. Idini. Marble plaque, Santa Maria sopra Minerva, cl. M. Marzot, *Christ*, Michelangelo, marble, Santa Maria sopra Minerva © Scala. **261** *Piazza della Minerva*, A. Pinelli, watercolor, c. 1835, Museo di Roma, cl. B. Brizzi. Bernini's elephant bearing an obelisk, cl. M. Marzot. The trompe l'oeil dome of Sant'Ignazio, A. Pozzo, fresco, 1685 © Scala. **262–3** Domes © G.-C. Gasponi. **264** *Dedication of the Pantheon*, engraving, all rights reserved. **264–5** *View of the Pantheon*, Marchi, oil on canvas, 1754, private coll., Rome © L. Pedicini, Naples. **265** Aerial view of the Pantheon © ICCD. Dome of the Pantheon, view of the interior, cl. A. Idini. Interior of the Pantheon, cl. W. Louvet. **266** *Pantheon*, G. C. Chédanne, watercolor, watercolor, 1891 © ENSBA. Interior of the Pantheon © Scala. **267** *The Temple of Hadrian*, G. B. Piranesi, engraving © Bibl. Nat. Paris.

475

◆ LIST OF ILLUSTRATIONS

Bocconi Stores, early 20th century, postcard, private coll. The top of Trajan's Column, cl. A. Idini. *The Column of Marcus Aurelius,* Piazza Colonna, colored photograph, early 20th century, Museo di Storia della fotografia © Alinari. **268** *Reliefs on the Column of Marcus Aurelius,* G. Guerra, drawings, © Statens Museum for Kunst, Copenhagen. Commemorative base of the Column of Antoninus Pius, Cortile delle Corazze, Vatican © Scala. **269** Views of the façades of Palazzo Montecitorio, cl. A. Idini. Palazzo Chigi, cl. *idem.* Galleria Colonna, cl. *idem.* Palazzo Montecitorio © ENIT. **270** Piazza delle Coppelle, cl. A. Idini. Santa Maria in Campo Marzio, cl. *idem. St Cecilia in Paradise,* Domenichino, fresco, San Luigi dei Francesi © Scala. **270–1** *The Vocation of St Matthew,* Caravaggio, oil on canvas, 1599-1602, *idem.* **271** The salamander, emblem of Francis I, façade of San Luigi dei Francesi, cl. M. Marzot. *St Matthew and the Angel,* detail, Caravaggio, oil on canvas, San Luigi dei Francesi © Scala. Virgin, votive aedicule, Piazza San Luigi dei Francesi, cl. M. Marzot. **272** Palazzo Madama, A. Specchi, engraving, all rights reserved. Cupola of Sant'Ivo, cl. M. Marzot. **273** Market on Piazza Navona, T. Cuccioni, photo, 1860 © Bibl. nat., Paris. **274** Via dei Coronari, cl. G. Peyrot. Map of Rome, 1637 © Bibl. nat., Paris. **276** *Piazza Navona Flooded,* J.-B. A. Thomas, watercolored litho, in *Un an à Rome* © Bibl. nat., Paris. **276–7** *Piazza Navona,* G. Van Wittel, oil on canvas, private coll. © Ugo Bozzi Editore. **277** Fontana dei Quattro Fiumi, cl. G. Peyrot. **278** Nostra Signora al Sacro Cuore Church, cl. G. Peyrot. *Section of Sant'Agnese in Agone,* engraving, Bibl. nat., Paris. **279** Palazzo Pamphili, cl. M. Marzot, *Portrait of Innocent X,* detail, D. Velázquez, oil on canvas, 17th century, Palazzo Doria Pamphili © Scala. Palazzo Massimo, cl. G. Peyrot. Via di Pasquino, street name, cl. *idem.* Pasquino, talking statue, cl. G. Peyrot. **280** Façade of the Church of Santa Maria della Pace, cl. G. Peyrot. Via di S. Maria dell'Anima, street name, cl. *idem.* **280–1** *Sibyls,* Raphael, fresco, Chigi Chapel, Santa Maria della Pace, early 16th century © Scala. **281** Cloister of Santa Maria dell'Anima, cl. G. Peyrot. Piazza della Pace, cl. *idem.* Terrina Fountain, cl. *idem. St Philip Neri,* engraving © Bibl. nat., Paris. **282** Oratorio dei Filippini, cl. G. Peyrot. Detail of San Salvatore in Lauro, bas-relief, cl. M. Marzot. **282–3** *Church and Oratory of Santa Maria in Vallicella,* G. B. Falda, engraving, all rights reserved. **283** Torre dell' Orologio, Chiesa Nuova, photo © ENIT. Via dei Coronari, cl. G. Peyrot. Façade of Palazzo Lancelotti, cl. *idem.* **284** Sign of the Albergo dell'Orso, J. H. Parker, photo, 1868 © Bibl. nat., Paris. Torre della Scimmia, cl. G. Peyrot. *The Prophet Isaiah,* Raphael, fresco, Sant'Agostino Church © Scala. **285** *Madonna of the Pilgrims,* Caravaggio, oil on canvas, Sant'Agostino © Scala. Façade of Sant'Apollinare Church, cl. M. Marzot. **286** Views of façades 6 cl. J.-L.Malroux, 2 cl. M. Marzot, 1 cl. S. Bottani, 1 cl. W. Louvet. **287** *The Trevi Fountain,* G. Rohner, oil on canvas, Subes coll., Paris, 1966 © Scala. **289** *Montecavallo,* engraving, P. Bril, ink, Gabinetto degli Stampi, Florence © Scala. **290** Carriages parked on Piazza Barberini, photo, Ceccarius coll. © bibl. naz., Rome. **290–1** *The Triumph of Divine Providence,* P. da Cortona, fresco, Palazzo Barberini © Scala. **291** *Palazzo Barberini,* engravings, all rights reserved. *St Michael overcoming the Devil,* G. Reni, oil on canvas, Church of the Cappuchins © G. Nimatallah/Ricciarini, Milan. Church of Santa Maria della Concezione, crypt of the Cappuchins' Church, photo early 20th century © Alinari-Giraudon. **292** Emblem of the Barberini, stained-glass window in Santa Maria in Aracoeli, cl. J. L. Malroux. *La Fornarina,* Raphael, oil on canvas, Galleria Nazionale dell'Arte Antica © Scala. **292–3** *Judith Beheading Holofernes,* Caravaggio, oil on canvas, *idem.* **293** *Madonna of Tarquinia,* F. Lippi, painting on wood, *idem. Portrait of Stefano Sciarra-Colonna,* A. di Cosimo, *idem.* **294** *Piazza delle Quattro Fontane,* L. Cruyl, engraving, 17th century © The Cleveland Museum of Art. Fountain representing the Nile, sculpture, cl. W. Louvet.

294–5 *Ecstasy of St Teresa,* Bernini, marble, Santa Maria della Vittoria © Scala. **295** Fountains representing the Tiber, Strength or Juno, Fidelity or Diana, sculptures, 1st century, cl. W. Louvet, 2nd and 3rd century, A. Idini. Dome of San Bernardo, cl. A. Idini. **296** Façade of San Carlo alle Quattro Fontane, cl. A. Idini. Façade of Sant'Andrea al Quirinale, cl. A. Idini. Dome of San Carlo alle Quattro Fontane, cl. G. Berengo Gardin © TCI. **296–297** *Piazza del Quirinale,* G. Van Wittel, oil on canvas, Galleria Nazionale dell'Arte Antica © Scala. **297** Piazza del Quirinale, aerial view, photo © ENIT. The Presidential Guard, State Room, Palazzo del Quirinale, © ENIT. Spiral staircase, Palazzo del Quirinale, cl. G. Berengo Gardin © TCI. **298** Anita Ekberg in front of the Trevi Fountain, in *La Dolce Vita,* F. Fellini, private coll., Paris. Virgin indicating the source of the spring to soldiers, bas-relief, Trevi Fountain, cl. A. Idini. **299** *Aurora,* G. Reni, fresco, Accademia di San Luca © Scala. *St Luke painting the Virgin Mary,* Raphael, oil on canvas, *idem.* © Scala. Trevi Fountain, cl. H. Simone Huber © SIE. **300** Galleria Colonna, cl. G. Berengo Gardin © TCI. *Peasant Eating Beans,* Annibale Carracci, oil on canvas, Galleria Colonna © Scala. Basilica dei Santi Apostoli, cl. A. Idini. **301** Galleria Sciarra, cl. G. Berengo Gardin © TCI. Via della Pilotta, photo, early 20th century © Alinari-Giraudon. Trasteverian figure, Ceccarius coll. © Bibl. naz., Rome. **302** Façade of San Silvestro in Capite, cl. *idem.* Paparazzo in Via Veneto in *La Dolce Vita,* F. Fellini © P. Praturlon. Via Veneto, postcard, private coll. **303** Trinità dei Monti, watercolor, Y. Brayer, private coll., Paris © Giraudon/A.D.A.G.P. **305** Via Peregrinorum, street name, cl. G. Peyrot. View of the twin churches, cl. G. Peyrot. **306** Bust of G. Valadier, cl. G. Peyrot. **306–307** Piazza del Popolo looking onto the Pincio, photo 20th century © Alinari-Brogi-Giraudon. **307** Antique dealers, Via del Babuino, cl. G. Peyrot. Caffè Canova cl. *idem.* Piazza del Popolo © cl. *idem. The Prophet Daniel,* Bernini, marble, Santa Maria del Popolo © Scala. **308** Fountain of Silenus, cl. G. Peyrot. *Horse race down the Via del Corso,* engraving, private coll. **309** Artists, Via Margutta, photos © ENIT. Façades, Via del Corso, cl. W. Louvet. Palazzo Bonaparte cl. G. Peyrot. Façade of the Church of Santi Ambrogio e Carlo, cl. *idem.* Kiosk on the Via del Corso, cl. *idem.* **310** *Res Gestae,* façade of the pavilion housing the Ara Pacis, cl. *idem. Mausoleum of Augustus,* engraving, private coll., Paris. Mausoleum of Augustus, cl. G. Peyrot. Bas-relief, detail of the Ara Pacis, cl. *idem.* **310–311** Ara Pacis, overall view, cl. *idem.* **311** *Earth with her two children,* bas-relief, Ara Pacis, cl. *idem.* Stands selling prints and engravings on Piazza Borghese, *idem.* Loggia di Palazzo BorGhese, cl. *idem.* **312** *The Caffè Greco,* L. Passini, oil on canvas, 19th century, Hamburg Kunsthalle © AKG, Berlin. **312–13** Carriages for rent, Piazza di Spagna, cl. G. Peyrot. **313** Pediment, façade of the Collegio di Propaganda Fide, cl. G. Peyrot. Piazza di Spagna, Collegio di Propaganda Fide, photo © Bibl. nat., Paris. Casina Rossa, cl. G. Peyrot. San Lorenzo in Lucina, cl. G. Peyrot. **314** Piazza di Spagna © ENIT. Barcaccia Fountain, cl. G. Peyrot. Church of the Trinità dei Monti, cl. *idem.* **314–15** *Church of Trinità dei Monti and Villa Medici,* F.-M. Granet, oil on canvas, musée du Louvre © RMN. **315** Doorway, Via Gregoriana, cl. M. Marzot. Villa Medici, garden side, cl. W. Louvet. Villa Medici, *idem.* **316** Front cover of the first edition of *Promenades dans Rome,* Stendhal, Paris, 1829, Bibl. nat., Paris. Casina Valadier, cl. G. Peyrot. Henrico Toti Monument, cl. *idem.* The Pincio, A. Léon, colored photo, 1921 © musée Albert-Kahn, Dépt. des Hauts-de-Seine. **317** Via Appia © V. Giannella. **318** Via Appia Antica, photo, early 20th century © Electa, Milan. **319** Via Appia Antica, cl. G. Peyrot. **320** *Mosaic of the athletes,* detail, Museo Gregoriano Profano, Vatican © Scala. Caracalla, coin, 3rd C. AD © Bibl. nat., Paris. *Farnese Hercules,* Museo Nazionale, Naples © Scala. **320–1** Baths of Caracalla, ground plan of its present state, J.-E. A. Duquesne, watercolor, 1901 © ENSBA. **321** Paving, lored mosaics of the Baths of Caracalla, cl. M. Marzot. *osaic of the athletes,* detail, Museo Gregoriano rofano, Vatican © Scala. House of Cardinal Bessarione, . G. Peyrot. **322** *Colombarium of Pomponius Hylas,* ampana, print, 1843 © Bibl. nat., Paris. **322–3** Stone arcophagus of Scipio Barbatus, Museo Pio-Clementino, atican © Scala. **323** Brickwork of Aurelian Wall and aths of Caracalla, cl. M. Marzot. Porta Latina, cl. G. eyrot. **324** Via di Porta San Sebastiano, street name, cl. . Peyrot. Porta di San Sebastiano, photo, Cecc arius oll. © Bibl. naz., Rome. Milestone, cl. G. Peyrot. **324–5** *uo Vadis* film poster, private coll. Paris. **25** Section of a atacomb, De Rossi, engraving, in *Roma sotterranea istiana* © Bibl. nat., Paris. The crypt of the popes, atacombs of San Callisto, *idem.* **326** Symbols in the atacombs, all rights reserved. The Crypt of the Popes, atacombs of San Callisto © Scala. Symbols in the atacombs, all rights reserved. **327** *Felicitas,* inscription, atacombs of Priscilla Comisscione di archeologia sacra. eacock, fresco, Catacombs of Priscilla, *idem.* Miracle the spring, Catacombs of Commodilla, *idem.* Eel, atacombs of Priscilla, *idem.* The Good Shepherd, ordani cemetery, *idem.* Symbols of the catacombs, all ghts reserved. View of three tombs, Catacombs of San ebastiano © Scala. **328** Church of Sant'Urbano alla affarella, cl. G. Peyrot. *Circus of Maxentius,* present ate, A. Recoura, atercolor, 1899 © ENSBA. **328–9** em., reconstruction of main façade. *Idem.,* main façade s it was at the time. **329** Circus of Maxentius, cl. G. eyrot. **330** Tomb of Cecilia Metella, details, cl. G. eyrot. Tomb of Cecilia Metella, photo, early 20th century Alinari-Giraudon. **331** View of the interior of the asilica of Santa Maria Maggiore, G. B. Piranesi, ngraving, 18th century © Bibl. nat., Paris. **333** Piazza ella Repubblica and details of the Fountain of the aiads, cl. G. Peyrot. Piazza Esedra with Termini Station nd the Fountain of the Naiads © Alinari-Brogi-Giraudon. **34** *St Bruno,* A. Houdon, sculpture, Santa Maria degli ngeli, cl. *idem.* The meridian of Santa Maria degli Angeli, cl. *idem.* View of the *caldarium,* entrance of the Church Santa Maria degli Angeli, cl. G .Peyrot. **334–5** econstruction of the Baths of Diocletian, E. Paulin, atercolor, 1880 © ENSBA. **335** Baths of the Ancient arden of the Diocletian, cl. M. Marzot. **336** *Young girl of nzio,* statue, Museo delle Terme © Scala. *Battle of the omans and the Germans,* sarcophagus, *idem.* **336–7** he Birth of Venus, high relief, *idem.* **337** Maenads ancing before an urn for ashes, funerary stele, *idem.* arden, fresco, *idem. Niobid,* marble, *idem.* **338** Termini ation, cl. G. Peyrot. Obelisk of the Cinquecento, cl. em. Bernich's Aquarium, cl. G. Peyrot. **338–9** Termini ation, S. Bianchi, photo, early 20th century © Alinari- raudon. **339** The first Termini Station, ©. H. Parker, hoto 1866 © Bibl. Nat., Paris. *Ruins of the Temple of inerva Medica in Rome,* G. B. Busiri, oil on canvas, ational Trust Photographic Library/Christopher Hurst © elbrigg Hall, Norfolk. **340** *Bas-relief of the Baker's Tomb,* ngraving, all rights reserved. The Tomb of Eurysaces, cl. . Peyrot. Basilica of Porta Maggiore, stucco bas-relief © cala. Piazza Vittorio Emanuele II © Alinari-Giraudon. **41** The water tower of the Aqua Giulia, reconstruction, M. Garnaud, watercolor, 1821 © ENSBA. *Idem.,* ctual state. *Trophies of Marius, idem.* **342** *Basilica of anta Maria Maggiore,* G.P. Pannini, oil on canvas, 18th entury, Palazzo del Quirinale, © Giraudon. **343** *The oronation of the Virgin,* J. Torriti, mosaic, Santa Maria aggiore © Scala. *The Dormition of the Virgin, idem. erusalem, idem.* **344** *Christ teaching the Apostles,* osaic, apse of Santa Pudenziana, cl. G. Peyrot. ampanile and door of Santa Pudenziana, cl. G. Peyrot. rchitectural ornament, Santa Pudenziana, cl. M. Marzot. **45** The heavenly Jerusalem, mosaic on the triumphal rch of San Prassede © Scala. Christ and saints, apse osaic, *idem. Madonna and Child with St Praxedes and Pudentiana,* mosaic, St Zeno Chapel © Scala. **346** azza San Pietro in Vincoli, F. Roesler, 19th century, oil n canvas, Museo di Roma, cl. C. Bernoni. The Salita di

Borgia, cl. M. Marzot. **346–7** *Moses,* tomb of Julius II, Michelangelo, marble, Basilica di San Pietro in Vincoli © Scala. **347** Via Leonina, Via dei Ciancaleoni, Via Panisperna, cl. G. Peyrot. Via degli Zingari, street name, cl. G. Peyrot. Portrait of E. Majorana, photo © Roger-Violiet, Paris. **348** Statues of the Palazzo delle Esposizioni, cl. M. Marzot. San Paolo entro le Mura, cl. G. Peyrot. Piccolo Eliseo, *idem.* Interior of the Teatro dell'Opera, photo © ENIT. Bottle of wine: *Est Est Est,* cl. Gallimard. **349** *Banks of the Tiber near the Regola,* F. Roesler, oil on canvas, 19th century, Museo di Roma, cl. C. Bernoni. **351** Danish artists in a Trastevere inn, D. C. Blunck, oil on canvas, © Thorsvaldsens Museum, Copenhagen. *Saltarello,* F. D. Soiron, watercolored engraving, cabinet communal des Estampes. **352** San Bartolomeo, cl. A. Idini. View of Isola Tiberina, cl. G. Rossi © The Image Bank, Milan. The Tiber, cl. M. Marzot **353** The Ponte Rotto, cl. A. Idini. Basilica of Santa Cecilia, cl. A. Idini. Monumental gate to the basilica, *idem. Medieval houses in the Santa Cecilia neighborhood,* F. Roesler, oil on canvas, Museo di Roma, cl. C. Bernoni. *St Cecilia,* S. Maderno, marble, Santa Cecilia in Trastevere © Scala. **354** Madonna dell'Orto Church, cl. A. Idini. Seraphim, details from *The Last Judgment,* P. Cavallini, fresco, Santa Cecilia © Scala. *The Blessed Lodovica Albertoni,* Bernini, marble, Madonna dell'Orto © Scala. **355** Porta Portese flea market, cl. M. Marzot. *Mamma Roma,* P. P. Pasolini, still from the film © Archivio S.A.C. Port of Ripagrande, postcard, private coll. Façade of San Michele, cl. J.-L. Malroux. **356** Cloister of San Cosimato, Ceccarius coll. © Bibl. naz., Rome. The Excubitorium, cl. A. Idini. *Medieval house in Via della Lungaretta,* F. Roesler, oil on canvas, Museo di Roma, cl. C. Bernoni. **357** Trasteverian figures, Ceccarius coll. © Bibl naz., Rome. *Santa Maria in Trastevere,* anon., oil on canvas, 19th century, Museo di Roma. **358** *The Dormition of the Virgin,* P. Cavallini, mosaic, Santa Maria in Trastevere © Scala. *Innocent II,* apse mosaic, *idem* © Scala. **359** *Christ and the Virgin, idem,* Santa Maria della Scala, Pinelli, watercolor, 19th century, Museo di Roma, cl. B. Brizzi. **360** *Juno,* Raphael, fresco in the Loggia di Amore e Psiche, Palazzo della Farnesina, photo © ENIT. Graffiti between two trompe l'oeil columns, B. Peruzzi, fresco in the Salone delle Prospettive, Palazzo della Farnesina © Accademia dei Lincei. **361** *Loggia della Farnesina,* F. Roesler, 19th century, oil on canvas, Museo di Roma, cl. C. Bernoni. Salone delle Prospettive, B. Peruzzi, frescoes, Palazzo della Farnesina © Scala. *Triumph of Galatea,* Raphael, *idem.* **362** Emblem of the Accademia dei Lincei, all rights reserved. *Venus and Adonis,* detail, J. de Ribera, oil on canvas, 1637, Galleria Nazionale d'Arte Antica, Palazzo Corsini. **362–3** *St John the Baptist,* Caravaggio, oil on canvas, *idem.* © Scala. **363** The Orto Botanico, cl. A. Idini. Trilussa, sculpture, Piazza Trilussa, *idem. Ponte Sisto Fountain,* F. Roesler, oil on canvas, 19th century Museo di Roma, cl. C. Bernoni. **364** Aqua Paola Fountain, photo, early 20th century © Alinari-Giraudon. Tempietto, Bramante, B. Berengo Gardin © TCI. **364–5** View from the Janiculum, cl. M. Marzot. **365** Tasso's oak, postcard, private coll. Garibaldi Monument, postcard, private coll. **366** 11 cl. M. Marzot, 3 cl. S. Grandadan, 2 cl. S. Bottani, 1 cl. J.-L. Malroux. **367** *Male Head,* Etruscan art, Villa Giulia © Scala. **368** *Portrait of J. J. Winckelmann,* engraving, all rights reserved. **368–9** Villa Doria-Pamphili, photo, early 20th century © Alinari-Giraudon. **370** Villa Giulia, aerial photograph, cl. G. Rossi © Image Bank, Milan. Crater with figure of a hoplite, glazed terracotta, 460–70 BC, Villa Giulia © Scala. Crater of Aurora, ceramic, *idem.* **370–1** *Apollo,* terracotta statue, late 6th century BC, *idem.* **371** Corner ornament, Etruscan art, *idem* © Scala. Ficoroni Cista, marriage casket, Novius Plautius, bronze, 4th century BC, Villa Giulia © Scala. Lid of cista, Etruscan art, bronze © Scala. *The Sarcophagus of the Bride and Bridegroom,* terracotta, 6th century, Villa Giulia © Scala. **372** View of the Villa Borghese, J. W. Baur, oil on canvas, Galleria Borghese © Scala. *Pauline Borghese,* A.Canova,

marble, *idem* © Scala. **373** Statues of animals in the park of Villa Borghese, cl. M. Marzot. *Apollo and Daphne*, Bernini, Galleria Borghese © Scala. *The Rape of Proserpina*, *idem* © Scala. **374** *Sacred Love and Profane Love*, Titian, oil on canvas 1514, *idem*. *The Palefrenieri Madonna* or *Madonna of the Serpent*, Caravaggio, oil on canvas, 1605, *idem*. **375** *The Deposition*, Raphael, oil on canvas, 1604, *idem*. *Danaë*, Correggio, oil on canvas, *idem*. **376–7** The statues of athletes at the Stadio di Marmo, cl. M. Marzot. **377** Fountain of the Sphere and the mosaic pavement, Ponte Milvio, cl. A. Idini. Stadio dei Marmi cl. M. Marzot. **378** Accademia per l'educazione fisica, cl. A. Idini. Loggia of the Villa Madama, G. Volpato, watercolor, private coll. **379** *The major churches of Rome*, engraving © Bibl. nat., Paris. **380** *St Agnes and Honorius I*, detail, apse mosaic of Sant' Agnese © Scala. **381** *Basilica of San Lorenzo fuori le Mure*, G. Vasi, engraving, all rights reserved. **381** Mausoleum of Santa Costanza, Villa Torlonia and the Peroni Brewery, cl. G. Peyrot. **382** *The Story of Adam and Eve*, miniature, Charles the Bald Bible, monastery library, San Paolo fuori le Mure, © Scala. *The Sarcophagus of the Grape Harvest*, detail, San Lorenzo fuori le Mura, cl. G. Peyrot. Views of the cloister of San Paolo fuori le Mure, cl. G. Peyrot. **383** *The Story of Adam and Eve*, detail, *op. cit*. Façade of San Paolo fuori le Mura © ENIT. **384** Fascist propaganda poster © Cinecittà archives. **384–5** Laying the first stone of the Istituto Luce © Istituto Luce. **385** Filming Fellini's *Roma*, photo of the set © Franco Pinna. *Cleopatra*, Mankiewicz, poster, private coll. **386** Mussolini, photo, 1937 © Roger-Viollet, Paris. Palazzo della Civiltà del Lavoro, EUR., cl. W. Louvet. **387** Signature of Giorgio de Chirico, © Roger-Viollet, Paris. *The Melancholy of the Politician*, G. de Chirico, oil on canvas, 1913, Basel Museum © Giraudon/ SPADEM. Piazza Marconi, cl. G. Peyrot. **388** Model of the Teatro di Marcello, Museo della Civiltà Romana © Scala. The Ferris wheel at Luna Park, cl. M. Marzot. Abbazia delle Tre Fontane, postcard private coll. **389** General view of the Cascatelle, Tivoli, photo © Alinari-Giraudon. **390** Medieval houses, cl. G. Peyrot.
391 Santa Maria Maggiore, cl. G. Peyrot. *The Temple of the Sibyl in Tivoli*, C. Labruzzi, wash, late 18th century, Ashby coll. © Biblioteca Vaticana. **392** Villa d'Este, mosaic, cl. G. G. Peyrot. *Portrait of Ippolito d'Este*, engraving © Bibl. nat., Paris. The Water-Organ Fountain, cl. Gallimard. *Idem.*, cl. G. Peyrot. Fountains, cl. Gallimard. **393** View of the Villa d'Este, cl. G. Peyrot. Proserpina's Fountain, cl. G. Peyrot. Frescoes, Villa d'Este, cl. G. Peyrot. The Avenue of a Hundred Fountains, photo © ENIT. **394** Image of Hadrian, coin, 2nd century AD © Bibl. nat., Paris. Title page of the book *Map of Hadrian's Villa*, Pirro Ligorio, all rights reserved. Model of Hadrian's villa, Museo della Civiltà Romana © Scala. **395** Bust of Antinous, Museo Gregoriano Egizio, Vatican © Scala. **396** Cariatyd and crocodile on the Canopus, Villa Adriana, cl. G. Peyrot. The cypress trees planted by Conte Fede, cl. G. Peyrot. **396–7** Colonnade of the Canopus, cl. G. Peyrot. **397** Cariatyds on the Canopus, photo © ENIT. **398** The right exedra of the Terrace of the Hemicycles, cl. G. Peyrot. **399** Cista from a princely tomb, Museo della Villa Giulia © Scala. Palestrina, S. Pomardi, charcoal, late 17th century, Ashby coll. © Biblioteca Vaticana. **400–1** The Nile in flood, mosaic, 2nd century BC, Museo Archeologico di Palestrina © Scala. **402** Statue of G. Pier Luigi da Palestrina, Piazza Regina Margherita, and Sant'Agapito church cl. G. Peyrot. G. Lollobrigida on her donkey, film: *Pane, amore e Fantasia*, L. Comencini, 1953, private coll. Paris. **403** Theatrical mask, Ostia cl. J.-L. Malroux. **404** *The carters' journey*, mosaic cl. A. de Luca. **405** Statue of Minerva as a winged Victory, Piazzale della Vittoria, cl. *idem*. **406** Inscription of the Firemen's Barracks, cl. *idem*. **406–407** Theater and Piazzale delle Corporazioni © ENIT. **407** *Roman ship with a cargo of wheat*, 3rd century, fresco, Bibl. Vaticana © Michael Dixon. **408** Mosaic showing the Ostia lighthouse, cl. A

. de Luca. **408–409** General view and details of the Merchants' mosaics, cl. *idem*. **409** *Idem*., details. **410** *Mithras killing the bull*, marble, Museo d'Ostia © Scala. **410–411** Model of an *insula*, Museo de la Civiltà Romana © Scala. **411** Bar decoration of the Thermopolium, 4th century AD, Museo di Ostia © Scala. Via dei Molini, Casa di Diana and Forum, cl. A. de Luca. **412** Temple of Hercules, cl. A. di Luca. Latrines, Temple of Rome and Augustus, pavement of colored marble in the Casa di Psiche e Amore and Casa degli Aurigi, cl. *idem*. **413** Terme dei Sette Sagi and the Serapeum, cl. A. de Luca. *Cupid and Psyche*, statue, cl. *idem*. Carnet d'Auguste © Bibl. nat., Paris. **414** Mithraeum of Felicissimus, cl. A. de Luca. Fresco in the Insula degli Volte Dipinte, cl. A. de Luca. *Naval Combat*, frieze of the Tomb of Cartilius Poplicola, bas-relief © Scala. **414–15** Horrea of Hortensius, cl. *idem*. **415** *Dyer's workshop*, engraving in *La Vie des Grecs et des Romains*, 1894, all rights reserved. Campo Magna Mater, postcard, all rights reserved. Fish market, cl. A. de Luca. **416** Castello di Giulio © ENIT. *Una Domenica in Agosto*, L. Emmer, 1949, private coll., Paris. Lido d'Ostia, cl. S. Grandadan. Via Severiana crossing the Isola Sacra © Luisa Ricciarini, Milan. **418** Colisuem, DR. Railtracks, cl. It Dagherrotipo/G. Rinaldi. **421** Bus, DR. Haorse and carriage, DR. **422** Market in Porta Portese, DR. Hostaria Farnese, via dei Baulari, cl. M. Marzot. **424** San Giovanni in Laterano, cl. A. Idini. Colisuem, DR. Ice cream and cold drink kiosk, cl. Gallimard. **427** Teatro Eliseo, cl. G. Peyrot. Open-air play © ENIT.

List of illustrators:

Cover: H. Dixon, J.-M. Guillou, R. Hutchins. Nature:
16–17 : J. Chevallier, J.-M. Kacédan, P. Robin, F. Desbordes. 18–19 : F. Desbordes, J. Chevallier, C. Felloni.
20–1 : A. Bodin, J. Wilkinson, C. Felloni, J. Chevallier.
22–3 : F. Desbordes, J. Chevallier, C. Felloni.
24 : F. desbordes, C. Felloni, J. Wilkinson.
History: 35 : B. Lenormand. 38–9 : J.-P.Chabot.
Architecture :
59 : J.-C. Séné.
60–1 : O. Hubert.
62–3 : P. Poulain.
64–5 : C. Quiec.
66–7 : M. Sinier.
68–9 : P. Lhez.
70–1 : J.-C. Séné.
71 : Gallimard.
72–3 :J.-B. Héron.
74–5 : J.-M. Kacédan.
76–7 : P. de Hugo.
78–9 : T. Townsend.
80–1 : H. Dixon.
82 : R. Hutchins.
83 : T. Hill.
84–5 : N. Castle.
86–7 : M. Shoebridge, J.-M. Guillou.
88–9 : J.-M. Guillou.
90–1 : S. Doyle, M. Morlacchi.
92-93 : R. Hutchins, J.-M. Guillou, B. Lenormand.
94 : Philippe Mignon.
Itineraries:
136–7 : J.-P. Poncabare.
146–7 : B. Lenormand.
163 : J.-M. Guillou.
180 : C. Quiec.
189 : H. Goger.
192–3, 202, 205 : C. Quiec.
208 : T. Hill.
216–7 : O. Hubert.
234–5 : J.-P. Poncabare.
246, 251 : J.-M. Guillou.
394–5 : C. Quiec.
405 and 407 : P. Montagut.

LIST OF ILLUSTRATIONS ◆

Maps: The itinerary maps have been taken from the *Pianta monumentale di Roma,* Centro Culturale Cicerone, Roma © Armando Ravaglioli and Luigi Piffero, with the exception of the map of the area and the itinerary maps for the Via Appia, the Villas, Tivoli, Palestrina and Ostia, which are by Eric Gillion.
Computer graphics: Olivier Brunot. Emmanuel Calamy. Paul Coulbois. Nathalie Pujebet.
Map section
08-525 *Maps,* © Touring Editore/Nouveaux Loisirs, adaptation Édigraphie. **526-528** *Plans*© Nouveaux Loisirs/Édigraphie.

We would like to thank the following people for their help:
Mme G. de Aldécoat.
M. C. Bernoni.
Mme L. Bianciani (cons. Bibl. nat., Rome).
M. S. Bottani.
M. B. Brizzi.
M. L. Ceccarelli.
M. Hinard.
Mme A. Hubrecht (agence Giraudon).
M. Christian Landes (cons. Musée archéologique de Lattes)
M. J.-L. Malroux.
M. P. Pinon.
Mme Portelance (ENSBA).
Mlle N. Sassaro (ENIT).
Mme L. Schaetzel (Institut catholique).
M. L. Ugiano (Istituto Luce).

◆ GLOSSARY

A

◆ ACANTHUS: Classical ornament based on the stylized leaves of the acanthus plant which adorn the capitals of Corinthian columns.

◆ ACCOLADE: A curved ornamental molding, especially one having the shape of an ogee arch.

◆ AEDICULE: Small niche or alcove framed by two columns, originally used in classical architecture.

◆ AEDILE: Roman magistrate in charge of the city's administration.

◆ AISLE: Lateral division in a church parallel to the nave.

◆ AMBULATORY: Aisle for walking around the back of a church; also, the gallery of a cloister.

◆ ANNONA: Food supplies in ancient Rome.

◆ APOTHEOSIS: Ceremony elevating an emperor to the rank of a god (deification).

◆ APSE: Rounded end of a church nave or aisle, generally behind the choir or containing it.

◆ ARCH: Curve formed by a vault. The Roman arch is semicircular, as opposed to the pointed Gothic arch.

◆ ARCHITRAVE: Lowest level of an entablature which rests horizontally on columns.

◆ ARCHIVOLT: Curved arch resting on columns.

◆ ATLAS OR TELEMON: Sculpted male figure supporting an architectural element.

◆ ATRIUM: Entrance courtyard surrounded by a covered gallery.

◆ ATTIC: Topmost level of a classical building.

B

◆ BALDACCHINO: A canopy, supported by columns, over an altar.

◆ BARREL VAULT: Vault created by a round or Roman arch.

◆ BASILICA: Ancient Roman building, with nave and aisles, designed for commercial and legal activities. Its architecture served as a model for the first Christian churches.

◆ BASIN: Shallow stone bowl-shaped water container found in Roman baths; later used for fountains.

◆ BASKET OR BELL: the flared and decorated part of a capital.

◆ BOSSAGE: Construction technique using large rough-hewn blocks of stone.

◆ BUCRANE: Classical decorative motif based on an ox's head.

C

◆ CAMPANILE: Bell tower, not usually attached to the main part of a church.

◆ CAPITAL: Architectural element which crowns the shaft of a column. Each of the five architectural orders has its own style of capital. Three of these are classical: Doric, Ionic and Corinthian.

◆ CAPITOLINE TRIAD: A group of three gods, Jupiter, Juno and Minerva, which replaced the triad of Jupiter, Mars and Quirinus and was worshipped on all the capitols throughout the whole Roman world.

◆ CARTOON: From cartone, meaning large sheet of paper. A full-size preparatory drawing for a painting or a fresco.

◆ CARYATID: Sculpted female figure used as a supporting column.

◆ CELLA: Innermost space in a temple which enclosed the statue of the divinity.

◆ CHANCEL: Part of a church containing the altar, sanctuary and choir, usually separated from the nave by an arch.

◆ CHEVET: The extremity of an apse.

◆ CIBORIUM: A baldacchino covering the tabernacle of a high altar.

◆ CISTA: A casket or basket used to store ritual objects.

◆ COFFER: An ornamental sunk panel in a ceiling.

◆ COMITIA: Assemblies of the Roman people, of which there were three types: curiata, centuriata and tributa.

◆ COMPOSITE: Architectural order of columns combining the Ionic and the Corinthian.

◆ CONFESSIO: Tomb of a martyr, or an altar built over a tomb of a martyr. Also used to refer to the altar of a basilica.

◆ CONSULS: Two magistrates vested with supreme power under the Republic.

◆ CORBELING: Projecting or overhanging piece or part of a building.

◆ CORINTHIAN: One of the three classical orders of columns, characterized by sculpted acanthus leaves on the capital.

◆ CROSSING: The space created by the intersection of the nave and the transept in a church.

◆ CRYPT: Underground chapel, usually containing the tomb of a saint.

◆ CRYPTOPORTICUS: Vaulted subterranean corridor.

◆ CUL-DE-FOUR: Vault in the shape of half a cupola.

D

◆ DAMNATIO MEMORIAE: Measures taken by the Senate to punish crimes against the state, especially "bad" emperors. Included erasing names from inscriptions and refusing apotheosis.

◆ DICTATOR: Roman magistrate vested with supreme powers for a fixed length of time.

◆ DORIC: One of the three classical orders of columns. It does not have a base, the shaft is sometimes fluted and the capital is a geometric shape, suggesting a corbeling.

◆ DRUM: Cylindrical base of a cupola.

E

◆ EMBRASURE: Oblique or splayed opening of a bay or window.

◆ ENTABLATURE: Combination of the main components of a classical façade supported by columns (architrave, frieze and cornice).

◆ EXEDRA: A semi-rotunda, usually with bench or seats.

◆ EXTRADOS: External or covering surface of a vault or cupola.

F

◆ FASCES: An axe bound by a bundle of rods; it was a symbol of a Roman magistrate's power. The fasces were carried by the lictor.

◆ FATHERS OF THE CHURCH: Early theologians who established the doctrine of the Church.

◆ FORUM: Public space designed for major activities in a Roman town (religion, trade, justice and politics).

◆ FRIEZE: Horizontal decorative band between the cornice and the architrave of a classical façade.

G

◆ GROTESQUES: Mural decorations composed of plants and mythical figures.

◆ GROUND PLANS OF CHRISTIAN CHURCHES: Basilical plan, with a nave and two or more aisles; Greek-cross plan, with four equal branches; Latin-cross plan, with two shorter transversal branches (transepts).

H

◆ HARUSPEX: A priest, originally of an Etruscan priesthood, who specialized in divination using the entrails of sacrificed animals.

◆ HERM: A sculpted male figure used instead of a column to support an architectural element.

◆ HILLS: According to tradition Rome was built on top of seven hills (the Capitol, Palatine, Aventine, Coelian, Quirinal, Viminal and Esquiline).

◆ HOLY YEAR: A Jubilee Year celebrated by the Roman Catholic Church every 25 years since the time of Pope Paul II. Pilgrims from all over the world visit the holy places in Rome, particularly the four major basilicas whose Holy Doors, normally bricked up, are opened.

◆ HYPOGEUM: Underground burial chamber.

I

◆ IDES: The 15th day of March, May, July and October and the 13th day of the other months in the Roman calendar.

◆ IMPERIUM: Sovereign, civil and military power which belonged to superior magistrates (praetors and consuls) and to the emperor in Imperial times.

◆ IONIC: One of the three classical orders of columns. The capital has symmetrical volutes on either side.

J

◆ JUBILEE: Plenary indulgence granted by the pope during Holy Year to the faithful who accomplish certain acts of devotion.

K

◆ KALENDS: 1st day of the Roman month.
◆ KEYSTONE: Central stone at the top of an arch.

L

◆ LARARIUM: Altar or shrine dedicated to the *lares*, household gods.

M

◆ MAGISTRATES: Generic term for the political leaders of Rome who had a variety of specialized and collegial duties. In ascending order of seniority they were: quaestor, aedile, praetor and consul. There were also the censors, in charge of the census and the tribunes of the people (defenders of the plebs).
◆ MANDORLA: Almond-shaped medallion in which Christ and sometimes Mary are portrayed triumphant.
◆ MANES: Spirits of the dead which became the object of a Roman cult.
◆ MAUSOLEUM: A large stately tomb.
◆ METOPE: Square space in Doric friezes, often plain but sometimes decorated with a bucrane or other ornamental motif.
◆ MOLDINGS: Reliefs on the façade of a building.

N

◆ NARTHEX: Vestibule or entrance hall of a Christian basilica.
◆ NAVE: The main elongated space inside a church.
◆ NONES: The 7th day of March, May, July and October and the 5th day of the other months of the Roman calendar.
◆ NYMPHAEUM: Natural or artificial grotto decorating a garden, usually with a fountain.

O

◆ OCULUS: Round opening in a wall or cupola.
◆ ORDERS: The architectural system of antiquity. The term is also used to refer to the elements which make up a column (base, shaft and capital) and the entablature (architrave, frieze and cornice). There are five architectural orders of columns: the three classical orders (Doric, Ionic and Corinthian) and the Tuscan and Composite.
◆ OVOLO MOLDINGS: An oval decorative motif used in the Doric order.

P

◆ PENDENTIVE: Vaulted surface between the rectangular wall and the domed cupola.
◆ PERISTYLE: Colonnade surrounding a building or courtyard.
◆ PIER: Rectangular pillar that bears the weight of a cupola.
◆ PILASTER: Visible part of a column attached to a wall.
◆ PODIUM: Stone platform of a Roman temple.
◆ POMERIUM: Furrow or trench marking the sacred boundary of the city, within which the army, the dead and temples of foreign gods were not allowed.
◆ PONTIFF: Minister of the Roman cult and member of the college of priests, headed by the high priest (*pontifex maximus*). In Imperial Rome the emperor was the supreme pontiff.
◆ PORTICO: Generally a covered passage with columns. The term is also used with reference to a porch supported by columns in front of a building.
◆ PRAETOR: Magistrate in charge of justice.
◆ PRONAOS: The space in classical temples, between the entrance colonnade and the actual sanctuary (*cella*).
◆ PUTTO (PLURAL, PUTTI): Naked child, without wings.

Q

◆ QUAESTOR: Magistrate in charge of public funds.
◆ QUIRITES: Another name for the citizens of Rome.

R

◆ RAISED ARCH: An arch, the height of which is greater than half the span.
◆ RETICULAR OR RETICULATED: Laid out in the form of a net.
◆ RIBBED DOME: A dome with projecting bands on the underside of the vault or ceiling.
◆ ROMAN PAINTING: Roman mural paintings are generally classified under four distinct styles according to criteria established by the excavations in Pompeii. The first style (2nd century and early 1st century BC) is essentially architectural and of Greek influence. The second style (end of the Roman Republic) is characterized by the use of trompe l'oeil (vanishing perspectives and false architecture). In the third style (period of Augustus and Claudius) decorative motifs are depicted against solid backgrounds on which small framed works are set. Finally, in the fourth style (period of Nero to 79 AD), the painting becomes more "impressionistic" in its brush strokes and introduces more imaginary elements.
◆ ROSTRA: Podium or platform for speakers in the Roman Forum.

S

◆ SACRISTY: Side-room in a church where religious objects such as chalices and vestments are kept.
◆ SALII: Salian priests of Mars and Quirinus whose ceremonies opened the warring season (in March) and closed it (in October).
◆ SCHOLA CANTORUM: The school of choristers of a church, or the choir itself set as an architectural or musical ensemble.
◆ SENATUS CONSULTUM: Decision of the Roman Senate.
◆ STEREOBATE: An undecorated platform of masonry forming the foundation of a colonnade.
◆ STUCCO: A mixture of plaster and marble dust used to decorate surfaces; the term also refers to the decorative

motifs made from the mixture.
◆ STYLOBATE: A molded platform of masonry forming the foundation of a colonnade.
◆ SUBSTRUCTION: A term, derived from Latin, used specifically with reference to classical architecture, to define the supporting structures of theaters and temples.
◆ SUOVETAURILE: Sacrifice of a pig (*sus*), a ram (*ovis*) or a bull (*taurus*).
◆ SURBASED ARCH: An arch, the height of which is less than half the span.

T

◆ TABERNACLE: A small ornamented cupboard or box placed in the center of the altar containing the Blessed Sacrament.
◆ TERM OR TERMINAL FIGURE: A sculpted belted or banded limbless figure or animal on top of a pillar.
◆ TITULUS: Place of Christian worship in a private dwelling.
◆ TRIBUNE: Apse of a Christian church containing the bishop's throne. In ancient Rome the term referred to a person elected to represent the people (plebs).
◆ TRIFORIUM: Upper arcaded gallery over the nave, choir or transept of a church, originally a triple-arched window.
◆ TRIUMPHAL ARCH: Monumental gate. Also, in Christian basilicas the arch separating the narthex from the nave.
◆ TYMPANUM: In temples it is the surface enclosed by the cornices of a pediment, particularly ones that are a triangular shape; in churches it is the surface enclosed by the lintel and the archivolt of a portal.

V

◆ VAULTING: Curved surface or element of an arch or a vault.
◆ VENT: Manhole or gauge in a pipe or aqueduct.
◆ VOLUTE: Ornamental spiral.

◆ BIOGRAPHICAL INDEX

FIGURES OF ANTIQUITY

Aeneas, hero of Troy who, according to legend, sailed to Italy: *146, 163, 310*

Agrippa (M. Vipsanius Agrippa), 63–12 BC, general, politician, Augustus' adviser and son-in-law: *142, 264, 298*

Ammianus Marcellinus, c. 330–400, Roman historian, saw himself as Tacitus' successor: *116, 166*

Ancus Marcius, 640–16 BC, according to legend, he was the fourth king of Rome: *404*

Antinous, the Emperor Hadrian's favorite: *317, 395*

Antony or Mark Antony (Marcus Antonius), 83–30 BC, general and politician, triumvir with Octavian and Lepidus, then Octavian's rival, husband of Cleopatra: *28, 143*

Apollodorus of Damascus, active in the 2nd century AD, architect of Syrian origin, brought to Rome by Trajan: *146, 165, 167, 174*

Appius Claudius Caecus, 4th–3rd century BC, politician, censor in 312, consul in 307 and 296, built the Via Appia and Rome's first aqueduct, Aqua Appia: *158, 318*

Caesar, Julius (Caius Julius Caesar), born in Rome c. 100 BC, Roman general and statesman, assassinated in 44 BC: *28, 138, 157, 163*

Caius Flaminius, Roman politician and general, tribune of the people in 232 BC, censor in 217, beaten by Hannibal at Lake Trasimene, built the Via Flaminia: *157*

Caius Socius, governor of Syria, consul in 32 BC, restored the Temple of Apollo which he enriched with many works of art brought back from the East: *158*

Camillus, (M. Furius Camillus), end of the 5th century–365 BC, general and politician, five times dictator, censor in 403 BC, conquered Veii, liberated Rome from the Gauls in 390 BC: *141*

Cecilia Metella, Roman woman of the 1st century BC, member of the illustrious family of the Metelli: *330*

Cicero, (Marcus Tullius Cicero), 106–43 BC, Latin author, lawyer, politician, consul in 63 BC, his throat was cut on Mark Antony's orders: *140, 141, 163, 398, 399*

Cybele, Asia Minor divinity, goddess of fertility whose initiatory cult was introduced in Rome: *147, 148, 324, 355, 415*

Fabullus, Roman painter active c. 64–68 AD: *172*

Gracchi, (Tiberius Sempronius Gracchus), 162–133 BC, and Caius his brother, 154–21 BC, tribunes, proposed agrarian reforms in favor of the plebeians. They were assassinated.

Hannibal, c. 247–183 BC, Carthaginian general, finally vanquished during the Second Punic War (218–202) by Scipio Africanus at Zama: *322*

Hortensius Hortalus Quintus, 114–50 BC, Roman orator: *148*

Jugurtha, c. 160–104 BC, king of Numidia, defeated by Marius: *131*

Kephisodotos the Younger, 4th–3rd century BC, Greek sculptor: *149*

Lucullus (Lucius Licinius Lucullus), c. 106–56 BC, Roman general, consul in 74 BC, deposed by Pompey during the war against Mithridates, retired to his villa where he lived a life of refinement: *315*

Lutatius (Catulus Quintus), Roman general, consul in 101 BC, was victorious at Vercellae with Marius, who later had him executed in 87 BC: *251*

Maecenas (Caius Clinius Maecenas), 69–8 BC, minister of Augustus, patron of artists and writers: *341*

Marcellus (Marcus Claudius Marcellus), c. 43–23 BC, Augustus' nephew, son-in-law and heir designate, died aged 19: *158, 310*

Marcus Aemilius Lepidus, censor in 179 BC, dedicated the temple, promised by M. Aemilius Regillus, on the occasion of his victory over Antiochus the Great in 190 BC: *137, 251*

Marcus Fulvius

Nobilior, Roman politician, tribune of the people in 199 BC, consul in 189 and censor in 179 BC: *137*

Marius (Caius Marius), 157–86 BC, general and politician, tribune of the people in 119, praetor in 116, pro-praetor of Spain, seven times consul, Sulla's rival: *27, 377*

Mark Antony (see Antony)

Martial (M. Valerius Marcialis), Bilbilis (Spain) c. 40–c. 104 AD, Latin satirical poet; his *Epigrams* are famous: *288*

Metellus (Quintus Metellus Macedonius), conqueror of Macedonia (148 BC), consul in 143 BC: *159*

Mithras, Iranian god whose initiatory cult spread to Rome in the 2nd century AD: *181, 194, 406*

Munatius Plancus Lucius, 1st century BC, Roman orator and general; pro-consul in Gaul, founded Lyon in 43 BC, consul, censor in 22 BC: *140*

Nikias, 4th century BC, painter born in Athens: *148*

Numa Pompilius, 717–673 BC, according to tradition he was the second king of Rome: *143*

Octavia, c. 70–11 BC, Augustus' sister: *159, 310*

Ovid (Publius Ovidius Naso), Sulmona 43 BC–17/18 AD, Latin poet, author of *Amores*, *Metamorphoses* and *Fasti*. Banished to Tomi (Scythia) in 8 AD: *106*

Piso, Roman family, branch of the "gens" Calpurnia. Caius Calpurnius Piso was involved in a plot against Nero (65 AD). He committed suicide when it was betrayed: *196*

Plotina (Plotina Pompeia), Trajan's wife, died 129 AD: *166*

Pompey (Cn. Pompeius Magnus), 106–48 BC, Roman general and politician. Consul in 70 and 55, victorious over Mithridates (66), triumvir with Caesar and Crassus (60), sole consul (52), beaten by Caesar at Pharsalus (48). Assassinated: *28, 248*

Remus, legendary twin of Romulus, founder of Rome: *26, 147*

Romulus, legendary twin of Remus, founded Rome in 753 BC, king of Rome 753–17 BC: *26, 147, 177, 288*

Romulus, son of Emperor Maxentius, died 309 AD: *144, 329*

Scipios, great family of ancient Rome, branch of the "gens" Cornelia. Important in politics from the 3rd century to the beginning of the 2nd century BC: *322*

Scopas the Elder, 3rd century BC, Greek sculptor: *149*

Servius Tullius, 578–34 BC, according to legend he was the sixth king of Rome: *26, 128, 156, 176*

Sulla (L. Cornelius Sulla), 138–78 BC, Roman general and politician, consul in 88, Marius' rival, dictator 82–79 BC: *398, 404*

Tarquinius Priscus (616–579 BC, according to legend): *128, 136, 177*

Tarquinius Superbus (534–9 BC, according to legend): *148, 352*

Tarquins, Etruscan kings of Rome: *238*

Timotheos, 4th century BC, Greek sculptor: *149*

Vercingetorix, c. 72–42 BC, chief of the Gauls, conquered by Caesar in 52 BC: *131*

Virgil, (Publius Virgilius Maro), Mantua c. 70–19 BC, Roman poet, author of *Georgics*, *Eclogues* and the *Aeneid*: *142, 155*

Vitruvius, (Marcus Vitruvius Pollio), 1st century BC, Roman architect, author of *De Architectura*: *139*

ROMAN EMPERORS AND IMPERIAL FAMILIES

Agrippina the Younger (Julia Agrippina), c. 16–59 AD, daughter of Germanicus and Agrippina the Elder, mother of Nero, second wife of Emperor Claudius: *133, 189*

Antonines, dynasty of six Roman emperors 96–192 AD: Nerva, Trajan, Hadrian, Antoninus, later Commodus: *233, 239*

Antoninus Pius (Titus Aurelius Fulvus Boionius Arrius Antoninus, later Titus Aelius Hadrianus Antoninus), born 86 AD,

oman emperor
38–61: *145*

ugustus (Caius
ctavius; after he was
dopted by Caesar
nown as C. Julius
aesar Octavianus,
ook the name of
ugustus in 27 BC),
orn Rome 63 BC, first
oman emperor (27
c–14 AD): *28, 138, 140,
49, 157, 163, 164,
09–311*

urelian (Lucius
omitius Aurelianus)
orn c. 214 AD, Roman
mperor 270–5: *128,
23*

aligula (popular name
f C. Julius Caesar
ermanicus), born 12
D, son of Germanicus
nd Agrippina; Roman
mperor 37–41: *28, 149*

aracalla (Marcus
urelius Antonius
assianus), born in
yon 188 AD, Roman
mperor 211–17: *139,
41, 298, 320*

laudius II Gothicus
Marcus Aurelius
alerius Claudius), born
19 AD, Roman emperor
68–70: *416*

laudius (Tiberius
laudius Nero
ermanicus), born in
yons 10 BC, Roman
mperor 41–54 AD: *189,
51, 339, 405*

ommodus (Lucius
elius Aurelius
ommodus Antoninus),
orn 161 AD, Roman
mperor 180–92: *133,
30*

onstantius II (Flavius
ulius Constantius),
orn 317, son of
onstantine the Great,
mperor of the East
37–50, sole Roman
mperor 350–61: *156,
66, 178*

onstantine I, the
reat (Flavius Valerius
laudius Constantinus),
orn c. 280 AD, Roman
mperor 306–37, sole
oman emperor from
24: *130, 145, 169, 192,
96, 200, 206, 377, 381*

iocletian (Caius
alerius Aurelius
iocletianus), born in
almatia 245 AD,
oman emperor
84–305: *29, 139*

omitian (Titus Flavius
omitianus), born 51
D, Roman emperor
1–96: *149, 150, 165,
39, 276*

austina, empress, wife
f the emperor
ntoninus Pius, died
41 AD: *145, 268, 329*

lavians, dynasty of
hree Roman emperors:
espasian and his two

sons, Titus and
Domitian (69–96): *146,
162*

Gallienus (Publius
Licinius Egnatius
Gallienus), born c. 218
AD, Roman emperor
253–68: *29, 340*

Geta (Publius Septimius
Geta), born 189 AD,
Roman emperor
211–12. Shared Imperial
power for a few months
with his brother
Caracalla who had him
murdered: *139*

Hadrian (Publius Aelius
Hadrianus), born 76 AD,
Roman emperor
117–38: *29, 132, 146,
200, 233, 239, 264, 267,
394*

**Heliogabalus or
Elagabalus** (Varius
Avitus Bassianus), born
204, high priest from
Emesa, Roman emperor
218–22: *151, 321*

Honorius (Flavius
Honorius),
Constantinople
384–Ravenna 423,
emperor of the West
395–423: *234, 339, 380*

Julia Domna, wife of
Septimius Severus: *139,
156*

Julian the Apostate
(Flavius Claudius
Julianus), born at
Constantinople 331 AD,
married to Helen,
daughter of
Constantine, Roman
emperor 361–63, tried
to restore paganism:
188

Livia (Livia Drusilla), 58
BC–29 AD, wife of
Augustus. Had two
children from a previous
marriage, Tiberius and
Drusus: *311*

Marcus Aurelius
(Marcus Annius Verus,
then Marcus Aelius
Aurelius Antonius),
Rome 121, Roman
emperor 161–80: *130,
267*

Maxentius (Marcus
Valerius Aurelius
Maxentius), son of
Maximian, Roman
emperor 306–12,
beaten by Constantine
at the Milvian Bridge
(312): *145, 328*

Maximian (Marcus
Aurelius Maximianus),
born c. 250, Roman
emperor 286–305 (with
Domitian) and 307–8
(tetrarchy):
334

Nero (Lucius Domitius
Ahenobarbus, then
Claudius Nero), born 37
AD, Roman emperor
54–68: *165*

Nerva (Marcus
Cocceius Nerva), born

26 AD, Roman emperor
96–8: *165*

Octavian (see
Augustus)

Septimius Severus
(Lucius Septimius
Severus), born in Leptis
Magna (Africa) 146 AD,
Roman emperor
193–211: *139, 141, 156,
158, 164*

Theodosius (Flavius
Theodosius), born 347
AD, Roman emperor
379–95, the last to rule
the whole empire: *29,
206*

Tiberius (Tiberius
Claudius Nero), born 42
BC, Roman emperor
14–37 AD: *28, 141, 149,
335*

Titus (Titus Flavius
Vespasianus), born
c. 40, Roman emperor
79–81: *146, 169, 170,
339*

Trajan (Marcus Ulpius
Traianus), born 53 AD,
Roman emperor
98–117: *29, 139, 165,
405*

Valerian (Publius
Licinius Valerianus),
Roman emperor
253–60: *29, 326*

Vespasian (Titus
Flavius Vespasianus),
born 9 AD, Roman
emperor 69–79: *132,
164, 170, 339*

SAINTS

Adalbertus (saint),
c. 956–97, Bishop of
Prague, martyred in
Prussia, stayed several
times in the monastery
of St Boniface on the
Aventine: *180*

Agapitus (saint), young
man martyred at
Praeneste in the reign of
Aurelian, 274 AD. Patron
saint of the town: *402*

Agnes (saint), young girl
martyred in the middle
of the 3rd century. The
details of her passion
were already legendary
in the 4th century:
278, 380

Alexis (saint), his
legend, which
originated in the East
spread to the West only
in the 10th century: *180*

Ambrose (saint), Trier c.
330/40–97, Bishop of
Milan. Father and
Doctor of the Roman
Church: *309*

Aurea (saint and
martyr), 3rd century,
from a great family,
owned a villa in Ostia.
Was thrown into the sea
with a millstone tied to
her neck: *419*

Benoît-Joseph Labre
(saint), Amettes

1748–Rome 1783,
French, penitent mystic,
mendicant pilgrim,
traveled through
Europe: *347*

Bibiana (saint), virgin
venerated in Rome from
the end of the 5th
century. According to a
late passion, she was
tied to a column and
whipped to death
during the reign of
Julian the Apostate (4th
century). It is said in a
popular tradition that
powder from the
column and the grass
growing around her
church provides a cure
for epilepsy: *339*

Bridget of Sweden
(saint), c. 1303–c. 1373,
mystic. A Swedish lady
of means, widow,
foundress of the Order
of the Blessed
Sacrament (Bridgetines).
Died in Rome.

Catherine of Sienna
(saint), (Catherine
Benincasa), 1347–80,
member of the
Dominican Third Order,
mystic, played a
decisive role in the
return of the popes from
Avignon. Doctor of the
Church: *260*

Cecilia (saint and
martyr), 3rd century, the
church that is dedicated
to her was founded by a
certain Roman matron
named Caecilia in the
4th century: *326, 354*

Charles Borromeo
(saint), 1538–84,
Cardinal-archbishop of
Milan, key figure of the
Italian Counter-
Reformation: *247, 309,
345*

Chrysogonus (saint),
not much is known
about this person who
was probably martyred
under Diocletian. Often
confused with St
Chrysogonus of
Aquileia (4th century):
356

Constantinia, 4th
century, daughter of the
emperor Constantine,
tradition gradually
transformed her into a
saint (St Constance):
380

Cosmas and Damian
(saints), brothers, Syrian
doctors, probably
martyred under
Diocletian. The cult of
these saints had a
major iconographic
impact: *168*

Dominic Guzman
(saint), came from
Castile, 1170–1221,
founder of the Order of
Friars Preachers

◆ BIOGRAPHICAL INDEX

(Dominicans): *179, 321*
Eligius (saint), born near Limoges c. 580, Bishop of Noyon 641–60 when he died. King Dagobert's treasurer. Goldsmith and patron of goldsmiths: *243*
Four Crowned Saints (Santi Quattro Coronati), their legend: *192*
Francesca Romana (saint), Rome 1384–1440, Francesca Buzzi, widow of the noble Ponziani, foundress of the Oblates of Tor de'Specchi (Benedictine rule): *159, 169*
Francis of Assisi (Il Poverello), 1181–1226, founder of the Order of Franciscans: *354*
Francis of Paola (saint), Paola, Calabria 1416–1507, founder of the Order of Minims, died in France where he was summoned by Louis XI.
Gaetano di Thiene (saint), Vicenza 1480–1547, founder of the Theatine Fathers: *250*
Helen (saint), c. 255–338, mother of Emperor Constantine. According to tradition, she discovered the True Cross in Jerusalem and brought relics of Christ's passion back to Rome: *199*
Ignatius of Loyola (saint), born 1491, a Spanish gentleman, founder of the Society of Jesus (Jesuits), died in Rome 1556: *383*
Jerome (saint), c. 341–420, Doctor of the Church, translated the Bible into Latin (Vulgate). Was a hermit in Palestine, often portrayed in the company of a lion. Venerated in Rome where he spent many years: *231*
John and Paul (saints), venerated as martyrs since the 4th century, a church on the Coelian Hill is dedicated to them.There is no historical proof of their existence: *188*
Lawrence (saint), Deacon of the Church of Rome, martyred in 258. According to a late version of his passion he was burnt on a grid: *381*
Lodovica Albertoni (Blessed) 1474–1553, widow, Tertiary of St

Francis, died in Rome: *354*
Monica (saint), Carthage c. 331–84, mother of St Augustine. Died at Ostia as she was about to return to Africa with her son: *285*
Nereus and Achilleus (saints), according to one legend they were soldiers in charge of persecuting Christians, miraculously converted and themselves martyred, either under Nero (1st century) or under Diocletian (end of 3rd century). Legend of their church: *321*
Pantaleon (saint), doctor who treated patients free, apparently martyred in Nicomedia 305: *279*
Paul (saint), apostle, born at Tarsus, martyred in Rome c. 65 AD: *192, 247, 327, 328, 344, 382*
Peter (saint), apostle, martyred in Rome between 64 and 67 AD: *131, 181, 206, 209, 212, 321, 324, 327, 344*
Petronilla (saint), Roman virgin venerated as a martyr of the 1st century. According to her legend she was St Peter's daughter. Protectress of Frankish kings and the kings of France since the 8th century: *206*
Philip Neri (saint), Florence 1515–Rome 1595, popular saint, priest founder of the Congregation of the Oratory (Oratorians), sometimes referred to as the "Second Apostle of Rome": *190, 240, 279, 281*
Praxedes (saint), (1st–2nd century), Roman virgin, daughter of Pudens, sister of Pudentiana (see these names): *344*
Prisca (saint), founder of a church on the Aventine, honored as a 1st century martyr. Her legend: *181*
Pudens, martyr (1st century), Roman senator converted by St Peter, father of Praxedes and Pudentiana (see these names). Possibly confused with another Pudens who founded a church in his house in the 3rd century: *344*
Pudentiana (saint), (1st–2nd century), virgin died aged 16. Daughter of Pudens, sister of Praxedes (see these

names): *344*
Sabina (saint), founder of the basilica which bears her name, in the 5th century. A Sabina has been honored as a 2nd-century martyr since the 4th century. Her legend: *179*
Sebastian (saint), Roman martyr (end of 3rd century–beginning of 4th). The details of his legend were developed in the 5th century, officer of Diocletian, he was shot with arrows, survived and then beaten to death: *151, 180, 327*
Stanislaus Kostka (saint), 1550–68, Polish saint, died aged 18 in Rome while a novice with the Jesuits: *296*
Tarcisius (saint and deacon), 3rd century martyr. Known because of an inscription by Pope Damasus. Rather than surrender the Eucharist that he was taking to captive Christians he let himself be murdered. The legend often portrays him as a child: *326*
Teresa of Avila (saint), Avila, 1515–82, Spanish Carmelite nun, mystic, Doctor of the Church: *294*

POPES

Alexander III Bandinelli, Sienese, pope 1159–81: *358*
Alexander VI Borgia, Jativa (Spain), pope 1492–1503: *215, 243, 252, 343*
Alexander VII Chigi, Sienna, pope 1655–67: *210, 212, 213, 280, 307, 308, 382*
Anterus (saint), Greek, pope 235–6: *326*
Benedict III, Roman, pope 855–8: *343*
Benedict XIV Lambertini, Bologna 1675, pope 1740–58: *281, 342*
Boniface IX Tomacelli, Neapolitan, pope 1389–1404: *130*
Calixtus I (saint), Roman, pope 217–22, ex-slave became a deacon in charge of the cemetery that bears his name, then pope: *326, 358*
Celestine I (saint), Campania, pope 422–32: *179*
Clement I (saint), pope 91–101: *193, 194*
Clement XI Albani, Urbino 1649, pope 1700–21: *264*

Clement VIII Aldobrandini, Fano 1536, pope 1592–1605: *168, 343*
Clement X Altieri, Rome 1590, pope 1670–6: *344*
Clement XII Corsini, Florence 1652, pope 1730–40: *297*
Clement XIV Ganganelli, Sant'Arcangelo di Romagna 1705, pope 1769–74: *215, 301*
Clement VII Medici, Florence 1478, pope 1523–34: *234, 239, 274, 378*
Clement XIII Rezzonico, Venice 1693, pope 1758–69: *213*
Clement IX Rospigliosi, Pistoia 1600, pope 1667–9: *32, 240*
Cornelius (saint), Roman, pope 251–3: *326*
Eugenius III Paganelli, Montemagno, pope 1145–53: *214, 343*
Eugenius IV Condulmer, Venice 1383, pope 1431–47: *274*
Eusebius (saint), Greek, pope 309–10: *326*
Eutychian (saint), Luni (Tuscany), pope 275–83: *326*
Fabian (saint), Roman, pope 236–50: *326*
Felix IV (saint), Benevento, pope 526–30: *168, 191*
Gelasius I (saint), African, pope 492–6: *323*
Gregory I the Great (saint), Rome c. 540, pope 590–604, Doctor of the Church. Turned his family home on the Coelian Hill into a monastery: *182, 187, 235*
Gregory III (saint), Syrian, pope 731-41: *356*
Gregory IV, Roman, pope 827–44: *162, 358*
Gregory VI Graziano, Roman, pope 1045–6 (abdication): *323*
Gregory VII Hildebrand (saint), Sovana (Tuscany) c. 1015–20, pope 1073–85: *234, 323*
Gregory IX Segni, Anagni c. 1145, pope 1227–41: *353*
Gregory XI de Beaufort, French, Maumont 1329, pope 1370–8. Last of the Avignon popes, returned to Rome in 1377: *197, 342*
Gregory XIII Boncompagni,

Bologna 1502, pope 1572–85: *191, 213, 281, 197, 342*
Gregory XVI Capellari, Belluno 1765, pope 1831–46: *391*
Adrian I, pope 772–95: *55, 358, 380, 382*
Adrian VI Florenz, Utrecht 1459, pope 1522–3, last non-Italian pope before John-Paul II: *280*
Honorius I, Campania, pope 625–38: *380*
Honorius III Savelli, Roman, pope 1216–27: *379, 382*
Honorius II Scannabecchi, Bologna, pope 1124–30: *157*
Innocent XIII Conti, Rome 1655, pope 1721–4: *314*
Innocent VIII Cybo, Genoa 1432, pope 1484–92: *214*
Innocent X Pamphili, Rome 1574, pope 1644–55: *209, 240, 269, 276, 278, 279, 368*
Innocent II Papareschi, Roman, pope 1130–43: *168*
Innocent XII Pignatelli, Spinazzola (Basilicata) 1615, pope 1691–1700: *69*
Innocent III Segni, Gavignano 1160, pope 1198–1216: *168, 199, 214, 321*
John I (saint), pope 523-6: *191*
John VII, Greek, pope 705–7: *142*
John X, Ravenna c. 860, pope 914–28: *179*
John XXIII Roncalli, Sotto il Monte (near Bergamo) 1881, pope 1958–63: *211*
John Paul ii Wotjila, Wadowice (Poland), 1920, pope 1978–2005: *14*
Julius III Ciocchi del Monte, Rome 1487, pope 1550-5: *370*
Julius II Della Rovere, Savona 1443, pope 1503–13: *209, 215, 235, 274, 240, 280, 346, 359, 360, 416*
Leo III (saint), Rome 750, pope 795–816: *197, 198, 321*
Leo IV (saint), Roman, pope 847-55: *192, 206, 234*
Leo XII Della Genga, Ancona 1760, pope 1823–9: *253*
Leo X Medici, Florence 1475, pope 1513-21: *161, 190, 197, 215, 241, 249, 274, 340, 360*
Leo XIII Pecci, Carpinetto Romano, pope 1878–1903
Liberius, Roman, pope

352–66: *342*
Lucius I (saint), Roman, pope 253–4: *326*
Mark (saint), Roman, pope January–October 366: *162*
Martin V Colonna, Genazzano 1368, pope 1417–31: *130, 197, 300, 416*
Miltiades (or Melchiades) (saint), African, pope 311–14: *196*
Nicholas IV Masci, Ascoli c. 1230, pope 1288–92: *343*
Nicholas III Orsini, Rome 1210/1220, pope 1277–80: *214, 234*
Nicholas V Parentucelli, Pisa 1398, pope 1447–55: *214, 234*
Paschal I (saint), Roman, pope 817–24: *190, 342, 343, 345*
Paschal II Raniero, Bieda (near Ravenna) c. 1050, pope 1099–1118: *192, 307, 312, 354*
Paul I (saint), Roman, pope 757–67: *142*
Paul II Barbo, Venice 1417, pope 1464–71: *161, 168, 274*
Paul V Borghese, Rome 1552, pope 1605–21: *52, 165, 209, 298, 311, 343, 357, 363, 364*
Paul IV Carafa, Naples 1476, pope 1555–9: *197, 252*
Paul III Farnese, Canino 1468, pope 1534–49: *31, 129, 215, 234, 244, 247, 252, 274*
Pelagius II, Rome 520, pope 579–90: *382*
Pius I (saint), Aquileia, pope 140–55: *344*
Pius VI Braschi, Cesena (Emilia) 1717, pope 1775–99: *318*
Pius VII Chiaramonti, Cesena (Emilia) 1742, pope 1800–23: *215*
Pius V Ghislieri (saint), Bosco Marengo (Lombardy) 1504, pope 1566–72: *343*
Pius IV Medici, Milan 1499, pope 1559–65: *161, 215, 247, 289, 294, 334*
Pius II Piccolomini, Corsignano, today Pienza 1405, pope 1458–64: *250, 391*
Pius IX Ratti, Desio (Lombardy) 1857, pope 1922–39: *198, 215*
Pius III Todeschini-Piccolomini, Sienna 1436, pope for 26 days, October–November 1503: *250*
Pontian (saint), Roman, pope 230–5, persecuted under Maximinus I, deported to Sardinia where he died: *326*

Sylvester I (saint), Roman, pope 314–35: *208, 346*
Simplicius (saint), Tivoli, pope 468–83: *191*
Sixtus II (saint), Greek, pope 257–8: *326*
Sixtus I (saint), Roman, pope 432–40: *179, 312, 342, 381*
Sixtus IV Della Rovere, Savona 1414, pope 1471–84: *214, 240, 274, 280, 306, 363*
Sixtus V Peretti, Grottamare 1520, pope 1585–90: *32, 197, 210, 215, 253, 289, 295, 306, 332, 343*
Stephen II, Roman, pope 752–7: *206*
Stephen III, Sicilian, pope 768–72: *159*
Symmachus (saint), Sardinian, pope 498–514: *206, 214, 346*
Urban VIII Barberini, Florence 1568, pope 1623–44: *32, 131, 132, 212, 230, 265, 290, 291, 314, 339*
Urban V de Grimoard (Blessed), French, born near Mende 1310, died in Avignon, pope 1362–70
Zephyrinus (saint), Roman, pope 195–217: *326*

CARDINALS AND PRIESTS

Bessarione, Cardinal Giovanni, Trebizond c. 1402–72, Byzantine humanist and theologian living in Rome: *321*
Corsini, Neri, Florence 1685–Rome 1770, cardinal, actually governed the Church during the last years of Clement XII's pontificate: *362*
Della Rovere (see Julius II, pope)
Este (Cardinal Ippolito d'-), 1509–72, humanist and patron of the arts, belonged to the illustrious Este family from Ferrara. Died in his villa at Tivoli: *392*
Luther, Martin, Eisleben (Thuringen) 1483–1546, Church reformer: *260*
Mazzarino, Cardinal Giulio, 1602–61, French statesman of Italian origin: *298, 314*
Peter of Illyria, Roman priest of Illyrian origin, appointed by Pope Celestine I (422–32) to direct the construction of the Basilica of Santa

Sabina on the Aventine: *179*
Ricci di Montepulciano, cardinal: *242, 315, 369*

KINGS AND QUEENS

Alaric I, king of the Visigoths 395–412, captured and sacked Rome (410): *177*
Albericus I, Marchese of Camerino, Duke of Spoleto, died c. 925 during an assault against Pope John X: *179*
Charlemagne, 742–814, king of the Francs in 768, crowned emperor of the Western Empire in 800 at Rome: *197, 206*
Charles V, born 1500, King of Spain in 1516, emperor of Germany in 1519. His troops captured and sacked Rome in 1527. He abdicated in 1556: *129*
Christina of Sweden, born 1626, queen of Sweden 1632–54, converted to Roman Catholicism, abdicated and opted for exile in Rome where she died in 1689: *214, 306, 362, 364*
Cleopatra VII, queen of Egypt 51–30 BC who committed suicide after the Battle of Actium in 31: *143*
Henry IV, born 1050, German emperor 1056–1106. In his fight against the papacy he captured Rome in 1084: *234*
Louis XIV, born 1638, king of France 1643–1715: *316*
Napoleon I, Ajaccio St Helena 1769–1821, emperor of the French 1804–15: *40, 161, 315, 372*
Otto III, Paterno (near Viterbo) 980, German emperor 983–1002. Dreamed of reconstituting the Christian empire. Asserted his authority over Italy and settled in Rome from which he was finally expelled: *180, 352*
Phocas, Byzantine emperor 602–10: *141, 257, 262*
Theodoric the Great, c. 455–Ravenna 526, king of the Ostrogoths 474–526: *170*
Totila, king of the Ostrogoths 541–52, seized Rome in 546: *183, 234*
Umberto I, born in Turin 1844, second king of Italy 1878–1900,

◆ BIOGRAPHICAL INDEX

murdered by an anarchist: *302*
Victor Emmanuel II, Turin 1820, king of Piedmont-Sardinia 1849–61, first king of unified Italy from 1861–78: *160, 266*
Witigis, king of the Ostrogoths 526–40: *234*

GREAT FAMILIES

Aldobrandini, famous family, originally from Florence: 258, 372 (see Clement VII, pope)
Anguillara, family name comes from their fiefdom on the Lake of Bracciano. Known in the 11th–12th centuries. Extinct by the 18th century: *351, 356, 357*
Barberini, great Roman family originally from Barberino, near Florence: *265, 289–92, 398* (see Urban VIII, pope)
Bonaparte (family): *260, 309*
Borghese, noble Roman family originally from Sienna; Cardinal Camillo elected pope in 1605 (see Paul V, pope); Cardinal Scipione: *188, 311, 372*
Borgia, family originally from Aragon (12th century) moved to Rome when Alfonso became Pope Calixtus III in 1455. (See Alexander VI, pope)
Caetani, noble family originally from Gaeta, mentioned since the 12th century. Pope Boniface VIII 1294–1303. Still extinct: *168, 318, 330, 352*
Capocci, noble Roman family in the Middle Ages, known since the 11th century: *346*
Cenci, noble Roman family known especially because of the tragic story of Beatrice Cenci (16th century): *234, 254*
Chigi, family of bankers originally from Sienna, which asserted itself in Rome in the 15th–16th centuries. Agostino: *307, 360, 363, 378* (see Alexander VIII, pope)
Colonna, Roman princely family mentioned as early as the 11th century. Very influential in Rome 13th–17th centuries: *298, 300, 310, 398*
Cybo, family originally from Genoa, influential from the 15th century, now extinct: *307* (see Innocent VIII, pope)

Falconieri, great family originally from Tuscany which settled in Rome in the 16th century: *244*
Farnese, noble family from upper Lazio, extinct by 1731; Cardinal Alexander (1468–1549) became Pope Paul III; Cardinal Alexander (1520–89), known as the Great Cardinal: *257, 360*
Frangipani, noble Roman family played a major role in the Middle Ages, extinct by the 17th century: *146, 168, 284*
Mattei, noble Roman family extinct by 1801: *190, 253, 351*
Medici, merchants and bankers from Florence who became princes. Very influential 15th–18th centuries, especially in Tuscany. In Rome: 329, 347, 378; Cardinal Ferdinand de' Medici (1548–1609): *315* (see Clement VII and Leo X, popes)
Odescalchi, family originally from Como, already mentioned in the 13th century. Settled in Rome when Benedetto Odescalchi was elected pope, taking the name of Innocent XI: *301*
Orsini, powerful Roman family known since the 10th century, rivals of the Colonna, three of its members were made pope: *31* (see Nicholas III, pope)
Pamphili, noble Roman family originally from Gubbio whose direct lineage became extinct in 1760; title inherited by the Doria branch: *278* (see Innocent X, pope)
Papareschi, noble Roman family established in Trastevere, very powerful in the 12th–13th centuries, extinct by the 15th century: *351, 353* (see Innocent II, pope)
Pierleoni, noble Roman family settled on the Isola Tiberina: *352*
Sacchetti, Florentine family, a branch of which settled in Rome in the 16th century: *242*
Savelli, noble Roman family, powerful in the Middle Ages, became extinct in 1712. Two of its members became pope: *179* (see Honorius III, pope)
Spada, originally from Gubbio this family is now extinct: *243, 246*

ARTISTS AND ARCHITECTS

Albani, Francesco, Bologna 1578–1660, painter: *259*
Alberti, Leon Battista, Genoa 1404–72, architect: *233*
Algardi, Alessandro, Bologna 1595–1654, sculptor, architect and painter: *133, 261, 368*
Ameli, Paolo, active in Rome 1730–49, architect: *259*
Ammanati, Bartolomeo, Settignano (Florence) 1511–92, sculptor and architect: *312, 370*
Andrea del Sarto, Florence 1486–1531, painter: *292*
Angelico (Fra) (Guido di Pietro, as a monk he was known as Fra Giovanni da Fiesole or Il Beato) Vicchio c. 1387–1455, painter: *214, 226, 260*
Armanni, Osvaldo, Perugia 1855–1929, architect: *254*
Arnolfo di Cambio, Colle Val d'Elsa, Sienna c. 1245–1302, architect and sculptor: *132, 354, 383*
Baciccia or **Baciccio** (Giovanni Battista Gaulli), Genoa 1639–1709, painter: *258, 278, 301, 354*
Baglione, Giovanni, Rome 1573–1644, painter
Bandinelli, Baccio, Florence 1493–1560, sculptor: *378*
Baratta, Giovanni Maria, Massa Carrara, 17th century, architect: *285*
Barocci, Federico, Urbino c. 1535–1612, painter: *281*
Basile, Ernesto, Palermo 1857–1932, architect: *269*
Bassano, Francesco (da Ponte) the Younger, Bassano del Grappa, 1549–92, painter: *233*
Batoni, Pompeo, Lucca 1707–87, painter: *335*
Bazzani, Cesare, Rome 1873–1939, architect: *215*
Bernich, Ettore, Rome 1845 or 1848–1914, architect: *339*
Bernini, Gian Lorenzo, Naples 1598–1680, architect, painter and sculptor: *133, 209, 210, 212, 213, 215, 260, 261, 265, 269, 276, 277, 285, 290, 291, 295–297, 301, 306, 307, 312, 313, 339, 356, 373, 393*

Bernini, Pietro, (father of Gian Lorenzo), Sesto Fiorentino (Florence) 1562–1629, sculptor: *314*
Bianchi, Salvatore, Rome 1821–84, architect: *338*
Bigot, Paul, 1870–1942, French architect, Prix de Rome 1900, designed the model of Rome in the 4th century: *388*
Borgognone, see: Courtois Guillaume
Borromini, Francesco, Bissone (Ticino) 1599–1667, architect: *198, 241, 244, 246, 272, 278, 282, 283, 291, 295, 299, 313, 323*
Bracci, Filippo, Rome (?) 1727–after 1746, painter: *213*
Bracci, Pietro, Rome 1700–73, sculptor: *298*
Bramante (Donato di Pascuccio), Monte Asdruvaldo (near Urbino) 1444–1514, architect and painter: *145, 167, 209, 215, 235, 249, 263, 281, 364*
Brandi, Giacinto, Poli (Rome) 1623–91, painter: *302, 309*
Bregno, Andrea, Osteno (Como) 1418/1421–1503/1506 architect and sculptor: *306*
Bronzino, Agnolo di Cosimo, Florence 1503–72, painter: *259, 293, 299*
Burne-Jones, Sir Edward Coley, Birmingham 1833–98, British painter: *348*
Caffi, Ippolito, Belluno (Veneto) 1809–66, painter: *103, 279*
Calandra, Davide, Turin 1856–1915, sculptor: *270*
Calderini, Guglielmo, Perugia 1837–1916, architect: *236, 383*
Canova, Antonio, Possagno (Treviso) 1757–1822, sculptor: *40, 213, 279, 284, 301*
Caravaggio, Il (Michelangelo Merisi), Caravaggio (Bergamo) 1571/1572–1610, painter: *230, 259, 271, 285, 292, 293, 307, 359, 362, 369*
Carimini, Luca, Rome 1830–90, architect: *333*
Carracci, family of painters from Bologna; Annibale, 1560–1609: *244, 245, 259, 266, 300, 307*; Agostino (his brother) 1557–1602: *245*
Castelli, Domenico, known as Il Fontanino,

Melide (Ticino), architect active in Rome 1619–58: 243

Cavaliere d'Arpino, (Giuseppe Cesari), Arpino (Frosinone) 1568–1640, painter: 198, 301, 322, 343, 365, 372

Cavallini, Pietro, painter and mosaic artist, active in Rome 1273–1321: 130, 354, 356, 358, 359

Cellini, Benvenuto, Florence 1500–71, sculptor and goldsmith: 234

Cellini, Giuseppe, Rome 1855–1940, painter: 301

Chiaradia, Enrico, Caneva (Pordenone) 1851–1901, sculptor: 161

Ciampelli, Agostino, Florence 1577–1642, painter: 339

Cigoli, Il (Ludovico Cardi), Cigoli di San Miniato (Pisa) 1559–1613, painter and architect: 272

Cioli, Giacomo, Rome (?)–1734, architect: 247

Cipolla, Antonio, Naples 1822–74, architect: 242

Cirilli, Guido, Ancona 1871–1954, architect: 161

Cordier, Nicolas known as Il Franciosino, 1567–1612, sculptor from Lorraine: 198

Cornacchini, Agostino, Pescia (Pistoia) 1683–1740, sculptor: 211

Corot, Jean-Baptiste Camille, Paris 1796–1875, French painter: 101

Cosmati, family of marble cutters, mosaic artists and sculptors, active in Rome 12th–13th centuries: 131, 343, 356

Costa, Vincenzo, 1899–1944, architect: 254

Courtois, Guillaume (known as Il Borgognone), 1628–79, French painter: 258

Daniele da Volterra, (Daniele Ricciarelli), Volterra 1509–66, painter: 314; school of: 279

David, Jacques-Louis, Paris 1748–1825, painter: 314

De Angelis, Giulio 1850–1906, Roman architect: 269, 301

De Chirico, Giorgio, Volos (Greece) 1888–1974, painter: 377

De Haan, David, Rotterdam 1602–22, painter: 364

De Renzi, Mario, Rome 1897–1967, architect: 184

De Rossi, Giovanni Antonio, Rome 1637–95, architect: 270, 279

De Rossi, Mattia, Rome 1637–95, architect: 302, 355

De Rossi, Vincenzo, Fiesole 1525–87, sculptor and architect: 159

De Sanctis, Francesco, Rome 1693–1740, architect: 247, 314

Decq, Odette, Laval born 1955, architect: 380

Del Debbio, Enrico, Carrara 1891–1973, architect: 377, 378

Del Duca, Jacopo, Cefalù (Sicily), c. 1520–c. 1601, sculptor and architect: 190

Del Grande, Antonio, Rome 1622–71, architect: 259, 313

Della Greca, Felice, Rome 1626–77, architect: 268

Della Porta, Giacomo, Genoa c. 1533–1602, architect and sculptor: 129, 157, 241, 245, 250, 254, 257, 268, 272, 278

Della Porta, Guglielmo, Porlezzo (Como) 1500–77, sculptor and architect: 213

Della Valle, Filippo, Florence 1697–1768, sculptor: 298

Dérizet, Antoine, Lyon 1697–1768, architect: 271, 302

Domenichino, Il (Domenico Zampieri), Bologna 1581–1641, painter: 188, 212, 243, 247, 270, 283, 291, 294, 335, 346, 358, 372

Dughet, Gaspard (Poussin), Rome 1615–75, painter: 346

Duquesnoy, François, known as Il Fiammingo, Brussels 1597–1643, sculptor: 167, 213

Ersoch, Gioacchino, 1815–1902, architect: 184

Fanzago, Cosimo, Clusone (Bergamo) 1591–1678, architect: 260

Ferrari, Ettore, Rome 1845–1929, sculptor and painter: 178

Ferri, Ciro, Rome 1634–89, painter: 278

Filarete, Il (Antonio Averulino), Florence c 1400–c. 1469, sculptor and architect: 211

Fontana, Carlo, Brusata (Ticino) 1634–1714, architect: 214, 269, 270, 300, 301, 307, 357

Fontana, Domenico, Melide (Ticino) 1543–1607, architect: 196, 197, 198, 210, 215, 242, 271, 295, 314, 343

Fontana, Francesco, Rome 1668–1708, architect: 300

Fontana, Giovanni, Melide (Ticino) 1540–1614, architect: 364

Francesco da Volterra (Francesco Capriano), c. 1535– 88, architect and sculptor: 243, 283, 301, 302, 309, 344, 359

Fuga, Ferdinando, Florence 1699–1781, architect: 244, 285, 297, 342, 343, 362

Galilei, Alessandro, Florence 1691–1736, architect: 198, 241

Gallori, Emile, Florence 1846–1924, sculptor: 365

Giacomo da Pietra Santa, Lucca, earliest known work c. 1452, died c. 1497, architect: 284

Giaquinto, Corrado, Molfetta (Puglia) 1703–65, painter: 200, 280

Giardoni, Francesco, 1692–1757, cast the bronze angel for Castel Sant'Angelo (1742) designed by the Flemish sculptor P. A. Verschaffelt: 235

Giotto or **Giotto di Bondone**, Vespignano di Vicchio (Florence) c. 1267–1337, painter: 211

Giovanni da San Giovanni (Giovanni Mannozzi), San Giovanni Valdarno (Arezzo) 1592–1636, painter: 192

Giovanni da Udine (Giovanni Nanni), Udine 1487–1564, painter: 360, 378

Giovenale, Giovanni Battista, Rome 1849–1564, architect: 155

Gismondi, Italo, Rome 1887, architect: 388

Giulio Romano (Giulio Pippi), Rome 1499–1546, painter and architect: 108, 374

Gozzoli, Benozzo (Benozzo di Lese), Florence c. 1420–97, painter: 159

Grassi, Orazio, Savona 1583–1654, architect: 261

Graziani, Ercole, Bologna 1688–1765, painter: 285

Gregorini, Domenico, Rome 1700–77, architect: 200

Guercino, Il (Giovanni Francesco Barbieri), Cento (Ferrara) 1591–1666, painter: 246, 254, 283, 285, 294, 369

Guerra, Giovanni, Modena 1540/4–1618, painter and architect: 268

Guerrini, Giovanni, Bagnara di Romagna 1887, painter and architect: 387

Guglielmetti, Camillo, architect active in Rome c. 1857–62: 283

Gui, Enrico, 1841–1905, architect: 249

Guidetti, Guidetto, Lombard architect, active in Rome from 1550, died in 1564: 254

Hennebique, François, Neuville-Saint-Vaast 1843–1921, French architect: 376

Holbein, Hans the Younger, Augsburg 1497–1543, German painter: 292

Honthorst, Gerrit van, known as Gherardo delle Notti, Utrecht 1590–1656, painter: 246, 359

Houdon, Jean-Antoine, Versailles 1741–Paris 1828, sculptor: 334

Juvara, Filippo, Messina 1678–1736, architect: 243

Klimt, Gustav, Vienna 1862–1918, Austrian painter: 376

Koch, Gaetano, Rome 1849–1910, architect: 160, 302, 334, 348

Lambardi, Carlo, Arezzo 1554–1620, architect: 181

Landini, Taddeo, Florence 1550–96, architect and sculptor: 254

Lanfranco, Giovanni, Terenzo (Parma) 1582–1647, painter: 247, 250, 285, 291, 343

La Padula, Ernesto Bruno, Pisticci (Matera) 1902–68, architect: 387

Legros, Pierre (the Younger), Paris 1666–1719, French sculptor: 258, 261, 286, 297

Libera, Adalberto, Villa Lagrani (Trento) 1903–63, architect and town planner: 184, 387

Ligorio, Pirro, Naples c. 1510–83, architect and painter: 214, 215, 272, 318, 392, 394

Lippi, Annibale, worked in Rome during the second half of the 16th century: 315, 369

Lippi, Filippino, Prato (Florence) c. 1457– 1504, painter: 260

◆ BIOGRAPHICAL INDEX

Lippi, Fra Filippo, Florence c. 1406–69, painter: *292, 293*

Longhi (the Elder), Viggiù (Varese) c. 1520–91, architect: *129, 130, 281, 284, 311*

Longhi, Martino (the Younger), Rome 1602–60, architect: *309*

Lorenzetto (Lorenzo Lotti), Florence 1490–1541, architect and sculptor: *240, 307*

Lorrain, Claude (Claude Gellée), Chamagne (Vosges), 1600–82, French painter, died in Rome where he spent part of his life: *259, 272*

Lotto, Lorenzo, Venice 1480–c. 1556, painter: *292*

Lutyens, Edwin Landseer, London 1869–1944, British architect: *376*

Maccari, Cesare, Sienna 1840–1919, painter: *236*

Maderno, Carlo, Capolago (Ticino), 1556–1629, architect: *209, 241, 250, 268, 291, 294, 302, 309, 314, 342*

Maderno, Stefano, Bissone (Ticino) 1576–1636, sculptor: *167, 326, 353*

Maini, Giovanni Battista, Cassano Magnano (Varese) 1690–1752, sculptor: *278*

Manfredi, Manfredo, Piacenza 1859–1927, architect: *160, 365*

Manzù, Giacomo, Bergamo 1908–91, sculptor: *211*

Maratta, Carlo, Camerano (Ancona) 1625–1713, painter: *258, 300, 307, 335, 362*

Marucelli, Paolo, Rome 1594–1649, architect: *272*

Mascherino or **Mascarino**, Ottaviano (Ottaviano Nonni), Bologna 1524–1606, painter and architect: *283, 297*

Masolino da Panicale (Tommaso di Cristoforo Fini), Panicale in Valdarno (Florence) c. 1383–1440, painter: *193*

Matteo da Città di Castello (Matteo Bartolini), Città di Castello (Perugia) c. 1525/1530–89 or 1597, architect: *281*

Maturino da Firenze, Florence 1490–1527/1528, painter: *243*

Mazzoni, Giulio, Piacenza c. 1525–1618, architect, painter and sculptor: *246*

Mazzoni del Grande, Angiolo, 1894–after 1934, architect: *338*

Meier, Richard, Newark (New Jersey), born 1934, architect: *310*

Melozzo da Forlì (Melozzo degli Ambrosi), Forlì 1438–94, painter: *214, 226*

Mengs, Anton Raphael, Aussig (Bohemia) 1728–79, painter: *368*

Metsys, Quentin, Louvain c. 1465–1530, Flemish painter: *292*

Michelangelo (Michelangelo Buonarroti), Caprese (Arezzo) 1475–1564, sculptor, painter and architect: *129, 130, 209, 210, 212, 214, 215, 218, 245, 260, 263, 298, 318, 334, 346, 347*

Mochi, Francesco, Montevarchi (Arezzo) 1580–1654, sculptor

Momo, Giuseppe, Vercelli 1875–1940, architect: *215*

Moreau, Gustave, Paris 1826–98, French painter, engraver and draftsman: *98*

Morelli, Cosimo, Imola (Bologna) 1732–1812, architect: *279*

Morris, William, Elm-House 1834–96, British painter: *348*

Murena, Carlo, Rieti 1713–64, architect: *279*

Muziano, Girolama, Acquafredda (Brescia) 1528/1532–92, painter: *393*

Muzio, Giovanni, Milan 1893–1982, architect: *387*

Nanni di Baccio Bigio (Giovanni Lippi), Florence (?)–1568, architect and sculptor: *242*

Natoire, Charles-Joseph, Nimes 1700–77, French painter: *271*

Nebbia, Cesare, Orvieto c. 1536–1614, painter

Nervi, Pier Luigi, Sondrio, 1891–1979, engineer and architect: *388*

Nicolò di Angelo, active 1170–80, Roman sculptor: *383*

Ojetti, Raffaele, Rome 1845–1924, architect: *284*

Pagano, Giuseppe, Parenzo (Istria) 1896–1945, architect and town planner: *386*

Paniconi, Mario, Rome 1904–1973, architect: *387*

Pannini, Giovanni Paolo, Piacenza 1691–1765, painter and architect: *299*

Parmigianino, Il (Girolamo Francesco Maria Mazzola), Parma 1503–40, painter: *259*

Parodi, Giovanni Battista, Genoa 1674–1730, painter: *346*

Passignano (Domenico Cresti), Passignano (Florence) 1559–1638, painter: *181*

Pediconi, Giulio, Rome 1906, architect: *387*

Penni, Giovanni Francesco, known as Il Fattore, Florence 1488–after 1528, painter: *360*

Perin del Vaga (Pietro Buonaccorsi), Florence 1501–47, painter: *235, 266, 301*

Perugino, Il (Pietro Vannucci), Città della Pieve (Perugia) c. 1450–1523, painter: *227, 292*

Peruzzi, Baldassare, Sienna 1481–1536, architect and painter: *157, 209, 266, 279, 280, 360, 361, 378*

Piacentini, Marcello, 1881–1960, architect and town planner: *233, 236, 302, 382, 386, 388*

Piacentini, Pio, Rome 1846–1928, architect: *160, 348*

Piano, Renzo, Genova, born in 1937, architect: *376*

Piccinato, Luigi, Legnago (Verona) 1899–1983, architect and town planner: *386*

Piero della Francesca, Borgo San Sepolcro (Arezzo) c. 1415–92, painter: *214*

Pietro da Cortona (Pietro Berrettini), Cortona 1596–1669, painter and architect: *131, 230, 260, 278, 280, 283, 291, 309, 346*

Pinelli, Achille, Rome 1809–41, painter: *359*

Pinelli, Bartolomeo, Rome 1781–1835, painter: *359*

Pinturicchio (Bernardino di Betto), Perugia c. 1454–1513, painter: *131, 215, 226, 307*

Piranesi, Giovanni Battista, Maiano di Mestre (Veneto) 1720–78, engraver and architect: *180, 299, I–XIII*

Poletti, Luigi, Modena 1792–1869, architect: *313, 383*

Polidoro da Caravaggio (Polidoro da Caldara), Caravaggio (Lombardy) c. 1500–46, painter: *243*

Pollaiuolo (Antonio Benci), Florence c.

1431–98, painter and sculptor: *213, 214*

Pomarancio, (Cristoforo Roncalli), Pomarance (Pisa) 1552–1626, painter: *167, 191, 257, 302*

Pontelli, Baccio, Florence c. 1450–92, architect and sculptor: *232, 280, 300, 306, 353*

Ponzio, Flaminio, Viggiù (Varese) c. 1560–1613, architect: *311, 343, 364*

Poussin, Nicolas, Les Andelys 1594–1665, French painter: *292, 299, 312*

Pozzi, Stefano, Rome 1699–1768, painter: *285*

Pozzo, Fra Andrea, Trento, 1642–1709, Jesuit, painter and architect: *82–3, 258*

Preti, Mattia, also known as Il Calabrese, Taverna 1613–99, painter: *250*

Prospero Bresciano (Prospero Antichi), Brescia (?)–1592, sculptor: *295*

Raffaello da Montelupo (Raffaello di Bartolomeo Sinibaldi), Montelupo Fiorentino (Florence) c. 1505–67, sculptor and architect: *235, 347*

Raggi, Ercole Antonio, Vico Morcote (Ticino) 1624–86, sculptor: *252*

Raguzzini, Filippo, Naples c. 1680–1771, architect: *261, 321*

Rainaldi, Carlo, Rome 1611–91, architect: *159, 242, 250, 300, 301, 307, 309, 311*

Rainaldi, Girolamo, Rome 1570–1655, architect: *278*

Raphael (Raffaello Sanzio), Urbino 1483–1520, painter and architect: *215, 228, 243, 266, 281, 284, 285, 292, 299, 307, 309, 318, 360, 361, 375, 378*

Reni, Guido, Bologna 1575–1642, painter: *188, 231, 243, 247, 291, 298, 299, 343, 363*

Rinaldi, Rinaldo, Padua 1793–1873, sculptor: *283*

Roesler Franz, Ettore, Rome 1852–1907, painter: *233, 359*

Romano, Mario, Rome 1898, architect: *387*

Rosa, Ercole, San Severino (Marche) 1846–93, sculptor: *316*

Rosa, Salvator, Naples 1615–73, painter: *242, 335, 363*

Rosati, Rosato, Montalto delle Marche (Ascoli Piceno) 1559–1622, architect: *247*

ossi, Ettore, Fano (Marche) 1894, architect: 386

ossini, Luigi, Ravenna 1790–1857, painter and engraver: 299

ubens, Peter Paul, Siegen (Westphalia) 1577–1640, Flemish painter: 282

ughesi, Fausto, Montepulciano (Sienna) active c. 1593–1606, architect: 281

usconi Sassi, Lodovico, Rome 1678–1736, architect: 283

usuti, Filippo, painter and mosaic artist, active in Rome 13th–14th centuries: 342

utelli, Mario, Palermo 1850–1941, sculptor: 4, 341

acchi, Andrea, Nettuno (Rome) 1599–1661, painter: 198

acconi, Giuseppe, Montalto delle Marche (Ascoli Piceno) 1854–1905, architect: ?0

alvi, Nicolà, Rome 1697–1751, architect: 7, 298, 301

alviati, Francesco (Francesco de' Rossi), Florence c. 1510–63, painter: 242, 245, 283, 1

angallo, Antonio da, the Elder (Antonio Giamberti), Florence 1455–1534, architect: 3

angallo, Antonio da, the Younger, Florence 1484–1546, architect: 7, 215, 235, 241, 242, 4, 249, 263, 279, 378

angallo, Giuliano da (Giuliano Giamberti), Florence c. 1445–16, architect: 209, 0, 343

ansovino II (Andrea Contucci), Monte San Savino (Arezzo) 1460–1629, architect and sculptor: 190, 280, 1

ansovino, Jacopo (Jacopo Tatti), Florence 1486–1570, architect and sculptor: 241, 243, 5, 301

araceni, Carlo, Venice c. 1579–1620, painter: 9

rdi, Giuseppe, Sant'Angelo in Vado (Marche) 1680–1753, architect: 247, 270

rti, Antonio, Budrio (Bologna) 1797–1880, architect: 305, 356

rtorio, Giulio Aristide, Rome 1860–1932, painter: 270

bastiano, Fiorentino, architect active in Rome 1479–83: 284

Sebastiano del Piombo (Sebastiano Luciani), Venice c. 1485–1547, painter: 307, 361, 364

Sodoma, Il (Giovanni Antonio Bazzi), Vercelli 1477–1549, painter: 361

Soffici, Ardengo, Rignano sull'Arno (Florence) 1879–1964, painter: 377

Soria, Giambattista, Rome 1581–1651, architect: 187, 188, 294, 356

Spaccarelli, Attilio, Rome 1890–1975, architect: 233

Street, George Edmond 1824–81, British architect: 348

Tassi, Agostino, Ponzano Romano (Rome) c. 1566–1644, painter: 283

Théodon, Jean-Baptiste, 1646–1713, French sculptor: 258

Titian (Tiziano Vecelli), Pieve di Cadore (Venice) c. 1490–1576, painter: 259, 299, 374

Torriti, Jacopo, painter and mosaic artist active at the end of the 13th century: 198, 343

Trentacoste, Domenico, Palermo 1859–1933, sculptor: 270

Tripisciano, Michele, Caltanissetta (Sicily) 1860–1913, sculptor: 357

Vaccaro, Giuseppe, Bologna 1896–1934, architect: 302

Valadier, Giuseppe, Rome 1762–1839, architect and town planner: 40, 209, 279, 306, 316

Valentin, Le (Valentin de Boulogne) Coulommiers 1591–1632, French painter: 246

Valvassori, Gabriele, Rome 1683–1761, architect: 259

Van Baburen, Dirk, c. 1595–c. 1624, Dutch painter: 364

Vanvitelli, Luigi, Naples 1700–73, architect and painter: 285, 296, 335

Vasanzio, Giovanni (Jan Van Santen), Utrecht c. 1550–1621, Dutch architect: 372

Vasari, Giorgio, Arezzo 1511–74, painter, writer and architect: 249

Vassalletto, family of sculptors, marble cutters and mosaic artists (12th–13th century); Pietro Vassalletto, active in Rome during the 12th century: 199, 382, 383

Velázquez, Diego Rodriguez da Silva y Velázquez, Seville 1599–1660, Spanish painter: 259

Vespignani, Virginio, Rome 1808–82, architect: 301, 383

Vietti, Luigi, Novara 1903, architect and town planner: 386

Vignola, Jacopo Barozzi, Vignola (Modena) 1507–73, architect: 146, 249, 257, 354, 370

Vouet, Simon, Paris 1590–1649, French painter: 312, 355

Ximenes, Ettore, Palermo 1855–1926, sculptor: 236

Zanelli, Angelo, San Felice di Benaco (Brescia) 1879–1942, sculptor: 161

Zuccaro, Federico, Sant'Angelo in Vado (Marche) c. 1540–1609, painter: 245, 257, 301, 314, 393

Zuccaro, Taddeo, his brother, Sant'Angelo in Vado (Marche) 1529–66, painter: 253, 254

Zucchi, Jacopo, Florence 1542–89, painter: 312

POLITICAL FIGURES

Barracco, Baron Giovanni, 1829–1914, member of parliament, art collector, bequeathed his collection of ancient sculptures to the municipality of Rome: 249

Berlinguer, Enrico, Sassari (Sardinia) 1922–84, politician, General Secretary of the Italian Communist Party (PCI) from 1972 to his death: 196

Cola di Rienzo, Rome c. 1313–54, tribune of the people, instigated a revolution in 1347 with the aim of establishing a Republic: 31, 234, XV

Garibaldi, Giuseppe, 1807–82, a patriot who was a major figure in the movement for the unification of Italy: 33, 314, 365

Gramsci, Antonio, Ales (Sardinia) 1881–Rome 1937, Marxist thinker, one of the founders of the Italian Communist Party, murdered by a group of Fascists in 1924: 177

Guiscard, Robert (guiscardo – cunning), c. 1015–Salerno 1085, Count of Apulia (1057–1059), Duke of Apulia, Calabria and Sicily (1059–1085). He crushed the pontifical army in 1053, his troops sacked Rome in 1084: 30

Mazzini, Giuseppe, Genoa 1805–72, patriot, founder of the "La Giovane Italia" movement, fought for the unification of Italy and for republican ideals: 178

Moro, Aldo, Maglie (Puglia) 1916–78, leader of the Christian Democrat Party, kidnapped and assassinated by the Red Brigade: 234

Mussolini, Benito, "Il Duce", born in Varano dei Costa (Romagna) in 1883, executed by Partisans of the anti-Fascist resistance near Como in 1945: 162, 184, 233, 377, 384, 386

Primoli, Giuseppe, (Count), 1851–1927, scholar and art collector, related to the Bonaparte family, founder of the Museo Napoleonico in Rome: 284

Togliatti, Palmiro, Genoa 1893–1964, one of the founders of the Italian Communist Party in 1921: 196

WRITERS AND SCIENTISTS

Bosio, Antonio, Malta 1575–1629, engraver, Roman priest, explored the Catacombs: 325

Bruno, Giordano, 1548–1600, philosopher, burnt at the stake for heresy: 234, 249

Cagliostro, Alessandro Conte di (Giuseppe Balsamo), Palermo 1743–95. Occult scientist, founder of the "Egyptian" branch of Freemasons, condemned to death in 1789 by the Inquisition, sentence commuted to life imprisonment in 1791: 234

De Rossi, Gian Battista, 1822–94, archeologist, specialist in early Christianity: 41, 325, 326

Fermi, Enrico, Rome 1901–Chicago 1954, Italian physicist, specialized in nuclear physics: 347

Gadda, Carlo-Emilio, Milan 1893–Rome 1973, Italian novelist: 43

Keats, John, London 1795–Rome 1821,

◆ BIOGRAPHICAL INDEX

English Romantic poet: *313*

Kircher, Athanase, 1635–Rome 1680, Jesuit scholar from Germany: *258, 387*

Majorana, Ettore, Italian physicist who disappeared in 1938: *347*

Marconi, Guglielmo, Bologna 1874–Rome 1937, Italian physicist, established the first radio link using Hertz-waves. Nobel Prize in 1909: *387*

Morante, Elsa, Rome 1912–1985, novelist: *253, 381*

Tasso, (Torquato Tasso), Sorrento 1544– Rome 1595, poet: *365*

Winckelmann, Johann Joachim, Brandenburg 1717–Trieste 1768, German archeologist and art historian. Became librarian to Cardinal Albani, curator of Roman antiquities and librarian in the Vatican. He was a pioneer of archeology and art history. He was assassinated: *41, 368*

COMPOSERS

Berlioz, Hector, La Côte–Saint–André 1803–Paris 1869, French composer: *315*

Puccini, Giacomo, Lucca 1858–Brussels 1924, Italian composer. Originally an organist, his first opera, *Manon Lescaut* was produced in 1893. The works *La Bohème* (1896), *Tosca* (1900) and *Madame Butterfly* (1904) were enormously successful and earned him acclaim as the champion of *verismo*: *250*

Verdi, Giuseppe, La Roncole 1813–Milan 1901, Italian oomposer made famous by his opera *Nabucco* (1842), then *Rigoletto* (1851), *Il Trovatore* and *La Traviata* (1835). A romantic figure with humanist tendencies, he contributed to the unification of Italy and brought revolutionary innovations to the art of opera: *284*

FILM STARS AND DIRECTORS

De Sica, Vittorio, Sora 1902–Neuilly 1974, Italian actor and film director. As a director he was most influential between 1944 and 1952, always working with Zavattini. He provided one of the masterpieces of neo-Realism, *Ladri di Biciclette* and went on to paint a vast fresco of postwar Italy with *Sciuscià* (1946), *Miracolo a Milano* (1950), *Umberto D* (1952). His other major works include *La Ciociara* (1960), *Giardino dei Finzi Contini* (1970): *355*

Fellini, Federico, Rimini 1920–Rome 1993, Italian film director. Worked with Rossellini before making his own films. His major works include: *La Strada* (1954), *La Dolce Vita* (1960), *8 1/2* (1962), *Giulietta degli Spiriti* (1965), *Fellini Roma* (1971), *Amarcord* (1973), *Città delle Donne* (1980), *La Voce della Luna* (1990). His baroque and dream-like world is pervaded by a feeling of loneliness and portrays the decadence of society: *298, 385*

Le Roy, Mervyn, San Francisco 1900, American film director. One of the great film makers of the early talkies. His famous works include: *Little Caesar* (1931), *Escape* (1932) and the epic *Quo Vadis?* (1950): *325*

Lizzani, Carlo, Rome 1922, Italian director and scriptwriter. His works include: *Achtung Banditi* (1951), *Il Gobbo* (1960), *L'Oro di Roma* (1961): *402*

Lollobrigida, Gina, Subiaco 1927, her beauty, vivacity and charm won her worldwide popularity as an actress in films like *Pane, Amore e Fantasia* by Comencini (1953), *Fanfan la Tulipe* by Christian Jacques (1952): *402*

Magnani, Anna, Alexandria 1908–Rome 1973, one of the greatest Italian film actresses. She can be seen in *Roma, città aperta* by Rossellini (1945), *Bellissima* by Visconti (1951): *43*

Mankiewicz, Joseph L., Wilkes Barre 1909–93, American film director. Some of his famous works are *All About Eve* (1950), *The Cicero Affair* (1952), *The Barefoot Contessa* (1954), *Sleuth* (1972), and some grandiose epics such as *Julius Caesar* (1954) and the extravagant *Cleopatra* (1961–3): *385*

Pasolini, Pier Paolo, Bologna 1922–Rome 1975, Italian film director and author. His brilliant career in the cinema started with *Accattone* (1961) and *Mamma Roma* (1963). He blended the proletarian reality of the suburbs of Rome with great universal myths and texts from the Bible in works such as *Oedipus Rex* (1967) and *Il Vangelo secondo Matteo* (1964): *43*

Rossellini, Roberto, Rome 1906–77. With *Roma, città aperta* (1945), *Paisà* (1946) and *Germania anno zero* (1948) he established neo-Realism as the most important current in Italian postwar cinema. His meeting with Ingrid Bergman was to mark a turning point in his career: he made *Europa 51* (1952) and *Viaggio in Italia* (1953) with her: *43*

Scola, Ettore, Trevico 1931, Italian film director. He reconciled comedy with social comment. *Dramma della gelosia* (1970), *C'eravamo tanti amati* (1975), *Brutti, sporchi e cattivi* (1976), *Una giornata particolare* (1977), *La terrazza* (1980), *Splendore* (1989): *236*

INDEX ◆

A

Academy, The (Villa Adriana) 397
Academy, British 376
Academy, French 315
Academy, Spanish 364
Accademia di San Lucia, Galleria 299
Actium, Battle of 28
Adriana Villa 394
Aemilia, Basilica 136
Agrippa, Basilica of 266
Agrippa, Baths of 266
Agrippa, Temple of 264
Albani, Villa 368
Albergo Quirinale 348
Alessandro e Rossana, Sala delle Nozze di 361
Altemps, Cappella 358
Altemps, Palazzo 284, 336
Alto Medioevo, Museo dell' 387
America, Viale 388
Amore e Psiche, Casa di 412
Amore Sacro e Amore Profano, 374
Amphitheater, games in the 172
Angelica, Biblioteca 282
Anguillara Palazzo 356
Anguillara, Torre 356
Anime in Purgatorio, Museo delle 236
Antamoro, Cappella 243
Antoninus and Faustina, Temple of 144, 145
Antoninus Pius, Column of 268
Apollo and Daphne 373
Apollo Sosianus, Temple of 158
Apollo, Temple of 149, 156
Appia, Via 126, 318
Aqua Paola 363, 364
Aqua Virgo 266, 277, 298, 314
Ara Pacis Augustae 310
Arcadia, Accademia dell' 364
Architecture, House of 339
Archivio di Stato (State Archives) 272, 388
Argentina, Area Sacra dell' 250
Argonauti, Portico degli 266
Art, Etruscan 371
Arte Moderna, Galleria Nazionale d' 376
Arti e Tradizioni Popolari, Museo delle 387
Assicurazioni Generali di Venezia, Palazzo delle 161
Auditorium 388
Augustine, Convent of Saint 284
Augustus, Arch of 143

Augustus, Forum of 163
Augustus, House of 148
Augustus, Mausoleum of 309
Aurelian Wall, the 306, 323
Aventine, the 176

B

Babington's Tea Rooms 313
Babuino, Via del 308
Balbus, Theater of 253
Banca Nazionale del Lavoro 302
Bandiere, Museo delle 161
Bank of Italy 348
Barberini coat of arms XVI, 212, 292
Barberini, neighborhood 290
Barberini, Palazzo 291
Barberini, Piazza 290
Barberini, Villa 369
Barcaccia Fountain 314
Barracco, Museo 249
Bees, Fountain of the 290
Bellone, Temple of 158
Belvedere, Palazzo del 214
Bernich, Aquarium of 339
Bessarione, Casa del Cardinale 321
Biblicum, Biblioteca del 299
Biblioteca della Storia contemporanea 254
Biblioteche, Cortile delle 395
Bicchierone Fountain 393
Birra Peroni, Stabilimento della 381
birrerie 301
Boarium, Forum 155
Bocca della Verità, Piazza 155
Bocconi, Magazzini 267, 269
Bonaparte, Palazzo 309
Boncompagni-Piombino, Palazzo 302
Borghese, Villa 372
Borghese, Palazzo 311
Borgo 232
Bosco Parrasio 364
Botteghe Oscure, Via delle 253
Braccio Nuovo 133, 215
Braschi, Palazzo 279
Buticosus, Baths of 413

C

Caesar, Forum of 163
Caetani, Cappella 344
Caetani, Palazzo 253
Cafés, famous 308
Campidoglio 128
Campidoglio, Piazza del 129

Campidoglio, Pinacoteca del 133
Campo de' Fiori 125, 241, 247, 249
Campo Marzio 256, 274, 304
Campus Martins 238
Cancelleria, Palazzo della 249
Canopus 396
Canopus, caryatids 397
Canova, Caffè 306
Carabinieri 125
Caracalla, edict of 29
Caracalla, Baths of 319
Carnevale Romano 48
Cartilius Poplicola, Tomb of 414
Casa Romuli 148
Caseggiato dei Dipinti 410
Caseggiato del Larario 412
Casina di Pius IV 214
Casina Valadier 316
Castro Praetorio 335
Castrense Amphitheater, 200
Catacombs 324–8
Catholic Cultural Center 270
Cavalieri di Malta, Piazza dei 188
Cecilia Metella, Tomb of 330
Celimontana, park of the Villa 190, 369
Celimontana, Villa 190
Celio 186
Cemetery, Protestant 183
Cenci Bolognetti, Palazzo 254, 258
Cerasi, Cappella 307
Cestius, Ponte 353
Cestius, Pyramid of 182
Chamber of Deputies 269
Chiesa Nuova 281
Chigi, Cappella 280, 307
Chigi, Palazzo 268
Cimarra, Palazzo 347
Cinecittà, 384, 385
Cinquecento, Piazza dei 338
Circus Maximus 177
Circus of Maxentius 328
Cista Ficoroni 371
Civiltà del Lavoro, Palazzo della 122, 387
Civiltà Romana, Museo della 388
Claudius, Aqueduct of 339
Claudius, Temple of the Divine 189
Clivus Martis 324
Clivus Scauri 188
Cloaca Maxima 156
Coliseum 123, 170
Collegio di Propaganda Fide 313
Colonna, Galleria 268
Colonna, gardens of the Villa 298
Colonna, Palazzo and Galleria 300
Colonna, Piazza 267

Colonnade of Piazza San Pietro 210
Colosseo Quadrato 387
Comitium 34, 138
Conciliazione, Via della 122, 232
Concord, Temple of 141
Congressi, Palazzo dei 387
Conservatori, Palazzo dei 130, 132
Constantine, Arch of 169
Constantine, legend of 192
Consulta, Palazzo della 297
Contemporary Art Museum in Rome (MACRO) 184, 381
Conti, Torre dei 168
Coppelle, Piazza delle 270
Cornaro, Cappella 294
Coronari, Via dei 283
Corporations, Theater of the 406
Corporazioni, Piazzale delle 407, 408
Corsini, Galleria 292, 362
Corsini, Palazzo 362
Corso, Via del 307,308
Cortina, Terrazza della 399
Cosmati 76
Costaguti, Palazzo 254
Counter-Reformation 23, 281
Crypta Balbi, 253, 336
Cupolas 262, 263
Curia 31, 138
Cybo, Cappella 307

D

Dames du Sacré-Coeur, Convent of the 315
Danae 375
Dante, Casa di 357
Dei consentes, Portico of the 140
Deposition (The) 375
Diana, Via di 410, 411
Diocletian, Baths 288, 334, 336
Dioscuri, Temple of the 142
Dolabella, Arco di 190
Domine Quo Vadis, church 324
Dominicans 260
Domitian, buildings of 142
Domitian, Obelisk of 329
Domitian, Palace of 150
Domitian, Stadium of 276
Domus Augustana 150
Domus Aurea 40, 174
Domus Flavia 150
Domus Fulminata 414
Domus Severiana 151
Domus Tiberiana 149
Doria Pamphilj, Galleria 259
Doria Pamphilj, Palazzo 258

Doria Pamphilj, Villa 20, 368, 369
Dragons, Fountain of the 393
Drusus, Arch of 324
Duomo (Tivoli) 391

E

Educazione Fisica, Accademia di 378
English Pavilion 376
Esedra, Piazza 333
Esquilino, Piazza dell' 342, 344
Este, gardens of Villa d' 88, 392
Etruscans, 26
Etruscan Museum 370
EUR 386, 387
Europa, Viale 388
Eurysaces, Tomb of Virgilius 339
Excavations, archeological l40
Excubitorium 356
Exhibition of 1911 376, 388

F

Fabri Navales, Temple of the 414
Fabricio, Ponte 353
Facchino, Fontanella del 260
Falconieri, Palazzo 244
Farnese coat of arms XVI, 244
Farnese, Palazzo 244
Farnese, Villa 369
Farnesina, Villa della 360
Faro della Latinità 365
Festa de' Noantri 351
Fiano, Palazzo 309
Filippini, Oratorio dei 282
Finland, Academy of 365
Fiori, Campo de' 125, 241, 247, 249
Fiumi, Fontana dei 277
Fiumicino 416
Flaminia, Porta 306
Flaminia, Via 238, 308
Flaminius, Circus of 157
Foce, Via della 412
Fonseca, Cappella 312
Fontana del Mose 289, 294, 295
Fontanella di Borghese, Largo della 311
Forma Urbis 164
Fornarina, house of La 363
Fornarina, La 292
Foro Italico 377
Fortuna, Temple of (Palestrina) 398
Fortuna, Temple of (Rome) 156
Forty Martyrs, Oratory of the 142
Forum, Antiquarium of the 147
Forum, Roman 136
Forums, Imperial 162
Forum Transitorium 165
Fountains 366

Fregene 416

G

Gabinetto Nazionale delle Stampe 360
Galatea, Camera di 360
Gallienus, Arch of 340
Gesù, church 257
Gesù e Maria, church 309
Ghetto 252
Ghibellines 279
Gianicolo, see Janiculum
Giappone, Passeggiata del 388
Giovanni e Paolo, Casa di 188, 189
Giovanni Giolitti, Via 339
Gismondi, Italo 388
Giubbonari, Via de' 247
Giulia Via 240
Giulia, Villa 370
Giulio, Castello di 416
Giuturna, Fonte di 142
Gladiators 173
Goldoni, Largo 311
Governo Vecchio, Palazzo del 281
Grand Tour 97
Grattacielo Italia 387
Greco, Caffè 312
Gregorian Reform 323
Gregorian, University 299
Gregoriana, Villa 391
Griffins, House of the 150
Guadagnolo, 402
Guelphs 279

H

Hadrian, Mausoleum of 233, 235
Hadrian, quarter of 406
Hadrian, Temple of 267
Hadrian's Villa 394
Hans Christian Anderson museum 369
Heliogabalus, Temple of 151
Hemicycles, Terrace of the 399
Hercules Victor, Temple of (Rome) 155
Hercules Victor, Temple of (Tivoli) 390
Herodias Atticus Triopius of 329
Herziana, Biblioteca 314
Holitorium, Forum 154
Horatii and Curatii, Tomb of the 330
Horrea Agrippiana 142
Horrea Epagathiana and Epaphrodisiana 412
Horse races 308
Hospitalia 394

Hotels
Abruzzi 429
Albergo del Sole 429
Amalia 428

Antica Locanda 428
Arenula 429
Boccaccio 430
Bolivar 428
Bramante 428
Campo de'Fiori 429
Colors Hotel & Hostel 428
Domus Aventina 428
Grifo 429
Hotel Ercoli 431
Hotel Fiori 429
Hotel Florida 428
Hotel Galli 431
Hotel Kennedy 430
Hotel Parlamento 430
Hotel Trastevere 431
Navona 430
Pomezia 430
Nerva 429
Papà Germano 431
Pensione Barrett 429
Pensione di Rienzo 431
Pensione Panda 430
Perugia 429
Raphael 430
Rome à Volonté 430
Teatro de Pompeo 430
Villa San Pio 428
Viminale 431

Hundred Fountains, Alley of 393
Hypogeums 324, 327

I

Ignatius, altar of St 258
Immaculate Conception, Column of the 313
Independence, First War of 32
Independence, Second War of 33
Industry and Commerce, Ministry of 302
Instituto Nazionale per la Grafica 298
Insula dei Dipinti 411
Insula delle Volte Dipinte 414
Insula di Giove e Ganimede 411
Insulae 410
Isola Sacra 416
Isola Tiberina 352

J

Janiculum, 363
Janiculum, Passeggiata del 365
Janiculum, Syrian Sanctuary of the 355
Janiculum, view from the 122
Janus, Temple of 138
Janus, Arch of 156
Jewish Community, Museum of the 254
Julia, Basilica 141
Julius, Temple of the Divine 143
Julius II, Tomb of 346

K

Keats-Shelley Memorial House 313

Knights of Malta, Order of the 50, 180

L

Lacus Curtius 141
Lancellotti, Palazzo 283
Lante, Villa 365
Laocoön 40
Lapis Niger 138
Lares 413
Large Baths (Villa Adriana) 396
Lata, Via 238
Lateran Treaty 33, 198, 202, 232
Lateran, The 196
Laterano, Basilica of San Giovanni in 198
Laterano, Obelisk of 196
Legnano, Battle of 316
Lepanto, Battle of 300
Liberius 342
Lincei, Academia Nazionale dei 362
Livia, Casa di 148
Ludus Magnus 171
Luna Park 388
Lungara, Via della 359
Lupercalia, Feast of the 147
Luperci 147

M

MACRO (Museo di arte contemporanea di Roma) 184, 381
Madama, Palazzo 272
Madama, Villa 378
Madonna dell'Orto, church 354
Madonna dei Palefrenieri, 374
Maecenas, Auditorium of 341
Magna Mater, Piazzale della 415
Malta, the Knights of Order of 50, 180
Mamertine Prison 131
Mancini, Palazzo 309
Marcello, Teatro di 157
March on Rome 33, 386
Marconi, Piazza 387
Marcus Aurelius, Column of 267
Marcus Aurelius, restoration of the statue of 54
Marcus Aurelius, statue of 130
Margana, Piazza 159
Margani, Torre Medievale dei 159
Margutta, Via 308
Marius, Trophies of 130, 341
Marmorata, Via 184
Mars Ultor, Temple of 163
Marzio, Campo 256, 274, 304
Mascherone Fountain 244
Massimo alle Colonne, Palazzo 279
Mater Matuta, Temple of 156

Matidia, Temple of 267
Mattatoio (slaughterhouse) 184
Mattei di Giove, Palazzo 254
Mattei di Paganica, Palazzo di 253
Mattei, Piazza 254
Mattei, Villa 369
Maxentius and Constantine, Basilica of 145
Maxentius, Circus of 328
Maximus, Circus of 177
Mazzini, Giuseppe, statue of 178
Medici, gardens of the Villa 315
Medici, Villa 89, 315, 369
Medieval houses 391
Memoria Apostolorum 328
Merchants, Mosaics of the 408
Meta Remi 182
Metro, sign of the 124
Michael, Archangel 235
Michelangelo, *Pietà* 212
Milizie, Torre delle 168
Milliarium Aureum 140
Millina, Torre 279
Minerva Medica, Temple of 339
Minerva, Piazza della 260, 261
Ministero per i Bene Culturali e Ambientali 55
Ministry of Foreign Affairs 378
Mirabilia Urbis 40
Mithraeum 181, 196, 197, 406, 407
Mithraeum of the Seven Spheres 406, 407
Molini, Via dei 411
Money Changers, Arch of the 156
Monserrato, Via 240
Monte Mario 377
Monte di Pietà 247
Montecitorio 269
Montecitorio, Palazzo di 269
Montecitorio, Piazza di 269
Montegiordano, Palazzo 282
Moro, Fontana del 278
Mosaics 408
Mosè, Fontana del 295
Mostra, Augustea della Romanità 388
Municipal Gallery of Modern and Contemporary Art 290
Musei Capitolini 130, 132
Museo Astronomico e Copernicano 377
Museo Chiaramonti 215
Museo delle Terme (Museum of the Baths) 335
Museo di Roma in

Trastevere 359
Museo Geologico 302
Museo Napoleonico 284
Museo Nazionale Romano (National Roman Museum) 336
Museo Nuovo 133
Museo Preistorico ed Etnografico Pigorini 387
Museum, Contemporary Art (MACRO) 184, 381
Museum of the Baths (Museo delle Terme) 335
Mutilati, Casa dei 236

N
Naiads, Fountain of the 334
Nasi rossi 49
National Liberation Committee 33
National Roman Museum (Museo Nazionale Romano) 336
Naumachiae 276
Navicella Fountain of 190
Navona, Piazza 3, 239, 276
Nazioni Unite, Piazzale delle 387
Nazionale, Via 348
Necropoli del Vaticano 209
Nerva, Forum of 165
Neptune, Fountain of 123, 278
Neptune, the Baths of 406
Niches with Two Columns, Terrace of the 399
Nile Mosaic 400, 402
Nostra Signora al Sacro Cuore, church 278

O
Oblates, Congregation of 169
Odeon 239
Odescalchi, Palazzo 301
Olympic Games 33
Oratorians, Shrine of the 281
Oratorio, Confederazione del 281
Orotorio dei Filippini 281, 282
Oro, Piazza d' 395
Orso, Hostaria del 284
Orso, Via dell' 284
Orto Botanico 363
Osservatorio Astronomico e Meteorologico 377
Ostia 404
Ostia, Capitolium of 411
Ostia, Forum of 411
Ostia, mosaics of 408
Ostia, Republican Temples of 410

Ostia, Synagogue of 414
Ostia, village of 416
Ottavia, Portico di 158
Ottobrata 49

P
Pace, Piazza della 281
Palatine, Antiquarium of the 151
Palazzo di Giustizia 236
Palazzo Massimo 336
Palazzo Nuovo 130
Palazzo Senatorio 130
Palestrina 398
Palestrina, Museo di 402
Pamphilj, Palazzo 278
Panetteria, Via della 298
Panisperna, Via 347
Pantheon 264
Pantheon, dome of 265
Paolina, Cappella 215, 343
Paolina, Sala 234
Parilia, Feast of the 147
Passetto 234
Patriarchium 197
Patricians 26
Paul II, Tomb of 213
Peace, Temple of 164
Pellegrino, Via del 240
Peregrinorum, Via 305
Peretti coat of arms XVI
Peter, Chains of St 346
Peter, statue of St 167
Phocas, Column of 141
Piccolo Aventino 182
Piè di Marmo, Via 260
Pietà 212
Pigorini, Museo Preistorico ed Etnografico 387
Pincio 316
Pinturicchio 215
Piscinula, Piazza in 353
Pius IV, Casina of 214
Plebeians 26
Poikile, Stoa 396
Pomerium 176, 238, 319
Pompey, Theater of 248
Pompey, Porticos of 248
Pomponius Hylas, Columbarium of 322
Ponte Fabricio 353
Ponte Milvio 377
Ponte Rotto 352
Ponte Sisto 363
Ponzetti, Cappella 281
Popes, coats of arms of XVI
Popes, Crypt of the 326
Popolo, Piazza del 306
Popolo, Porta del 306
Porta Latina 323
Porta Maggiore 339
Porta Maggiore, Basilica sotterranea di 340
Porta Marina 414
Porta San Paolo 182, 183
Porta Ostiensis, Museo della 183

Porta Portese, Piazza di 355
Porta Romana 405
Portico d'Ottavia, Via del 253
Porticus Minucia Frumentaria 251
Portunus, Temple of 155
Praeneste 398
Prati 236
Presidency of the Council of Ministers 268
Primoli, Fondazione 284
Prospettive, Sala delle 361
Psyche, Loggia of 360
Punic Wars 27

Q
Quercia, Piazza della 246
Quintili, Villa dei 330
Quirinal, the 297
Quirinale, Palazzo del 297
Quirinus, Temple of 288

R
Raymondi, Cappella 364
Ramses II, Obelisk of 178
Rape of Proserpina (The) 373
Re Magi, church of the 313
Regia 143
Regia, Sala 215
Regina Margherita, Piazza 402
Reliquie, Cappella delle 200
Repubblica, Piazza della 333

Restaurants
Agata e Romeo 439
Alberto Ciarla 439
Antico Falcone 434
Boccon Divino 435
Boccondivino 435
Buccone 437
Cavour 313 435
Checchino dal 1887 434
Cul de Sac 435
Da Baffetto 435
Da Francesco 436
Da Franco Ar Vicoletto 439
Da Lucia 439
'Da Oio' a Casa Mia 434
Dal Pompiere 436
Dal Toscano 434
Dar Filettaro a Santa Barbara 436
Enoteca Antica di Via della Croce 437
Enoteca Ferrara 439
Fiaschetteria Beltramme 437
Giuseppe al 59 438
Gusto 438
Hotel-Ristorante Adriano 440
Il Convivio Troiani 436
La Casa Bleve 436
La Rosetta 436

◆ INDEX

Maccheroni 436
Margutta Vegetariano 438
Mario 438
Maticianella 438
Osteria Ar Galletto 437
Osteria dell' Angelo 434
Osteria Gensola 439
Piperno 437
Pizzeria Formula Uno 439
Pizzeria Montecarlo 437
Pizzeria Panattoni-I Marmi 440
Pizzeria Remo 434
Sabatini 440
Santa Lucia 437
Settimio all'Arancio 438
Taverna Romana 435
Tram-Tram 439
Trattoria Agustarello 434
Trattoria Augusto 435
Trattoria De Enzo 440
Trattoria Da Sergio 437
Trattoria Da Tonino 437

Restoration of art works 54
Rhodes, House of the Knights of 168
Ricci, Palazzo 243
Ripagrande 353
Ripetta, Via di 308
Risorgimento, Museo Centrale del 161
Rocca Pia 391
Roma, Museo di 279
Roma in Trastevere, Museo di 359
Roman dialect 42
Roman language 40
Roman Republic 32, 272, 363
Romanaccio 41
Romanesco 40
Rome and Augustus, Temple of 412
Rometta, Fountain of the 393
Romulus, Mausoleum of 329
Romulus, Temple of 144
Rondinini, Palazzo 309
Rosati, Caffè 306
Rospigliosi-Pallavicini, Palazzo 298
Rossa, Casina 313
Rostra, Imperial 140
Rotonda, Piazza della 264
Round-up of 1943 (Jews and Roman Resistance) 253
Rovatti, Magazzini 348
Rovere, Cappella della 307
Ruspoli, Palazzo 312

S

Sabines 26, 177
Sacchetti, Palazzo 242
Sack of Rome 36
San Bartolomeo, church 352
San Benedetto in Piscinula, basilica 353
San Bernardo alle Terme, church 295, 334
San Bernardo alle Terme, dome of 262
San Bonaventura, church 151
San Callisto, Catacombs of 326
San Callisto, church of 357
San Callisto, Palazzo di 357
San Carlo ai Catinari, church 247
San Carlo alle Quattro Fontane, church 295, 296
San Cesareo, church 322
San Clemente, basilica 193, 194
San Cosimato, Piazza 356
San Crisogno, church 356
San Francesco a Ripa, church 354
San Giacomo, church 309
San Giorgio in Velabro, church 156
San Giovanni, Festa di 49
San Giovanni a Porta Latina, church 323
San Giovanni Calibata, church 353
San Giovanni dei Fiorentini, church 241
San Giovanni in Fonte, baptistery 198
San Giovanni Battista dei Genovesi, church 353
San Giovanni in Oleo, oratory 323
San Girolamo della Carità, church 243
San Giuseppe ai Falegnami, church 131
San Gregorio Magno, church 187
San Lorenzo in Damaso, church 249
San Lorenzo fuori le Mura, basilica 381
San Lorenzo in Miranda, church 145
San Lorenzo in Panisperna, church 347
San Luca, Accademia Nazionale di 298
San Luigi dei Francesi, church 270, 271
San Luigi dei Francesi, dome of 262
San Marcello al Corso, church 301
San Marco, basilica 162
San Martino ai Monti, basilica 346
San Martino ai Monti, Piazza di 346
San Nicola, church 280
San Nicola a Capo di Bove, church 330
San Nicola in Carcere, church 156
San Pancrazio, Porta 364
San Pantaleo, church 279
San Paolo, cloister of 382
San Paolo entro le Mura (St Paul's Within the Walls), church 348
San Paolo fuori le Mura, basilica 382
San Paolo, Porta 183
San Paolo alla Regola, church 247
San Paolo alle Tre Fontane, church 388
San Pietro, basilica 209, 210, 262
San Pietro, dome of 210, 262
San Pietro in Montorio, church 364
San Pietro, Obelisk of 210
San Pietro, Piazza 210
San Pietro e San Paolo, basilica 388
San Pietro in Vincoli, basilica 346
San Pietro in Vincoli, Piazza 346
San Rocco, dome of 263
San Saba, church 182
San Sacramento, Capella del 356
San Salvatore in Lauro, church 283
San Sebastiano, basilica 327
San Sebastiano, Catacombs of 327
San Sebastiano, church 151
San Sebastiano, Crypt of 327
San Sebastiano, Porta 324
San Silvestro in Capite, church 302
San Silvestro, Cappella 192
San Silvestro al Quirinale, church 298, 392
San Silvestro, Piazza 301
San Sisto Vecchio, church 321
San Teodoro, church 142
San Tommaso dei Cenci, Cappella 254
San Zeno, Capella 345
Sant'Agapito, church 402
Sant'Agnese in Agone, church 278
Sant'Agnese fuori le Mura 380
Sant'Agostino, church 284
Sant'Alessio, church 180
Sant'Andrea delle Fratte, church 313
Sant'Andrea al Quirinale, church 296
Sant'Andrea della Valle, church 250
Sant'Andrea della Valle, dome of 262
Sant'Angelo, Castel 37, 233
Sant'Angelo in Pescheria, church 159
Sant'Angelo, Ponte 239
Sant'Anselmo, Via di 182
Sant'Antonio dei Portoghesi, church 284
Sant'Apollinare, church 285
Sant'Egidio, Piazza 359
Sant'Eligio degli Orefici, church 243
Sant'Ignazio, church 261
Sant'Ignazio, dome of 261
Sant'Ivo, church 272
Sant'Ivo, dome of 262
Sant'Omobono, church 156
Sant'Onofrio, Convent of 365
Sant'Urbano alla Caffarella, church 328
Santa Aurea, church 416
Santa Bibiana, Church 339
Santa Caterina dei Funari, church 254
Santa Cecilia, basilica 353
Santa Cecilia, Crypt of 326
Santa Costanza, Mausoleum of 380
Santa Croce in Gerusalemme, basilica of 200
Santa Dorotea 363
Santa Francesca Romana, church 169
Santa Lucia del Gonfalone, Oratorio di 242
Santa Maria degli Angeli, 334
Santa Maria dell' Anima, church 280
Santa Maria dell' Anima, cloister of 281
Santa Maria Antiqua, church 142
Santa Maria in Aracoeli, church 130
Santa Maria in Campitelli, church 159
Santa Maria in Campitelli, dome of 263
Santa Maria in Campo Marzio, church 353
Santa Maria della Concezione, church 290
Santa Maria in Cosmedin, church 154, 155
Santa Maria in Dominica, church 190
Santa Maria Liberatrice, Piazza 184
Santa Maria di Loreto, church 167
Santa Maria Maddalena, church

270

Santa Maria Maggiore, basilica 342

Santa Maria Maggiore, church 391

Santa Maria Maggiore, dome of 263

Santa Maria Maggiore, mosaics of 343

Santa Maria Maggiore, Piazza 342

Santa Maria dei Miracoli 307

Santa Maria in Monserrato, church 243

Santa Maria di Montesanto, church 307

Santa Maria dell'Orazione e Morte, oratory 244

Santa Maria della Pace, church 280

Santa Maria della Pace, cloister 280

Santa Maria del Popolo, church 306

Santa Maria del Popolo, dome of 262

Santa Maria del Priorato, church 180

Santa Maria della Scala, church 359

Santa Maria Scala Coeli, church 388

Santa Maria dei Sette Dolori, church 364

Santa Maria sopra Minerva, church 260

Santa Maria del Suffragio, church 242

Santa Maria in Trastevere, basilica 357

Santa Maria in Trastevere, Piazza 357

Santa Maria in Vallicella, church 281

Santa Maria in Via, church 301

Santa Maria in Via Lata, church 260

Santa Maria della Vittoria, church 294

Santa Maria della Vittoria, dome of 263

Santa Prassede, church 344

Santa Prisca, church 181

Santa Pudenziana, church 344

Santa Sabina, church 179

Santa Susanna, church 294

Santi Ambrogio e Carlo al Corso, church 263, 309

Santi Andrea Claudio dei Borgognoni, church 302

Santi Apostoli, basilica 300

Santi Bonifacio e Alessio, church 180

Santi Cosma e Damiano, church 168

Santi Giovanni e Paolo, church 188

Santi Luca e Martina,

church 131

Santi Nereo e Achilleo, church 321

Santi Quattro Coronati, church 192

Santi Vincenzo e Anastasio, church 388

Santissmo Nome di Maria, church 167

Santissima Trinità dei Pellegrini, church of the 246

Santo Bambino, legend of the 131

Santo Stefano Rotondo, church 191

Sapienza, Palazzo alla 272

Sarcophagus of the Bride and Bridegroom 371

Saturn, Temple of 140

Scala Regia 215

Scala Santa 199

Sciarra, Galleria 301

Scienze, Palazzo delle 387

Scimia, Torre della 284

Scipio Barbatus, Sarcophagus of 322

Scipios, Tomb of the 322

Secular Games 158

Senate (Italian) 272

Septimius Severus, Arch of 139

Serapeum 413

Sette Sagi, Termi dei 413

Settimiana, Porta 359

Seven Churches 240

Sibilla, Tempio della 391

Sistina, Capella (Sistine Chapel) 218, 243

Sistine Chapel, restoration of 55

Sisto, Ponte 363

Small Baths (Villa Adriana) 396

Spada, Cappella 243

Spada, Palazzo 246

Spagna, Palazzo di 313

Spagna, Piazza di 313

Spanish Steps (Trinità dei Monti) 313, 314

Sphere, Fountain of the 378

Spina 178

Spirito Santo dei Napoletani, church 242

Sport, Palazzo degli 388

S.P.Q.R. 152

Spring, Feast of 49

St Clement, miracle of 194

St Louis de France

Stadio dei Marmi 377

Stadio Olimpico 378

Stamperia, Via della 298

Statues, talking 46, 260, 279

Stazione Termini 338

Sublicius, Ponte 154

Synagogue 254

T

Tabularium

64, 128, 141

Tarpeian Rock 128

Tartarughe, Fontana delle (Tortoise Fountain) 253

Teatro Argentina 251

Teatro Eliseo 348

Teatro di Marcello 157

Tempe, Terrace of 394

Tempietto 364

Terme di Caracalla, see Baths

Terme di Diocleziano, see Baths

Terme, Museo delle 335

Terme, Palazzo delle 378

Terrina, Fontana della 281

Testaccio 184

Tetrarchy 29

Theater, Maritime 395

Theatines, Order of the 250

Tiberina, Isola 352

Tiberinus, Portus 154

Tibur 390

Tiburtina, Via 390

Titus, Arch of 146

Tivoli 390

Tobacco Factory 356

Tombs 319

Tor Sanguigna, Piazza 283

Torre di Roccabruna 397

Tortoise Fountain (Fontana delle Tartarughe) 253

Tosca 250

Trajan, Baths of 174

Trajan, Forum of 165

Trajan, Market of 167

Trajan's Column 166

Trappists 388

Trastevere 350

Trastevere, Viale 356

Tre Fontane, Abbazia delle 388

Treaty of Rome 33

Trent, Council of 31

Trevi Fountain 298, 299

Trevi Fountain, restoration of 55

Trevi River 298

Tribunes of the people 27

Trilussa, Piazza 363

Trinità dei Monti, church 314

Trinità dei Monti, Obelisk of the 294

Trinità dei Monti, steps of the 314

Tritone Fountain 290

Triumph of the Cross 193

Tullianum Prison 131

U

Ulpia, basilica 165

University Campus 382

Urban VIII, Tomb of 213

V

Valadier, Casina 316

Vallicelliana, Biblioteca 282

Vandals 29

Varianus, Circus of 200

Vatican, The 202–36

Vatican Council II 33

Vatican Pinacoteca (Picture Gallery) 215

Velabro River 136

Veneto, Via 302

Venezia, Museo del Palazzo 161

Venezia, Piazza 160

Venus Cloacina, shrine of 138

Venus Genitrix, Temple of 163

Venus Victrix, Temple of 248

Vespasian and Titus, Temple of 141

Vestals, House of the 144

Via della Foce, Republican Shrine of the 412

Via di Diana, Museo della 411

Via Ostiensis 404

Via Sacra 144

Vigiles, Barracks of the 406

Vigna 368

Villa Torlonia, gardens of the 381

Villino Ximenes 381

Vittoria, Piazzale della 405

Vittoriano 376

Vittorio Emanuele, Ponte di 122

Vittorio Emanuele, Biblioteca Nazionale 335

Vittorio Emanuele II, Piazza 340

Volte Dipinte, Via delle 414

WXZ

Well of the Sortes 399

Ximines, Villano 381

Zuccari, Palazzetto 314

◆ INDEX

MONUMENTS

Academy (accademia)
American
  Academy 365
dell'Arcadia 364
British School
  at Rome 376
di Educazione
  Fisica 378
di Finlandia 365
di Francia 315
dei Lincei 362
di Spagna 364
Nazionale di
  San Luca 299

Antiquarium
of the Forum 146
of the Palatine 151

Aqueducts
Aqua Claudia 339
Aqua Felice 289, 294
Aqua Paola 363, 364
Aqua Vergine 314
Aqua Virgo
  266, 277, 298

Ara Pacis
  Augustae 310
Area Sacra del Largo
Argentina 250

Arch (arco)
of Augustus
of Constantine 169
of Dolabella 190
of Drusus 324
of Gallienus 340
of Janus 156
of the Money
  Changers 156
of Septimius
  Severus 139
of Titus 146

Auditorium of
  Maecenas 341
Aurelian Wall,
  the 306, 323

Basilica (ancient)
Aemilia 136
Agrippa's 266
of Maxentius and
  Constantine 145
Ulpia 165

Basilica (Christian)
see **Church**

Baths (terme)
of Agrippa 266
of Buticosus 413
of Caracalla 179
of Diocletian 288, 334
of Neptune 406
of the Seven Sages 413
of Trajan 174

Bridge (ponte)
Cestius 353
Fabricius 353
Milvio 377
Rotto 352
Sant'Angelo 239
Sisto 363
Sublicius 154
Vittorio Emanuele II
  122

Canopus 397
Capitol
  (Campidoglio) 129
Capitolium of
  Ostia 411
Castra Praetoria 335

Catacombs
of San Callisto 326
of San Sebastiano 327

Cento Camerelle 396

Chapels (cappella)
Altemps 358
Antamoro 243
of the Blessed
  Sacrament 356
Caetani 344
Cenci 254
Cerasi 307
Chigi 280, 307
Cornaro 294
Cybo 307
Fonseca 312
Pauline 215, 343
Ponzetti 281
Raymondi 364
of the Relics 200
della Rovere 307
St Silvester 192
St Zeno 345
Sistine 218, 343
Spada 243

**Christian church
(chiesa) and
basilica (basilica)**
Chiesa Nuova 281
Domine Quo Vadis 324
Il Gesù 257
the Lateran 198
della Madonna
  dell'Orto 354
Nostra Signora al
  Sacro Cuore 278
dei Re Magi 313
San Bartolomeo 352
San Benedetto
  in Piscinula 353
San Bernardo
  alle Terme 295, 334
San Bonaventura 151
San Callisto 357
San Carlo ai
  Catinari 247
San Carlo alle
  Quattro Fontane
  295, 296
San Cesareo 322
San Claudio de'
  Borgognoni 302
San Clemente 193
San Crisogono 356
San Francesco
  a Ripa 354
San Giacomo 309
San Giorgio
  in Velabro 156
San Giovanni
  Calibita 353
San Giovanni
  dei Fiorentini 241
San Giovanni Battista
  dei Genovesi 353
San Giovanni in
  Laterano 198
San Giovanni in
  Porta Latina 323
San Girolamo
  della Carità 243

San Giuseppe
  ai Falegnami 131
San Gregorio
  Magno 187
San Lorenzo
  in Damaso 249
San Lorenzo
  fuori le Mura 381
San Lorenzo
  in Lucina 312
San Lorenzo
  in Miranda 145
San Lorenzo in
  Panisperna 347
San Luigi dei
  Francesi 271
San Marcello
  al Corso 301
San Marco 162
San Martino
  ai Monti 346
San Nicola 280
San Nicola a Capo
  di Bove 330
San Nicola
  in Carcere 156
San Pantaleo 279
San Paolo alla
  Regola 247
San Paolo,
  cloister of 382
San Paolo
  entro le Mura 348
San Paolo fuori le
  Mura 382
San Pietro 209–13
San Pietro in
  Montorio 364
San Pietro
  in Vincoli 346
San Saba 182
San Salvatore
  in Lauro 283
San Sebastiano,
  church 151
San Sebastiano,
  basilica 327
San Silvestro al
  Quirinale 298, 392
San Silvestro in
  Capite 302
San Sisto Vecchio 321
San Teodoro 142
San Tommaso dei
  Cenci 254
Sant'Agapito 402
Sant'Agnese fuori
  le Mura 380
Sant'Agnese in
  Agone 278
Sant'Agostino 284
Sant'Andrea delle
  Fratte 313
Sant'Andrea al
  Quirinale 296
Sant'Andrea della
  Valle 250
Sant'Angelo in
  Pescheria 159
Sant'Antonio dei
  Portoghesi 284
Sant'Apollinare 285
Sant'Eligio degli
  Orefici 243
Sant'Ignazio 261
Sant'Ivo 272
Sant'Omobono 156
Sant'Urbano alla
  Caffarella 328
Santa Aurea 416
Santa Bibiana 339
Santa Caterina dei

Funari 254
Santa Cecilia 353
Santa Croce in
  Gerusalemme 200
Santa Dorotea 363
Santa Francesca
  Romana 169
Santa Francesca in Tor
  de' Specchi 159
Santa Maria degli
  Angeli 334
Santa Maria
  Antiqua 143
Santa Maria
  dell'Anima 280
Santa Maria in
  Aracoeli 130
Santa Maria in
  Campitelli 159
Santa Maria in
  Campo Marzio 270
Santa Maria
  in Cappella 353
Santa Maria della
  Concezione 290
Santa Maria in
  Cosmedin 154, 155
Santa Maria in
  Domnica 190
Santa Maria di
  Loreto 167
Santa Maria
  Maddalena 270
Santa Maria
  Maggiore, basilica
  342
Santa Maria
  Maggiore, church 391
Santa Maria di
  Monserrato 243
Santa Maria di
  Montesanto 307
Santa Maria della
  Pace 280
Santa Maria della
  Pace, cloister of 281
Santa Maria del
  Popolo 306
Santa Maria
  del Priorato 180
Santa Maria
  della Scala 359
Santa Maria dei
  Sette Dolori 364
Santa Maria sopra
  Minerva 260
Santa Maria del
  Suffragio 242
Santa Maria in
  Trastevere 357
Santa Maria in
  Vallicella 281
Santa Maria in
  Via 301
Santa Maria
  della Vittoria 294
Santa Prassede 344
Santa Prisca 181
Santa Sabina 179
Santa Susanna 294
Santi Ambrogio e
  Carlo al Corso 309
Santi Apostoli 300
Santi Bonifacio e
  Alessio 180
Santi Cosma e
  Damiano 168
Santi Giovanni
  e Paolo 188
Santi Luca e Martina
  131
Santi Nereo e

Achilleo 321
anti Quattro
Coronati 192
anti Pietro e Paolo
388
anti Vincenzo e
Anastasio 388
antissimo Nome
di Maria 167
anto Stefano
Rotondo 191
pirito Santo dei
Napoletani 242
e Fontane, Abbazia
delle 388
nità dei Monti 314
nità dei Pellegrini
246

rcus (circo)
aminius 157
axentius 328
aximus 177
rianus 200

oaca Maxima 156
ollegio di
Propaganda Fide 313
ollegio Romano 258
oliseum 123, 170
olumbarium of
Pomponius Hylas 322

olumn (colonna)
Antoninus Pius 268
Marcus Aurelius
167
Phocas 141
Trajan 166

omitium 138

nvent (convento)
the Sacred
Heart 315

mus
gustana 150
rea 174
avia 150
lminata 414
veriana 151
eriana 149

rtico
gli Argonauti 266
i Dei Consentes 140
nucia
rumentaria 251
Ottavia 158
Pompeio (and
heater) 248

cubitorium 356

ro Italico 277

rum (foro)
Augustus 163
arium 155
Caesar 163
litorium 154
perial 162
Nerva 165
Ostia 411
man 136
Trajan 165
nsitorium 165

untain (fontana)
le Api (Bee
ountain 290

Aqua Felice 295
della Barcaccia (Boat
Fountain) 314
del Bicchierone 393
dei Draghi (Fountain
of the Dragons) 393
del Facchino 260
di Nettuno 123, 278
di Juturna 142
del Mascherone 244
del Moro 278
delle Naiadi 334
della Navicella 190
dei Fiumi (Rivers) 277
Roman fountains 366
dell'Organo Idraulico
393
della Rometta 393
della Sfera (Fountain
of the Sphere) 378
della Terrina 281
delle Tartarughe
(Tortoise Fountain)
254
di Trevi 298, 299
del Tritone (Triton
Fountain) 290
Villa d'Este 393

Galleria Sciarra 301

Gate (porta)
Appia (San
Sebastiano) 318
Flaminia 306
Latina 323
Maggiore 339, 340
Marina 414
Ostiensis 182, 183
del Popolo 306
Portese 355
Romana 405
Santa (Holy Door) 211
Settimiana 359

House (casa)
of Augustus (Domus
Augustana) 148
del Cardinale
Bessarione 321
Caseggiato del
Larario 412
dei Crescenzi 156
di Dante 357
dei Grifi (Griffins) 150
di Livia 148
Romulus 148
of the Vestals 144

Insula
dei Dipinti 411
di Giove e
Ganimede 411
delle Volte
Dipinte 414

Isola Sacra 416

Lacus Curtius 141

Library (biblioteca)
Angelica 282
of the Biblicum 299
of Contemporary
History 254
of the French School
at Rome 245
Herziana 314
Vallicelliana 282
Vittorio Emanuele
335

Mausoleum
(mausoleo)
of Augustus 309
of Hadrian 233, 235
of Romulus 329
of Santa Costanza 380

Mithraeum (mitreo)
of Felicissimus 414
of San Clemente 196
of Santa Prisca 181
delle Sette Sfere (of
the Seven Spheres)

Monastery
(monastero)
of the Augustinians
284
of Sant'Onofrio 365
Tor de' Specchi 159

Museum (museo);
gallery (galleria)
d'Arte Moderna 376
del Alto Medioevo 387
delle Anime in
Purgatorio 236
di arte
contemporanea di
Roma (MACRO)
184, 381
delle Arti e Tradizioni
Popolari 387
Astronomico e
Copernico 377
delle Bandiere 161
Barraco (Farnesina ai
Baullari) 249
of the Baths 335
della Calcografia
Nazionale 299
del Campidoglio
(Pinacoteca) 133
Capitolino 130, 132
Centrale del
Risorgimento 161
Chiaramonti 215
della Civiltà
Romana 388
Colonna 268
d'Arte Ebraica
(Jewish) 254
dei Conservatori 132
Doria Pamphilj 259
Etruscan 370
Geologico 302
Hans Christian
Andersen museum
369
Keats-Shelley
Memorial House 313
Municipal Gallery of
Modern and
Contemporary Art
290
Napoleonico 284
Nazionale d'Arte
Antica, palazzo
Corsini 292, 362
Nazionale d'Arte
Moderna 376
Nazionale Romano
delle Terme 335, 336
Nuovo 133
di Palazzo di Venezia
161
di Palestrina 402
de la Porta Ostiensis
183
Preistorico ed
Etnografico Pigorini

387
di Roma 279
di Roma in Trastevere
359
Rossa (Casina) 313
Spade 246
delle Stampe
(Gabinetto) 360
delle Terme 335
del Vaticano
(Pinacoteca) 157, 215
de la Via di Diana 411

Obelisks
of Domitian 329
of the Lateran 196
di Piazza San Pietro
210
of Ramses II 178
of the Trinità dei
Monti 294

Odeon 239

Oratory (oratorio)
dei Filippini 281
dei Quaranta Martiri
142
di San Giovanni in
Oleo 323
di Santa Lucia del
Gonfalone 242

Palace (palazzo)
Altemps 284
Anguillara 356
delle Assicurazioni
Generali di Venezia
161
Barberini 291
del Belvedere 214
Bonaparte 309
Borghese 311
Braschi 279
Caetani 253
della Cancelleria 249
Cenci Bolognetti
254, 258
Chigi 268
Cimarra 347
della Civiltà del
Lavoro 122, 387
Colonna (palace
and gallery) 300
dei Congressi 387
dei Conservatori
130, 132
de la Consulta 297
Corsini 362
Costaguti 254
of Domitian 150
Doria Pamphilj 258
delle Esposizioni 348
Falconieri 244
Farnese 244
Fiano 309
di Giustizia 236
del Governo Vecchio
281
Lancelotti 283
Madama 272
Mancini 309
Massimo alle
Colonne 279
Mattei di Giove 254
Mattei di Paganica
253
di Montecitorio 269
Odescalchi 301
Senatoriale 130
Pamphilj 278
dei Penitenzieri 232

◆ INDEX

Piombino 302
del Quirinale 297
Ricci 243
Rondini 309
Rospigliosi-Pallavicini 298
Ruspoli 312
Sacchetti 242
di San Callisto 357
della Sapienza 272
delle Scienze 387
Serristori 232
Spada 246
di Spagna 313
degli Sport 388
Taverna 283
delle Terme 378
Torlonia 232
di Venezia 161
Zuccaro 314

Portus Tiberinus 154
Pyramid of Cestius 182

Rostra, Imperial 140

Square (piazza)
Barberini 290
Bocca della Verità, 155
Borghese 311
del Campidoglio 129
Campo de' Fiori 125, 241, 247–249
dei Cavalieri di Malta 180
Colonna 267
dei Cinquecento 338
delle Coppelle 270
delle Corporazione 407
Esedra 333
dell'Esquilino 342, 344
Farnese 244
de la Magna Mater 415
Marconi 387
Margana 159
Mattei 254
della Minerva 260, 261
di Montecitorio 269
Navona 3, 239, 276
delle Nazioni Unite 387
d'Oro 395
dell'Orologio 282
della Pace 281
in Piscinula 353
del Popolo 306
di Porta Portese 355
delle Quattro Fontane 294
de la Quercia 246
del Quirinale 297
Regina Margherita 402
della Repubblica 333
della Rotonda 264
San Cosimato 356
di San Martino ai Monti 346
San Pietro 210
San Pietro in Vincoli 346
San Silvestro 301
Sant'Egidio 359
Sant'Ignazio 261
Santa Maria Liberatrice 184
Santa Maria

Maggiore 342
Santa Maria in Trastevere 357
di Spagna 313
Tor Sanguigna 283
Trilussa 363
Venezia 160
della Vittoria 405
Vittorio Emanuele II 340

Stadium of Domitian 276

Tabularium 64, 128

Temple (tempio); shrine (altare)
of Antoninus and Faustina 144, 145
of Apollo 149, 156
of Apollo Sosianus 158
of Bellona 158
of Concord 141
of the Dioscuri 142
of the Divine Claudius 189
of the Divine Julius 143
of the Fabri Navales 414
of Fortuna 1 (Rome) 56
of Fortuna (Praeneste) 398
of Hadrian 267
of Heliogabalus or Elagabalus 151
of Hercules Victor (Tivoli) 390
of the Janiculum (shrine) 355
of Janus 138
of the Magna Mater 148
of Mars Ultor 163
of Mater Matuta 156
of Matidia 267
of Minerva Medica 339
of Peace 164
Pantheon 264
of Portunus 155
of Quirinus 288
of Rome and Augustus 412
of Romulus 144
of Saturn 140
Serapeum 413
of the Sybil 391
of Venus Cloacina 138
of Venus Genitrix 163
of Venus Victrix 248
of Vespasian and Titus 141
of Vesta 144, 155
of Via della Foce (shrine) 412

Theater (teatro)
–Argentina 251
–of Balbus 253
–of the Corporations (Ostia) 406
–Eliseo 348
–di Marcello 157
–di Pompeo 248
–dei Pupi Siciliani dei

Tomb (tomba)
–of Cartilius Poplicola (Ostia) 414
–of Cecilia Metella 330
–of Eurysaces 339
–of the Horatii and the Curiatii 330
Meta Remi 182
of the Scipios 322

Tower (torre)
Anguillara 356
dei Conti 168
dei Margani 159
delle Milizie 168
Millina 279
di Roccabruna 397
della Scimmia 284

Trajan's market 167
Triopius of Heriodias Atticus 329
Trophies of Marius 130, 341
Tullianum Prison 131

Villa (villa)
Adriana 394
Albani 368
Barberini 369
Borghese 372, 374
Celimontana 190, 369
Colonna 298
Doria Pamphilj 20, 368, 369
d'Este 88, 89, 392
Farnese 369
Farnesina 88, 360
Giulia 370
Gregoriana 391
Lante 365
Madama 378
Mattei 369
Medici 89, 315, 369
Torlonia 368, 381

Map section

502 Street index

A Monte Mario

B Villa Borghese

C Villa Ada, Villa Torliona

D Vatican, Trastevere

E Historic center (Campo Marzio), Celio

F Pantheon, Il Quirinale

G Around Stazione Termini

H Testaccio, Ostiense

I Via Appia Antica

526 Metro plan

528 Bus map of the city center

Key

▬	Freeway
▣	Freeway under construction
▬	Expressway
▬	Main road
▬	Railroad
Ⓜ	Metro station
✚	Hospital
✈	Airport

◆ STREET INDEX

A

Acaia (via) **I** A 3
Acciaioli (via) **D** A 4
Acqua Acetosa (lungotevere dell')
B A 2-3
Acqua Acetosa (stazione) **B** A 3
Adda (via) **B** C 4
Addis Adeba (piazza) **C** A 3
Adriana (piazza) **D** A 4
Agri (via) **C** B 1
Albalonga (via) **I** A 4
Albania (piazza) **E** D 2
Albenga (via) **I** A 4
Albina (piazza) **E** D 2
Aldrovandi Ulisse (via) **B** B-C 2-3
Aleardi (via) **G** C 1
Alessandria (piazza) **B** D 4
Alessandria (via) **B** D 4
Algardi Alessandro (via) **D** D 3
Alma Alagi (piazza) **C** A 3
Alpino Prospero (via) **I** B 1
Amari Michele (via) **I** A-B 4
Amba Aradam (via dell') **E** D 4
Amendola (via) **E** A-B 4
Ammiragli (viale degli) **A** D 1
Anapo (via) **C** A-B 1
Anastasio II (via) **D** B 1
Ancona Jacopo (via d') **H** C 3-4
Andronico Livio (via) **A** D 1
Angelico (viale) **A** B-C 3
Anneo Lucano (via) **A** A-B 1
Annia Faustina (via) **H** A 4
Annibaldi (via degli) **E** B-C 3
Annibaliano (piazza) **C** B 2
Annio Felice (via) **I** D 2
Annunziatella (via dell') **I** D 3
Ansaldo Giovanni (via) **I** C 1
Antonelli Giovanni (via) **B** B 2-3
Aosta (via) **G** D 2
Apollodoro (piazza) **A** A 4
Appennini (via degli) **C** C 1-2
Appia (via) **G** D 2
Appia (circonvallazione) **I** A 4
Appia Antica (via) **I** C-D 3-4
Appiano (via) **A** C 1
Appia Nuova (via) **I** A 4
Appia Pignatelli (via) **I** D 4
Appio Latino (quartiere) **I** B 3-4
Apulia (via) **A** C-D 2
Aquila (via) **G** C 3
Aracoeli (piazza d') **F** D 3
Aracoeli (via di) **F** D 2-3
Ara Pacis (via) **E** A 1
Arcadia (via dell') **I** D 1-2
Archetto (via dell') **F** C 3

Archimede (via) **B** A 1-2
Arcione (via in) **F** B 4
Arcireale (via) **G** C 3
Ardeatina (circonvallazione) **I** C 2
Ardeatina (via) **I** C 3
Ardeatino (piazzale) **I** A 1
Ardeatino (quartiere) **I** D 3
Arduino (via) **C** D 3
Arenula (largo) **E** B 1
Arenula (via) **E** B-C 1
Arezzo Guido (via d') **B** B 3
Armeria (via) **I** A 3
Armi (lungotevere delle) **A** C 4
Arnaldo da Brescia (lungotevere) **B** C-D 1
Arrigo VII (largo) **E** D 2
Artigiani (lungotevere degli) **H** A-B 2
Asmara (via) **C** A 3
Astalli (via degli) **F** D 2
Augusto Imperatore (piazza) **E** A 1
Aurelia (via) **D** A 1
Aurelia Antica (via) **D** C 2-3
Aurelio (piazzale) **D** C 3
Ausoni (via degli) **G** B 2-3
Aventino (lungotevere) **E** D 1-2
Aventino (viale) **E** D 2
Avicenna (via) **H** C 2
Avieno Fiesto (via) **A** A-B 1
Avignonesi (via degli) **F** B 4
Azuni Domenico Alberto (via) **G** B C 1

B

Babuino (via del) **B** D 2
Baccarini Alfredo (via) **I** A-B 4
Baccelli Guido (viale) **I** A 1-2
Baccina (via) **E** B 3
Bainsizza (piazza) **A** B 3
Balbo Cesare (via) **E** B 3
Baldelli Ferdinando (viale) **H** D 3
Baldi Andrea (via) **A** B-C 1
Balduina (piazza della) **A** B 1
Balduina (via della) **A** A 1
Barberini (piazza) **E** A 3
Barberini (stazione metropolitana) **E** A 3
Barberini (via) **E** A 3
Bari (via) **C** D 2
Barletta (via) **A** D 3
Baronio Cesare (piazza) **I** B 4
Barrili Anton Giulio (via) **H** A 1
Bartolini Paolo (via) **B** B 1
Batteria Nomentana (via della) **C** A-B 3-4
Battisti Cesare (via) **F** D 3
Baullari (via dei) **F** D 1
Beccari Odoardo (via) **I** A-B 1
Beccaria Cesare (via) **B** C-D 1

Belle Arti (viale delle) **B** C 1-2
Belli Carlo (via) **A** A 1
Belli Giuseppe (piazza) **E** C 1
Bellini Vincenzo (via) **B** B 3-4
Bellotti Bon (via) **B** A 3
Belluzzo Giuseppe (via) **H** C 1
Belsiniana (via) **F** A 2
Benaco (via) **C** B 1
Bencivenga Generale Roberto (via) **C** A 4
Benzoni Gerolamo (via) **H** B 4
Berchet Giovanni (largo) **D** D 3
Bernini Gian Lorenzo (piazza) **H** A 4
Bertolini Antonio (via) **B** B 3
Bettolo Giovanni (via) **A** D 3
Bezzi Ergisto (via) **D** D 4
Biffi Eugenio (piazza) **I** C 1
Bignami Ugo (via) **A** B 1
Biondo Flavio (piazza) **H** B 2
Biscione (via del) **F** D 1
Bissolati Leonida (via) **E** A 3
Bitinia (via) **I** B 3
Bixio Nino (via) **G** C 1
Blaserna Pietro (via) **H** C 2
Bocca della Verità (piazza) **E** C 2
Bocca di Leone (via) **F** A 2-3
Boezio (via) **A** D 3-4
Bologna (piazza) **C** C 3
Bologna (stazione metropolitana) **C** C 3
Bompiani Benedetto (largo) **I** D 2
Boncompagni (via) **B** D 3-4
Bonghi Ruggero (via) **E** C 4
Bono Cairoli Adelaide (via) **H** D 4
Borelli Alfonso (via) **C** D 2
Borghese (piazza) **F** B 1-2
Borgognona (via) **E** A 2
Borgoncini Duca Francesco (piazza) **D** B 2
Borri Cristoforo (via) **I** C 1
Borsieri Pietro (via) **A** C 3
Boschetto (via del) **E** B 3
Botta Carlo (via) **E** C 4
Botteghe Oscure (via delle) **E** B 1-2
Braccio da Montone (via) **G** C 4
Bradano (via) **C** B 2
Branca Giovanni (via) **H** A 3
Brescia Arnaldo da (lungotevere) **B** C-D 1
Britannia (via) **I** A 3
Brofferio Angelo (via) **A** C 3
Brunelleschi Filippo (via) **A** A 3-4
Bruxelles (via) **B** B 4
Bufalo (via del) **F** B 3

Buozzi Bruno (viale) **B** B 2-3

C

Cadiolo Alberto (via) **A** B-C 2
Cadorna maresciallo (ungotevere) **A** A-B 3
Caffarella (via della) **I** C 3
Caffarelletta (via della) **I** B 4
Caffaro (via) **H** C 4
Caio Cestio (via) **H** A 3
Cairoli (piazza) **E** B 1
Cairoli (via) **G** B-C 1
Calandrelli (via) **D** D 3-4
Campanella Tommaso (via) **A** D 2
Campani (via dei) **G** B 2
Campania (via) **B** D 3-4
Campidoglio (piazza del) **E** B-C 2
Campitelli (piazza) **E** B 2
Campitelli (rione) **E** C 2-3
Campo Boario (viale del) **H** A 3
Campo dei Fiori **E** B 1
Campo Marzio (piazza in) **F** B 1-2
Campo Marzio (rione) **B** D 2
Campo Marzio (via di) **F** B 2
Candia (via) **A** D 2
Canestre (piazzale) delle **B** C-D 2
Canonica Pietro (viale) **B** C 2-3
Capitan Bavastro (via) **I** B 1
Capo d'Africa (via) **E** C 4
Capodistria (via) **C** C 2
Capo le Case (via) **F** B 3-4
Capponi Ciro (via) **I** B 4
Caprera (piazza) **C** C 1
Caravita (via) **F** C 3
Carcani Michele (via) **E** D 1
Cardano Gerolamo (via) **H** C 2
Cardinal Agostino Galamini (largo) **D** B 1
Carini Giacinto (via) **D** D 3
Carlo Alberto (via) **E** B 4
Carlo Felice (viale) **G** C-D 2
Caro Lucrezio (via) **A** D 4
Caroncini Alberto (via) **B** A 3
Carrozze (via delle) **F** A 2-3
Carso (viale) **A** B 3-4
Casal Bertone **G** B 4
Casale De Bustis Marcello (via) **A** A 1
Casale De Merode (via) **I** D 2-3
Casalmaggiore (piazza) **G** D 2
Casalmonferrato (via) **I** A 4
Caselli Giovanni (via) **H** B 1-2
Casilina (circonvallazione) **G** C 4

asilina (via) **G** C 3-4
asinò Algardi (viale)
C-D 3
astelfidardo (via) **B** D 4
astellini Gualtiero (via)
A-B 3
astello (lungotevere)
A 4
astel Sant'Angelo
A 4
astro Pretorio Rione
D 4
astro Pretorio (stazione
metropolitana) **G** A 1
astro Pretorio (via)
G A 1
atanzaro (via) **C** D 2-3
ava Aurelia (via della)
B 2
avalieri di Vittorio Veneto
(viale dei)
B-C 3
avazzi (via) **I** C 1
avour (piazza) **D** A 4
avour (ponte) **E** A 1
avour (stazione
metropolitana) **E** B 3
avour (via) **E** B 3
elano Tommaso da (via) **I** B

elimontana (piazza)
E-C-D 3-4
elio Rione **E** D 3
elio Vibenna (via)
E C 3
elsco Cornelio (via)
C D 2
enci (lungotevere dei)
E C 1
eneda (via) **I** A 3-4
erbara Giuseppe (via)
I D 2-3
ernaia (via) **E** A 4
erveteri (via) **G** D 2
esi Federico (via)
A D 4
estari (via dei) **E** B 1
estio (ponte) **E** C 1
helini Domenico (via)
B B 2
hiabrera Gabriele (via)
H D 3
hiana (via) **C** B 1
hiarini Giovanni (largo)
I A 1
hiavari (via dei) **E** B 1
hiesa Nuova (piazza della)
E B 1
higi (largo) **F** B 3
hini Eusebio (via)
I C 2
ialdi Alessandro (via)
H C 3-4
iappi Anselmo (via)
H C 1
icerone (via) **A** D 4
ilicia (via) **I** B 2-3
inque Vicolo del **E** C 1
inquecento (piazza dei)
E A 4
inque Giornate
(piazza delle) **A** C 4
ipro (via) **A** D 1-2
irco Massimo (stazione
metropolitana) **E** D 3
irco Massimo (via del)
E C-D 2
iterni Carlo (via) **I** B 1
ittà del Vaticano **D** A 2
ivinini Filippo (via)
B B 2
laudia (via) **E** C 3

Clementino (via del)
F B 1-2
Clitunno (via) **C** B-C 1
Clivio Rutario (via) **D** D 2
Clodia (circonvallazione)
A B-C 2-3
Clodio (piazzale) **A** C 3
Cloro Costanzo (via)
H D 4
Cola di Rienzo (piazza)
A D 4
Cola di Rienzo (via)
A D 4
Col di Lana (via) **A** C 4
Collazia (via) **I** A 3
Collegio (via) **F** B-C 2
Collegio Romano (piazza) **E**
B 2
Collina (via) **B** D 4
Colombo Cristoforo (via)
I B-D 1-2
Colonna (piazza) **E** A 2
Colonna (via) **E** A 1
Colonna Marcantonio (via)
A D 4
Colonna Antonina (via)
F C 2
Colosseo (piazza del)
E C 3
Colosseo (stazione
metropolitana) **E** C 3
Colosseo (via del) **E** C 3
Colossi (via) **H** D 3
Commercio (via del)
H B 3
Como (via) **C** D 2
Conciliazione (via della)
D A 3-4
Condotti (via) **E** A 2
Condottieri (piazza dei)
G C 4
Consolazione (via della)
E C 2
Conte Carmagnola (via del)
G C 4
Conti Rossini Carlo (via)
I C 2
Coppelle (via delle)
F B 1-2
Corallo (via del) **E** B 1
Cordonata (via della)
F D 4
Coronari (via dei) **D** A 4
Coronelli (via) **G** D 4
Corridoni Filippo (via)
A B 3
Corsica (via) **C** C 3
(corso) **E** A-B 2
Cossa Pietro (via) **F** A 1
Costantino (via) **H** D 4
Cottolengo (via del)
D B 2
Crati (piazza) **C** A 2
Crescenzio (via) **D** A 3-4
Crispi Francesco (via)
F A-B 4
Croce (via della) **B** D 2
Croce Rossa (piazza) della **C**
D 1
Crociate (piazzale delle)
C D 4
Crugnola Gaetano (via)
H D 1
Cubertin Pietro de (via)
B A 1
Cuccagna (vicolo della)
F C 1

D

Dalla Chiesa Carlo Alberto
(via) **A** D 3

Dall'Ongaro Francesco (via)
D D 4
Dalmazia (piazza) **C** C 1
Dalmazia (via) **C** C 1
Dandini Girolamo (via)
I A-B 1
Dandolo (via) **D** D 4
Dante (lungotevere)
H D 1-2
Dante (piazza) **G** C 1
Dardanelli (via) **A** C 3
Dataria (via della) **F** C 4
D'Avanzo Nicola (via)
G A-B 4
De Agostini Giovanni (via) **G**
D 4
De Carolis Ugo (via)
A C 1
De Jacobis (via) **I** C 1
De Mattias Beata Maria
(via) **I** A 2-3
De Nicola Enrico (viale)
E A 4
De Nobili Roberto (via)
I C 1
De Notaris Giuseppe (via) **B**
B 2
Denza Francesco (via)
B A-B 2
De' Renzi (piazza) **E** C 1
De Rossi Giovanni Battista
(via) **C** C 2-3
De Vecchi Pieralice Giacinto
(via) **D** A 1
Dionigi (via) **F** A 1
Di Pietro Angelo (via)
D B 1
Di Tullio (via) **A** D 1
Dogana Vecchia (via)
F C 1
Dolci Carlo (via) **B** B 1
Domizia Lucilla (via)
A D 1
Donatello (via) **A** B 4
Donizetti Gaetano (via)
B C 4
Don Minzoni Giovanni
(piazzale) **B** B 2
Donna Olimpia (via di)
H A 1
Don Orione (largo) **I** A 4
Doria Andrea (via) **A** D 2
Druso (via) **E** D 4
Duca d'Aosta (ponte)
A A 3
Due Macelli (via) **E** A 2
Dunant Enrico (piazzale)
H B 1
Durante Alfredo (via)
A A 1
Durazzo (via) **A** B 3
Duse Eleonora (via)
B A 3

E

Edison Tommaso (piazzale)
H D 2
Efeso (via) **H** D 3
Einstein Alberto (via)
H B 2
Eleliana (via) **G** C 2
Emanuele Filiberto (via)
G C 1
Emo Angelo (via)
D A 1-2
Empoli Giovanni da (via)
H B 3
Emporio (piazza dell')
E D 1
Epiro (piazza) **I** A 3
Equi (via degli) **G** B 2

Eritrea (viale) **C** A-B 2
Eroi (piazzale degli)
A D 2
Esquilino (piazza dell')
E B 4
Esquilino Rione **E** C 4
Esquilino (via dell')
E C 4
Etiopia (viale) **C** A 3
Etruria (via) **I** A 3-4
Etruschi (via degli)
G B 2
Euclide (piazza) **B** A 2
Ezio (via) **A** D 4

F

Fabio Massimo (via)
A D 3
Fabriano Gentile da (piazza)
A A 3
Fabricio (ponte) **E** C 2
Fabrizi Nicola (via)
D C-D 4
Falegnami (via dei)
E B 1
Farini (via) **E** B 4
Farnese (piazza) **E** B 1
Farnese Alessandro (via) **A** D
4
Farnesina (lungotevere
della) **D** B 4
Faro (piazza del) **D** B 3
Fauro Ruggero (via)
B A 3
Fea Carlo (via) **C** C 2
Febo (largo) **F** C 1
Fedro (via) **A** C 2
Feltre Bernardino da (piazza)
D D 4
Fermi Enrico (piazza)
H C 2
Fermi Enrico (via)
H C 2-3
Ferraris Galileo (via)
A C 4
Ferratella (via della)
E D 4
Fienili (via dei) **E** C 2
Filippi (via) **H** D 3
Filzi Fabio (via) **A** B 3
Finanza (piazza della)
E A 4
Fiori Mario de' (via)
F A 3
Fioritto Enzo (largo)
I A 1
Flaminio (lungotevere)
A B 4
Flaminio (quartiere)
A A 4
Flaminio (stazione
metropolitana) **B** C 1-2
Flavia (via) **B** D 4
Fochetti Angelo (largo)
I C 2
Foligno (via) **G** D 3
Fontana di Borghese
(largo) di **F** B 2
Fontanella di Borghese (via)
F A 2
Fonteiana (via) **D** D 2
Fori Imperiali (via dei)
E B-C 2-3
Forli (via) **C** D 2
Forli Melozzo da (piazza) **A**
A-B 4
Fornaci (via delle)
D B-C 3
Fornetto (via del)
H B 1-2
Fornovo (via) **A** C 4

◆ STREET INDEX

Foro Italico (quartiere)
A A 3
Foscolo (via) **G** C 1
Fracassini Cesare (via)
B B 1
Fra' Mauro (via) **G** D 4
Franchetti Raimondo (via)
I C-D 2
Francia (corso) di **B** A 1
Frangipane (via)
E B-C 3
Fratelli Bonnet (via)
D D 3
Frattina (via) **E** A 2
Fregene (via) **G** D 2
Frentani (via dei) **G** A 2
Frescobaldi Gerolamo (via)
B C 3
Frezza (via della)
B D 1-2
Friggeri Attilio (via)
A B 1

G

Gaeta (via) **E** A 4
Galamini Cardinal Agostino
(largo) **D** B 1
Galeria (piazza) **I** A-B 3
Galilei Galileo (via)
G C 1
Gallia (via) **E** D 4
Galvaligi (largo) **I** C 2
Galvani (via) **H** A 3
Garbatella (stazione
metropolitana) **H** C 4
Garbatella (via della)
H C 4
Garibaldi (ponte) **E** C 1
Garibaldi (via) **D** C 4
Garigliano (via) **C** B 1
Gastaldi Bartolomeo
(piazza) **B** B 2
Gelsomini Manlio (largo)
H A 3-4
Generale Bengivenga
Roberto (via) **C** A 4
Genocchi Giovanni (via)
I D 1-2
Genovesi (via dei) **E** C 1
Germanico (via) **A** D 3
Gesù (via del) **E** B 2
Gesù e Maria (via di)
B D 2
Gherzi Luigi (via) **A** A 1
Gianicolense
(circonvallazione) **H** B 1
Gianicolense (lungotevere)
D B 3-4
Gianicolense (quartiere)
H B 1
Gianicolo (passeggiata del)
D B-C 3
Gianicolo (via del) **D** B 3
Giardino maresciallo
(piazza) **A** B 3
Gigli Beniamino (piazza)
E A-B 4
Gioberti (via) **E** B 4
Giolitti Giovanni (via)
G B 1
Giorgi (via) **E** B-C 3
Giotto (viale) **I** A 1
Giovane Italia (piazza)
A C 3
Giovannelli Ruggero (via) **B**
C 4
Giovannipoli (via)
H C-D 4
Giubbonari (via dei)
E B 1
Giulia (via) **D** B 4

Giuliana (via della)
A C-D 2-3
Giuliani padre Reginaldo
(via) **I** C 1
Giulio Cesare (viale)
A D 3-4
Giustiniani (via) **F** C 1-2
Giustiniano Imperatore (via)
H D 4
Gladiatori (viale dei)
A A 3
Glorioso (viale) **D** D 4
Gobetti Piero (viale)
G A 2
Goito (via) **E** A 4
Goldoni (largo) **F** A 2
Gomenizza (via) **A** B 3
Gorizia (viale) **C** B-C 2
Governale (piazza)
A C 1
Governo Vecchio (via del) **D**
B 4
Gozzi Gaspare (via)
H D 3
Gracchi (via dei) **A** D 4
Gradisca (via) **C** B 2
Gramsci Antonio (via)
B B-C 2
Grazioli Lante (via)
A C 3
Gregorio VII (viale)
D B 1-2
Gregorovius (largo) **I** B 4
Grillo (piazza) del **F** D 4
Grimaldi Francesco (via)
H C 2
Grogoriana (via) **F** A 3-4
Grotta Pinta (via di)
F D 1
Guarnieri-Carducci Rosa
(via) **I** D 1
Gubbio Oderisi da (via)
H B-C 2
Guglia (via di) **F** C 2
Guidi Ignazio (via) **I** C 2
Guido d'Arezzo (via)
C B 3
Guidotti Obizzo (via)
I C 1
Guinizelli Guido (via)
H A 1

I

Iberia (via) **I** A 3
Imera (via) **I** A 3
IIndipendenza (piazza) **E** A 4
Industria (ponte dell') **H** B 2
Innocenzo III (via) **D** B 2
Inventori (lungotevere degli)
H C 2
Ippocrate (viale) **C** D 2-3
Ipponio (piazzale) **E** D 4
Ipponio (via) **E** D 4
Isola Tiberina **E** C 1
Isonzo (via) **B** C-D 3-4
Istria (piazza) **C** B 2
Italia (corso d') **B** D 3-4
Ivrea (via) **I** A 4

J

Jacopo d'Ancona (via)
H C 3-4
Josè de San Martin
(piazzale) **B** C 2

L

Labicana (via) **E** C 4
Lago di Lesina (via)
C A-B 2

La Goletta (via) **A** D 2
La Guardia Fiorello (viale) **B**
C 2
La Malfa Ugo (piazzale)
E D 2
Lanciani Rodolfo (via)
C B 3
Lancisi (via) **C** D 2
Lando Michele di (via)
C C 3
Lanza Giovanni (via)
E B 3-4
Lariana (via) **C** B 1
La Spezia (via) **G** D 2
Latina (via) **I** A 3
Latini (via dei) **G** B 2
Lattanzio (via) **A** C-D 1
Lavatore (via del) **F** B 3
Lazzerini (largo) **I** A 1
Lecce (piazza) **C** D 2
Lega Lombarda (via della) **C**
D 3
Leone IV (via) **A** D 3
Leone XIII (via) **D** C-D 1
Leopardi (largo) **E** B 4
Lepanto (stazione
metropolitana) **A** D 4
Lepanto (via) **A** C-D 4
Levi Civita Tullio (via)
H D 3
Libertà (piazza della)
B D 1
Libia (viale) **C** A 3
Licia (via) **I** A 3
Licinio Calvo (via)
A A-B 1-2
Lidia (via) **I** B 3
Liegi (viale) **B** B-C 4
Lima (via) **B** B 4
Lisbona (via) **B** B 4
Livorno (via) **C** C 3
Lodi (piazza) **C** C-D 3
Lombardi (largo dei)
F A 2
Lombardia (via) **B** D 3
Longobardi (piazza)
I C 1
Lorenzo il Magnifico (via)
C D 3-4
Loria Lamberto (largo)
I C 2
Lovanio (via) **B** B 4
Lucchesi (via dei) **F** C 3
Luce (via della) **E** C 1
Lucilio (via) **A** A-B 1-2
Lucio Fabio Cilone (via)
I A 1
Ludovico di Savoia (via)
E D 4
Ludovisi (rione) **B** D 3
Ludovisi (via) **B** D 3
Lungara (via della)
D B 4
Lungaretta (via della)
E C 1
Lupa (via della) **F** B 2
Lusitania (via) **I** A 3

M

Macedonia (via) **I** B 4
Machiavelli Nicolò (via)
G C 1
Macinghi Strozzi Alessandro
(via) **I** D 1
Macrobio Teodosio (via)
A B 1
Magliana (via della)
H D 1
Magliana Antica (via)
H C 1-2
Maglio (via del) **D** C 2

Magnaghi Giovan Battista
(via) **I** C 1
Magna Grecia (via)
G D 1
Magnanapoli (largo)
F D 4
Magni Cornelio (via)
I C 2
Magnifico Lorenzo il (via) **C**
D 3-4
Magnolie (viale delle)
B D 2
Majorana Quirino (via)
H B-C 1-2
Makalle (via) **C** A 3
Malfante (via) **I** C 2
Mameli Goffredo (via)
D C 4
Manara Luciano (via)
D C 4
Manfredi Eustachio (via)
B B 2
Mangili Giuseppe (via)
B B-C 2
Mantellini Giuseppe (via)
I B 4
Mantova (via) **B** D 4
Manunzio Aldo (via)
H A 3
Manzoni (stazione
metropolitana) **G** C 1
Manzoni Alessandro (viale)
G C 1
Marco Aurelio (via)
E C 3-4
Marco e Marcelliano (via) **I**
D 2
Marconi Guglielmo (ponte)
H D 2
Marconi Guglielmo (viale) **H**
B-C 2
Maresciallo Cadorna
(lungotevere) **A** A-B 3
Maresciallo Giardino
(piazza) **A** B 3
Maresciallo Pilsudski (viale)
B A 1-2
Margana (piazza) **F** D 2
Margutta (via) **B** D 2
Mario Alberto (via)
D D 3
Mario de' fiori (via) **F** A 3
Marmorata (via) **H** A 3
Marsala (via) **G** A-B 1
Marsi (via dei) **G** B 2
Martini Placido (via)
A C 1
Marzi Giovanni Battista
(largo) **H** A 2
Marzio (lungotevere)
E A 1
Masaccio (via) **A** A 4
Massaia Guglielmo (viale) **I**
C 1
Massi Francesco (via)
H A-B 1
Massimi (via) **A** A 1
Mastai (piazza) **E** C 1
Matera (via) **G** D 2-3
Mattei (piazza) **E** C 2
Matteotti Giacomo (ponte)
B C 1
Matteucci Pellegrino (via) **H**
B 4
Mazzarino (via) **F** D 4
Mazzini Giuseppe (piazza) **A**
C 4
Mazzini Giuseppe (ponte) **D**
B 4
Mazzini Giuseppe (viale)
A C 3-4
Mecenate (via) **E** C 4

Iedaglie d'Oro (piazzale)
B 2

edaglie d'Oro
iale delle) **A** B 1-2
1edici Giacomo (via)
C 3
ellini (lungotevere dei)
D 1
1eloria (via della)
D 1-2
1engarini Guglielmo (via)
C 1
1enotti Ciro (via) **A** C 4
1ercadante Saverio (via)
C 3
1ercalli Giuseppe (via)
B 2-3
1ercati Michele (via)
B-C 2
1ercede (via della)
B 3
1eropia (via) **I** D 3
1erulana (via) **E** B-C 4
1essina (via) **B** D 4
1etauro (via) **B** C 4
1etronio (viale) **I** A 2-3
1eucci Antonio (piazza)
C 1-2
1ichelangelo (lungotevere)
D 1
1ichele di Lando (via)
C 3
1icheli Pietro Antonio (via)
B 2
1ichelini Tocci Franco (via)
B 2
1ignanelli (piazza) **E** A 2
1ilano (via) **E** B 3
1ilizie (viale delle)
C-D 3-4
1inerva (piazza di)
C 2
1inghetti (via) **F** C 3
1irandola (via) **G** D 3
1oletta (via della)
B 4
1onserrato (via) **D** B 4
1ontecitorio (piazza di)
A 2
1onte del Gallo (via di)
B 2
1onte della Farina
via del) **F** D 1
1onte Grappa (piazza)
C 4
1onte Oppio (viale del)
C 3-4
1onterone (via) **E** B 1
1onte Santo (via) **A** C 3
1onte Testaccio (via)
C 3
1onte Zebio (via)
B-C 4
1onti **E** B 4
1onti Vincenzo (via)
A 1
1onti di Pietralata
via dei) **C** C D-4
1onti Parioli (via dei)
B 1-2
1onti Tiburtini (via dei)
B 4
1ordini Antonio (via)
C 4
1organgi Gian Battista (via)
C D 2
1oro Aldo (piazzale)
A 2
1oroni (via) **C** C 3
1oschea (viale della)
A 3
1uggia (via) **A** C 3

Mura Aurelie (viale delle)
D B 3
Mura Gianicolensi
(viale delle) **D** C-D 3
Mura Latine (viale delle)
I A-B 2-3
Muratte (via delle) **F** C 3
Muro Torto (viale del)
B D 2-3
Musa Antonio (via)
C D 2
Museo Borghese
(viale del) **B** C-D 3

N

Napoleone I (piazzale)
B D 2
Napoli (via) **E** A 3-4
Navi (lungotevere delle)
B C 1
Navicella (via della)
E D 4
Navigatori (piazza dei)
I C-D 2
Navona (piazza) **E** B 1
Nazareno (via) **F** B 3
Nazionale (via) **E** A-B 3
Negri Francesco (via)
H B 3-4
Nemorense (via) **C** A 2
Nenni Pietro (ponte)
B D 1
Nerazzini Cesare (piazza)
I C 2
Nibby Antonio (via)
C C 2
Nicolai Filippo (via)
A C 1
Nicosia (piazza) **F** B 1
Nicotera Giovanni (via)
A C 4
Nievo Ippolito (piazza)
D D 4
Nisco Nicola (via) **I** B 4
Nizza (via) **B** C-D 4
Nomentana
(circonvallazione)
C B-C 4
Nomentana (via)
C B-D 1-2
Nomentano (quartiere)
C C 3
Novella (via di) **C** A 2
Numa Pompilio (piazzale)
I A 2

O

Oberdan (lungotevere)
A B 4
Oderico da Pordenone
(piazza) **I** D 1-2
Odescalchi Carlo Tommaso
(viale) **I** D 2
Olimpiadi (viale delle)
A A 3
Omboni Tito (via) **I** C 2
Ombrone (via) **C** C 1
Oriani Barnaba (via)
B A-B 2-3
Oristano (via) **G** D 3
Orso (via dell') **F** B 1
Orti d'Alibert (via degli)
D B 3
Oslavia (via) **A** C 3
Ostiense (circonvallazione)
H B-C 4
Ostiense (piazzale)
H A 4
Ostiense (quartiere)
H D 4

Ostiense (via) **H** B-C 3
Ostilia (via) **E** C 3
Ottaviano (stazione
metropolitana) **A** D 3
Ottaviano (via) **A** D 3
Ottavilla (piazza)
D D 2
Otto Marzo (viale)
D C-D 1
Ovidio (via) **A** D 4
Oxilia Nino (via) **B** B 3

P

Pace (piazza della)
F D 4
Pace (via della) **D** D 4
Pacini Giovanni (via)
B C 4
Pacinotti Antonio (via)
H B 2
Padova (via) **C** D 3
Padre Semeria (via)
I C 2
Paisiello Giovanni (via)
B B-C 3
Paladini Ettore (via)
H C 1
Palatino (ponte) **E** C 2
Palestro (via) **D** B 4
Pallaro (largo del) **F** D 1
Panama (via) **B** B 4
Panaro (via) **C** B 2
Pancaldo Leon (via)
I C-D 2
Panetteria (via della)
F B 2
Panisperna (via) **E** B 3
Pannonia (via) **I** A 2
Pantera (piazza) **H** C 4
Paoli (piazza) **D** A 4
Paolo Emilio (via)
A D 3-4
Papa Achille (via) **A** B 4
Papareschi (lungotevere dei)
H B-C 3
Papi Lazzaro (piazza)
I B 4
Parini Giuseppe (via)
H A-B 2
Parioli (quartiere) **B** A 2-3
Parioli (viale dei) **B** B 3
Parione Rione **E** B 1
Parlamento (piazza del)
E A 1-2
Partigiani (piazzale dei)
H B 4
Passino Francesco (via)
H C 4
Pasubio (via) **A** C 4
Paulucci de' Calboli Fulcieri
(via) **A** C 3
Pavia (via) **C** C 2
Pellegrino (via del)
D B 4
Pellico Silvio (via)
A C 3
Penna (via della) **B** D 1
Percoto (via) **I** C 1
Pereira Romano Rodriguez
(via) **A** B-C 1
Persico Ignazio (via)
I C 1
Petrolini Ettore (via)
B A 3-4
Pettinari (via dei)
E B-C 1
Pezzana Giacinta (via)
B A 3-4
Piave (via) **B** D 4
Euclide Stazione (piazza)
B A 2

Piccolomini (via)
G C 3
Piccolomini Nicolò (via)
D C 1
Piè di Marmo (via) **F** C 2
Piemonte (via) **B** D 3
Pietra (piazza di) **F** C 2
Pietralata (via di) **C** A 4
Pietra Papa (lungotevere di)
H C 2-3
Pietri Dorando (via)
B A 1
Pietro de Cubertin (via)
B A 1
Pigafetta Antonio (via)
H B 4
Pigna Rione **E** B 2
Pigneto (via del)
G C-D 4
Pilo Rosolino (piazza)
D D 3
Pilotta (piazza della)
E B 2
Pilotta (via della) **F** C 3
Pilsudski maresciallo (viale)
B A 1-2
Pinciana (via) **B** D 3
Pinciano (quartiere)
B B 2-3
Pinturicchio (viale) **A** A 4
Pio Borgo **D** A 3
Pio IV (via) **D** B 1
Pio XII (piazza) **D** A 3
Piramide (stazione
metropolitana) **H** A 3-4
Piramide Cestia (viale della)
H A 4
Pisa (via) **C** C 3
Piscinula (piazza in)
E C 1
Pittore O. F. (via) **A** C 1
Platone (viale) **A** C 2
Plebiscito (via del) **E** B 2
Po (via) **B** C 4
Poerio Alessandro (via)
H A 1-2
Poggio Catino (via)
C A 2
Policlinico (stazione
metropolitana) **E** A 4
Policlinico (viale del)
C D 1-2
Pollio Alberto (via) **G** B 4
Polo Marco (viale)
H A-B 4
Pomezia (via) **I** A 3-4
Pompei (piazza) **I** A 3
Pompeo Magno (via)
A D 4
(ponte) Rione **D** A 4
(ponte) Lungo (piazza di)
I A 4
Ponte Lungo (stazione
metropolitana)
I A 4
Ponte Umberto I (piazza)
E A 1
Ponziani (piazza dei)
E C 1-2
Ponzio (via) **H** A 4
Popolo (piazza del)
B D 1
Populonia (via) **I** A 3
Porcari Stefano (via)
D A 3
Porro Gian Giacomo (via) **B**
A 3
Porta Ardeatina **I** B 2
Porta Ardeatina (viale di)
I B 2
Porta Asinara **G** D 2
Porta Capena **E** D 3

◆ STREET INDEX

Porta Capena (piazza di)
E D 3
Porta Cavalleggeri
D A 3
Porta Cavalleggeri (via)
D A 2-3
Porta del Popolo
B D 1
Porta Latina **I** A 2
Porta Latina (via di)
I A 2
Porta Maggiore **G** C 2
Porta Maggiore (piazza)
G C 2
Porta Maggiore (via di)
G C 2
Porta Metronia **E** D 4
Porta Metronia (piazza di)
E D 4
Porta Pia **B** D 4
Porta Pinciana **B** D 2-3
Porta Pinciana (via di)
B D 2-3
Porta Portese **E** D 1
Porta Portese (via di)
E D 1
Porta Portuense
(piazza di) **E** D 1
Porta San Giovanni
G D 1
Porta San Giovanni (piazza
di) **G** D 1
Porta San Lorenzo
G B 2
Porta San Paolo **H** A 4
Porta San Paolo (piazza di)
H A 4
Porta San Sebastiano
I B 2
Porta San Sebastiano
(via di) **I** A 2
Porta Tiburtina **G** B 2
Portico d'Ottavia (via)
E C 1-2
Porto di Ripetta
(piazza del) **F** A 1
Porto Fluviale (via del)
H B 3
Portuense (lungotevere)
E D 1
Portuense (quartiere)
H C 1-2
Portuense (via) **H** B 2
Prati (lungotevere) **E** A 1
Prati Rione **A** D 4
Prati degli Strozzi (piazza
dei) **A** C 3
Prefetti (via dei) **F** B 2
Premuda (via) **A** C 2
Prenestina (via) **G** C 3-4
Prenestino-Labicano
(quartiere) **G** C 4
Prestinari Marcello (via)
A B-C 4
Pretoriano (viale) **G** A-B 1
Principe Amedeo (via)
G B 1
Principe Amedeo Savoia
Aosta (ponte).
D B 3-4
Principe Umberto (via)
G B 1-2
Prisciano (via) **A** A-B 2
Priscilla (via) **C** A 2
Procida Giovanni da (via)
C C-D 3
Provincie (piazzale) delle
C D 3
Provincie (viale) delle
C D 3
Pullino Giacomo (via)
H C 4

Q

Quattro Cantoni (via)
E B 4
Quattro Fontane (via delle)
E A 3
Quattro Novembre (via)
F D 3-4
Quattro Venti (piazzale dei)
H A 1
Quattro Venti (viale dei)
H A 1
Quirinale (piazza del)
E B 3
Quirinale (via del) **F** C 4
Quiriti (piazza) dei **A** D 4

R

Radio (piazza) della
H B 2
Raimondi Pietro (via)
B C 3
Raimondi Garibaldi Rosa
(via) **I** D 1
Rammi (via dei) **G** B 2
Rasella (via) **F** B 4
Ravenna (via) **C** C-D 2-3
Recina Elvia (via) **I** A 3
Re di Roma (piazza dei)
G D 2
Re di Roma (stazione
metropolitana) **G** D 2
Regina Elena (viale)
G A 2-3
Regina Margherita (piazza)
C C 1
Regina Margherita (ponte) B
D 1
Regina Margherita (viale) **C**
C-D 1
Regola Rione **D** B 4
Reni Guido (via) **A** A 4
Repubblica (piazza della) **E**
A 4
Repubblica (stazione
metropolitana) **E** A 4
Reti (via delle) **G** B 2-3
Riari (via dei) **D** B 3-4
Riccardi Placido (largo)
H D 3
Ricciotti Nicola (via)
A C 4
Righi Augusto (piazza)
H C 2
Rinascimento (corso del) **E**
A-B 1
Ripa (lungotevere)
E C-D 1-2
Ripa Rione **E** D 2
Ripetta (passeggiata di)
B D 1
Ripetta (via di) **B** D 1
Risorgimento (piazza del)
A D 3
Risorgimento (ponte del)
A C 4
Rizzo Luigi (via) **A** D 1-2
Robbia Leonardo della (via)
H A 3
Rodi (via) **A** C 2
Roiti Antonio (via) **H** C 2
Rolli Ettore (via) **H** A-B 2
Roma-Lido di Ostia
(stazione) **H** A 4
Romania (viale) **B** B 3
Roma-Ostiense (stazione)
H B 4
Roma Termini (stazione
centrale) **G** B 1
Roma-Tiburtina (stazione)
C D 4

Romei Romeo (via)
A B-C 2
Romolo e Remo (largo)
E B 3
Rosa Ercole (via) **I** A 1
Roselle (piazza) **I** B 3
Rosetta (via della) **F** B 2
Rosini (via) **F** B 2
Rossetti Gabriele (via)
D D 3
Rossini Gioacchino (viale) **B**
B-C 3
Rotonda (piazza della)
F C 2
Rotonda (via) **F** C 2
Rotto (ponte) **E** C 2
Rovere (piazza della)
D A-B 3
Rozat Bartolomeo (viale)
D C 2
Rubens Pietro Paolo (via) **B**
B 1
Rubicone (via) **C** B-C 1
Rubino Antonio (via)
I C 1
Rufina Valeria (via) **I** D 2

S

Sabelli (via dei) **G** B 2
Sabotino (via) **A** C 3
Sacchi Andrea (via)
D C-D 4
Sacconi Giuseppe (via)
A A 4
Saffi Aurelio (viale)
D D 4
Sagrestia **D** A 2
Salaria (circonvallazione)
C A 3-4
Salaria (via) **B** C-D 4
Salario (quartiere) **C** C 1
Salentini (via dei) **G** B 2
Salento (via) **C** C 3
Sallustiana (via) **B** D 3-4
Sallustiano (rione)
B D 3-4
Sallustio (piazza) **B** D 4
Salvini Tommaso (via)
B A 3
San Bernardo (piazza)
E A 3-4
San Calisto (piazza)
E C 1
San Cipriano (via) **A** C 1
San Claudio (piazza)
F B 3
San Cosimato (piazza)
D C 4
San Filippo Martire (via)
B A 3-4
San Francesco a Ripa (via) **D**
C-D 4
San Francesco di Sales
(vicolo di) **D** B 3-4
San Giovanni (porta)
G D 2
San Giovanni (stazione
metropolitana) **G** D 2
San Giovanni in Laterano
(via di) **E** C 4
San Gregorio (via di)
E C-D 3
Sanità Militare (largo della)
E D 3-4
San Lorenzo (piazzale)
G A 3
San Lorenzo in Lucina
(piazza) **F** B 2
San Lucio (via) **D** B 1
San Marco (piazza)
F D 3

San Marco (via) **F** D 3
San Nicola da Tolentino (via)
E A 3
Sannio (via) **G** D 1
Sanniti (piazza dei)
G B 2
San Pancrazio (via di)
D C 3
San Paolo (lungotevere di)
H C-D 3
San Paolo (stazione
metropolitana) **H** D 3
San Paolo (viale di)
H D 3
San Paolo del Brasile (viale)
B D 2-3
San Pietro (basilica di)
D A 2
San Pietro (piazza)
D A 2
San Pietro (stazione di)
D B 2
San Quintino (via)
G C 1-2
San Roberto Bellarmino (via)
B B 3
San Silvestro (piazza)
E A 2
Santa Balbina (piazza di) **E**
D 3
Santa Costanza (piazza di)
C B 2
Santa Croce in
Gerusalemme (via)
G C 2
Santa Galla (via di) **I** B 1
Sant'Alessio (via) **E** D 2
Santa Maria alle Fornaci
(piazza) **D** B 3
Santa Maria dell'Anima
(via di) **E** A-B 1
Santa Maria delle Grazie
(piazza di) **A** D 2
Santa Maria in Trastevere
(piazza)
D C 4
Santa Maria Maggiore
(piazza) **E** B 4
Santa Maria Maggiore (via)
E B 3-4
Santa Maria Mediatrice
(via di) **D** A-B 1
Sant'Angela Merici (via di)
C B 3
Sant'Angelo (borgo)
F D 2
Sant'Angelo (ponte)
D A 4
Sant'Angelo (rione)
E B 2
Sant'Anselmo (piazza)
E D 2
Sant'Anselmo (via di)
E D 2
Santa Petronilla (via)
I D 2
Santa Prisca (via di)
E D 2
Santa Sabina (via di)
E D 2
Sant'Emerenziana (piazza
di) **C** A 2
San Teodoro (via)
E C 2
Sant'Eufemia (via) **F** D 3
Santiago del Cile (piazza)
B A-B 3
Sant'Ignazio (piazza)
F C 2
Sant'Ignazio (via) **F** C 2
Sant'Ippolito (via di)
C D 3

506

Santi Quattro (via dei) **E** C 4
Santissimi Apostoli (via dei) **F** C-D 3
Santo Stefano Rotondo (via di) **E** D 4
San Valentino (via di) **B** A-B 2
San Vincenzo (via) **F** C 3
San Vitale (via) **E** B 3
Sanzio Raffaello (lungotevere) **E** C 1
Sardegna (via) **B** D 3
Sarti Antonio (largo) **A** B 4
Sassari (piazza) **C** D 2
Sassia (lungotevere in) **D** A 3
Satrico (via) **I** A 3
Sauli Damiano (piazza) **H** C 4
Savoia (via) **B** C 4
Savoia Ludovico di (via) **G** C 1-2
Savonarola Girolamo (via) **A** C-D 2
Scala (via della) **D** C 4
Scalo di San Lorenzo (viale dello) **G** B-C 2-3
Scipione Ammirato (piazza) **I** A-B 4
Scipioni (via degli) **A** D 4
Scott Robert (via) **I** C 2
Scrofa (via della) **F** B-C 1
Scrota (via della) **E** A 1
Secchi Angelo (via) **B** B 3
Sediari (via dei) **F** C 1
Segesta (via) **I** B 3
Segre Corrado (via) **H** D 2
Seminario (via del) **F** C 2
Seneca (via) **A** B 1
Serpenti (via dei) **E** B 3
Serranti (via) **A** A 1
Servili (piazza dei) **E** D 2
Sette Chiese (largo delle) **H** C 4
Sette Chiese (via delle) **H** C 3-4
Settembrini Luigi (via) **A** C 4
Sette Sale (via delle) **E** B-C 4
Severano Giovanni (via) **C** C 2-3
Severo Alessandro (via) **B** B 3
Siacci Francesco (via) **B** B 3
Sicilia (via) **??D** 3-4
Sicilia Ruggero di (piazza) **C** D 3
Simoni Simone (via) **A** D 1
Siracusa (via) **C** D 2
Siria (via) **I** A-B 3
Sistina (via) **E** A 2-3
Sisto (ponte) **E** C 1
Sisto V (piazzale) **G** B 1-2
Socrate (piazzale) **A** C 2
Solunto (via) **I** A 3-4
Spagna (piazza di) **E** A 2
Spagna (stazione metropolitana) **E** A 2
Spallanzani Lazzaro (via) **C** C-D 2
Spinola Carlo (via) **I** C 1-2

Stadio Olimpico (viale dello) **A** A 3
Stalilia (via) **G** C 1-2
Stamperia (via della) **F** B 3
Stazione (via della) **D** B 2
Stazione Tuscolana (via della) **G** D 3
Stelletta (via della) **E** A 1
Sublicio (ponte) **E** D 1

T

Tabarrini Marco (via) **I** B 4
Tacchini Pietro (via) **B** B 2-3
Tacito (via) **A** D 4
Tagliamento (via) **C** B-C 1
Tajani Filippo (via) **H** C 1
Taranto (via) **G** D 2
Tata Giovanni (via) **I** A 1
Teatro di Marcello (via del) **E** B-C 2
Teatro Valle (via) **F** C 1
Tebaldi (lungotevere dei) **D** B 4
Tempio di Diana (piazza) **E** D 2
Terme Deciane (via delle) **E** D 2
Terme di Caracalla (largo delle) **I** B 2
Terme di Caracalla (viale delle) **I** B 2
Termini (stazione metropolitana) **E** A 4
Testaccio (lungotevere) **H** A 2
Testaccio (ponte) **H** A 2
Testaccio (rione) **H** A 2
Teulada (via) **A** B 3
Tevere (via) **B** C-D 4
Tiburtina (circonvallazione) **G** A-B 3-4
Tiburtina (stazione metropolitana) **C** D 4
Tiburtina (via) **G** B 2
Tiburtino (quartiere) **G** B 3-4
Tigre (via) **C** A 3
Timavo (via) **A** B 3
Tito Livio (via) **A** B-C 1
Tiziano (viale) **B** B 1
Tolmino (via) **C** B-C 2
Tomacelli (via) **E** A 1
Tommasini Oreste (via) **C** C 3
Tommaso da Celano (via) **I** B 4
Toniolo (largo) **F** C 1
Topino (via) **C** B 2
Tor de' Conti (via) **E** B 3
Tor di Nona (lungotevere) **D** A 4
Torino (via) **E** A-B 4
Torlonia Alessandro (via) **C** C 2
Tor Marancia (viale di) **I** D 2
Torre Federico (via) **D** D 3
Torre Argentina (largo di) **F** D 2
Torre Argentina (via di) **F** D 2
Toscana (via) **B** D 3
Traforo (via del) **F** B 4
Trastevere (rione) **D** C 4

Trastevere (stazione) **H** B 2
Trastevere (viale di) **H** A 2
Travicella (via della) **I** B 2
Trento (piazza) **C** C 1
Trevi (rione) **E** A 3
Trevis Giacomo (via) **I** C 2
Triboniano (via) **D** A 4
Tribunali (piazza dei) **E** A 1
Trieste (corso) **C** C 1
Trieste (quartiere) **C** A 2
Trilussa (piazza) **D** C 4
Trinità dei Monti (piazza) **F** A 3
Trinità dei Monti (viale) **B** D 2
Trionfale (circonvallazione) **A** C-D 2
Trionfale (largo) **A** D 3
Trionfale (via) **A** B-C 2
Tripoli (via) **C** A 3
Tripolitania (via) **C** A 3
Tritone (largo del) **F** B 4
Tritone (via del) **E** A 2
Tunisi (via) **A** D 2
Turati Filippo (via) **G** B 1
Tuscolo (piazza) **I** A 3

U

Uccelliera (viale dell') **B** C 3
Uffici del Vicario (via) **F** B 2
Ughelli Ferdinando (via) **I** B 4
Umberto I (ponte) **E** A 1
Umiltà (via dell') **F** C 3
Ungheria (piazza) **B** B 3
Unità (piazza dell') **A** D 3
Università (viale dell') **G** A 2
Usodimare Antoniotto (via) **I** B 1-2

V

Val d'Aosta (via) **C** A 3-4
Valla Lorenzo (via) **H** A 1-2
Vallati (lungotevere dei) **E** C 1
Valle Aurelia (via di) **D** A 1
Varese (via) **G** A 1
Vasca Navale (via della) **H** D 2
Vascello (via del) **D** D 3
Vaticano (lungotevere) **D** A 4
Vaticano (viale) **D** A 2
Veio (via) **G** D 1-2
Veneto (via) **F** A 4
Venezia (piazza) **E** B 2
Venosta (largo) **E** B 3
Ventiquattro Maggio (via) **E** B 3
Venti Settembre (via) **B** D 4
Ventuno Aprile (largo) **C** B-C 3
Ventuno Aprile (viale) **C** B-C 3
Verano (piazzale del) **G** A 3
Verbano (piazza) **C** B 1
Vercelli (via) **G** D 2

Verdi Giuseppe (piazza) **B** B-C 3-4
Verrazzano Giovanni (piazza) **I** B 1
Verri (via) **E** C 4
Vescia (via) **I** A 3
Vespucci Amerigo (via) **E** D 1
Vetulonia (via) **I** A 3
Vigna Mangani (via di) **C** B 4
Vigna Pia (viale di) **H** C 1
Vignola (viale del) **A** A-B 4
Villa Ada (via di) **B** A 4
Villa Albani (via di) **B** C 4
Villa di Lucina (via della) **H** D 4
Villa Fiorelli (piazza di) **G** D 3
Villa Glori (viale di) **B** B 2
Villa Grazioli (via di) **B** B 4
Villa Massimo (viale di) **C** C-D 2
Villa Pamphilij (viale di) **D** D 3
Villa Peretti (largo) **E** A 4
Villa San Filippo (via di) **B** A 3
Viminale (piazza del) **E** B 3
Viminale (via) **E** A-B 4
Vinci Leonardo da (largo) **H** D 3
Vinci Leonardo da (viale) **H** C-D 3
Virgilio (via) **A** D 4
Visconti Ennio Quirino (via) **A** D 4
Vite (via della) **E** A 2
Vitelleschi Giovanni (via) **D** A 3
Vitellia (via) **D** D 2
Vittoria (lungotevere della) **A** B 3-4
Vittoria (via) **B** D 2
Vittorio Borgo **D** A 3
Vittorio Emanuele (stazione metropolitana) **G** B 1
Vittorio Emanuele II (corso) **D** A-B 4
Vittorio Emanuele II (piazza) **G** B 1
Vittorio Emanuele II (ponte) **D** D 4
Vittorio Veneto (via) **B** D 3
Voghera (via) **G** D 3
Volsci (via dei) **G** B 2
Volsinio (via) **C** B 1-2

W

Washington (viale) **B** C-D 2
Winckelmann (piazza) **C** B 3

Z

Zabaglia Nicola (via) **H** A 3
Zama (piazza) **I** A 3
Zanardelli (via) **F** B 1
Zoccolette (via delle) **E** C 1

◆ MONTE MARIO

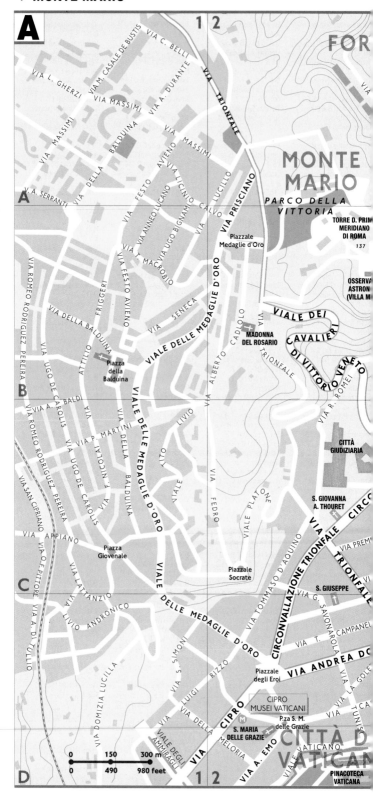

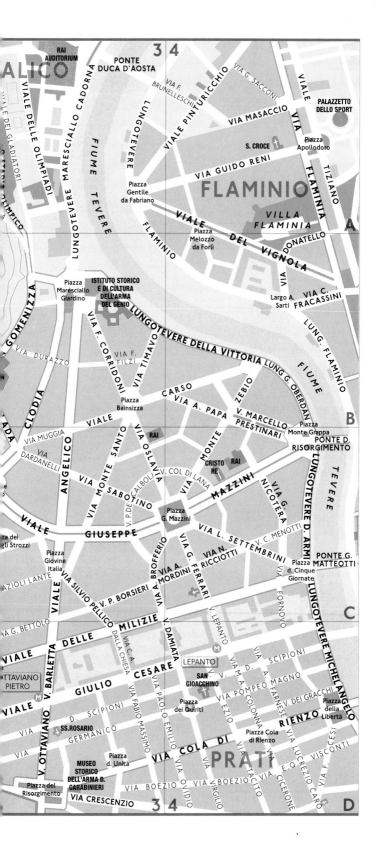

◆ VILLA BORGHESE

B

1 **2**

VILLAGGIO OLIMPICO

VILLA GLORI

VILLA GLORI

LUNG. DELL'AC.

CORSO DI FRANCIA

AUDITORIUM-PARCO DELLA MUSICA

VIALE PIETRO DE COUBERTIN

VIALE PIETRO DE COUBERTIN

PARCO DELLA RIMEMBRANZA

VIALE DI VILLA GLORI

PALAZZETTO DELLO SPORT

VIA PIETRO DE COUBERTIN

VIALE

VIA DORANDO PIETRI

VIA TIZIANO

VIALE MARESCIALLO PILSUDSKI

VIA ARCHIMEDE

SS. CUORE IMMACOLATO DI MARIA

VIA BARNABA ORIA

STADIO FLAMINIO

VIA DI S. VALENTINO

VILLA ELIA

Piazza Euclide

STAZIONE P.ZA EUCLIDE

VIA D. CHELINI

VIA DENZA

A

VILLA FLAMINIA

VIA DONATELLO

V. C. FRACASSINI

VIALE FLAMINIA

V. CARLO DOLCI

V.P. RUBENS

VIA P. BARTOLINI

VILLA BALESTRA

VIA DEI MONTI PARIOLI

VIA DEI MONTI PARIOLI

VIA ARCHIMEDE

VIA FILIPPO CIVININI

VIA P. A. MICHELI

VIA A. MANFREDI

VIA A. EMANFREDI

P.za B. Gastaldi

LUNGOTEVERE FLAMINIA

MONTI PARIOLI

VIA TIZIANO

VIA ANTONIO

P.le Don Minzoni

VIA G. DE NOTARIS

VIALE MICHELE MERC.

VIALE BRU

LUNG. G. OBERDAN

B

SCUOLA SUP. DI ARCHITETTURA

VIA G. MANGILI

Piazza Monte Grappa

PONTE DEL RISORGIMENTO

VIALE DELLE BELLE

VIA GRAMSCI

SANT'EUGENIO

ACCAD. BRITANNICA

LUNGOTEVERE DELLE ARMI

LUNGOTEVERE DELLE NAVI

FIUME

VIA

MUSEO NAZ. DI VILLA GIULIA

VILLA GIULIA

ACCAD. DI ROMANIA

P.za José de S. Martín

ACCAD. DI BELLE ARTI (GALL. NAZ. D'ARTE MODERNA)

PALAZZO D. BELLE ARTI

VIALE DELLE ARTI

ULIS

MINISTERO D. DIFESA (MARINA)

IST. STORICO OLANDESE

ACCAD. BELGA

VIA D.A. AZUNI

VILLA STROHL-FERN

V

BOR

Piazza d. Cinque Giornate

P.TE G. MATTEOTTI

FLAMINIA

VILLA RUFFO

TEMPIO DI ESCULAPIO

LUNGOTEVERE A. DA BRESCIA

VILLA RUFFO

FLAMINIO Ⓜ

VIALE LA GUARDIA

P.le Car

C

V.LE G. CESARE

LUNGOTEVERE MICHELANGELO

PONTE P. NENNI

VIA C. BECCARIA

VIALE WASHINGTON

VIALE DEL MURO

TORTO

P.LE DELLE MAGNOLIE

VIA L. DI SAVOIA

P.TA DEL POPOLO

S. MARIA D. POPOLO

P.le Napoleone I

V.LE DELLE MAGNOLIE

PONTE REG. MARGHERITA

VIA COLA DI RIENZO

Piazza della Libertà

Piazza del Popolo

TOURING CLUB ITALIANO

GALOPPA

VIA E. Q. VISCONTI

VIA L. CARO

PASS. DI RIPETTA

V. D. PENNA

S. M. DEI MIRACOLI

V. ANGELO BRUNETTI

S. M. DI MONTESANTO

PAL. RONDININI

CASA DI GOETHE

VIA MARGUTTA

VIA DEL BABUINO

VILLA MEDICI (ACCAD. DI FRANCIA)

V.LE TRINITÀ DEI M.

VIA DI RIPETTA

VIA DI RIPETTA

ACCAD. DI BELLE ARTI

OSPEDALE S. GIACOMO

V. D. FREZZA

GESÙ E MARIA

VIA D. CORSO

CAMPO MARZIO

VIA VITTORIA

SPAGNA Ⓜ

TRINITÀ D. MONTI

VIA DEI MONTI

0   150   300 m

1/15 000 - 1 cm = 150 m

MAUSOLEO DI AUGUSTO

V. DELLA CROCE

D

1 **2**

C

1 2

VILLA CHIGI

VILLA ADA

VIA SALARIA

VIA POGGIO CATINO

VIA DI NOVELLA

VIA PRISCILLA

NEMORENSE

Piazza S. Emere

SANTA EMERENZIA

VILLA ADA

VIA ANAPO

Piazza Crati

TRIESTE

VIA ERITREA

A

VIA LAGO DI LESINA

VIA SALARIA

VIA LARIANA

VIA BENACO

VIA NEMORENSE

PARCO VIRGILIANO

VIALE

VIA PANAMA

VIA

VIA CHIANA

VIA AGRI

VIA VOLSINIO

Piazza Verbano

S. SATURNINO

VIA BRADANO

Piaz Anniba

CORSO TRIESTE

Piazza Istria

VIA

VIA CHIANA

VIA TOPINO

VIALE TRIESTE

VIA PANARO

Piazza Costa

VIA GARIGLIANO

VIA TAGLIAMENTO

VIA CHIANA

VIA GRADISCA

VIA TOLMINO

B

VIA RUBICONE

VIA CLITUNNO

CORSO

VIA CORSICA

VIALE GORIZIA

VIA APPENNINI

VIA

VIA OMBRONE

DEGLI

VIA CAPODISTRIA

VIA MIR

VIALE SALARIO

Piazza Trento

Piazza Caprera

VILLA PAGANINI

NOMENTANA

VIA A. GUATTANI

VIA A. N

CORSO DALMAZIA

VIA

VIA G. B.

VILLA ALBANI

VIA REGINA

Piazza Dalmazia

VIA A. TORLONIA

VIA DI VILLA MASSIM

VIA SAVOIA

VIA NIZZA

Piazza Reg. Margherita

VILLA TORLONIA

C

VIA MANTOVA

VIA ALESSANDRIA

NOMENTANA

S. GIUSEPPE

VIA LAZZARO SPALLANZANI

V. C. CELSO

V. SIRACUSA

VIALE DI VILLA MASSIM

Piazza Lecce

Piazza Alessandria

VIA

VIA MARGHERITA

VIA A. MUSANZANI

VIA BARI

VIA FORLI

VIA COMO

CORPUS DOMINI

VIA G.B. MORGAGNI

Piazza Sassari

MINISTERO D. LAVORI PUBBLICI

MINISTERO DEI TRASPORTI

P.za della Croce Rossa

VIA LANCISI

VIALE REGINA ELENA

PORTA PIA

VIALE DEL POLICLINICO

VIALE DEL POLICLINICO

POLICLINICO Ⓜ

VIA A. BORELLI

CASTRO PRETORIO

D

BIBLIOTECA NAZ. CENTRALE VITT. EMANUELE II

POLICLINICO UMBERTO I

1 2

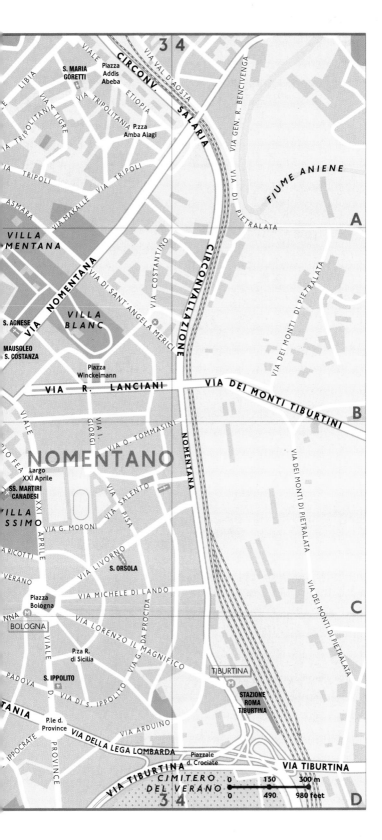

D

1 2

VALLE AURELIA

CITTA DEL VATICAN

VIA DI VALLE AURELIA

VIA ANASTASIO II

VIA ANGELO EMO

VIALE VATICANO

PONTIFICIA ACCADEMIA D. SCIENZE

V. G. DE VECCHI PIERALICE

PONTIFICIO SEM. ROMANA MINORE

VIA

COLLEGIO ETIOPICO

GOVERNATORATO

BASILI DI S. PI

RADIO VATICANA

TRIBUNALE

VIALE

VIA AURELIA

STAZIONE FERROVIARIA

SAGRE

V. DI S. M. MEDIATRICE

VATICANO

A

VIA AURELIA

VIA PORTA CA

VIA AURELIA

VIA INNOCE

VIA ANASTASIO II

V. DEL COTTOLENGO

VIA

L.go C. A. Galamini

GREGORIO

VII

STAZ DI S. P

VIA A. DI PIETRO

VIA D. CAVA AURELIA

VIA DI MONTE DEL GALLO

Piazza F. Borgoncini Duca

VIA PIO IV

VIA SAN LUCIO

B

VIA N. PICCOLOMINI

AURELIO

VILLA FLORIDIA

VIA AURELIA ANTICA

VIA

VILLA DORIA PAMPHILI

AURE

VIALE B. ROZAT

VIA LEONE XIII

MARZO

ALGARDI

VIALE DEL MAGLIO

C

VIALE III

CASINO

S. PANCRAZIO

VIA LEONE XIII

VILLA DORIA PAMPHILI

VIALE

VITELLIA

0   150   300 m
1/15 000 - 1 cm = 150 m

VIA FONTEIA

D

VIA VITELLIA

VIA CLIVIO RUTARIO

VIA

1 2

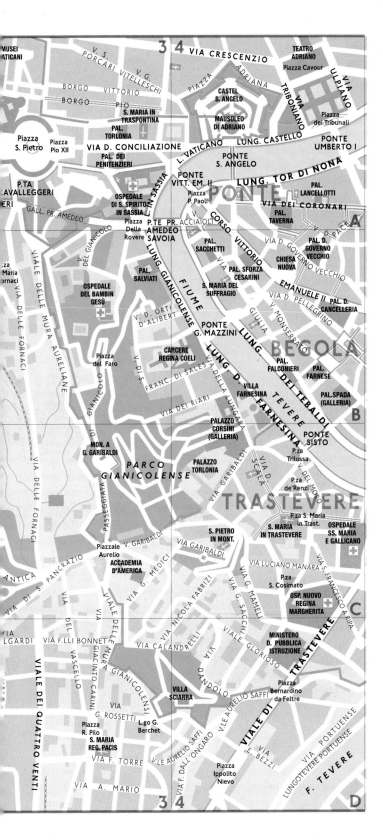

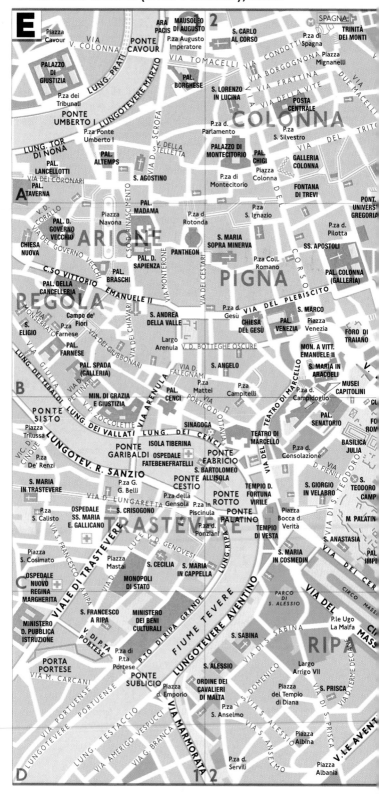

◆PANTHEON, IL QUIRINALE

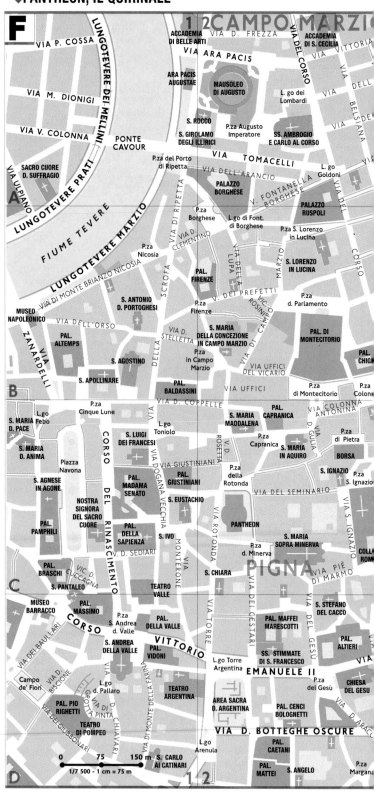

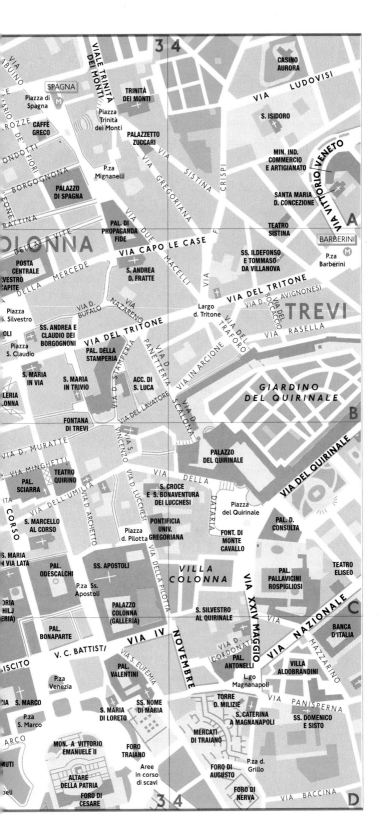

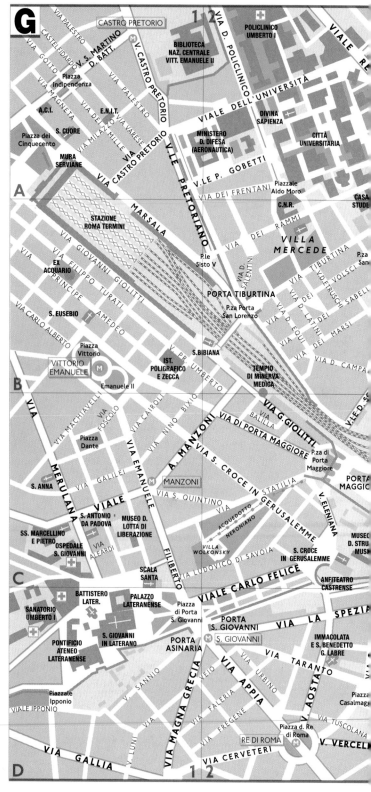

H

1 2

VIALE DI VILLA DI PAMPHILI

VENTI

Piazza d. Quattro Venti

VIA GUIDO GUINICELLI

VIA A. GIULIO BARRILI

V. F. DALL'ONGARO

VIA I. NIEVO

VIA PORTUENSE

LUNGOTEVERE PORTUENSE

VIALE DEI QUATTRO VENTI

VIA ALESSANDRO POERIO

VIA ALESSANDRO

VIA LORENZO VALLA

VIA DI TRASTEVERE

LUNGOTEVERE
L.
G.B

V. DI DONNA OLIMPIA

VIA F. MASSI

VIA VINCENZO MONTI

G. PARINI

VIA ETTORE ROLLI

PONTE TESTACCIO

A

SACRO CUORE

SS. PATR. D'ITALIA

Piazza F. Biondo

LUNG. DEGLI ARTIGIANI

GIANICOLENSE

GIANICOLENSE

STAZIONE TRASTEVERE

Piazzale E. Dunant

VIA DEL FORNETTO

VIA PORTUENSE

VIA ANTONIO PACINOTTI

PON INDUS

CIRCONV.

VIA QUIRINO MAJORANA

VIA G. CASELLI

Piazza della Radio

VIA CONSTANZI

OSPEDALE S. CAMILLO

VIA PORTUENSE

GESU DIVINO LAVORATORE

VIA DA GUBBIO

VIALE

B

VIA A. EINST

VIA GUGLIELMO

OSPEDALE SPALLANZANI

VIA PORTUENSE

VIALE DI VIGNA PIA

VIA MAGLIANA ANTICA

VIA ODERISI DA

VIA F. GRIMALDI

VIA P. BLAS

VIA E. PALADINI

Piazza Enrico Fermi

VIA EN

VIA GEROLAMO CARDANO

MARCONI

VIA GUGLIELMO

VIA F. TAJANI

GIUSEPPE

BELLUZZO

VIA ANTONIO ROITI

VIA ANSELMO CIAPPI

MENGARINI

Piazza Antonio Meucci

LUNGOTEVERE DEGLI INVENTORI

Piazza A. Righi

LU

C

VIA A. CUCCHINI

PORTUENSE

PONTE G. MARCONI

VIA G. CRUGNOLA

VIA DELLA MAGLIANA

Piazzale T. Edison

V. GUGLIELMO

F. TEVERE

LUNGOTEVERE DANTE

VIA DELLA VASCA NAVALE

V. GUGLIELMO

VIA CORRADO SEGRE

0	150	300 m
0	490	980 feet

D

1 2

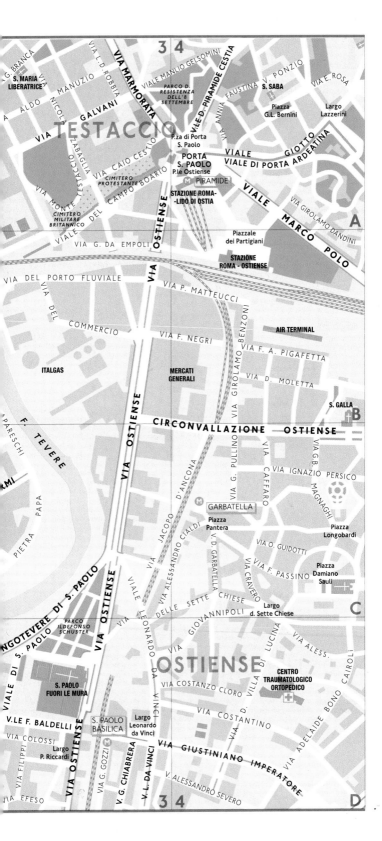

◆ VIA APPIA ANTICA

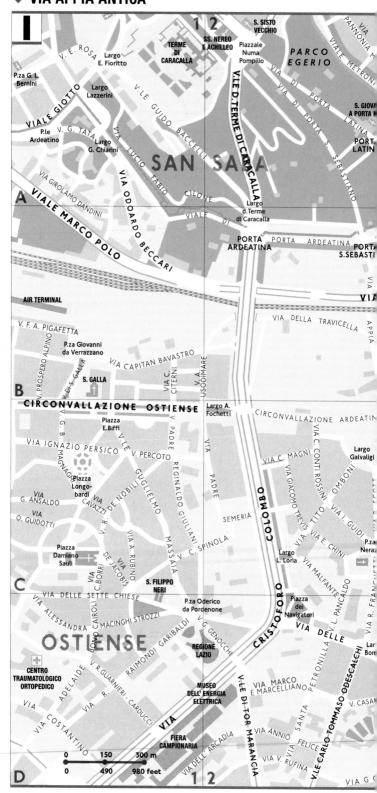

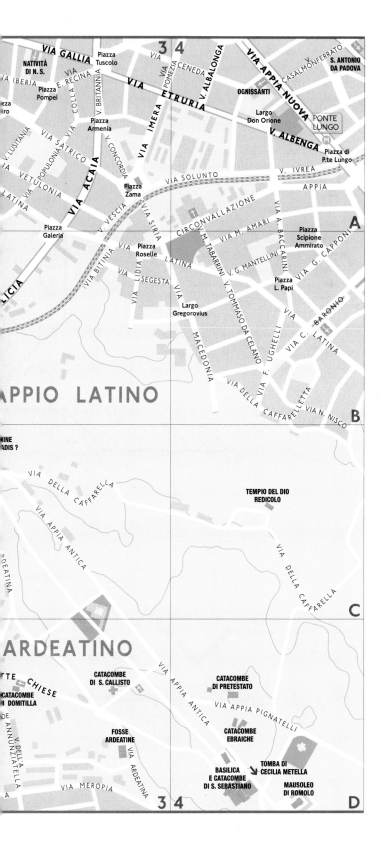

◆ METRO PLAN

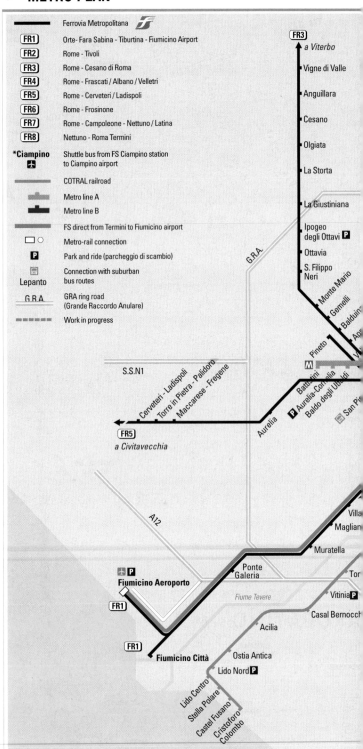

▬▬▬	Ferrovia Metropolitana
FR1	Orte- Fara Sabina - Tiburtina - Fiumicino Airport
FR2	Rome - Tivoli
FR3	Rome - Cesano di Roma
FR4	Rome - Frascati / Albano / Velletri
FR5	Rome - Cerveteri / Ladispoli
FR6	Rome - Frosinone
FR7	Rome - Campoleone - Nettuno / Latina
FR8	Nettuno - Roma Termini
*Ciampino ✈	Shuttle bus from FS Ciampino station to Ciampino airport
	COTRAL railroad
	Metro line A
	Metro line B
	FS direct from Termini to Fiumicino airport
▢ ○	Metro-rail connection
P	Park and ride (parcheggio di scambio)
Lepanto	Connection with suburban bus routes
G.R.A.	GRA ring road (Grande Raccordo Anulare)
▬ ▬ ▬	Work in progress

FR3
a Viterbo
Vigne di Valle
Anguillara
Cesano
Olgiata
La Storta
La Giustiniana
Ipogeo degli Ottavi P
Ottavia
S. Filippo Neri
Monte Mario
Gemelli
Balduina
G.R.A.
Pineto
Ap...
M
Battistini
Aurelia-Cornelia P
Baldo degli Ubaldi
San Pie...

S.S.N1
Cerveteri - Ladispoli
Torre in Pietra - Palidoro
Maccarese - Fregene
Aurelia
FR5
a Civitavecchia

A12
Villa
Maglian
Muratella
Ponte Galeria
Tor
Vitinia P
Casal Bernocc...
Fiume Tevere
Acilia
Fiumicino Aeroporto ✈ P
FR1
Casal Bernocc...
Ostia Antica
Lido Nord P
FR1
Fiumicino Città
Lido Centro
Stella Polare
Castel Fusano
Cristoforo Colombo

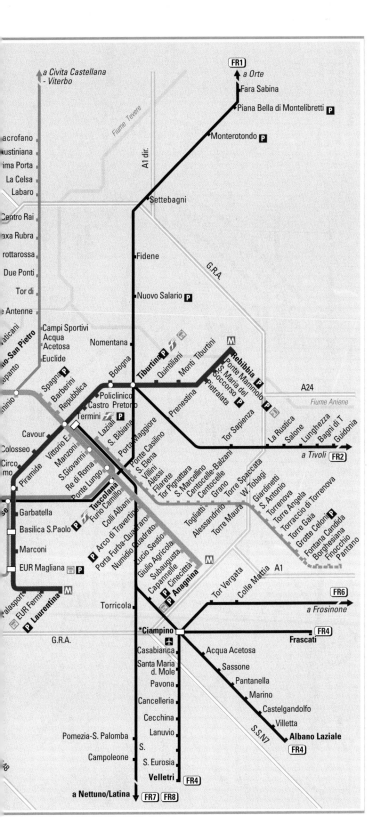

◆ BUS MAP OF THE CITY CENTER

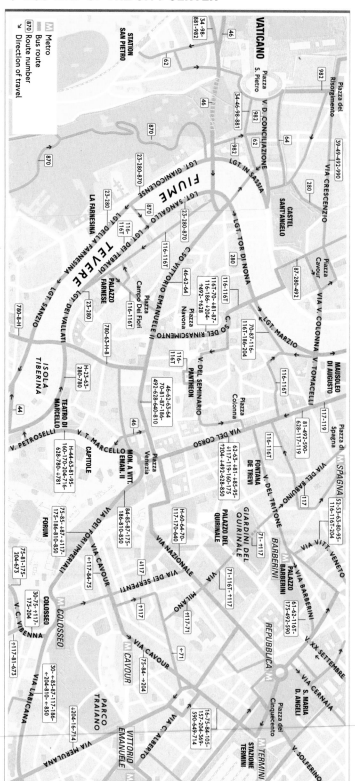

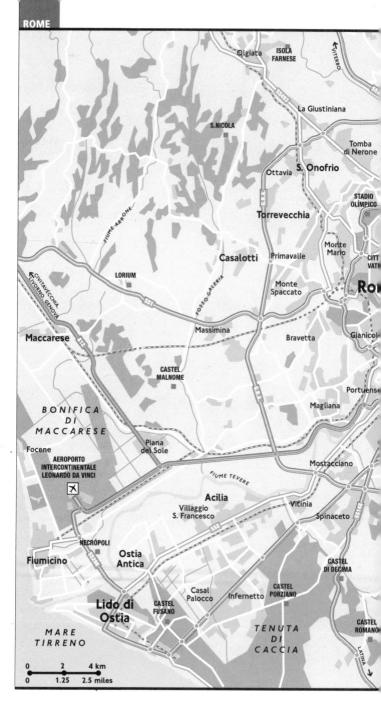

ROMAN FACTS AND FIGURES

Capital of Italy, Rome is the national center of politics and the media. The city's economy is now focused mainly on three areas: tourism, telecommunications and electronics. Within Rome is the world's smallest country, Vatican City.

■ **AREA**
580 square miles. Population density: 4,833 people per square mile; 1,839 people per square mile in the province of Rome.

■ **POPULATION**
2,655,000 in the Eternal City; 3,800,000 in the province of Rome.

■ **TOURISM IN THE PROVINCE OF ROME**
20.4 million tourists per year, of which 7 million are Italian. Museum visitors: 905,800 per year. Visitors to archeological sites and monuments: 514,4000 per year. Hotels: 1,095 (or